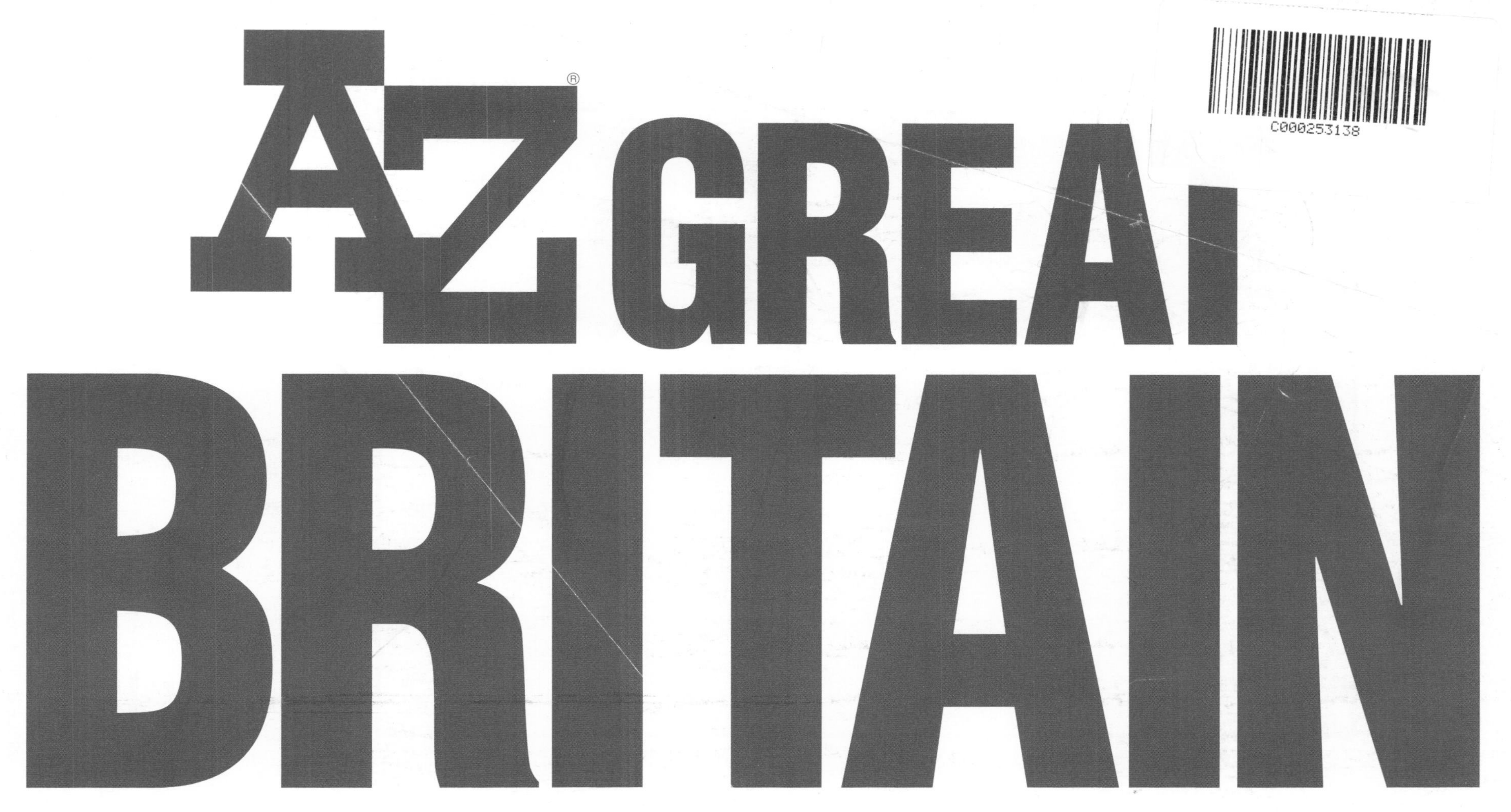

AZ GREAT BRITAIN
and Northern Ireland

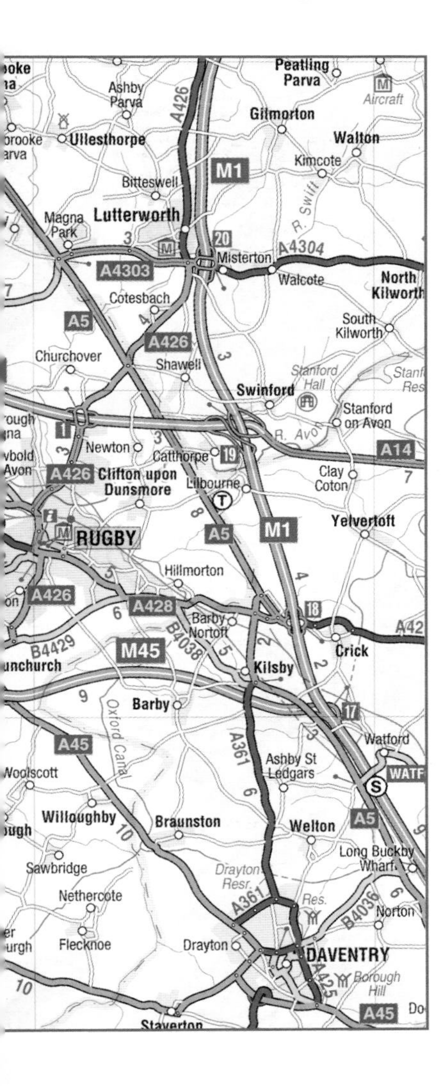

EDITION 1 2019
Copyright © Geographers' A-Z Map Company Ltd.

A-Z AZ AtoZ
registered trade marks of
Geographers' A-Z Map Company Ltd

www./az.co.uk

Contains OS data © Crown copyright and database rights 2018

Northern Ireland: This is Based upon Crown Copyright and is reproduced with the permission of Land & Property Services underdelegated authority from the Controller of Her Majesty's Stationery Office, © Crown copyright and database right 2018 PMLPA No 100508. The inclusion of parts or all of the Republic of Ireland is by permission of the Government of Ireland who retain copyright in the data used. © Ordnance Survey Ireland and Government of Ireland.

Land & Property Services
Paper Map Licensed Partner   This is a registered Trade Mark of
                              Department of Finance and Personnel.

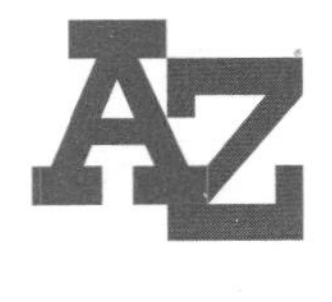

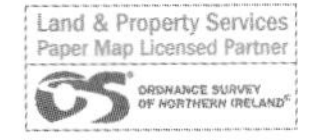

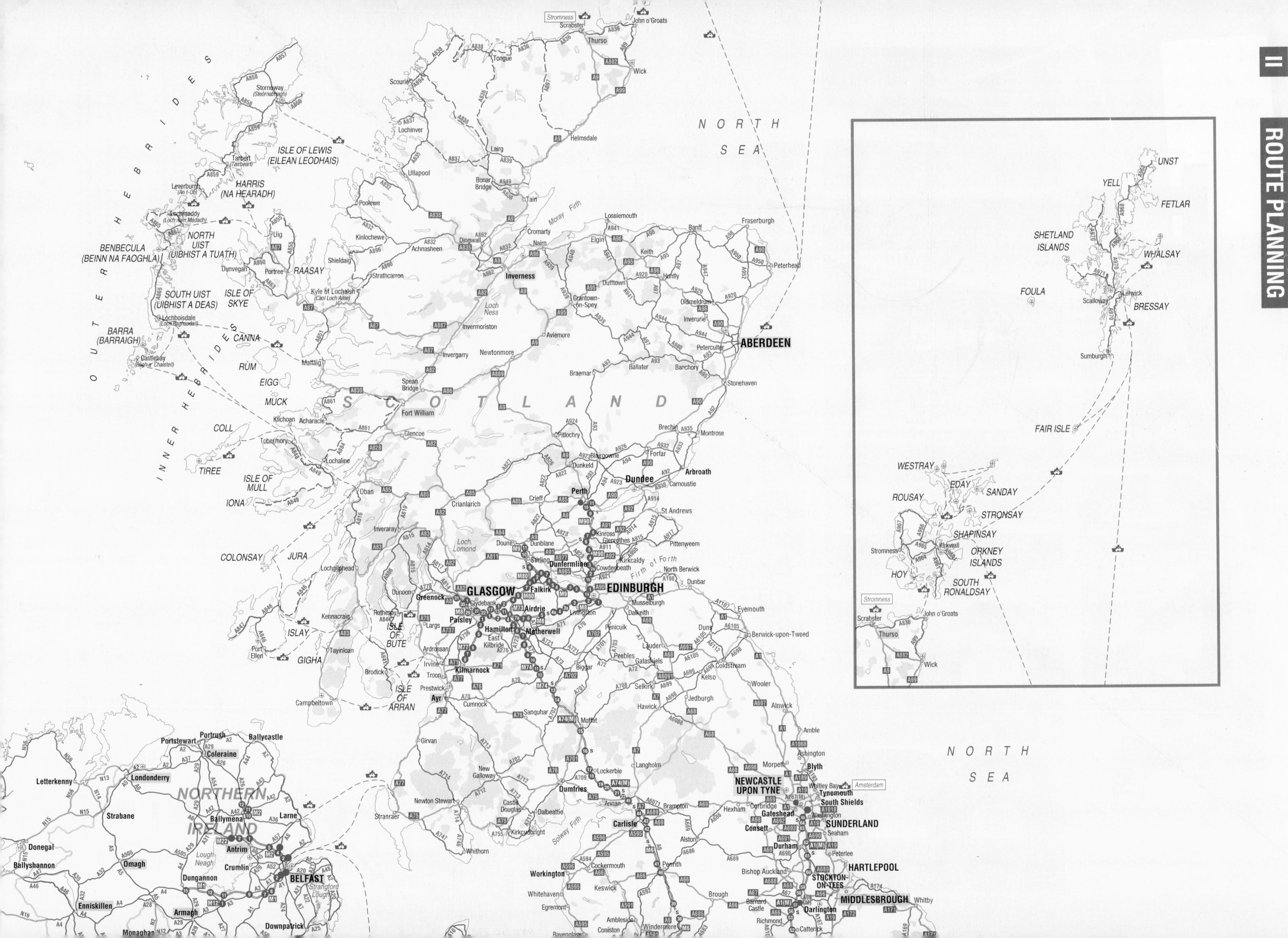
NORTH SEA
UNST
YELL
FETLAR
SHETLAND ISLANDS
WHALSAY
FOULA
Lerwick
Scalloway
BRESSAY
Sumburgh
FAIR ISLE
WESTRAY
EDAY
SANDAY
ROUSAY
STRONSAY
SHAPINSAY
Kirkwall
Stromness
ORKNEY ISLANDS
HOY
SOUTH RONALDSAY
John o'Groats
Scrabster
Thurso
Wick
Tongue
Helmsdale
Scourie
Lochinver
Ullapool
Lairg
Bonar Bridge
Tain
Stornoway (Steòrnabhagh)
ISLE OF LEWIS (EILEAN LEODHAIS)
Tarbert (Tairbeart)
HARRIS (NA HEARADH)
Leverburgh (An t-Ob)
Lochmaddy (Loch nam Madadh)
NORTH UIST (UIBHIST A TUATH)
BENBECULA (BEINN NA FAOGHLA)
SOUTH UIST (UIBHIST A DEAS)
Lochboisdale (Loch Baghasdail)
BARRA (BARRAIGH)
Castlebay (Bàgh a' Chaisteil)
OUTER HEBRIDES
INNER HEBRIDES
Uig
Dunvegan
Portree
RAASAY
ISLE OF SKYE
Kyle of Lochalsh (Caol Loch Aillse)
CANNA
RÙM
EGG
MUCK
COLL
TIREE
ISLE OF MULL
IONA
COLONSAY
JURA
ISLAY
Port Ellen
GIGHA
Mallaig
Kilchoan
Acharacle
Tobermory
Lochaline
Oban
Poolewe
Kinlochewe
Achnasheen
Shieldaig
Strathcarron
Dingwall
Cromarty
Moray Firth
Nairn
Inverness
Loch Ness
Invermoriston
Invergarry
Newtonmore
Aviemore
Spean Bridge
Fort William
Glencoe
SCOTLAND
Lossiemouth
Elgin
Banff
Fraserburgh
Keith
Huntly
Dufftown
Grantown-on-Spey
Peterhead
Oldmeldrum
Inverurie
Peterculter
ABERDEEN
Ballater
Banchory
Braemar
Stonehaven
Brechin
Montrose
Forfar
Arbroath
Pitlochry
Blairgowrie
Dunkeld
Dundee
Carnoustie
Perth
Crieff
Crianlarich
St Andrews
Kinross
Glenrothes
Pittenweem
Kirkcaldy
Firth of Forth
North Berwick
Dunbar
Doune
Dunblane
Stirling
Dunfermline
Cowdenbeath
Inveraray
Loch Lomond
Lochgilphead
Dunoon
Greenock
GLASGOW
Clydebank
Falkirk
EDINBURGH
Musselburgh
Dalkeith
Livingston
Airdrie
Paisley
Hamilton
Motherwell
East Kilbride
Largs
Rothesay
ISLE OF BUTE
Kennacraig
Tayinloan
Ardrossan
Irvine
Troon
Kilmarnock
Brodick
ISLE OF ARRAN
Prestwick
Ayr
Campbeltown
Cumnock
Sanquhar
Moffat
Biggar
Penicuik
Peebles
Lauder
Galashiels
Selkirk
Hawick
Jedburgh
Kelso
Coldstream
Duns
Eyemouth
Berwick-upon-Tweed
Wooler
Alnwick
Amble
Ashington
Morpeth
Blyth
Whitley Bay
Tynemouth
South Shields
Amsterdam
NEWCASTLE UPON TYNE
Hexham
Corbridge
Gateshead
Washington
Consett
SUNDERLAND
Seaham
Durham
Peterlee
HARTLEPOOL
Bishop Auckland
STOCKTON-ON-TEES
MIDDLESBROUGH
Whitby
Barnard Castle
Darlington
Richmond
Catterick
Brough
Alston
Brampton
Langholm
Lockerbie
Annan
Carlisle
Dumfries
Dalbeattie
Castle Douglas
Kirkcudbright
Solway Firth
New Galloway
Newton Stewart
Girvan
Stranraer
Whithorn
Workington
Cockermouth
Keswick
Penrith
Whitehaven
Egremont
Ambleside
Coniston
Windermere
Ravenglass
Portstewart
Portrush
Ballycastle
Coleraine
Londonderry
Letterkenny
Strabane
NORTHERN IRELAND
Ballymena
Larne
Antrim
Lough Neagh
Crumlin
BELFAST
Strangford Lough
Donegal
Ballyshannon
Omagh
Dungannon
Enniskillen
Armagh
Downpatrick
Monaghan

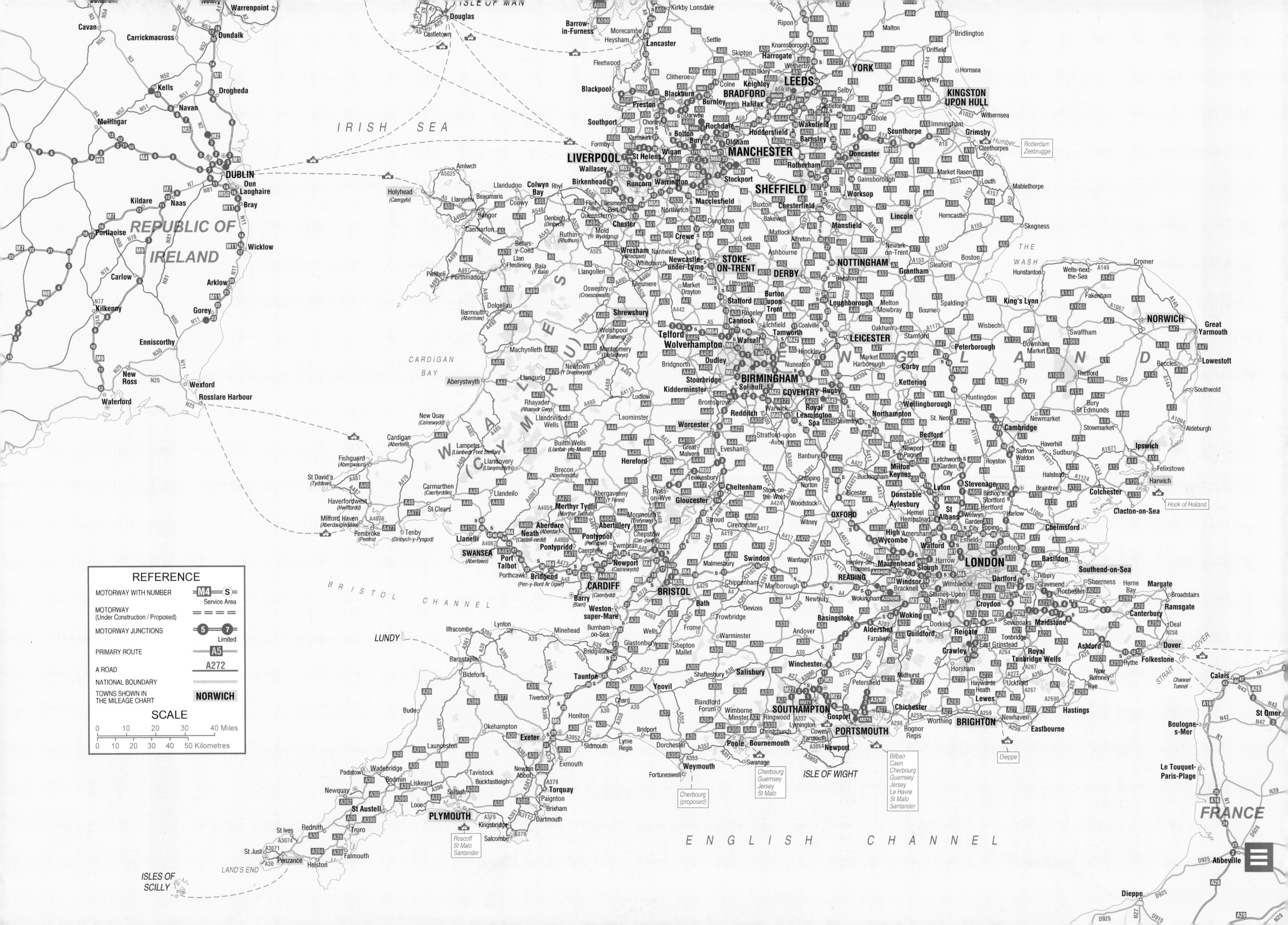

REFERENCE
MOTORWAY WITH NUMBER
M4
S
Service Area
MOTORWAY (Under Construction / Proposed)
MOTORWAY JUNCTIONS
5
7
Limited
PRIMARY ROUTE
A5
A ROAD
A272
NATIONAL BOUNDARY
TOWNS SHOWN IN THE MILEAGE CHART
NORWICH
SCALE
0 10 20 30 40 Miles
0 10 20 30 40 50 Kilometres
REPUBLIC OF IRELAND
IRISH SEA
ISLE OF MAN
WALES (CYMRU)
ENGLAND
FRANCE
ENGLISH CHANNEL
BRISTOL CHANNEL
CARDIGAN BAY
THE WASH
STRAIT OF DOVER
ISLE OF WIGHT
ISLES OF SCILLY
LAND'S END
LUNDY
DUBLIN
Dundalk
Drogheda
Wicklow
Arklow
Wexford
Rosslare Harbour
Waterford
Kilkenny
Douglas
LIVERPOOL
MANCHESTER
LEEDS
BRADFORD
YORK
KINGSTON UPON HULL
SHEFFIELD
NOTTINGHAM
DERBY
STOKE-ON-TRENT
LEICESTER
BIRMINGHAM
COVENTRY
NORWICH
LONDON
BRISTOL
CARDIFF
SWANSEA
PLYMOUTH
SOUTHAMPTON
PORTSMOUTH
BRIGHTON
Holyhead (Caergybi)
Fishguard (Abergwaun)
Pembroke (Penfro)
Rotterdam Zeebrugge
Hook of Holland
Dieppe
Cherbourg (proposed)
Cherbourg Guernsey Jersey St Malo
Bilbao Caen Cherbourg Guernsey Jersey Le Havre St Malo Santander
Roscoff St Malo Santander
Channel Tunnel
Calais
Boulogne-s-Mer
Le Touquet-Paris-Plage
Abbeville
Dover
Folkestone

Mileage Chart and Journey Times

This chart shows the distance in miles and journey time between two cities or towns in Great Britain. Each route has been calculated using a combination of motorways, primary routes and other major roads. This is normally the quickest, though not always the shortest route.

Average journey times are calculated whilst driving at the maximum speed limit. These times are approximate and do not include traffic congestion or convenience breaks.

To find the distance and journey time between two cities or towns, follow a horizontal line and vertical column until they meet each other.

For example, the 285 mile journey from London to Penzance is approximately 4 hours and 59 minutes.

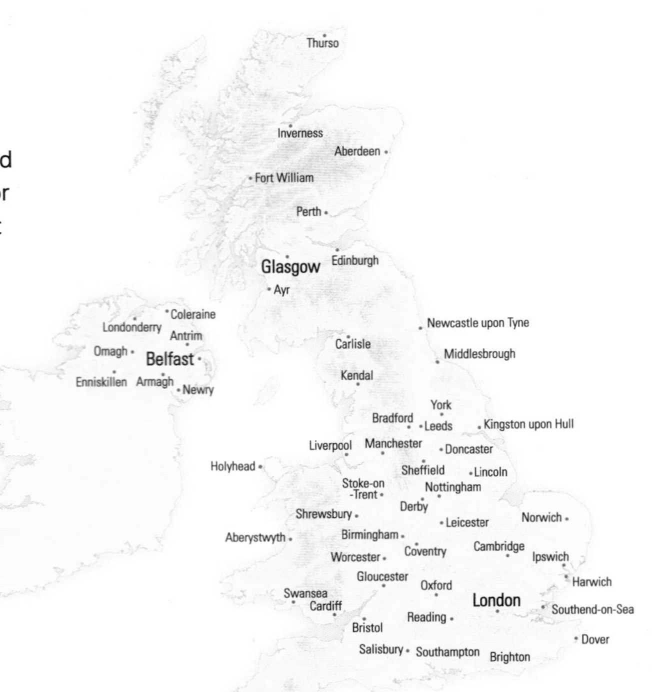

Northern Ireland

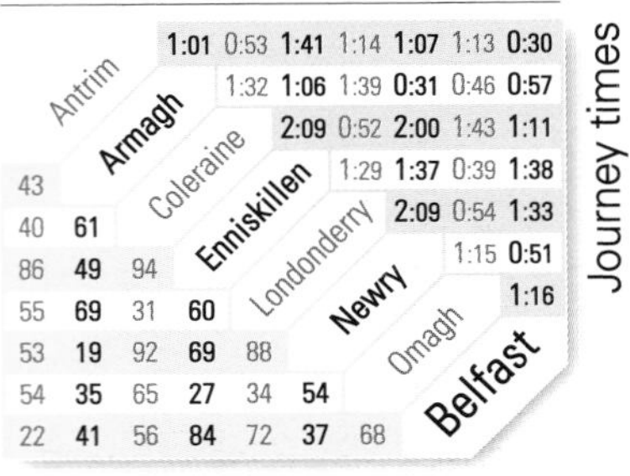

Journey times

	Armagh	Coleraine	Enniskillen	Londonderry	Newry	Omagh	Belfast
Antrim	1:01	0:53	1:41	1:14	1:07	1:13	0:30
Armagh		1:32	1:06	1:39	0:31	0:46	0:57
Coleraine			2:09	0:52	2:00	1:43	1:11
Enniskillen				1:29	1:37	0:39	1:38
Londonderry					2:09	0:54	1:33
Newry						1:15	0:51
Omagh							1:16

Distance in miles

	Antrim	Armagh	Coleraine	Enniskillen	Londonderry	Newry	Omagh
Armagh	43						
Coleraine	40	61					
Enniskillen	86	49	94				
Londonderry	55	69	31	60			
Newry	53	19	92	69	88		
Omagh	54	35	65	27	34	54	
Belfast	22	41	56	84	72	37	68

Belfast to London = 440m / 9:46h (excluding ferry)
Belfast to Glasgow = 104m / 4:46h (excluding ferry)

Great Britain

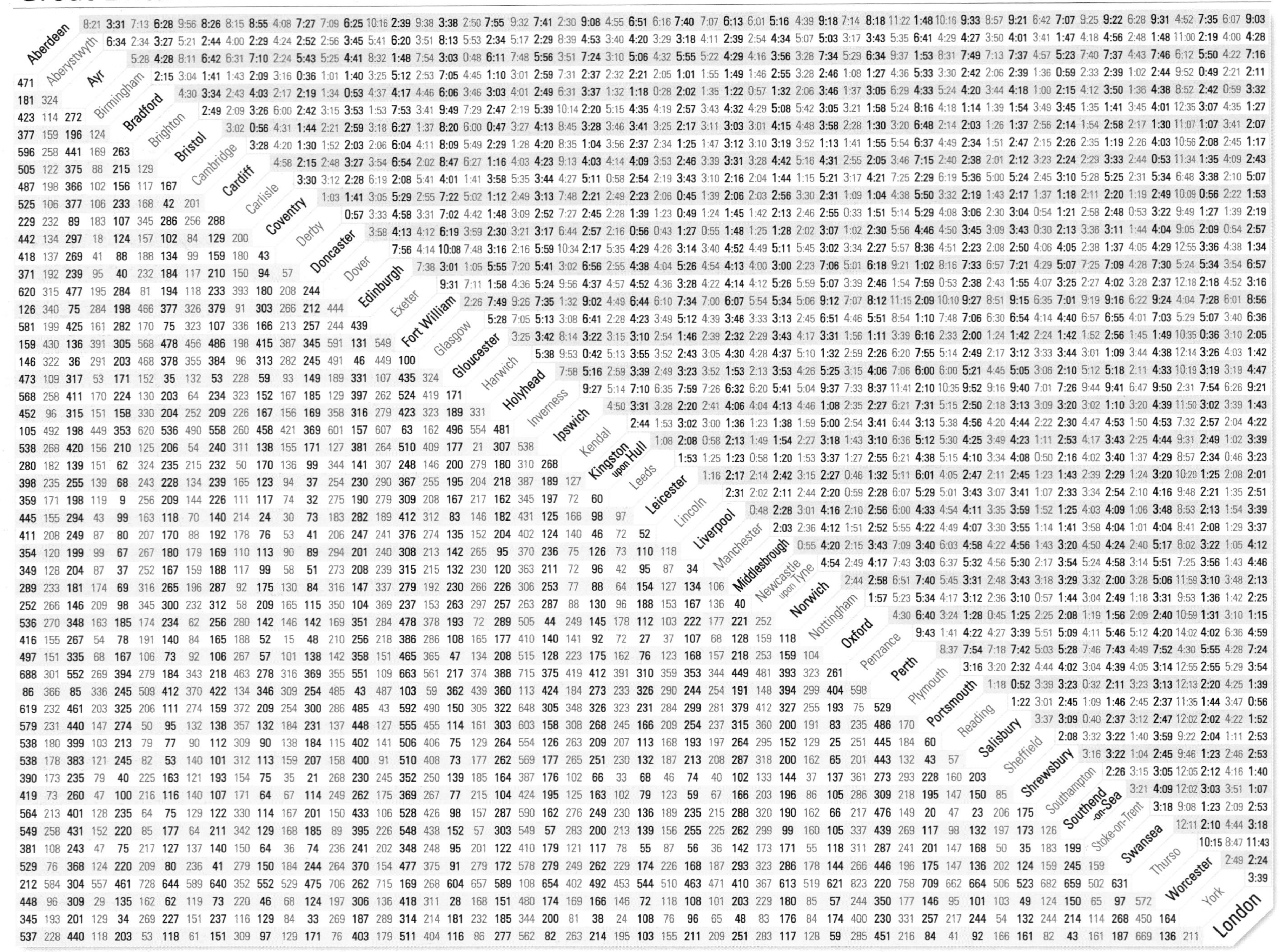

Journey times

	Aberystwyth	Ayr	Birmingham	Bradford	Brighton	Bristol	Cambridge	Cardiff	Carlisle	Coventry	Derby	Doncaster	Dover	Edinburgh	Exeter	Fort William	Glasgow	Gloucester	Harwich	Holyhead	Inverness	Ipswich	Kendal	Kingston upon Hull	Leeds	Leicester	Lincoln	Liverpool	Manchester	Middlesbrough	Newcastle upon Tyne	Norwich	Nottingham	Oxford	Penzance	Perth	Plymouth	Portsmouth	Reading	Salisbury	Sheffield	Shrewsbury	Southampton	Southend-on-Sea	Stoke-on-Trent	Swansea	Thurso	Worcester	York	London
Aberdeen	8:21	3:31	7:13	6:28	9:56	8:26	8:15	8:55	4:08	7:27	7:09	6:25	10:16	2:39	9:38	3:38	2:50	7:55	9:32	7:41	2:30	9:08	4:55	6:51	6:16	7:40	7:07	6:13	6:01	5:16	4:39	9:18	7:14	8:18	11:22	1:48	10:16	9:33	8:57	9:21	6:42	7:07	9:25	9:22	6:28	9:31	4:52	7:35	6:07	9:03
Aberystwyth		6:34	2:34	3:27	5:21	2:44	4:00	2:29	4:24	2:52	2:56	3:45	5:41	6:20	3:51	8:13	5:53	2:34	5:17	2:29	8:39	4:53	3:40	4:20	3:29	3:18	4:11	2:39	2:54	4:34	5:07	5:03	3:17	3:43	5:35	6:41	4:29	4:27	3:50	4:01	3:41	1:47	4:18	4:56	2:48	1:48	11:00	2:19	4:00	4:28
Ayr			5:28	4:28	8:11	6:42	6:31	7:10	2:24	5:43	5:25	4:41	8:32	1:48	7:54	3:03	0:48	6:11	7:48	5:56	3:51	7:24	3:10	5:06	4:32	5:55	5:22	4:29	4:16	3:56	3:28	7:34	5:29	6:34	9:37	1:53	8:31	7:49	7:13	7:37	4:57	5:23	7:40	7:37	4:43	7:46	6:12	5:50	4:22	7:16
Birmingham				2:15	3:04	1:41	1:43	2:09	3:16	0:36	1:01	1:40	3:25	5:12	2:53	7:05	4:45	1:10	3:01	2:59	7:31	2:37	2:32	2:21	2:05	1:01	1:55	1:49	1:46	2:55	3:28	2:46	1:08	1:27	4:36	5:33	3:30	2:42	2:06	2:39	1:36	0:59	2:33	2:39	1:02	2:44	9:52	0:49	2:21	2:11
Bradford					4:30	3:34	2:43	4:03	2:17	2:19	1:34	0:53	4:37	4:17	4:46	6:06	3:46	3:03	4:01	2:49	6:31	3:37	1:32	1:18	0:28	2:02	1:35	1:22	0:57	1:32	2:06	3:46	1:37	3:05	6:29	4:33	5:24	4:20	3:44	4:18	1:00	2:15	4:12	3:50	1:36	4:38	8:52	2:42	0:59	3:32
Brighton						2:49	2:09	3:26	6:00	2:42	3:15	3:53	1:53	7:53	3:41	9:49	7:29	2:47	2:19	5:39	10:14	2:20	5:15	4:35	4:19	2:57	3:43	4:32	4:29	5:08	5:42	3:05	3:21	1:58	5:24	8:16	4:18	1:14	1:39	1:54	3:49	3:45	1:35	1:41	3:45	4:01	12:35	3:07	4:35	1:27
Bristol							3:02	0:56	4:31	1:44	2:21	2:59	3:18	6:27	1:37	8:20	6:00	0:47	3:27	4:13	8:45	3:28	3:46	3:41	3:25	2:17	3:11	3:03	3:01	4:15	4:48	3:58	2:28	1:30	3:20	6:48	2:14	2:03	1:26	1:37	2:56	2:14	1:54	2:58	2:17	1:30	11:07	1:07	3:41	2:07
Cambridge								3:28	4:20	1:30	1:52	2:03	2:06	6:04	4:11	8:09	5:49	2:29	1:28	4:20	8:35	1:04	3:56	2:37	2:34	1:25	1:47	3:12	3:10	3:19	3:52	1:13	1:41	1:55	5:54	6:37	4:49	2:34	1:51	2:47	2:15	2:26	2:35	1:19	2:26	4:03	10:56	2:08	2:45	1:17
Cardiff									4:58	2:15	2:48	3:27	3:54	6:54	2:02	8:47	6:27	1:16	4:03	4:23	9:13	4:03	4:14	4:09	3:53	2:46	3:39	3:31	3:28	4:42	5:16	4:31	2:55	2:05	3:46	7:15	2:40	2:38	2:01	2:12	3:23	2:24	2:29	3:33	2:44	0:53	11:34	1:35	4:09	2:43
Carlisle										3:30	3:12	2:28	6:19	2:08	5:41	4:01	1:41	3:58	5:35	3:44	4:27	5:11	0:58	2:54	2:19	3:43	3:10	2:16	2:04	1:44	1:15	5:21	3:17	4:21	7:25	2:29	6:19	5:36	5:00	5:24	2:45	3:10	5:28	5:25	2:31	5:34	6:48	3:38	2:10	5:07
Coventry											1:03	1:41	3:05	5:29	2:55	7:22	5:02	1:12	2:49	3:13	7:48	2:21	2:49	2:23	2:06	0:45	1:39	2:06	2:03	2:56	3:30	2:31	1:09	1:04	4:38	5:50	3:32	2:19	1:43	2:17	1:37	1:18	2:11	2:20	1:19	2:49	10:09	0:56	2:22	1:53
Derby												0:57	3:33	4:58	3:31	7:02	4:42	1:48	3:09	2:52	7:27	2:45	2:28	1:39	1:23	0:49	1:24	1:45	1:42	2:13	2:46	2:55	0:33	1:51	5:14	5:29	4:08	3:06	2:30	3:04	0:54	1:21	2:58	2:48	0:53	3:22	9:49	1:27	1:39	2:19
Doncaster													3:58	4:13	4:12	6:19	3:59	2:30	3:21	3:17	6:44	2:57	2:16	0:56	0:43	1:27	0:55	1:48	1:25	1:28	2:02	3:07	1:02	2:30	5:56	4:46	4:50	3:45	3:09	3:43	0:30	2:13	3:36	3:11	1:44	4:04	9:05	2:09	0:54	2:57
Dover														7:56	4:14	10:08	7:48	3:16	2:16	5:59	10:34	2:17	5:35	4:29	4:26	3:14	3:40	4:52	4:49	5:11	5:45	3:02	3:34	2:27	5:57	8:36	4:51	2:23	2:08	2:50	4:06	4:05	2:38	1:37	4:05	4:29	12:55	3:36	4:38	1:34
Edinburgh															7:38	3:01	1:05	5:55	7:20	5:41	3:02	6:56	2:55	4:38	4:04	5:26	4:54	4:13	4:00	3:00	2:23	7:06	5:01	6:18	9:21	1:02	8:16	7:33	6:57	7:21	4:29	5:07	7:25	7:09	4:28	7:30	5:24	5:34	3:54	6:57
Exeter																9:31	7:11	1:58	4:36	5:24	9:56	4:37	4:57	4:52	4:36	3:28	4:22	4:14	4:12	5:26	5:59	5:07	3:39	2:46	1:54	7:59	0:53	2:38	2:43	1:55	4:07	3:25	2:27	4:02	3:28	2:37	12:18	2:18	4:52	3:16
Fort William																	2:26	7:49	9:26	7:35	1:32	9:02	4:49	6:44	6:10	7:34	7:00	6:07	5:54	5:34	5:06	9:12	7:07	8:12	11:15	2:09	10:10	9:27	8:51	9:15	6:35	7:01	9:19	9:16	6:22	9:24	4:04	7:28	6:01	8:56
Glasgow																		5:28	7:05	5:13	3:08	6:41	2:28	4:23	3:49	5:12	4:39	3:46	3:33	3:13	2:45	6:51	4:46	5:51	8:54	1:10	7:48	7:06	6:30	6:54	4:14	4:40	6:57	6:55	4:01	7:03	5:29	5:07	3:40	6:36
Gloucester																			3:25	3:42	8:14	3:22	3:15	3:10	2:54	1:46	2:39	2:32	2:29	3:43	4:17	3:31	1:56	1:11	3:39	6:16	2:33	2:00	1:24	1:42	2:24	1:42	1:52	2:56	1:45	1:49	10:35	0:36	3:10	2:05
Harwich																				5:38	9:53	0:42	5:13	3:55	3:52	2:43	3:05	4:30	4:28	4:37	5:10	1:32	2:59	2:26	6:20	7:55	5:14	2:49	2:17	3:12	3:33	3:44	3:01	1:09	3:44	4:38	12:14	3:26	4:03	1:42
Holyhead																					7:58	5:16	2:59	3:39	2:49	3:23	3:52	1:53	2:13	3:53	4:26	5:25	3:15	4:06	7:06	6:00	6:00	5:21	4:45	5:05	3:06	2:10	5:12	5:18	2:11	4:33	10:19	3:19	3:19	4:47
Inverness																						9:27	5:14	7:10	6:35	7:59	7:26	6:32	6:20	5:41	5:04	9:37	7:33	8:37	11:41	2:10	10:35	9:52	9:16	9:40	7:01	7:26	9:44	9:41	6:47	9:50	2:31	7:54	6:26	9:21
Ipswich																							4:50	3:31	3:28	2:20	2:41	4:06	4:04	4:13	4:46	1:08	2:35	2:27	6:21	7:31	5:15	2:50	2:18	3:13	3:09	3:20	3:02	1:10	3:20	4:39	11:50	3:02	3:39	1:43
Kendal																								2:44	1:53	3:02	3:00	1:36	1:23	1:38	1:59	5:00	2:54	3:41	6:44	3:13	5:38	4:56	4:20	4:44	2:22	2:30	4:47	4:53	1:50	4:53	7:32	2:57	2:04	4:22
Kingston upon Hull																									1:08	2:08	0:58	2:13	1:49	1:54	2:27	3:18	1:43	3:10	6:36	5:12	5:30	4:25	3:49	4:23	1:11	2:53	4:17	3:43	2:25	4:44	9:31	2:49	1:02	3:39
Leeds																										1:53	1:25	1:23	0:58	1:20	1:53	3:37	1:27	2:55	6:21	4:38	5:15	4:10	3:34	4:08	0:50	2:16	4:02	3:40	1:37	4:29	8:57	2:34	0:46	3:23
Leicester																											1:16	2:17	2:14	2:42	3:15	2:27	0:46	1:32	5:11	6:01	4:05	2:47	2:11	2:45	1:23	1:43	2:39	2:29	1:24	3:20	10:20	1:25	2:08	2:01
Lincoln																												2:31	2:02	2:11	2:44	2:20	0:59	2:28	6:07	5:29	5:01	3:43	3:07	3:41	1:07	2:33	3:34	2:54	2:10	4:16	9:48	2:21	1:35	2:51
Liverpool																													0:48	2:28	3:01	4:16	2:10	2:56	6:00	4:33	4:54	4:11	3:35	3:59	1:52	1:25	4:03	4:09	1:06	3:48	8:53	2:13	1:54	3:39
Manchester																														2:03	2:36	4:12	1:51	2:52	5:55	4:22	4:49	4:07	3:30	3:55	1:14	1:41	3:58	4:04	1:01	4:04	8:41	2:08	1:29	3:37
Middlesbrough																															0:55	4:20	2:15	3:43	7:09	3:40	6:03	4:58	4:22	4:56	1:43	3:20	4:50	4:24	2:40	5:17	8:02	3:22	1:05	4:12
Newcastle upon Tyne																																4:54	2:49	4:17	7:43	3:03	6:37	5:32	4:56	5:30	2:17	3:54	5:24	4:58	3:14	5:51	7:25	3:56	1:43	4:46
Norwich																																	2:44	2:58	6:51	7:40	5:45	3:31	2:48	3:43	3:18	3:29	3:32	2:00	3:28	5:06	11:59	3:10	3:48	2:13
Nottingham																																		1:57	5:23	5:34	4:17	3:12	2:36	3:10	0:57	1:44	3:04	2:49	1:18	3:31	9:53	1:36	1:42	2:25
Oxford																																			4:30	6:40	3:24	1:28	0:45	1:25	2:25	2:08	1:19	1:56	2:09	2:40	10:59	1:31	3:10	1:15
Penzance																																				9:43	1:41	4:22	4:27	3:39	5:51	5:09	4:11	5:46	5:12	4:20	14:02	4:02	6:36	4:59
Perth																																					8:37	7:54	7:18	7:42	5:03	5:28	7:46	7:43	4:49	7:52	4:30	5:55	4:28	7:24
Plymouth																																						3:16	3:20	2:32	4:44	4:02	3:04	4:39	4:05	3:14	12:55	2:55	5:29	3:54
Portsmouth																																							1:18	0:52	3:39	3:23	0:32	2:11	3:23	3:13	12:13	2:20	4:25	1:39
Reading																																								1:22	3:01	2:45	1:09	1:46	2:45	2:37	11:35	1:44	3:47	0:56
Salisbury																																									3:37	3:09	0:40	2:37	3:12	2:47	12:02	2:02	4:22	1:52
Sheffield																																										2:08	3:32	3:22	1:40	3:59	9:22	2:04	1:11	2:53
Shrewsbury																																											3:16	3:22	1:04	2:45	9:46	1:23	2:46	2:53
Southampton																																												2:26	3:15	3:05	12:05	2:12	4:16	1:40
Southend-on-Sea																																													3:21	4:09	12:02	3:03	3:51	1:07
Stoke-on-Trent																																														3:18	9:08	1:23	2:09	2:53
Swansea																																															12:11	2:10	4:44	3:18
Thurso																																																10:15	8:47	11:43
Worcester																																																	2:49	2:24
York																																																		3:39

Distance in miles

	Aberdeen	Aberystwyth	Ayr	Birmingham	Bradford	Brighton	Bristol	Cambridge	Cardiff	Carlisle	Coventry	Derby	Doncaster	Dover	Edinburgh	Exeter	Fort William	Glasgow	Gloucester	Harwich	Holyhead	Inverness	Ipswich	Kendal	Kingston upon Hull	Leeds	Leicester	Lincoln	Liverpool	Manchester	Middlesbrough	Newcastle upon Tyne	Norwich	Nottingham	Oxford	Penzance	Perth	Plymouth	Portsmouth	Reading	Salisbury	Sheffield	Shrewsbury	Southampton	Southend-on-Sea	Stoke-on-Trent	Swansea	Thurso	Worcester	York
Aberystwyth	471
Ayr	181	324
Birmingham	423	114	272
Bradford	377	159	196	124
Brighton	596	258	441	169	263
Bristol	505	122	375	88	215	129
Cambridge	487	198	366	102	156	117	167
Cardiff	525	106	377	106	233	168	42	201
Carlisle	229	232	89	183	107	345	286	256	288
Coventry	442	134	297	18	124	157	102	84	129	200
Derby	418	137	269	41	88	188	134	99	159	180	43
Doncaster	371	192	239	95	40	232	184	117	210	150	94	57
Dover	620	315	477	195	284	81	194	118	233	393	180	208	244
Edinburgh	126	340	75	284	198	466	377	326	379	91	303	266	212	444
Exeter	581	199	425	161	282	170	75	323	107	336	166	213	257	244	439
Fort William	159	430	136	391	305	568	478	456	486	198	415	387	345	591	131	549
Glasgow	146	322	36	291	203	468	378	355	384	96	313	282	245	491	46	449	100
Gloucester	473	109	317	53	171	152	35	132	53	228	59	93	149	189	331	107	435	324
Harwich	568	258	411	170	224	130	203	64	234	323	152	167	185	129	397	262	524	419	171
Holyhead	452	96	315	151	158	330	204	252	209	226	167	156	169	358	316	279	423	323	189	331
Inverness	105	492	198	449	353	620	536	490	558	260	458	421	369	601	157	607	63	162	496	554	481
Ipswich	538	268	420	156	210	125	206	54	240	311	138	155	171	127	381	264	510	409	177	21	307	538
Kendal	280	182	139	151	62	324	235	215	232	50	170	136	99	344	141	307	248	146	200	279	180	310	268
Kingston upon Hull	398	235	255	139	68	243	228	134	239	165	123	94	37	254	230	290	367	255	195	204	218	387	189	127
Leeds	359	171	198	119	9	256	209	144	226	111	117	74	32	275	190	279	309	208	167	217	162	345	197	72	60
Leicester	445	155	294	43	99	163	118	70	140	214	24	30	73	183	282	189	412	312	83	146	182	431	125	166	98	97
Lincoln	411	208	249	87	80	207	170	88	192	178	76	53	41	206	247	241	376	274	135	152	204	402	124	140	46	72	52
Liverpool	354	120	199	99	67	267	180	179	169	110	113	90	89	294	201	240	308	213	142	265	95	370	236	75	126	73	110	118
Manchester	349	128	204	87	37	252	167	159	188	117	99	58	51	273	208	239	315	215	132	230	120	363	211	72	96	42	95	87	34
Middlesbrough	289	233	181	174	69	316	265	196	287	92	175	130	84	316	147	337	279	192	230	266	226	306	253	77	88	64	154	127	134	106
Newcastle upon Tyne	252	266	146	209	98	345	300	232	312	58	209	165	115	350	104	369	237	153	263	297	257	263	287	88	130	96	188	153	167	136	40
Norwich	536	270	348	163	185	174	234	62	256	280	142	146	142	169	351	284	478	378	193	72	289	505	44	249	145	178	112	103	222	177	221	252
Nottingham	416	155	267	54	78	191	140	84	165	188	52	15	48	210	256	218	386	286	108	165	177	410	140	141	92	72	27	37	107	68	128	159	118
Oxford	497	151	335	68	167	106	73	92	106	267	57	101	138	142	358	151	465	365	47	134	208	515	128	223	175	162	76	123	168	157	218	253	159	104
Penzance	688	301	552	269	394	279	184	343	218	463	278	316	369	355	551	109	663	561	217	374	388	715	375	419	412	391	310	359	353	344	449	481	393	323	261
Perth	86	366	85	336	245	509	412	370	422	134	346	309	254	485	43	487	103	59	362	439	360	113	424	184	273	233	326	290	244	254	191	148	394	299	404	598
Plymouth	619	232	461	203	325	206	111	274	159	372	209	254	300	286	485	43	592	490	150	305	322	648	305	348	326	323	231	284	299	281	379	412	327	255	193	75	529
Portsmouth	579	231	440	147	274	50	95	132	138	357	132	184	231	137	448	127	555	455	114	161	303	603	158	308	268	245	166	209	254	237	315	360	200	191	83	235	486	170
Reading	538	180	399	103	213	79	77	90	112	309	90	138	184	115	402	141	506	406	75	129	264	554	126	263	209	207	113	168	193	197	264	295	152	129	25	251	445	184	60
Salisbury	538	178	383	121	245	82	53	140	101	312	113	159	207	158	400	91	510	408	73	177	262	569	177	265	251	230	132	187	213	208	287	318	200	162	65	201	443	132	43	57
Sheffield	390	173	235	79	40	225	163	121	193	154	75	35	21	268	230	245	352	250	139	185	164	387	176	102	66	33	68	46	74	40	102	133	144	37	137	361	273	293	228	160	203
Shrewsbury	419	73	260	47	100	216	116	140	107	171	64	67	114	249	262	175	369	267	77	215	104	424	195	125	163	102	79	123	59	67	166	203	196	86	105	286	309	218	195	147	150	85
Southampton	564	213	401	128	235	64	75	129	122	330	114	167	201	150	433	106	528	426	98	157	287	590	162	276	249	230	136	189	235	215	288	320	190	162	66	217	476	149	20	47	23	206	175
Southend-on-Sea	549	258	431	152	220	85	177	64	211	342	129	168	185	89	395	226	548	438	152	57	303	549	57	283	200	213	139	156	255	225	262	299	99	160	105	337	439	269	117	98	132	197	173	126
Stoke-on-Trent	381	108	243	47	75	217	127	137	140	150	64	36	74	236	241	202	348	248	95	201	122	410	179	121	117	78	55	87	56	36	142	173	171	55	118	311	287	241	201	147	168	50	35	183	199
Swansea	529	76	368	124	220	209	80	236	41	279	150	184	244	264	370	154	477	375	91	279	172	578	279	249	262	229	174	226	168	187	293	323	286	178	144	266	446	196	175	147	136	202	124	159	245	159
Thurso	212	584	304	557	461	728	644	589	640	352	552	529	475	706	262	715	169	268	604	657	589	108	654	402	492	453	544	510	463	471	410	367	613	519	621	823	220	758	709	662	664	506	523	682	659	502	631
Worcester	448	96	309	29	135	162	62	119	73	220	46	68	124	197	306	136	418	311	28	168	151	480	174	169	166	146	72	118	108	101	203	229	180	85	57	244	350	177	146	95	101	103	49	124	150	65	97	572
York	345	193	201	129	34	269	227	151	237	116	129	84	33	269	187	289	314	214	181	232	185	344	200	81	38	24	108	76	96	65	48	83	176	84	174	400	230	331	257	217	244	54	132	244	214	114	268	450	164
London	537	228	440	118	203	53	118	61	151	309	97	129	171	76	403	179	511	404	116	86	277	562	82	263	214	195	103	155	211	209	251	283	117	128	59	285	451	216	84	41	92	166	161	82	43	161	187	669	136	211

Scales to Map Pages

BRITAIN
1:221,760 = 3.5 miles to 1 inch (2.54 cm)
2.2 km to 1 cm

0 1 2 3 4 5 10 15 20 25 Miles
0 1 2 3 4 5 10 15 20 25 30 35 40 Kilometres

NORTHERN IRELAND
1:380,160 = 6 miles to 1 inch (2.54 cm)
3.8 km to 1 cm

0 1 2 3 4 5 10 15 20 25Miles
0 1 2 3 4 5 10 15 20 25 30 35 40 Kilometres

Limited Interchange Motorway Junctions

Limited Interchange Motorway Junctions are shown on the mapping pages by red junction indicators 2

M1

Junction		
2	Northbound	No exit, access from A1 only
	Southbound	No access, exit to A1 only
4	Northbound	No exit, access from A41 only
	Southbound	No access, exit to A41 only
6a	Northbound	No exit, access from M25 only
	Southbound	No access, exit to M25 only
17	Northbound	No access, exit to M45 only
	Southbound	No exit, access from M45 only
19	Northbound	Exit to M6 only, access from A14 only
	Southbound	Access from M6 only, exit to A14 only
21a	Northbound	No access, exit to A46 only
	Southbound	No exit, access from A46 only
24a	Northbound	No exit
	Southbound	Access from A50 only
35a	Northbound	No access, exit to A616 only
	Southbound	No exit, access from A616 only
43	Northbound	Exit to M621 only
	Southbound	Access from M621 only
48	Eastbound	Exit to A1(M) northbound only
	Westbound	Access from A1(M) southbound only

M2

Junction		
1	Eastbound	Access from A2 eastbound only
	Westbound	Exit to A2 westbound only

M3

Junction		
8	Eastbound	No exit, access from A303 only
	Westbound	No access, exit to A303 only
10	Northbound	No access from A31
	Southbound	No exit to A31
13	Southbound	No access from A335 to M3 leading to M27 Eastbound

M4

Junction		
1	Eastbound	Exit to A4 eastbound only
	Westbound	Access from A4 westbound only
21	Eastbound	No exit to M48
	Westbound	No access from M48
23	Eastbound	No access from M48
	Westbound	No exit to M48
25	Eastbound	No exit
	Westbound	No access
25a	Eastbound	No exit
	Westbound	No access
29	Eastbound	No exit, access from A48(M) only
	Westbound	No access, exit to A48(M) only
38	Westbound	No access, exit to A48 only
39	Eastbound	No access or exit
	Westbound	No exit, access from A48 only
42	Eastbound	No access from A48
	Westbound	No exit to A48

M5

Junction		
10	Northbound	No exit, access from A4019 only
	Southbound	No access, exit to A4019 only
11a	Southbound	No exit to A417 westbound
18a	Northbound	No access from M49
	Southbound	No exit to M49

M6

Junction		
3a	Eastbound	No exit to M6 Toll
	Westbound	No access from M6 Toll
4	Northbound	No exit to M42 northbound No access from M42 southbound
	Southbound	No exit to M42 No access from M42 southbound
4a	Northbound	No exit, access from M42 southbound only
	Southbound	No access, exit to M42 only
5	Northbound	No access, exit to A452 only
	Southbound	No exit, access from A452 only
10a	Northbound	No access, exit to M54 only
	Southbound	No exit, access from M54 only
11a	Northbound	No exit to M6 Toll
	Southbound	No access from M6 Toll
20	Northbound	No exit to M56 eastbound
	Southbound	No access from M56 westbound
24	Northbound	No exit, access from A58 only
	Southbound	No access, exit to A58 only
25	Northbound	No access, exit to A49 only
	Southbound	No exit, access from A49 only
30	Northbound	No exit, access from M61 northbound only
	Southbound	No access, exit to M61 southbound only
31a	Northbound	No access, exit to B6242 only
	Southbound	No exit, access from B6242 only
45	Northbound	No access onto A74(M)
	Southbound	No exit from A74(M)

M6 Toll

Junction		
T1	Northbound	No exit
	Southbound	No access
T2	Northbound	No access or exit
	Southbound	No access
T5	Northbound	No exit
	Southbound	No access
T7	Northbound	No access from A5
	Southbound	No exit
T8	Northbound	No exit to A460 northbound
	Southbound	No exit

M8

Junction		
6	Eastbound	No exit, access only
	Westbound	No access, exit only
6a	Eastbound	No access, exit only
	Westbound	No exit, access only
7	Eastbound	No access, exit only
	Westbound	No exit, access only
7a	Eastbound	No exit, access from A725 Northbound only
	Westbound	No access, exit to A725 Southbound only
8	Eastbound	No exit to M73 northbound
	Westbound	No access from M73 southbound
9	Eastbound	No access, exit only
	Westbound	No exit, access only
13	Eastbound	No access from M80 southbound
	Westbound	No exit to M80 northbound
14	Eastbound	No access, exit only
	Westbound	No exit, access only
16	Eastbound	No exit, access only
	Westbound	No access, exit only
17	Eastbound	No exit, access from A82 only
	Westbound	No access, exit to A82 only
18	Westbound	No exit, access only
19	Eastbound	No exit to A814 eastbound
	Westbound	No access from A814 westbound
20	Eastbound	No exit, access only
	Westbound	No access, exit only
21	Eastbound	No access, exit only
	Westbound	No exit, access only
22	Eastbound	No exit, access from M77 only
	Westbound	No access, exit to M77 only
23	Eastbound	No exit, access from B768 only
	Westbound	No access, exit to B768 only
25	Eastbound & Westbound	Access from A739 southbound only Exit to A739 northbound only
25a	Eastbound	Access only
	Westbound	Exit only
28	Eastbound	No exit, access from airport only
	Westbound	No access, exit to airport only

M9

Junction		
2	Northbound	No exit, access from B8046 only
	Southbound	No access, exit to B8046 only
3	Northbound	No access, exit to A803 only
	Southbound	No exit, access from A803 only
6	Northbound	No exit, access only
	Southbound	No access, exit to A905 only
8	Northbound	No access, exit to M876 only
	Southbound	No exit, access from M876 only

M11

Junction		
4	Northbound	No exit, access from A406 eastbound only
	Southbound	No access, exit to A406 westbound only
5	Northbound	No access, exit to A1168 only
	Southbound	No exit, access from A1168 only
8a	Northbound	No access, exit only
	Southbound	No exit, access only
9	Northbound	No access, exit only
	Southbound	No exit, access only
13	Northbound	No access, exit only
	Southbound	No exit, access only
14	Northbound	No access from A428 eastbound No exit to A428 westbound
	Southbound	No exit, access from A428 eastbound only

M20

Junction		
2	Eastbound	No access, exit to A20 only (access via M26 Junction 2a)
	Westbound	No exit, access only (exit via M26 Jun.2a)
3	Eastbound	No exit, access from M26 eastbound only
	Westbound	No access, exit to M26 westbound only
11a	Eastbound	No access from Channel Tunnel
	Westbound	No exit to Channel Tunnel

M23

Junction		
7	Northbound	No exit to A23 southbound
	Southbound	No access from A23 northbound

M25

Junction		
5	Clockwise	No exit to M26 eastbound
	Anti-clockwise	No access from M26 westbound
Spur to A21	Northbound	No exit to M26 eastbound
	Southbound	No access from M26 westbound
19	Clockwise	No access, exit only
	Anti-clockwise	No exit, access only
21	Clockwise & Anti-clockwise	No exit to M1 southbound No access from M1 northbound
31	Northbound	No access, exit only (access via Jun.30)
	Southbound	No exit, access only (exit via Jun.30)

M26

Junction with M25 (M25 Jun.5)	Eastbound	No access from M25 clockwise or spur from A21 northbound
	Westbound	No exit to M25 anti-clockwise or spur to A21 southbound
Junction with M20 (M20 Jun.3)	Eastbound	No exit to M20 westbound
	Westbound	No access from M20 eastbound

M27

Junction		
4	Eastbound & Westbound	No exit to A33 southbound (Southampton) No access from A33 northbound
10	Eastbound	No exit, access from A32 only
	Westbound	No access, exit to A32 only

M40

Junction		
3	N.W bound	No access, exit to A40 only
	S.E bound	No exit, access from A40 only
7	N.W bound	No access, exit only
	S.E bound	No exit, access only
13	N.W bound	No access, exit only
	S.E bound	No exit, access only
14	N.W bound	No exit, access only
	S.E bound	No access, exit only
16	N.W bound	No exit, access only
	S.E bound	No access, exit only

M42

Junction		
1	Eastbound	No exit
	Westbound	No access
7	Northbound	No access, exit to M6 only
	Southbound	No exit, access from M6 northbound only
8	Northbound	No exit, access from M6 southbound only
	Southbound	Exit to M6 northbound only Access from M6 southbound only

M45

Junction with M1 (M1 Jun.17)	Eastbound	No exit to M1 northbound
	Westbound	No access from M1 southbound
Junction with A45 east of Dunchurch	Eastbound	No access, exit to A45 only
	Westbound	No exit, access from A45 northbound only

M48

Junction with M4 (M4 Jun.21)	Eastbound	No exit to M4 westbound
	Westbound	No access from M4 eastbound
Junction with M4 (M4 Jun.23)	Eastbound	No access from M4 westbound
	Westbound	No exit to M4 eastbound

M53

Junction		
11	Northbound & Southbound	No access from M56 eastbound, no exit to M56 westbound

M56

Junction		
1	Eastbound	No exit to M60 N.W bound No exit to A34 southbound
	S.E bound	No access from A34 northbound
	Westbound	No access from M60
2	Eastbound	No exit, access from A560 only
	Westbound	No access, exit to A560 only
3	Eastbound	No access, exit only
	Westbound	No exit, access only
4	Eastbound	No exit, access only
	Westbound	No access, exit only
7	Westbound	No access, exit only
8	Eastbound	No access or exit
	Westbound	No exit, access from A556 only
9	Eastbound	No access from M6 northbound
	Westbound	No exit to M60 southbound
10a	Northbound	No exit, access only
	Southbound	No access, exit only
15	Eastbound	No exit to M53
	Westbound	No access from M53

M57

Junction		
3	Northbound	No exit, access only
	Southbound	No access, exit only
5	Northbound	No exit, access from A580 westbound only
	Southbound	No access, exit to A580 eastbound only

M58

Junction		
1	Eastbound	No exit, access from A506 only
	Westbound	No access, exit to A506 only

M60

Junction		
2	N.E bound	No access, exit to A560 only
	S.W bound	No exit, access from A560 only
3	Eastbound	No access from A34 southbound
	Westbound	No exit to A34 northbound
4	Eastbound	No exit to M56 S.W bound No exit to A34 northbound
	Westbound	No access from A34 southbound No access from M56 eastbound
5	N.W bound	No access from or exit to A5103 southbound
	S.E bound	No access from or exit to A5103 northbound
14	Eastbound	No exit to A580 No access from A580 westbound
	Westbound	No exit to A580 eastbound No access from A580
16	Eastbound	No exit, access from A666 only
	Westbound	No access, exit to A666 only
20	Eastbound	No access from A664
	Westbound	No exit to A664
22	Westbound	No access from A62
25	S.W bound	No access from A560 / A6017
26	N.E bound	No access or exit
27	N.E bound	No access, exit only
	S.W bound	No exit, access only

M61

Junction		
2&3	N.W bound	No access from A580 eastbound
	S.E bound	No exit to A580 westbound
Junction with M6 (M6 Jun.30)	N.W bound	No exit to M6 southbound
	S.E bound	No access from M6 northbound

M62

Junction		
23	Eastbound	No access, exit to A640 only
	Westbound	No exit, access from A640 only

M65

Junction		
9	N.E bound	No access, exit to A679 only
	S.W bound	No exit, access from A679 only
11	N.E bound	No exit, access only
	S.W bound	No access, exit only

M66

Junction		
1	Northbound	No access, exit to A56 only
	Southbound	No exit, access from A56 only

M67

Junction		
1	Eastbound	Access from A57 eastbound only
	Westbound	Exit to A57 westbound only
1a	Eastbound	No access, exit to A6017 only
	Westbound	No exit, access from A6017 only
2	Eastbound	No exit, access from A57 only
	Westbound	No access, exit to A57 only

M69

Junction		
2	N.E bound	No exit, access from B4669 only
	S.W bound	No access, exit to B4669 only

M73

Junction		
1	Southbound	No exit to A721 eastbound
2	Northbound	No access from M8 eastbound No exit to A89 eastbound
	Southbound	No exit to M8 westbound No access from A89 westbound
3	Northbound	No exit to A80 S.W bound
	Southbound	No access from A80 N.E bound

M74

Junction		
1	Eastbound	No access from M8 Westbound
	Westbound	No exit to M8 Westbound
3	Eastbound	No exit
	Westbound	No access
7	Northbound	No exit, access from A72 only
	Southbound	No access, exit to A72 only
9	Northbound	No access or exit
	Southbound	No access, exit to B7078 only
10	Southbound	No exit, access from B7078 only
11	Northbound	No exit, access from B7078 only
	Southbound	No access, exit to B7078 only
12	Northbound	No access, exit to A70 only
	Southbound	No exit, access from A70 only

M77

Junction		
Junction with M8 (M8 Jun.22)	Northbound	No exit to M8 westbound
	Southbound	No access from M8 eastbound
4	Northbound	No exit
	Southbound	No access
6	Northbound	No exit to A77
	Southbound	No access from A77
7	Northbound	No access from A77 No exit to A77

M80

Junction		
1	Northbound	No access from M8 westbound
	Southbound	No exit to M8 eastbound
4a	Northbound	No access
	Southbound	No exit
6a	Northbound	No exit
	Southbound	No access
8	Northbound	No access from M876
	Southbound	No exit to M876

M90

Junction		
1	Northbound	No exit
	Southbound	No access from A90
2a	Northbound	No access, exit to A92 only
	Southbound	No exit, access from A92 only
7	Northbound	No exit, access from A91 only
	Southbound	No access, exit to A91 only
8	Northbound	No access, exit to A91 only
	Southbound	No exit, access from A91 only
10	Northbound	No access from A912 Exit to A912 northbound only
	Southbound	No exit to A912 Access from A912 southbound only

M180

Junction		
1	Eastbound	No access, exit only
	Westbound	No exit, access from A18 only

M606

Junction		
2	Northbound	No access, exit only

M621

Junction		
2a	Eastbound	No exit, access only
	Westbound	No access, exit only
4	Southbound	No exit
5	Northbound	No access, exit to A61 only
	Southbound	No exit, access from A61 only
6	Northbound	No exit, access only
	Southbound	No access, exit only
7	Eastbound	No access, exit only
	Westbound	No exit, access only
8	Northbound	No access, exit only
	Southbound	No exit, access only

M876

Junction		
Junction with M80 (M80 Jun.5)	N.E bound	No access from M80 southbound
	S.W bound	No exit to M80 northbound
Junction with M9 (M9 Jun.8)	N.E bound	No exit to M9 northbound
	S.W bound	No access from M9 southbound

A1(M)

Junction		
Hertfordshire Section		
2	Northbound	No access, exit only
	Southbound	No exit, access from A1001 only
3	Southbound	No access, exit only
5	Northbound	No exit, access only
	Southbound	No access or exit
Cambridgeshire Section		
14	Northbound	No exit, access only
	Southbound	No access, exit only
Leeds Section		
40	Southbound	Exit to A1 southbound only
43	Northbound	Access from M1 eastbound only
	Southbound	Exit to M1 westbound only
Durham Section		
57	Northbound	No access, exit to A66(M) only
	Southbound	No exit, access from A66(M)
65	Northbound	Exit to A1 N.W bound and to A194(M) only
	Southbound	Access from A1 S.E bound and from A194(M) only

A3(M)

Junction		
4	Northbound	No access, exit only
	Southbound	No exit, access only

Aston Expressway A38(M)

Junction with Victoria Road, Aston	Northbound	No exit, access only
	Southbound	No access, exit only

A48(M)

Junction		
Junction with M4 (M4 Jun.29)	N.E bound	Exit to M4 eastbound only
	S.W bound	Access from M4 westbound only
29a	N.E bound	Access from A48 eastbound only
	S.W bound	Exit to A48 westbound only

Mancunian Way A57(M)

Junction with A34 Brook Street, Manchester	Eastbound	No access, exit to A34 Brook Street, southbound only
	Westbound	No exit, access only

Leeds Inner Ring Road A58(M)

Junction with Park Lane / Westgate	Southbound	No access, exit only

Leeds Inner Ring Road A64(M) (continuation of A58(M))

Junction with A58 Clay Pit Lane	Eastbound	No access
	Westbound	No exit

A66(M)

Junction with A1(M) (A1(M) Jun.57)	N.E bound	Access from A1(M) northbound only
	S.W bound	Exit to A1(M) southbound only

A74(M)

Junction		
18	Northbound	No access
	Southbound	No exit

Newcastle Central Motorway A167(M)

Junction with Camden Street	Northbound	No exit, access only
	Southbound	No access or exit

A194(M)

Junction with A1(M) (A1(M) Jun. 65) and A1 Gateshead Western By-Pass	Northbound	Access from A1(M) only
	Southbound	Exit to A1(M) only

Northern Ireland

M1

Junction		
3	Northbound	No exit, access only
	Southbound	No access, exit only
7	Westbound	No access, exit only

M2

Junction		
2	Eastbound	No access to M5 northbound
	Westbound	No exit to M5 southbound

M5

Junction		
2	Northbound	No access from M2 eastbound
	Southbound	No exit to M2 westbound

Motorway
Autoroute
Autobahn
M1

Motorway Under Construction
Autoroute en construction
Autobahn im Bau

Motorway Proposed
Autoroute prévue
Geplante Autobahn

Motorway Junctions with Numbers
Unlimited Interchange **4**
Limited Interchange **5**
Autoroute échangeur numéroté
Echangeur complet
Echangeur partiel
Autobahnanschlußstelle mit Nummer
Unbeschränkter Fahrtrichtungswechsel
Beschränkter Fahrtrichtungswechsel

Motorway Service Area (with fuel station)
with access from one carriageway only
Aire de services d'autoroute (avec station service)
accessible d'un seul côté
Rastplatz oder Raststätte (mit tankstelle)
Einbahn

Major Road Service Area (with fuel station) with 24 hour facilities
Primary Route **S**   Class A Road **S**
Aire de services sur route prioritaire (avec station service) Ouverte 24h sur 24
Route à grande circulation   Route de type A
Raststätte (mit tankstelle) Durchgehend geöffnet
Hauptverkehrsstraße   A- Straße

Major Road Junctions   Detailed **4**
Jonctions grands routiers   Détaillé
Hauptverkehrsstraße Kreuzungen   Ausführlich
    Other   Autre   Andere

Truckstop (selection of) **T**
Sélection d'aire pour poids lourds
Auswahl von Fernfahrerrastplatz

Primary Route **A41**
Route à grande circulation
Hauptverkehrsstraße

Primary Route Junction with Number **5**
Echangeur numéroté
Hauptverkehrsstraßenkreuzung mit Nummer

Primary Route Destination **DOVER**
Route prioritaire, direction
Hauptverkehrsstraße Richtung

Dual Carriageways (A & B roads)
Route à double chaussées séparées (route A & B)
Zweispurige Schnellstraße (A- und B- Straßen)

Class A Road **A129**
Route de type A
A-Straße

Class B Road **B177**
Route de type B
B-Straße

Narrow Major Road (passing places)
Route prioritaire étroite (possibilité de dépassement)
Schmale Hauptverkehrsstraße (mit Überholmöglichkeit)

Major Roads Under Construction
Route prioritaire en construction
Hauptverkehrsstraße im Bau

Major Roads Proposed
Route prioritaire prévue
Geplante Hauptverkehrsstraße

Gradient 1:7 (14%) **& steeper** »»
(descent in direction of arrow)
Pente égale ou supérieure à 14% (dans le sens de la descente)
14% Steigung und steiler (in Pfeilrichtung)

Toll *Toll*
Barrière de péage
Gebührenpflichtig

Dart Charge **C**
www.gov.uk/pay-dartford-crossing-charge

Park & Ride **P+R**
Parking avec Service Navette
Parken und Reisen

Mileage between markers 8
Distence en miles entre les flèches
Strecke zwischen Markierungen in Meilen

Airport ⊕
Aéroport
Flughafen

Airfield +
Terrain d'aviation
Flugplatz

Heliport Ⓗ
Héliport
Hubschrauberlandeplatz

Ferry   Bac   Fähre
(vehicular, sea)   (véhicules, mer)   (auto, meer)
(vehicular, river)   (véhicules, rivière)   (auto, fluß)
(foot only)   (piétons)   (nur für Personen)

Railway and Station
Voie ferrée et gare
Eisenbahnlinie und Bahnhof

Level Crossing and Tunnel
Passage à niveau et tunnel
Bahnübergang und Tunnel

River or Canal
Rivière ou canal
Fluß oder Kanal

County or Unitary Authority Boundary
Limite de comté ou de division administrative
Grafschafts- oder Verwaltungsbezirksgrenze

National Boundary
Frontière nationale
Landesgrenze

Built-up Area
Agglomération
Geschloßene Ortschaft

Town, Village or Hamlet
Ville, Village ou hameau
Stadt, Dorf oder Weiler

Wooded Area
Zone boisée
Waldgebiet

Spot Height in Feet · 813
Altitude (en pieds)
Höhe in Fuß

Relief above 400' (122m)
Relief par estompage au-dessus de 400' (122m)
Reliefschattierung über 400' (122m)

National Grid Reference (kilometres) ¹00
Coordonnées géographiques nationales (Kilomètres)
Nationale geographische Koordinaten (Kilometer)

Page Continuation
Suite à la page indiquée **48**
Seitenfortsetzung

---

i

Tourist Information

Information
Touristeninformationen

Abbey, Church, Friary, Priory +
Abbaye, église, monastère, prieuré
Abtei, Kirche, Mönchskloster, Kloster

Animal Collection
Ménagerie
Tiersammlung

Aquarium
Aquarium
Aquarium

Arboretum, Botanical Garden
Jardin Botanique
Botanischer Garten

Aviary, Bird Garden
Volière
Voliere

Battle Site and Date
Champ de bataille et date *1066*
Schlachtfeld und Datum

Blue Flag Beach
Plage Pavillon Bleu
Blaue Flagge Strand

Bridge
Pont
Brücke

Butterfly Farm
Ferme aux Papillons
Schmetterlingsfarm

Castle (open to public)
Château (ouvert au public)
Schloß / Burg (für die Öffentlichkeit zugänglich)

Castle with Garden (open to public)
Château avec parc (ouvert au public)
Schloß mit Garten (für die Öffentlichkeit zugänglich)

Cathedral ✝
Cathédrale
Kathedrale

Cidermaker
Cidrerie (fabrication)
Apfelwein Hersteller

Country Park
Parc régional
Landschaftspark

Distillery
Distillerie
Brennerei

Farm Park, Open Farm
Park Animalier
Bauernhof Park

Fortress, Hill Fort ※
Château Fort
Festung

Garden (open to public)
Jardin (ouvert au public)
Garten (für die Öffentlichkeit zugänglich)

Historic Building (open to public)
Monument historique (ouvert au public)
Historisches Gebäude (für die Öffentlichkeit zugänglich)

Historic Building with Garden (open to public)
Monument historique avec jardin (ouvert au public)
Historisches Gebäude mit Garten (für die Öffentlichkeit zugänglich)

Horse Racecourse
Hippodrome
Pferderennbahn

Industrial Monument ☼
Monument Industrielle
Industriedenkmal

Leisure Park, Leisure Pool
Parc d'Attraction, Loisirs Piscine
Freizeitpark, Freizeit pool

Lighthouse
Phare
Leuchtturm

Mine, Cave
Mine, Grotte
Bergwerk, Höhle

Monument
Monument
Denkmal

Motor Racing Circuit
Circuit Automobile
Automobilrennbahn

Museum, Art Gallery Ⓜ
Musée
Museum, Galerie

National Park
Parc national
Nationalpark

National Trail
Sentier national
Nationaler weg

National Trust Property
National Trust Property
National Trust- Eigentum

Natural Attraction ★
Attraction Naturelle
Natürliche Anziehung

Place of Interest *Craft Centre* •
Site, curiosité
Sehenswürdigkeit

Prehistoric Monument
Monument Préhistorique
Prähistorisches Denkmal

Railway, Steam or Narrow Gauge
Chemin de fer, à vapeur ou à voie étroite
Eisenbahn, Dampf- oder Schmalspurbahn

Roman Remains
Vestiges Romains
Römischen Ruinen

Theme Park
Centre de loisirs
Vergnügungspark

Tourist Information Centre
Office de Tourisme
Touristeninformationen

Viewpoint   (360 degrees)
Vue panoramique   (360 degrés)
Aussichtspunkt   (360 Grade)
    (180 degrees)
    (180 degrés)
    (180 Grade)

Vineyard
Vignoble
Weinberg

Visitor Information Centre **V**
Centre d'information touristique
Besucherzentrum

Wildlife Park
Réserve de faune
Wildpark

Windmill
Moulin à vent
Windmühle

Zoo or Safari Park
Parc ou réserve zoologique
Zoo oder Safari-Park

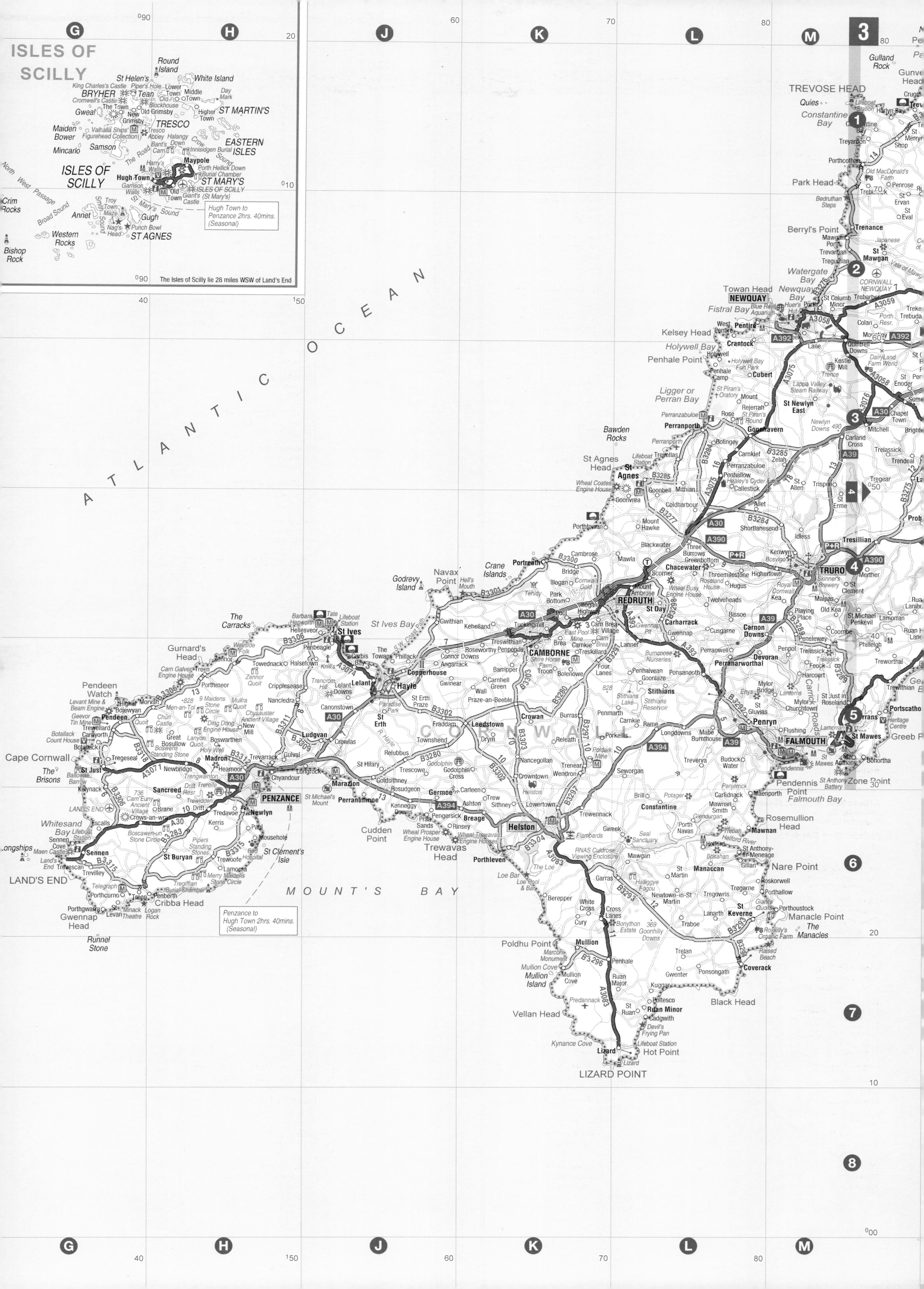

3
ISLES OF SCILLY
Round Island
St Helen's
White Island
BRYHER
Tean
ST MARTIN'S
TRESCO
EASTERN ISLES
Samson
Maiden Bower
Mincarlo
Gweal
ISLES OF SCILLY
Maypole
Hugh Town
ST MARY'S
Crim Rocks
Annet
Gugh
ST AGNES
Western Rocks
Bishop Rock
Hugh Town to Penzance 2hrs. 40mins. (Seasonal)
The Isles of Scilly lie 28 miles WSW of Land's End
ATLANTIC OCEAN
TREVOSE HEAD
Constantine Bay
Park Head
Berryl's Point
Trenance
St Mawgan
Watergate Bay
Towan Head
NEWQUAY
Newquay Bay
Fistral Bay
Pentire
Crantock
Kelsey Head
Holywell Bay
Penhale Point
Cubert
Ligger or Perran Bay
Perranporth
Goonhavern
St Newlyn East
Mitchell
Bawden Rocks
St Agnes Head
St Agnes
Porthtowan
Chacewater
TRURO
Tresillian
Godrevy Island
Navax Point
Crane Islands
Portreath
REDRUTH
St Day
CAMBORNE
The Carracks
St Ives Bay
St Ives
Lelant
Hayle
Copperhouse
Gurnard's Head
Zennor
Pendeen Watch
Pendeen
Cape Cornwall
St Just
The Brisons
Madron
PENZANCE
Newlyn
Marazion
Sancreed
St Buryan
Sennen
Whitesand Bay
Longships
LAND'S END
Gwennap Head
Runnel Stone
Cribba Head
St Clement's Isle
MOUNT'S BAY
Penzance to Hugh Town 2hrs. 40mins. (Seasonal)
Cudden Point
Trewavas Head
Porthleven
Breage
Germoe
Helston
CORNWALL
Crowan
Leedstown
Stithians
Carharrack
Penryn
FALMOUTH
St Mawes
Zone Point
Pendennis Point
Falmouth Bay
Rosemullion Head
Nare Point
Manaccan
St Keverne
Manacle Point
The Manacles
Coverack
Black Head
Mullion
Poldhu Point
Mullion Island
Vellan Head
Kynance Cove
Lizard
Hot Point
LIZARD POINT
Constantine
Mawnan
Gweek
G
H
J
K
L
M
40
50
60
70
80

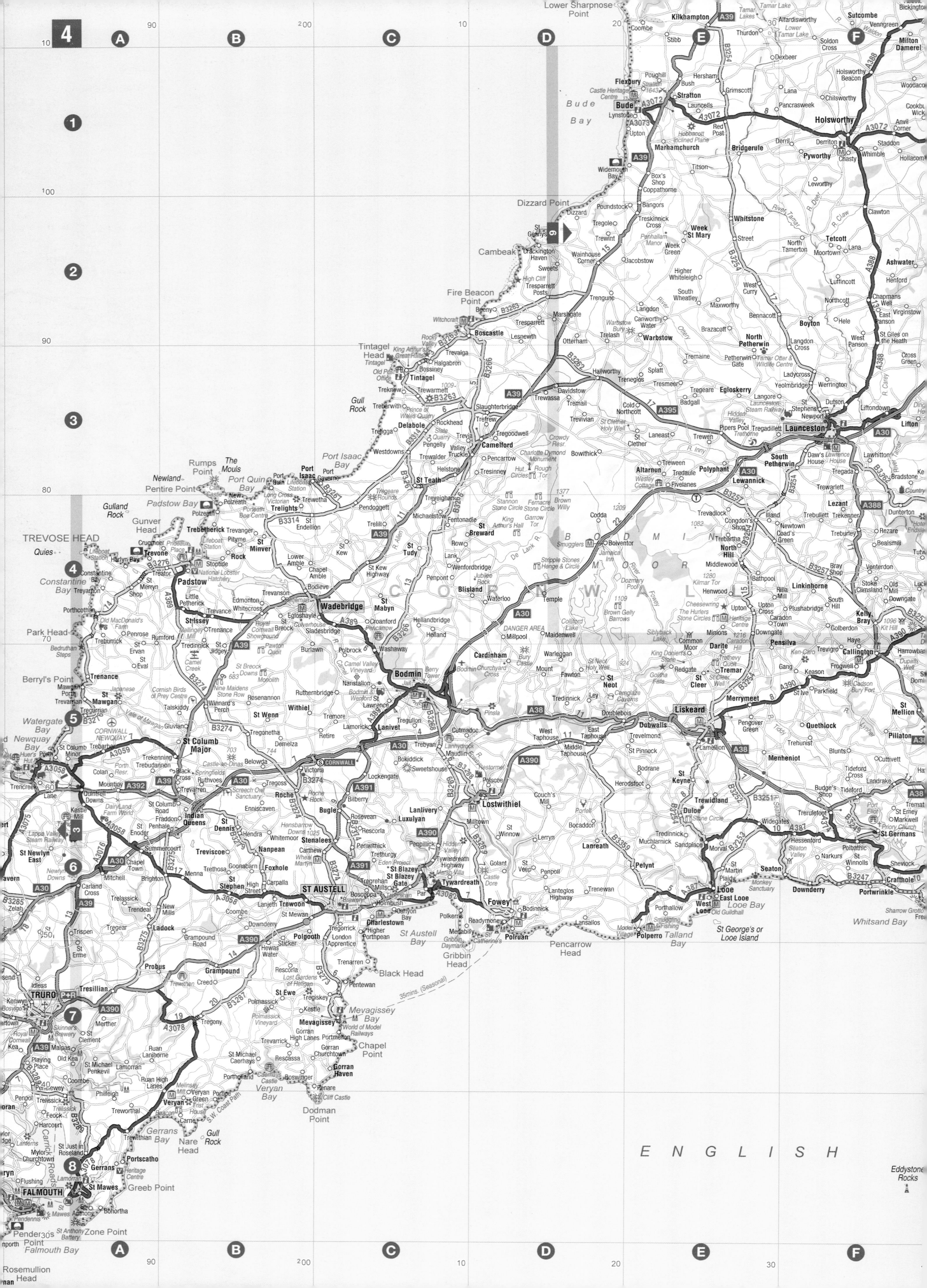
A
B
C
D
E
F
1
2
3
4
5
6
7
8
90
200
10
20
30
100
80
70
Lower Sharpnose Point
Kilkhampton
Tamar Lakes
Alfardisworthy
Sutcombe
Venngreen
Bickington
Coombe
Stibb
Thurdon
Lower Tamar Lake
Soldon Cross
Milton Damerel
Dexbeer
Poughill
Hersham
Flexbury
Bush
Stratton
Grimscott
Lana
Holsworthy Beacon
Woodacott
Bude
Launcells
Pancrasweek
Chilsworthy
Lynstone
Bude Bay
Holsworthy
Anvil Corner
Hobbacott Inclined Plane
Red Post
Upton
Derril
Derriton
Staddon
Marhamchurch
Bridgerule
Pyworthy
Chasty
Whimble
Hollacombe
Widemouth Bay
Titson
Box's Shop
Coppathorne
Leworthy
Dizzard Point
Dizzard
Poundstock
Bangors
Trегole
Treskinnick Cross
Whitstone
Clawton
St Gennys
Week St Mary
Cambeak
Crackington Haven
Wainhouse Corner
Jacobstow
Street
Tetcott
North Tamerton
Mortown
Lana
Ashwater
Sweets
Higher Whiteleigh
Luffincott
Henford
Fire Beacon Point
Trengune
South Wheatley
Trесparrett Posts
Northcott
Chapmans Well
Virginstow
Boscastle
Marshgate
Maxworthy
Bennacott
Boyton
Hele
Canworthy Water
Warbstow
Brazacott
East Panson
Tintagel Head
Tintagel
Trevalga
Lesnewth
Otterham
Treiash
North Petherwin
Langdon Cross
West Panson
St Giles on the Heath
Halgabron
Bossiney
Cross Green
Hallworthy
Splatt
Tremaine
Petherwin Gate
Ladycross
Trewarmett
Davidstow
Trenegios
Tresmeer
Tregeare
Egloskerry
Yeolmbridge
Werrington
Gull Rock
Trebarwith
Slaughterbridge
Trewassa
Tremail
Cold Northcott
Badgall
Langore
Launceston Steam Railway
St Stephens
Newport
Dutson
Liftondown
Lifton
Delabole
Rockhead
Trefrew
Trevivian
St Clether Holy Well
Hidden Valley
Pipers Pool
Tregadillett
Launceston
Trebarwith
Trevia
Tregoodwell
Crowdy Resr
Laneast
Trewen
Port Isaac Bay
Westdowns
Trewalder
Valley Truckle
Camelford
St Clether
Lawhitton
Pengelly
Charlotte Dymond Monument
Bowithick
South Petherwin
Daw's House
Tregadan
Rumps Point
The Mouls
Port Isaac
Port Gaverne
Helstone
Pencarrow
Rough Tor
Treween
Altarnun
Tredaule
Polyphant
Lewannick
Bradstone
Newland
Port Quin
Port Quin Bay
Pentire Point
Trewetha
St Teath
Tresinney
Fivelanes
Trewarlett
Padstow Bay
New Polzeath
Polzeath
Trelights
Pendoggett
Treveighan
Stannon Stone Circle
Fernacre Stone Circle
Brown Willy
Trevadlock
Congdon's Shop
Lezant
Gulland Rock
Trebetherick
St Endellion
Michaelstow
Fentonadle
King Arthur's Hall
Garrow Tor
Codda
Illand
Trebullett
Trekenner
Dunterton
Gunver Head
Trevanger
Pityme
St Minver
Trelill
St Breward
Newtown
Coad's Green
Treburley
Trevose Head
Quies
Trevone
Rock
St Kew
Row
Smugglers
Bolventor
Trebartha
Rezare
Constantine Bay
Harlyn Bay
Treator
Stoptide
Lower Amble
Chapel Amble
St Tudy
Lank
Jamaica Inn
North Hill
Bealsmill
Padstow
St Merryn
Shop
St Kew Highway
Wenfordbridge
Stripple Stones Henge & Circle
Middlewood
Bray Shop
Venterdon
Treyarnon
Little Petherick
Edmonton
Whitecross
Trevanson
Wadebridge
Penpont
Blisland
Dozmary Pool
Kilmar Tor
Bathpool
Linkinhorne
Stoke Climsland
Old Mill
Downgate
Porthcothan
Trevance
St Mabyn
Waterloo
Temple
Henwood
Rilla Mill
South Hill
Egloshayle
Croanford
Cheesewring
Upton Cross
Plushabridge
Kelly Bray
Park Head
Penrose
St Issey
Trenance
Rumford
Royal Cornwall Showground
St Breock
Sladesbridge
Helland
Hellandbridge
Brown Gelly Barrows
Colliford Lake
The Hurlers Stone Circles
Caradon Town
Golberdon
Kit Hill
Treburrick
St Ervan
Tredinnick
St Jidgey
Burlawn
Polbrock
Washaway
DANGER AREA
Millpool
Maidenwell
Siblyback Lake
Minions
Common Moor
Darite
Caradon Hill
Pensilva
Haye
Callington
Harrowbarrow
Bedruthan Steps
St Eval
Pawton Quoit
Camel Creek
Camel Valley Vineyard
Cardinham
Bury Castle
Warleggan
St Neot Holy Well
Trevigro
Berryl's Point
Trenance
St Breock Downs
Monolith
Bodmin
Berry Tower
Bodmin Churchyard Cross
Mount
Fawton
St Neot
Redgate
Tremar
St Cleer
Golitha Falls
Kearson
Frogwell
Dupath Well
Mawgan Porth
St Mawgan
Trevarrian
Cornish Birds of Prey Centre
Nine Maidens Stone Row
Rosenannon
Nanstallion
Rutherbridge
Withiel
Tredinnick
Ley
Canglaze Caverns
Merrymeet
St Ive
Parkfield
Cadson Bury Fort
Tregurrian
Watergate Bay
Talskiddy
Winnard's Perch
St Wenn
Lanivet
Tregullon
Pinsla
Doublebois
Liskeard
Pengover Green
Quethiock
St Mellion
Newquay Bay
Tremore
Lamorick
Cutmadoc
West Taphouse
East Taphouse
Dobwalls
Trehunist
Pillaton
Cornwall Newquay
Gluvian
Tregonetha
Retire
Trebyan
Lanhydrock House
Maudlin
Middle Taphouse
Trevelmond
Blunts
St Columb Minor
Trebarber
St Columb Major
Demelza
Lamellion
Menheniot
Cuttivett
Trekenning
Trebudannon
Castle-an-Dinas
Belowda
Victoria
Bokiddick
Sweetshouse
St Pinnock
Tideford Cross
Landrake
Colan
Porth Resr
Black Cross
Springfields
Ruthvoes
Lockengate
Restormel
Bodrane
Trencreek
Mountjoy
Trevarren
Tregoss
Roche
Roche Rock
Polscoe
Herodsfoot
St Keyne
Tideford
Budge's Shop
Quintrell Downs
Dairyland Farm World
Screech Owl Sanctuary
Enniscaven
Bilberry
Lostwithiel
Couch's Mill
Trewidland
Trerulefoot
St Germans
Port Eliot
St Erney
Kestle Mill
St Columb Road
Indian Queens
St Dennis
Bugle
Lanlivery
Duloe
Stone Circle
Markwell
Fraddon
St Enoder
Penhale
Hendra
Whitemoor
Luxulyan
Rosevean
Milltown
Tredinnick
Widegates
Hessenford
Lappa Valley Steam Railway
Hensbarrow Downs
Stenalees
Rescorla
St Winnow
Bocaddon
Lerryn
Muchlarnick
Sandplace
St Newlyn East
Summercourt
Treviscoe
Nanpean
Penwithick
Hidden Valley
Tywardreath Highway
Lanreath
Morval
Seaton Valley
Narkurs
Polbathic
St Winnolls
Sheviock
Chapel Town
Trethosa
Carthew
Wheal Martyn
Trethurgy
St Blazey
Golant
Pelynt
St Martin
Plaidy
Seaton
Menna
Goonabarn
Foxhole
St Blazey Gate
Marsh Villa
Tywardreath
St Veep
Penpoll
Monkey Sanctuary
Downderry
Crafthole
Mitchell
Brighton
Carpalla
Tregrehan Mills
Castle Dore
Lanteglos Highway
Trenewan
Looe
East Looe
Portwrinkle
Carland Cross
St Stephen
High Street
Eden Project
Par
Fowey
West Looe
Looe Bay
Trelassick
New Mills
St Austell
Boscoppa
Bodinnick
Porthallow
Old Guildhall
Sharrow Grotto
Zelah
Trendeal
Lanjeth
Trewoon
Holmbush
Charlestown
Polkerris
Readymoney
Lansallos
Smuggling & Fishing
Whitsand Bay
Coombe
St Mewan
Duporth
Menabilly
Polruan
Model Village
Polperro
Talland Bay
St George's or Looe Island
Trispen
Tregear
Ladock
Downderry
Tregorrick
Higher Porthpean
St Austell Bay
Gribbin Daymark
St Catherine's Castle
Pencarrow Head
Grampound Road
Polgooth
London Apprentice
Gribbin Head
St Erme
Hewas Water
Sticker
Probus
Grampound
Trenarren
Idless
Trewithen
Creed
Rescorla
Lost Gardens of Heligan
Black Head
Tresillian
Pentewan
Truro
Kenwyn
Merther
B3287
Polmassick
St Ewe
Tregiskey
35mins. (Seasonal)
Tregony
Polmassick Vineyard
Kestle
Mevagissey
Mevagissey Bay
World of Model Railways
Skinner's Brewery
St Clement
Royal Cornwall
Malpas
Gorran High Lanes
Portmellon
Trevarrick
Gorran Churchtown
Chapel Point
Ruan Lanihorne
Kea
Old Kea
Playing Place
St Michael Penkevil
Lamorran
St Michael Caerhays
Rescassa
Gorran Haven
Ruan High Lanes
Porthalland
Caerhays Castle
Boswinger
Penare
Cliff Castle
Pengelly
Coombe
Philleigh
Melinsey Mill
Veryan
Veryan Green
Portloe
Veryan Bay
Dodman Point
Penpol
Trelissick
Treworthal
Trist House
Feock
Carne
S.W. Coast Path
Harcourt
Gerrans Bay
Nare Head
Gull Rock
Carrick Roads
Trewithian
Mylor Churchtown
St Just in Roseland
Portscatho
Flushing
Gerrans
Heritage Centre
Falmouth
Lamorran
St Mawes
Greeb Point
Pendennis
St Anthony
Bohortha
Pendennis Point
St Anthony Battery
Zone Point
Falmouth Bay
Rosemullion Head
ENGLISH
Eddystone Rocks
C O R N W A L L
B O D M I N
M O O R
A39
A3072
A3073
B3254
A388
B3263
B3266
B3262
B3314
B3267
B3276
B3274
A389
A395
A30
B3257
A390
A38
B3268
B3269
B3359
B3252
B3253
A387
B3251
B3247
A3059
A3058
A392
A3075
A3076
A391
B3273
B3275
B3287
A3078
B3289
A3082
B3285
B3249
B3254

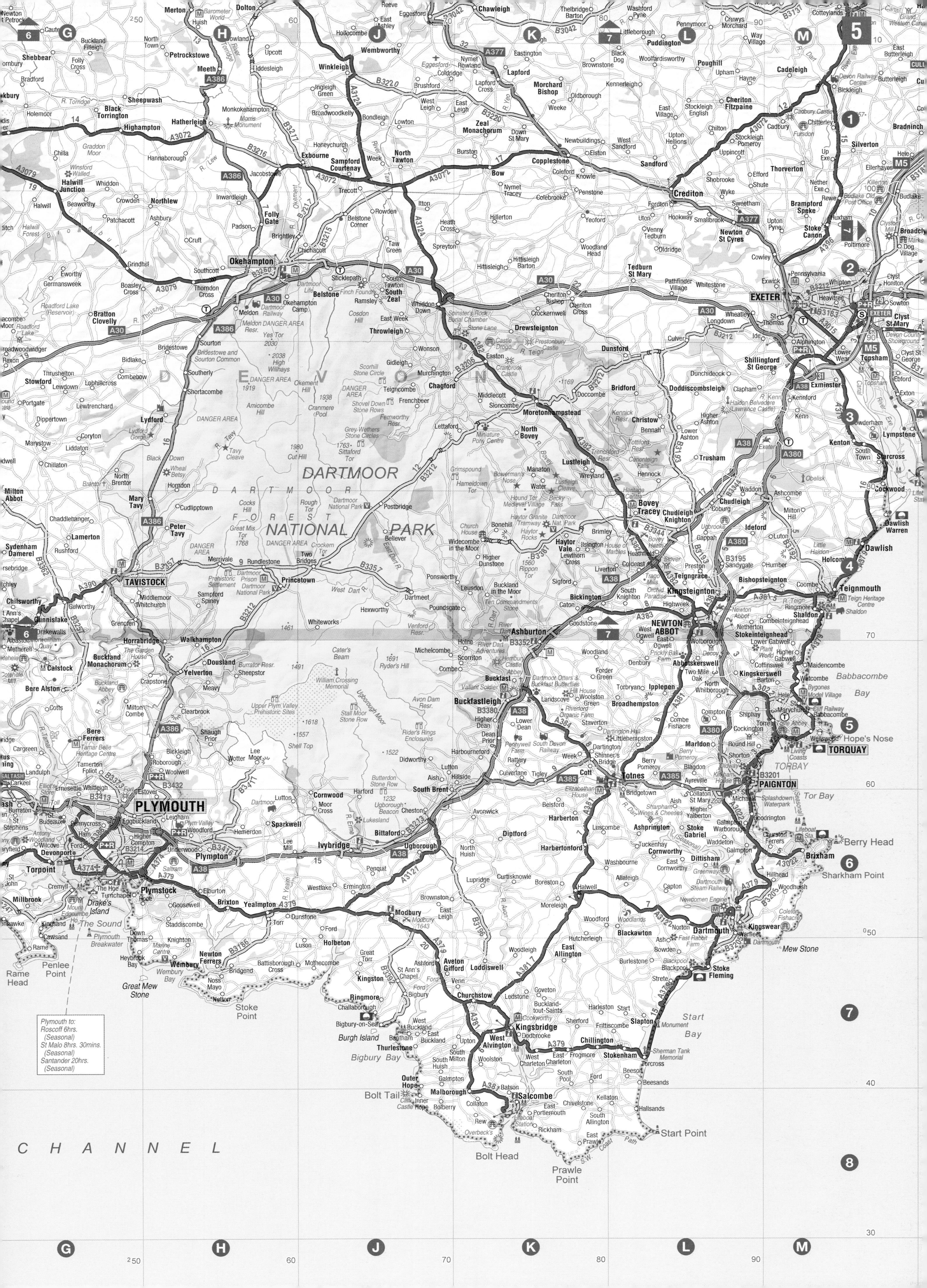
5
G
H
J
K
L
M
Merton
Dolton
Chawleigh
Eggesford
Wembworthy
Winkleigh
Shebbear
Petrockstowe
Meeth
Black Torrington
Highampton
Hatherleigh
Sheepwash
Halwill Junction
Northlew
Exbourne
Sampford Courtenay
North Tawton
Bow
Zeal Monachorum
Lapford
Morchard Bishop
Puddington
Poughill
Cadeleigh
Cheriton Fitzpaine
Silverton
Bradninch
Copplestone
Crediton
Sandford
Thorverton
Brampford Speke
Stoke Canon
Newton St Cyres
Tedburn St Mary
Okehampton
Belstone
South Zeal
Sticklepath
Meldon
Bratton Clovelly
Folly Gate
EXETER
Topsham
Clyst St Mary
Shillingford St George
Exminster
Kenton
Starcross
Lympstone
Cockwood
Dawlish Warren
Dawlish
Teignmouth
Shaldon
Drewsteignton
Dunsford
Chagford
Moretonhampstead
Bridford
Christow
Doddiscombsleigh
Trusham
North Bovey
Lustleigh
Manaton
Bovey Tracey
Chudleigh
Chudleigh Knighton
Ideford
Haytor Vale
Ilsington
Kingsteignton
Teigngrace
Bishopsteignton
NEWTON ABBOT
Kingskerswell
Ipplepen
Abbotskerswell
DARTMOOR
DARTMOOR FOREST
DARTMOOR NATIONAL PARK
DEVON
Lydford
Mary Tavy
Peter Tavy
Horndon
Lamerton
TAVISTOCK
Princetown
Two Bridges
Postbridge
Widecombe in the Moor
Ashburton
Buckfast
Buckfastleigh
Yelverton
Horrabridge
Walkhampton
Dousland
Buckland Monachorum
Bere Alston
Bere Ferrers
Calstock
Gunnislake
PLYMOUTH
Plympton
Plymstock
Devonport
Torpoint
Saltash
Ivybridge
Ugborough
Bittaford
South Brent
Cornwood
Sparkwell
Yealmpton
Brixton
Wembury
Newton Ferrers
Modbury
Aveton Gifford
Loddiswell
Kingsbridge
West Alvington
Salcombe
Malborough
Thurlestone
Kingston
Ringmore
Bigbury-on-Sea
Burgh Island
Bigbury Bay
Bolt Tail
Bolt Head
Prawle Point
Start Point
Start Bay
Stokenham
Chillington
Slapton
Stoke Fleming
Dartmouth
Kingswear
Blackawton
East Allington
Halwell
Dittisham
Cornworthy
Ashprington
Harbertonford
Harberton
Diptford
Totnes
Dartington
Staverton
Marldon
Berry Pomeroy
Broadhempston
PAIGNTON
TORQUAY
TORBAY
Tor Bay
Brixham
Berry Head
Sharkham Point
Hope's Nose
Babbacombe Bay
Mew Stone
Rame Head
Penlee Point
Great Mew Stone
Stoke Point
The Sound
Drake's Island
CHANNEL
Plymouth to:
Roscoff 6hrs. (Seasonal)
St Malo 8hrs. 30mins. (Seasonal)
Santander 20hrs. (Seasonal)
A30
A38
A380
A381
A382
A385
A386
A3072
A377
A379
A384
A390
A3079
A3122
B3212
B3357
B3344
B3352
M5
50
60
70
80
90
40
30
1
2
3
4
6
7
8

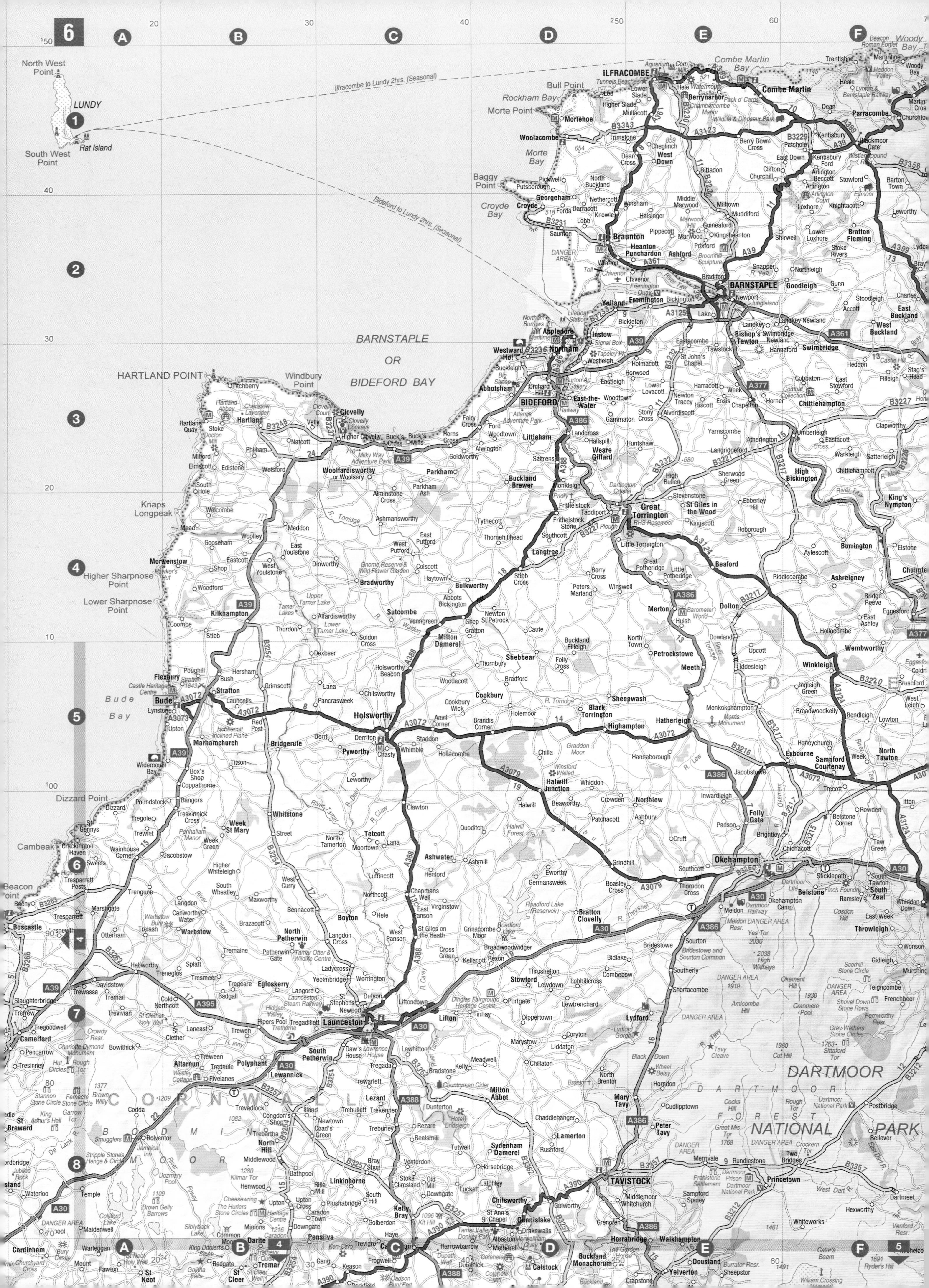
6
A
B
C
D
E
F
North West Point
LUNDY
Rat Island
South West Point
Ilfracombe to Lundy 2hrs. (Seasonal)
Bideford to Lundy 2hrs. (Seasonal)
ILFRACOMBE
Combe Martin Bay
Combe Martin
Bull Point
Rockham Bay
Morte Point
Mortehoe
Woolacombe
Morte Bay
Baggy Point
Croyde Bay
Croyde
Georgeham
Braunton
West Down
Berrynarbor
Parracombe
Blackmoor Gate
BARNSTAPLE
Fremington
Instow
Appledore
Northam
Westward Ho!
BIDEFORD
BARNSTAPLE OR BIDEFORD BAY
HARTLAND POINT
Windbury Point
Hartland
Hartland Quay
Clovelly
Woolfardisworthy or Woolsery
Abbotsham
Littleham
Parkham
Buckland Brewer
Great Torrington
Chittlehampton
High Bickington
King's Nympton
Swimbridge
Bishop's Tawton
Knaps Longpeak
Morwenstow
Higher Sharpnose Point
Lower Sharpnose Point
Kilkhampton
Bradworthy
Sutcombe
Milton Damerel
Shebbear
Langtree
Beaford
Merton
Dolton
Winkleigh
Burrington
Ashreigney
Flexbury
Bude
Bude Bay
Stratton
Holsworthy
Black Torrington
Highampton
Hatherleigh
Sampford Courtenay
North Tawton
Widemouth Bay
Marhamchurch
Bridgerule
Pyworthy
Halwill Junction
Northlew
Dizzard Point
Week St Mary
Whitstone
Cambeak
Crackington Haven
Ashwater
Okehampton
Belstone
South Zeal
Folly Gate
Beacon Point
Boscastle
Warbstow
North Petherwin
Boyton
Bratton Clovelly
Bridestowe
Camelford
Launceston
Egloskerry
Lifton
Lydford
Altarnun
Polyphant
Lewannick
South Petherwin
Lezant
Milton Abbot
Mary Tavy
Peter Tavy
CORNWALL
BODMIN MOOR
DARTMOOR
DARTMOOR FOREST
NATIONAL PARK
St Breward
Temple
North Hill
Linkinhorne
Kelly Bray
Callington
Gunnislake
Chilsworthy
Calstock
Sydenham Damerel
Lamerton
TAVISTOCK
Princetown
Two Bridges
Horrabridge
Walkhampton
Yelverton
Dousland
Buckland Monachorum
Cardinham
Pensilva
Darite
Tremar
St Cleer
St Neot
Mount
A39
A361
A386
A388
A3072
A3079
A30
A377
A395
A390
B3254
B3257
B3357
5
4

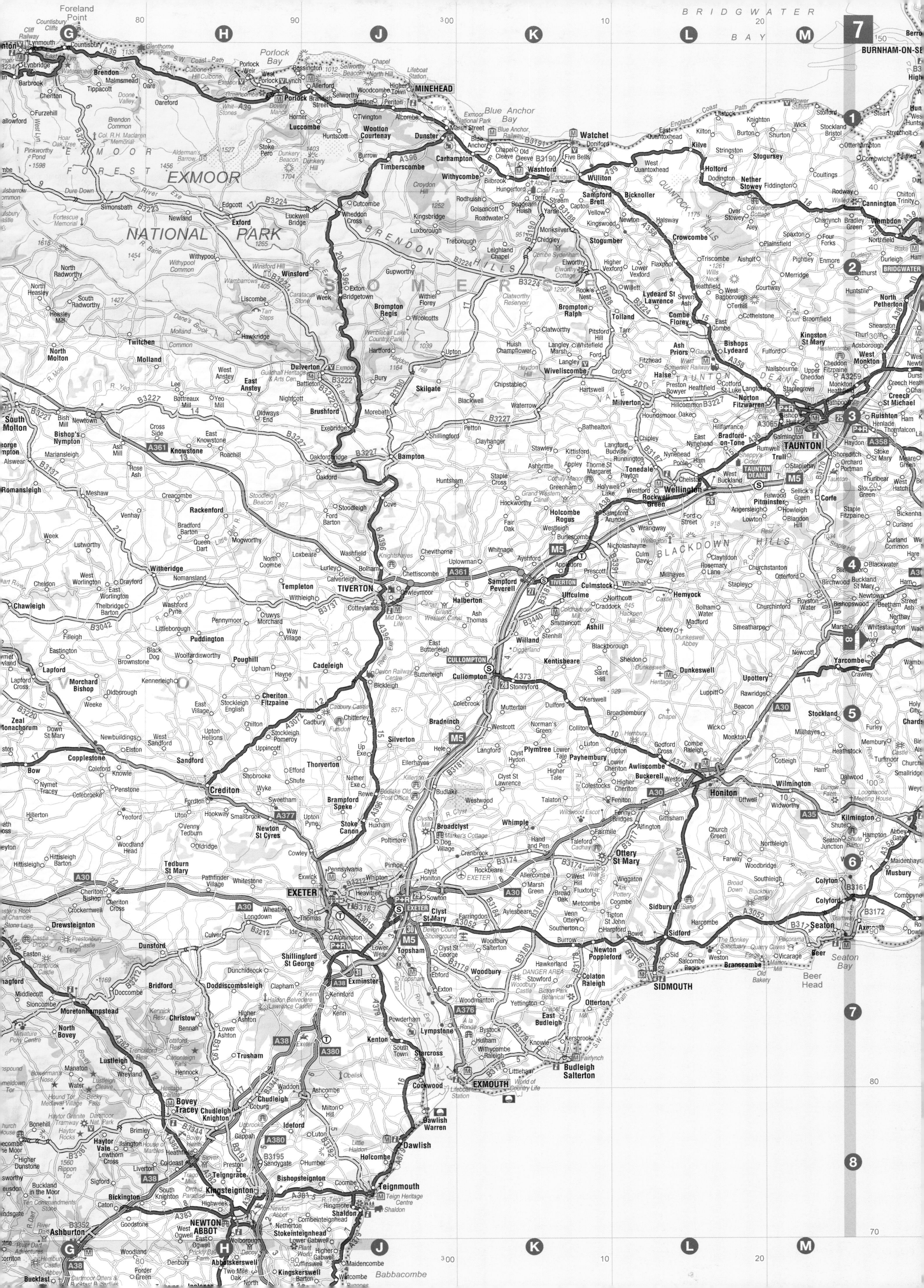
BRIDGWATER BAY
Foreland Point
EXMOOR
NATIONAL PARK
EXMOOR FOREST
BRENDON HILLS
QUANTOCK HILLS
BLACKDOWN HILLS
VALE OF TAUNTON DEANE
SOMERSET
DEVON
MINEHEAD
Porlock
Porlock Bay
Dunster
Watchet
Blue Anchor Bay
Williton
Carhampton
Washford
Wootton Courtenay
Luccombe
Timberscombe
Exford
Simonsbath
Winsford
Withypool
Dulverton
Exebridge
Bampton
Wiveliscombe
Milverton
Bishops Lydeard
Crowcombe
Stogumber
Nether Stowey
Stogursey
Kilve
Cannington
BURNHAM-ON-SEA
North Petherton
TAUNTON
Wellington
Wellington Monument
Rockwell Green
Sampford Arundel
Sampford Peverell
Halberton
TIVERTON
Uffculme
Culmstock
Hemyock
Cullompton
Bradninch
Silverton
Thorverton
Crediton
Copplestone
Morchard Bishop
Witheridge
Rackenford
Knowstone
Bishop's Nympton
South Molton
Molland
Twitchen
North Molton
Chulmleigh
Chawleigh
Lapford
Cheriton Fitzpaine
Stoke Canon
Broadclyst
Whimple
Ottery St Mary
Honiton
Awliscombe
Dunkeswell
Upottery
Yarcombe
Stockland
Wilmington
Kilmington
Axminster
Colyton
Colyford
Seaton
Seaton Bay
Beer
Beer Head
Branscombe
Sidford
Sidbury
SIDMOUTH
Otterton
East Budleigh
Budleigh Salterton
EXMOUTH
Lympstone
Topsham
Clyst St Mary
Woodbury
EXETER
Exeter Airport
Alphington
Exminster
Kenton
Starcross
Cockwood
Dawlish Warren
Dawlish
Holcombe
Teignmouth
Shaldon
Bishopsteignton
Kingsteignton
Teigngrace
NEWTON ABBOT
Ashburton
Bickington
Bovey Tracey
Chudleigh
Chudleigh Knighton
Christow
Dunsford
Moretonhampstead
North Bovey
Lustleigh
Haytor Vale
Ideford
Shillingford St George
Doddiscombsleigh
Tedburn St Mary
Newton St Cyres
Drewsteignton
Babbacombe
M5
A30
A38
A39
A358
A361
A373
A375
A376
A377
A379
A380
A396
A3052
B3227
B3224
G
H
J
K
L
M
1
2
3
4
5
6
7
8
80
90
300
10
20

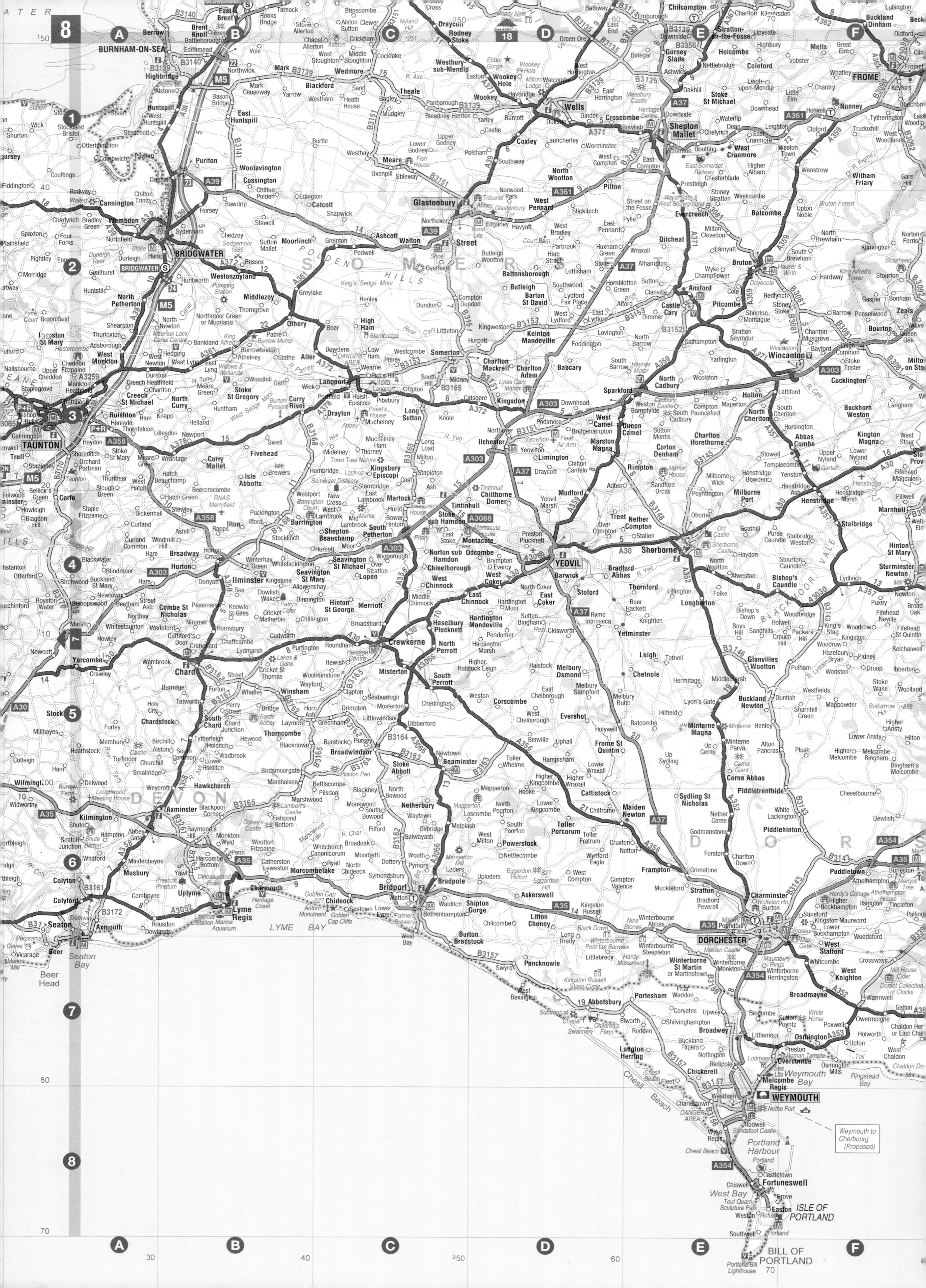

8
BURNHAM-ON-SEA
Berrow
Brent Knoll
East Brent
Highbridge
Huntspill
East Huntspill
Mark
Wedmore
Blackford
Theale
Wookey Hole
Wookey
Wells
Westbury-sub-Mendip
Rodney Stoke
Draycott
Chilcompton
Stratton-on-the-Fosse
Gurney Slade
Holcombe
Coleford
Mells
Buckland Dinham
FROME
Nunney
Shepton Mallet
Croscombe
Stoke St Michael
West Cranmore
Doulting
Evercreech
Pilton
North Wootton
West Pennard
Glastonbury
Street
Meare
Woolavington
Cossington
Puriton
Cannington
Wembdon
BRIDGWATER
Westonzoyland
Middlezoy
Othery
North Petherton
West Monkton
TAUNTON
Creech St Michael
North Curry
Stoke St Gregory
Curry Rivel
Langport
Aller
Somerton
Charlton Mackrell
Keinton Mandeville
Baltonsbury
Butleigh
Barton St David
Castle Cary
Ansford
Bruton
Pitcombe
Wincanton
Bourton
Zeals
Sparkford
North Cadbury
Queen Camel
West Camel
Marston Magna
Ilchester
Kingsdon
Long Sutton
Martock
Kingsbury Episcopi
Ilminster
Isle Abbotts
Curry Mallet
Ilton
Horton
Broadway
Barrington
Shepton Beauchamp
South Petherton
Seavington St Michael
Seavington St Mary
Hinton St George
Merriott
Crewkerne
Misterton
Haselbury Plucknett
North Perrott
South Perrott
Stoke sub Hamdon
Montacute
Odcombe
West Coker
East Coker
YEOVIL
Barwick
Stoford
Sherborne
Milborne Port
Henstridge
Stalbridge
Marnhull
Sturminster Newton
Bishop's Caundle
Longburton
Yetminster
Leigh
Chetnole
Melbury Osmond
Evershot
Corscombe
Beaminster
Stoke Abbott
Broadwindsor
Netherbury
Bridport
Bradpole
Chideock
Charmouth
Lyme Regis
Uplyme
Axminster
Axmouth
Seaton
Colyton
Colyford
Musbury
Kilmington
Chard
Chardstock
South Chard
Winsham
Thorncombe
Combe St Nicholas
Yarcombe
Corfe
Maiden Newton
Toller Porcorum
Powerstock
Frampton
Cattistock
Frome St Quintin
Minterne Magna
Buckland Newton
Cerne Abbas
Piddletrenthide
Sydling St Nicholas
Charminster
DORCHESTER
Puddletown
Winterborne St Martin or Martinstown
Broadmayne
West Knighton
Osmington
Preston
Overcombe
Chickerell
WEYMOUTH
Portesham
Abbotsbury
Puncknowle
Burton Bradstock
Shipton Gorge
Litton Cheney
Askerswell
LYME BAY
Chesil Beach
Portland Harbour
Fortuneswell
ISLE OF PORTLAND
Easton
Southwell
BILL OF PORTLAND
Portland Bill Lighthouse
Weymouth to Cherbourg (Proposed)
DEVON
M5
A39
A303
A30
A37
A35
A358
A354
A352
A371
A361
A372
A356
A3066
A3088
A357
A3030
A359
A3052
A3259
A378

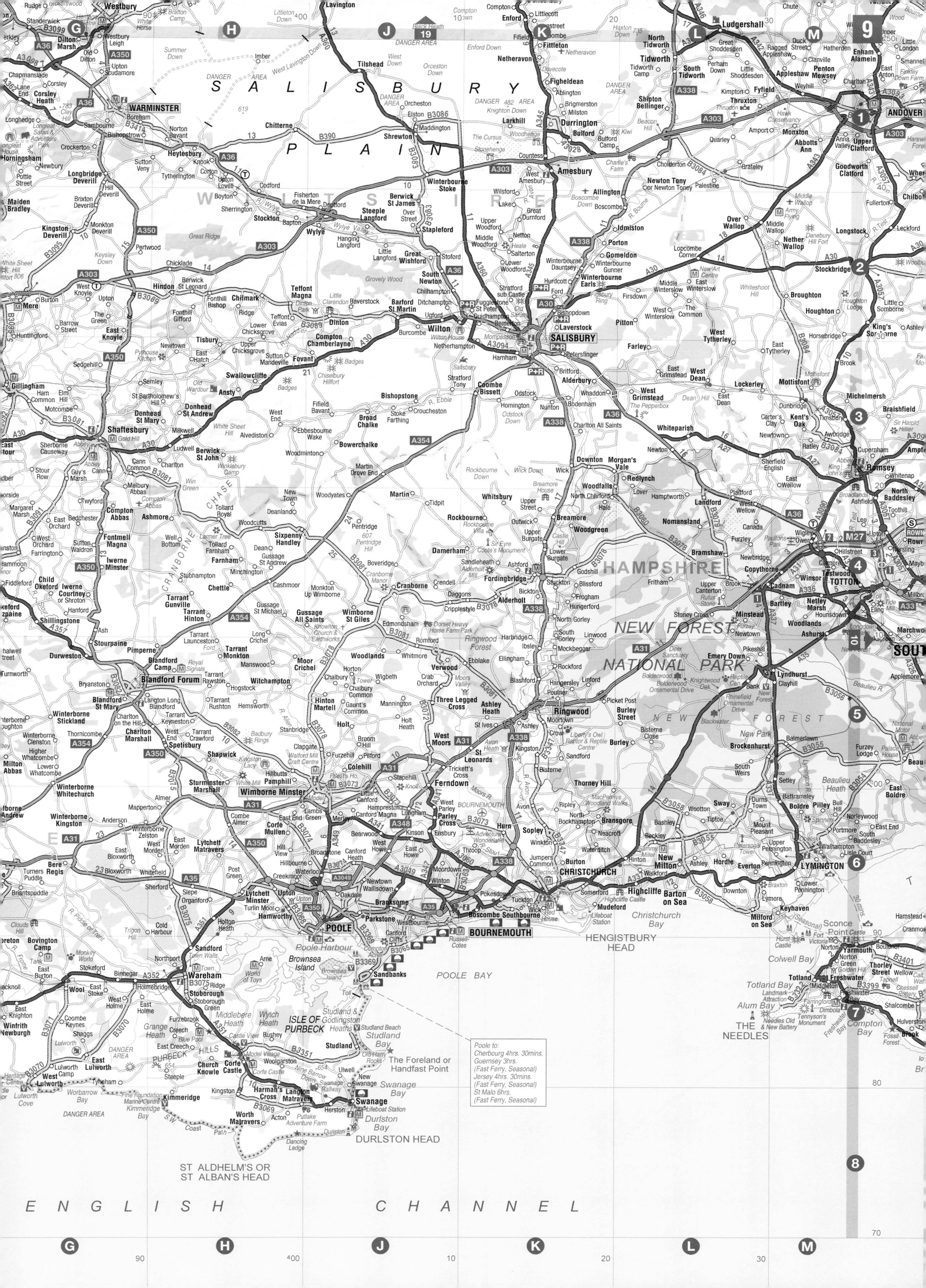

9
G
H
J
K
L
M
SALISBURY PLAIN
WILTSHIRE
HAMPSHIRE
NEW FOREST NATIONAL PARK
ENGLISH CHANNEL
POOLE BAY
Poole Harbour
Christchurch Bay
HENGISTBURY HEAD
ISLE OF PURBECK
PURBECK HILLS
The Foreland or Handfast Point
DURLSTON HEAD
ST ALDHELM'S OR ST ALBAN'S HEAD
THE NEEDLES
Colwell Bay
Totland Bay
Alum Bay
Compton Bay
Brownsea Island
Poole to:
Cherbourg 4hrs. 30mins.
Guernsey 3hrs.
(Fast Ferry, Seasonal)
Jersey 4hrs. 30mins.
(Fast Ferry, Seasonal)
St Malo 6hrs.
(Fast Ferry, Seasonal)
Westbury
WARMINSTER
Tilshead
Ludgershall
ANDOVER
Tidworth
Durrington
Amesbury
Stonehenge
Larkhill
Shrewton
Wylye
Wilton
SALISBURY
Shaftesbury
Gillingham
Blandford Forum
Fordingbridge
Ringwood
Verwood
Ferndown
Wimborne Minster
Romsey
TOTTON
Lyndhurst
Brockenhurst
LYMINGTON
CHRISTCHURCH
BOURNEMOUTH
POOLE
Wareham
Swanage
Corfe Castle
Lulworth
Yarmouth
Freshwater
Stockbridge
Whiteparish
Downton
Cranborne
Sixpenny Handley
Highcliffe
Barton on Sea
New Milton
Milford on Sea
A36
A303
A30
A350
A354
A338
A31
A35
A36
A348
A351
A352
A3049
A27
A337
M27
B3081
B3078
1
2
3
4
5
6
7
8
90
400
10
20
30
80
70

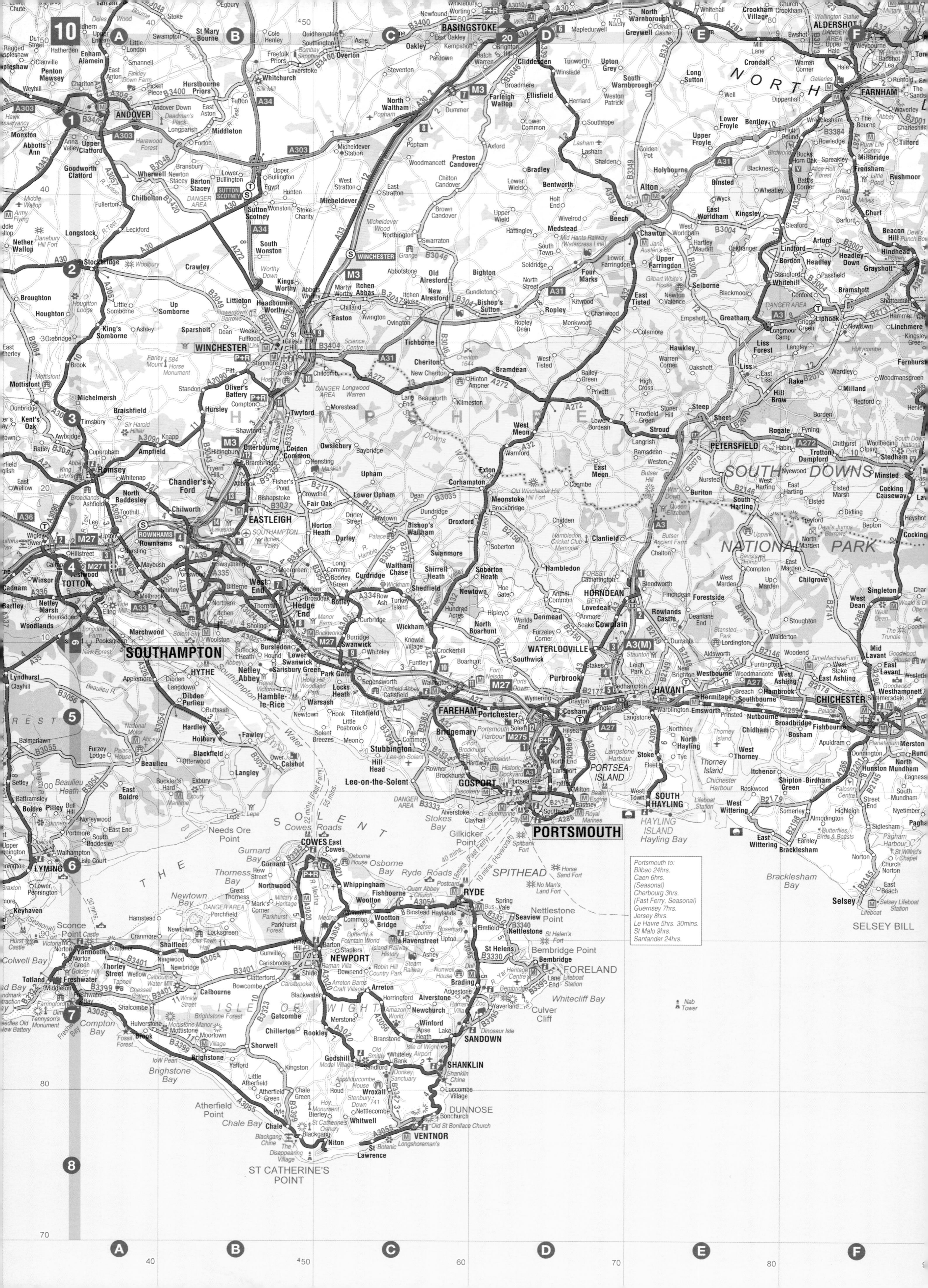

10
A
B
C
D
E
F
BASINGSTOKE
ANDOVER
WINCHESTER
ALDERSHOT
FARNHAM
NORTH
Alton
Petersfield
PETERSFIELD
HAMPSHIRE
SOUTH DOWNS
NATIONAL PARK
EASTLEIGH
Romsey
TOTTON
SOUTHAMPTON
HYTHE
Hamble-le-Rice
FAREHAM
GOSPORT
PORTSMOUTH
PORTSEA ISLAND
HAVANT
WATERLOOVILLE
HORNDEAN
CHICHESTER
SOUTH HAYLING
HAYLING ISLAND
Hayling Bay
Selsey
SELSEY BILL
LYMINGTON
Lee-on-the-Solent
THE SOLENT
SPITHEAD
COWES
RYDE
NEWPORT
ISLE OF WIGHT
SANDOWN
SHANKLIN
VENTNOR
Yarmouth
Freshwater
FORELAND
Bembridge Point
Culver Cliff
Whitecliff Bay
DUNNOSE
ST CATHERINE'S POINT
Atherfield Point
Chale Bay
Brighstone Bay
Compton Bay
Colwell Bay
Osborne Bay
Bracklesham Bay
Portsmouth to:
Bilbao 24hrs.
Caen 6hrs.
(Seasonal)
Cherbourg 3hrs.
(Fast Ferry, Seasonal)
Guernsey 7hrs.
Jersey 8hrs.
Le Havre 5hrs. 30mins.
St Malo 9hrs.
Santander 24hrs.
40
50
60
70
80

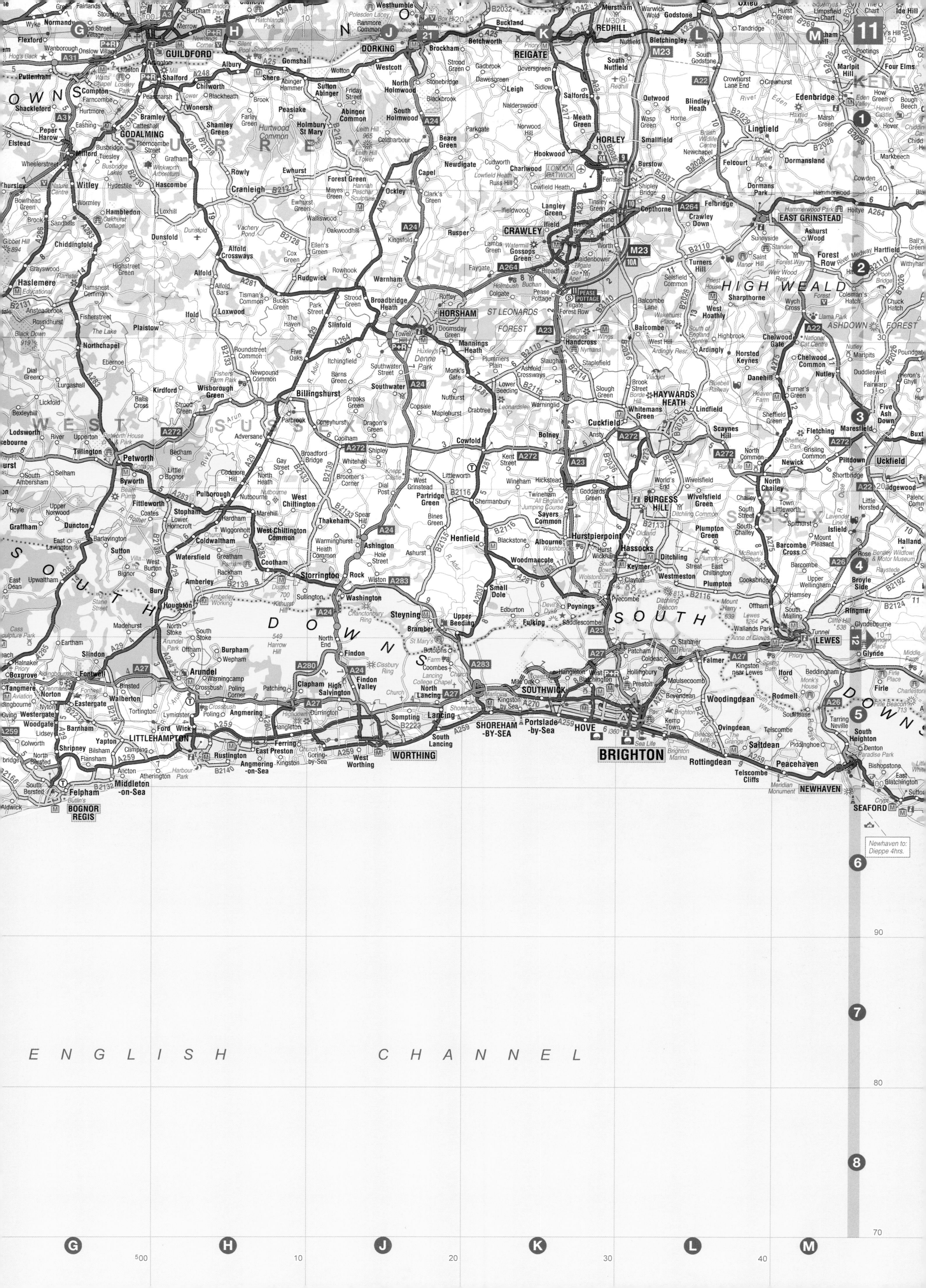

11
GUILDFORD
DORKING
REIGATE
REDHILL
GODALMING
HORLEY
CRAWLEY
EAST GRINSTEAD
HORSHAM
HAYWARDS HEATH
BURGESS HILL
LEWES
WORTHING
SHOREHAM -BY-SEA
SOUTHWICK
HOVE
BRIGHTON
NEWHAVEN
SEAFORD
LITTLEHAMPTON
BOGNOR REGIS
Uckfield
S U R R E Y
KENT
W E S T S U S S E X
EAST SUSSEX
HIGH WEALD
ASHDOWN FOREST
ST LEONARDS FOREST
S O U T H D O W N S
SOUTH DOWNS
E N G L I S H C H A N N E L
M23
A23
A24
A27
A264
A272
A283
A259
Newhaven to: Dieppe 4hrs.
G
H
J
K
L
M
1
2
3
4
5
6
7
8
500
10
20
30
40
90
80
70

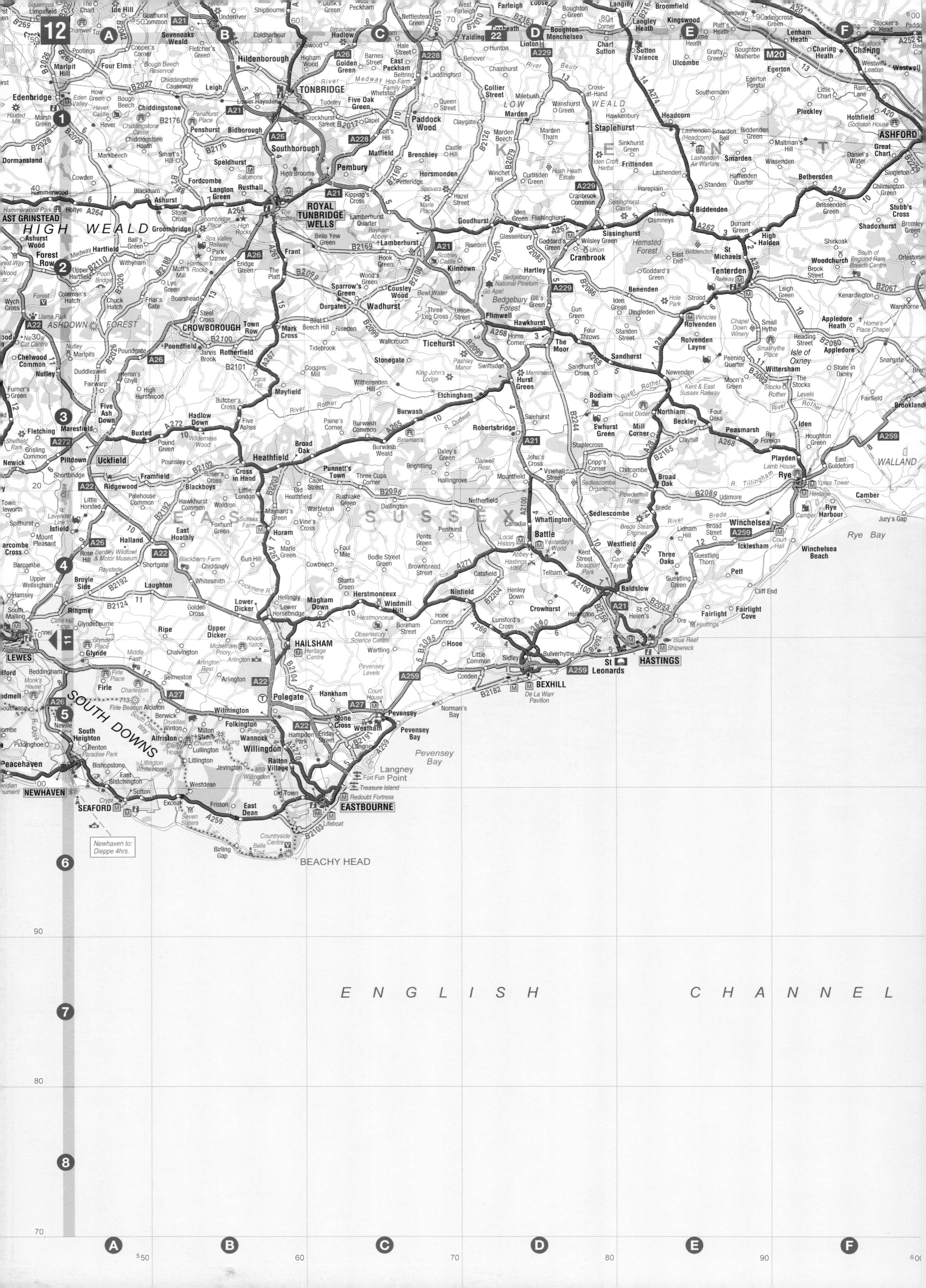
12
A
B
C
D
E
F
1
2
3
4
5
6
7
8
Edenbridge
Hildenborough
TONBRIDGE
Chiddingstone
Penshurst
Bidborough
Southborough
Pembury
Paddock Wood
Brenchley
Horsmonden
Matfield
Marden
Staplehurst
Headcorn
Sutton Valence
Ulcombe
Charing
ASHFORD
Yalding
Linton
Hadlow
Leigh
Dormansland
Speldhurst
Langton Green
Rusthall
Fordcombe
Groombridge
ROYAL TUNBRIDGE WELLS
AST GRINSTEAD
HIGH WEALD
Hartfield
Forest Row
Goudhurst
Lamberhurst
Cranbrook
Sissinghurst
Biddenden
Bethersden
High Halden
Tenterden
St Michaels
Benenden
Hawkhurst
Flimwell
Kilndown
Wadhurst
Frant
Crowborough
Rotherfield
Mayfield
Ticehurst
Stonegate
Etchingham
Burwash
Hurst Green
Robertsbridge
Bodiam
Sandhurst
Newenden
Northiam
Beckley
Peasmarsh
Rolvenden
Wittersham
Appledore
Rye
Playden
Camber
Winchelsea
Icklesham
Winchelsea Beach
Rye Bay
WALLAND
Heathfield
Cross in Hand
Uckfield
Maresfield
Buxted
Framfield
Hadlow Down
Nutley
Fletching
Newick
Isfield
Halland
East Hoathly
Horam
Battle
Sedlescombe
Westfield
Three Oaks
Fairlight
Pett
Guestling Green
Baldslow
HASTINGS
St Leonards
BEXHILL
Sidley
Ninfield
Crowhurst
Catsfield
Herstmonceux
Windmill Hill
Magham Down
HAILSHAM
Hellingly
Lower Dicker
Upper Dicker
Laughton
Ringmer
Ripe
Chalvington
Glynde
Firle
LEWES
Selmeston
Berwick
Wilmington
Polegate
Alfriston
Folkington
Wannock
Willingdon
Litlington
Westham
Pevensey
Pevensey Bay
Stone Cross
Hankham
Langney Point
Pevensey Levels
EASTBOURNE
East Dean
Friston
Exceat
SEAFORD
NEWHAVEN
Peacehaven
South Heighton
Denton
Bishopstone
SOUTH DOWNS
ASHDOWN FOREST
EAST SUSSEX
KENT
LOW WEALD
BEACHY HEAD
Birling Gap
Newhaven to: Dieppe 4hrs.
ENGLISH CHANNEL
A21
A26
A22
A27
A28
A229
A259
A267
A268
A264
A265
A271
A272
A262
A2100
M20
90
80
70
50
60

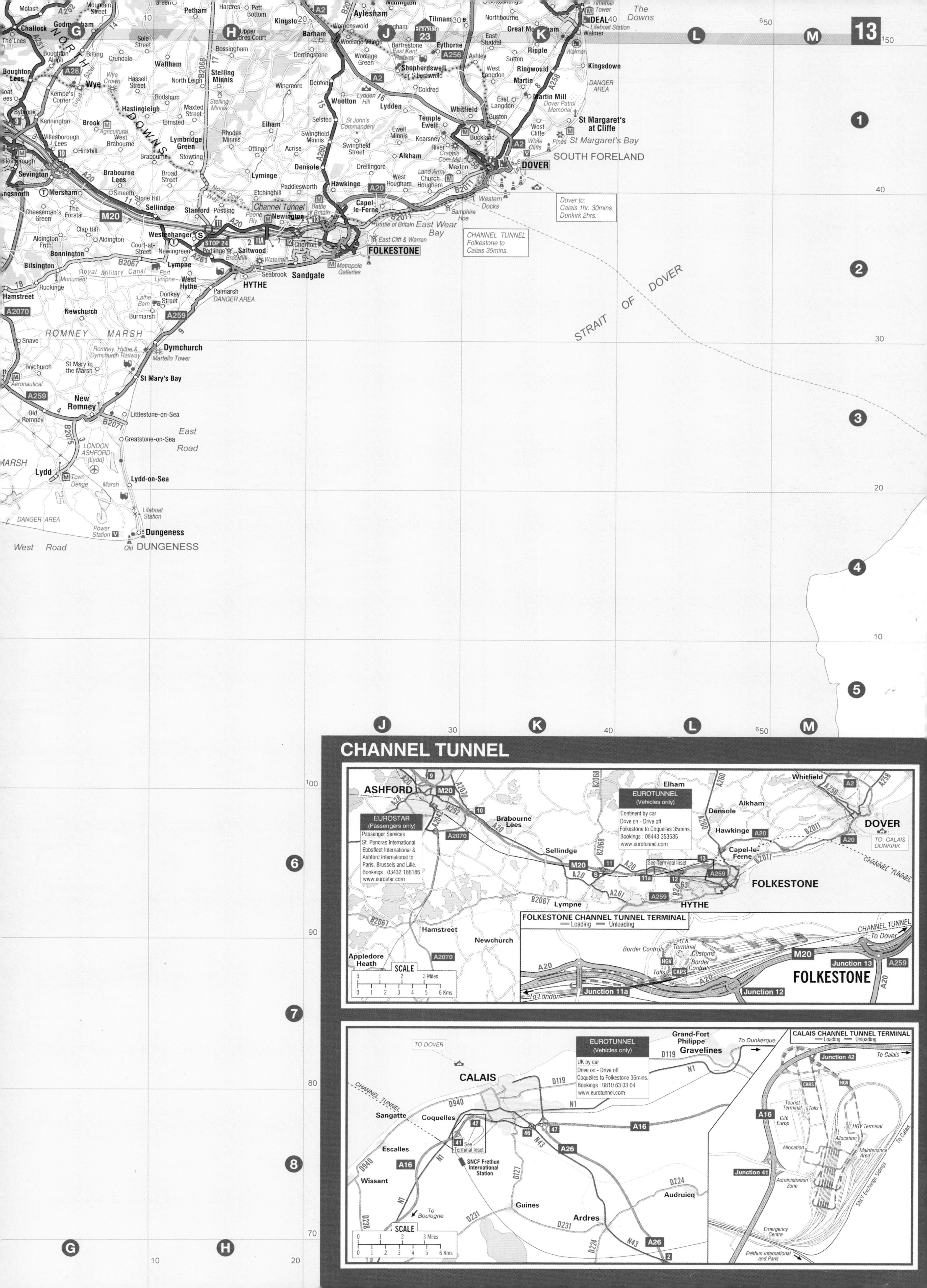
G
H
J
K
L
M
1
2
3
4
5
6
7
8
Molash
Challock
Godmersham
The Lees
Petham
Hardres
Pett Bottom
Kingston
Barham
Aylesham
Womenswold
Tilmanstone
Northbourne
DEAL
Timeball Tower
Lifeboat Station
Walmer
The Downs
Upper Hardres Court
Sole Street
Bossingham
Derringstone
Woolage Village
Woolage Green
Barfrestone
East Kent Railway
Eythorne
East Studdal
Great Mongeham
Ripple
Sutton
Ashley
Kingsdown
DANGER AREA
Boughton Lees
Boughton Aluph
Bilting
Crundale
Waltham
Stelling Minnis
North Leigh
Wingmore
Denton
Shepherdswell or Sibertswold
Coldred
West Langdon
Ringwould
Martin
Martin Mill
Dover Patrol Memorial
Wye
Wye Crown
Hassell Street
Kempe's Corner
Great Stour
NORTH DOWNS
Bodsham
Hastingleigh
Maxted Street
Elmsted
Wootton
Lydden Hill
Lydden
Whitfield
East Langdon
Guston
St Margaret's at Cliffe
Kennington
Brook
Agricultural
West Brabourne
Willesborough Lees
Hinxhill
Lymbridge Green
Rhodes Minnis
Elham
Selsted
St John's Commandery
Swingfield Minnis
Swingfield Street
Temple Ewell
Ewell Minnis
Kearsney
River
Crabble Corn Mill
Buckland
West Cliffe
White Cliffs
Pines
St Margaret's Bay
SOUTH FORELAND
Willesborough
Sevington
Brabourne
Stowting
Ottinge
Acrise
Densole
Drellingore
Alkham
Maxton
DOVER
Brabourne Lees
Smeeth
Broad Street
Lyminge
Etchinghill
Paddlesworth
Hawkinge
West Hougham
Land Army Church
Hougham
Mersham
Stone Hill
Sellindge
Stanford
Postling
North Downs Way
Channel Tunnel
Peene Rly
Newington
Battle of Britain
Capel-le-Ferne
Western Docks
Samphire Hoe
Cheeseman's Green
The Forstal
M20
Westenhanger
Clap Hill
Aldington
Aldington Frith
Court-at-Street
Newingreen
STOP 24
Pedlinge
Saltwood
Brockhill
Cheriton
FOLKESTONE
Battle of Britain
East Wear Bay
East Cliff & Warren
Metropole Galleries
Dover to:
Calais 1hr. 30mins.
Dunkirk 2hrs.
CHANNEL TUNNEL
Folkestone to
Calais 35mins.
Bonnington
Bilsington
B2067
Royal Military Canal
Monument
Lympne
Port Lympne
West Hythe
HYTHE
Seabrook
Sandgate
Waterman
Ruckinge
Hamstreet
Lathe Barn
Donkey Street
Palmarsh
DANGER AREA
Newchurch
Burmarsh
A2070
A259
ROMNEY MARSH
Romney, Hythe & Dymchurch Railway
Dymchurch
Martello Tower
Snave
Ivychurch
St Mary in the Marsh
St Mary's Bay
Aeronautical
New Romney
Old Romney
Littlestone-on-Sea
Greatstone-on-Sea
East Road
LONDON ASHFORD (Lydd)
MARSH
Lydd
Town
Denge Marsh
Lydd-on-Sea
Lifeboat Station
DANGER AREA
Power Station
Dungeness
Old
DUNGENESS
West Road
STRAIT OF DOVER
CHANNEL TUNNEL
ASHFORD
EUROSTAR
(Passengers only)
Passenger Services
St. Pancras International
Ebbsfleet International &
Ashford International to:
Paris, Brussels and Lille.
Bookings : 03432 186186
www.eurostar.com
EUROTUNNEL
(Vehicles only)
Continent by car
Drive on - Drive off
Folkestone to Coquelles 35mins.
Bookings : 08443 353535
www.eurotunnel.com
Elham
Whitfield
Densole
Alkham
Hawkinge
DOVER
TO: CALAIS DUNKIRK
Brabourne Lees
Sellindge
See Terminal Inset
Capel-le-Ferne
FOLKESTONE
Lympne
HYTHE
Hamstreet
Newchurch
Appledore Heath
SCALE
3 Miles
6 Kms
FOLKESTONE CHANNEL TUNNEL TERMINAL
Loading
Unloading
CHANNEL TUNNEL
To Dover
Border Controls
U.K. Terminal
Customs
Border Controls
HGV
CARS
Tolls
To London
Junction 11a
Junction 12
Junction 13
FOLKESTONE
TO DOVER
EUROTUNNEL
(Vehicles only)
UK by car
Drive on - Drive off
Coquelles to Folkestone 35mins.
Bookings : 0810 63 03 04
www.eurotunnel.com
Grand-Fort Philippe
Gravelines
To Dunkerque
CALAIS
Sangatte
Coquelles
See Terminal Inset
SNCF Frethun International Station
Escalles
Wissant
To Boulogne
Guines
Ardres
Audruicq
CALAIS CHANNEL TUNNEL TERMINAL
Loading
Unloading
Junction 42
To Calais
CARS
HGV
Tourist Terminal
Tolls
Cité Europ
HGV Terminal
Allocation
Maintenance Area
Junction 41
Administration Zone
SNCF Exchange Sidings
Emergency Centre
Fréthun International and Paris

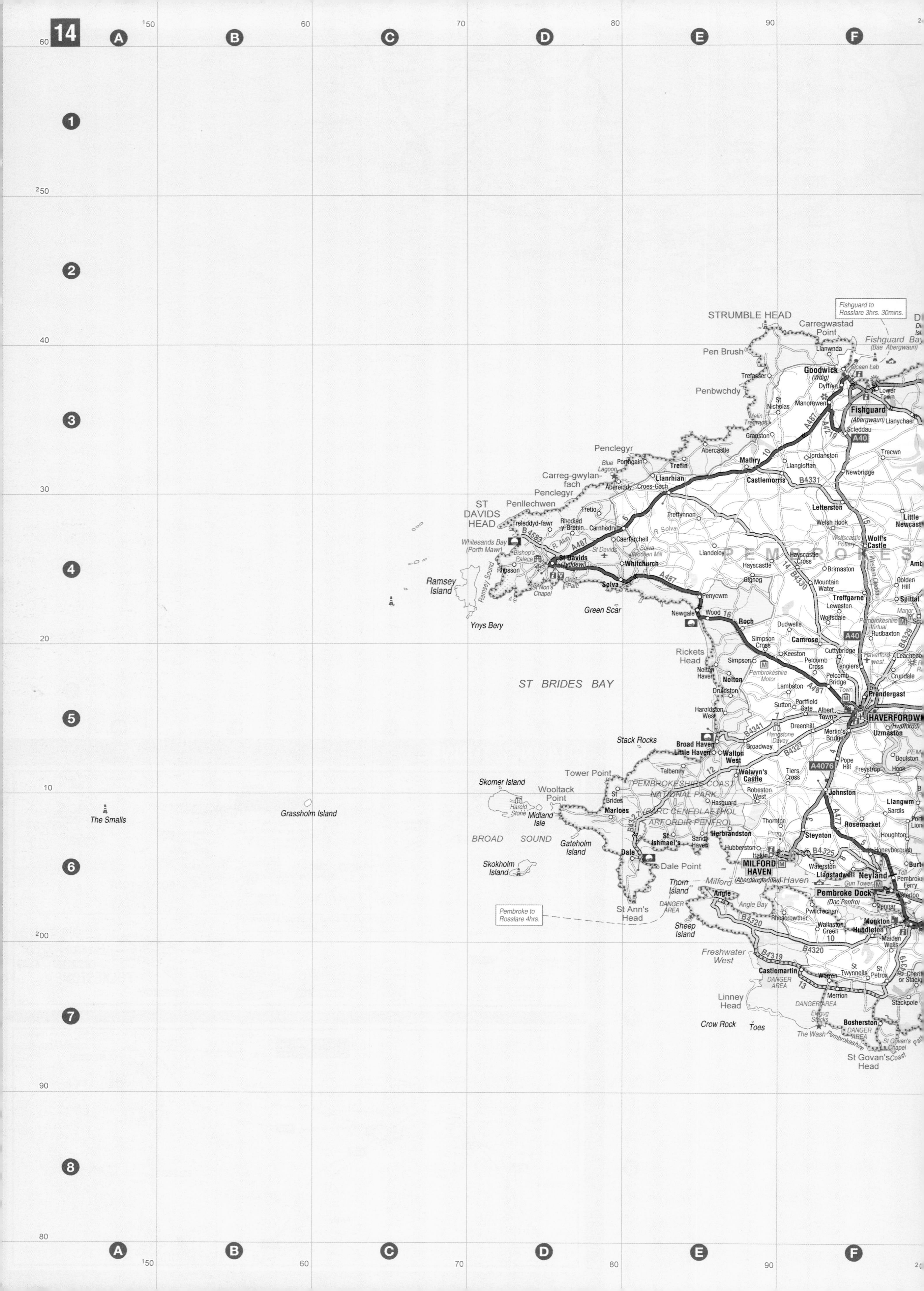

14
A B C D E F
1 2 3 4 5 6 7 8
Fishguard to Rosslare 3hrs. 30mins.
STRUMBLE HEAD
Carregwastad Point
Fishguard Bay (Bae Abergwaun)
Pen Brush
Llanwnda
Goodwick (Wdig)
Ocean Lab
Trefasser
Dyffryn
Lower Town
Penbwchdy
St Nicholas
Manorowen
Fishguard (Abergwaun)
Llanychaer
Melin Tregwynt
Scleddau
Granston
A40
Abercastle
Jordanston
Trecwn
Penclegyr
Porthgain
Mathry
Blue Lagoon
Trefin
Llangloffan
Newbridge
Carreg-gwylan-fach
Llanrhian
Abereiddy
Croes-Goch
Castlemorris
B4331
Penclegyr
ST DAVIDS HEAD
Penllechwen
Tretio
Letterston
Treleddyd-fawr
Rhodiad -y-Brenin
Carnhedryn
Treffynnon
Welsh Hook
Little Newcastle
Whitesands Bay (Porth Mawr)
Caerfarchell
R. Solva
Wolf's Castle
Bishop's Palace
St Davids (Tyddewi)
Whitchurch
Llandeloy
PEMBROKES
Hayscastle Cross
Brimaston
Ramsey Island
Ramsey Sound
Rhosson
St Non's Chapel
Solva
Hayscastle
Mountain Water
Golden Hill
Treffgarne
Spittal
Penycwm
Green Scar
Leweston
Wolfsdale
Ynys Bery
Newgale
Roch
Dudwells
Camrose
Rudbaxton
Rickets Head
Simpson Cross
Keeston
Cuttybridge
Nolton Haven
Simpson
Pelcomb Cross
Tangiers
ST BRIDES BAY
Nolton
Pelcomb Bridge
Prendergast
Druidston
Lambston
Sutton
Portfield Gate
Haroldston West
Albert Town
HAVERFORDWEST (Hwlffordd)
Dreenhill
Merlin's Bridge
Uzmaston
Stack Rocks
Broad Haven
Little Haven
Walton West
B4341
Broadway
B4327
Talbenny
Pope Hill
Freystrop
Hook
Boulston
A4076
Tower Point
Walwyn's Castle
Tiers Cross
Skomer Island
Wooltack Point
PEMBROKESHIRE COAST NATIONAL PARK
(PARC CENEDLAETHOL ARFORDIR PENFRO)
Robeston West
Johnston
St Brides
Marloes
Hasguard
Llangwm
Sardis
Harold Stone
Midland Isle
The Smalls
Grassholm Island
Thornton
Rosemarket
BROAD SOUND
St Ishmael's
Herbrandston
Steynton
Houghton
Gateholm Island
Sandy Haven
Hubberston
Hakin
Honeyborough
Dale
B4325
Dale Point
MILFORD HAVEN (Aberdaugleddau)
Waterston
Llanstadwell
Neyland
Skokholm Island
Thorn Island
Milford Haven
Gun Tower
Pembroke Ferry
Angle
Pembroke Dock (Doc Penfro)
DANGER AREA
Angle Bay
Pembroke to Rosslare 4hrs.
St Ann's Head
Rhoscrowther
Pwllcrochan
Pennar
B4320
Sheep Island
Wallaston Green
Monkton
Hundleton
Maiden Wells
Freshwater West
B4319
B4320
Castlemartin
St Twynnells
St Petrox
Warren
DANGER AREA
Merrion
Linney Head
Stackpole
Crow Rock
Toes
Bosherston
The Wash
Pembrokeshire Coast Path
St Govan's Chapel
St Govan's Head
A487
B4583
B4330
B4329
A477
B4332
A40
150 60 70 80 90
60 250 40 30 20 10 200 90 80

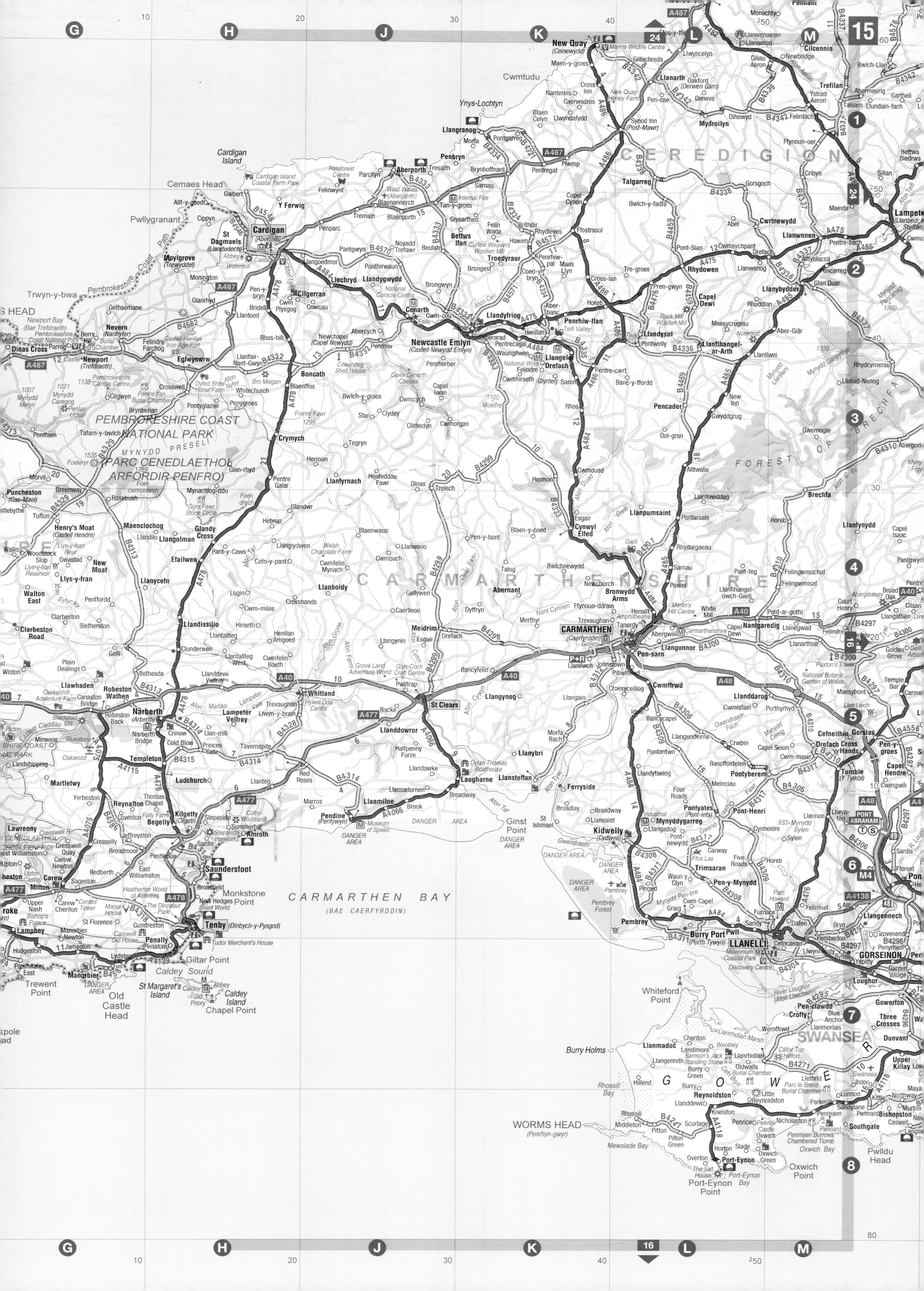
G
H
J
K
L
M
10
20
30
40
50
60
24
New Quay
(Ceinewydd)
Marine Wildlife Centre
Cwmtudu
Ynys-Lochtyn
Llangranog
Llanarth
Oakford
(Derwen Gam)
Synod Inn
(Post-Mawr)
Cilcennin
Trefilan
Talsarn
Llundain-fach
Ystrad
Aeron
Mydroilyn
Felinfach
CEREDIGION
Lampeter
(Llanbedr Pont Steffan)
Cardigan
Island
Cemaes Head
Pwllygranant
Aberporth
Tresaith
Penbryn
Brynhoffnant
Pentregat
Plwmp
Talgarreg
Gorsgoch
Cwrtnewydd
Llanwnnen
St
Dogmaels
(Llandudoch)
Cardigan
(Aberteifi)
Y Ferwig
Gwbert
Moylgrove
(Trewyddel)
Monington
Trwyn-y-bwa
Pembrokeshire Coast Path
Newport Bay
(Bae Trefdraeth)
Dinas Cross
Newport
(Trefdraeth)
Nevern
(Nanhyfer)
Eglwyswrw
Felindre
Farchog
Llechryd
Cilgerran
Llandygwydd
Cenarth
Newcastle Emlyn
(Castell Newydd Emlyn)
Adpar
Llandyfriog
Henllan
Penrhiw-llan
Llangeler
Drefach
Llandysul
Pontwelly
Llanfihangel-
ar-Arth
Rhydowen
Capel
Dewi
Llanybydder
Pencarreg
Troedyraur
Bettws
Ifan
Rhydlewis
Beulah
Boncath
Crymych
Rhos-hill
Blaenffos
PEMBROKESHIRE COAST
NATIONAL PARK
MYNYDD PRESELI
PARC CENEDLAETHOL
ARFORDIR PENFRO
Mynachlog-ddu
Glan-rhyd
Pentre
Galar
Rosebush
Puncheston
(Cas-Mael)
Henry's Moat
(Castell Hendre)
Maenclochog
Llangolman
Glandy
Cross
Efailwen
Llanycefn
Walton
East
Llys-y-fran
New
Moat
Clarbeston
Road
Llandissilio
Clunderwen
CARMARTHENSHIRE
Llanfyrnach
Hebron
Llanboidy
Cwmbach
Trelech
Dinas
Cynwyl
Elfed
Cwmduad
Alltwalis
Pencader
Gwyddgrug
Llanpumsaint
Bronwydd
Arms
Abernant
Meidrim
Drefach
FOREST OF BRECHFA
Brechfa
Llanfynydd
Nantgaredig
CARMARTHEN
(Caerfyrddin)
Pen-sarn
Llangunnor
Johnstown
Whitland
St Clears
Llanddowror
Laugharne
Llansteffan
Llangynog
Bancyfelin
Narberth
(Arberth)
Robeston
Wathen
Templeton
Ludchurch
Lampeter
Velfrey
Kilgetty
(Cilgeti)
Begelly
Saundersfoot
Amroth
Tenby
(Dinbych-y-Pysgod)
Penally
(Penalun)
Manorbier
Lamphey
Carew
Milton
Pendine
(Pentywyn)
Llanmiloe
CARMARTHEN BAY
(BAE CAERFYRDDIN)
Caldey Sound
St Margaret's
Island
Caldey
Island
Chapel Point
Giltar Point
Old
Castle
Head
Trewent
Point
Ferryside
Kidwelly
(Cydweli)
Mynyddygarreg
Pontyates
(Pont-iets)
Pontyberem
Trimsaran
Pen-y-Mynydd
Pembrey
Burry Port
(Porth Tywyn)
Pwll
LLANELLI
Cwmffrwd
Llanddarog
Cross Hands
Drefach
Gorslas
Cefneithin
Tumble
(Y Tymbl)
Llangennech
GORSEINON
Loughor
Pen-clawdd
Crofty
SWANSEA
Three
Crosses
Dunvant
Whiteford
Point
Burry Holms
Llanmadoc
Cheriton
Llangennith
Llanrhidian
Reynoldston
GOWER
Rhossili
Bay
Rhossili
WORMS HEAD
(Penrhyn-gwyr)
Port-Eynon
Port-Eynon
Point
Oxwich
Point
Pwlldu
Head
Bishopston
Southgate
Upper
Killay
Ginst
Point
St
Ishmael
DANGER AREA
Pembrey
Forest
A40
A48
A477
A478
A484
A485
A486
A487
A475
A4066
M4
1
2
3
4
5
6
7
8
16
80

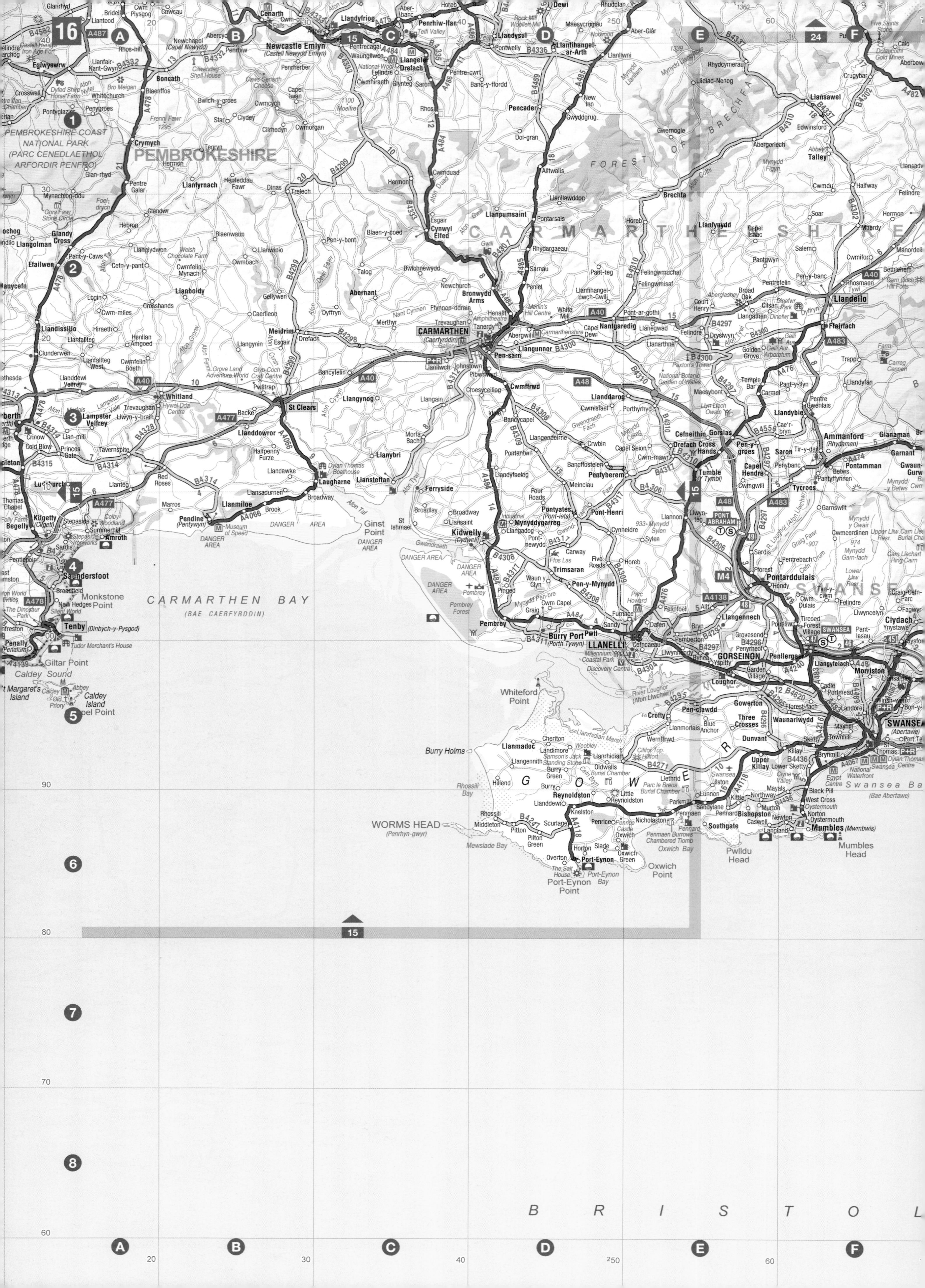

16
A
B
C
D
E
F
1
2
3
4
5
6
7
8
PEMBROKESHIRE COAST NATIONAL PARK (PARC CENEDLAETHOL ARFORDIR PENFRO)
PEMBROKESHIRE
CARMARTHENSHIRE
FOREST OF BRECHFA
SWANSEA
CARMARTHEN BAY
(BAE CAERFYRDDIN)
GOWER
BRISTOL
Swansea Bay
(Bae Abertawe)
Newcastle Emlyn
(Castell Newydd Emlyn)
Cenarth
Llandyfriog
Penrhiw-llan
Llandysul
Llanfihangel-ar-Arth
Dewi
Boncath
Crymych
Llanfyrnach
Glandy Cross
Efailwen
Llanboidy
Whitland
St Clears
Lampeter Velfrey
Narberth
Llanddowror
Laugharne
Llansteffan
Pendine
(Pentywyn)
Llanmiloe
Kilgetty
Begelly
Amroth
Saundersfoot
Tenby
(Dinbych-y-Pysgod)
Penally
Giltar Point
Caldey Sound
Caldey Island
St Margaret's Island
Monkstone Point
Meidrim
Cynwyl Elfed
Bronwydd Arms
CARMARTHEN
(Caerfyrddin)
Pen-sarn
Llangunnor
Cwmffrwd
Llangynog
Ferryside
Kidwelly
(Cydweli)
Mynyddygarreg
Pontyates
(Pont-iets)
Pont-Henri
Trimsaran
Pen-y-Mynydd
Pembrey
Burry Port
(Porth Tywyn)
Pwll
LLANELLI
Pontyberem
Llanddarog
Nantgaredig
Brechfa
Llanfynydd
Talley
Llansawel
Pencader
Llandeilo
Ffairfach
Llandybie
Ammanford
(Rhydaman)
Pontamman
Garnant
Tycroes
Pen-y-groes
Gorslas
Cefneithin
Drefach
Cross Hands
Tumble
(Y Tymbl)
Capel Hendre
Saron
Pontarddulais
Hendy
Llangennech
GORSEINON
Penllergaer
Loughor
Gowerton
Three Crosses
Dunvant
Waunarlwydd
Llangyfelach
Morriston
SWANSEA
(Abertawe)
Upper Killay
Bishopston
Mumbles
(Mwmbwls)
Mumbles Head
Pwlldu Head
Oxwich Point
Port-Eynon
Port-Eynon Point
Reynoldston
Llanmadoc
Penclawdd
Crofty
Whiteford Point
Burry Holms
Rhossili Bay
WORMS HEAD
(Penrhyn-gwyr)
Mewslade Bay
Ginst Point
DANGER AREA
Millennium Coastal Park
Discovery Centre
National Botanic Garden of Wales
A40
A48
A477
A478
A484
A485
A483
A4138
M4
15
24
10
20
30
40
50
60
70
80
90
250

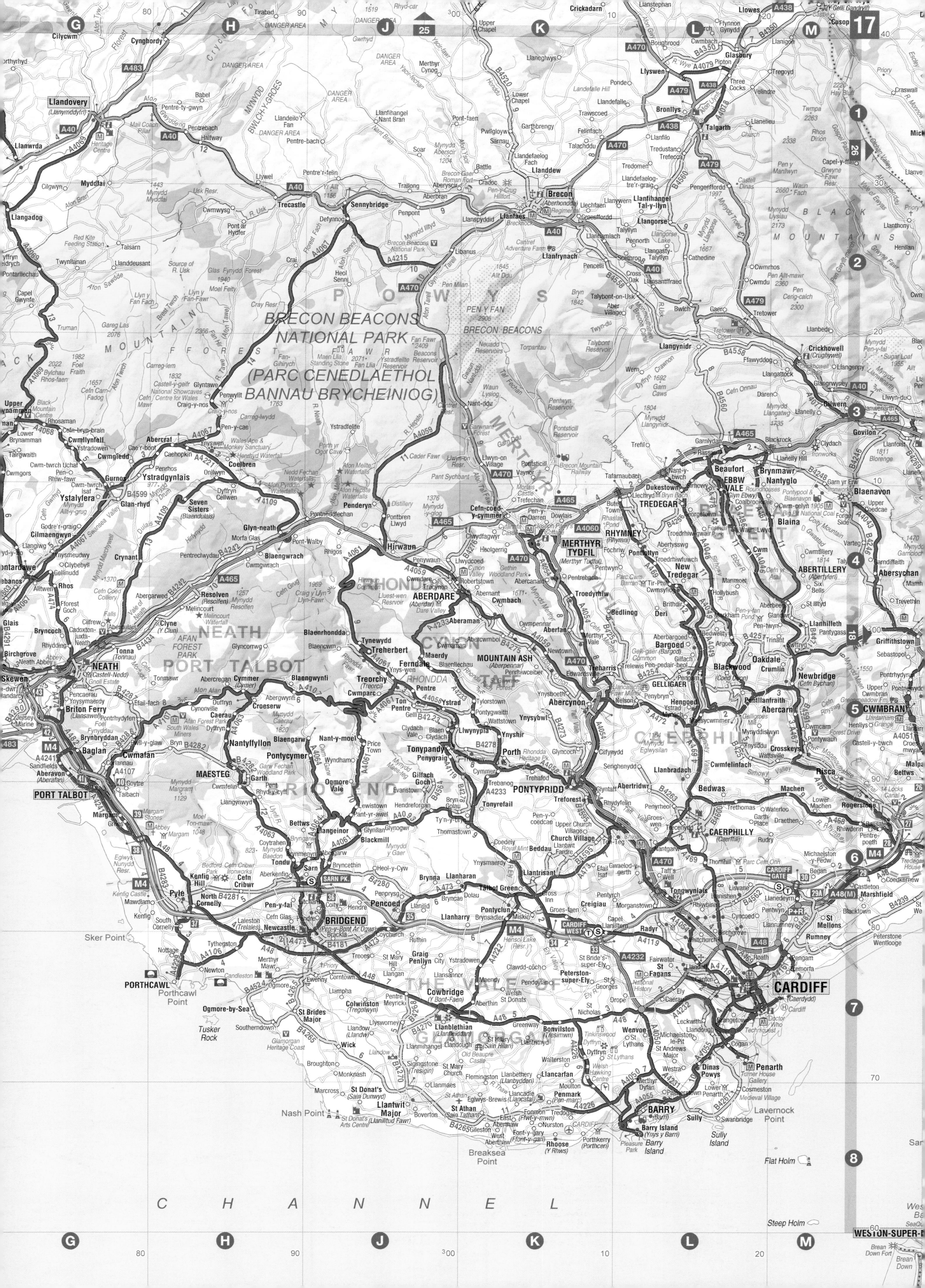

BRECON BEACONS
NATIONAL PARK
(PARC CENEDLAETHOL
BANNAU BRYCHEINIOG)
P O W Y S
BRECON BEACONS
PEN Y FAN
2906
BLACK MOUNTAINS
NEATH
PORT TALBOT
RHONDDA
CYNON TAF
MERTHYR TYDFIL
CAERPHILLY
BLAENAU GWENT
BRIDGEND
THE VALE OF GLAMORGAN
CARDIFF
C H A N N E L
Llandovery
(Llanymddyfri)
Llangadog
Myddfai
Trecastle
Sennybridge
Brecon
(Aberhonddu)
Llanfaes
Talgarth
Bronllys
Glasbury
Llyswen
Hay Bluff
Llanfrynach
Talybont-on-Usk
Llangynidr
Crickhowell
(Crughywel)
Gilwern
Govilon
Blaenavon
Brynmawr
Nantyglo
Beaufort
EBBW VALE
TREDEGAR
RHYMNEY
(Rhymni)
MERTHYR TYDFIL
(Merthyr Tudful)
Dowlais
Cefn-coed-y-cymmer
Hirwaun
Penderyn
Glyn-neath
Ystradgynlais
Abercraf
Ystalyfera
Pontardawe
Seven Sisters
(Blaendulais)
Resolven
(Resolfen)
Crynant
NEATH
(Castell-Nedd)
Skewen
Briton Ferry
(Llansawel)
Baglan
PORT TALBOT
Aberavon
(Aberafan)
Margam
Cymmer
(Cymer)
MAESTEG
Caerau
Nantyffyllon
Treorchy
(Treorci)
Treherbert
Ferndale
Maerdy
Pentre
Tonypandy
Porth
PONTYPRIDD
ABERDARE
(Aberdâr)
MOUNTAIN ASH
(Aberpennar)
Abercynon
Aberfan
Treharris
Bargoed
GELLIGAER
Blackwood
(Coed Duon)
Oakdale
Crumlin
New Tredegar
ABERTILLERY
(Abertyleri)
Abersychan
Newbridge
(Cefn Bychan)
CWMBRAN
Abercarn
Risca
Crosskeys
Rogerstone
Bedwas
CAERPHILLY
(Caerffili)
Machen
Llanharan
Llantrisant
Beddau
Church Village
Tonyrefail
Pencoed
BRIDGEND
(Pen-y-Bont Ar Ogwr)
Pyle
Kenfig Hill
North Cornelly
PORTHCAWL
Porthcawl Point
Ogmore-by-Sea
Tusker Rock
St Brides Major
Wick
Llantwit Major
(Llanilltud Fawr)
St Donat's
Nash Point
Cowbridge
(Y Bont-Faen)
Llanblethian
St Athan
(Sain Tathan)
Rhoose
(Y Rhws)
Breaksea Point
BARRY
(Barri)
Barry Island
(Ynys y Barri)
Dinas Powys
Penarth
Sully
Sully Island
Lavernock Point
Flat Holm
Steep Holm
Radyr
St Fagans
Tongwynlais
CARDIFF
(Caerdydd)
Marshfield
St Mellons
Rumney
WESTON-SUPER-
Llanelly
Clydach
Sker Point
M4
A40
A470
A465
A48
A4119
A4232

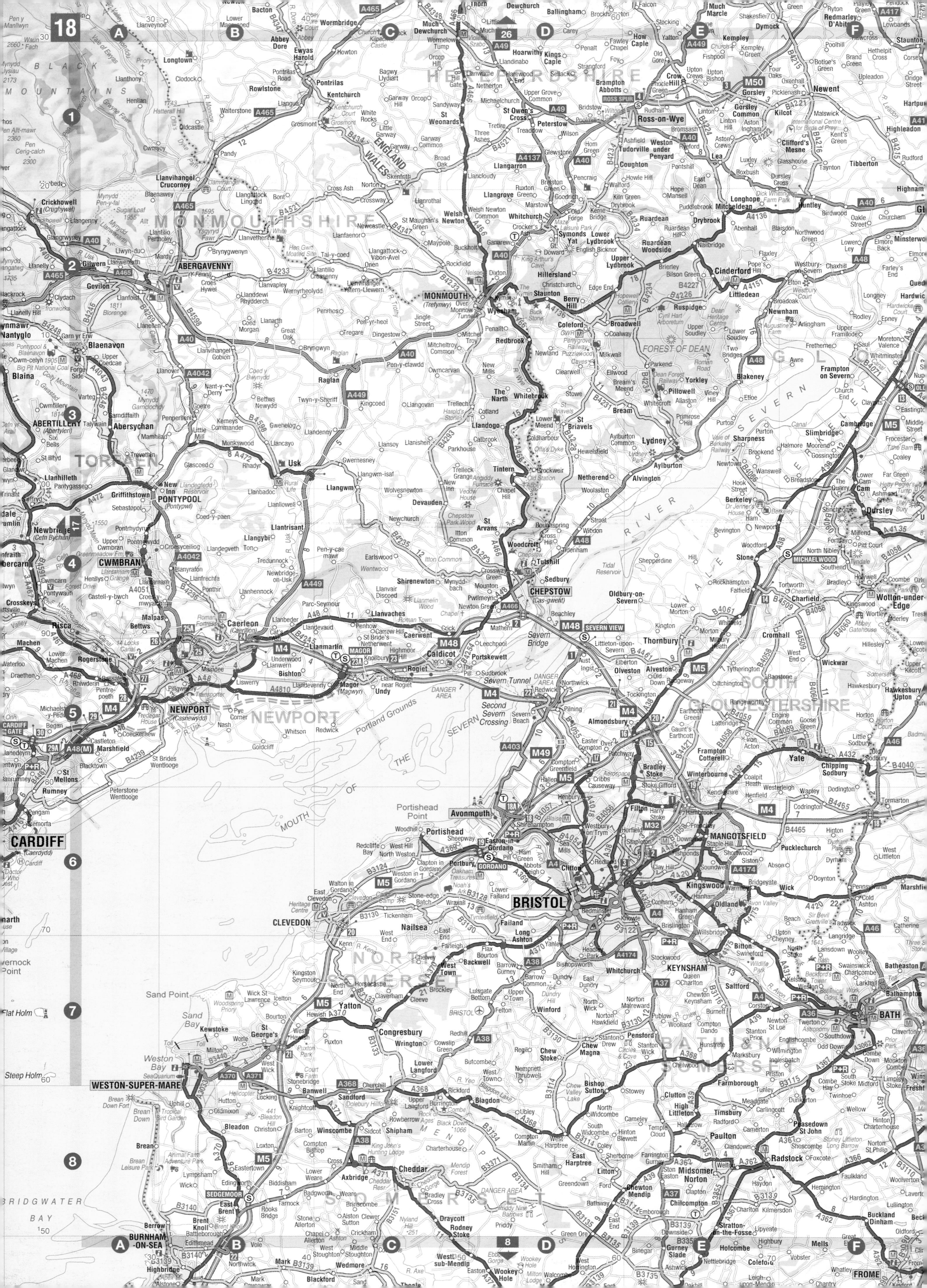
A
B
C
D
E
F
1
2
3
4
5
6
7
8
BLACK MOUNTAINS
HEREFORDSHIRE
MONMOUTHSHIRE
TORFAEN
NEWPORT
SOUTH GLOUCESTERSHIRE
NORTH SOMERSET
BATH & NE SOMERSET
SOMERSET
MENDIP
ENGLAND
WALES
FOREST OF DEAN
RIVER SEVERN
VALE OF BERKELEY
MOUTH OF THE SEVERN
BRIDGWATER BAY
Ross-on-Wye
Newent
Monmouth
Abergavenny
Crickhowell
Blaenavon
Abertillery
Pontypool
Cwmbran
Usk
Raglan
Chepstow
Lydney
Cinderford
Coleford
Newport
Caerleon
Risca
Cardiff
Caldicot
Magor
Portishead
Avonmouth
Clevedon
Bristol
Nailsea
Keynsham
Kingswood
Yate
Chipping Sodbury
Thornbury
Dursley
Wotton-under-Edge
Bath
Weston-super-Mare
Burnham-on-Sea
Cheddar
Yatton
Congresbury
Midsomer Norton
Radstock
Chew Magna
Flat Holm
Steep Holm
Second Severn Crossing
Severn Bridge
M4
M5
M48
M49
M50
M32
A40
A48
A449
A465
A466
A38
A37
A368
A370
A4
A46
8

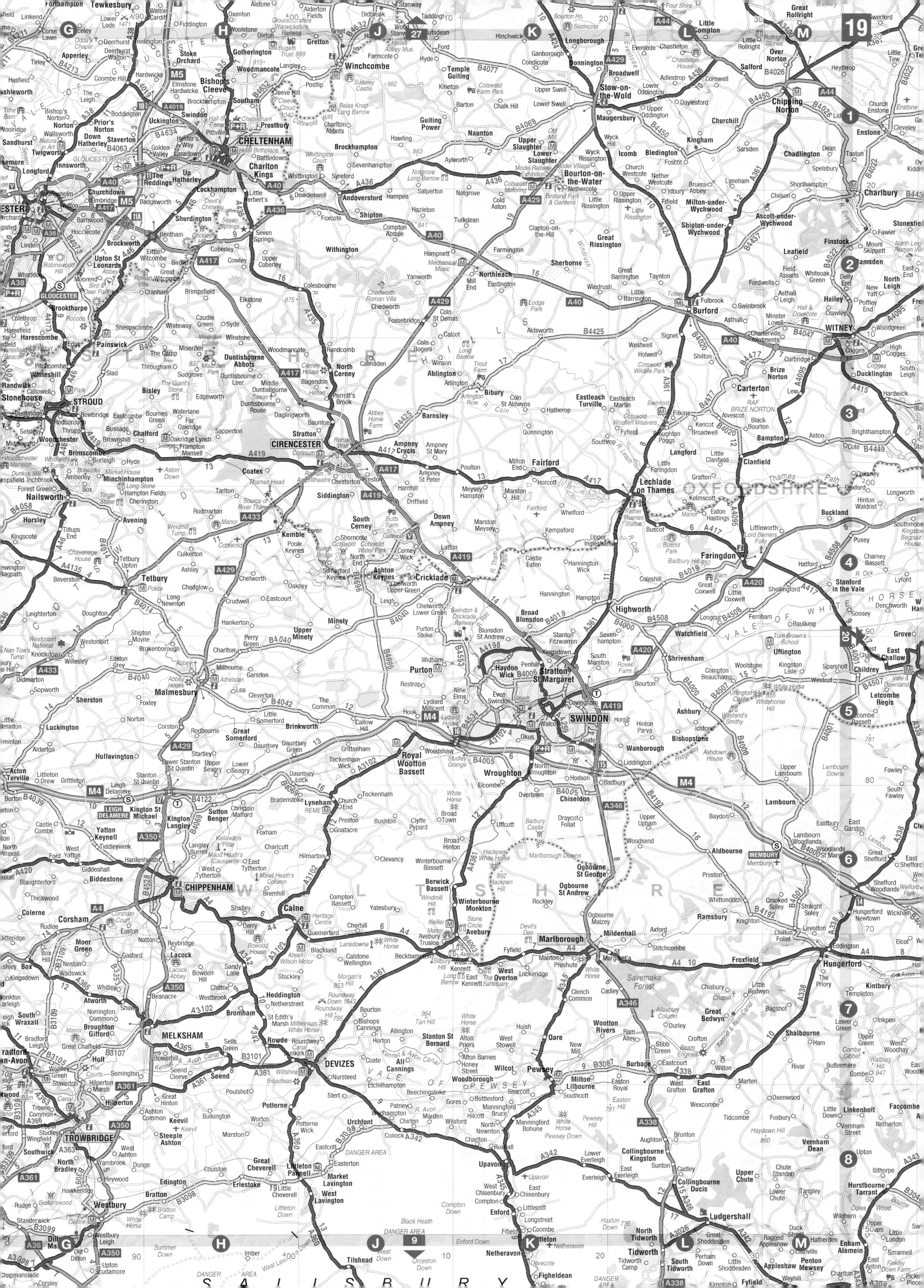

19
G
H
J
K
L
M
1
2
3
4
5
6
7
8
27
20
9
CHELTENHAM
GLOUCESTER
STROUD
CIRENCESTER
SWINDON
CHIPPENHAM
MELKSHAM
TROWBRIDGE
DEVIZES
WITNEY
Tewkesbury
Winchcombe
Bishop's Cleeve
Stow-on-the-Wold
Chipping Norton
Bourton-on-the-Water
Northleach
Burford
Charlbury
Carterton
Bampton
Lechlade on Thames
Fairford
Faringdon
Highworth
Tetbury
Malmesbury
Cricklade
Nailsworth
Royal Wootton Bassett
Wroughton
Calne
Corsham
Marlborough
Hungerford
Lambourn
Pewsey
Ludgershall
Tidworth
Westbury
Upavon
Netheravon
Tilshead
Market Lavington
Stratton St Margaret
OXFORDSHIRE
Thames Path
VALE OF WHITE HORSE
VALE OF PEWSEY
Savernake Forest
SALISBURY

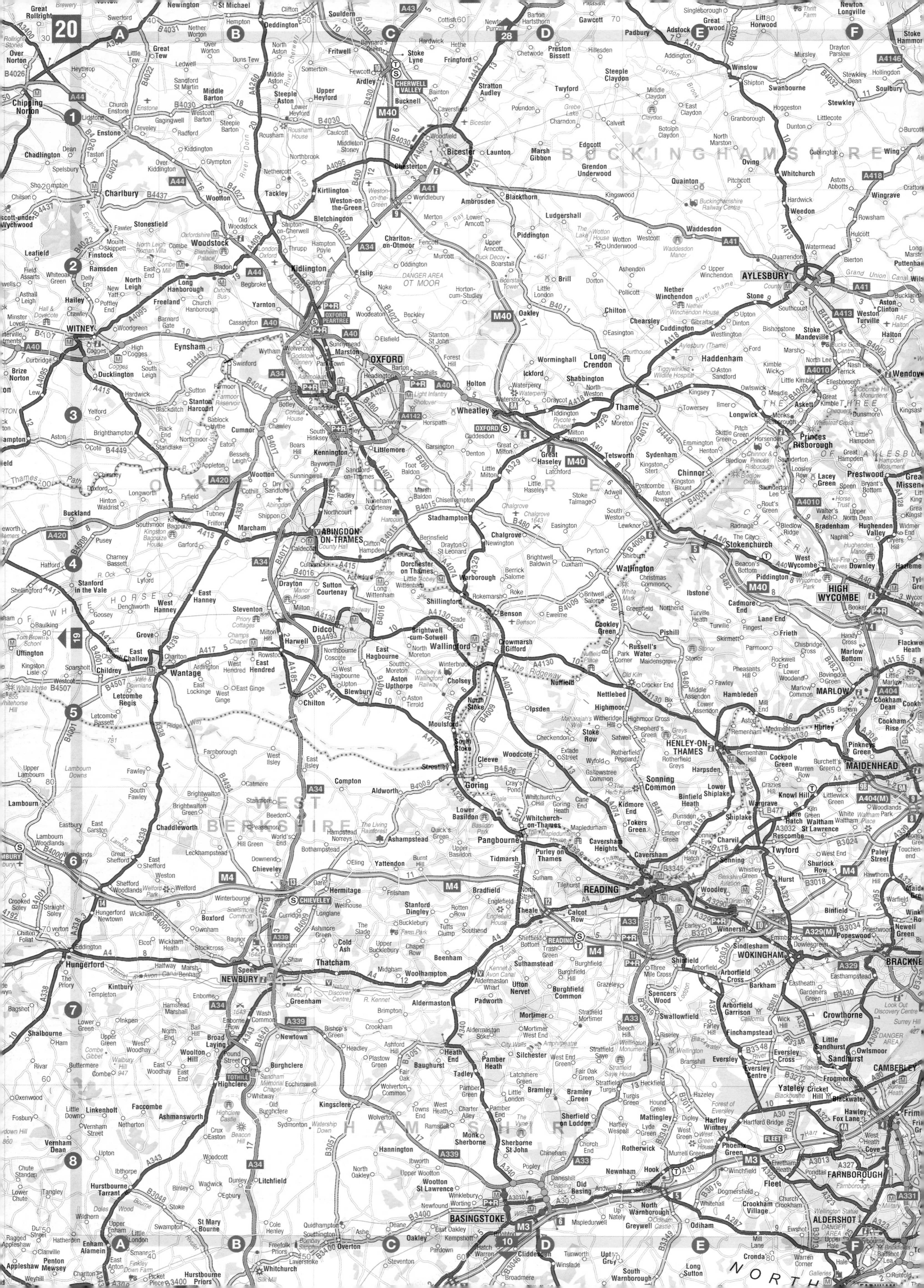
20
A
B
C
D
E
F
1
2
3
4
5
6
7
8
28
19
10
BUCKINGHAMSHIRE
OXFORDSHIRE
WEST BERKSHIRE
HAMPSHIRE
VALE OF WHITE HORSE
THE CHILTERNS
VALE OF AYLESBURY
OT MOOR
Chipping Norton
Charlbury
Witney
Woodstock
Kidlington
Bicester
Oxford
Abingdon-on-Thames
Wantage
Didcot
Wallingford
Thame
Aylesbury
Princes Risborough
High Wycombe
Marlow
Maidenhead
Henley-on-Thames
Reading
Wokingham
Bracknell
Newbury
Hungerford
Thatcham
Basingstoke
Camberley
Farnborough
Fleet
Aldershot
Tadley
Kingsclere
Whitchurch
Overton
Odiham
Wheatley
Watlington
Chinnor
Haddenham
Long Crendon
Eynsham
Faringdon
Stanford in the Vale
Steventon
Harwell
Cholsey
Goring
Pangbourne
Theale
Twyford
Sonning
Winslow
Wendover
Stokenchurch
M40
M4
M3
A34
A40
A41
A44
A4
A33
A339
A338
A329(M)
A404(M)
A413
A418
A4074
A4130
A420
A415
A417

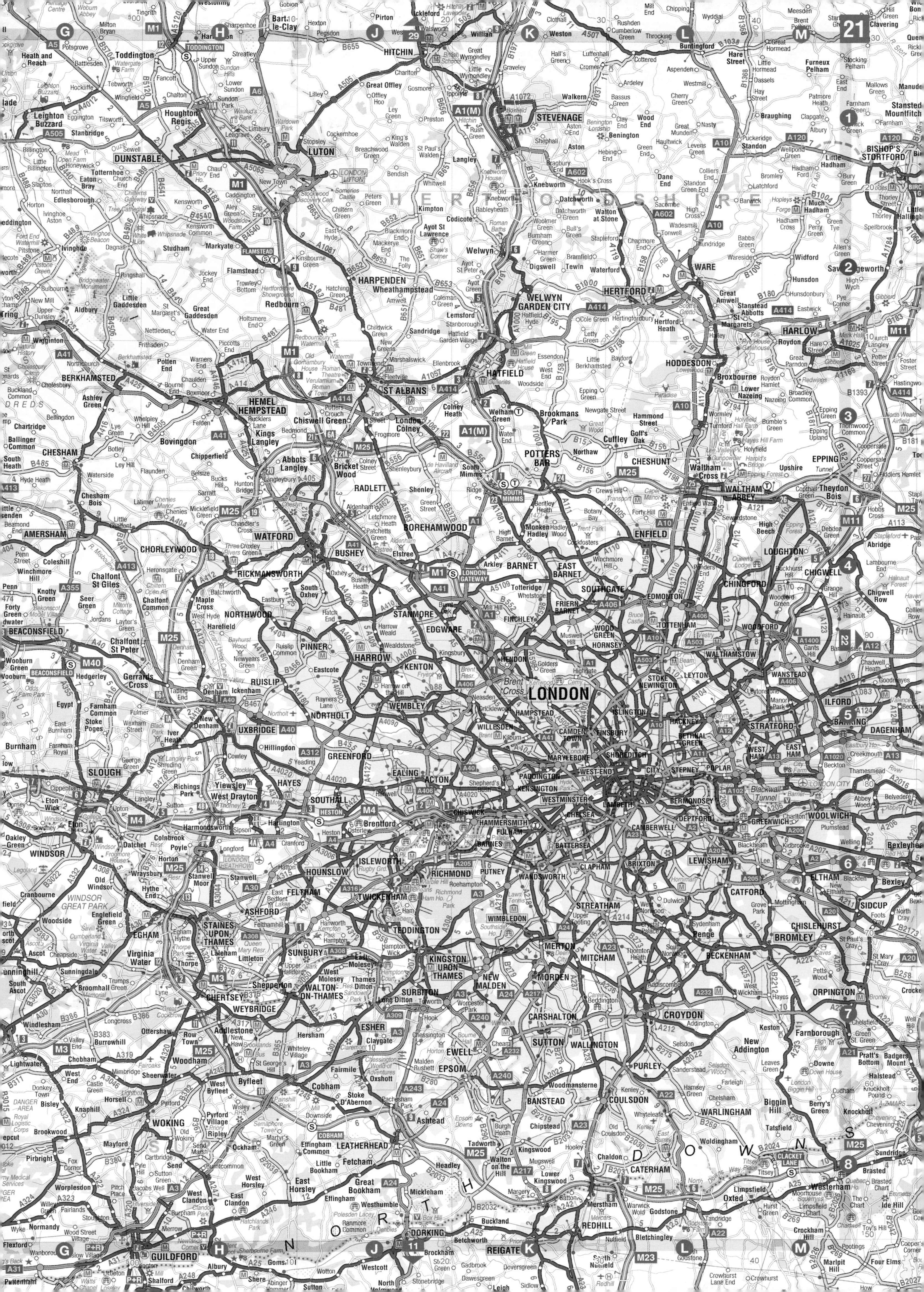

21
G
H
J
K
L
M
1
2
3
4
5
6
7
8
HERTFORDSHIRE
SURREY
NORTH DOWNS
LONDON
LEIGHTON BUZZARD
DUNSTABLE
LUTON
HITCHIN
STEVENAGE
BISHOP'S STORTFORD
HARPENDEN
HERTFORD
WARE
WELWYN GARDEN CITY
HATFIELD
ST ALBANS
HEMEL HEMPSTEAD
BERKHAMSTED
HARLOW
HODDESDON
CHESHUNT
WALTHAM ABBEY
EPPING
POTTERS BAR
BOREHAMWOOD
WATFORD
CHESHAM
AMERSHAM
RICKMANSWORTH
BARNET
ENFIELD
LOUGHTON
CHINGFORD
BEACONSFIELD
UXBRIDGE
SLOUGH
HARROW
WEMBLEY
ILFORD
STRATFORD
DAGENHAM
WINDSOR
STAINES-UPON-THAMES
HOUNSLOW
RICHMOND
KINGSTON UPON THAMES
CROYDON
BROMLEY
SIDCUP
WOOLWICH
WOKING
WEYBRIDGE
EPSOM
SUTTON
LEATHERHEAD
DORKING
REIGATE
REDHILL
CATERHAM
GUILDFORD
ORPINGTON

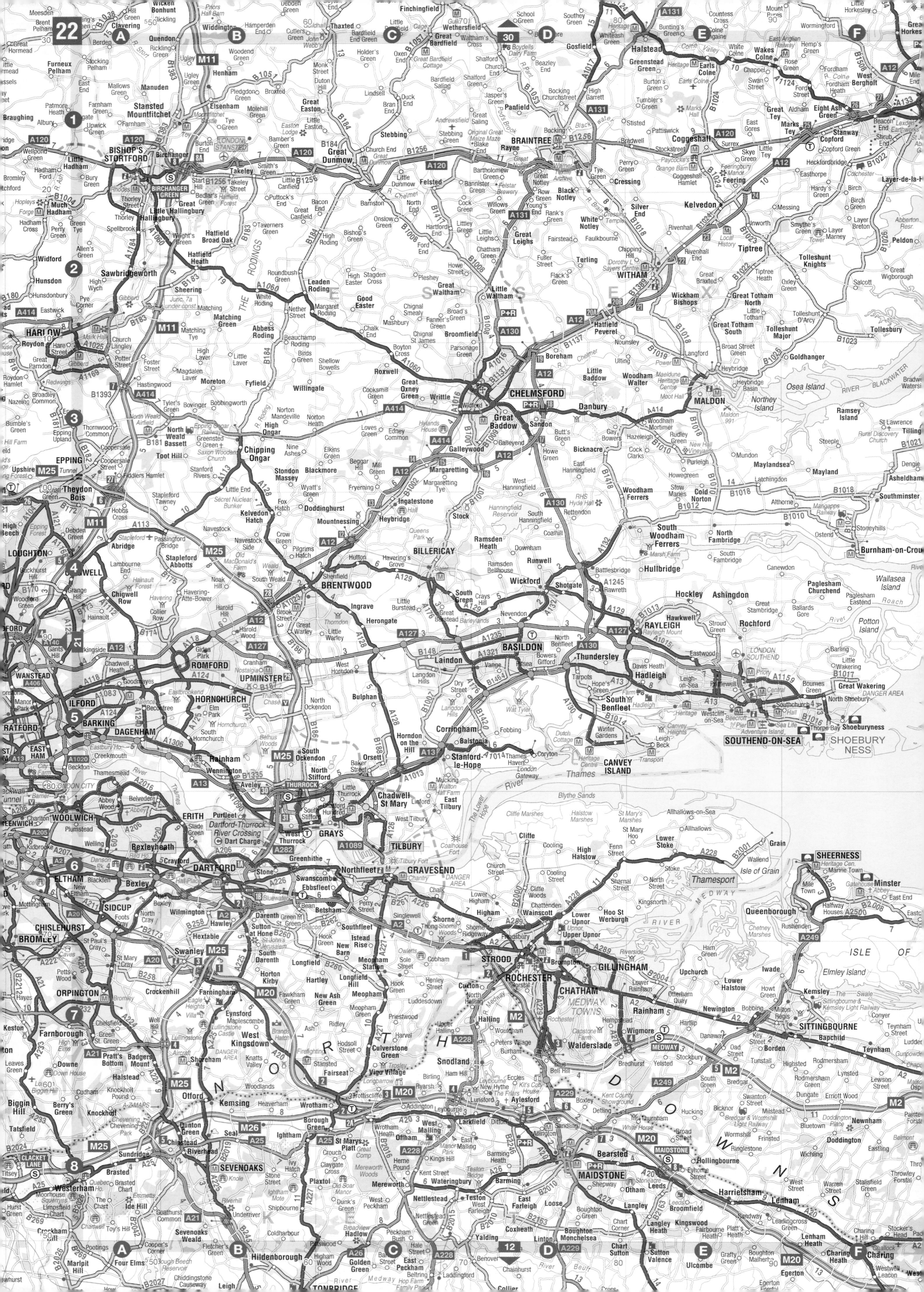
22
30
12
A
B
C
D
E
F
1
2
3
4
5
6
7
8
BISHOP'S STORTFORD
Stansted Mountfitchet
LONDON STANSTED
Great Dunmow
Thaxted
Finchingfield
Wethersfield
Great Bardfield
BRAINTREE
Halstead
Gosfield
Earls Colne
Coggeshall
Kelvedon
WITHAM
Tiptree
Feering
Marks Tey
Copford
Stanway
Great Tey
Wakes Colne
Sawbridgeworth
Much Hadham
Little Hadham
HARLOW
Roydon
Hatfield Heath
Hatfield Broad Oak
Great Hallingbury
Takeley
Felsted
Great Waltham
Little Waltham
Terling
Hatfield Peverel
Boreham
CHELMSFORD
Great Baddow
Writtle
Danbury
Sandon
Galleywood
Margaretting
Ingatestone
Stock
Chipping Ongar
High Ongar
North Weald Bassett
EPPING
Theydon Bois
LOUGHTON
Abridge
Stapleford Abbotts
Kelvedon Hatch
Doddinghurst
BRENTWOOD
Shenfield
Hutton
BILLERICAY
Wickford
Shotgate
Runwell
MALDON
Heybridge
Tollesbury
Tolleshunt Knights
Goldhanger
Osea Island
Northey Island
Mayland
Maylandsea
Burnham-on-Crouch
South Woodham Ferrers
Woodham Ferrers
Hullbridge
Rayleigh
Rochford
Hockley
Ashingdon
Hadleigh
Thundersley
BASILDON
Laindon
Pitsea
Vange
Canvey Island
SOUTHEND-ON-SEA
Leigh-on-Sea
Shoeburyness
SHOEBURY NESS
Great Wakering
Wallasea Island
Potton Island
Corringham
Stanford-le-Hope
Horndon on the Hill
Orsett
Chadwell St Mary
Grays
TILBURY
East Tilbury
THURROCK
Dartford-Thurrock River Crossing
Dart Charge
South Ockendon
Aveley
Rainham
UPMINSTER
HORNCHURCH
ROMFORD
DAGENHAM
BARKING
ILFORD
WANSTEAD
Chigwell
WOOLWICH
ERITH
Bexleyheath
Crayford
DARTFORD
Stone
Greenhithe
Swanscombe
Northfleet
GRAVESEND
Ebbsfleet
Bexley
SIDCUP
ELTHAM
CHISLEHURST
BROMLEY
ORPINGTON
Swanley
Farnborough
Biggin Hill
Westerham
Sundridge
Chipstead
Riverhead
SEVENOAKS
Otford
Kemsing
Shoreham
Eynsford
West Kingsdown
Wrotham
Borough Green
Ightham
Hildenborough
TONBRIDGE
Hadlow
Kings Hill
West Malling
East Malling
Aylesford
Snodland
Larkfield
Ditton
MAIDSTONE
Bearsted
Hollingbourne
Harrietsham
Lenham
Charing
Headcorn
Sutton Valence
Ulcombe
Coxheath
Yalding
Linton
Loose
Barming
Teston
Wateringbury
Mereworth
Meopham
Hartley
Longfield
Culverstone Green
Vigo Village
Higham
Shorne
Cliffe
High Halstow
Hoo St Werburgh
Upper Upnor
STROOD
ROCHESTER
CHATHAM
MEDWAY TOWNS
GILLINGHAM
Rainham
Walderslade
Wigmore
Upchurch
Newington
SITTINGBOURNE
Teynham
Bapchild
Borden
Milton Regis
Kemsley
Iwade
Queenborough
SHEERNESS
Minster
Eastchurch
ISLE OF
Elmley Island
Isle of Grain
Grain
Allhallows
Thamesport
NORTH DOWNS
ESSEX
KENT
THE RODINGS
Thames
River Medway
M11
M25
M20
M26
M2
A12
A120
A130
A127
A13
A2
A20
A414
A131
A1060
A228
A229
A249
A25
A21
A26
A228

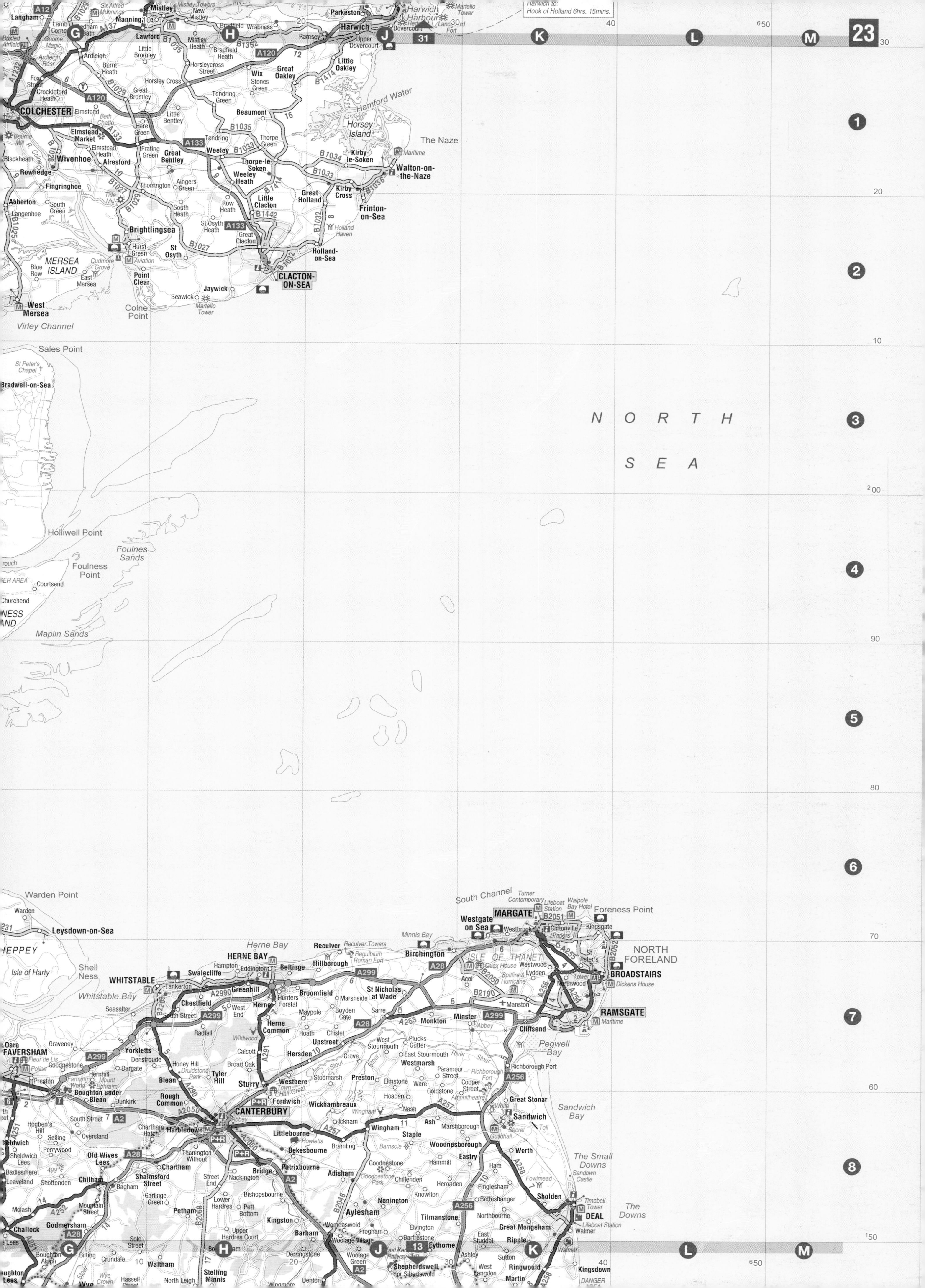
Harwich to:
Hook of Holland 6hrs. 15mins.
NORTH
SEA
Langham
Mistley
Manningtree
Lawford
Parkeston
Harwich
Harwich Harbour
Dovercourt
Upper Dovercourt
Ramsey
Wrabness
Bradfield
Bradfield Heath
Mistley Heath
Horsleycross Street
Horsley Cross
Little Bromley
Great Bromley
Ardleigh
Ardleigh Resr.
Burnt Heath
Great Oakley
Little Oakley
Wix
Stones Green
Tendring Green
Tendring
Beaumont
Hamford Water
Horsey Island
The Naze
Kirby-le-Soken
Walton-on-the-Naze
Kirby Cross
Frinton-on-Sea
Great Holland
Holland-on-Sea
Holland Haven
Thorpe Green
Thorpe-le-Soken
Weeley
Weeley Heath
Little Clacton
Great Clacton
Clacton-on-Sea
Jaywick
Seawick
Martello Tower
Colne Point
St Osyth
St Osyth Heath
Row Heath
South Heath
Aingers Green
Thorrington
Great Bentley
Frating Green
Little Bentley
Hare Green
Alresford
Elmstead Market
Elmstead Heath
Elmstead
Colchester
Crockleford Heath
Fox Street
Wivenhoe
Rowhedge
Fingringhoe
Blackheath
Abberton
Langenhoe
South Green
Brightlingsea
Point Clear
Mersea Island
East Mersea
West Mersea
Blue Row
Cudmore Grove
Virley Channel
Sales Point
St Peter's Chapel
Bradwell-on-Sea
Holliwell Point
Foulness Sands
Foulness Point
Courtsend
Churchend
Maplin Sands
Warden Point
Warden
Leysdown-on-Sea
Isle of Harty
Shell Ness
Whitstable Bay
Whitstable
Seasalter
Tankerton
Swalecliffe
Chestfield
Greenhill
Herne Bay
Hampton
Eddington
Beltinge
Herne
Herne Common
Hunters Forstal
Reculver
Reculver Towers
Regulbium Roman Fort
Hillborough
Broomfield
Marshside
St Nicholas at Wade
Sarre
Minnis Bay
Birchington
Westgate on Sea
Margate
Westbrook
Cliftonville
Kingsgate
Foreness Point
North Foreland
South Channel
Isle of Thanet
Acol
Quex House
Westwood
Lydden
Northwood
St Peter's
Broadstairs
Dickens House
Manston
Minster
Monkton
Ramsgate
Cliffsend
Pegwell Bay
Richborough Port
Richborough Fort
Sandwich Bay
Sandwich
Great Stonar
Worth
The Small Downs
Sandown Castle
Sholden
Deal
Timeball Tower
Walmer
The Downs
Kingsdown
Ripple
Great Mongeham
Northbourne
Betteshanger
Finglesham
Ham
Eastry
Woodnesborough
Marshborough
Ash
Staple
Wingham
Ickham
Littlebourne
Bekesbourne
Patrixbourne
Bridge
Adisham
Goodnestone
Chillenden
Knowlton
Nonington
Aylesham
Tilmanstone
Eythorne
Elvington
Barfrestone
Frogham
Womenswold
Woolage Village
Woolage Green
Shepherdswell or Sibertswold
Barham
Kingston
Derringstone
Denton
Canterbury
Harbledown
Thanington Without
Chartham
Chartham Hatch
Petham
Street End
Nackington
Lower Hardres
Upper Hardres Court
Pett Bottom
Bishopsbourne
Fordwich
Sturry
Westbere
Hersden
Upstreet
Chislet
Hoath
Maypole
Boyden Gate
Grove
Preston
Elmstone
Hoaden
Westmarsh
Stourmouth
Plucks Gutter
Wickhambreaux
Tyler Hill
Blean
Rough Common
Broad Oak
Calcott
Honey Hill
Radfall
Yorkletts
Dargate
Denstroude
Faversham
Oare
Graveney
Goodnestone
Hernhill
Boughton under Blean
Dunkirk
South Street
Oversland
Selling
Perrywood
Old Wives Lees
Chilham
Shalmsford Street
Bagham
Mountain Street
Godmersham
Challock
Shottenden
Leaveland
Badlesmere
Sheldwich
Molash
Crundale
Waltham
Sole Street
Bilting
North Leigh
Stelling Minnis
Wye
Hassell Street
East Studdal
Ashley
Sutton
Ringwould
West Langdon
Martin

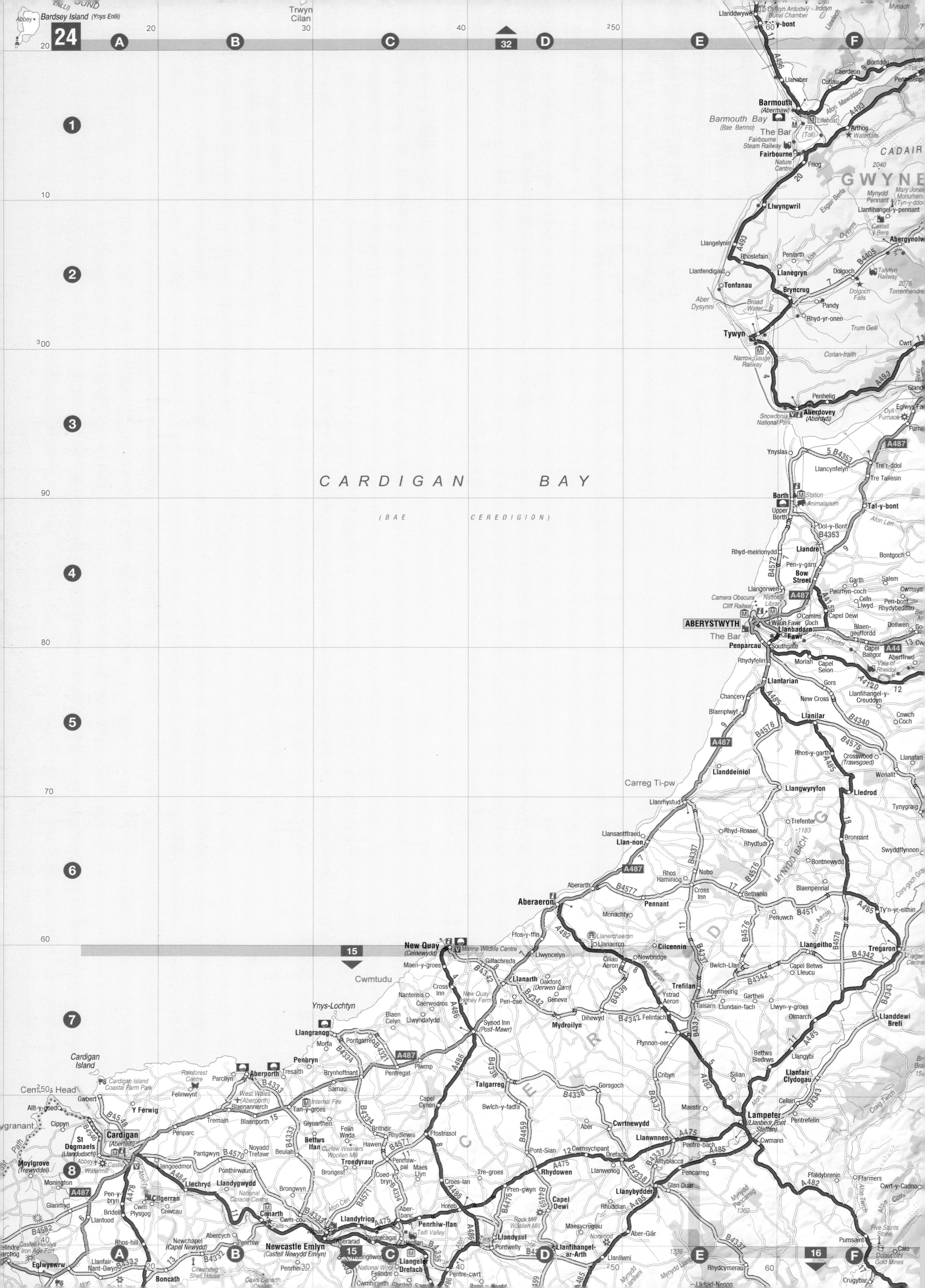

24
32
15
16
A
B
C
D
E
F
1
2
3
4
5
6
7
8
Bardsey Island (Ynys Enlli)
Trwyn Cilan
CARDIGAN BAY
(BAE CEREDIGION)
Barmouth (Abermaw)
Barmouth Bay (Bae Bermo)
The Bar
Fairbourne Steam Railway
Fairbourne
Friog
Llanaber
Arthog
CADAIR
GWYNE
Llwyngwril
Llangelynin
Rhoslefain
Llanfendigaid
Tonfanau
Llanegryn
Bryncrug
Peniarth
Dolgoch
Talyllyn Railway
Dolgoch Falls
Pandy
Rhyd-yr-onen
Aber Dysynni
Broad Water
Tywyn
Narrow Gauge Railway
Corlan-fraith
Trum Gelli
Penhelig
Aberdovey (Aberdyfi)
Snowdonia National Park
Ynyslas
Llancynfelyn
Tre'r-ddol
Tre Taliesin
Borth
Upper Borth
Tal-y-bont
Dol-y-Bont
Llandre
Rhyd-meirionydd
Pen-y-garn
Bow Street
Bontgoch
Llangorwen
Camera Obscura
Cliff Railway
National Library
ABERYSTWYTH
The Bar
Penparcau
Llanbadarn Fawr
Waun Fawr
Comins Coch
Capel Dewi
Southgate
Rhydyfelin
Capel Bangor
Aberffrwd
Vale of Rheidol
Capel Seion
Llanfarian
Chancery
Blaenplwyf
Gors
New Cross
Llanfihangel-y-Creuddyn
Llanilar
Cnwch Coch
Rhos-y-garth
Crosswood (Trawsgoed)
Llanafan
Wenallt
Llanddeiniol
Carreg Ti-pw
Llangwyryfon
Lledrod
Llanrhystud
Tynygraig
Trefenter
Rhyd-Rosser
Rhydfudr
Bronnant
Llansantffraed
Llan-non
Swyddffynnon
Bontnewydd
Rhos Haminiog
Nebo
MYNYDD BACH
Aberarth
Aberaeron
Cross Inn
Bethania
Blaenpennal
Pennant
Monachty
Penuwch
Ty'n-y-re-eithin
Ffos-y-ffin
Llanerchaeron
Llanaeron
Cilcennin
Llangeitho
Tregaron
New Quay (Cenewydd)
Marine Wildlife Centre
Maen-y-groes
Gilfachreda
Llwyncelyn
Ciliau Aeron
Newbridge
Bwlch-Llan
Capel Betws Lleucu
Cwmtudu
Llanarth
Oakford (Derwen Gam)
Trefilan
Ystrad Aeron
Abermeurig
Gartheli
Nanternis
Cross Inn
Caerwedros
Pen-cae
Geneva
Talsarn
Llundain-fach
Llwyn-y-groes
Olmarch
Llanddewi Brefi
Ynys-Lochtyn
Blaen Celyn
Llwyndafydd
Synod Inn (Post-Mawr)
Mydroilyn
Dihewyd
Felinfach
Ffynnon-oer
Llangranog
Morfa
Pontgarreg
Penbryn
Cardigan Island
Aberporth
Tresaith
Brynhoffnant
Pentregat
Plwmp
Llangybi
Llanfair Clydogau
Talgarreg
Betws Bledrws
Silian
Cemaes Head
Gwbert
Cardigan Island Coastal Farm Park
Felinwynt
Parcllyn
Sarnau
Gorsgoch
Y Ferwig
Blaenannerch
Tan-y-groes
Capel Cynon
Bwlch-y-fadfa
Cribyn
Cellan
Allt-y-goed
Cippyn
St Dogmaels (Llandudoch)
Cardigan (Aberteifi)
Penparc
Tremain
Blaenporth
Glynarthen
Felin Wnda
Brithdir
Rhydlewis
Hawen
Ffostrasol
Aber
Cwrtnewydd
Maestir
Lampeter (Llanbedr Pont Steffan)
Pentrefelin
Cwmann
Moylgrove (Trewyddel)
Pantgwyn
Noyadd Trefawr
Beulah
Bettws Ifan
Troedyraur
Penrhiw-pal
Pont-Sian
Cwmsychpant
Drefach
Llanwnnen
Pentre-bach
Alltyblacca
Llangoedmor
Ponthirwaun
Brongest
Coed-y-bryn
Maes Llyn
Tre-groes
Rhydowen
Llanwenog
Pencarreg
Ffaldybrenin
Ffarmers
Cwrt-y-Cadno
Monington
Pen-y-bryn
Cilgerran
Llechryd
Llandygwydd
National Coracle Centre
Brongwyn
Croes-lan
Pren-gwyn
Capel Dewi
Llanybydder
Glan Duar
Glanrhyd
Bridell
Cwm Plysgog
Cnwcau
Cenarth
Cwm-cou
Llandyfriog
Aber-banc
Penrhiw-llan
Horeb
Rhuddlan
Llantood
Rhos-hill
Newchapel (Capel Newydd)
Abercych
Penrhiw
Newcastle Emlyn (Castell Newydd Emlyn)
Adpar
Aberarad
Pentrecagal
Henllan
Teifi Valley
Llangeler
Drefach
Llandysul
Pontwelly
Llanfihangel-ar-Arth
Maesycrugiau
Aber-Giâr
Pumsaint
Five Saints Stone
Caio
Dolaucothi Gold Mines
Eglwyswrw
Llanfair-Nant-Gwyn
Boncath
Cilwendeg Shell House
Penrherber
Felindre
Cwmhiraeth
Llanllwni
Rhydcymerau
Crugybar
Mynydd Pencarreg
A496
A493
A487
A44
A485
A4120
A482
A486
A475
A484
A478
A4159
B4405
B4353
B4572
B4340
B4575
B4576
B4577
B4578
B4337
B4342
B4339
B4334
B4321
B4333
B4338
B4459
B4476
B4571
B4570
B4548
B4546
B4582
B4332
B4343

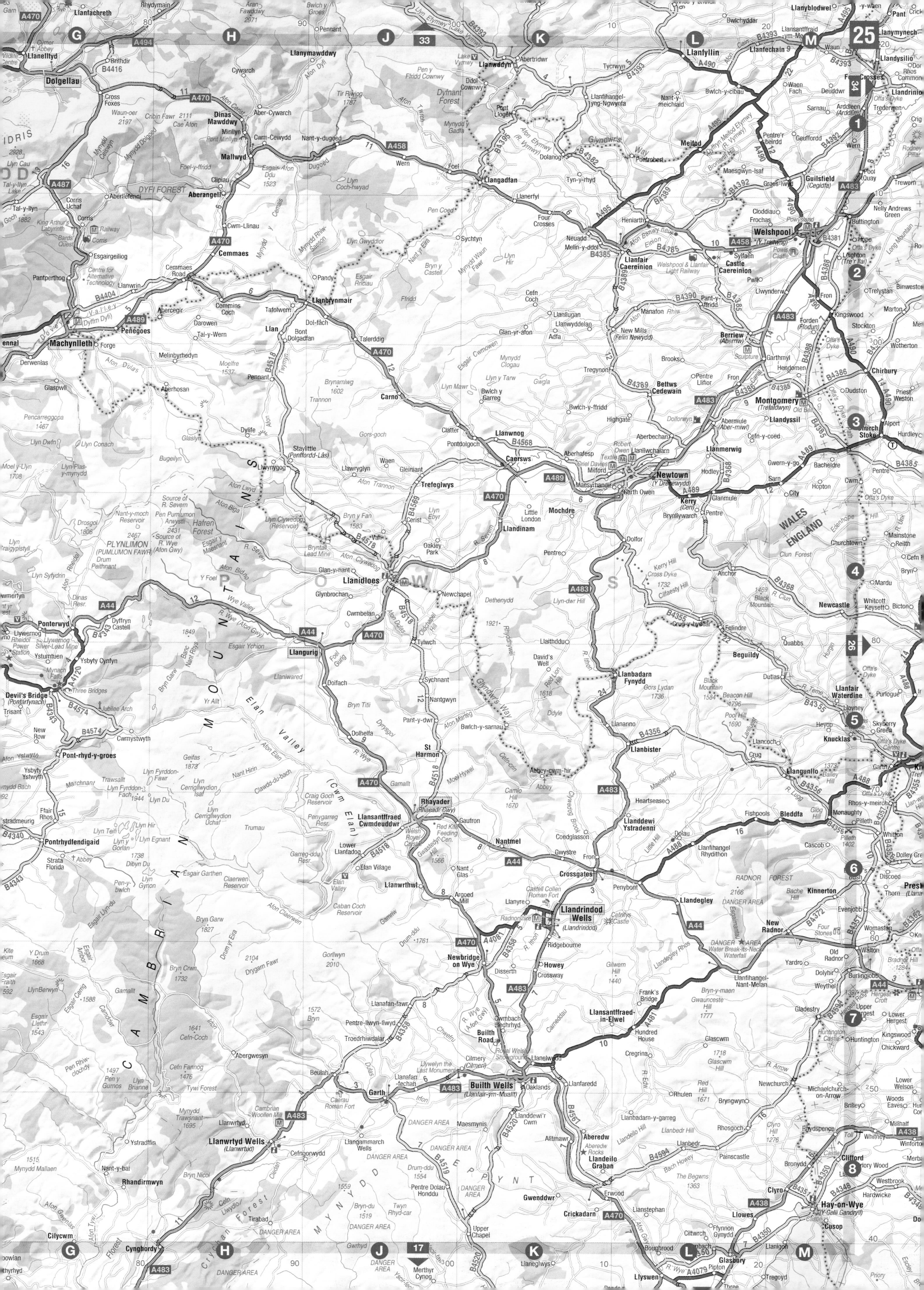
G
H
J
K
L
M
33
34
26
17
1
2
3
4
5
6
7
8
A470
A494
A487
A458
A489
A44
A495
A490
A483
A488
A481
A4081
A438
A4079
A489
A458
B4416
B4404
B4393
B4395
B4382
B4389
B4385
B4390
B4568
B4569
B4518
B4574
B4343
B4340
B4355
B4356
B4368
B4386
B4388
B4381
B4372
B4357
B4358
B4520
B4519
B4567
B4594
B4350
B4351
B4348
Llanfachreth
Llanelltyd
Dolgellau
Cross Foxes
Dinas Mawddwy
Mallwyd
Llanymawddwy
Lake Vyrnwy
Llanwddyn
Abertridwr
Llanfyllin
Llanfechain
Llanymynech
Llansantffraid-ym-Mechain
Meifod
Pontrobert
Llangadfan
Llanerfyl
Foel
Cwm-Cewydd
Nant-y-dugoed
Wern
Aberangell
Corris
Corris Uchaf
Aberllefenni
Cemmaes
Cemmaes Road
Tal-y-llyn
Esgairgeiliog
Pantperthog
Llanwrin
Machynlleth
Penegoes
Forge
Derwenlas
Abercegir
Commins Coch
Darowen
Tal-y-Wern
Llanbrynmair
Tafolwern
Dol-fâch
Llan
Bont Dolgadfan
Talerddig
Pennant
Carno
Glaspwll
Aberhosan
Dylife
Staylittle (Penffordd-Lâs)
Llwynygog
Trefeglwys
Caersws
Llanwnog
Pontdolgoch
Clatter
Llanidloes
Llandinam
Little London
Mochdre
Newtown (Y Drenewydd)
Llanllwchaiarn
Aberhafesp
Milford
Maesyrhandir
Garth Owen
Kerry (Ceri)
Glanmule
Welshpool (Y Trallwng)
Guilsfield (Cegidfa)
Pool Quay
Buttington
Llanfair Caereinion
Castle Caereinion
Sylfaen
Manafon
New Mills (Felin Newydd)
Berriew (Aberriw)
Garthmyl
Forden (Ffodun)
Kingswood
Montgomery (Trefaldwyn)
Llandyssil
Abermule (Aber-miwl)
Llanmerewig
Bettws Cedewain
Tregynon
Chirbury
Church Stoke
Sarn
WALES
ENGLAND
Clun Forest
Churchtown
Mainstone
Newcastle
Bicton
Felindre
Beguildy
Llanfair Waterdine
Knucklas
Llangunllo
Bleddfa
Monaughty
Pilleth
Whitton
Kinnerton
New Radnor
Old Radnor
Walton
Gladestry
Huntington
Kington
Clyro
Hay-on-Wye (Y Gelli Gandryll)
Clifford
Cusop
Glasbury
Llyswen
Boughrood
Llowes
Llanigon
Ponterwyd
Devil's Bridge (Pontarfynach)
Ysbyty Cynfyn
Pont-rhyd-y-groes
Ysbyty Ystwyth
Pontrhydfendigaid
Strata Florida
Cwmystwyth
Llangurig
Rhayader (Rhaeadr Gwy)
Llansantffraed Cwmdeuddwr
Elan Village
St Harmon
Llanwrthwl
Nantmel
Crossgates
Llandrindod Wells
Howey
Newbridge on Wye
Disserth
Builth Road
Builth Wells (Llanfair-ym-Muallt)
Llanelwedd
Garth
Beulah
Abergwesyn
Llanwrtyd Wells (Llanwrtud)
Llangammarch Wells
Rhandirmwyn
Cynghordy
Cilycwm
Upper Chapel
Erwood
Aberedw
Llandeilo Graban
Gwenddwr
Crickadarn
Llanbister
Llananno
Llanbadarn Fynydd
Abbey-cwm-hir
Llanddewi Ystradenni
Penybont
Llandegley
Llansantffraed-in-Elwel
Llanfihangel-Nant-Melan
Painscastle
Llanbedr
PLYNLIMON (PUMLUMON FAWR)
CAMBRIAN MOUNTAINS
POWYS
MYNYDD EPPYNT
DYFI FOREST
Hafren Forest
Elan Valley
RADNOR FOREST
Glyndŵr's Way
Offa's Dyke
DANGER AREA

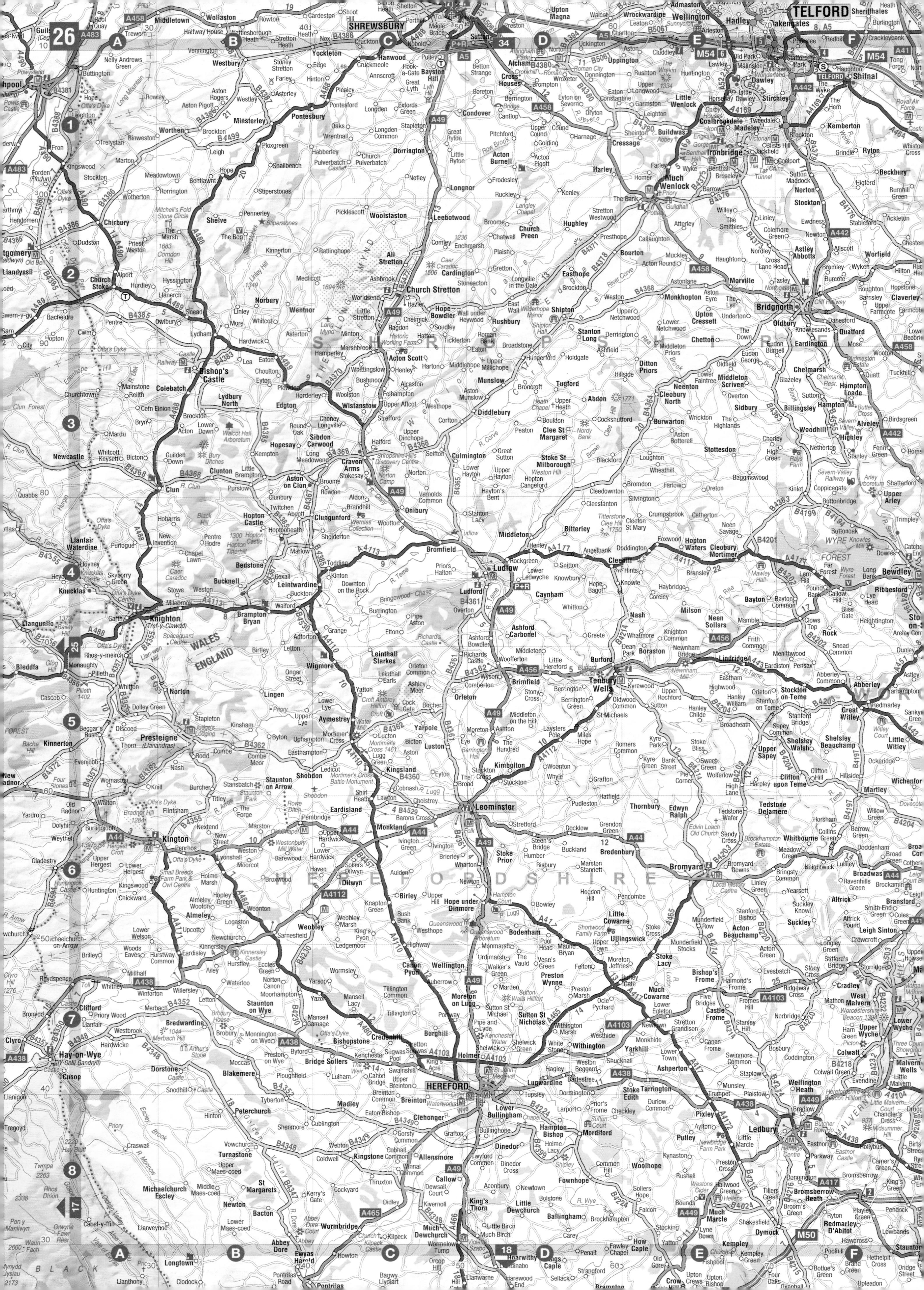

26
A
B
C
D
E
F
1
2
3
4
5
6
7
8
17
18
25
34
TELFORD
SHREWSBURY
Wellington
Hadley
Oakengates
Shifnal
Dawley
Stirchley
Madeley
Ironbridge
Coalbrookdale
Much Wenlock
Broseley
Bridgnorth
Pontesbury
Minsterley
Westbury
Hanwood
Bayston Hill
Condover
Dorrington
Cressage
Buildwas
Chirbury
Church Stoke
Montgomery
Bishop's Castle
Lydham
Norbury
Wentnor
Church Stretton
All Stretton
Little Stretton
Acton Scott
Leebotwood
Longnor
Cardington
Shipton
Easthope
Morville
Oldbury
Quatford
Eardington
Kinlet
Upper Arley
Highley
Alveley
Stottesdon
Burwarton
Cleobury North
Ditton Priors
Clun
Clunton
Colebatch
Lydbury North
Edgton
Hopesay
Aston on Clun
Craven Arms
Sibdon Carwood
Wistanstow
Onibury
Culmington
Diddlebury
Munslow
Hopton Castle
Clungunford
Bucknell
Leintwardine
Bedstone
Bromfield
Ludlow
Ludford
Caynham
Middleton
Cleobury Mortimer
Hopton Wafers
Cleehill
Bewdley
Ribbesford
Rock
Knighton
Knucklas
Llanfair Waterdine
Brampton Bryan
Newcastle
WALES
ENGLAND
Presteigne
Kinnerton
Norton
Lingen
Wigmore
Aymestrey
Yarpole
Luston
Orleton
Richards Castle
Brimfield
Burford
Tenbury Wells
Leominster
Kingsland
Shobdon
Staunton on Arrow
Pembridge
Eardisland
Kington
Monkland
Stoke Prior
Docklow
Bredenbury
Bromyard
Whitbourne
Tedstone Delamere
Edwyn Ralph
Thornbury
Great Witley
Stockton on Teme
Abberley
Shelsley Beauchamp
Martley
Clifton upon Teme
Upper Sapey
HEREFORDSHIRE
Dilwyn
Weobley
Birley
Hope under Dinmore
Bodenham
Ullingswick
Stoke Lacy
Much Cowarne
Bishop's Frome
Acton Beauchamp
Suckley
Cradley
West Malvern
Malvern Wells
Colwall
Ledbury
Wellington Heath
Eastnor
Bosbury
Castle Frome
Ashperton
Yarkhill
Withington
Sutton St Nicholas
Moreton on Lugg
Marden
Wellington
Canon Pyon
Burghill
Credenhill
Mansell Lacy
Staunton on Wye
Bredwardine
Eardisley
Almeley
Kinnersley
Sarnesfield
Clifford
Hay-on-Wye
Cusop
Bridge Sollers
Bishopstone
Madley
Blakemere
Dorstone
Peterchurch
HEREFORD
Holmer
Lugwardine
Stoke Edith
Tarrington
Mordiford
Hampton Bishop
Lower Bullingham
Clehonger
Allensmore
Kingstone
Callow
Much Dewchurch
Little Dewchurch
Fownhope
Woolhope
Putley
Pixley
Ballingham
Much Marcle
Kempley
Dymock
Redmarley D'Abitot
Bromsberrow Heath
Wormbridge
Abbey Dore
Ewyas Harold
Longtown
Michaelchurch Escley
St Margarets
Newton
Bacton
Turnastone
Vowchurch
Hoarwithy
Kings Caple
How Caple
SHROPSHIRE
M54
M50
A5
A49
A458
A483
A488
A489
A4113
A4117
A456
A44
A4112
A4110
A417
A465
A4103
A438
A449
A4172
A466
A480
A4111
A443
A451
A442
A4169

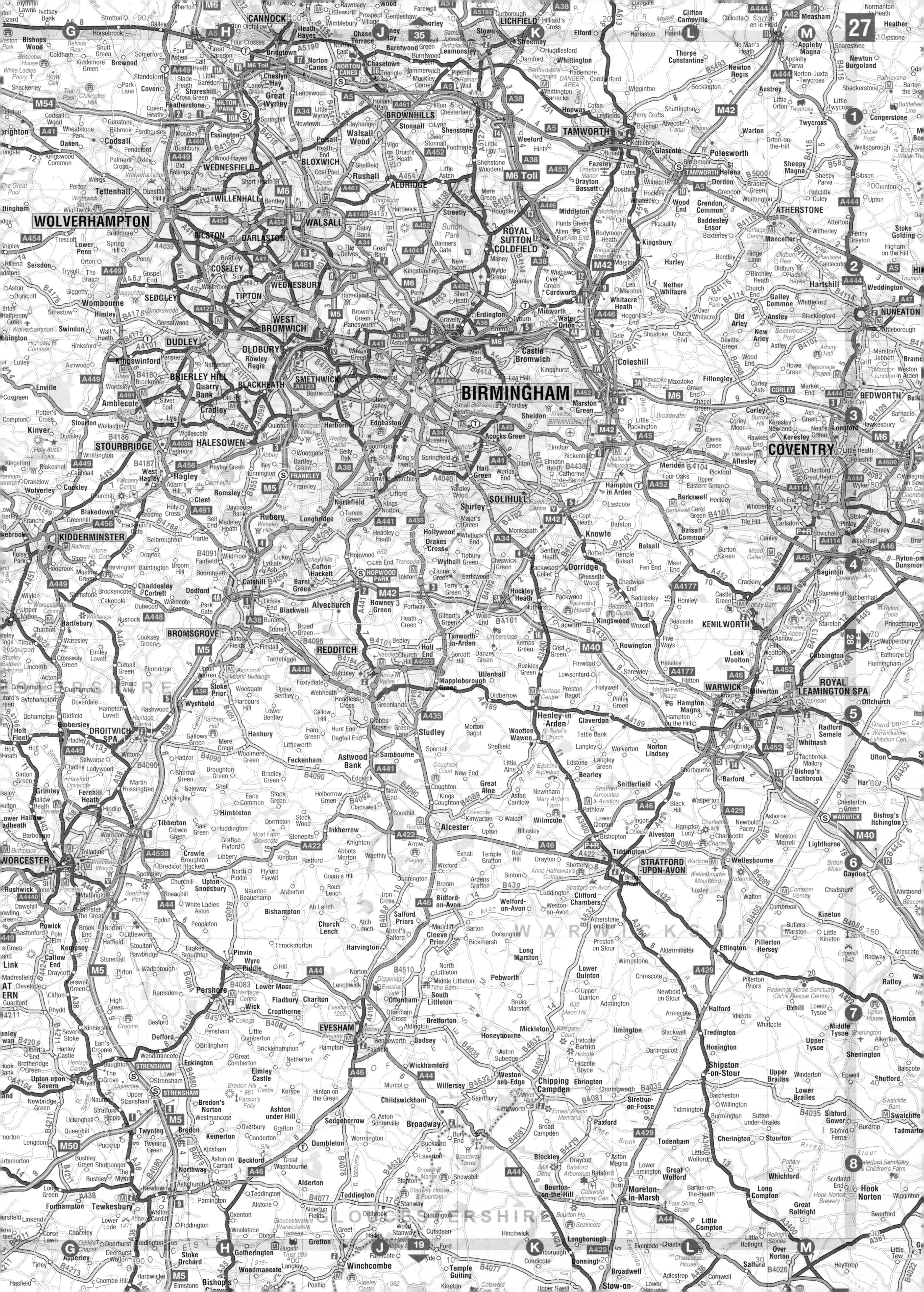
27
28
35
19
G
H
J
K
L
M
1
2
3
4
5
6
7
8
CANNOCK
LICHFIELD
TAMWORTH
WOLVERHAMPTON
WALSALL
WEDNESFIELD
WILLENHALL
BLOXWICH
BROWNHILLS
ALDRIDGE
BILSTON
DARLASTON
COSELEY
WEDNESBURY
TIPTON
SEDGLEY
WEST BROMWICH
DUDLEY
OLDBURY
SMETHWICK
BRIERLEY HILL
BLACKHEATH
STOURBRIDGE
HALESOWEN
ROYAL SUTTON COLDFIELD
BIRMINGHAM
SOLIHULL
NUNEATON
BEDWORTH
COVENTRY
KENILWORTH
WARWICK
ROYAL LEAMINGTON SPA
KIDDERMINSTER
BROMSGROVE
REDDITCH
DROITWICH SPA
WORCESTER
STRATFORD-UPON-AVON
EVESHAM
ATHERSTONE
Coleshill
Alcester
Pershore
Tewkesbury
Broadway
Chipping Campden
Shipston-on-Stour
Moreton-in-Marsh
Winchcombe
WARWICKSHIRE
GLOUCESTERSHIRE
M6
M6 Toll
M5
M42
M40
M50
M54

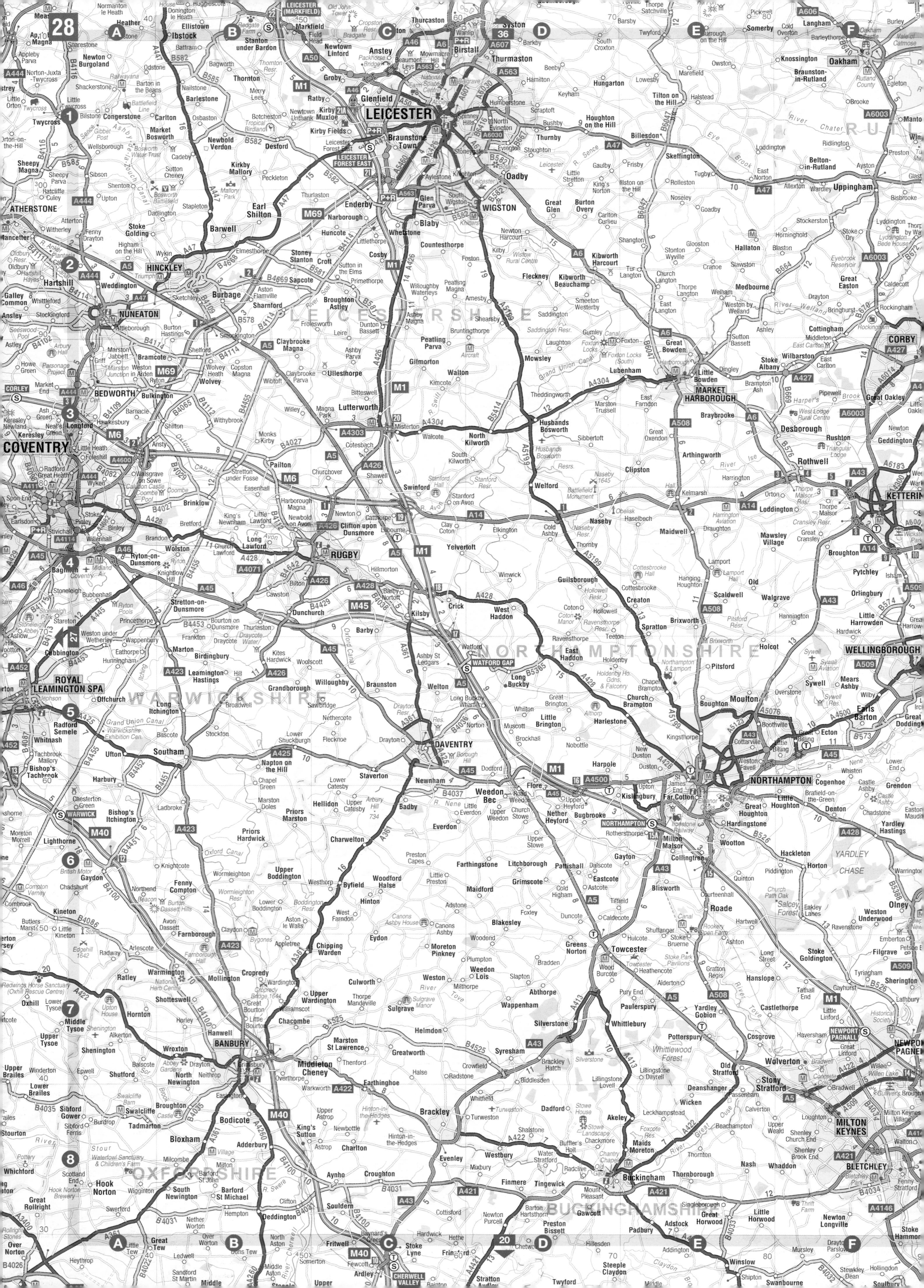
28
36
20
A
B
C
D
E
F
1
2
3
4
5
6
7
8
LEICESTERSHIRE
WARWICKSHIRE
NORTHAMPTONSHIRE
OXFORDSHIRE
BUCKINGHAMSHIRE
LEICESTER
COVENTRY
NUNEATON
HINCKLEY
BEDWORTH
RUGBY
ROYAL LEAMINGTON SPA
WARWICK
BANBURY
DAVENTRY
NORTHAMPTON
MARKET HARBOROUGH
KETTERING
CORBY
WELLINGBOROUGH
MILTON KEYNES
BLETCHLEY
ATHERSTONE
Oakham
Uppingham
Wigston
Oadby
Lutterworth
Towcester
Brackley
Buckingham
Southam
Bicester
Rothwell
Desborough
Stony Stratford
Wolverton
Olney
M1
M6
M40
M45
M69
A5
A43
A45
A14
A6
A47
A422
A423
A361
A426
A428
A508
A5199
A4303
A4304
WATFORD GAP
CHERWELL VALLEY
NEWPORT PAGNELL
LEICESTER FOREST EAST
LEICESTER (MARKFIELD)
CORLEY

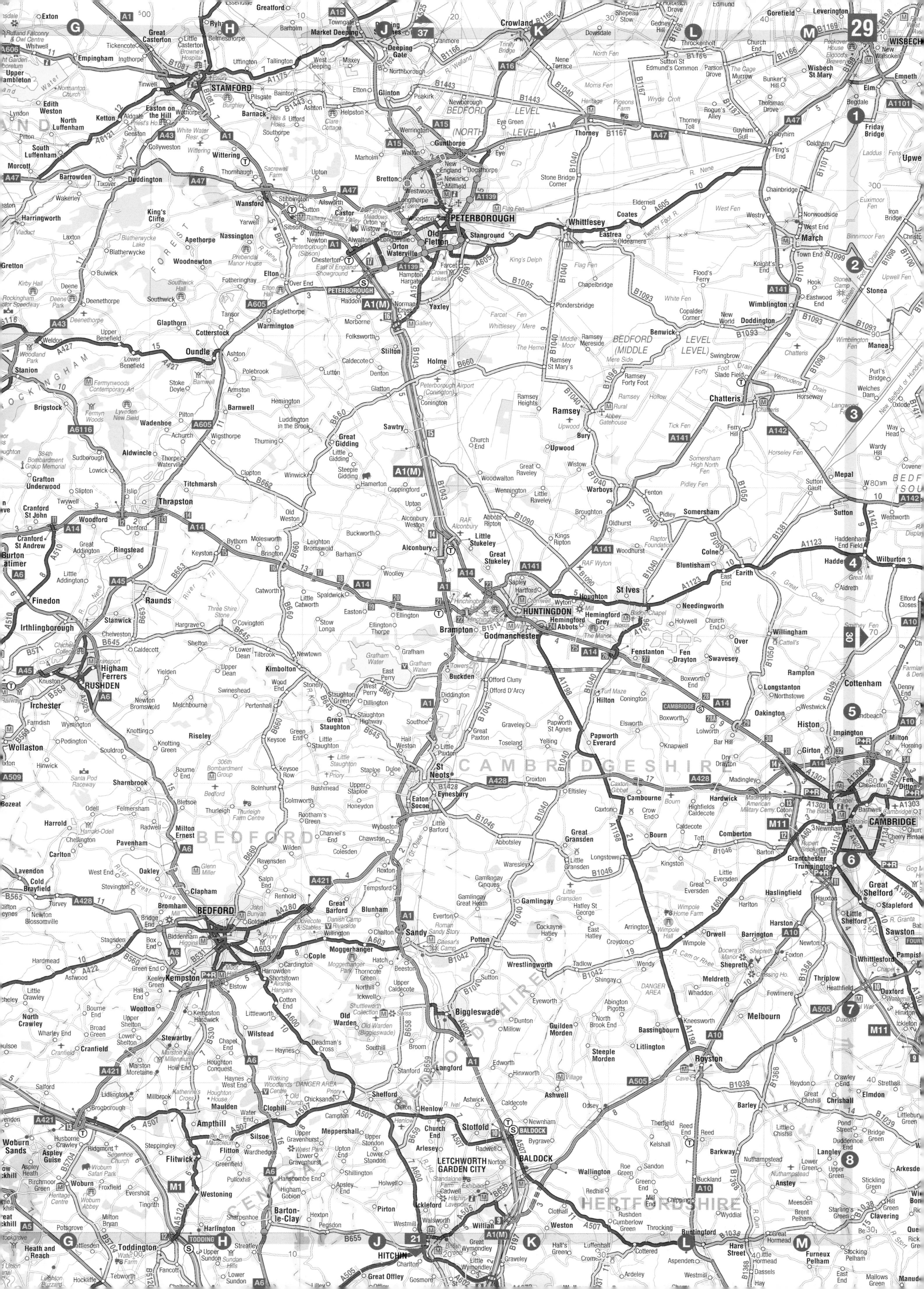

29
STAMFORD
PETERBOROUGH
WISBECH
Whittlesey
March
Chatteris
Ramsey
Oundle
Thrapston
HUNTINGDON
St Ives
Godmanchester
St Neots
Eaton Socon
Sandy
BEDFORD
Kempston
Biggleswade
Royston
Baldock
LETCHWORTH GARDEN CITY
HITCHIN
CAMBRIDGE
RUSHDEN
Higham Ferrers
Irthlingborough
Raunds
Finedon
Ampthill
Flitwick
Shefford
Stotfold
Potton
Toddington
Barton-le-Clay
Market Deeping
Deeping Gate
Crowland
Thorney
Eye
Yaxley
Stilton
Sawtry
Alconbury
Brampton
Buckden
Kimbolton
Somersham
Sutton
Cottenham
Histon
Girton
Melbourn
Sawston
Great Shelford
Harston
Bassingbourn
Gamlingay
Hemingford Grey
Fenstanton
Papworth Everard
Cambourne
Comberton
Great Gransden
Wrestlingworth
Guilden Morden
Steeple Morden
Ashwell
Arlesey
Henlow
Clophill
Silsoe
Westoning
Harlington
Cranfield
Wootton
Clapham
Oakley
Riseley
Sharnbrook
Wollaston
Irchester
Woodnewton
Nassington
Wansford
Elton
Warmington
Barnwell
Brigstock
Aldwincle
Woodford
Ringstead
Molesworth
Catworth
Spaldwick
Ellington
Great Gidding
Holme
Upwood
Warboys
Bury
Earith
Bluntisham
Colne
Willingham
Swavesey
Longstanton
Oakington
Haddenham
Wilburton
Doddington
Wimblington
Benwick
Manea
Stonea
Friday Bridge
Elm
Emneth
Barkway
Barley
Langley
Elmdon
Clavering
Anstey
CAMBRIDGESHIRE
BEDFORD
BEDFORDSHIRE
HERTFORDSHIRE
ROCKINGHAM FOREST
BEDFORD (NORTH LEVEL)
BEDFORD (MIDDLE LEVEL)
A1
A1(M)
A14
A428
A421
A6
A45
A47
A605
A141
A142
A10
A505
A507
A600
A603
M1
M11
G
H
J
K
L
M
1
2
3
4
5
6
7
8
37
30

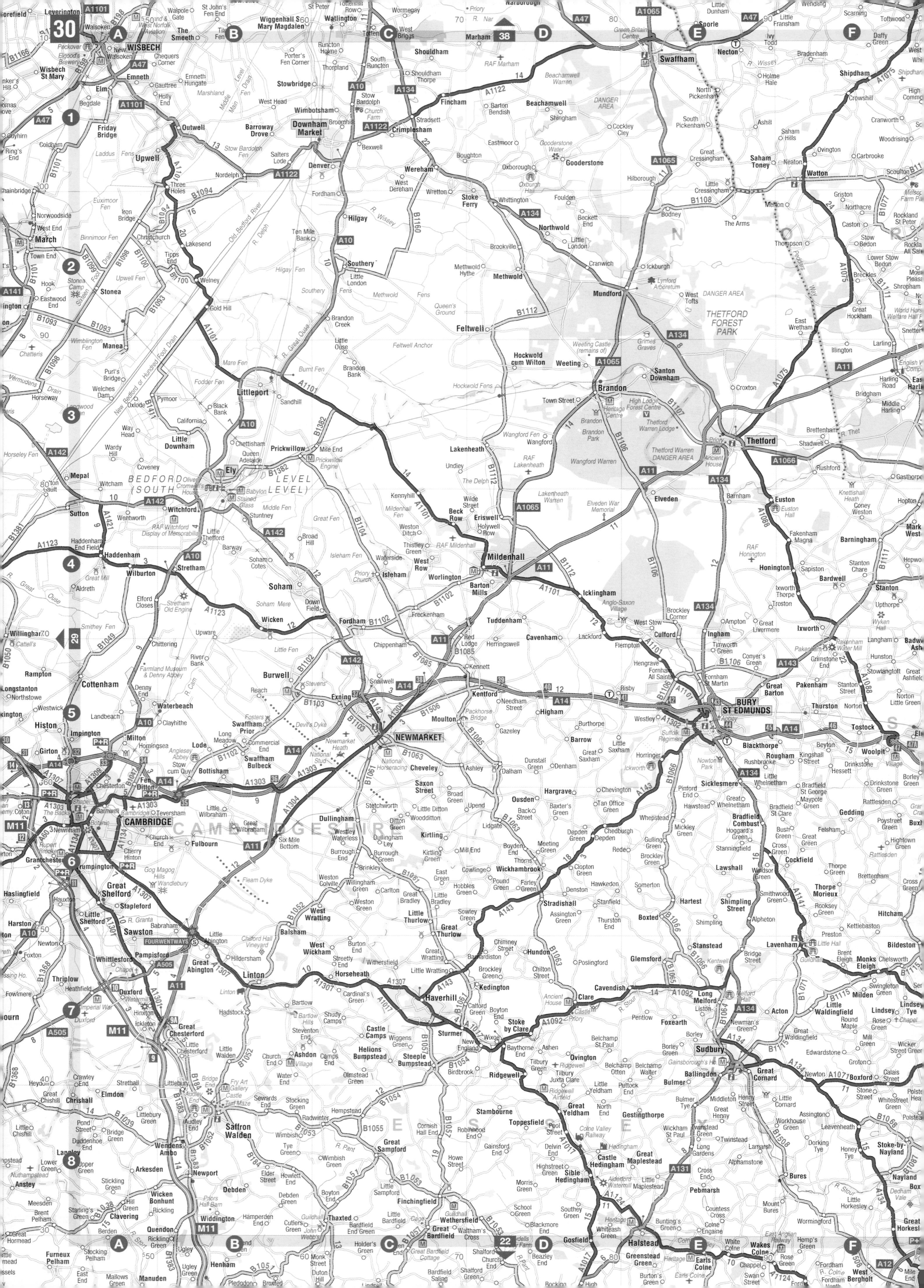
30
38
29
22
A
B
C
D
E
F
1
2
3
4
5
6
7
8
WISBECH
Wisbech St Mary
Walsoken
Emneth
Elm
Outwell
Upwell
Downham Market
Denver
Wimbotsham
Stow Bardolph
Crimplesham
Fincham
Shouldham
Marham
RAF Marham
Beachamwell
Swaffham
Sporle
Necton
Shipdham
Watton
Saham Toney
South Pickenham
North Pickenham
Gooderstone
Oxborough
Stoke Ferry
Wereham
Hilgay
Southery
March
Manea
Stonea
Welney
Littleport
Feltwell
Hockwold cum Wilton
Weeting
Methwold
Mundford
Brandon
Santon Downham
Thetford
THETFORD FOREST PARK
Elveden
Lakenheath
RAF Lakenheath
Mildenhall
Barton Mills
Worlington
Icklingham
Euston
Honington
Ixworth
Bardwell
Stanton
Ely
Witchford
Sutton
Mepal
Haddenham
Wilburton
Stretham
Soham
Isleham
Fordham
Wicken
Burwell
Exning
NEWMARKET
Kentford
Higham
BURY ST EDMUNDS
Woolpit
Tostock
Great Barton
Pakenham
Thurston
Cottenham
Histon
Impington
Milton
Waterbeach
CAMBRIDGE
Fulbourn
Grantchester
Trumpington
Great Shelford
Sawston
Linton
Haverhill
Clare
Cavendish
Long Melford
Lavenham
Sudbury
Great Cornard
Saffron Walden
Newport
Thaxted
Great Bardfield
Finchingfield
Wethersfield
Castle Hedingham
Sible Hedingham
Halstead
Great Yeldham
Ridgewell
Steeple Bumpstead
Helions Bumpstead
Ashdon
Great Sampford
Radwinter
Clavering
Elmdon
Great Chesterford
Duxford
Sawston
Balsham
West Wickham
West Wratting
Kedington
Stradishall
Glemsford
Hartest
Lawshall
Boxford
Nayland
Bures
Earls Colne
Wakes Colne
Greenstead Green
Gosfield
CAMBRIDGESHIRE
BEDFORD LEVEL (SOUTH LEVEL)
DANGER AREA
FOURWENTWAYS
A10
A11
A14
A47
A134
A142
A143
A505
A1065
A1066
A1101
A1122
A1123
A1307
M11

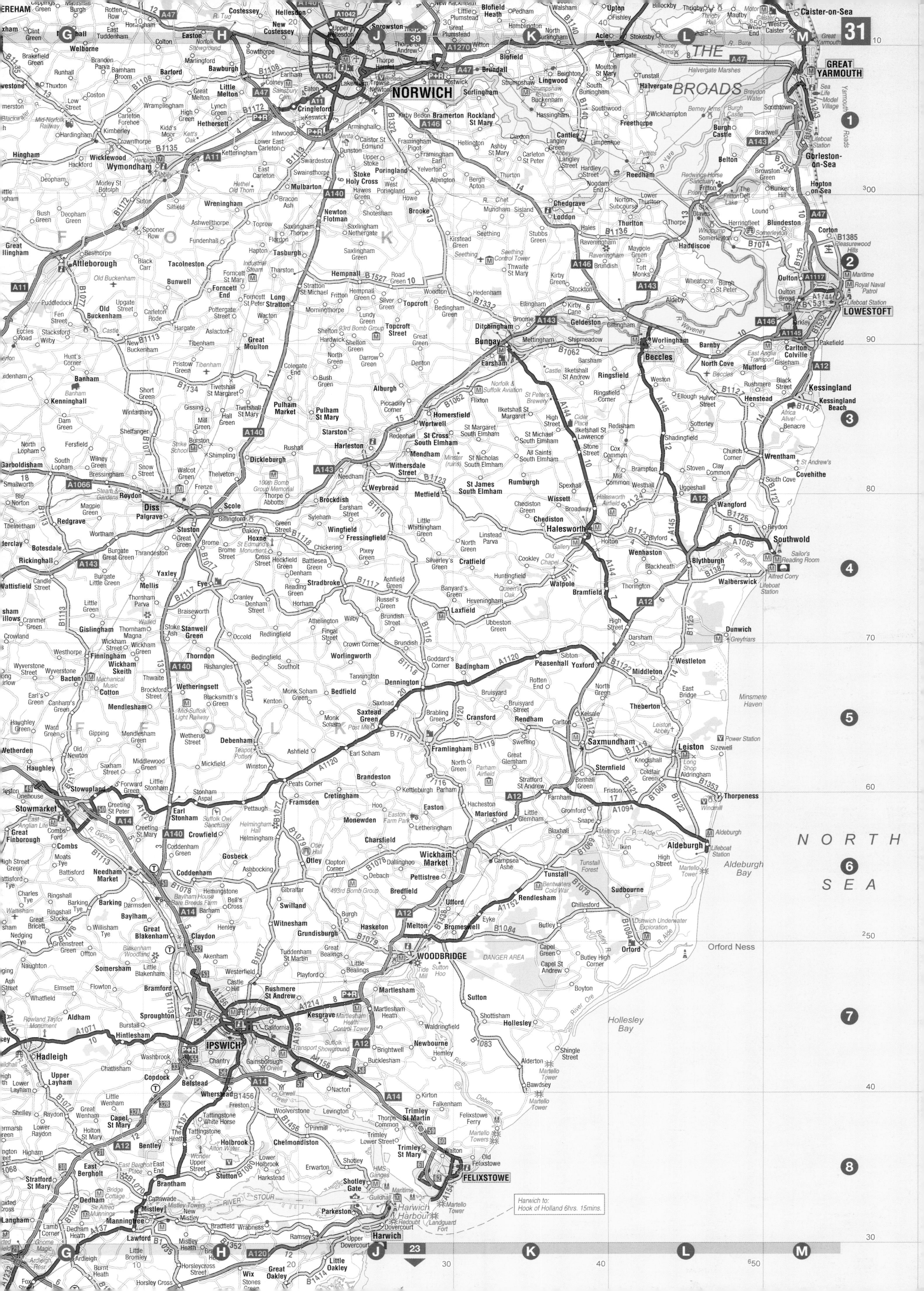
31
G
H
J
39
K
L
M
NORWICH
GREAT YARMOUTH
THE BROADS
LOWESTOFT
Caister-on-Sea
Gorleston-on-Sea
Hopton on Sea
Corton
Oulton Broad
Carlton Colville
Kessingland
Wymondham
Attleborough
Hingham
Diss
Scole
Eye
Harleston
Bungay
Beccles
Halesworth
Southwold
Walberswick
Blythburgh
Wrentham
Covehithe
Dunwich
Westleton
Yoxford
Saxmundham
Leiston
Sizewell
Thorpeness
Aldeburgh
Aldeburgh Bay
Orford
Orford Ness
Hollesley Bay
Framlingham
Wickham Market
Debenham
Stowmarket
Needham Market
Woodbridge
Melton
IPSWICH
Kesgrave
Hadleigh
FELIXSTOWE
Harwich
Dovercourt
Manningtree
Mistley
Shotley Gate
Trimley St Martin
Trimley St Mary
Harwich to: Hook of Holland 6hrs. 15mins.
NORTH SEA
1
2
3
4
5
6
7
8
23
10
20
30
40
50
60
70
80
90
300
250

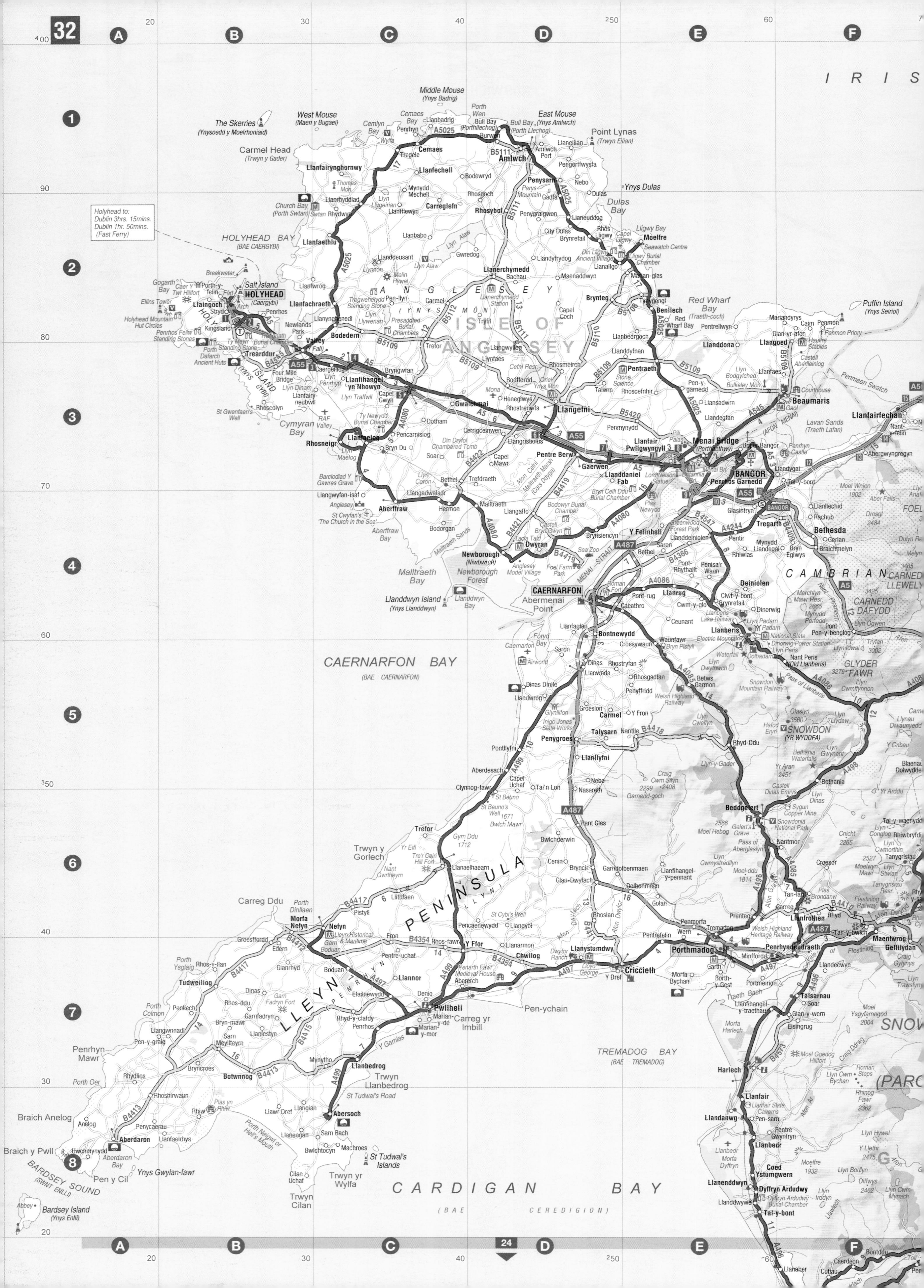

IRIS
Middle Mouse
(Ynys Badrig)
West Mouse
(Maen y Bugael)
The Skerries
(Ynysoedd y Moelrhoniaid)
Carmel Head
(Trwyn y Gader)
East Mouse
(Ynys Amlwch)
Point Lynas
(Trwyn Eilian)
Cemaes Bay
Llanbadrig
Porth Wen
Bull Bay
(Porthllechog)
Cemlyn Bay
Wylfa
Penrhyn
A5025
Cemaes
Tregele
Burwen
Amlwch
Amlwch Port
Llaneilian
Penygorffwysfa
Llanfairynghornwy
Llanfechell
Bodewryd
Penysarn
Nebo
Ynys Dulas
Dulas
Dulas Bay
Parys Mountain
Gadfa
Mynydd Mechell
Rhosgoch
Church Bay
(Porth Swtan)
Swtan
Rhydwyn
Llanrhyddlad
Llanfflewyn
Carreglefn
Rhosybol
Penygraigwen
Llaneuddog
Holyhead to:
Dublin 3hrs. 15mins.
Dublin 1hr. 50mins.
(Fast Ferry)
HOLYHEAD BAY
(BAE CAERGYBI)
Llanbabo
City Dulas
Lligwy Bay
Rhos Lligwy
Moelfre
Llantaethlu
Brynrefail
Seawatch Centre
Llanddeusant
Llyn Alaw
Gwredog
Din Lligwy Ancient Village
Llanallgo
Lligwy Burial Chamber
Llandyfrydog
Llanerchymedd
Bachau
Maenaddwyn
Marian-glas
Breakwater
Salt Island
Gogarth Bay
Porth-y-felin
Llanfwrog
Holyhead Mountain Hut Circles
Ellins Tower
HOLYHEAD
(Caergybi)
Llaingoch
Penrhos
Stryd
Llanfachraeth
Pen-llyn
Brynteg
Tynygongl
Benllech
Red Wharf Bay
(Traeth-coch)
Red Wharf Bay
Capel Coch
Kingsland
Penrhos Feilw Standing Stones
Porth Dafarch
Trearddur
Valley
(Fali)
Bodedern
ANGLESEY
(YNYS MÔN)
ISLE OF ANGLESEY
Trefor
Llanbedrgoch
Pentrellwyn
Llanddona
Mariandyrys
Glan-yr-afon
Llangoed
Penmon Priory
Puffin Island
(Ynys Seiriol)
Penmon
Llangwyllog
Llynfaes
Llanddyfnan
Rhosmeirch
Pentraeth
Four Mile Bridge
Rhoscolyn
Llanfihangel yn Nhowyn
Caergeiliog
Bryngwran
Bodffordd
Talwrn
Rhoscefnhir
Llanfaes
Beaumaris
Capel Gwyn
Gwalchmai
Llangefni
Penmaen Swatch
Llanfairfechan
Cymyran Bay
RAF Valley
Ty Newydd Burial Chamber
Rhosneigr
Llanfaelog
Dotham
Pencarnisiog
Cerrigceinwen
Llangristiolus
Penmynydd
Llandegfan
Lavan Sands
(Traeth Lafan)
Menai Bridge
(Porthaethwy)
Llanfair Pwllgwyngyll
Pentre Berw
Gaerwen
Llanddaniel Fab
Bryn Celli Ddu Burial Chamber
Plas Newydd
BANGOR
Penrhos Garnedd
Penrhyn Castle
Llandygai
Tal-y-bont
Abergwyngregyn
Barclodiad Y Gawres Grave
Llangwyfan-isaf
Aberffraw
Llangadwaladr
Bethel
Trefdraeth
Malltraeth
Hermon
Bodorgan
Llangaffo
Brynsiencyn
Glasinfryn
Tregarth
Bethesda
Moel Wnion
Aber Falls
Drosgl
Llanllechid
Rachub
Gerlan
Aberffraw Bay
Y Felinheli
Llanddeiniolen
Pentir
Rhiwlas
Mynydd Llandegai
Bryn Eglwys
Braichmelyn
Malltraeth Bay
Newborough
(Niwbwrch)
Newborough Forest
Dwyran
Sea Zoo
Anglesey Model Village
Foel Farm Park
MENAI STRAIT
Bethel
Saron
Pont-Rhythallt
Penisa'r Waun
CAMBRIAN
CARNEDD LLEWELYN
Llanddwyn Island
(Ynys Llanddwyn)
Llanddwyn Bay
CAERNARFON
Abermenai Point
Pont-rug
Llanrug
Deiniolen
Clwt-y-bont
Brynrefail
Cwm-y-glo
Caeathro
Ceunant
Dinorwig
CARNEDD DAFYDD
Llanberis
Llanfaglan
Bontnewydd
Pen-y-benglog
Llyn Ogwen
Foryd Bay
Saron
Croesywaun
Waunfawr
Electric Mountain
Dinorwig Power Station
Llyn Idwal
Tryfan
Nant Peris
(Old Llanberis)
GLYDER FAWR
CAERNARFON BAY
(BAE CAERNARFON)
Dinas
Rhostryfan
Llanwnda
Rhosgadfan
Betws Garmon
Llyn Cwellyn
Dinas Dinlle
Llandwrog
Penyffridd
Welsh Highland Railway
Snowdon Mountain Railway
Pass of Llanberis
Glynllifon
Inigo Jones Slate Works
Groeslon
Carmel
Y Fron
Talysarn
Nantlle
Penygroes
SNOWDON
(YR WYDDFA)
Pontllyfni
Llanllyfni
Rhyd-Ddu
Aberdesach
Capel Uchaf
Clynnog-fawr
Tai'n Lon
Nebo
Nasareth
Garnedd-goch
Bethania
St Beuno's Well
Bwlch Mawr
Beddgelert
Sygun Copper Mine
Snowdonia National Park
Pant Glas
Moel Hebog
Pass of Aberglaslyn
Trefor
Gym Ddu
Bwlchderwin
Nantmor
Trwyn y Gorlech
Tre'r Ceiri Hill Fort
Llanaelhaearn
PENINSULA
(LLYN)
Cenin
Bryncir
Garndolbenmaen
Llanfihangel-y-pennant
Moel-ddu
Nant Gwrtheyrn
Glan-Dwyfach
Dolbenmaen
Carreg Ddu
Porth Dinllaen
Llithfaen
Pistyll
Golan
Morfa Nefyn
Nefyn
St Cybi's Well
Rhoslan
Prenteg
Tan-lan
Llanfrothen
Lleyn Historical & Maritime
Pencaenewydd
Llangybi
Penmorfa
Wern
Tremadog
Groesffordd
Edern
Fron
B4354
Rhos-fawr
Y Ffor
Llanarmon
Pentrefelin
Welsh Highland Heritage Railway
Penrhyndeudraeth
Maentwrog
Gellilydan
Porth Ysglaig
Rhos-y-llan
Garnfadryn
Glanrhyd
Pentre-uchaf
Chwilog
Llanystumdwy
Porthmadog
Minffordd
Tudweiliog
Boduan
Penarth Fawr Medieval House
Abererch
Criccieth
Y Dref
Morfa Bychan
Borth-y-Gest
Portmeirion
Llandecwyn
Llannor
Dinas
Garn Fadryn Fort
Efailnewydd
Denio
LLEYN
Porth Colmon
Penllech
Rhos-ddu
Pwllheli
Carreg yr Imbill
Pen-ychain
Llanfihangel-y-traethau
Talsarnau
Soar
Glan-y-wern
Eisingrug
Moel Ysgyfarnogod
SNOW
Llangwnnadl
Bryn-mawr
Rhyd-y-clafdy
Penrhos
Marian-y-de
Marian-y-mor
Morfa Harlech
Pen-y-graig
Sarn Meyllteyrn
Llaniestyn
Y Gamlas
TREMADOG BAY
(BAE TREMADOG)
Moel Goedog Hillfort
Penrhyn Mawr
Bryncroes
Botwnnog
Mynytho
Llanbedrog
Trwyn Llanbedrog
Harlech
Porth Oer
Rhydlios
St Tudwal's Road
Llanfair
Llanfair Slate Caverns
Pen-sarn
Llyn Cwm Bychan
Rhinog Fawr
Rhoshirwaun
Rhiw
Plas yn Rhiw
Lawr Dref
Llangian
Abersoch
Llandanwg
Pentre Gwynfryn
Braich Anelog
Anelog
Penycaerau
Porth Neigwl or Hell's Mouth
Llanengan
Sarn Bach
Aberdaron
Llanfaelrhys
Machroes
Llanbedr
Morfa Dyffryn
Llyn Hywel
Y Llethr
Braich y Pwll
Uwchmynydd
Aberdaron Bay
Bwlchtocyn
St Tudwal's Islands
Moelfre
Llyn Bodlyn
Coed Ystumgwern
Diffwys
Ynys Gwylan-fawr
Pen y Cil
Cilan Uchaf
Trwyn yr Wylfa
Llanenddwyn
Dyffryn Ardudwy
Dyffryn Ardudwy Burial Chamber
Llyn Irddyn
BARDSEY SOUND
(SWNT ENLLI)
CARDIGAN BAY
(BAE CEREDIGION)
Trwyn Cilan
Llanddwywe
Tal-y-bont
Abbey
Bardsey Island
(Ynys Enlli)
Llanaber
Bontddu
Cutiau
Caerdeon
A
B
C
D
E
F
1
2
3
4
5
6
7
8
24

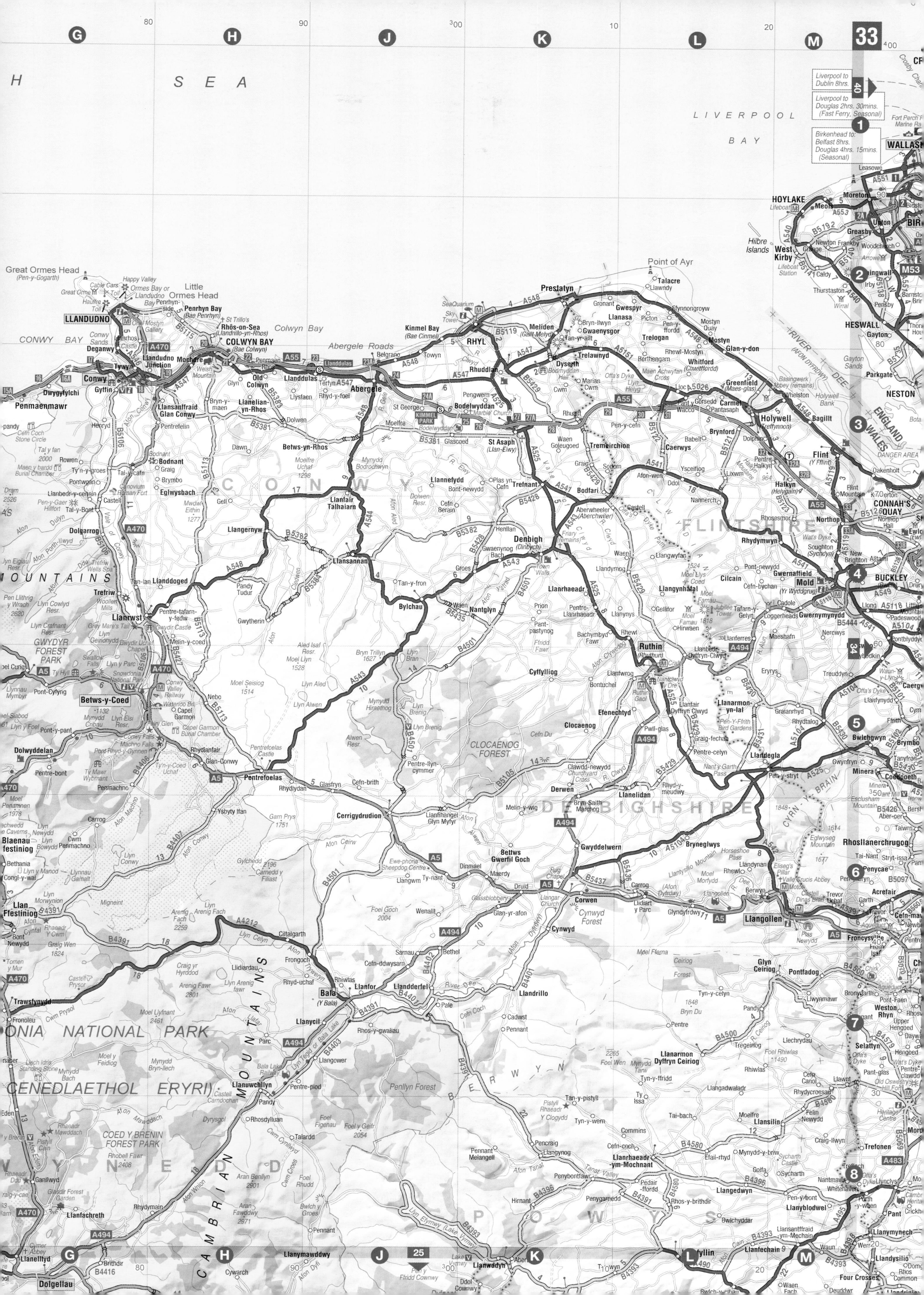

G
H
J
K
L
M
80
90
300
10
20
400
SEA
LIVERPOOL
BAY
Liverpool to Dublin 8hrs.
Liverpool to Douglas 2hrs. 30mins. (Fast Ferry, Seasonal)
Birkenhead to: Belfast 8hrs. Douglas 4hrs. 15mins. (Seasonal)
40
WALLASEY
HOYLAKE
Meols
Moreton
Leasowe
Upton
Greasby
Hilbre Islands
West Kirby
Caldy
Irby
Thurstaston
Pensby
HESWALL
Gayton
Gayton Sands
Parkgate
NESTON
Bagillt
ENGLAND
WALES
Flint (Y Fflint)
Oakenholt
Flint Mountain
CONNAH'S QUAY
Northop
Northop Hall
Soughton (Sychdyn)
New Brighton
Buckley
BUCKLEY (Bwcle)
Mold (Yr Wyddgrug)
Gwernaffield
Gwernymynydd
Loggerheads
Cadole
Maeshafn
Nercwys
Treuddyn
Pontblyddyn
Llanfynydd
Rhydtalog
Bwlchgwyn
Brymbo
Minera
Coedpoeth
Gwynfryn
Llandegla
Point of Ayr
Talacre
Llawndy
Prestatyn
Gronant
Gwespyr
Llanasa
Picton
Ffynnongroyw
Mostyn
Mostyn Quay
Glan-y-don
Trelogan
Whitford (Chwitffordd)
Greenfield (Maes-glas)
Holywell (Treffynnon)
Brynford
Carmel
Gorsedd
Pantasaph
Lloc
Halkyn (Helygain)
Rhosesmor
Rhydymwyn
Cilcain
Pont-newydd
Cefn-bychan
Gellifor
Llanferres
Llanbedr Dyffryn-Clwyd
Ruthin (Rhuthun)
Eryrys
Llanarmon-yn-Ial
Graianrhyd
Pwll-glas
Graig-fechan
Pentre-celyn
Clocaenog
Cyffylliog
Efenechtyd
Llanfwrog
Bontuchel
Derwen
Llanelidan
Rhyd-y-meudwy
Bryn Saith Marchog
Melin-y-wig
Gwyddelwern
Bryneglwys
Corwen
Carrog
Llidiart y Parc
Glyndyfrdwy
Llangollen
Froncysyllte
Glyn Ceiriog
Pontfadog
Llanarmon Dyffryn Ceiriog
Tregeiriog
Llanrhaeadr-ym-Mochnant
Llansilin
Llangedwyn
Llanyblodwel
Penybontfawr
Pennant Melangell
Llanwddyn
Abertridwr
Lake Vyrnwy
Llanfyllin
Llanfechain
Selattyn
Weston Rhyn
Chirk
Trefonen
Llandysilio
Four Crosses
Meliden (Gallt Melyd)
Gwaenysgor
Dyserth
Trelawnyd
Rhuddlan
RHYL
Kinmel Bay (Bae Cinmel)
Towyn
Belgrano
Abergele
Llanddulas
Old Colwyn
Llanelian-yn-Rhos
Bodelwyddan
St George
St Asaph (Llan-Elwy)
Tremeirchion
Trefnant
Bodfari
Henllan
Denbigh (Dinbych)
Llannefydd
Llansannan
Llangernyw
Llanfair Talhaiarn
Betws-yn-Rhos
Bylchau
Nantglyn
Llanrhaeadr
Llanynys
Cerrigydrudion
Pentrefoelas
Bala (Y Bala)
Llanfor
Llandderfel
Llandrillo
Cynwyd
Betws Gwerfil Goch
Llanycil
Llanuwchllyn
Llangower
Penllyn Forest
Rhos-y-gwaliau
Great Ormes Head (Pen-y-Gogarth)
Little Ormes Head
LLANDUDNO
Deganwy
Llandudno Junction
Conwy
Penrhyn Bay (Bae Penrhyn)
Rhôs-on-Sea (Llandrillo-yn-Rhos)
COLWYN BAY (Bae Colwyn)
Mochdre
Colwyn Bay
CONWY BAY
Abergele Roads
Penmaenmawr
Dwygyfylchi
Gyffin
Llansanffraid Glan Conwy
Tal-y-Cafn
Eglwysbach
Bodnant
Graig
Brymbo
Dolgarrog
Llanddoged
Trefriw
Llanrwst
Betws-y-Coed
Dolwyddelan
Pentre-bont
Blaenau Ffestiniog
Llan Ffestiniog
Trawsfynydd
Dolgellau
Llanelltyd
Llanfachreth
Rhydymain
Llanymawddwy
Dinas Mawddwy
CONWY
FLINTSHIRE
DENBIGHSHIRE
POWYS
GWYNEDD
BERWYN
CAMBRIAN MOUNTAINS
CLOCAENOG FOREST
GWYDYR FOREST PARK
COED Y BRENIN FOREST PARK
SNOWDONIA NATIONAL PARK
PARC CENEDLAETHOL ERYRI
MOUNTAINS
RIVER DEE
A55
A5
A470
A494
A541
A543
A544
A548
A525
A547
A5104
A483
A495
A4212
B4391
B4401
B5105
B5113
B5382
B5381
B5428
B5429
25
34

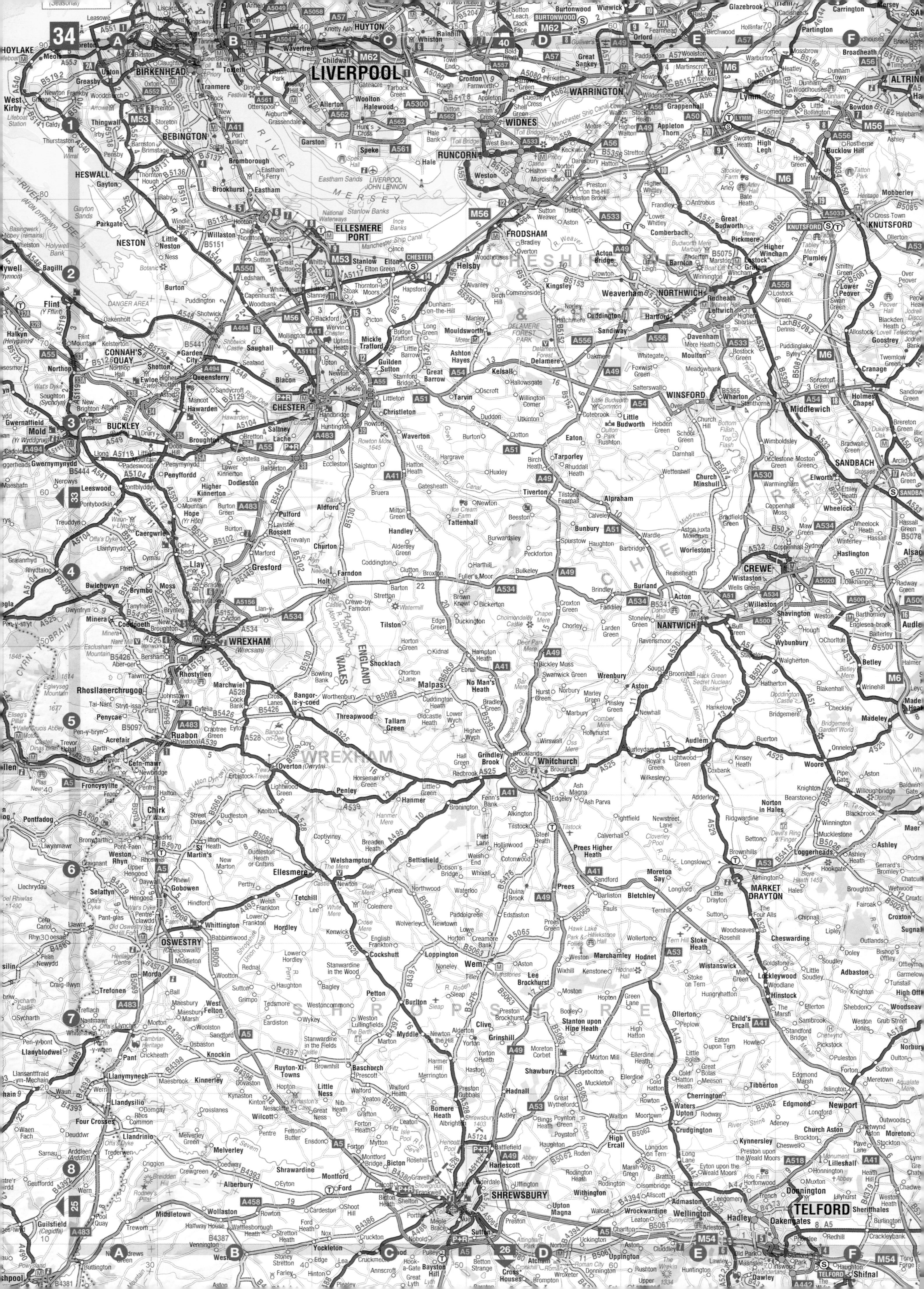
34
HOYLAKE
West Kirby
BIRKENHEAD
LIVERPOOL
HUYTON
Wavertree
Childwall
Allerton
Garston
Speke
LIVERPOOL JOHN LENNON
Halewood
WIDNES
RUNCORN
WARRINGTON
Great Sankey
Orford
Birchwood
Lymm
Carrington
Partington
Broadheath
ALTRINCHAM
Bowdon
Dunham Town
Mobberley
KNUTSFORD
Plumley
Over Peover
Goostrey
Cranage
Holmes Chapel
Middlewich
SANDBACH
Elworth
Wheelock
Haslington
CREWE
Shavington
Wybunbury
Betley
Madeley
Audlem
Woore
Onneley
NANTWICH
Acton
Burland
Wrenbury
Aston
Newhall
WINSFORD
Wharton
NORTHWICH
Weaverham
Barnton
Hartford
Cuddington
Sandiway
Davenham
Moulton
Kingsley
Frodsham
Helsby
Alvanley
Mouldsworth
Manley
Delamere
Kelsall
Tarvin
Tarporley
Eaton
Little Budworth
Bunbury
Beeston
Tattenhall
Tiverton
Alpraham
CHESTER
Christleton
Waverton
Huntington
Saltney
Broughton
Hawarden
Queensferry
Shotton
CONNAH'S QUAY
Flint
Halkyn
Northop
Buckley
Mold
Gwernaffield
Leeswood
Penyffordd
Dodleston
Pulford
Aldford
Rossett
Marford
Gresford
Caergwrle
Hope
Llay
Cefn-y-bedd
Ffrith
WREXHAM
Brymbo
Minera
Coedpoeth
Rhostyllen
Marchwiel
Bangor-is-y-coed
Overton
Ruabon
Cefn-mawr
Acrefair
Chirk
Froncysyllte
Penley
Hanmer
Whitchurch
Malpas
No Man's Heath
Tilston
Holt
Farndon
Churton
Broxton
Bickerton
Ellesmere
Welshampton
Tetchill
Cockshutt
Wem
Prees
Whixall
Market Drayton
Hodnet
Stoke Heath
Child's Ercall
Shawbury
Harlescott
SHREWSBURY
Upton Magna
Withington
Atcham
Bayston Hill
Sutton
Meole Brace
Hanwood
Yockleton
Ford
Montford
Bicton
Baschurch
Ruyton-XI-Towns
Myddle
Burlton
Loppington
Clive
Grinshill
Hadnall
High Ercall
Crudgington
Waters Upton
Tibberton
Edgmond
Newport
Church Aston
Lilleshall
Donnington
TELFORD
Oakengates
Wellington
Hadley
Shifnal
OSWESTRY
Whittington
Gobowen
St Martin's
Weston Rhyn
Morda
Trefonen
Llanymynech
Pant
Knockin
Kinnerley
West Felton
Melverley
Alberbury
Middletown
Wollaston
Four Crosses
Llandysilio
Guilsfield
Welshpool
Pontfadog
Selattyn
Penycae
Rhosllanerchrugog
Johnstown
HESWALL
Neston
Parkgate
Willaston
Little Neston
Thurstaston
Greasby
Upton
Meols
Thingwall
Irby
Pensby
Bebington
Bromborough
Eastham
Ellesmere Port
Hooton
Great Sutton
Stanlow
Thornton-le-Moors
Saughall
Blacon
Mollington
Backford
Upton
Mickle Trafford
Guilden Sutton
Great Barrow
Ashton Hayes
CHESHIRE
WREXHAM
SHROPSHIRE
WALES
ENGLAND
RIVER MERSEY
RIVER DEE
M53
M56
M62
M6
M54
A41
A49
A51
A55
A5
A483
A525
A534
A530
A53
A442
A458
33
25
40
26
A
B
C
D
E
F
1
2
3
4
5
6
7
8

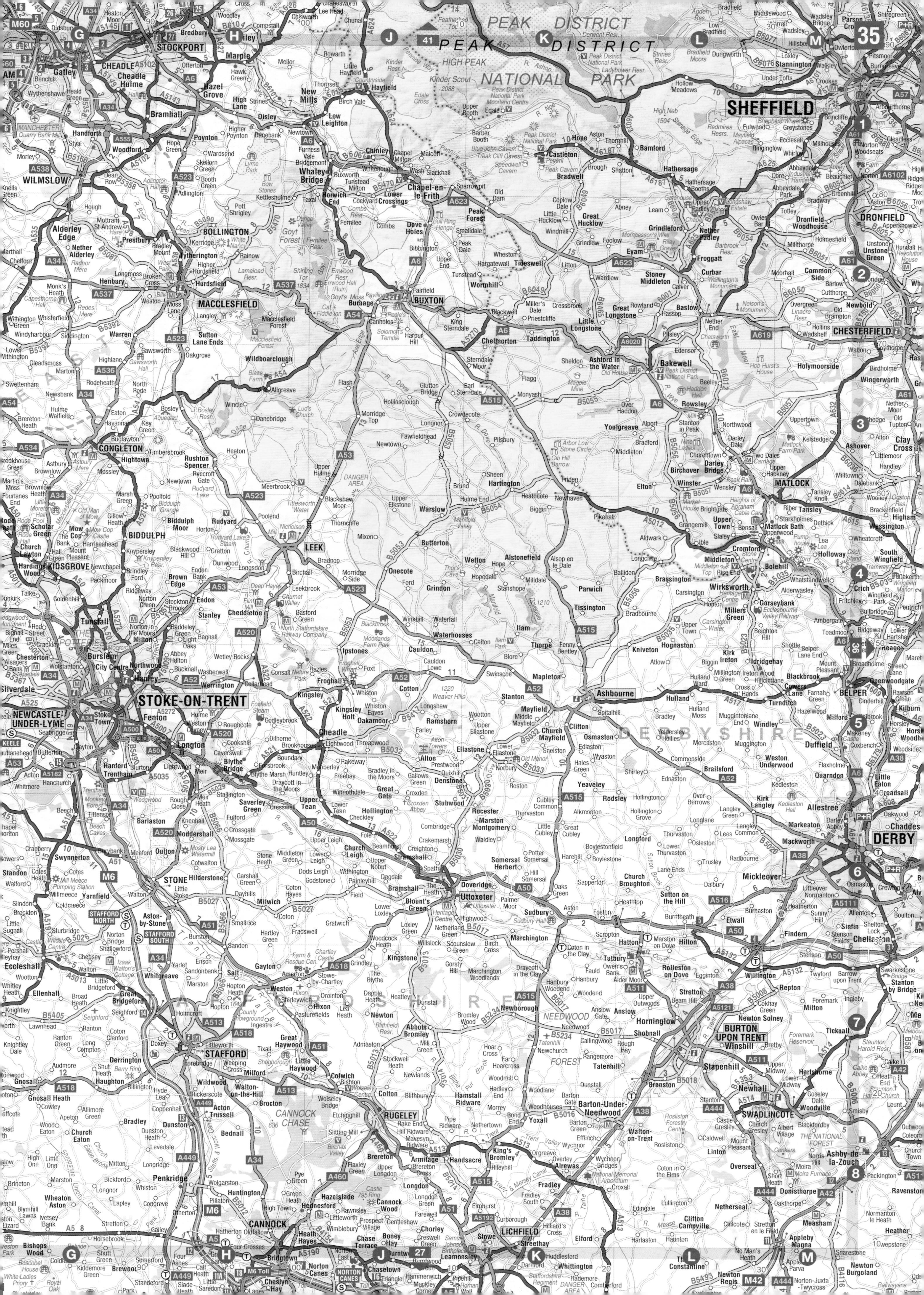

35
PEAK DISTRICT
PEAK DISTRICT NATIONAL PARK
41
SHEFFIELD
STOCKPORT
CHEADLE
Cheadle Hulme
Gatley
Hazel Grove
Marple
Bramhall
Poynton
WILMSLOW
Alderley Edge
BOLLINGTON
MACCLESFIELD
New Mills
Hayfield
Chinley
Whaley Bridge
Chapel-en-le-Frith
BUXTON
Castleton
Hope
Hathersage
Bamford
Bradwell
Tideswell
Eyam
Stoney Middleton
Baslow
Bakewell
Ashford in the Water
Rowsley
DRONFIELD
CHESTERFIELD
Holymoorside
Ashover
MATLOCK
Matlock Bath
Darley Dale
Cromford
Wirksworth
Youlgreave
Hartington
Warslow
Longnor
CONGLETON
BIDDULPH
KIDSGROVE
LEEK
Cheddleton
Endon
Tunstall
Burslem
Hanley
STOKE-ON-TRENT
Fenton
Longton
NEWCASTLE-UNDER-LYME
Cheadle
Alton
Ashbourne
Mayfield
Tissington
Parwich
Ilam
Waterhouses
Uttoxeter
Rocester
DERBYSHIRE
Belper
Duffield
Milford
Allestree
DERBY
Mickleover
Hilton
Etwall
Tutbury
Sudbury
Marchington
STONE
STAFFORD
Eccleshall
Great Bridgeford
Rugeley
Cannock Chase
CANNOCK
Hednesford
Penkridge
LICHFIELD
Alrewas
BURTON UPON TRENT
Stapenhill
SWADLINCOTE
Ashby-de-la-Zouch
Repton
Willington
Melbourne
Barton-Under-Needwood
Yoxall
Abbots Bromley
STAFFORDSHIRE
NEEDWOOD FOREST
36
27
M6
M42
M60
A34
A50
A38
A6
A515
A52
A53
A523
A54
A619
A61
A632
A444
A42
A51
A513
A518

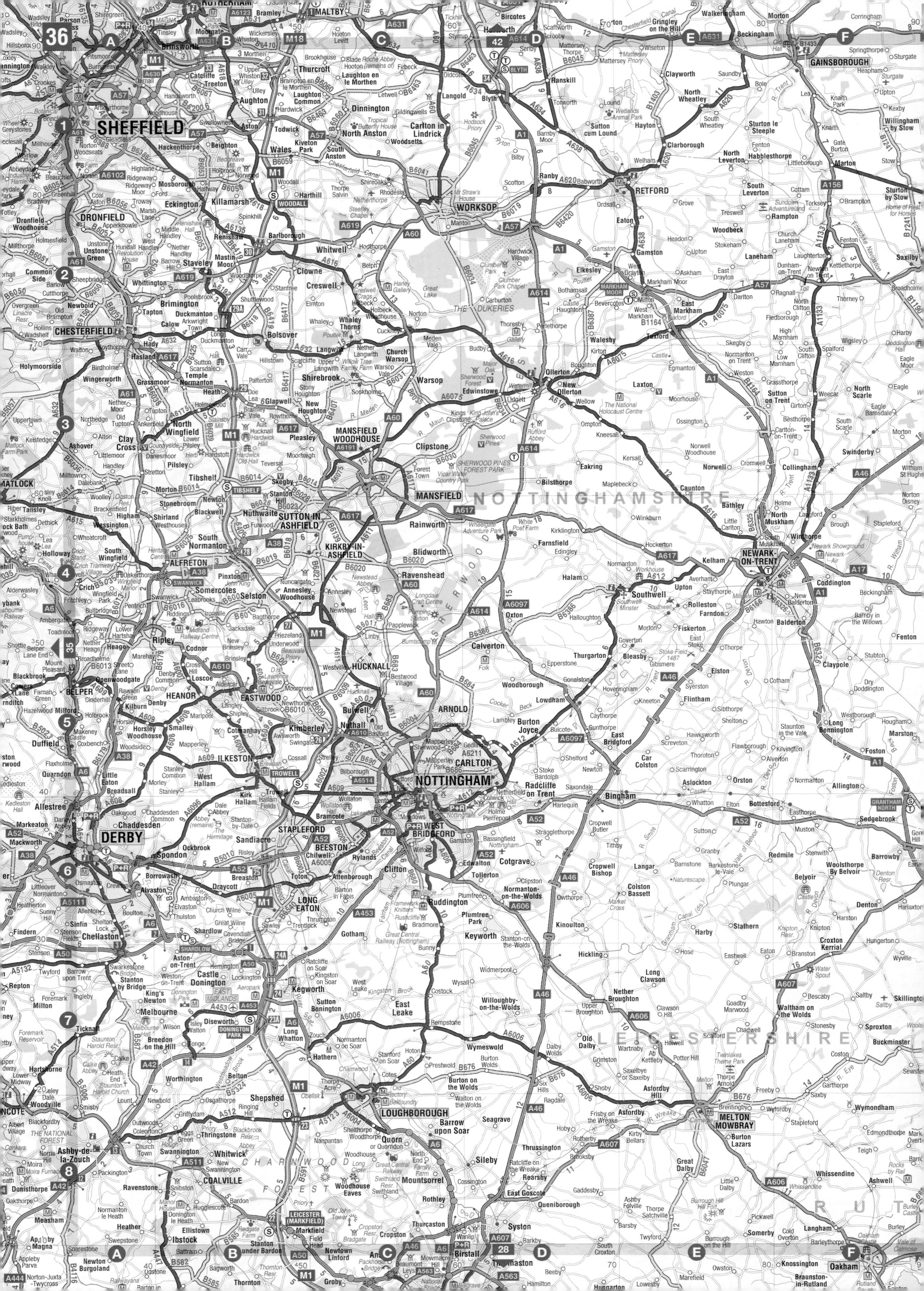

36
SHEFFIELD
ROTHERHAM
MALTBY
DRONFIELD
CHESTERFIELD
WORKSOP
RETFORD
GAINSBOROUGH
MANSFIELD
MANSFIELD WOODHOUSE
SUTTON IN ASHFIELD
KIRKBY-IN-ASHFIELD
ALFRETON
NOTTINGHAMSHIRE
NEWARK-ON-TRENT
MATLOCK
BELPER
HEANOR
EASTWOOD
ILKESTON
DERBY
NOTTINGHAM
ARNOLD
CARLTON
WEST BRIDGFORD
STAPLEFORD
BEESTON
LONG EATON
HUCKNALL
LOUGHBOROUGH
MELTON MOWBRAY
COALVILLE
LEICESTERSHIRE
Ashby-de-la-Zouch
Oakham
THE DUKERIES
SHERWOOD
CHARNWOOD FOREST
EAST MIDLANDS
35
42
28
A
B
C
D
E
F
1
2
3
4
5
6
7
8

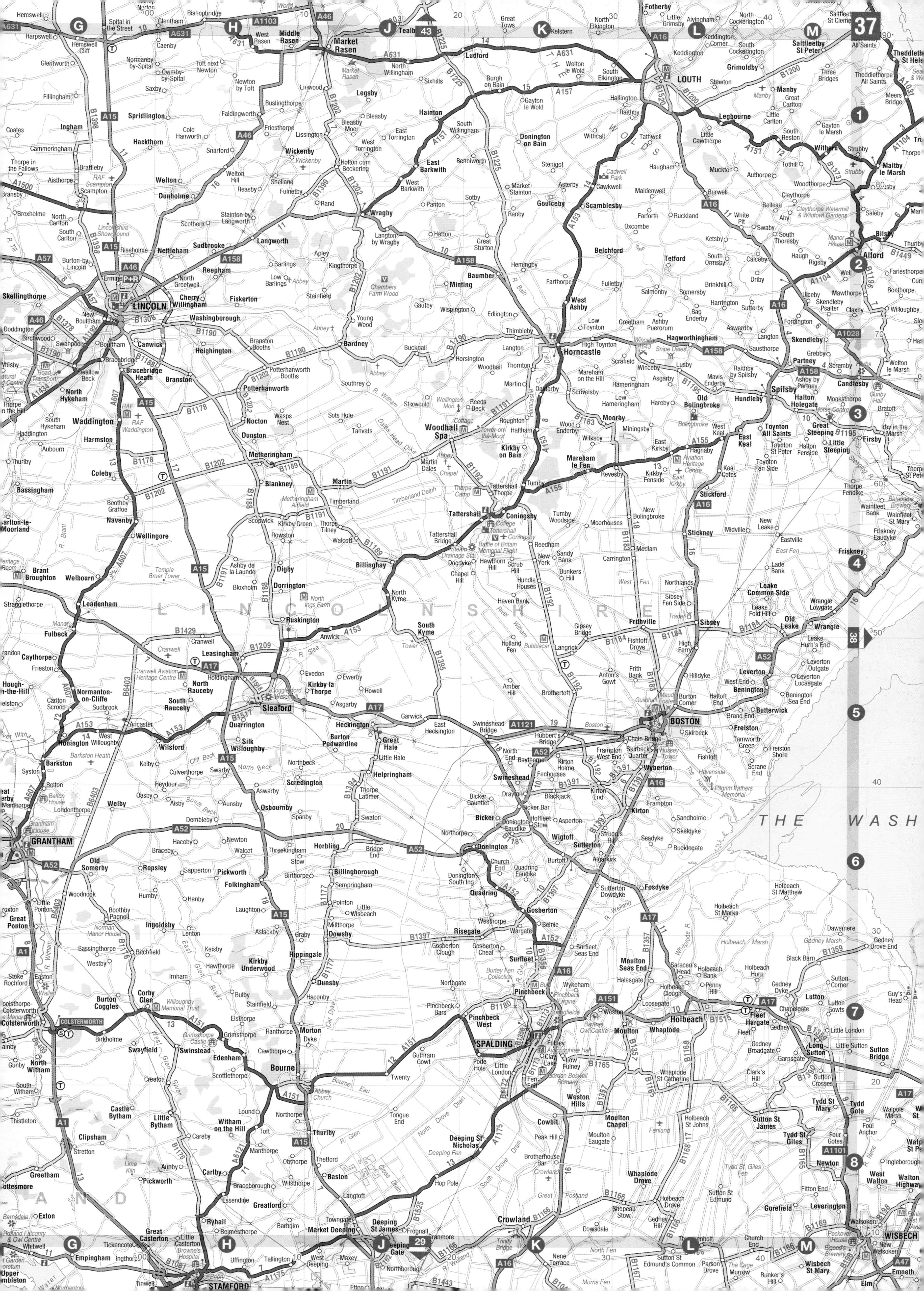

37
G
H
J
K
L
M
43
29
38
1
2
3
4
5
6
7
8
L I N C O L N S H I R E
THE WASH
LINCOLN
GRANTHAM
BOSTON
SPALDING
STAMFORD
WISBECH
LOUTH
Market Rasen
Horncastle
Sleaford
Woodhall Spa
Coningsby
Tattershall
Alford
Spilsby
Bourne
Holbeach
Long Sutton
Market Deeping
Crowland
Wragby
Ludford
Legbourne
Saltfleetby St Peter
Middle Rasen
West Rasen
Welton
Nettleham
Sudbrooke
Reepham
Fiskerton
Washingborough
Bracebridge Heath
Branston
Waddington
North Hykeham
Skellingthorpe
Navenby
Wellingore
Leadenham
Fulbeck
Caythorpe
Ancaster
Barkston
Honington
Wilsford
Ruskington
Leasingham
Heckington
Swineshead
Kirton
Sutterton
Donington
Gosberton
Pinchbeck
Moulton
Whaplode
Fleet Hargate
Sutton Bridge
Tydd St Mary
Deeping St Nicholas
Thurlby
Baston
Langtoft
Deeping St James
Edenham
Swinstead
Corby Glen
Colsterworth
North Witham
Castle Bytham
Little Bytham
Witham on the Hill
Carlby
Ryhall
Great Casterton
Empingham
Kirkby la Thorpe
Billinghay
Digby
Dorrington
Metheringham
Martin
Timberland
Tumby
Revesby
Mareham le Fen
East Kirkby
Stickney
Stickford
Sibsey
Frithville
Old Leake
Wrangle
Friskney
Leverton
Benington
Butterwick
Freiston
Wyberton
Fosdyke
Quadring
Surfleet
Hundleby
Partney
Candlesby
Toynton All Saints
Great Steeping
Firsby
Skendleby
Willoughby
Bilsby
Maltby le Marsh
Manby
Grimoldby
Withern
Strubby
Tetford
Belchford
West Ashby
Scamblesby
Goulceby
Donington on Bain
Hainton
East Barkwith
Baumber
Minting
Langworth
Wickenby
Legsby
Spridlington
Ingham
Hackthorn
Dunholme
Bardney
Potterhanworth
Nocton
Dunston
Blankney
Heighington
Canwick
Harmston
Coleby
Bassingham
Brant Broughton
Welbourn
Leverton
A15
A16
A17
A46
A52
A151
A153
A155
A157
A158
A631
A1

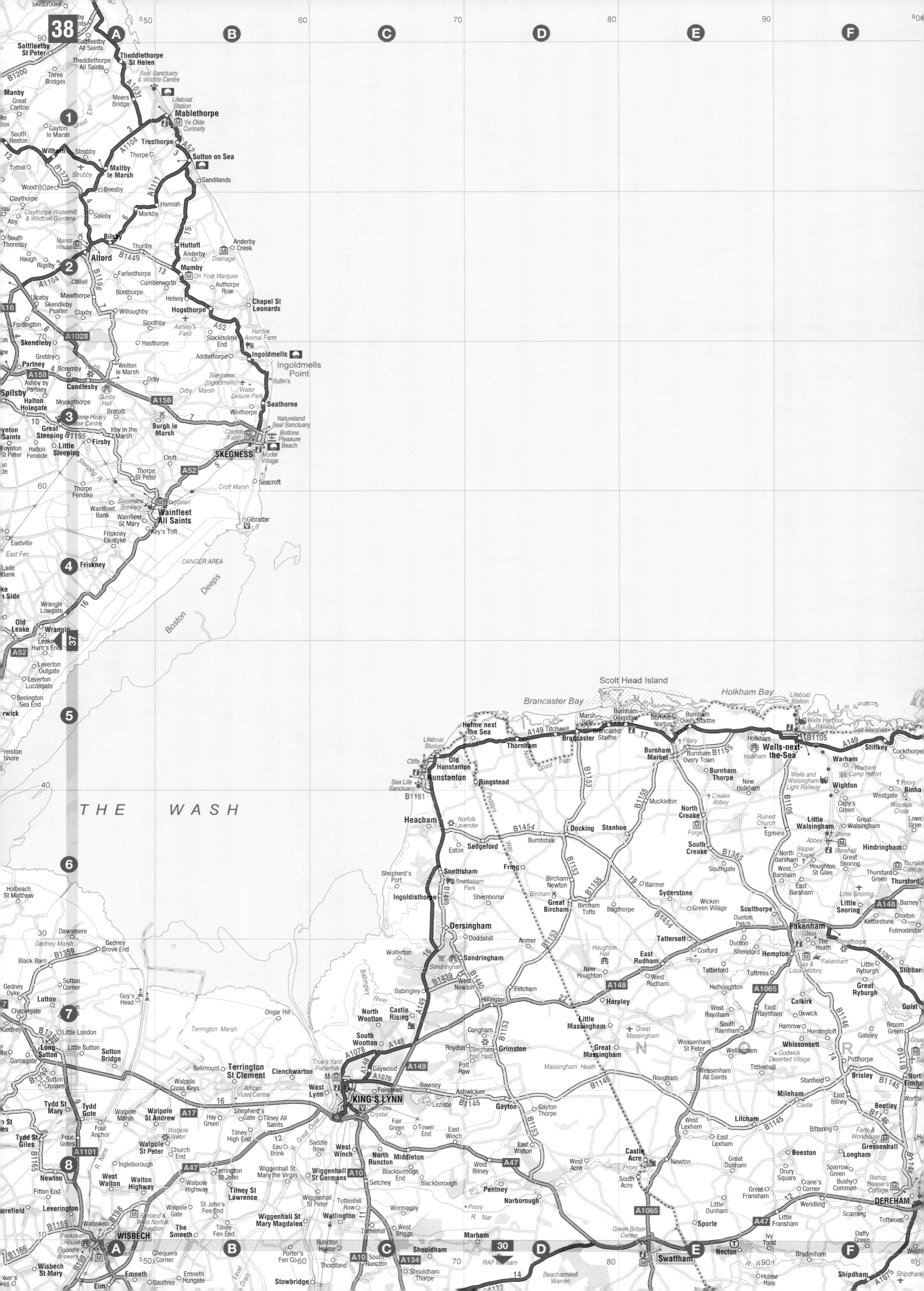

38
A
B
C
D
E
F
50
60
70
80
90
Saltfleetby St Peter
Theddlethorpe St Helen
Theddlethorpe All Saints
Three Bridges
Seal Sanctuary & Wildlife Centre
Manby
Great Carlton
Meers Bridge
Lifeboat Station
Mablethorpe
Ye Olde Curiosity
Gayton le Marsh
South Reston
Withern
Strubby
Trusthorpe
Thorpe
Sutton on Sea
Tothill
Maltby le Marsh
Sandilands
Beesby
Claythorpe
Claythorpe Watermill & Wildfowl Gardens
Hannah
Markby
Saleby
Aby
South Thoresby
Manor House
Bilsby
Huttoft
Anderby
Anderby Creek
Drainage
Haugh
Rigsby
Alford
Thurlby
Mumby
On Your Marques
Farlesthorpe
Cumberworth
Authorpe Row
Well
Bonthorpe
Ulceby
Mawthorpe
Skendleby Psalter
Claxby
Willoughby
Helsey
Hogsthorpe
Chapel St Leonards
Sloothby
Ashley's Field
Hardys Animal Farm
Fordington
Slackholme End
Hasthorpe
Skendleby
Grebby
Addlethorpe
Ingoldmells
Ingoldmells Point
Partney
Scremby
Welton le Marsh
Butlin's
Orby
Skegness (Ingoldmells)
Water Leisure Park
Candlesby
Orby Marsh
Spilsby
Ashby by Partney
Gunby Hall
Halton Holegate
Monksthorpe
Bratoft
Winthorpe
Seathorne
Natureland Seal Sanctuary
Irby in the Marsh
Great Steeping
Burgh le Marsh
Church Farm
Bottons Pleasure Beach
Little Steeping
Firsby
SKEGNESS
Model Village
Halton Fenside
Steeping R.
Croft
Thorpe St Peter
Thorpe Fendike
Croft Marsh
Seacroft
Batemans Brewery
Magdalen
Wainfleet Bank
Wainfleet All Saints
Wainfleet St Mary
Key's Toft
Gibraltar
Friskney Eaudyke
Eastville
East Fen
Friskney
DANGER AREA
Lade Bank
Deeps
Wrangle Lowgate
Boston
Old Leake
Wrangle
Leake Hurn's End
37
Leverton Outgate
Leverton Lucasgate
Benington Sea End
Freiston Shore
THE WASH
Holbeach St Matthew
Dawsmere
Gedney Marsh
Gedney Drove End
Black Barn
Gedney Dyke
Sutton Corner
Lutton
Guy's Head
Chapelgate
Gedney
Little London
Ongar Hill
Terrington Marsh
Long Sutton
Little Sutton
Sutton Bridge
Bellmount
Terrington St Clement
Clenchwarton
True's Yard Fisherfolk
Walpole Cross Keys
African Violet Centre
West Lynn
KING'S LYNN
Tydd St Mary
Tydd Gote
Walpole Marsh
Walpole St Andrew
Shepherd's Gate
Tilney All Saints
Hay Green
Foul Anchor
Walpole Water
Tilney High End
Tydd St Giles
Four Gotes
Walpole St Peter
Church End
Eau Brink
Saddle Bow
West Winch
Ingleborough
Terrington St John
Wiggenhall St Mary the Virgin
Wiggenhall St Germans
Newton
West Walton
Walton Highway
Walpole Highway
Tilney St Lawrence
Wiggenhall St Peter
Fitton End
Leverington
Walpole Gate
St John's Fen End
Wiggenhall St Mary Magdalen
Tottenhill Row
Walsoken
Fenland & West Norfolk Aviation
The Smeeth
Tilney Fen End
Watlington
WISBECH
Peckover House
Elgood's Brewery
Chequers Corner
Runcton Holme
Tottenhill
Porter's Fen Co
South Runcton
Wisbech St Mary
Emneth
Emneth Hungate
Gaultree
Thorpland
Stowbridge
Elm
Scolt Head Island
Brancaster Bay
Holkham Bay
Lifeboat Station
Marsh Side
Burnham Deepdale
Burnham Norton
Burnham Overy Staithe
Wells Harbour Railway
Holme next the Sea
Titchwell
Brancaster
Brancaster Staithe
Salt Marshes
Thornham
Norfolk Coast Path
Friary
Burnham Market
Burnham Overy Town
Holkham
Wells-next-the-Sea
Stiffkey
Cockthorpe
Cliffs
Old Hunstanton
Hunstanton
Ringstead
Sea Life Sanctuary
Burnham Thorpe
New Holkham
Warham
Warham Camp Hillfort
Wells and Walsingham Light Railway
Wighton
Binham
Creake Abbey
Muckleton
Peddars Way
Heacham
Norfolk Lavender
North Creake
Forge
Ruined Church
Little Walsingham
Great Walsingham
Wayside Cross
Copy's Green
Westgate
Docking
Stanhoe
Burntstalk
Egmere
Eaton
Sedgeford
South Creake
Abbey
Shrine
Shirehall
Hindringham
Fring
Southgate
North Barsham
West Barsham
Houghton St Giles
Great Snoring
Thursford Green
Thursford
Shepherd's Port
Snettisham
Snettisham Park
Bircham Newton
Barmer
East Barsham
Little Snoring
Ingoldisthorpe
Shernborne
Bircham
Great Bircham
Bircham Tofts
Syderstone
Bagthorpe
Wicken Green Village
Sculthorpe
Dunton Patch
Barney
Kettlestone
Croxton
Fulmodeston
Dersingham
Doddshill
Tattersett
Fakenham
Glass
Anmer
Houghton Hall
Coxford
Dunton
Shereford
The Heath
Pensthorpe
Wolferton
Sandringham
East Rudham
Hempton
Fakenham
Priory
Little Ryburgh
Stibbard
New Houghton
West Rudham
Tatterford
Toftrees
Gas & Local History
Great Ryburgh
Babingley
West Newton
Flitcham
Helhoughton
Hillington
Harpley
Colkirk
Guist
North Wootton
Castle Rising
River
Little Massingham
East Raynham
West Raynham
Oxwick
Congham
Great Massingham
South Raynham
Hamrow
Horningtoft
Broom Green
Gateley
South Wootton
Roydon
Grimston
Congham Hall Herb
Weasenham St Peter
Wellingham
Whissonsett
Gaywood
Great Massingham
Godwick Deserted Village
Potthorpe
Pott Row
Massingham Heath
Weasenham All Saints
Tittleshall
Fairstead
Bawsey
Rougham
Brisley
Stanfield
North Elmham
Ashwicken
Leziate
Gayton
Gayton Thorpe
Mileham
Castle
East Bilney
Beetley
Caithness Crystal
Fair Green
Tower End
East Winch
Litcham
West Lexham
East Lexham
Bittering
Farm & Workhouse
Gressenhall
East Walton
Castle Acre
Priory
Newton
Great Dunham
Beeston
Longham
North Runcton
Middleton
West Acre
West Bilney
Blackborough End
Setchey
Blackborough
Pentney
Narborough
South Acre
Drury Square
Sparrow Green
Crane's Corner
Bushy Common
Bishop Bonner's Cottage
Wormegay
Priory
Great Fransham
Little Dunham
Wendling
DEREHAM
R. Nar
Little Fransham
Scarning
Toftwood
West Briggs
Marham
Green Britain Centre
Sporle
Ivy Todd
Daffy Green
Shouldham
30
RAF Marham
Swaffham
Necton
Bradenham
Shouldham Thorpe
Beachamwell Warren
Holme Hale
Shipdham

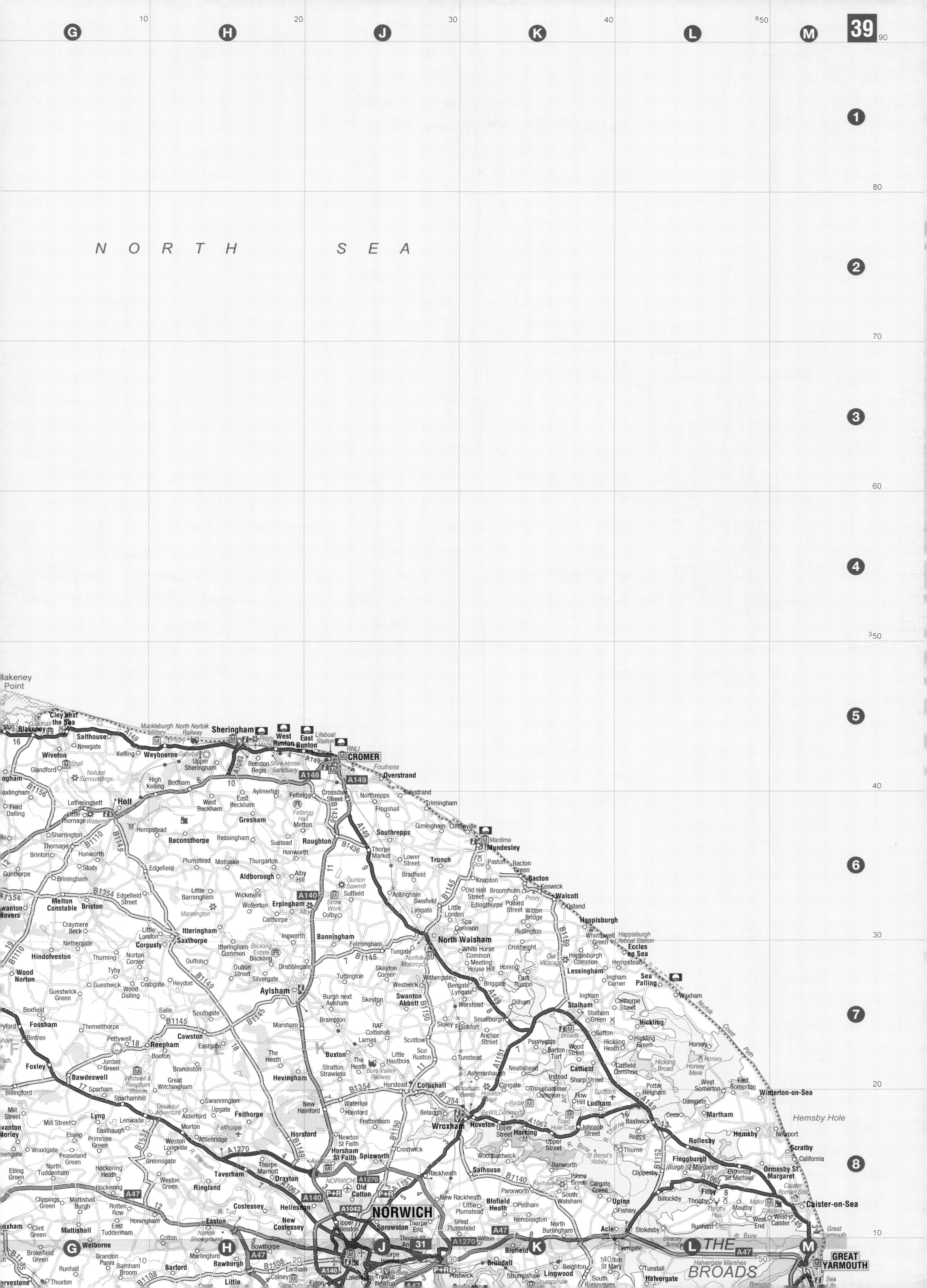

NORTH SEA

Blakeney
Point

Cley next
the Sea
Blakeney
16
ston

Muckleburgh North Norfolk
Military Railway
Sheringham
West East
Runton Runton
Lifeboat
Station
RNLI
CROMER
Foulness
Overstrand

Salthouse
Newgate
Wiveton
Weybourne
Kelling
Shell
Glandford
Natural
Surroundings
Gazebo
Maze
Upper
Sheringham
Beeston
Regis
Shire Horse
Sanctuary
A148
A149
A149

gham
axlingham
Field
Dalling
B1156
High
Kelling
Bodham
Holt
West Beckham
East
Beckham
Aylmerton
Felbrigg
Felbrigg
Hall
Crossdale
Street
Northrepps
Sidestrand
Trimingham

Letheringsett
Little
Thornage
Watermill
Hempstead
Gresham
Sustead
Metton
Roughton
Gimingham
Cliftonville
Maritime
Mundesley

Thornage
Brinton
Sharrington
Baconsthorpe
Bessingham
Hanworth
Thorpe
Market
Lower
Street
Trunch
Paston
Knapton
Bacton
Green
Bacton
Keswick
Walcott
Ostend

354
Melton
Constable
Briston
wanton
Novers
Edgefield
Street
Plumstead
Matlaske
Thurgarton
Aldborough
Alby
Hill
Wickmere
Wolterton
Erpingham
Alby
Colby
Swafield
Antingham
Old Hall
Street
Suffield
Broomholm
Priory
Edingthorpe
Pollard
Street
Witton
Bridge
Happisburgh

Craymere
Beck
Edgefield
Little
London
Nethergate
Thurning
Saxthorpe
Itteringham
Common
Blickling
Estate
Banningham
Felmingham
Tungate
Little
London
Spa
Common
Ridlington
Happisburgh
Common
Hempstead
Whimpwell
Green
Happisburgh
Lifeboat Station
Eccles
on Sea

Hindolveston
Wood
Norton
Corpusty
Itteringham
Oulton
Street
Silvergate
Drabblegate
Blickling
Skeyton
Corner
Westwick
Withergate
Bengate
Honing
Briggate
East
Ruston
Lessingham
Ingham
Corner
Sea
Palling

Guestwick
Green
Guestwick
Wood
Dalling
Aylsham
Burgh next
Aylsham
Skeyton
Swanton
Abbott
Worstead
Dilham
Ingham
Calthorpe
Street
Waxham
Norfolk
Coast
Path

Bexfield
Foulsham
Themelthorpe
Salle
Southgate
Marsham
Brampton
RAF
Coltishall
Lamas
Sloley
Frankfort
Smallburgh
Stalham
Staltham
Green
Sutton
Hickling
Horsey

ryford
Billingford
Pettywell
Cawston
Eastgate
Buxton
The
Heath
Little
Hautbois
Sco
Ruston
Anchor
Street
Pennygate
Wood
Street
Hickling
Heath
Hickling
Green

Bintree
Booton
Brandiston
Stratton
Strawless
Scottow
Tunstead
Barton
Turf
Catfield
Catfield
Common
Hickling
Mere
Horsey
Mere

Foxley
Reepham
18
Bawdeswell
Whitwell &
Reepham
Station
Great
Witchingham
Hevingham
Horstead
Coltishall
Ashmanhaugh
Neatishead
Sharp Street
West
Somerton
East
Somerton
Winterton-on-Sea

wanton
orley
Sparham
Dinosaur
Adventure
Alderford
Swannington
Upgate
New
Hainford
Waterloo
Hainford
Belaugh
Hoveton
Hall
How
Hill
Potter
Heigham
Damgate
Martham
Hemsby Hole

Mill
Street
Lyng
Lenwade
Felthorpe
Frettenham
Wroxham
Hoveton
Upper
Street
Ludham
Cess
Repps
Hemsby
Newport
Scratby
California

Elsing
Primrose
Green
Weston
Longville
Attlebridge
Horsford
Horsham
St Faith
Crostwick
Rackheath
BeWILDerwood
Toad
Hole Cott
Johnson
Street
Bastwick
Rollesby
Ormesby St
Margaret

Woodgate
Peaseland
Green
Hockering
Heath
Taverham
Drayton
Spixworth
Woodbastwick
Ranworth
St Benet's
Abbey
Thurne
Clippesby
Fleggburgh
(Burgh St Margaret)
Ormesby St
Michael
Filby
Caister
Roman Site

Etting
Green
North
Tuddenham
Hockering
Ringland
Weston
Green
NORWICH
Old
Catton
Sprowston
Salhouse
Pilson
Green
Cargate
Green
Billockby
Thrigby
Thrigby
Hall
Mautby
West
Caister
Caister-on-Sea

Clippings
Green
Mattishall
Burgh
Rotten
Row
Honingham
Costessey
Hellesdon
New
Rackheath
Little
Plumstead
North
Burlingham
Upton
Runham

Clint
Green
Mattishall
Easton
Colton
Norfolk
Showground
New
Costessey
Upper
Hellesdon
Thorpe
End
Great
Plumstead
Hemblington
Acle
Stokesby
Great
Yarmouth

xham
rstone
Welborne
Marlingford
Bawburgh
Bowthorpe
Blofield
Heath
Blofield
Strumpshaw
Lingwood
Olton
St Mary
Ormesby St
Margaret
GREAT
YARMOUTH
THE
BROADS

Runhall
Brandon
Parva
Barford
Earlham
Colney
Postwick
Brundall
Beighton
Halvergate Marshes
Halvergate

Brakefield
Green
Barnham
Broom
B1108
Thuxton
Little
Bawburgh
Lakenham Trowse
Newton
Strumpshaw
South
Burlingham
Reedham
Stracey
Arms
Sea

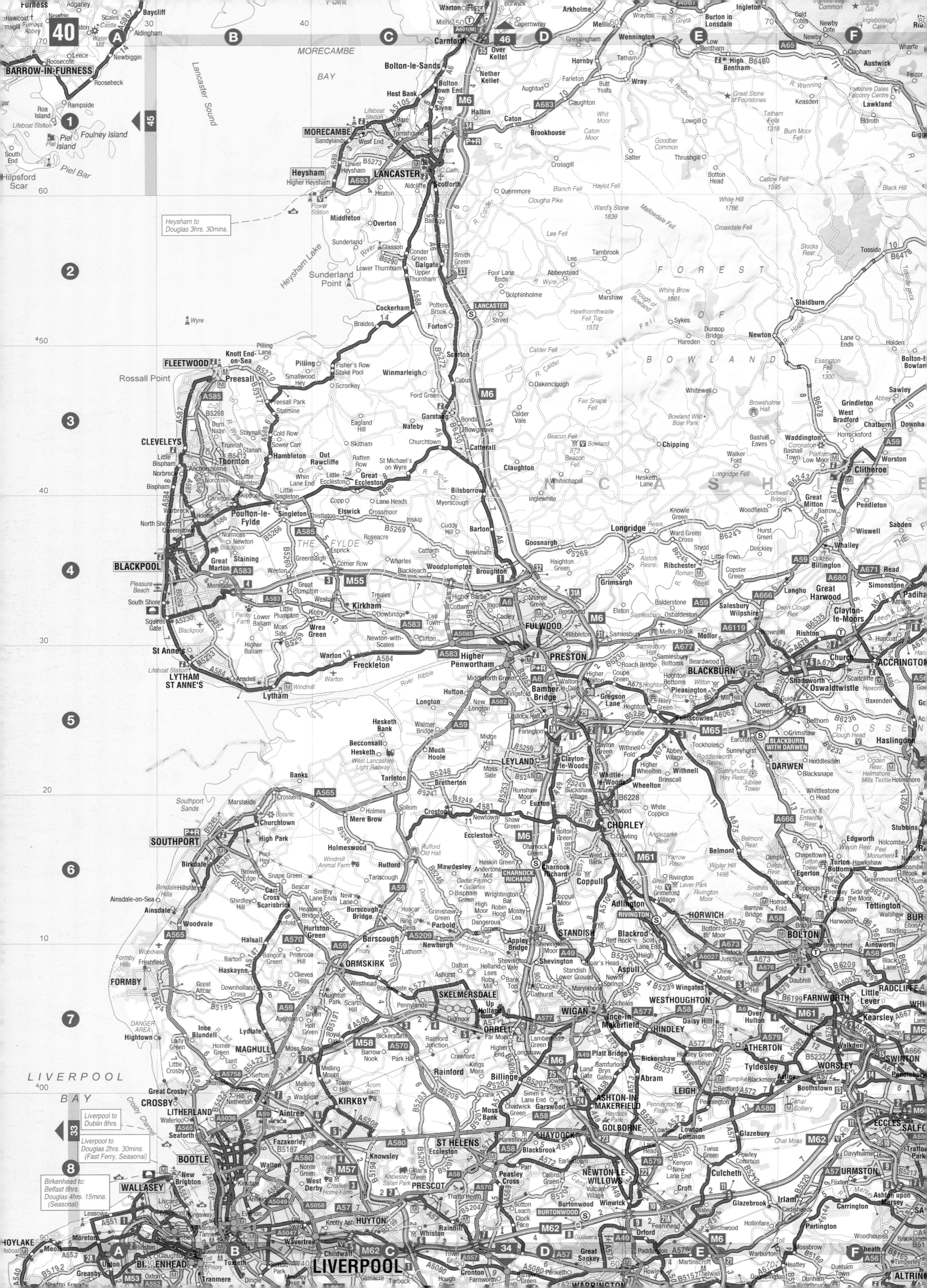
40
BARROW-IN-FURNESS
MORECAMBE BAY
Lancaster Sound
45
MORECAMBE
Heysham
LANCASTER
Heysham to Douglas 3hrs. 30mins.
Heysham Lake
Sunderland Point
Carnforth
Bolton-le-Sands
Galgate
Cockerham
Garstang
FOREST OF BOWLAND
LANCASHIRE
FLEETWOOD
Rossall Point
Preesall
CLEVELEYS
Thornton
Poulton-le-Fylde
BLACKPOOL
THE FYLDE
Kirkham
St Anne's
LYTHAM ST ANNE'S
Lytham
Freckleton
FULWOOD
PRESTON
Longridge
Clitheroe
BLACKBURN
ACCRINGTON
Oswaldtwistle
DARWEN
Haslingden
LEYLAND
CHORLEY
Southport Sands
SOUTHPORT
Birkdale
Ainsdale
FORMBY
Ormskirk
SKELMERSDALE
WIGAN
STANDISH
HORWICH
BOLTON
FARNWORTH
WESTHOUGHTON
HINDLEY
LEIGH
MAGHULL
KIRKBY
CROSBY
LITHERLAND
BOOTLE
LIVERPOOL BAY
33
Liverpool to Dublin 8hrs.
Liverpool to Douglas 2hrs. 30mins. (Fast Ferry, Seasonal)
Birkenhead to: Belfast 8hrs. Douglas 4hrs. 15mins. (Seasonal)
WALLASEY
HOYLAKE
BIRKENHEAD
LIVERPOOL
ST HELENS
HUYTON
PRESCOT
NEWTON-LE-WILLOWS
ASHTON-IN-MAKERFIELD
GOLBORNE
HAYDOCK
ECCLES
URMSTON
WORSLEY
SWINTON
RADCLIFFE
ALTRINCHAM
WARRINGTON
34
46
M6
M55
M65
M61
M58
M62
M57

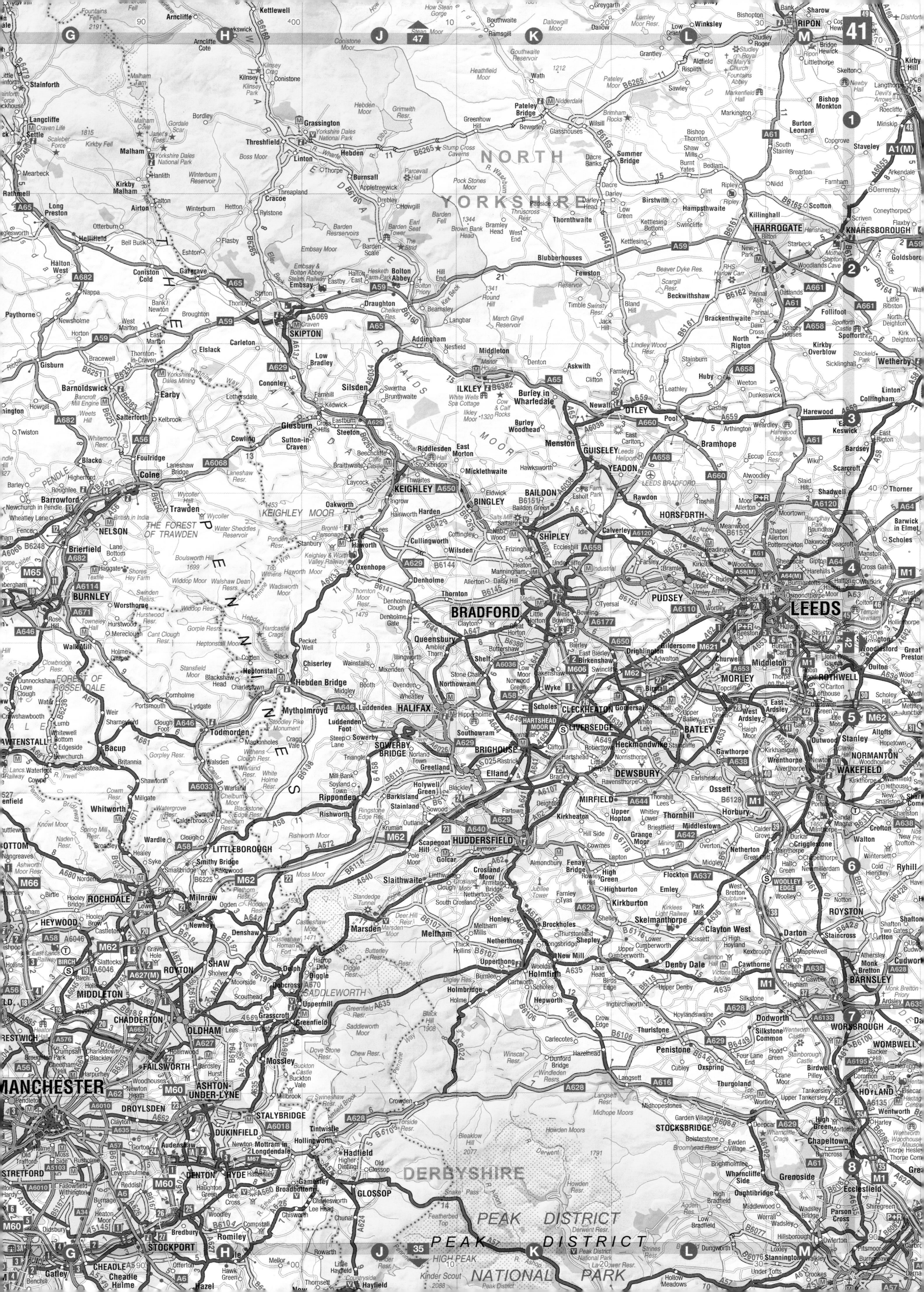

41
G
H
J
47
K
L
M
NORTH
YORKSHIRE
RIPON
HARROGATE
KNARESBOROUGH
Wetherby
SKIPTON
ILKLEY
OTLEY
Burley in Wharfedale
KEIGHLEY
BINGLEY
BAILDON
SHIPLEY
GUISELEY
YEADON
HORSFORTH
PUDSEY
BRADFORD
LEEDS
HALIFAX
BRIGHOUSE
Elland
HUDDERSFIELD
DEWSBURY
BATLEY
MORLEY
ROTHWELL
WAKEFIELD
NORMANTON
CLECKHEATON
LIVERSEDGE
Heckmondwike
MIRFIELD
Ossett
Horbury
Holmfirth
Denby Dale
BARNSLEY
ROYSTON
Darton
Penistone
STOCKSBRIDGE
Grenoside
Chapeltown
Ecclesfield
HOYLAND
WOMBWELL
WORSBROUGH
Dodworth
Todmorden
Hebden Bridge
Mytholmroyd
SOWERBY BRIDGE
Ripponden
Marsden
Meltham
Slaithwaite
LITTLEBOROUGH
ROCHDALE
Milnrow
HEYWOOD
MIDDLETON
CHADDERTON
OLDHAM
ROYTON
SHAW
FAILSWORTH
ASHTON-UNDER-LYNE
MANCHESTER
DROYLSDEN
STALYBRIDGE
DUKINFIELD
HYDE
DENTON
STRETFORD
STOCKPORT
CHEADLE
Romiley
Mossley
Hadfield
GLOSSOP
Hayfield
DERBYSHIRE
PEAK DISTRICT
NATIONAL PARK
SADDLEWORTH
NELSON
BURNLEY
Colne
Barnoldswick
Earby
Settle
Grassington
Malham
Pateley Bridge
Bacup
Whitworth
RAWTENSTALL
FOREST OF ROSSENDALE
THE FOREST OF TRAWDEN
KEIGHLEY MOOR
PENDLE
35
M62
M1
M60
M66
M65
A1(M)
A59
A65
A629
A61
A58
A62
A635
A628
A616
A6024
A646
A56
A682
A6068

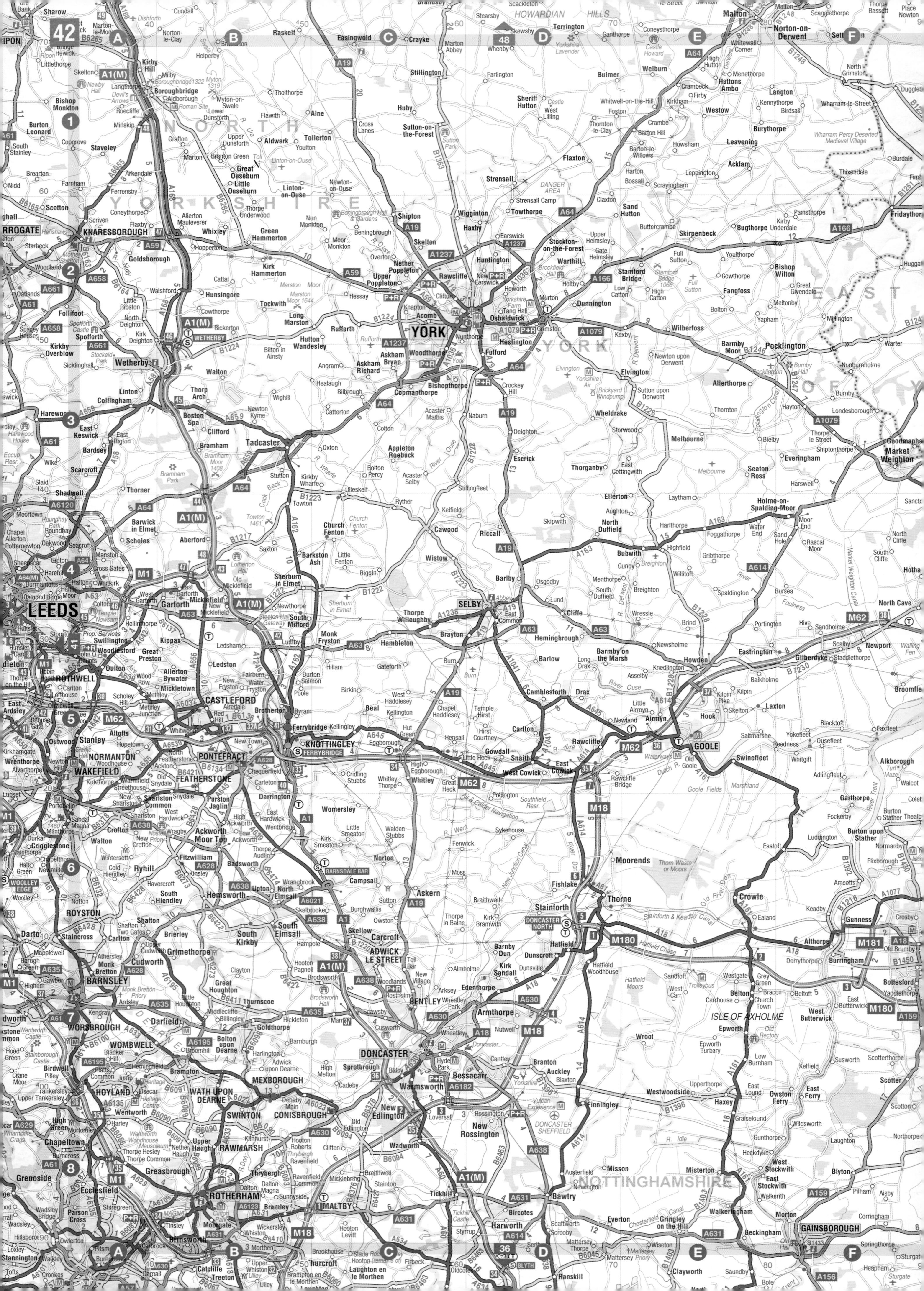
42
48
36
A
B
C
D
E
F
1
2
3
4
5
6
7
8
HOWARDIAN HILLS
NORTH YORKSHIRE
EAST OF YORK
NOTTINGHAMSHIRE
ISLE OF AXHOLME
YORK
LEEDS
KNARESBOROUGH
Wetherby
Tadcaster
SELBY
Malton
Norton-on-Derwent
Pocklington
Market Weighton
Howden
GOOLE
CASTLEFORD
PONTEFRACT
KNOTTINGLEY
FEATHERSTONE
NORMANTON
WAKEFIELD
ROTHWELL
BARNSLEY
WORSBROUGH
WOMBWELL
HOYLAND
MEXBOROUGH
CONISBROUGH
SWINTON
RAWMARSH
ROTHERHAM
DONCASTER
BENTLEY
ADWICK LE STREET
Thorne
Crowle
GAINSBOROUGH
Bawtry
MALTBY
Tickhill
Boroughbridge
Garforth
Sherburn in Elmet
Easingwold
Haxby
Stamford Bridge
Epworth
Hatfield
Snaith
Askern
Hemsworth
A1(M)
M1
M62
M18
M180
M181
A64
A19
A1079
A63
A614
A18
A638
A161

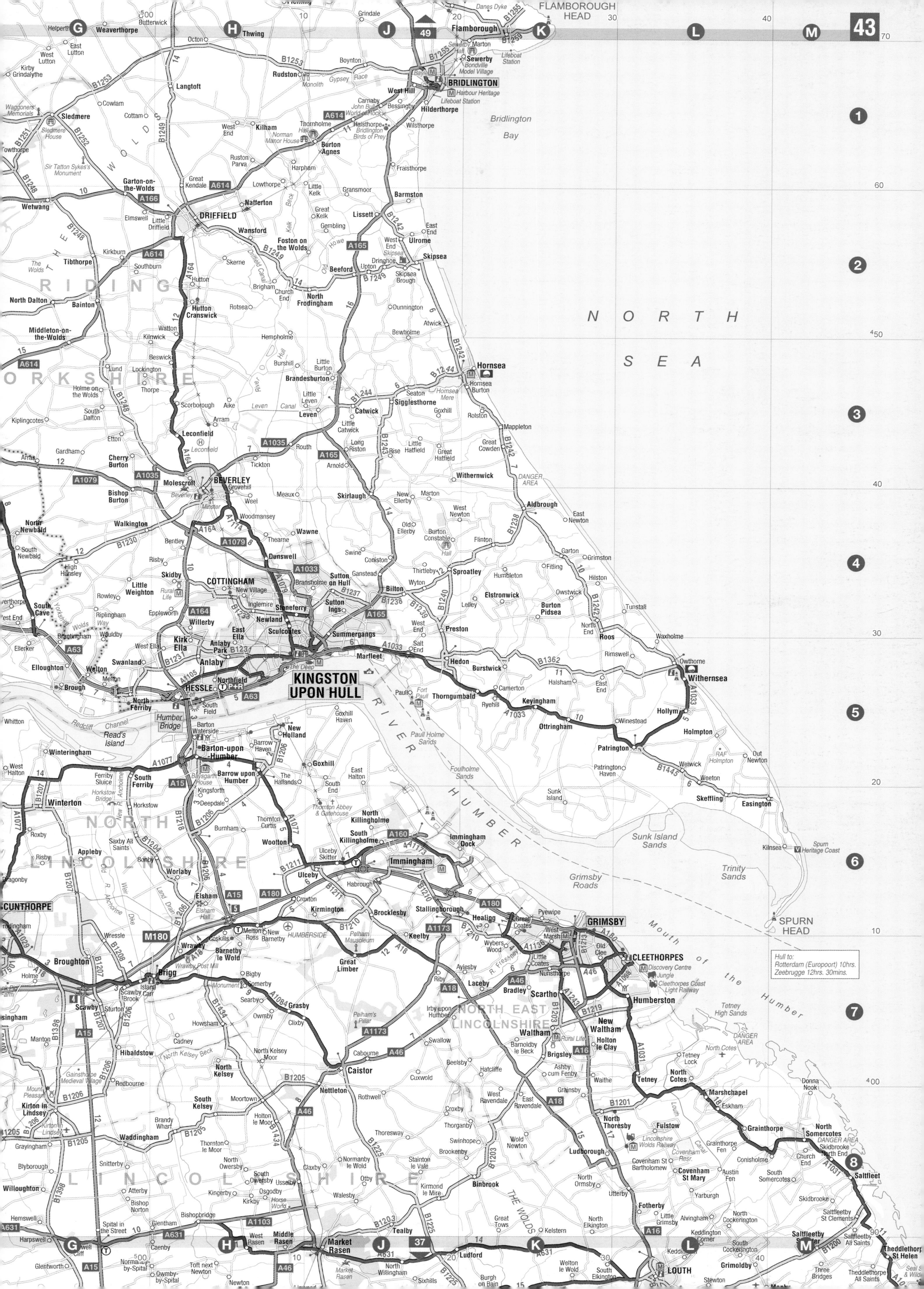
FLAMBOROUGH HEAD
Flamborough
BRIDLINGTON
Bridlington Bay
NORTH SEA
Hornsea
Withernsea
SPURN HEAD
KINGSTON UPON HULL
RIVER HUMBER
BEVERLEY
DRIFFIELD
COTTINGHAM
HESSLE
Humber Bridge
Barton-upon-Humber
Immingham
GRIMSBY
CLEETHORPES
SCUNTHORPE
Brigg
Caistor
Market Rasen
LOUTH
Saltfleet
Sunk Island Sands
Grimsby Roads
Mouth of the Humber
Tetney High Sands
NORTH LINCOLNSHIRE
NORTH EAST LINCOLNSHIRE
LINCOLNSHIRE
RIDING
YORKSHIRE
THE WOLDS
Hull to:
Rotterdam (Europoort) 10hrs.
Zeebrugge 12hrs. 30mins.
49
37
G H J K L M
1 2 3 4 5 6 7 8

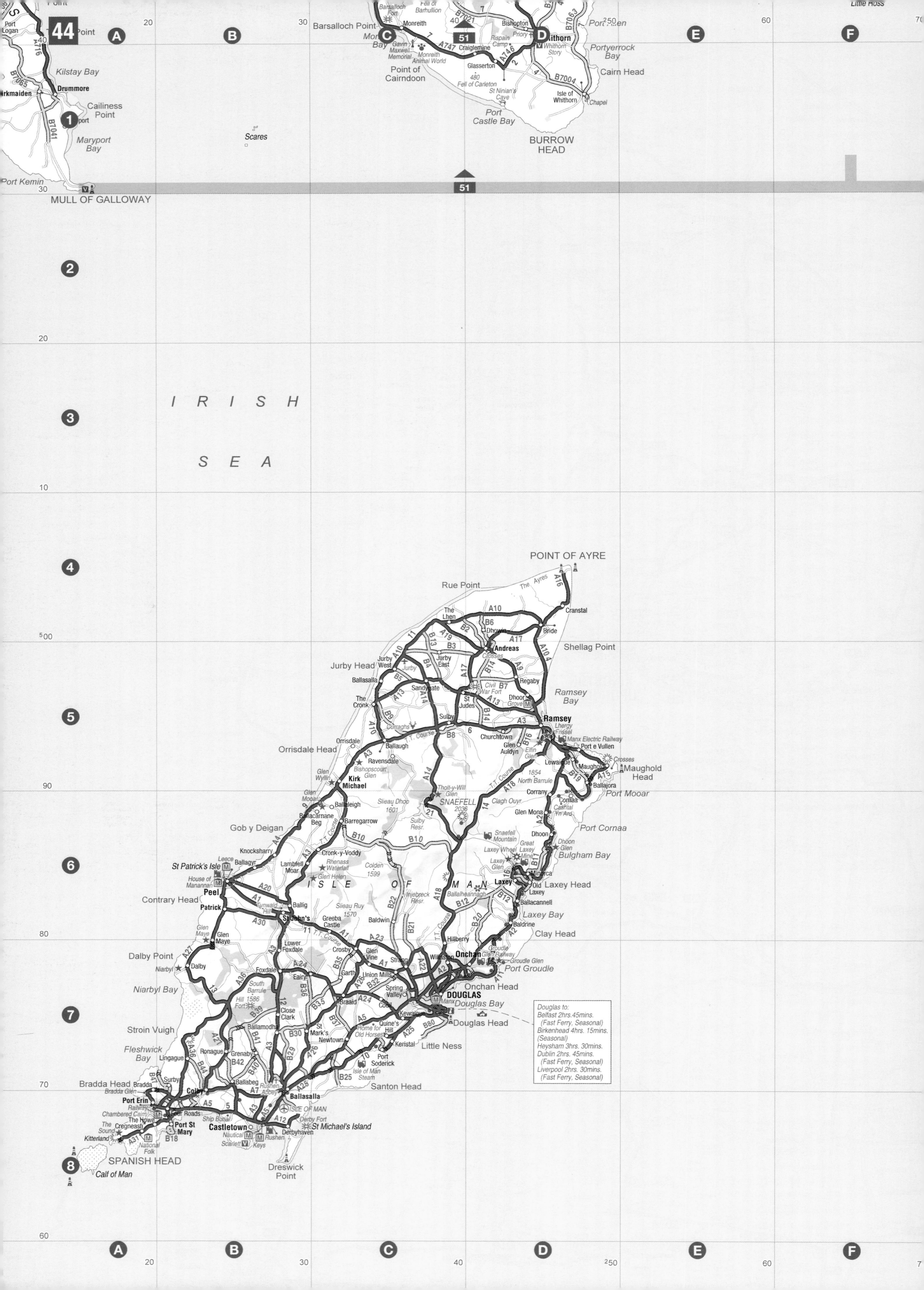
44
51
Port Logan
Kilstay Bay
Drummore
Cailiness Point
Maryport Bay
Port Kemin
MULL OF GALLOWAY
Scares
Barsalloch Point
Monreith
Gavin Maxwell Memorial
Monreith Animal World
Point of Cairndoon
Craiglemine
Glasserton
Fell of Carleton
St Ninian's Cave
Port Castle Bay
BURROW HEAD
Bishopton
Rispain Camp
Whithorn Story
Portyerrock Bay
Cairn Head
Isle of Whithorn
Chapel
Little Ross
IRISH SEA
POINT OF AYRE
Rue Point
The Ayres
Cranstal
The Lhen
Bride
Andreas
Shellag Point
Jurby Head
Jurby West
Jurby East
Ballasalla
Regaby
Ramsey Bay
The Cronk
Sandygate
St Judes
Dhoor
Sulby
Churchtown
Ramsey
Manx Electric Railway
Port e Vullen
Orrisdale
Orrisdale Head
Ballaugh
Ravensdale
Bishopscourt Glen
Glen Auldyn
Maughold
Maughold Head
Ballajora
Port Mooar
Kirk Michael
Glen Wyllin
Sleiau Dhoo 1601
SNAEFELL 2036
Tholt-y-Will Glen
North Barrule
Corrany
Cornaa
Port Cornaa
Glen Mona
Dhoon
Dhoon Glen
Bulgham Bay
Ballaleigh
Ballacarnane Beg
Barregarrow
Sulby Resr.
Gob y Deigan
Snaefell Mountain
Laxey Wheel
Great Laxey Mine
Laxey Glen
Laxey
Old Laxey
Laxey Head
Minorca
Knocksharry
Ballagyr
St Patrick's Isle
Cronk-y-Voddy
Rhenass Waterfall
Glen Helen
Colden 1599
ISLE OF MAN
Lambfell Moar
Peel
House of Manannan
Contrary Head
Patrick
Ballig
St John's
Slieau Ruy 1570
Greeba Castle
Baldwin
Ballacannell
Laxey Bay
Baldrine
Clay Head
Hillberry
Glen Maye
Dalby Point
Niarbyl
Dalby
Lower Foxdale
Crosby
Glen Vine
Strang
Onchan
Groudle Glen
Port Groudle
Foxdale
South Barrule
Union Mills
Garth
Spring Valley
Onchan Head
DOUGLAS
Douglas Bay
Niarbyl Bay
Hill Fort 1586
Close Clark
Braaid
Kewaigue
Douglas Head
Douglas to:
Belfast 2hrs.45mins. (Fast Ferry, Seasonal)
Birkenhead 4hrs. 15mins. (Seasonal)
Heysham 3hrs. 30mins.
Dublin 2hrs. 45mins. (Fast Ferry, Seasonal)
Liverpool 2hrs. 30mins. (Fast Ferry, Seasonal)
Stroin Vuigh
Ballamodha
St Mark's
Newtown
Quine's Hill
Keristal
Little Ness
Fleshwick Bay
Lingague
Ronague
Grenaby
Port Soderick
Isle of Man Steam
Santon Head
Bradda Head
Bradda
Bradda Glen
Surby
Ballabeg
Rushen Abbey
Colby
Ballasalla
Port Erin
Four Roads
ISLE OF MAN
Chambered Cairn
The Howe
Cregneash
Port St Mary
Castletown
Derby Fort
St Michael's Island
The Sound
Kitterland
Nautical
Scarlett
Rushen
Keys
Derbyhaven
National Folk
SPANISH HEAD
Calf of Man
Dreswick Point
A3
A4
A1
A2
A5
A10
A18
A20
A23
A27
A30
B10
B12
B22
B8

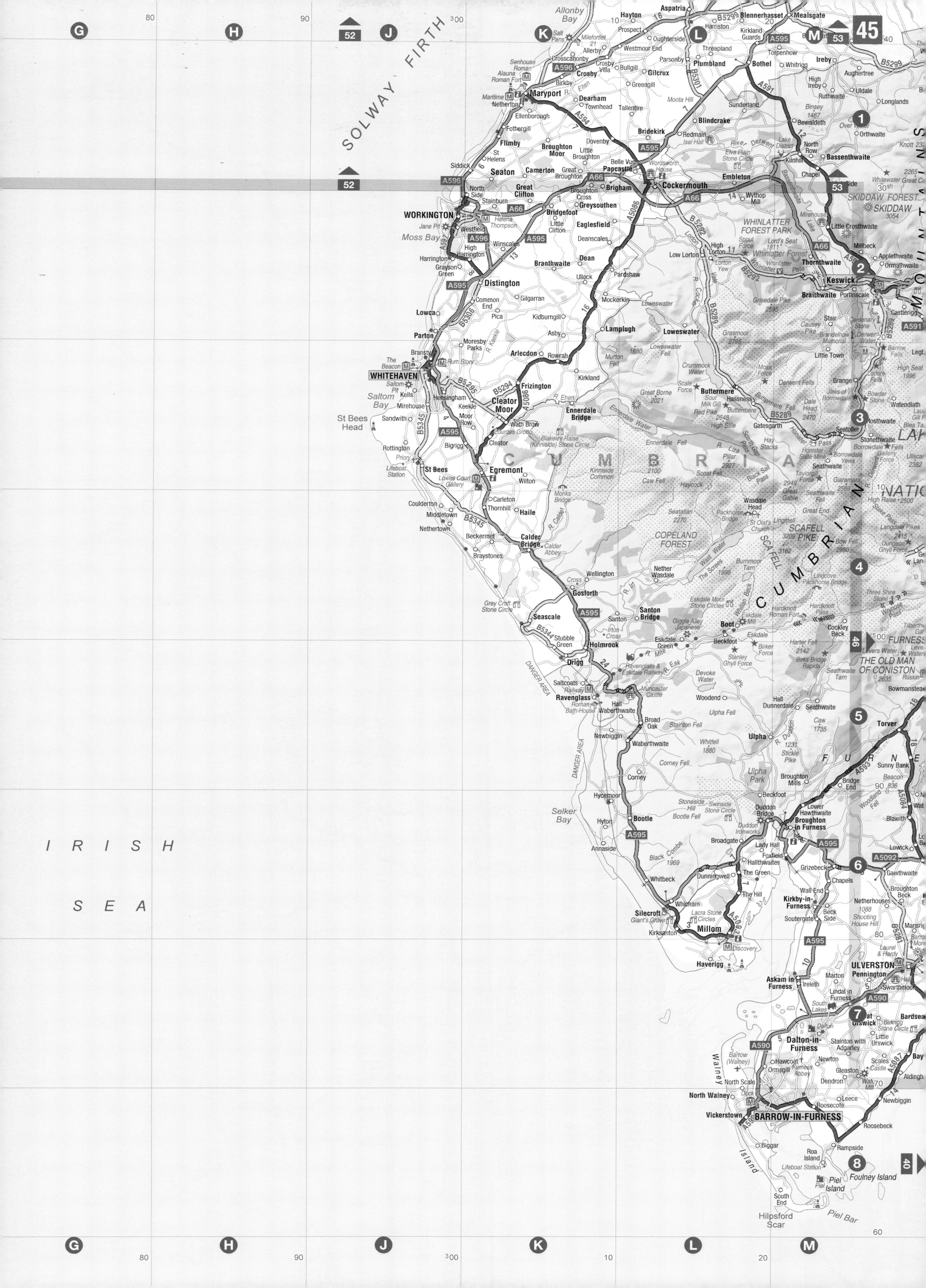

45
G
H
J
K
L
M
80
90
300
10
20
40
60
52
53
46
40
SOLWAY FIRTH
IRISH
SEA
CUMBRIA
CUMBRIAN
MOUNTAINS
NATIONAL
FURNESS
Allonby Bay
Hayton
Aspatria
Blennerhasset
Mealsgate
Prospect
Harriston
Kirkland Guards
Oughterside
Mawbray
Salt Pans
Milefortlet 21
Allerby
Westmoor End
Threapland
Torpenhow
Crosscanonby
Parsonby
Plumbland
Bothel
Ireby
Whitrigg
Senhouse Roman Museum
Alauna Roman Fort
Crosby
Crosby Villa
Bullgill
Gilcrux
High Ireby
Aughertree
Birkby
Greengill
Uldale
Maryport
Maritime Museum
Netherton
Dearham
Townhead
Tallentire
Moota Hill
Sunderland
Ruthwaite
Longlands
Ellenborough
Binsey 1467
Bewaldeth
Fothergill
Blindcrake
Over Water
Orthwaite
Flimby
Dovenby
Bridekirk
Redmain
Isel Hall
Lake District
Broughton Moor
Little Broughton
River Derwent
Kilnhill
North Row
Bassenthwaite
St Helens
Belle Vue
Elva Plain Stone Circle
Siddick
Seaton
Camerton
Great Broughton
Papcastle
Wordsworth House
Embleton
Chapel
Whitewater Great Cockup
SKIDDAW FOREST
SKIDDAW 3054
North Side
Great Clifton
Broughton Cross
Brigham
Cockermouth
Wythop Mill
Stainburn
Greysouthen
WORKINGTON
Jane Pit
Westfield
Helena Thompson
Bridgefoot
Little Clifton
Eaglesfield
WHINLATTER FOREST PARK
Lord's Seat 1811
Mirehouse
Little Crosthwaite
Moss Bay
Winscales
Deanscales
Spout Force
Whinlatter Forest
Millbeck
Harrington
High Harrington
Dean
Low Lorton
High Lorton
Lorton Yew
Thornthwaite
Applethwaite
Ormathwaite
Grayson Green
Branthwaite
Ullock
Pardshaw
Keswick
Portinscale
Braithwaite
Distington
Grisedale Pike 2595
Castlerigg
Common End
Gilgarran
Mockerkin
Loweswater
Stair
Lowca
Pica
Kidburngill
Causey Pike
Centenary Stone
Lamplugh
Loweswater
Grasmoor 2795
Derwent Water
Parton
Asby
Moresby Parks
Brandelhow Memorial
Barrow Falls
Branstу
The Beacon
Rum Story
Arlecdon
Rowrah
Murton Fell
Loweswater Fell
Little Town
WHITEHAVEN
Saltom Pit
Kells
Crummock Water
Moss Force
Lodore Falls
High Seat 1996
Frizington
Kirkland
Scale Force
Buttermere
Hassness
Derwent Fells
Grange
Saltom Bay
Mirehouse
Hensingham
Cleator Moor
Great Borne 2021
Red Pike
Sour Milk Gill
Jaws of Borrowdale
Bowder Stone
Watendlath
St Bees Head
Sandwith
Keekle
Ennerdale Bridge
Ennerdale Water
High Stile
Dale Head 2470
Moor Row
Wath Brow
Lourdes Grotto
Gatesgarth
Seatoller
Rosthwaite
Stonethwaite
Bigrigg
Cleator
Blakeley Raise (Kinniside) Stone Circle
Ennerdale Fell
Hay Stacks
Honister Slate Mine
Borrowdale Yews
Rottington
Priory
Pillar 2927
Lifeboat Station
St Bees
Egremont
Kinniside Common
Scoat Fell
Black Sail Pass
Seathwaite
Lowes Court Gallery
Caw Fell
Haycock
Taylorgill Force
Glaramara 2569
Wilton
Great Gable
Seathwaite Fell
High Raise 2500
Coulderton
Carleton
Monks Bridge
Wasdale Head
Great End
Thornhill
Haile
Middletown
Seatallan 2270
Packhorse Bridge
St Olaf's Church
Lingmell
Nethertown
Beckermet
Calder Bridge
Calder Abbey
COPELAND FOREST
SCAFELL PIKE 3209
3162
Bow Fell 2960
Langdale Pikes 2415
Dungeon Ghyll Force
Braystones
Wast Water
Burnmoor Tarn
Nether Wasdale
Wellington
The Screes 1998
Lingcove Packhorse Bridge
Cross
Gosforth
Eskdale Moor Stone Circles
Hardknott Roman Fort
Hardknott Pass
Three Shire Stone
Wrynose Pass
Grey Croft Stone Circle
Seascale
Santon
Santon Bridge
Giggle Alley Japanese
Eskdale Mill
Boot
Cockley Beck
Irton Cross
Eskdale
Stubble Green
Eskdale Green
Beckfoot
Birker Force
Harter Fell 2142
Holmrook
Stanley Ghyll Force
Birks Bridge Rapids
Levers Water
THE OLD MAN OF CONISTON 2635
Drigg
Ravenglass & Eskdale Railway
R. Esk
Seathwaite Tarn
DANGER AREA
Saltcoats
Railway
Devoke Water
Ruskin
Ravenglass
Muncaster Castle
Bowmanstead
Roman Bath-House
Hall Waberthwaite
Woodend
Hall Dunnerdale
Seathwaite
Broad Oak
Ulpha Fell
Torver
Stainton Fell
Caw 1735
Newbiggin
Waberthwaite
Whitfell 1880
Ulpha
Stickle Pike 1231
Corney Fell
Sunny Bank
Beacon 836
Corney
Ulpha Park
Broughton Mills
Bridge End
Woodland Fell
Hycemoor
Beckfoot
Selker Bay
Stoneside Hill
Swinside Stone Circle
Lower Hawthwaite
Hyton
Bootle
Bootle Fell
Duddon Bridge
Broughton in Furness
Blawith
Duddon Ironworks
Broadgate
Lady Hall
Lowick
Annaside
Black Combe 1969
Foxfield
Hallthwaites
Grizebeck
Gawthwaite
The Green
Chapels
Dunningwell
Whitbeck
Wall End
Broughton Beck
The Hill
Kirkby-in-Furness
Netherhouses
Whicham
Beck Side
1088
Shooting House Hill
Silecroft
Giant's Grave
Lacra Stone Circles
Soutergate
Kirksanton
Millom
Discovery
Laurel & Hardy
Haverigg
ULVERSTON
Marton
Pennington
Askam in Furness
Ireleth
Lindal in Furness
Swarthmoor
South Lakes
Urswick
Bardsea
Birkrigg Stone Circle
Dalton
Little Urswick
Dalton-in-Furness
Stainton with Adgarley
Barrow (Walney)
Hawcoat
Newton
Scales
Ormsgill
Furness Abbey
Gleaston
Castle
Aldingham
Walney
North Scale
Wat Mill
Dendron
North Walney
Dock Museum
Leece
Newbiggin
Roosecote
Vickerstown
BARROW-IN-FURNESS
Rosebeck
Rampside
Biggar
Roa Island
Lifeboat Station
Island
Piel Island
Foulney Island
South End
Piel Bar
Hilpsford Scar
A595
A596
A594
A591
A66
A5086
A590
A593
A5092
A5093
A5084
A5087
B5299
B5301
B5292
B5289
B5306
B5294
B5295
B5345
B5344
B5281

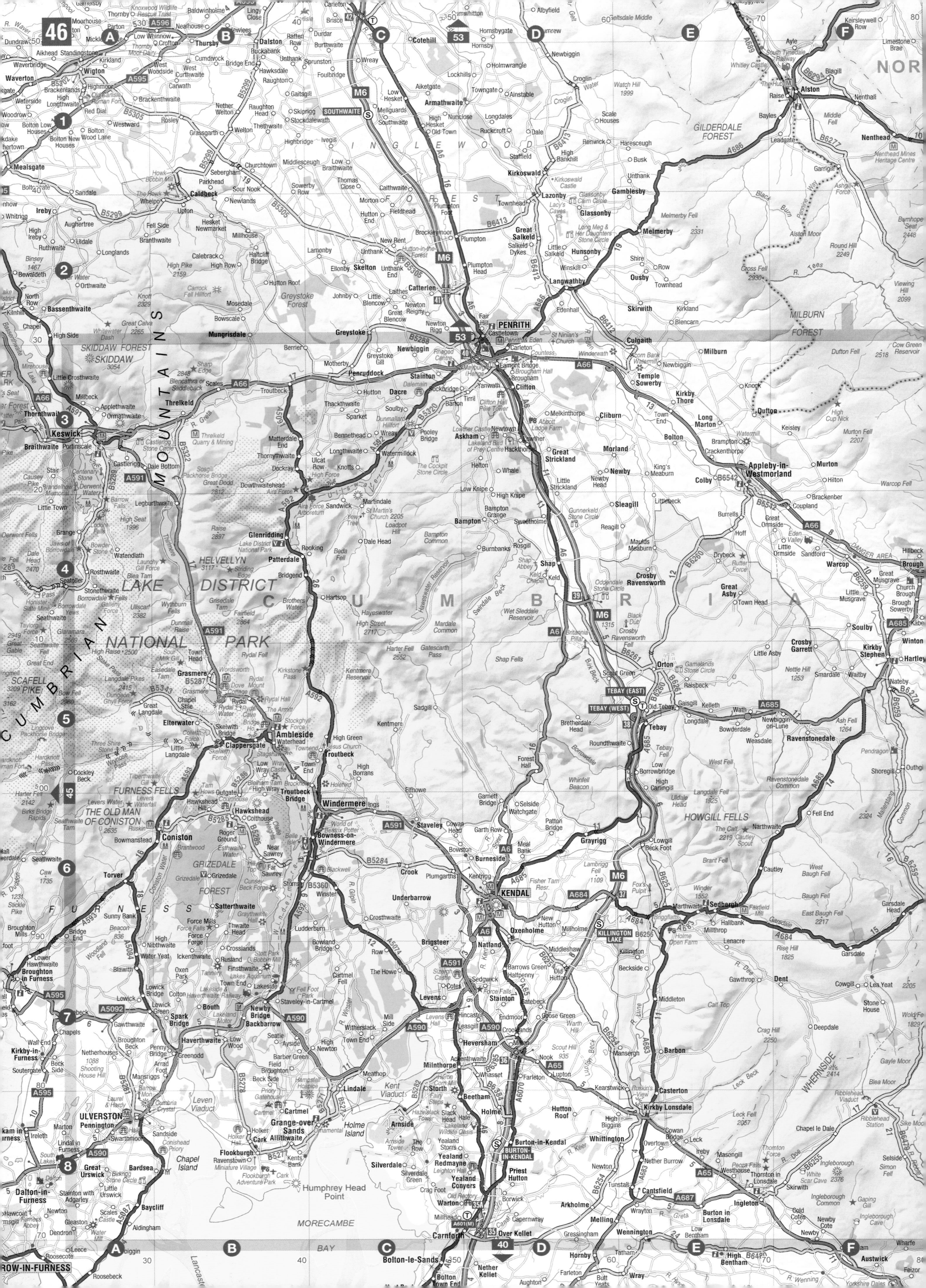
46
A
B
C
D
E
F
1
2
3
4
5
6
7
8
53
45
40
M6
A66
A6
A591
A592
A593
A595
A590
A65
A683
A684
A685
A686
A689
A596
A5092
A5074
A687
A601(M)
B5305
B5299
B6413
B6412
B5288
B5320
B5285
B5284
B5360
B6260
B6261
B6254
B6255
B6256
B6257
B6542
SOUTHWAITE
TEBAY (EAST)
TEBAY (WEST)
KILLINGTON LAKE
BURTON-IN-KENDAL
Wigton
Thursby
Dalston
Carlisle
Cotehill
Armathwaite
Kirkoswald
Lazonby
Melmerby
Alston
Nenthead
Caldbeck
Hesket Newmarket
Skelton
Catterlen
PENRITH
Greystoke
Mungrisdale
Bassenthwaite
Keswick
Threlkeld
Penruddock
Stainton
Dacre
Eamont Bridge
Clifton
Askham
Temple Sowerby
Kirkby Thore
Culgaith
Langwathby
Appleby-in-Westmorland
Great Strickland
Morland
Bampton
Shap
Orton
Tebay
Glenridding
Patterdale
Grasmere
Ambleside
Windermere
Bowness-on-Windermere
Hawkshead
Coniston
Torver
Staveley
Burneside
KENDAL
Oxenholme
Sedbergh
Kirkby Stephen
Warcop
Brough
Ravenstonedale
Dent
Garsdale
Kirkby Lonsdale
Casterton
Barbon
Ingleton
Bentham
Carnforth
Milnthorpe
Heversham
Levens
Grange-over-Sands
Cartmel
Newby Bridge
ULVERSTON
Dalton-in-Furness
Broughton in Furness
Kirkby-in-Furness
Arnside
Silverdale
Burton-in-Kendal
Holme
Bolton-le-Sands
Over Kellet
Hornby
Wennington
Austwick
SKIDDAW
HELVELLYN
SCAFELL PIKE
LAKE DISTRICT NATIONAL PARK
CUMBRIAN MOUNTAINS
C U M B R I A
I N G L E W O O D F O R E S T
F U R N E S S
GRIZEDALE FOREST
HOWGILL FELLS
GILDERDALE FOREST
MILBURN FOREST
FURNESS FELLS
THE OLD MAN OF CONISTON
WHERNSIDE
Cross Fell 2930
Humphrey Head Point
Chapel Island
Holme Island
MORECAMBE BAY
NOR

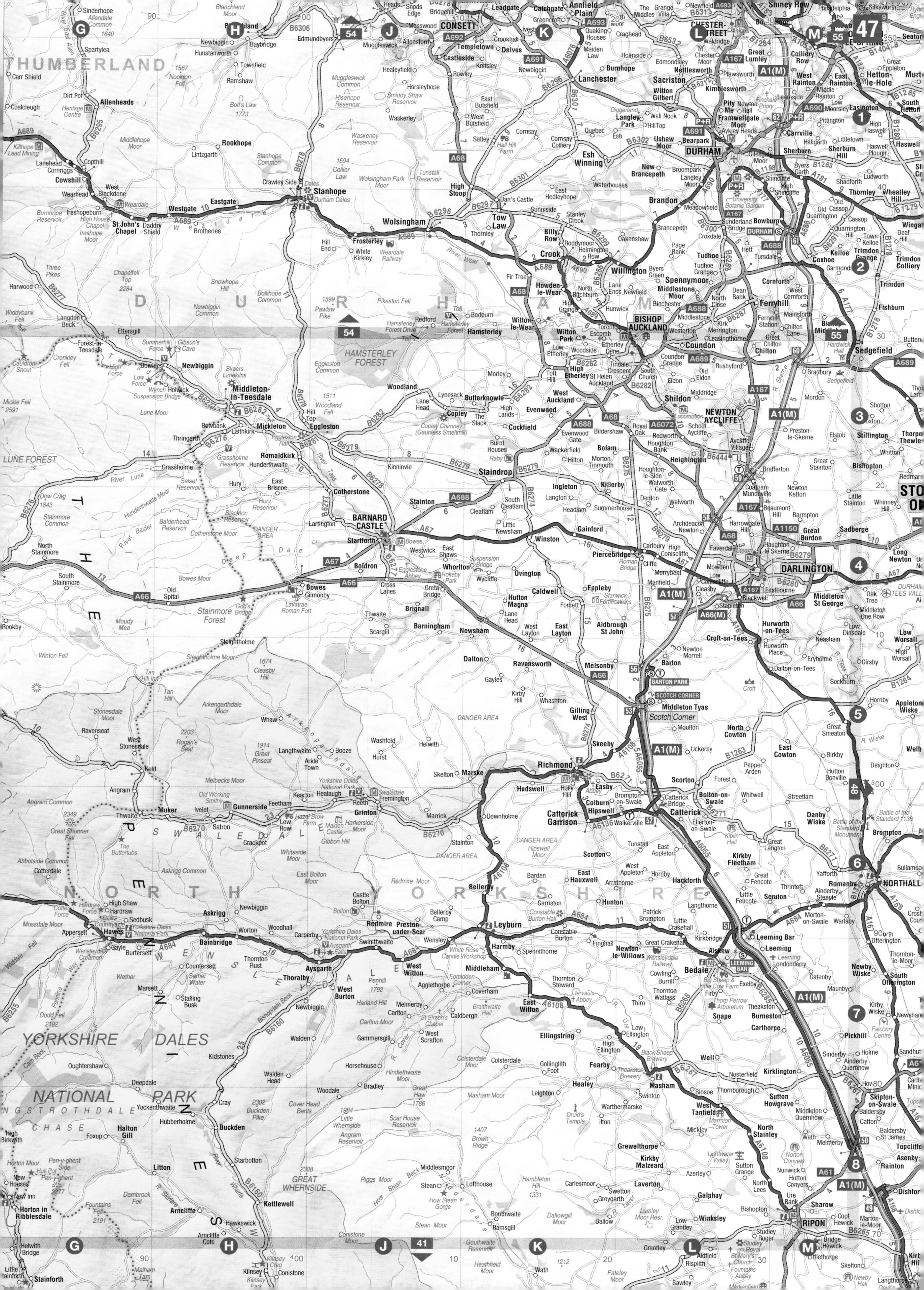

47
THUMBERLAND
CONSETT
Lanchester
Sacriston
CHESTER-LE-STREET
DURHAM
Stanhope
Wolsingham
Allenheads
St John's Chapel
Westgate
Eastgate
Tow Law
Crook
Willington
Spennymoor
Ferryhill
Sedgefield
BISHOP AUCKLAND
Shildon
NEWTON AYCLIFFE
DURHAM
HAMSTERLEY FOREST
Middleton-in-Teesdale
Eggleston
Staindrop
BARNARD CASTLE
LUNE FOREST
DARLINGTON
Piercebridge
Gainford
Bowes
Stainmore Forest
Richmond
Scotch Corner
Catterick Garrison
Catterick
Leyburn
Hawes
Askrigg
Bainbridge
Aysgarth
Middleham
Bedale
Northallerton
NORTHALLERTON
Masham
West Tanfield
RIPON
Kettlewell
Buckden
Horton in Ribblesdale
NORTH YORKSHIRE
YORKSHIRE DALES NATIONAL PARK
PENNINES
SWALEDALE
WENSLEYDALE
A1(M)
A66
A68
A689
A684
A6108
A167
54
55
48
41
G
H
J
K
L
M

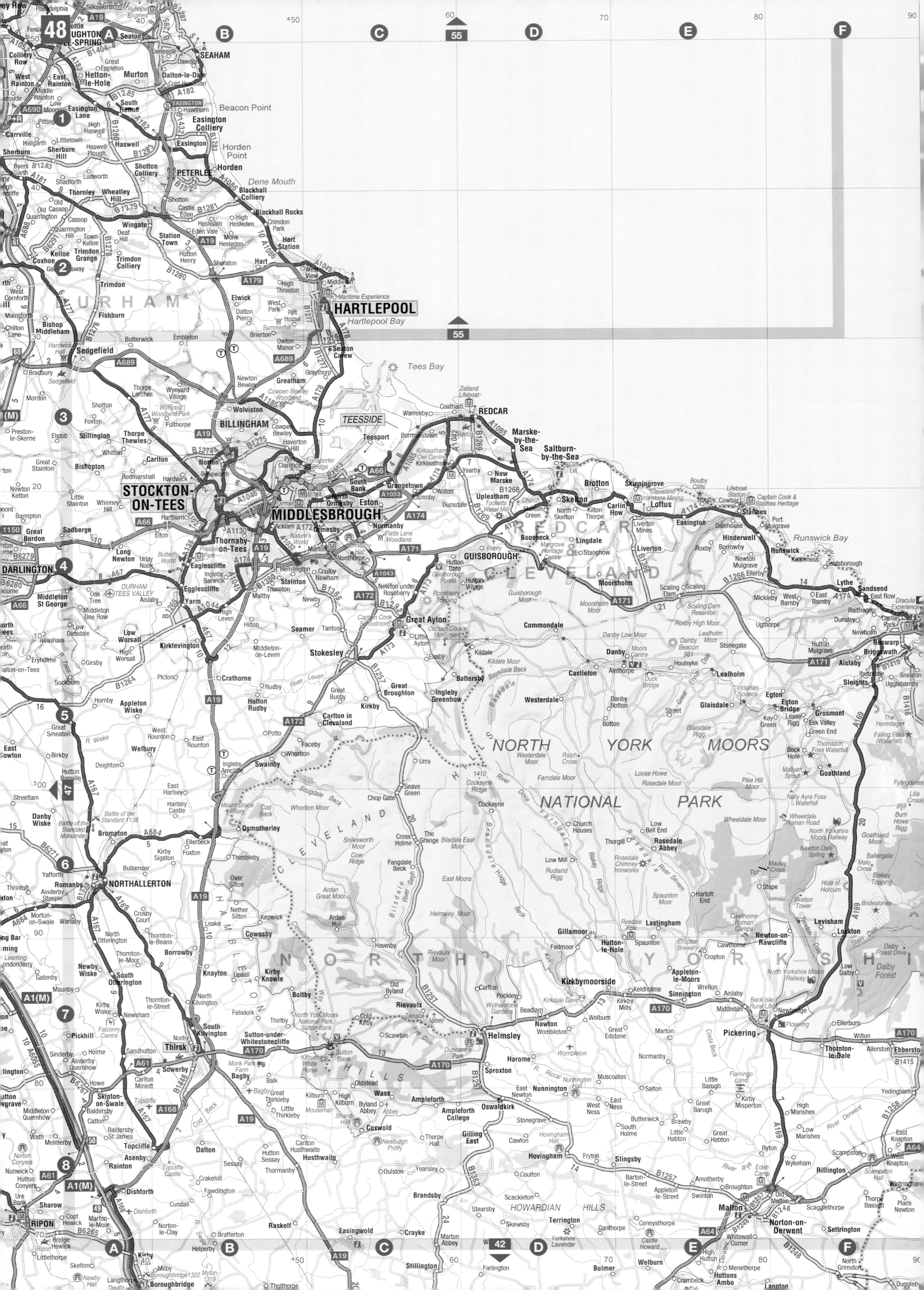

48
55
47
42
DURHAM
HARTLEPOOL
Hartlepool Bay
Tees Bay
TEESSIDE
REDCAR
Marske-by-the-Sea
Saltburn-by-the-Sea
STOCKTON-ON-TEES
MIDDLESBROUGH
BILLINGHAM
DARLINGTON
NORTHALLERTON
Thirsk
RIPON
GUISBOROUGH
REDCAR & CLEVELAND
NORTH YORK MOORS
NATIONAL PARK
NORTH YORKSHIRE
HOWARDIAN HILLS
HAMBLETON HILLS
CLEVELAND HILLS
CLEVELAND WAY
Runswick Bay
Beacon Point
Horden Point
Dene Mouth
Blackhall Rocks
SEAHAM
Seaton
Murton
Hetton-le-Hole
Easington
Easington Colliery
Horden
PETERLEE
Shotton Colliery
Wingate
Station Town
Hart
Trimdon
Sedgefield
Fishburn
Bishop Middleham
Elwick
Greatham
Wolviston
Norton
Thornaby-on-Tees
Eaglescliffe
Yarm
Stainton
Marton
Ormesby
Nunthorpe
Eston
Normanby
Grangetown
South Bank
Teesport
Warrenby
Coatham
Dormanstown
Kirkleatham
New Marske
Upleatham
Skelton
Brotton
Skinningrove
Loftus
Carlin How
Easington
Staithes
Port Mulgrave
Hinderwell
Runswick
Kettleness
Goldsborough
Lythe
Sandsend
Whitby
Ruswarp
Sleights
Grosmont
Egton
Egton Bridge
Glaisdale
Lealholm
Danby
Castleton
Commondale
Westerdale
Kildale
Great Ayton
Stokesley
Great Broughton
Ingleby Greenhow
Carlton in Cleveland
Swainby
Osmotherley
Seamer
Hutton Rudby
Crathorne
Kirklevington
Low Worsall
Hilton
Welbury
Brompton
Romanby
Yafforth
Thornton-le-Beans
Borrowby
Knayton
Kirby Knowle
Boltby
Sutton-under-Whitestonecliffe
Sowerby
Bagby
Topcliffe
Dishforth
Rainton
Asenby
Dalton
Coxwold
Husthwaite
Byland Abbey
Wass
Ampleforth
Ampleforth College
Oswaldkirk
Gilling East
Hovingham
Slingsby
Terrington
Malton
Norton-on-Derwent
Old Malton
Pickering
Middleton
Thornton-le-Dale
Ebberston
Levisham
Lockton
Goathland
Newton-on-Rawcliffe
Sinnington
Kirkbymoorside
Helmsley
Rievaulx
Nawton
Beadlam
Gillamoor
Hutton-le-Hole
Lastingham
Spaunton
Cropton
Appleton-le-Moors
Rosedale Abbey
Church Houses
Low Mill
Cockayne
Chop Gate
Seave Green
Hawnby
Fangdale Beck
Bilsdale
Sheriff Hutton
Easingwold
Crayke
Brandsby
Stillington
Raskelf
Sessay
Thormanby
Helperby
Brafferton
Kirby Hill
Skipton-on-Swale
Carlton Miniott
Sandhutton
Pickhill
Kirby Wiske
Newby Wiske
South Otterington
North Otterington
Thornton-le-Moor
Great Smeaton
Hutton Bonville
Danby Wiske
Middleton St George
Hurworth
Neasham
Girsby
Sockburn
Low Dinsdale
A1(M)
A19
A66
A67
A167
A168
A170
A171
A172
A173
A174
A178
A179
A181
A182
A689
A690
A1085
A1086
A169
A64

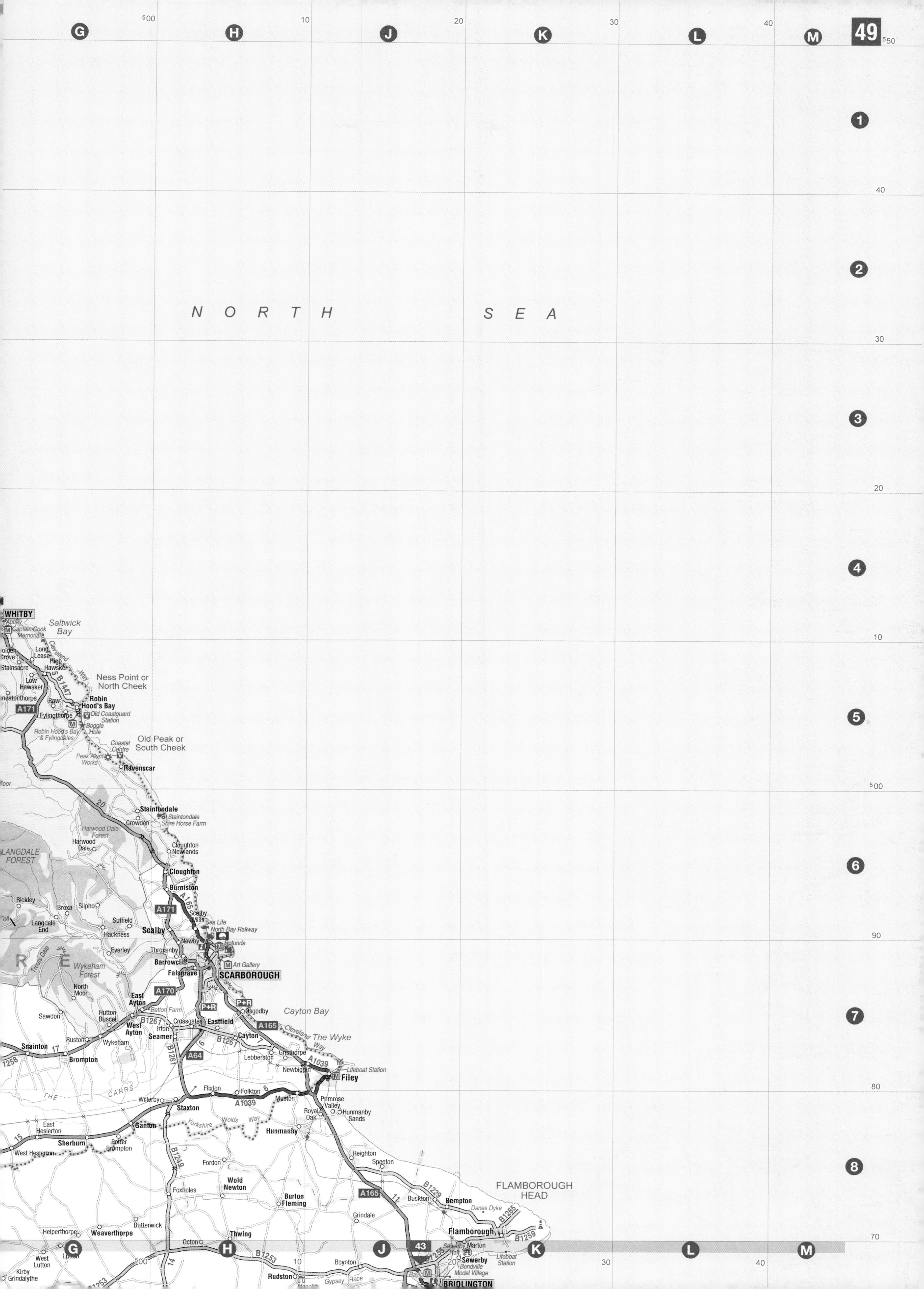

N O R T H   S E A

WHITBY
Saltwick Bay
Captain Cook Memorial
Abbey
Golden Grove
Long Lease
Stainsacre
Low Hawsker
High Hawsker
Cleveland Way
B 1447
Ness Point or North Cheek
Sneatonthorpe
Raw
Robin Hood's Bay
Fylingthorpe
Old Coastguard Station
A171
Boggle Hole
Robin Hood's Bay & Fylingdales
Old Peak or South Cheek
Coastal Centre
Peak Alum Works
Ravenscar
oor

20

Staintondale
Staintondale Shire Horse Farm
Crowdon
Harwood Dale Forest
Harwood Dale
Cloughton Newlands
LANGDALE FOREST
Cloughton
Burniston
Bickley
Broxa
Silpho
Scalby Mills
Sea Life
A171
A165
North Bay Railway
Suffield
Scalby
Hackness
Langdale End
Newby
Rotunda
Everley
Throxenby
Art Gallery
R E
Wykeham Forest
Barrowcliff
Falsgrave
North Moor
SCARBOROUGH
Sawdon
Hutton Buscel
East Ayton
A170
P+R
Betton Farm
Cayton Bay
West Ayton
Crossgates
Eastfield
Osgodby
B1261
Irton
P+R
Ruston
Seamer
Cayton
A165
Cleveland Way
The Wyke
Wykeham
B1261
Snainton
17
Lebberston
Gristhorpe
A1039
Brompton
A64
Newbiggin
Lifeboat Station
T1258
Muston
A1039
Filey
THE   CARRS
Flixton
Folkton
Primrose Valley
Staxton
Willerby
A1039
Royal Oak
Hunmanby Sands
East Heslerton
Ganton
Yorkshire Wolds
Hunmanby
15
Sherburn
Potter Brompton
West Heslerton
Reighton
Speeton
Foxholes
Fordon
B1249
FLAMBOROUGH HEAD
Wold Newton
A165
B1229
Burton Fleming
Buckton
Bempton
Danes Dyke
Helperthorpe
Weaverthorpe
Thwing
Grindale
B1255
West Lutton
Octon
Flamborough
B1259
Kirby Grindalythe
H
B1253
J
43
K
Sewerby Hall
L
M
Boynton
Marton
Lifeboat Station
Rudston
Gypsey Race
Bondville Model Village
BRIDLINGTON

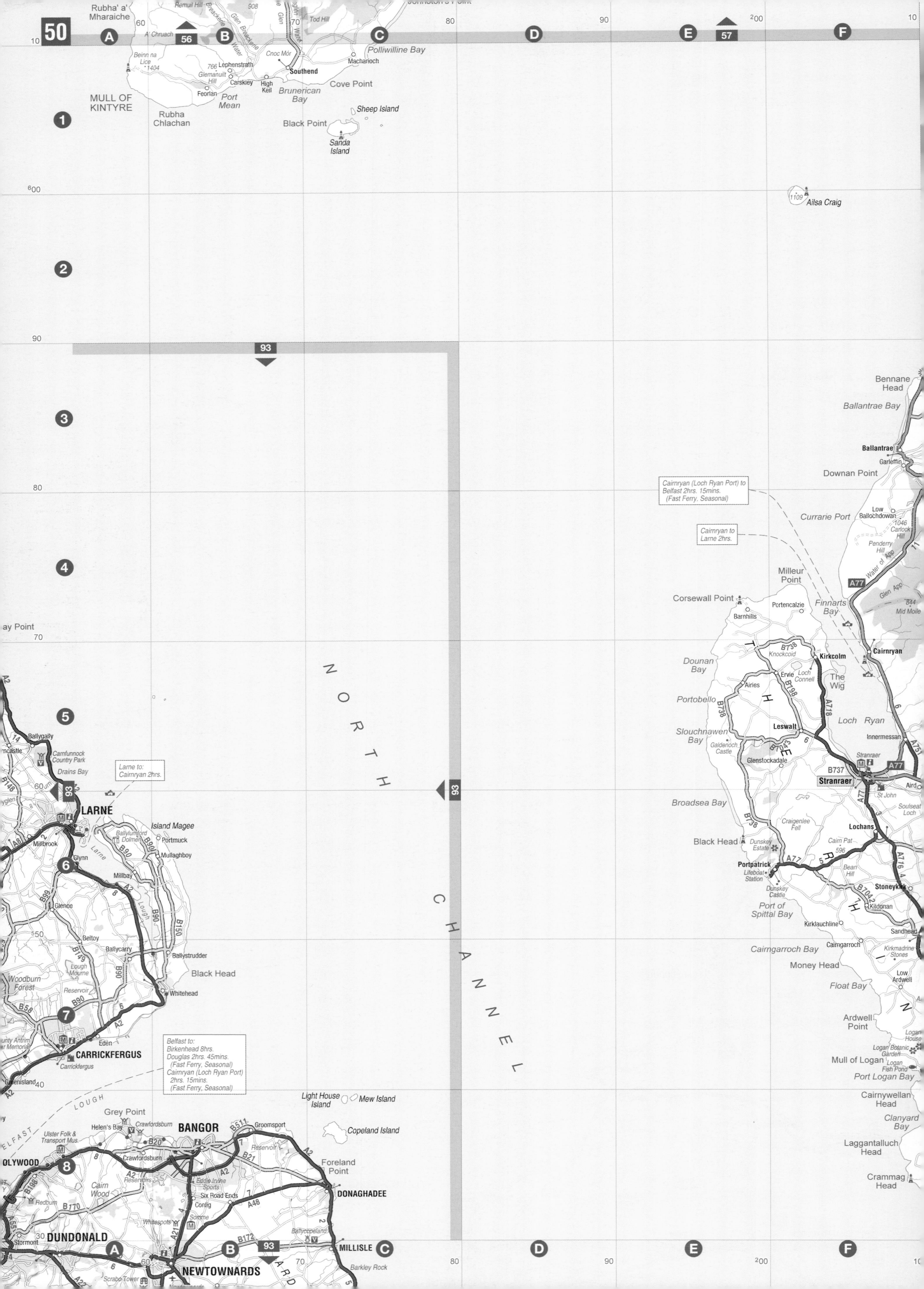

MULL OF KINTYRE

Rubha' a' Mharaiche
Remuil Hill
A' Chruach
Beinn na Lice *1404
Glemanuilt Hill
Feorlan
766 Lephenstrath
Carskiey
High Keil
Cnoc Mór
Macharioch
Southend
Polliwilline Bay
Cove Point
Port Mean
Bruherican Bay
Rubha Chlachan
Black Point
Sheep Island
Sanda Island

Ailsa Craig 1109

NORTH CHANNEL

Bennane Head
Ballantrae Bay
Ballantrae
Garleffin
Downan Point
Low Ballochdowan
Currarie Port
1046 Carlock Hill
Penderry Hill
Finnarts Bay
344 Mid Moile
Glen App
Milleur Point
A77

Corsewall Point
Portencalzie
Barnhills
Dounan Bay
Knockcoid
Kirkcolm
B738
Ervie
Loch Connell
Cairnryan
The Wig
Airies
Portobello
B738
Leswalt
Loch Ryan
B704
Galdenoch Castle
Innermessan
Slouchnawen Bay
Stranraer
B737
Glenstockadale
Aird
St John
Broadsea Bay
Soulseat Loch
Craigenlee Fell
Lochans
A77
Black Head
Dunskey Estate
Cairn Pat 596
Portpatrick
Lifeboat Station
Bean Hill
Stoneykirk
B7042
Dunskey Castle
Kildonan
Port of Spittal Bay
Kirklauchline
Sandhead
Cairngarroch Bay
Cairngarroch
Kirkmadrine Stones
Money Head
Low Ardwell
Float Bay
Ardwell Point
Logan House
Logan Botanic Garden
Mull of Logan
Logan Fish Pond
Port Logan Bay
Cairnywellan Head
Clanyard Bay
Laggantalluch Head
Crammag Head

Cairnryan (Loch Ryan Port) to Belfast 2hrs. 15mins. (Fast Ferry. Seasonal)

Cairnryan to Larne 2hrs.

Larne to: Cairnryan 2hrs.

Ballygally
Carnfunnock Country Park
Drains Bay
93
LARNE
Millbrook
Glynn
Island Magee
Ballylumford Dolmen
Portmuck
Mullaghboy
Millbay
B90
B150
Glenoe
Ballycarry
Ballystrudder
Black Head
Beltoy
Ballyhill
Whitehead
Woodburn Forest
Reservoir
B90
B58
County Antrim War Memorial
CARRICKFERGUS
Eden
Greenisland

Belfast to:
Birkenhead 8hrs.
Douglas 2hrs. 45mins.
(Fast Ferry. Seasonal)
Cairnryan (Loch Ryan Port)
2hrs. 15mins.
(Fast Ferry. Seasonal)

Light House Island
Mew Island
Copeland Island
Foreland Point

BELFAST LOUGH
Grey Point
Helen's Bay
Ulster Folk & Transport Mus.
Crawfordsburn
BANGOR
Groomsport
B511
B20
B21
A2
Reservoir
HOLYWOOD
Crawfordsburn
Cairn Wood
Redburn
B170
Eddie Irvine Sports
Six Road Ends
Conlig
DONAGHADEE
B172
Ballycopeland
MILLISLE
Whitespots
Somme
Stormont
DUNDONALD
A22
Scrabo Tower
NEWTOWNARDS
Barkley Rock
93

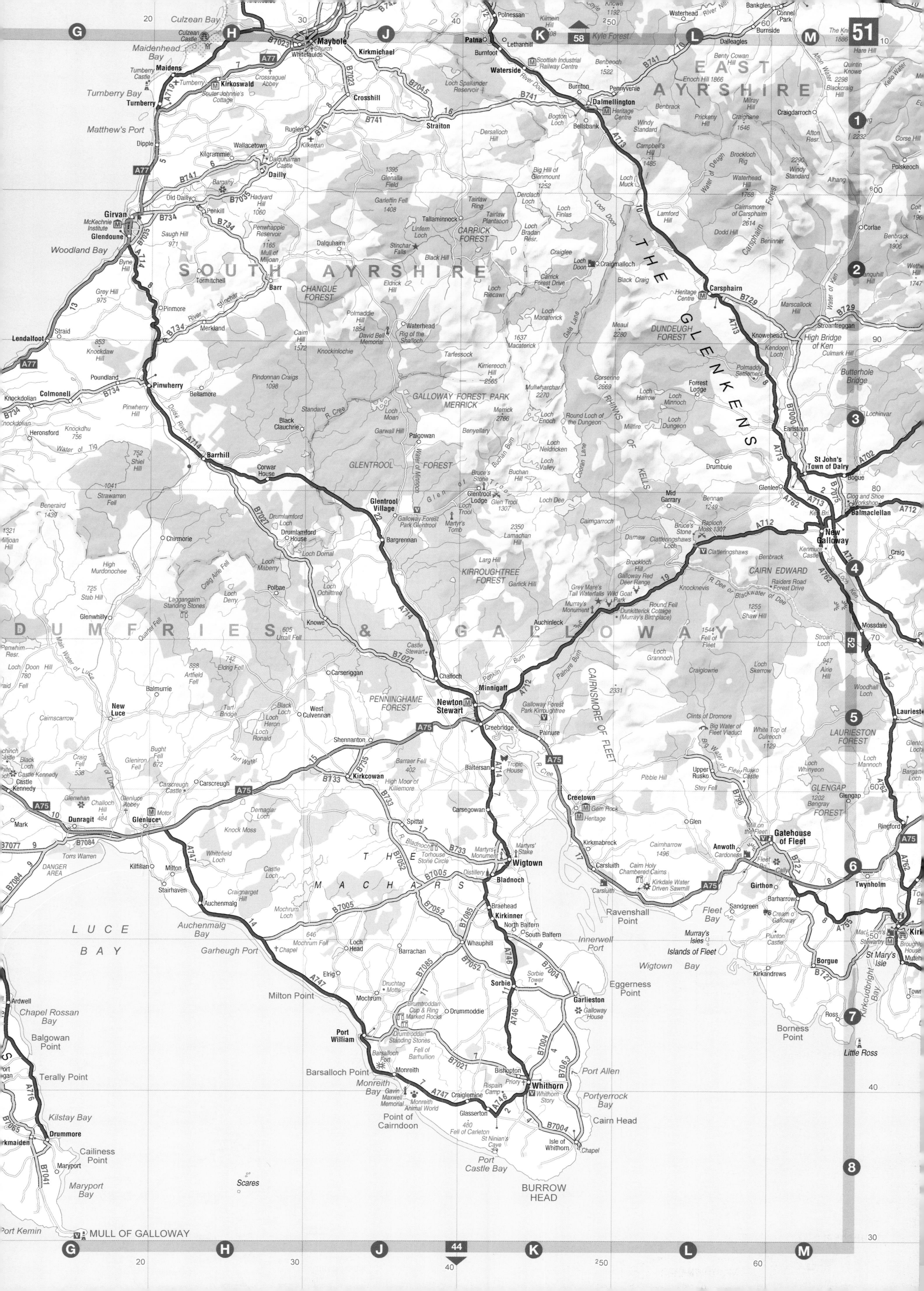

51
G
H
J
K
L
M
20
30
40
50
60
58
44
52
1
2
3
4
5
6
7
8
EAST AYRSHIRE
SOUTH AYRSHIRE
DUMFRIES & GALLOWAY
THE GLENKENS
RHINNS OF KELLS
CAIRNSMORE OF FLEET
THE MACHARS
LUCE BAY
GALLOWAY FOREST PARK MERRICK
GLENTROOL FOREST
CARRICK FOREST
CHANGUE FOREST
KIRROUGHTREE FOREST
PENNINGHAME FOREST
DUNDEUGH FOREST
CAIRN EDWARD
LAURIESTON FOREST
GLENGAP FOREST
Culzean Bay
Culzean Castle
Maidenhead Bay
Maybole
Kirkmichael
Patna
Polnessan
Lethanhill
Kyle Forest
Dalleagles
Waterside
Burnfoot
Scottish Industrial Railway Centre
Loch Spallander Reservoir
Maidens
Turnberry Castle
Turnberry
Kirkoswald
Crossraguel Abbey
Souter Johnnie's Cottage
Turnberry Bay
Crosshill
Straiton
Dalmellington
Bellsbank
Burnton
Pennyvenie
Benbeoch 1522
Matthew's Port
Dipple
Ruglen
Kilkerran
Wallacetown
Kilgrammie
Dalquharran Castle
Dailly
Bargany
Old Dailly
Girvan
McKechnie Institute
Glendoune
Penkill
Hadyard Hill 1060
Penwhapple Reservoir
Saugh Hill 971
Woodland Bay
Byne Hill
Tormitchell
Barr
Dalquhairn
Tallaminnock
Linfern Loch
Stinchar Falls
Black Hill
Eldrick Hill
Grey Hill 975
Pinmore
Merkland
Lendalfoot
Straid
Knockdaw Hill
Poundland
Pinwherry
Colmonell
Bellamore
Knockdolian
Heronsford
Knockdhu 756
Water of Tig
Shiel Hill
Barrhill
Corwar House
Pinwherry Hill
Black Clauchrie
Waterhead
Rig of the Shalloch
Polmaddie Hill 1854
David Bell Memorial
Tarfessock
Kirriereoch Hill 2565
Merrick 2766
Benyellary
Loch Moan
Garwall Hill
Palgowan
Water of Minnoch
Glentrool Village
Galloway Forest Park Glentrool
Glentrool Lodge
Glen Trool 1307
Loch Trool
Martyr's Tomb
Bruce's Stone
Buchan Hill
Bargrennan
Drumlamford Loch
Drumlamford House
Loch Dornal
Chirmorie
Strawarren Fell
Beneraird 1439
Loch Maberry
Polbae
Loch Ochiltree
Laggangairn Standing Stones
Loch Derry
Stab Hill
Glenwhilly
Knowe
Urrall Fell
Castle Stewart
Challoch
Newton Stewart
Minnigaff
Carseriggan
Eldrig Fell
Artfield Fell
Balmurrie
New Luce
Cairnscarrow
Tarf Bridge
Black Loch
Loch Heron
Loch Ronald
West Culvennan
Shennanton
Creebridge
Palnure
Galloway Forest Park Kirroughtree
Kirkcowan
Barraer Fell 402
High Moor of Killiemore
Baltersan
Tropic House
Craig Fell 538
Gleniron Fell
Bught Fell 672
Castle Kennedy
Carscreugh Castle
Carscreugh
Glenwhan
Challoch Hill 484
Glenluce Abbey
Glenluce
Motor
Dunragit
Mark
Torrs Warren
DANGER AREA
Knock Moss
Dernaglar Loch
Spittal
Torhouse Stone Circle
Martyrs' Monument
Martyrs' Stake
Wigtown
Bladnoch
Distillery
Carsegowan
Creetown
Gem Rock
Heritage
Kirkmabreck
Carsluith
Kilfillan
Milton
Stairhaven
Whitefield Loch
Castle Loch
Craignarget Hill
Auchenmalg
Auchenmalg Bay
Garheugh Port
Chapel
Mochrum Loch
Mochrum Fell
Loch Head
Barrachan
Braehead
Kirkinner
North Balfern
South Balfern
Innerwell Port
Ravenshall Point
Whauphill
Sorbie
Sorbie Tower
Garlieston
Galloway House
Eggerness Point
Wigtown Bay
Elrig
Druchtag Motte
Mochrum
Drumtroddan Cup & Ring Marked Rocks
Drumtroddan Standing Stones
Drummoddie
Milton Point
Port William
Barsalloch Fort
Barsalloch Point
Monreith
Fell of Barhullion
Monreith Bay
Gavin Maxwell Memorial
Monreith Animal World
Craiglemine
Glasserton
Point of Cairndoon
Fell of Carleton
St Ninian's Cave
Port Castle Bay
Bishopton
Priory
Whithorn
Whithorn Story
Rispain Camp
Port Allen
Portyerrock Bay
Cairn Head
Isle of Whithorn
Chapel
BURROW HEAD
Ardwell
Chapel Rossan Bay
Balgowan Point
Terally Point
Kilstay Bay
Drummore
Cailiness Point
Maryport
Maryport Bay
Scares
MULL OF GALLOWAY
Port Kemin
Carsphairn
Heritage Centre
Black Craig
Craigmalloch
Loch Doon
Craiglee
Loch Riecawr
Loch Bradan Resr.
Carrick Forest Drive
Loch Finlas
Derclach Loch
Tairlaw Ring
Tairlaw Plantation
Garleffin Fell 1408
Glenalla Fell
Big Hill of Glenmount 1252
Bogton Loch
Dersalloch Hill
Loch Muck
Windy Standard
Campbell's Hill 1485
Benbrack
Prickeny Hill
Craighane 1646
Enoch Hill 1866
Benty Cowan Hill
Millray Hill
Lamford Hill
Dodd Hill
Cairnsmore of Carsphairn 2614
Beninner
Waterhead Hill 1768
Brockloch Rig
Water of Deugh
Afton Resr.
Craigdarroch
Blackcraig Hill
Windy Standard
Alhang
Polskeoch
Corlae
Benbrack 1906
Marscallock Hill
Knowehead
Kendoon Loch
Stroanfreggan
High Bridge of Ken
Culmark Hill
Butterhole Bridge
Lochinvar
Polmaddy Settlement
Forrest Lodge
Loch Harrow
Loch Minnoch
Loch Dungeon
Millfire
Corserine 2669
Round Loch of the Dungeon
Mullwharchar 2270
Loch Enoch
Loch Macaterick
Macaterick 1637
Meaul 2280
Loch Neldricken
Loch Valley
Loch Dee
Cooran Lane
Gala Lane
Drumbuie
Earlstoun
St John's Town of Dalry
Bogue
Glenlee
Mid Garrary
Bennan 1249
Clog and Shoe Workshop
Balmaclellan
Ken Bri
New Galloway
Kenmure Castle
Craig
Cairngarroch
Lamachan Hill 2350
Larg Hill
Garlick Hill
Darnaw
Clatteringshaws Loch
Clatteringshaws
Bruce's Stone
Raploch Moss 1307
Brockloch Hill
Galloway Red Deer Range
Benbrack
Raiders Road Forest Drive
Knocknevis
Grey Mare's Tail Waterfalls
Wild Goat Park
Murray's Monument
Round Fell
Dunkitterick Cottage (Murray's Birthplace)
Shaw Hill
Auchinleck
Fell of Fleet 1544
Loch Grannoch
Loch Skerrow
Craiglowrie
Stroan Loch
Aine Hill
Mossdale
Woodhall Loch
Laurieston
Clints of Dromore
Big Water of Fleet Viaduct
White Top of Culreoch 1129
Loch Whinyeon
Loch Mannoch
Upper Rusko
Rusko Castle
Stey Fell
Pibble Hill
Bengray 1202
Glengap
Ringford
Glen
Mill on the Fleet
Gatehouse of Fleet
Anwoth
Cardoness
Cally
Cairnharrow 1496
Cairn Holy Chambered Cairns
Kirkdale Water Driven Sawmill
Carsluith
Girthon
Twynholm
Barharrow
Sandgreen
Cream o' Galloway
Fleet Bay
Murray's Isles
Islands of Fleet
Plunton Castle
Borgue
Kirkandrews
St Mary's Isle
Kirkcudbright Bay
Ross
Borness Point
Little Ross

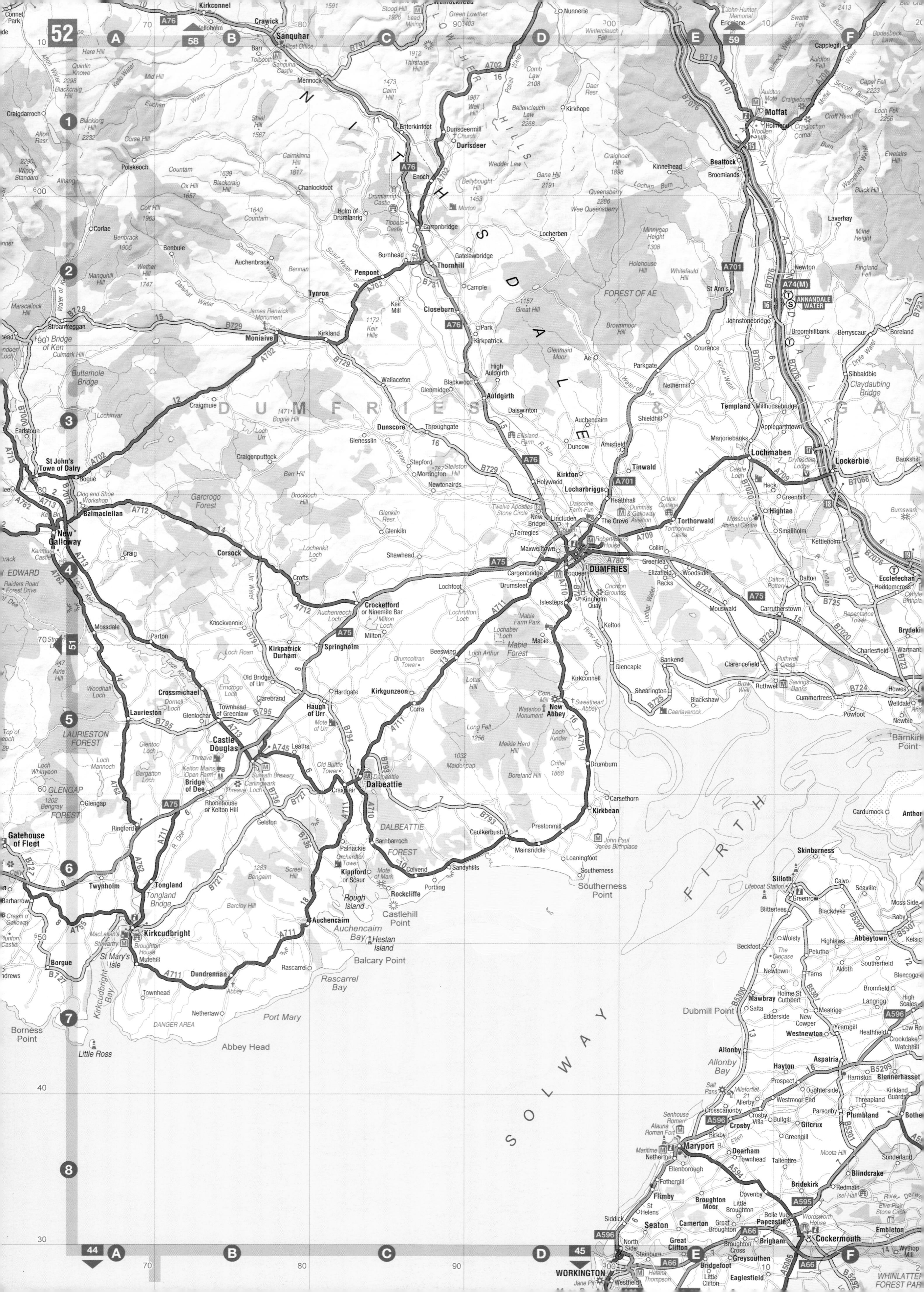
58
59
51
44
45
A
B
C
D
E
F
1
2
3
4
5
6
7
8
Kirkconnel
Crawick
Sanquhar
Mennock
Enterkinfoot
Durisdeermill
Durisdeer
Enoch
Drumlanrig Castle
Holm of Drumlanrig
Tibbers Castle
Carronbridge
Morton
Thornhill
Burnhead
Penpont
Gatelawbridge
Tynron
Keir Mill
Closeburn
Cample
Kirkland
Moniaive
Stroanfreggan
Bridge of Ken
Polskeoch
Chanlockfoot
Craigdarroch
Corlae
Benbuie
Auchenbrack
Craigmuie
St John's Town of Dalry
Earlstoun
Bogue
Balmaclellan
New Galloway
Kenmure Castle
Raiders Road Forest Drive
Mossdale
Parton
Corsock
Crofts
Crocketford or Ninemile Bar
Milton
Knockvennie
Kirkpatrick Durham
Springholm
Old Bridge of Urr
Clarebrand
Haugh of Urr
Hardgate
Kirkgunzeon
Corra
Crossmichael
Laurieston
Townhead of Greenlaw
Glenlochar
Castle Douglas
Threave
Bridge of Dee
Rhonehouse or Kelton Hill
Leaths
Craignair
Dalbeattie
Gelston
Glengap
Ringford
Tongland
Twynholm
Gatehouse of Fleet
Kirkcudbright
Borgue
Mutehill
Townhead
Dundrennan
Abbey
Netherlaw
Rascarrel
Auchencairn
Palnackie
Orchardton Tower
Kippford or Scaur
Rockcliffe
Barnbarroch
Colvend
Sandyhills
Portling
Rough Island
Castlehill Point
Hestan Island
Balcary Point
Rascarrel Bay
Port Mary
Abbey Head
DANGER AREA
Little Ross
Borness Point
St Mary's Isle
Kirkcudbright Bay
LAURIESTON FOREST
GLENGAP FOREST
DALBEATTIE FOREST
Garcrogo Forest
Mabie Forest
Mabie
Kirkconnell
New Abbey
Sweetheart Abbey
Loch Kindar
Criffel 1868
Drumburn
Carsethorn
Kirkbean
Prestonmill
Mainsriddle
Caulkerbush
Loaningfoot
Southerness
Southerness Point
Beeswing
Lochfoot
Drumsleet
Cargenbridge
Maxwelltown
Troqueer
DUMFRIES
Kingholm Quay
Islesteps
Kelton
Glencaple
Shearington
Caerlaverock
Bankend
Blackshaw
Ruthwell
Clarencefield
Cummertrees
Powfoot
Annan
Howes
Newbie
Barnkirk Point
Terregles
New Bridge
Lincluden
Holywood
Kirkton
Locharbriggs
Heathhall
The Grove
Torthorwald
Collin
Greenlea
Racks
Mouswald
Carrutherstown
Dalton
Hoddomcross
Ecclefechan
Lockerbie
Lochmaben
Hightae
Heck
Greenhill
Smallholm
Kettleholm
Templand
Millhousebridge
Applegarthtown
Marjoriebanks
Shieldhill
Tinwald
Amisfield
Duncow
Auchencairn
Dalswinton
Auldgirth
Blackwood
Glenmidge
Wallaceton
Dunscore
Throughgate
Stepford
Morrington
Newtonairds
Glenkiln
Shawhead
Kirkpatrick
Park
Ae
Parkgate
Nethermill
Courance
Johnstonebridge
St Ann's
Beattock
Moffat
Broomlands
Kinnelhead
Locherben
Kirkhope
Nunnerie
Laverhay
Newton
Boreland
Berryscaur
Broomhillbank
Sibbaldbie
Claydaubing Bridge
Bankshill
Brydekirk
Charlesfield
Ericstane
Capplegill
FOREST OF AE
ANNANDALE WATER
NITHSDALE
LOWTHER HILLS
DUMFRIES & GALLOWAY
SOLWAY FIRTH
Skinburness
Silloth
Greenrow
Calvo
Seaville
Blitterlees
Blackdyke
Wolsty
Beckfoot
Abbeytown
Mawbray
Dubmill Point
Westnewton
Allonby
Allonby Bay
Aspatria
Hayton
Prospect
Crosscanonby
Crosby
Maryport
Netherton
Ellenborough
Dearham
Flimby
Broughton Moor
Great Broughton
Seaton
Camerton
Great Clifton
Papcastle
Brigham
Cockermouth
Bridekirk
Blindcrake
Plumbland
Gilcrux
Bridgefoot
Greysouthen
Eaglesfield
Stainburn
WORKINGTON
Westfield
Embleton
Blennerhasset
A76
A702
A701
A74(M)
A709
A75
A710
A711
A712
A713
A762
A745
A755
A780
A596
A594
A595
A66
B729
B797
B7076
B7020
B724
B725
B793
B794
B795
B727
B736
B5300
B5301
B5302
B7068
B723
70
80
90
10
60
50
40
30
300
600

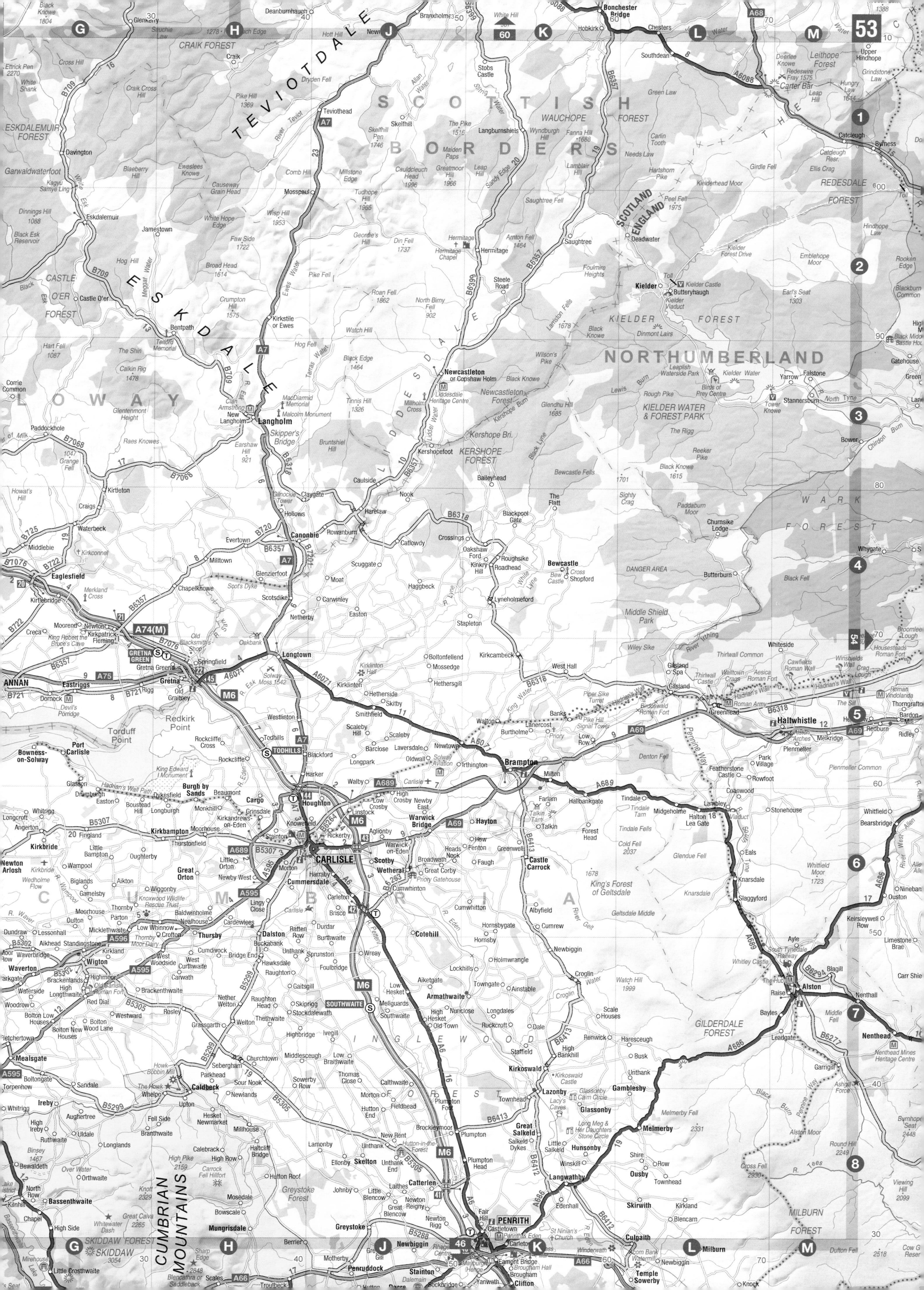
TEVIOTDALE
SCOTTISH BORDERS
CRAIK FOREST
WAUCHOPE FOREST
ESKDALEMUIR FOREST
ESKDALE
CASTLE O'ER FOREST
LIDDESDALE
SCOTLAND
ENGLAND
KIELDER FOREST
NORTHUMBERLAND
KIELDER WATER & FOREST PARK
REDESDALE FOREST
WARK FOREST
KERSHOPE FOREST
Newcastleton Forest
DANGER AREA
Middle Shield Park
King's Forest of Geltsdale
GILDERDALE FOREST
MILBURN FOREST
CUMBRIA
INGLEWOOD FOREST
CUMBRIAN MOUNTAINS
SKIDDAW FOREST
Deanburnhaugh
Bonchester Bridge
Hobkirk
Chesters
Southdean
Carter Bar
Catcleugh
Byrness
Teviothead
Skelfhill
Langburnshiels
Craik
Davington
Eskdalemuir
Jamestown
Mosspaul
Hermitage
Steele Road
Saughtree
Deadwater
Kielder
Butteryhaugh
Kielder Castle
Castle O'er
Bentpath
Kirkstile or Ewes
Newcastleton or Copshaw Holm
Langholm
New Langholm
Kershopefoot
Kershope Bri.
Falstone
Yarrow
Stannersburn
Bower
Whygate
Gatehouse
Kirtleton
Craigs
Waterbeck
Middlebie
Eaglesfield
Kirtlebridge
Canonbie
Rowanburn
Harelaw
Claygate
Hollows
Caulside
Nook
Baileyhead
Catlowdy
Crossings
Roughsike
Roadhead
Bewcastle
Shopford
Lyneholmeford
Butterburn
Evertown
Milltown
Glenzierfoot
Chapelknowe
Scotsdike
Moat
Carwinley
Easton
Netherby
Scuggate
Haggbeck
Stapleton
Longtown
Kirkcambeck
West Hall
Gilsland
Greenhead
Haltwhistle
Whiteside
Bardon Mill
Melkridge
Plenmeller
Annan
Eastriggs
Dornock
Gretna
Gretna Green
Springfield
Rigg
Kirkpatrick-Fleming
Newton
Moorend
Creca
A74(M)
M6
A7
A6071
A69
A689
A686
A595
A596
A6
A66
Westlinton
Smithfield
Kirklinton
Hethersgill
Boltonfellend
Mossedge
Skitby
Scaleby
Laversdale
Newtown
Irthington
Brampton
Milton
Lanercost
Banks
Walton
Low Row
Denton Fell
Featherstone Castle
Park Village
Rockcliffe
Todhills
Blackford
Harker
Port Carlisle
Bowness-on-Solway
Glasson
Drumburgh
Burgh by Sands
Beaumont
Cargo
Houghton
Crosby
Linstock
Warwick Bridge
Hayton
Farlam
Hallbankgate
Talkin
Tindale
Midgeholme
Lambley
Halton Lea Gate
Coanwood
Kirkbride
Kirkbampton
Fingland
Carlisle
Scotby
Wetheral
Cumwhinton
Great Corby
Heads Nook
Castle Carrock
Cumrew
Knarsdale
Slaggyford
Alston
Nenthall
Nenthead
Garrigill
Leadgate
Dalston
Thursby
Wigton
Waverton
Cotehill
Armathwaite
Kirkoswald
Lazonby
Glassonby
Gamblesby
Melmerby
Ousby
Skirwith
Kirkland
Blencarn
Culgaith
Milburn
Temple Sowerby
Renwick
Croglin
Newbiggin
Caldbeck
Sebergham
Hesket Newmarket
Ireby
Skelton
Plumpton
Great Salkeld
Little Salkeld
Hunsonby
Langwathby
Edenhall
Catterlen
Greystoke
Newbiggin
Penrith
Eamont Bridge
Clifton
Stainton
Penruddock
Motherby
Berrier
Mungrisdale
Bassenthwaite
High Side
Mealsgate
Sandale
Torpenhow
Skiddaw 3054

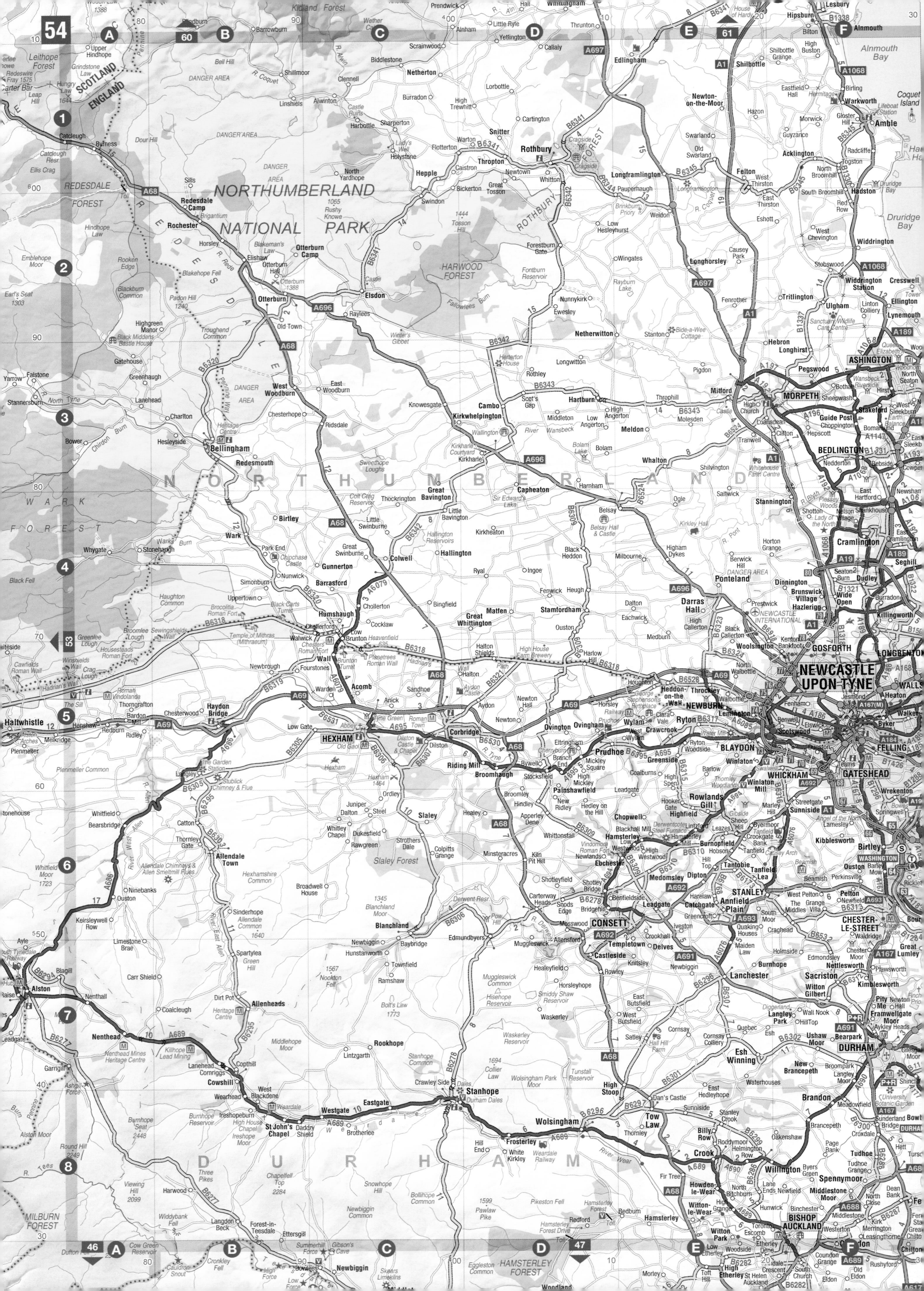

54
A
B
C
D
E
F
60
61
46
47
53
1
2
3
4
5
6
7
8
SCOTLAND
ENGLAND
NORTHUMBERLAND
NATIONAL PARK
REDESDALE FOREST
WARK FOREST
N O R T H U M B E R L A N D
D U R H A M
HARWOOD FOREST
MILBURN FOREST
HAMSTERLEY FOREST
Slaley Forest
Kidland Forest
Leithope Forest
Carter Bar
Catcleugh
Byrness
Redesdale Camp
Rochester
Horsley
Elishaw
Otterburn
Otterburn Camp
Elsdon
Rothbury
Thropton
Snitter
Netherton
Alwinton
Harbottle
Sharperton
Holystone
Hepple
Whitton
Edlingham
Whittingham
Alnham
Prendwick
Callaly
Thrunton
Shilbottle
Hipsburn
Alnmouth
Alnmouth Bay
Lesbury
Bilton
High Buston
Warkworth
Amble
Coquet Island
Acklington
Felton
Longframlington
Newton-on-the-Moor
Swarland
Old Swarland
Hadston
Druridge Bay
Widdrington
Widdrington Station
Longhorsley
Tritlington
Ulgham
Ellington
Cresswell
Lynemouth
Linton Colliery
Hebron
Longhirst
ASHINGTON
Pegswood
MORPETH
Mitford
Stakeford
Guide Post
BEDLINGTON
Stannington
Cramlington
Seghill
Dudley
Seaton Burn
Wide Open
Killingworth
Dinnington
Brunswick Village
Hazlerigg
Ponteland
Darras Hall
GOSFORTH
LONGBENTON
NEWCASTLE UPON TYNE
Jesmond
Heaton
Walker
Byker
Fenham
Benwell
Scotswood
FELLING
GATESHEAD
Dunston
Whickham
Blaydon
Winlaton
Winlaton Mill
Rowlands Gill
Highfield
Sunniside
Wrekenton
Kibblesworth
Birtley
WASHINGTON
Ouston
Pelton
Stanley
Annfield Plain
Tanfield
Tanfield Lea
Tantobie
Burnopfield
Hamsterley
Chopwell
Ebchester
Medomsley
Leadgate
Dipton
Catchgate
CONSETT
Castleside
Delves
Templetown
Lanchester
Burnhope
Sacriston
Witton Gilbert
CHESTER-LE-STREET
Great Lumley
Nettlesworth
Kimblesworth
Pity Me
Framwellgate Moor
DURHAM
Ushaw Moor
Bearpark
Esh
Esh Winning
New Brancepeth
Brandon
Langley Park
Quebec
Cornsay
Cornsay Colliery
Satley
Tow Law
High Stoop
Wolsingham
Frosterley
Stanhope
Eastgate
Westgate
St John's Chapel
Daddry Shield
Ireshopeburn
Cowshill
Allenheads
Nenthead
Alston
Garrigill
Nenthall
Crook
Billy Row
Willington
Spennymoor
Tudhoe
Middlestone Moor
Howden-le-Wear
Witton-le-Wear
Hamsterley
BISHOP AUCKLAND
Witton Park
Escomb
Etherley
Toft Hill
Newbiggin
Forest-in-Teesdale
Langdon Beck
Harwood
Bellingham
Redesmouth
Wark
Birtley
Stonehaugh
Gunnerton
Barrasford
Colwell
Humshaugh
Chollerton
Chollerford
Wall
Acomb
Hexham
Corbridge
Dilston
Riding Mill
Broomhaugh
Stocksfield
Prudhoe
Ovingham
Ovington
Wylam
Crawcrook
Ryton
Newburn
Lemington
Throckley
Heddon-on-the-Wall
Horsley
Stamfordham
Matfen
Great Whittington
Belsay
Capheaton
Kirkharle
Kirkwhelpington
Cambo
Scot's Gap
Hartburn
Whalton
Meldon
Netherwitton
Rothley
Great Bavington
Little Bavington
Thockrington
Haydon Bridge
Bardon Mill
Haltwhistle
Henshaw
Melkridge
Allendale Town
Catton
Whitfield
Langley
Slaley
Blanchland
Edmundbyers
Muggleswick
Hunstanworth
Rookhope
Ninebanks
Falstone
Stannersburn
Greenhaugh
Gatehouse
Charlton
Lanehead
A1
A68
A69
A695
A696
A697
A689
A686
A692
A691
A693
A167
A189
A19
A1068
B6341
B6342
B6343
B6318
B6320
B6306
B6278
B6296

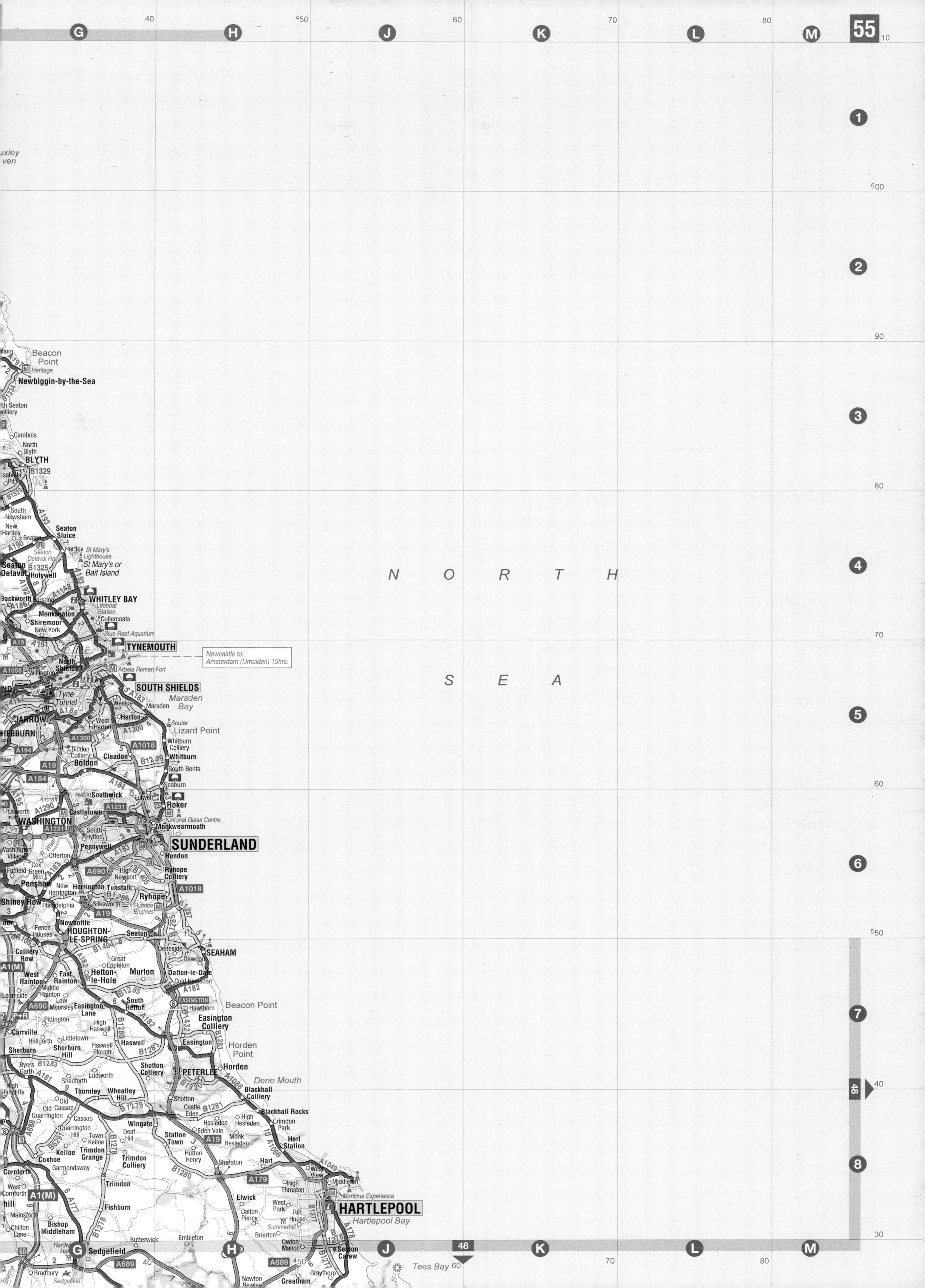
55
G
H
J
K
L
M
1
2
3
4
5
6
7
8
40
450
60
70
80
10
600
90
80
70
60
550
40
30
48
Beacon Point
Heritage
Newbiggin-by-the-Sea
Cambois
North Blyth
BLYTH
B1329
South Newsham
New Hartley
Seaton Sluice
Hartley
St Mary's Lighthouse
St Mary's or Bait Island
Seaton Delaval
Holywell
B1325
WHITLEY BAY
Lifeboat Station
Cullercoats
Monkseaton
Shiremoor
New York
Blue Reef Aquarium
TYNEMOUTH
Newcastle to: Amsterdam (IJmuiden) 15hrs.
North Shields
Arbeia Roman Fort
SOUTH SHIELDS
Marsden Bay
Marsden
Westoe
Tyne Tunnel
JARROW
HEBBURN
West Harton
Harton
A1300
Souter Lighthouse
Lizard Point
Whitburn Colliery
Whitburn
A1018
Boldon Colliery
Boldon
Cleadon
B1299
South Bents
Seaburn
A19
A194
A184
Southwick
Fulwell
Roker
A1231
Castletown
National Glass Centre
Monkwearmouth
WASHINGTON
South Hylton
Pennywell
SUNDERLAND
Hendon
Offerton
A183
A690
High Newport
Ryhope Colliery
Penshaw
New Herrington
Herrington
Tunstall
Ryhope
Silksworth
Shiney Row
Philadelphia
Newbottle
HOUGHTON-LE-SPRING
Fence Houses
Seaton
SEAHAM
Deneside
Dawdon
Colliery Row
A1(M)
Great Eppleton
Hetton-le-Hole
Murton
Dalton-le-Dale
Cold Hesledon
West Rainton
East Rainton
Middle Rainton
Low Moorsley
Easington Lane
A182
EASINGTON
Hawthorn
Beacon Point
South Hetton
Pittington
High Haswell
Easington Colliery
Easington
Horden Point
Haswell
Haswell Plough
Carrville
Littletown
Sherburn
Sherburn Hill
Shotton Colliery
PETERLEE
Horden
Ludworth
Shadforth
Dene Mouth
Blackhall Colliery
Thornley
Wheatley Hill
Shotton
Castle Eden
Old Cassop
Quarrington
Cassop
Quarrington Hill
Town Kelloe
Wingate
Deaf Hill
Station Town
Hesleden
Eden Vale
High Hesleden
Blackhall Rocks
Crimdon Park
Monk Hesleden
Hart Station
Kelloe
Trimdon Grange
Coxhoe
Garmondsway
Trimdon Colliery
Hutton Henry
Sheraton
Hart
West View
Cornforth
West Cornforth
Trimdon
A179
High Throston
Middleton
Maritime Experience
HARTLEPOOL
Hartlepool Bay
Fishburn
Elwick
West Park
Dalton Piercy
Rift House
Bishop Middleham
Summerhill
Brierton
Butterwick
Embleton
Owton Manor
Seaton Carew
Sedgefield
A689
Bradbury
Tees Bay
Newton Bewley
Greatham
Graythorp
N O R T H
S E A

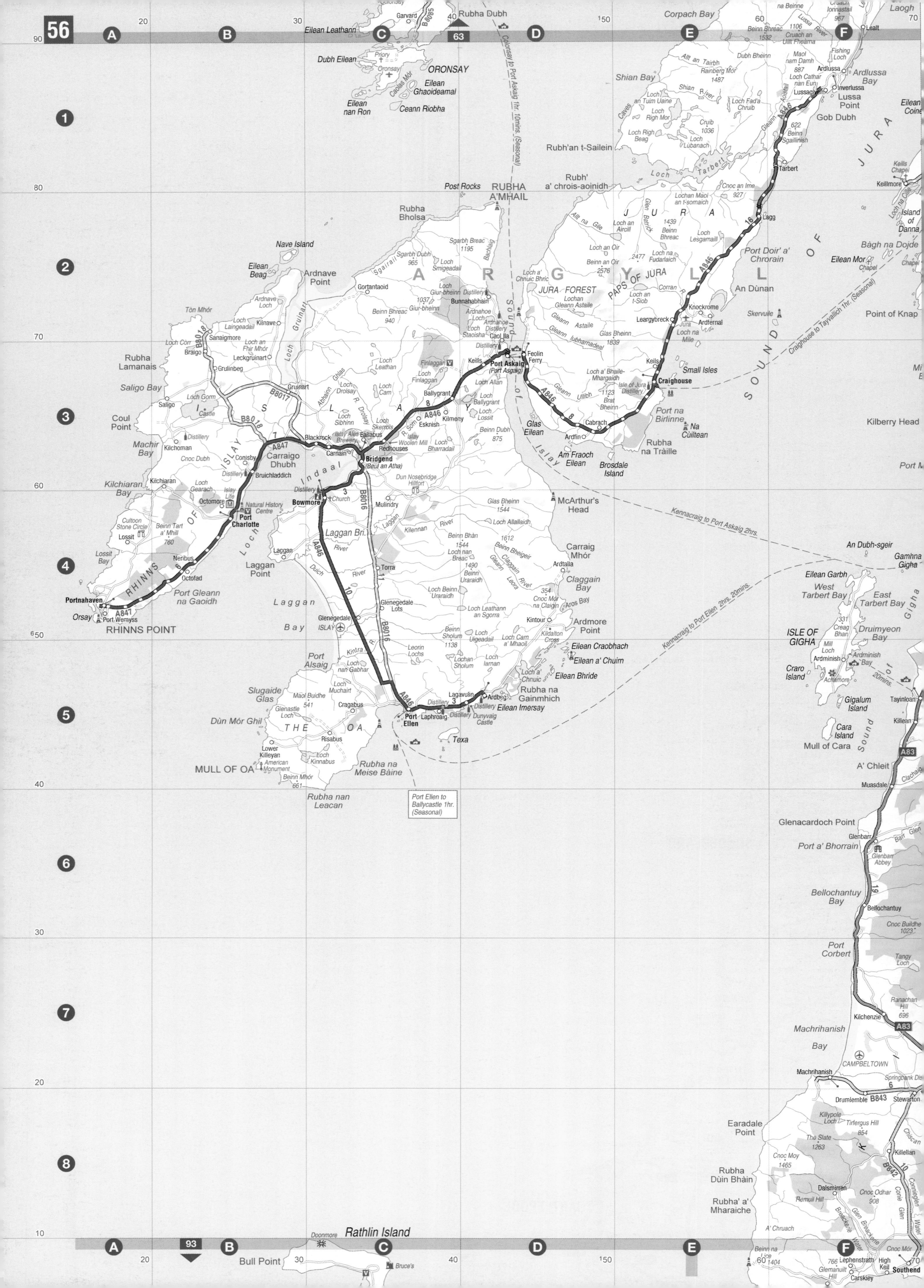
A
B
C
D
E
F
63
93
Rubha Dubh
Eilean Leathann
Garvard
Corpach Bay
Laogh
Lealt
Dubh Eilean
Priory
Oronsay
ORONSAY
Eilean Ghaoideamal
Eilean nan Ron
Ceann Riobha
Colonsay to Port Askaig 1hr. 10mins (Seasonal)
Shian Bay
Ardlussa
Ardlussa Bay
Inverlussa
Lussa Point
Lussagiven
Gob Dubh
Fishing Loch
Beinn Bhreac 532
Dubh Bheinn
Rainberg Mòr 1487
Shian River
Loch an Tuim Uaine
Loch Righ Mor
Loch Righ Beag
Cruib 1036
Loch Lùbanach
Loch Fad'a Chruib
Caves
Rubh'an t-Sailein
Rubh' a' chrois-aoinidh
Loch Tarbert
Tarbert
JURA
Keills Chapel
Keillmore
Loch na Cille
Island of Danna
Post Rocks
RUBHA A'MHAIL
Rubha Bholsa
Cnoc an Ime 927
Lochan Maol an t-sornaich
Glen Batrick
Loch an Aircill
1439 Beinn Bhreac
Loch Lesgamaill
Lagg
Nave Island
Sgarbh Breac 1195
Sgarbh Dubh 965
Loch Smigeadail
Bàgh na Dojde
Port Doir' a' Chrorain
Eilean Mor
Chapel
Eilean Beag
Ardnave Point
Ardnave Loch
Tòn Mhór
Gortantaoid
Beinn Bhreac 940
1037 Giur-bheinn
Loch Giur-bheinn
Bunnahabhain
Distillery
ARGYLL
Loch an Oir
Beinn an Oir 2576
2477
Loch na Fudarlaich
PAPS OF JURA
Corran
Loch an t-Siob
An Dùnan
Loch a' Chnuic Bhric
JURA FOREST
Lochan Gleann Astaile
Gleann Astaile
Gleann Iubharnadeal
Glas Bheinn 1839
Knockrome
Ardfernal
Leargybreck
Jura Loch na Mile
Skervuile
Point of Knap
Craighouse to Tayvallich 1hr. (Seasonal)
Sound of Jura
Loch Corr
B8018
Sanaigmore
Braigo
Loch Laingeadail
Kilnave
Loch an Fhir Mhòir
Leckgruinart
Loch Gruinart
Rubha Lamanais
Grulinbeg
Ardnahoe Loch
Ardnahoe Distillery
Loch Staoisha
Caol Ila
Sound of Islay
Feolin Ferry
Port Askaig (Port Asgaig)
Keills
Finlaggan
Loch Finlaggan
Loch Leathan
Loch Cam
Loch Drolsay
Abhainn Ghlas
Saligo Bay
Loch Gorm
Saligo
Castle
Gruinart
B8017
Ballygrant
Loch Ballygrant
Loch Allan
Small Isles
Craighouse
Isle of Jura Distillery
Loch a' Bhaile-Mhargaidh
Gleann Ullibh
1123 Brat Bheinn
Cabrach
Port na Birlinne
Na Cùiltean
Coul Point
B8018
Loch Sibhinn
Loch Skerrols
River Sorn
Kilmeny
Loch Lossit
Eskinish
Glas Eilean
Ardfin
Kilberry Head
Machir Bay
Distillery
Kilchoman
Cnoc Dubh
A847
Carraigo Dhubh
Blackrock
Carnain
Islay Ales Brewery
Eallabus
Redhouses
Islay Woolen Mill
Loch Bharradail
Beinn Dubh 875
Am Fraoch Eilean
Rubha na Tràille
Brosdale Island
Conisby
Bruichladdich
Bridgend (Beul an Atha)
Loch Indaal
Dun Nosebridge Hillfort
Kilchiaran Bay
Kilchiaran
Loch Gearach
Islay Life
Octomore
Natural History Centre
Port Charlotte
Bowmore
Church
B8016
Mulindry
Glas Bheinn 1544
McArthur's Head
Kennacraig to Port Askaig 2hrs.
Cultoon Stone Circle
Lossit
Beinn Tart a' Mhill 760
Laggan Bri.
Laggan River
Loch Allallaidh
Kilennan River
Beinn Bhàn 1544
Loch nan Breac
1612 Beinn Bheigeir
Claggain River
Gleann Leora
1490 Beinn Uraraidh
Carraig Mhór
Ardtalla
Claggain Bay
An Dubh-sgeir
Gamhna Gigha
Lossit Bay
Rhinns of Islay
Neribus
Octofad
Laggan
Laggan Point
Duich River
Torra
Eilean Garbh
West Tarbert Bay
East Tarbert Bay
Portnahaven
Port Gleann na Gaoidh
Loch Beinn Uraraidh
354 Cnoc Mòr na Claigin
Aros Bay
Orsay
Port Wemyss
A847
RHINNS POINT
Laggan Bay
Glenegedale
Glenegedale Lots
ISLAY
Loch Leathann an Sgorra
Kintour
Ardmore Point
331 Creag Bhan
Druimyeon Bay
ISLE OF GIGHA
Beinn Sholum 1138
Loch Uigeadail
Loch Cam a' Mhaoil
Kildalton Cross
Eilean Craobhach
Eilean a' Chuirn
Kennacraig to Port Ellen 2hrs. 20mins.
Mill Loch
Ardminish
Ardminish Bay
Achamore
Craro Island
Port Alsaig
Kintra
Loch nan Gabhar
Leorin Lochs
Lochan Sholum
Loch Iarnan
Loch a' Chnuic
Eilean Bhride
Rubha na Gainmhich
Slugaide Glas
Màol Buidhe 541
Loch Muchairt
Cragabus
Lagavulin
Ardbeg
Distillery
Laphroaig
Dunyvaig Castle
Eilean Imersay
Gigalum Island
Tayinloan
Dùn Mór Ghil
Glenastle Loch
THE OA
Port Ellen
Texa
Cara Island
Sound of Gigha
Killean
Mull of Cara
Lower Killeyan
Risabus
American Monument
Loch Kinnabus
MULL OF OA
Beinn Mhór 661
Rubha na Meise Bàine
A83
A' Chleit
Clachaig
Muasdale
Rubha nan Leacan
Port Ellen to Ballycastle 1hr. (Seasonal)
Glenacardoch Point
Glenbarr
Barr Glen
Port a' Bhorrain
Glenbarr Abbey
Bellochantuy Bay
Bellochantuy
Cnoc Buidhe 1023
Port Corbert
Tangy Loch
Ranachan Hill 696
Kilchenzie
A83
Machrihanish Bay
CAMPBELTOWN
Machrihanish
Springbank Distillery
Drumlemble
B843
Stewarton
Earadale Point
Killypole Loch
Tirfergus Hill 854
The Slate 1263
Chiscan
Cnoc Moy 1465
Killellan
B842
Rubha Dùin Bhàin
Dalsmirren
Cnoc Odhar 908
Conieglen Water
Remuil Hill
Rubha' a' Mharaiche
Glen Breackerie
A' Chruach
Cnoc Mór
Rathlin Island
Doonmore
Bull Point
Bruce's
Beinn na Lice 1404
766
Lephenstrath
High Keil
Southend
Glemanuilt Hill
Carskiey
10
20
30
40
50
60
70
80
90
150

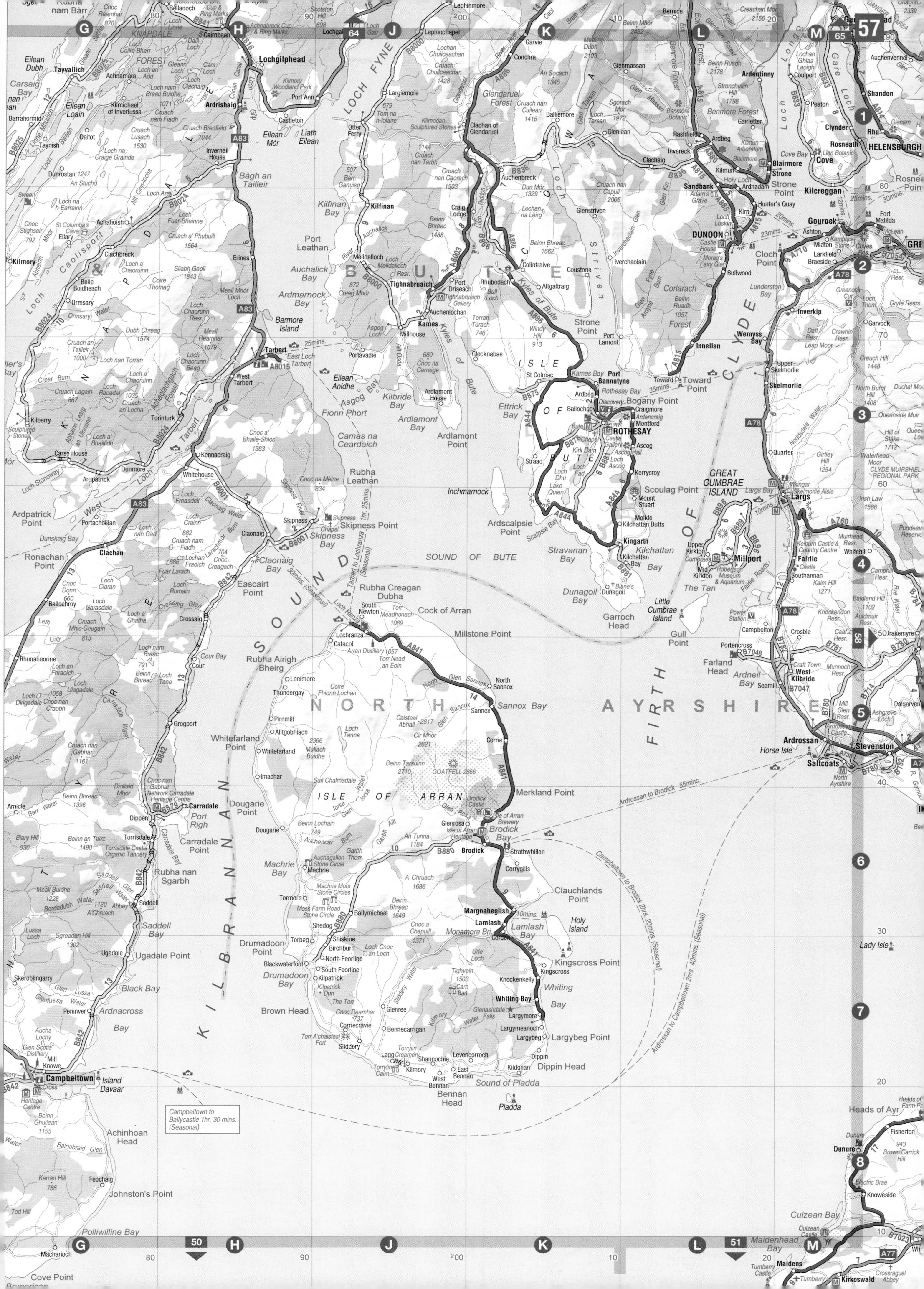

G
H
J
K
L
M
64
65
KNAPDALE
FOREST
Lochgilphead
Ardrishaig
Tayvallich
Eilean Dubh
Carsaig Bay
Eilean Loain
Kilmichael of Inverlussa
Crinan Canal
LOCH FYNE
Eilean Mòr
Liath Eilean
Castleton
Port Ann
Kilmory Woodland Park
Largiemore
Otter Ferry
Kilmodan Sculptured Stones
Clachan of Glendaruel
Glendaruel Forest
Garvie
Conchra
Glenmassan
Benmore Forest
Ardentinny
Shandon
Rhu
HELENSBURGH
Rosneath
Cove
Kilcreggan
Clynder
Gare Loch
Strone
Blairmore
Kilmun
Ardbeg
Rashfield
Inverneil House
Bàgh an Tailleir
Kilfinan Bay
Kilfinan
Port Leathan
Auchalick Bay
Millhouse
Kames
Tighnabruaich
Ardmarnock Bay
Barmore Island
Portavadie
Kyles of Bute
Colintraive
Altgaltraig
Coustonn
Strone Point
Port Lamont
Sandbank
Hunter's Quay
DUNOON
Kirn
Gourock
Fort Matilda
Cloch Point
Bullwood
Corlarach Forest
Innellan
Toward Point
Toward
Inverkip
Wemyss Bay
Skelmorlie
Upper Skelmorlie
Tarbert
East Loch Tarbert
West Tarbert
Kennacraig
Whitehouse
Dunmore
Carse House
Ardpatrick
Ardpatrick Point
Kilberry
Loch Stornoway
West Loch Tarbert
Ronachan Point
Clachan
Claonaig
Skipness
Skipness Point
Skipness Bay
Eilean Aoidhe
Asgog Bay
Fionn Phort
Kilbride Bay
Ardlamont Bay
Ardlamont Point
Camas na Ceardaich
Rubha Leathan
Inchmarnock
ISLE OF BUTE
Port Bannatyne
Kames Bay
Rothesay Bay
Bogany Point
Craigmore
ROTHESAY
Ettrick Bay
Straad
Ascog
Kerrycroy
Scoulag Point
Mount Stuart
Kilchattan Bay
Kingarth
Ardscalpsie Point
Stravanan Bay
Dunagoil Bay
Garroch Head
SOUND OF BUTE
GREAT CUMBRAE ISLAND
Millport
Little Cumbrae Island
Largs
Largs Bay
Fairlie
FIRTH OF CLYDE
Gull Point
Farland Head
Portencross
West Kilbride
Ardneil Bay
Seamill
Ardrossan
Saltcoats
Stevenston
Horse Isle
NORTH AYRSHIRE
Eascairt Point
Claonaig Bay
Crossaig
Cour Bay
Cour
Grogport
Carradale
Port Righ
Carradale Point
Dippen
Torrisdale
Rubha nan Sgarbh
Saddell
Saddell Bay
Ugadale
Ugadale Point
Black Bay
Ardnacross Bay
Peninver
KILBRANNAN SOUND
Rubha Creagan Dubha
Cock of Arran
Lochranza
Catacol
Millstone Point
Rubha Airigh Bheirg
North Sannox
Sannox Bay
Sannox
Corrie
NORTH
Whitefarland Point
Whitefarland
Pirnmill
Imachar
Dougarie Point
Dougarie
ISLE OF ARRAN
GOATFELL 2866
Merkland Point
Brodick Castle
Brodick Bay
Brodick
Strathwhillan
Corrygills
Clauchlands Point
Machrie Bay
Machrie
Tormore
Shedog
Shiskine
Drumadoon Point
Drumadoon Bay
Blackwaterfoot
Lamlash
Lamlash Bay
Holy Island
Kingscross Point
Whiting Bay
Brown Head
Sliddery
Largybeg Point
Dippin Head
Kildonan
Sound of Pladda
Bennan Head
Pladda
Ardrossan to Brodick 55mins.
Campbeltown to Brodick 2hrs. 20mins. (Seasonal)
Ardrossan to Campbeltown 2hrs. 40mins. (Seasonal)
Tarbert to Lochranza 1hr. 25mins. (Seasonal)
Claonaig to Lochranza 30mins. (Seasonal)
Campbeltown
Island Davaar
Campbeltown to Ballycastle 1hr. 30 mins. (Seasonal)
Achinhoan Head
Johnston's Point
Polliwilline Bay
Macharioch
Cove Point
Lady Isle
Heads of Ayr
Dunure
Fisherton
Knoweside
Culzean Bay
Maidenhead Bay
Maidens
Kirkoswald
58
50
51

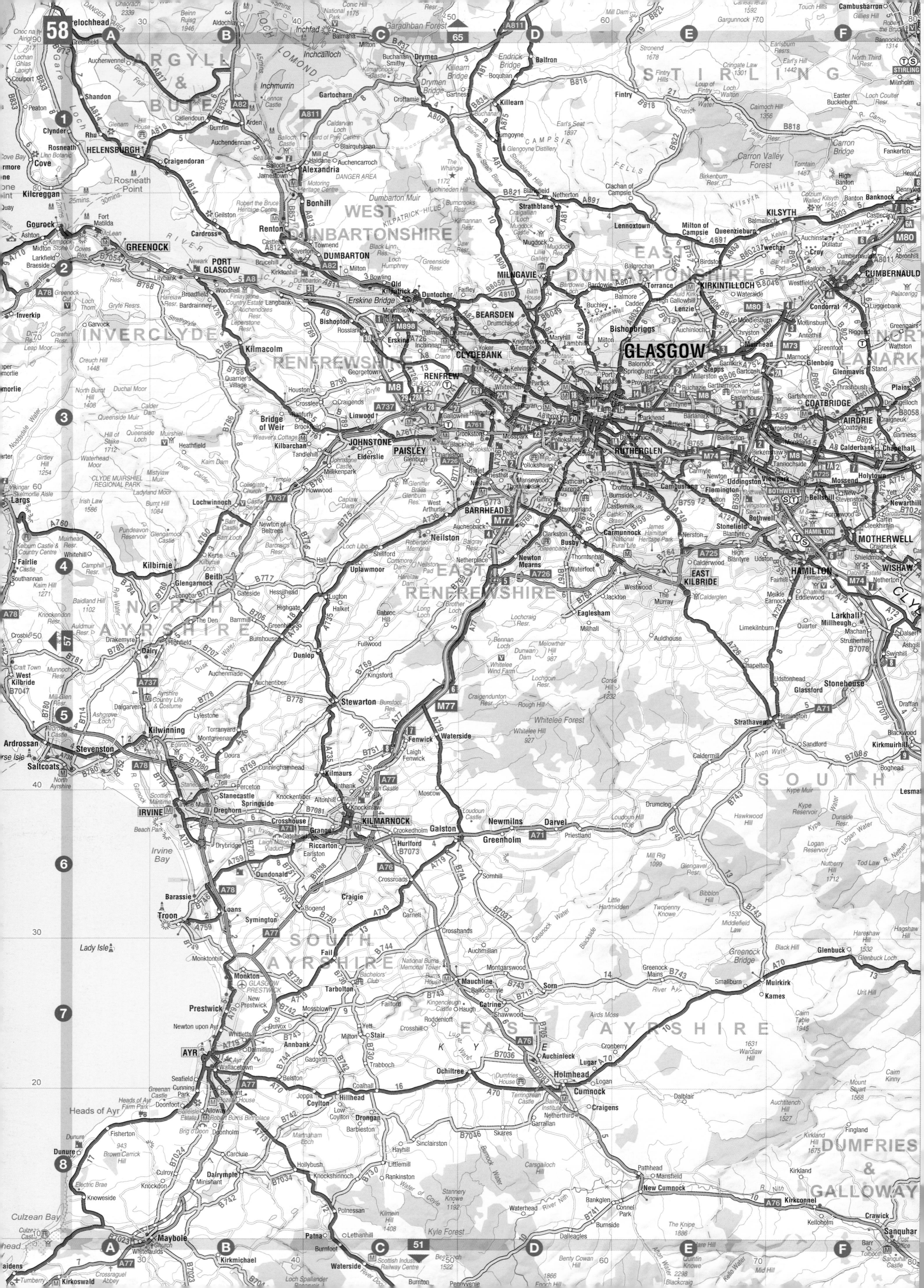
58
A
B
C
D
E
F
65
57
51
ARGYLL & BUTE
STIRLING
WEST DUNBARTONSHIRE
EAST DUNBARTONSHIRE
INVERCLYDE
RENFREWSHIRE
EAST RENFREWSHIRE
NORTH LANARKSHIRE
NORTH AYRSHIRE
SOUTH AYRSHIRE
EAST AYRSHIRE
SOUTH LANARKSHIRE
DUMFRIES & GALLOWAY
KYLE
GLASGOW
HELENSBURGH
GREENOCK
PORT GLASGOW
DUMBARTON
CLYDEBANK
BEARSDEN
MILNGAVIE
KIRKINTILLOCH
KILSYTH
CUMBERNAULD
COATBRIDGE
AIRDRIE
RUTHERGLEN
PAISLEY
JOHNSTONE
RENFREW
BARRHEAD
EAST KILBRIDE
HAMILTON
MOTHERWELL
WISHAW
BOTHWELL
KILMARNOCK
IRVINE
AYR
Loch Lomond
Inchmurrin
Campsie Fells
Kilpatrick Hills
Irvine Bay
Heads of Ayr
Culzean Bay
Lady Isle
Whitelee Forest
Carron Valley Forest
Kyle Forest
Clyde Muirshiel Regional Park
Erskine Bridge
Alexandria
Balloch
Bonhill
Gourock
Largs
Ardrossan
Saltcoats
Stevenston
Kilwinning
Troon
Prestwick
Maybole
Dalry
Kilbirnie
Beith
Stewarton
Fenwick
Newmilns
Darvel
Galston
Strathaven
Mauchline
Catrine
Auchinleck
Cumnock
New Cumnock
Muirkirk
Sanquhar
Kirkconnel
Patna
Dalrymple
Tarbolton
Ochiltree
Eaglesham
Neilston
Kilmacolm
Lochwinnoch
Bridge of Weir
Strathblane
Killearn
Fintry
Drymen
Balfron
M8
M73
M74
M77
M80
M898
A77
A78
A71
A70
A76
A82
A737
A736
A726

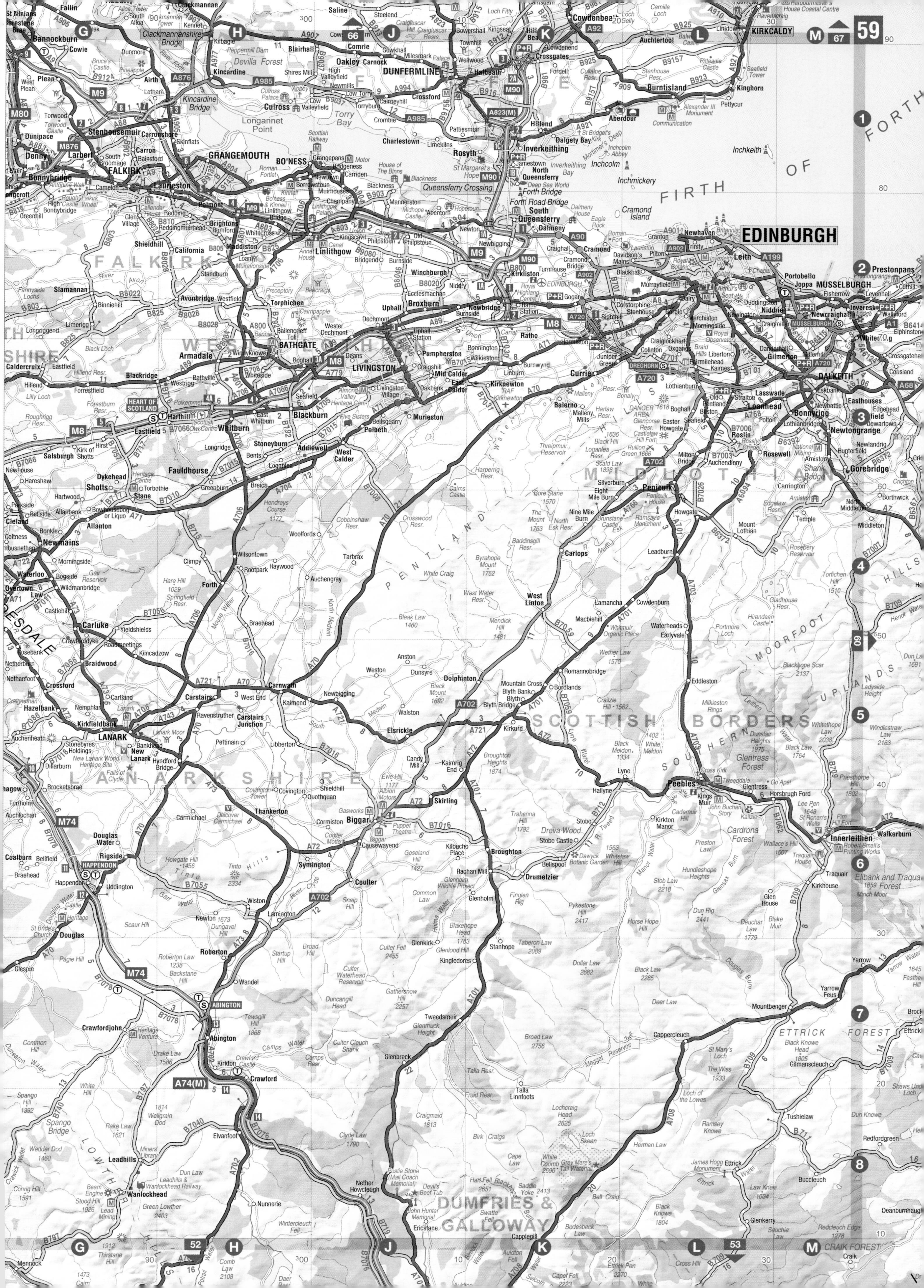

59
66
67
52
53
G
H
J
K
L
M
FIRTH OF FORTH
EDINBURGH
KIRKCALDY
DUNFERMLINE
GRANGEMOUTH
FALKIRK
BO'NESS
LIVINGSTON
BATHGATE
LANARK
DALKEITH
MUSSELBURGH
Prestonpans
Leith
Portobello
Newhaven
Musselburgh
Inverkeithing
Rosyth
Queensferry
South Queensferry
North Queensferry
Forth Road Bridge
Forth Bridge
Queensferry Crossing
Burntisland
Kinghorn
Aberdour
Dalgety Bay
Inchkeith
Inchcolm
Inchmickery
Cramond Island
Cramond
Dalmeny
Kirkliston
Ratho
Currie
Balerno
Penicuik
Loanhead
Lasswade
Bonnyrigg
Newtongrange
Gorebridge
Roslin
Gilmerton
Linlithgow
Broxburn
Uphall
Winchburgh
Whitburn
Blackburn
West Calder
Mid Calder
East Calder
Kirknewton
Armadale
Shotts
Carluke
Carstairs
Carnwath
Biggar
Peebles
Innerleithen
Walkerburn
Broughton
Tweedsmuir
Abington
Crawford
Leadhills
Wanlockhead
Douglas
Lamington
Symington
Coulter
Skirling
West Linton
Carlops
Dolphinton
Leadburn
Eddleston
Yarrow
Ettrick
Cappercleuch
Stanhope
Drumelzier
Stobo
Lyne
Larbert
Stenhousemuir
Denny
Bonnybridge
Polmont
Kincardine
Culross
Clackmannan
Cowdenbeath
Bannockburn
Newmains
Wishaw
Forth
Wilsontown
Braidwood
Crossford
Kirkfieldbank
New Lanark
Hyndford Bridge
Thankerton
Roberton
Wiston
Elsrickle
Kirkurd
Romannobridge
Mountbenger
Traquair
FALKIRK
WEST LOTHIAN
MIDLOTHIAN
SCOTTISH BORDERS
SOUTH LANARKSHIRE
DUMFRIES & GALLOWAY
PENTLAND HILLS
MOORFOOT HILLS
LOWTHER HILLS
ETTRICK FOREST
TINTO HILLS
CRAIK FOREST
M8
M9
M90
M74
A74(M)
A70
A71
A72
A701
A702
A703
A708
A720
A721
A1
Glentress Forest
Cardrona Forest
Talla Resr.
Fruid Resr.
Megget Reservoir
St Mary's Loch
Loch of the Lowes
Tinto 2334
Broad Law 2756
Dollar Law 2682
Culter Fell 2455
Scald Law 1898

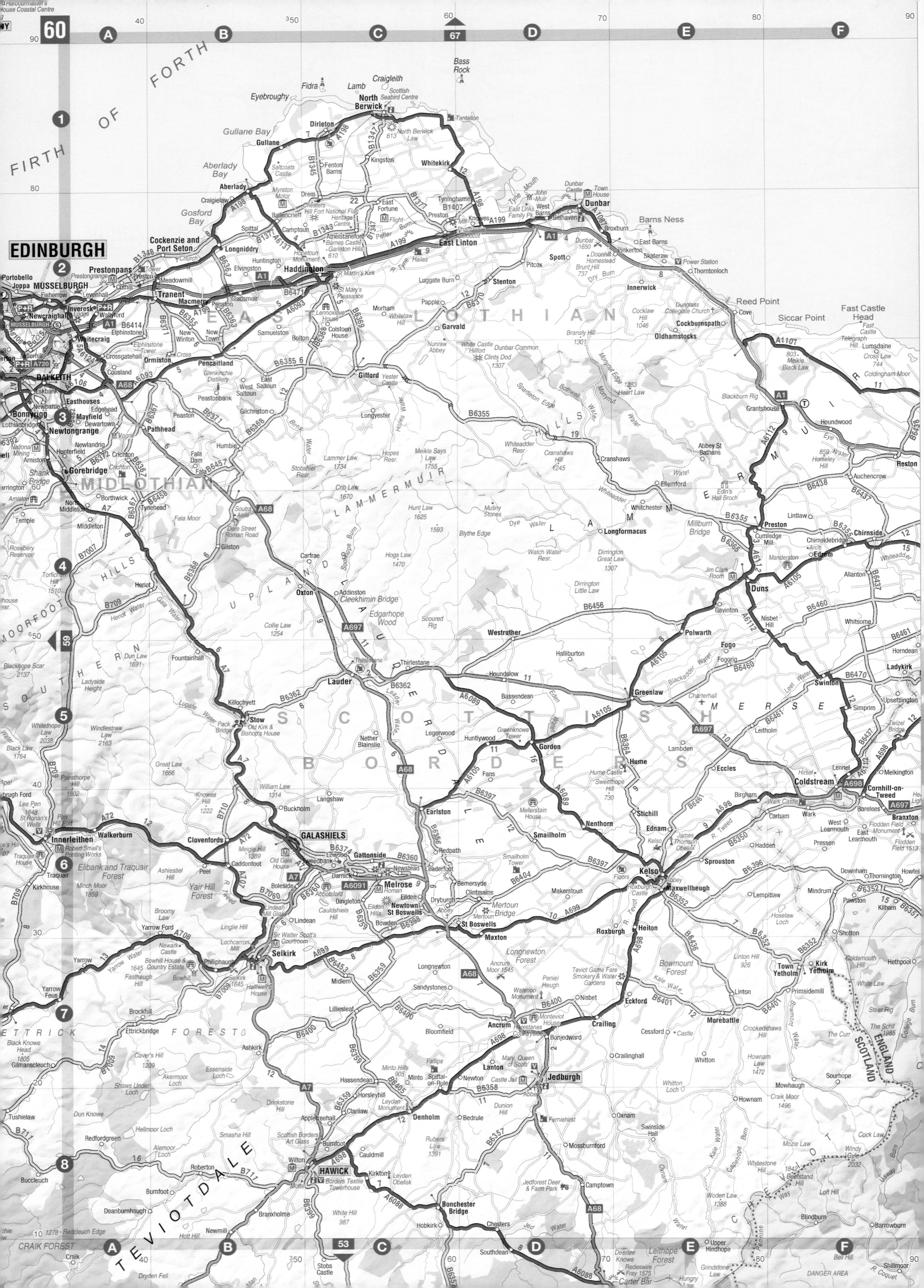
FIRTH OF FORTH
EDINBURGH
Bass Rock
Fidra
Lamb
Craigleith
Eyebroughy
North Berwick
Scottish Seabird Centre
Tantallon
Dirleton
Gullane Bay
Gullane
North Berwick Law
Kingston
Whitekirk
Aberlady Bay
Aberlady
Saltcoats Castle
Fenton Barns
Craigielaw
Myreton Motor
Drem
East Fortune
Tyninghame
Dunbar Castle
Town House
Dunbar
John Muir
West Barns
Belhaven
Gosford Bay
Ballencrieff
Chesters Hill Fort
National Flag Heritage Centre
Flight
Preston
Knowes
East Links Family Pk
Barns Ness
Broxburn
Spittal
Camptoun
Athelstaneford
East Linton
Cockenzie and Port Seton
Longniddry
Barnes Castle
Hopetoun Monument
Hailes
Dunbar 1650
Pinkerton
East Barns
Skateraw
Power Station
Thorntonloch
Prestonpans
Tower
Elvingston
Huntington
Haddington
St Martin's Kirk
Pitcox
Spott
Doonhill Homestead
Brunt Hill 737
Portobello
Joppa
MUSSELBURGH
Meadowmill
Luggate Burn
Stenton
Innerwick
Reed Point
Cove
Fisherrow
Levenhall
Tranent
Gladsmuir
St Mary's Pleasance
Papple
Dunglass Collegiate Church
Siccar Point
Fast Castle Head
Inveresk
Wallyford
Macmerry
Penston
Morham
EAST LOTHIAN
Cocklaw Hill 1046
Cockburnspath
Newcraighall
Elphinstone
Lennoxlove House
Whitelaw Hill
Garvald
Oldhamstocks
Telegraph Hill
Lumsdaine
Whitecraig
New Winton
New Town
Samuelston
Colstoun House
Nunraw Abbey
White Castle Hillfort
Dunbar Common
Bransly Hill 1301
803 Meikle Black Law
Cross Law 744
Elphinstone Tower
Bolton
Clints Dod 1307
Crossgatehall
Ormiston
Cross
Pencaitland
Gifford
Yester Castle
Coldingham Moor
Cousland
Glenkinchie Distillery
East Saltoun
Monynut Edge
DALKEITH
West Saltoun
1283 Heart Law
Blackburn Rig
Grantshouse
Eskbank
Peastonbank
Bothwell
Easthouses
Newbattle
Edgehead
Gilchriston
Bonnyrigg
Mayfield
Longyester
Hopes Water
Houndwood
Dewartown
Peaston
Lothianbridge
Newtongrange
Pathhead
HILLS
Whiteadder Resr.
Cranshaws Hill 1245
Abbey St Bathans
Newlandrig
Humbie
Cranshaws
Horseley Hill
Reston
Hunterfield
Crichton
Arniston
Fala
Fala Dam
Lammer Law 1734
Hopes Resr.
Meikle Says Law 1755
Auchencrow
Gorebridge
Stobshiel Resr.
MIDLOTHIAN
Ellemford
Crib Law 1670
LAMMERMUIR
Edin's Hall Broch
Borthwick
North Middleton
Tynehead
Whitchester
Fala Moor
Soutra Aisle
Dere Street Roman Road
Hunt Law 1625
Mutiny Stones
Lintlaw
Temple
Middleton
Blythe Edge
Dye Water
Longformacus
Millburn Bridge
Preston
Chirnside
Cumledge Mill
Chirnsidebridge
Rosebery Reservoir
Gilston
Watch Water Resr.
Dirrington Great Law 1307
Manderston
Edrom
Carfrae
Hogs Law 1470
Allanton
Torfichen Hill 1510
HILLS
Jim Clark Room
Duns
Heriot
Oxton
Addinston
Cleekhimin Bridge
UPLAND
Dirrington Little Law
Edgarhope Wood
Scoured Rig
Gavinton
MOORFOOT
Westruther
Polwarth
Nisbet Hill
Whitsome
Collie Law 1254
Fogo
Fogorig
Horndean
Fountainhall
Dun Law 1691
SOUTHERN
Halliburton
Ladykirk
Blackhope Scar 2137
Thirlestane
Lauder
Houndslow
Swinton
Ladyside Height
Bassendean
Greenlaw
Charterhall
Simprim
Upsettlington
Killochyett
Stow
Old Kirk & Bishop's House
Pack Bridge
SCOTTISH
MERSE
Whitehope Law 2038
Windlestraw Law 2163
Legerwood
Greenknowe Tower
Huntlywood
Gordon
Leitholm
Twizel Bridge
Nether Blainslie
Black Law 1764
Lambden
BORDERS
Hume
Great Law 1666
Hume Castle
Eccles
Fans
Sweethope Hill 730
Hirsel
Lennel
Coldstream
Melkington
Priesthorpe Hill 1802
William Law 1314
Cornhill-on-Tweed
Birgham
Knowes Hill 1222
Langshaw
Buckholm
Earlston
Mellerstain House
Wark Castle
Barelees
Lee Pen 1648
Wark
Carham
Branxton
Stichill
St Ronan's Wells
Pirn Hill Fort
Nenthorn
Innerleithen
Walkerburn
Robert Smail's Printing Works
Clovenfords
GALASHIELS
Smailholm
Ednam
Flodden Field Monument
Flodden Field 1513
Meigle Hill 1389
Lowood
Gattonside
James Thomson Obelisk
West Learmouth
East Learmouth
Pressen
Traquair House
Elibank and Traquair Forest
Ashiestiel Hill
Peel
Caddonfoot
Old Gala House
Tweedbank
Newstead
Redpath
Leaderfoot
Smailholm Tower
Hadden
Traquair
Darnick
Melrose
Kelso
Sprouston
Downham
Thornington
Kirkhouse
Minch Moor 1859
Yair Hill Forest
Boleside
Abbotsford
Roman
Bemersyde
Clintmains
Floors
Roxburgh Castle
Maxwellheugh
Mindrum
Pawston
Kilham
Dingleton
Eildon
Eildon Hills
Newtown St Boswells
Dryburgh Abbey
Makerstoun
Lempitlaw
Broomy Law
Lindean Mill Glass
Lindean
Cauldshiels Hill
Mertoun Bridge
St Boswells
Hoselaw Loch
Yarrow Ford
Linglie Hill
Sir Walter Scott's Courtroom
Bowden
Maxton
Roxburgh
Heiton
Shotton
Newark Castle
Lochcarron Mill
Selkirk
Longnewton Forest
Linton Hill 926
Coldsmouth Hill
Hethpool
Yarrow
Bowhill House & Country Estate
Philiphaugh
Longnewton
Ancrum Moor 1545
Teviot Game Fare Smokery & Water Gardens
Bowmount Forest
Town Yetholm
Kirk Yetholm
Fastheugh Hill
Bowhill
Selkirk 1645
Halliwell's House
Midlem
Peniel Heugh
White Law
Yarrow Feus
Sandystones
Waterloo Monument
Nisbet
Prinsidemill
Linton
Lilliesleaf
Eckford
Steer Rig
ETTRICK FOREST
Brockhill
Ancrum
Monteviot House
Harestanes Countryside Centre
Crailing
Cessford Castle
Morebattle
Crookedshaws Hill
The Schil 1985
Ettrickbridge
Bloomfield
Bonjedward
The Curr
Ashkirk
Black Knowe Head 1805
Gilmanscleuch
Caver's Hill 1209
Essenside Loch
Crailinghall
Whitton
Hownam Law 1472
SCOTLAND
ENGLAND
Akermoor Loch
Fatlips
Minto Hills 905
Minto
Mary, Queen of Scots'
Lanton
Hassendean
Spittal-on-Rule
Newton
Castle Jail
Jedburgh
Shaws Under Loch
Sourhope
Whitton Loch
Mowhaugh
Horsleyhill
Drinkstone Hill
Abbey
Clarilaw
Leyden Monument
Dunion Hill
Hownam
Craik Moor 1496
Tushielaw
Dun Knowe
Appletreehall
Denholm
Bedrule
Ferniehirst
Oxnam
Hellmoor Loch
Swinside Hall
Smasha Hill
Scottish Borders Art Glass
Redfordgreen
Alemoor Loch
Burnfoot
Cauldmill
Rubers Law 1391
Mossburnford
Cock Law
Mozie Law
Windy Gyle 2032
Wilton
Roberton
HAWICK
Borders Textile Towerhouse
Kirkton
Leyden Obelisk
Whitestone Hill
Beefstand Hill
Buccleuch
Burnfoot
Jedforest Deer & Farm Park
Camptown
Loft Hill
TEVIOTDALE
Deanburnhaugh
Branxholme
White Hill 987
Bonchester Bridge
Woden Law 1388
Hobkirk
Chesters
Blindburn
Newmill
Hott Hill
Barrowburn
1278 Redcleuch Edge
CRAIK FOREST
Southdean
Upper Hindhope
Leithope Forest
Deerlee Knowe
Redeswire Fray 1575
Carter Bar
Craik
Dryden Fell
Stobs Castle
Grindstone Law
DANGER AREA
Shillmoor
Bell Hill
Hungry Law
Pennine Way
CHEVIOT
Coquet

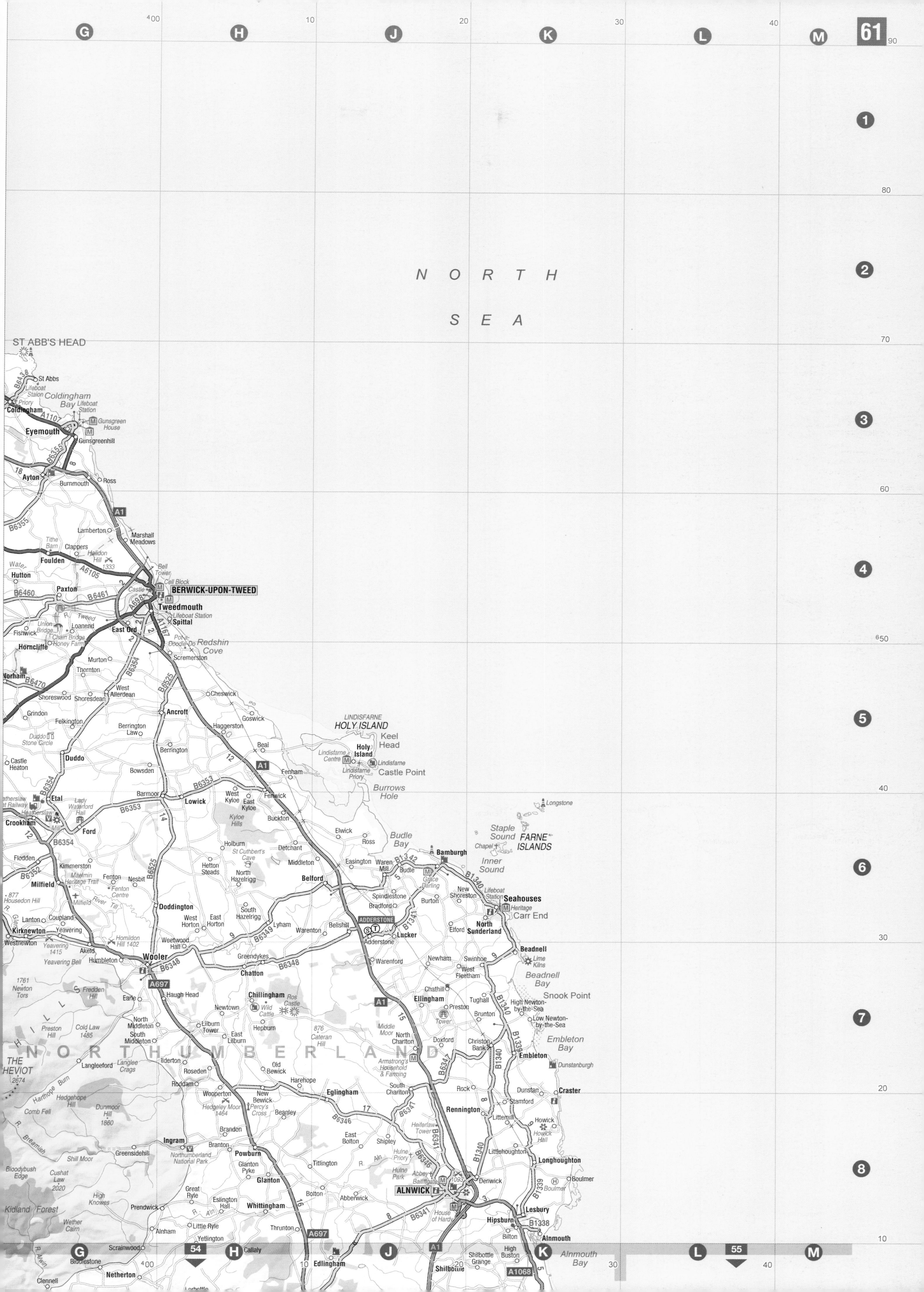
NORTH SEA
ST ABB'S HEAD
St Abbs
Coldingham Bay
Coldingham
Eyemouth
Gunsgreen House
Gunsgreenhill
Ayton
Burnmouth
Ross
Lamberton
Marshall Meadows
Foulden
Clappers
Hutton
Paxton
BERWICK-UPON-TWEED
Tweedmouth
Spittal
East Ord
Horncliffe
Murton
Thornton
Norham
Redshin Cove
Scremerston
Cheswick
Goswick
Haggerston
Ancroft
Grindon
Felkington
Berrington Law
Duddo
Castle Heaton
Beal
Berrington
Bowsden
Fenham
LINDISFARNE
HOLY ISLAND
Holy Island
Keel Head
Castle Point
Burrows Hole
Etal
Barmoor
Lowick
West Kyloe
East Kyloe
Fenwick
Kyloe Hills
Buckton
Crookham
Ford
Elwick
Ross
Budle Bay
Bamburgh
Longstone
Staple Sound
FARNE ISLANDS
Inner Sound
Flodden
Kimmerston
Holburn
Detchant
Middleton
Easington
Waren Mill
Budle
Milfield
Fenton
Nesbit
Hetton Steads
North Hazelrigg
Belford
Spindlestone
Bradford
Burton
New Shoreston
Seahouses
Carr End
Doddington
South Hazelrigg
Lanton
Coupland
Kirknewton
Yeavering
West Horton
East Horton
Lyham
Warenton
Bellshill
ADDERSTONE
Lucker
Adderstone
Elford
North Sunderland
Beadnell
Westnewton
Akeld
Humbleton
Weetwood Hall
Wooler
Greendykes
Chatton
Warenford
Newham
Swinhoe
West Fleetham
Beadnell Bay
Yeavering Bell
Earle
Haugh Head
Chillingham
Ros Castle
Newtown
Chathill
Ellingham
Tughall
Snook Point
High Newton-by-the-Sea
Low Newton-by-the-Sea
Preston
Brunton
Embleton Bay
North Middleton
South Middleton
Lilburn Tower
East Lilburn
Hepburn
Middle Moor
North Charlton
Doxford
Christon Bank
Embleton
Dunstanburgh
NORTHUMBERLAND
THE HEVIOT
Langleeford
Ilderton
Roseden
Old Bewick
Harehope
Eglingham
South Charlton
Rock
Dunstan
Craster
Roddam
Wooperton
New Bewick
Beanley
Rennington
Stamford
Littlemill
Howick
Howick Hall
Brandon
Ingram
Branton
Powburn
Glanton Pyke
Glanton
East Bolton
Shipley
Titlington
Littlehoughton
Longhoughton
Greensidehill
Boulmer
Denwick
ALNWICK
Great Ryle
Eslington Hall
Whittingham
Bolton
Abberwick
Lesbury
Prendwick
Little Ryle
Thrunton
Hipsburn
Alnham
Yetlington
Bilton
Alnmouth
Alnmouth Bay
Callaly
Edlingham
Shilbottle
Shilbottle Grange
High Buston
Biddlestone
Netherton
Clennell
Kidland Forest
Bloodybush Edge
A1
A697
A1068
B6341
B1340
B1339
B1342
B6348
B6353
B6354
B6525
54
55

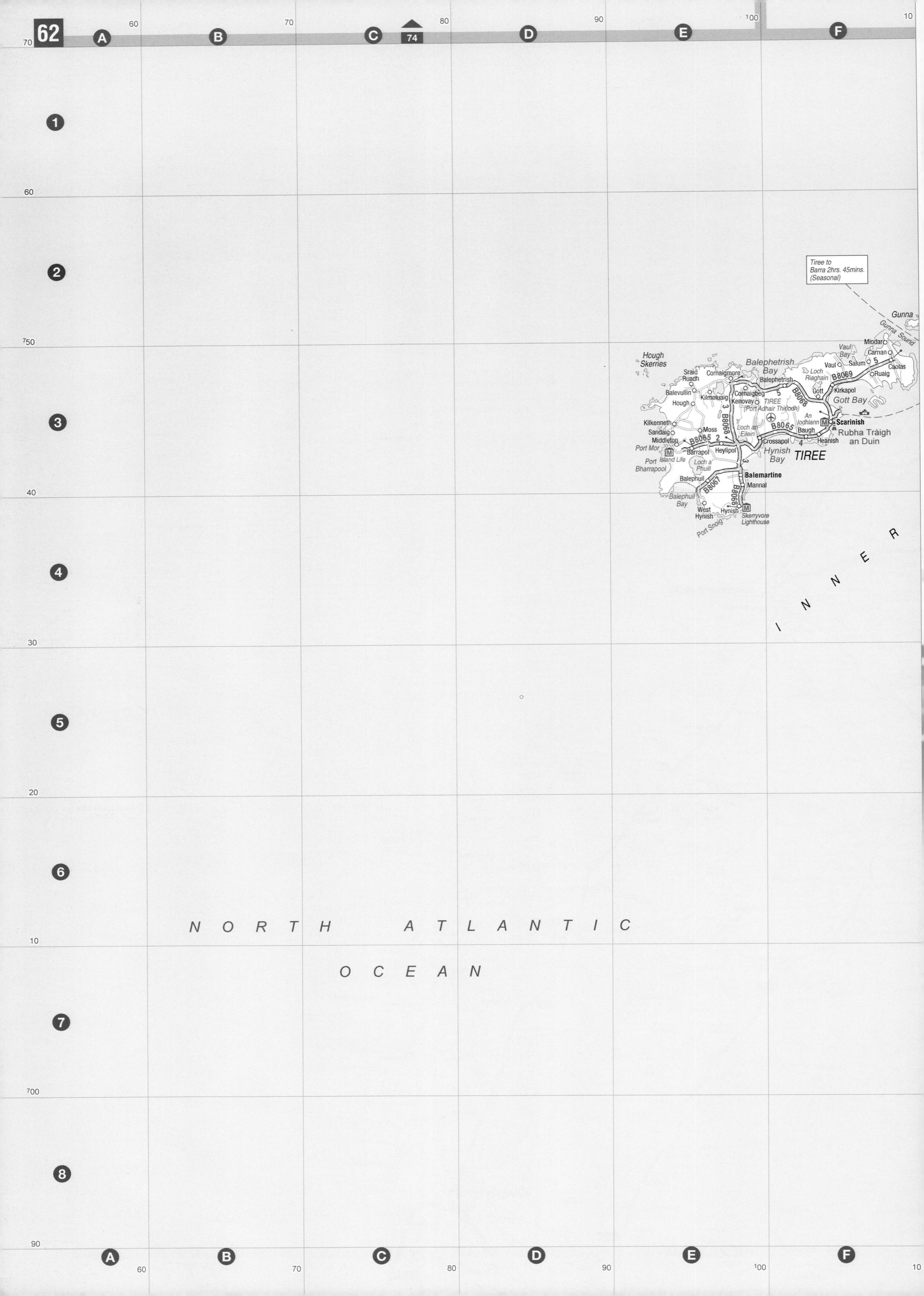

Tiree to
Barra 2hrs. 45mins.
(Seasonal)

Gunna

Gunna Sound

Hough Skerries

Balephetrish Bay

Miodar
Carnan

Vaul Bay

Vaul · Salum · Caolas

Sraid Ruadh · Cornaigmore

Balephetrish

Loch Riaghain · Gott · Ruaig

Balevullin · Kilmoluaig

Cornaigbeg

Hough

Kirkapol

Gott Bay

Kilkenneth · Moss

TIREE
(Port Adhair Thiriodh)

An Iodhlann

Sandaig

Loch an Eilein

Baugh

Scarinish

Middleton

Crossapol · Heanish

Rubha Tràigh an Duin

Port Mor · Barrapol · Heylipol

Island Life

Loch a' Phuill

Hynish Bay

TIREE

Port Bharrapool

Balephuil

Balemartine

Mannal

Balephuil Bay

West Hynish · Hynish

Skerryvore Lighthouse

Port Snoig

I N N E R

N O R T H   A T L A N T I C

O C E A N

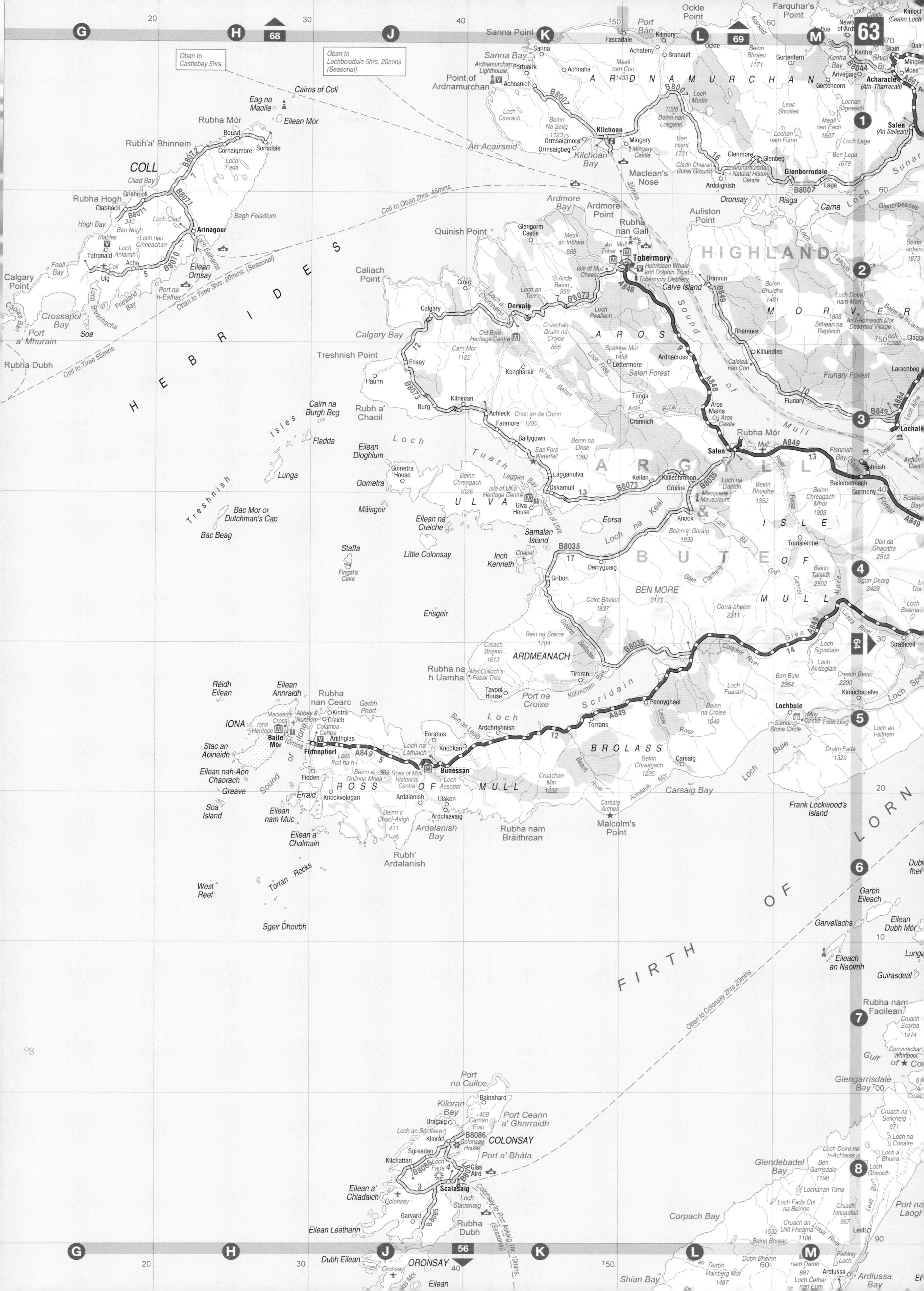

G
H
68
J
K
L
69
M
20
30
40
150
60
Oban to Castlebay 5hrs.
Oban to Lochboisdale 5hrs. 20mins. (Seasonal)
Sanna Point
Port Bàn
Ockle Point
Farquhar's Point
Fascadale
Kilmory
Achateny
Branault
Ockle
Sanna Bay
Sanna
Portuairk
Achnaha
Point of Ardnamurchan
Ardnamurchan Lighthouse
Achosnich
A R D N A M U R C H A N
Meall nan Con 1433
Beinn Bhreac 1171
Gortenfern
Kentra Bay
Kentra
Arivegaig
Gorteneorn
Acharacle (Ath-Tharracail)
Shiel Br.
B8044
Blain
Mingary
Moss
Cairns of Coll
Eag na Maoile
Eilean Mór
Rubha Mór
Bousd
Sorisdale
Cornaigmore
Rubh'a' Bhinnein
Loch Fada
COLL
B8072
Cliad Bay
B8071
Grishipoll
Clabhach
Rubha Hogh
Hogh Bay
Ben Hogh
Loch Cliad
Bagh Feisdlum
Arinagour
Stables
Loch nan Cinneachan
Loch Anlaimh
Totronald
Acha
Coll
Uig
Feall Bay
B8070
Loch Eathàrna
Eilean Ornsay
Port na h-Eathar
Calgary Point
Friesland Bay
Loch Breachacha
Crossapol Bay
Port a' Mhurain
Soa
Rubha Dubh
Coll to Tiree 55mins.
Oban to Tiree 3hrs. 20mins. (Seasonal)
Coll to Oban 2hrs. 45mins.
H E B R I D E S
Loch Caorach
B8007
Beinn Na Seilg 1123
Kilchoan
Ormsaigmore
Ormsaigbeg
Kilchoan Bay
An Acairseid
Mingary
Mingary Castle
Maclean's Nose
35mins.
B8007
Loch Mudle
1026 Beinn nan Losgann
Ben Hiant 1731
Cladh Chiaran Burial Ground
Ardslignish
Glenmore
Glenbeg
Ardnamurchan Natural History Centre
Glenborrodale
Leac Shoilleir
Lochan nam Fiann
Meall nan Each 1607
Lochan Sligneach
Loch Laga
Ben Laga 1679
Salen (An Sailean)
Laga
Oronsay
Risga
Carna
Loch Sunart
Glencripesdale
Auliston Point
Ardmore Bay
Ardmore Point
Rubha nan Gall
Quinish Point
Glengorm Castle
Meall an Inbhire 865
Mull
An Tobar
Tobermory
Hebridean Whale and Dolphin Trust
Tobermory Distillery
Isle of Mull Cheese
Calve Island
HIGHLAND
Drimnin
B849
Beinn Bhuidhe 1481
M O R V E R N
Loch Doire nam Mart
1806 Sithean na Raplaich
An t-Aoineadh Mór Deserted Village
Rhemore
Killundine
Caisteal nan Con
Fiunary Forest
Larachbeg
Fiunary
B849
Lochaline
Caliach Point
Croig
Loch a' Chumhainn
Dervaig
Loch an Torr
'S Airde Beinn 959
B8073
Loch Peallach
A848
Calgary
Calgary Bay
Old Byre Heritage Centre
Cruachan Druim na Croise 866
A R O S
Sound of Mull
Carn Mor 1122
Treshnish Point
Ensay
Speinne Mór 1458
Lettermore
Loch Frisa
Salen Forest
Ardnacross
Haunn
B8073
Kengharair
River Bellart
Tenga
Aros
Aros Mains
Aros Castle
Crannich
Cairn na Burgh Beg
Rubh a' Chaoil
Burg
Kilninian
Achleck
Fanmore
Cnoc an da Chinn 1280
Rubha Mór
Mull
A849
Salen
Fishnish Bay
Fishnish
Fladda
Eilean Dioghlum
Loch Tuath
Ballygown
Eas Fors Waterfall
Beinn na Drise 1392
A R G Y L L
Lunga
Treshnish Isles
Gometra House
Gometra
Beinn Chreagach 1026
Isle of Ulva Heritage Centre
Laggan Bay
Lagganulva
Oskamull
Kellan
Killiechronan
Gruline
B8035
Loch na Dairidh
Macquarie Mausoleum
Beinn Bhuidhe 1352
Beinn Chreagach Mhor 1903
Bailemeanach
Garmony
Bac Mor or Dutchman's Cap
Bac Beag
Màisgeir
U L V A
Ulva House
Sound of Ulva
Eilean na Creiche
Eorsa
Loch na Keal
Knock
Beinn a' Ghraig 1939
& I S L E
Tomsléibhe
Staffa
Fingal's Cave
Little Colonsay
Samalan Island
Chapel
Inch Kenneth
B8035
Gribun
Derryguaig
B U T E O F
Glen Clachaig
Beinn Talaidh 2502
Dùn da Ghaoithe 2512
Sgurr Dearg 2429
BEN MORE 3171
Coirc Bheinn 1837
Corra-bheinn 2311
M U L L
Erisgeir
Bein na Srèine 1704
Creach Bheinn 1613
ARDMEANACH
B8035
Glen More
A849
Coladoir River
Loch Sguabain
Loch Airdeglais
Creach Beinn 2290
Strathcoil
Rubha na h Uamha
MacCulloch's Fossil Tree
Tiroran
Tavool House
Port na Croise
Kilfinichen Bay
Loch Scridain
Pennyghael
Loch Fuaran
Ben Buie 2354
Kinlochspelve
Loch Spelve
Lochbuie
Moy Castle
Loch Uisg
Standing Stone Circle
Réidh Eilean
Eilean Annraidh
Rubha nan Cearc
Garbh Phort
Kintra
Creich
Columba Centre
Ardhglas
IONA
Iona Heritage
Maclean's Cross
Abbey & Nunnery
Baile Mór
10mins.
Fionnphort
Sound of Iona
Stac an Aoineidh
Eilean nah-Aon Chaorach
Greave
Soa Island
Fidden
Erraid
Knockvologan
Eilean nam Muc
Eilean a' Chalmain
Bun an Leoib
Eorabus
Ardchrishnish
Knockan
Loch na Làthaich
Bunessan
Ross of Mull Historical Centre
Loch Assopol
Ardalanish
Uisken
Ardchiavaig
Ardalanish Bay
Rubh' Ardalanish
R O S S O F M U L L
Torrans
B R O L A S S
Beinn na Croise 1649
Beinn Chreagach 1235
Carsaig
Cruachan Min 1232
Carsaig Arches
Malcolm's Point
Rubha nam Bràithrean
Carsaig Bay
Loch Buie
Druim Fada 1329
Frank Lockwood's Island
West Reef
Torran Rocks
Sgeir Dhoirbh
FIRTH OF LORN
Garbh Eileach
Garvellachs
Eilean Dubh Mór
Eileach an Naoimh
Guirasdeal
Rubha nam Faoilean
Cruach Scarba 1474
Corryvreckan Whirlpool
Gulf of Corryvreckan
Glengarrisdale Bay
Oban to Colonsay 2hrs. 20mins.
Port na Cuilce
Balnahard
Kiloran Bay
Uragaig
Carnan Eoin
Port Ceann a' Gharraidh
Loch an Sgoltaire
Kiloran
B8086
Colonsay House
COLONSAY
Port a' Bhàta
Sgreadan
Kilchattan
Loch Fada
Glas Aird
Eilean a' Chladaich
Colonsay
Scalasaig
Loch Staosnaig
Colonsay to Port Askaig 1hr. 10mins. (Seasonal)
Garvard
B8085
Rubha Dubh
Eilean Leathann
Dubh Eilean
ORONSAY
56
Eilean
Shian Bay
Glendebadel Bay
Cruach na Seilcheig 971
Loch Doire na h-Achlaise
Ben Garrisdale 1198
Lochan Tana
Loch Fada Cul na Beinne
Cruach Ionnastail 967
Cruach an Uillt Fhearna 1106
Beinn Bhreac
Corpach Bay
Lussa River
Lealt
Dubh Bheinn
Rainberg Mòr 1487
Fishing Loch
Ardlussa
Ardlussa Bay
Port na Laogh
1
2
3
4
5
6
7
8
64

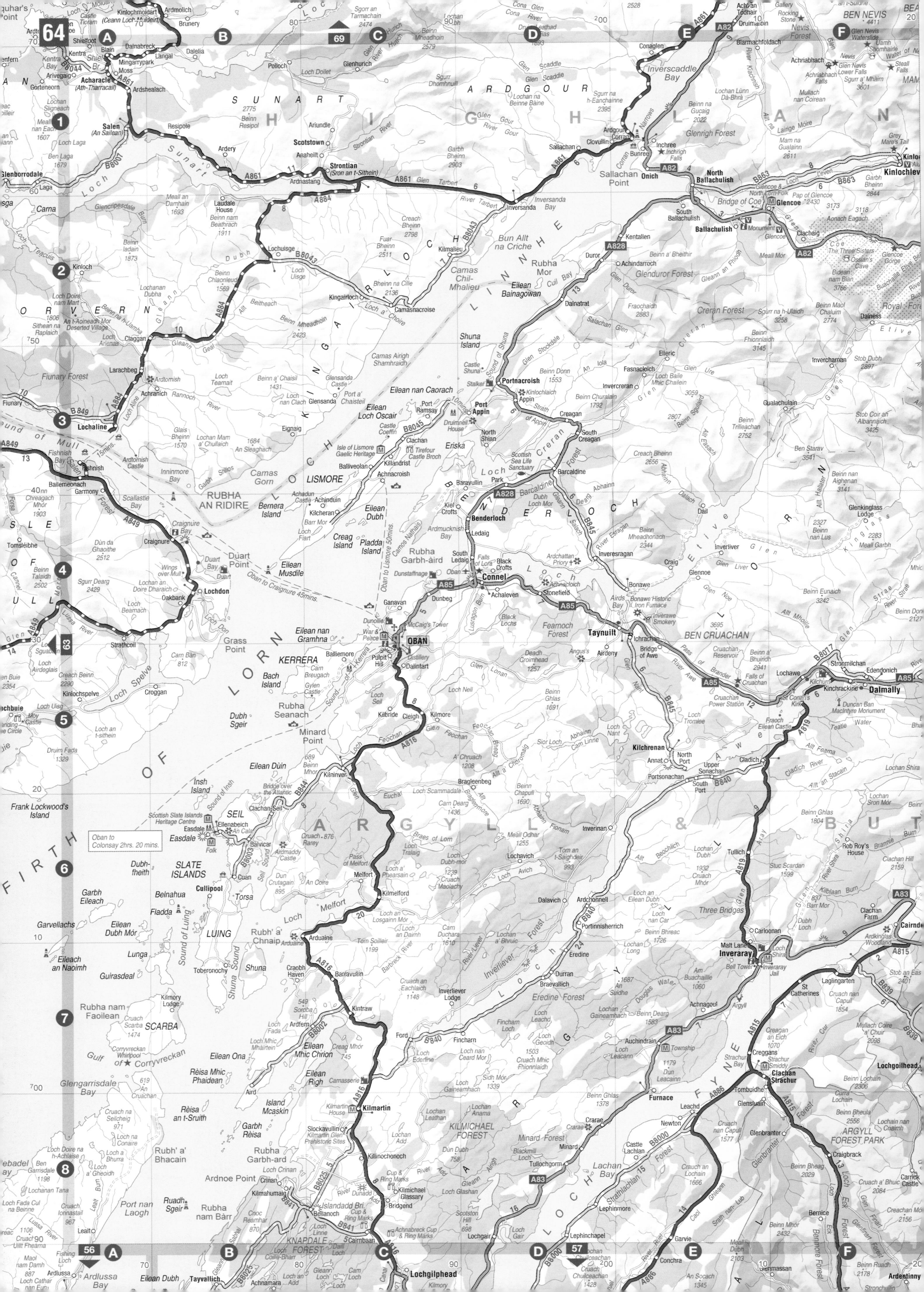

64
69
63
56
57
A
B
C
D
E
F
1
2
3
4
5
6
7
8
Kinlochmoidart
Ardmolich
Brunery
Shielfoot
Kentra
Dalnabreck
Mingarrypark
Langal
Dalelia
Acharacle (Ath-Tharracail)
Ardshealach
Arivegaig
Gorteneorn
SUNART
Salen (An Sailean)
Resipole
Ariundle
Scotstown
Anaheilt
Strontian (Sron an t-Sithein)
Ardery
Ardnastang
Glenborrodale
Laga
Loch Sunart
Polloch
Loch Doilet
Glenhurich
ARDGOUR
HIGHLAND
Glen Gour
Glen Scaddle
Ardgour
Corran
Clovullin
Sallachan
Sallachan Point
Onich
Inchree
Bunree
Corran Narrows
Inverscaddle Bay
Conaglen
Blarmachfoldach
Achriabhach
Glen Nevis
Nevis Forest
BEN NEVIS
4411
Glen Nevis Waterslide
Steall Falls
Glenrigh Forest
North Ballachulish
South Ballachulish
Ballachulish
Bridge of Coe
Glencoe
Kinlochleven
Clachaig
Aonach Eagach
The Three Sisters
Ossian's Cave
Glencoe Gorge
Buachaille Etive Mor
Royal Forest
Kentallen
Duror
Achindarroch
Glenduror Forest
Dalnatrat
Creran Forest
Inversanda
Inversanda Bay
Glen Tarbert
Laudale House
Lochuisge
Kilmalieu
Kingairloch
Camasnacroise
Bun Allt na Criche
Camas Chil-Mhalieu
Rubha Mor
Eilean Bainagowan
Cuil Bay
LOCH LINNHE
LOCH KINGAIRLOCH
MORVERN
Kinloch
Claggan
Larachbeg
Ardtornish
Achranich
Funiary Forest
Lochaline
Fiunary
Sound of Mull
Fishnish Bay
Fishnish
Garmony
Ardtornish Castle
Glensanda
Glensanda Castle
Port a' Chaisteil
Eilean nan Caorach
Eilean Loch Oscair
Port Ramsay
Port Appin
Appin
Portnacroish
Castle Stalker
Shuna Island
Sound of Shuna
Castle Coeffin
Clachan
Tirefour Castle Broch
Isle of Lismore Gaelic Heritage
Balliveolan
Achnacroish
Kilcheran
LISMORE
Bernera Island
RUBHA AN RIDIRE
Eilean Dubh
Creag Island
Pladda Island
Eilean Musdile
Oban to Lismore 50mins.
Oban to Craignure 45mins.
Eriska
North Shian
Creagan
South Creagan
Loch Creran
Barcaldine
Scottish Sea Life Sanctuary
Benderloch
Ledaig
South Ledaig
Falls of Lora
Connel
Black Crofts
Dunstaffnage
Dunbeg
Achaleven
Stonefield
Ardchattan Priory
Loch Etive
Bonawe
Bonawe Historic Iron Furnace
Inverawe Smokery
Airds Bay
Taynuilt
Ichrachan
Bridge of Awe
Pass of Brander
Falls of Cruachan
BEN CRUACHAN
Cruachan Reservoir
Cruachan Power Station
Lochawe
Kilchurn
Stronmilchan
Edendonich
Dalmally
Kinchrackine
Glen Etive
Glen Kinglass
Glen Strae
Craignure
Craignure Bay
Duart Bay
Duart Point
Duart
Lochdon
Oakbank
Strathcoil
Grass Point
Kinlochspelve
Loch Spelve
Croggan
Loch Buie
ISLE OF MULL
Ganavan
Dunollie
War & Peace
McCaig's Tower
OBAN
Pulpit Hill
Dalintart
Balliemore
KERRERA
Sound of Kerrera
Bach Island
Gylen Castle
Rubha Seanach
Dubh Sgeir
Minard Point
Kilbride
Cleigh
Kilmore
Loch Feochan
Loch Nell
Glen Lonan
Deadh Choimhead
Loch Tromlee
Kilchrenan
Annat
North Port
Portsonachan
Upper Sonachan
South Port
Cladich
Frach Eilean Castle
St Conan's Kirk
Loch Awe
FIRTH OF LORN
Eilean Dùin
Insh Island
Kilninver
Bridge over the Atlantic
Clachan-Seil
SEIL
Scottish Slate Islands Heritage Centre
Ellenabeich
Easdale
Balvicar
Ardmaddy Castle
SLATE ISLANDS
Cullipool
Cuan
Torsa
LUING
Fladda
Belnahua
Garvellachs
Eileach an Naoimh
Lunga
Shuna
Toberonochy
Sound of Luing
Shuna Sound
Oban to Colonsay 2hrs. 20 mins.
Frank Lockwood's Island
ARGYLL & BUTE
Loch Scammadale
Braes of Lorn
Pass of Melfort
Melfort
Kilmelford
Loch Melfort
Arduaine
Rubh' a' Chnaip
Craobh Haven
Barravullin
Kintraw
Ardfern
Loch Craignish
Eilean Mhic Chrion
Eilean Righ
Carnasserie
Kilmartin
Kilmartin House
Slockavullin
Kilmartin Glen Prehistoric Sites
Kilmichael Forest
Kilmichael Glassary
Kilninochonoch
Crinan
Loch Crinan
Cairnbaan
Achnabreck Cup & Ring Marks
Bellanoch
Islandadd Bri.
Bridgend
KNAPDALE FOREST
Lochgilphead
Tayvallich
Achnamara
Ardnoe Point
Rubha nam Barr
Port nan Laogh
Ruadh Sgeir
Garbh Rèisa
Rèisa an t-Sruith
Rèisa Mhic Phaidean
Eilean Ona
Rubha nam Faoilean
SCARBA
Kilmory Lodge
Gulf of Corryvreckan
Glengarrisdale Bay
Lussa River
Ardlussa
Ardlussa Bay
Eilean Dubh
Inverliever Forest
Inverliever Lodge
Dalavich
Lochavich
Loch Avich
Ardchonnell
Portinnisherrich
Eredine
Eredine Forest
Durran
Braevallich
Ford
Fincharn
Loch Ederline
Inverinan
Tullich
Glen Aray
Inveraray
Inveraray Jail
Bell Tower
Loch Shira
Three Bridges
Carloonan
Rob Roy's House
Achnagoul
Auchindrain
Township
Furnace
Crarae
Minard
Minard Forest
Tullochgorm
Lachan Bay
Castle Lachlan
Newton
Leachd
Strathlachlan
Lephinmore
Lephinchapel
Lochgair
LOCH FYNE
Strachur
Clachan Strachur
Creggans
St Catherines
Laglingarten
Cairndow
Ardkinglas Woodland
Glenbranter
ARGYLL FOREST PARK
Craigbrack
Lochgoilhead
Benmore Forest
Loch Eck
Glenmassan
Ardentinny
Garvie
Conchra
A82
A861
A884
A849
A828
A85
A816
A819
A83
A815
A886
B8044
B8007
B863
B8043
B8045
B849
B845
B8077
B840
B844
B8003
B8002
B8025
B841
B8000
B839

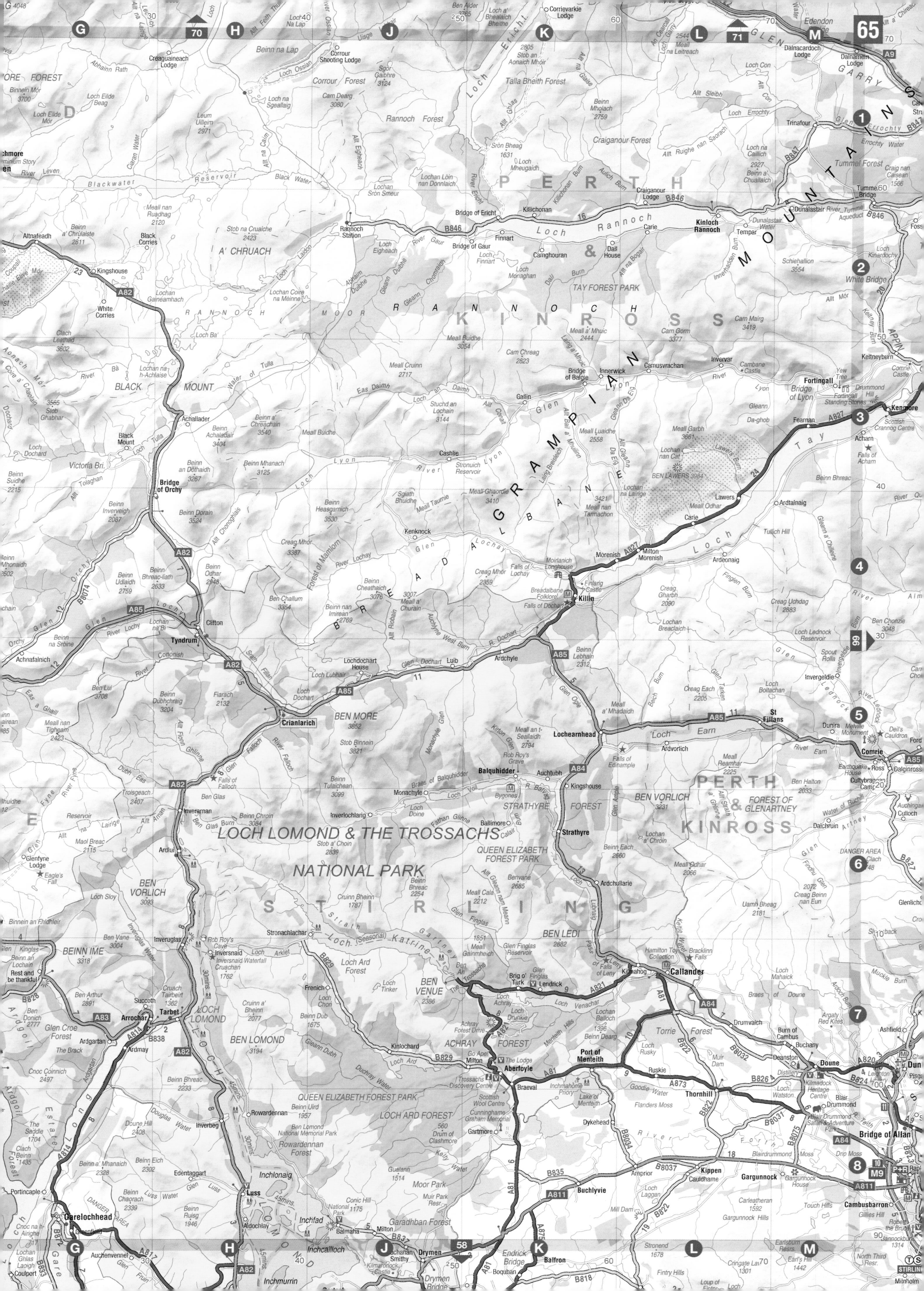
G
H
J
K
L
M
70
71
1
2
3
4
5
6
7
8
69
58
P E R T H
&
K I N R O S S
PERTH
&
KINROSS
G R A M P I A N
M O U N T A I N S
B R E A D
A L B A N E
R A N N O C H
R A N N O C H   M O O R
S T I R L I N G
LOCH LOMOND & THE TROSSACHS
NATIONAL PARK
Corrievarkie Lodge
Ben Alder 3765
Edendon Water
Dalnacardoch Lodge
Dalnamein Lodge
A9
GLEN GARRY
Beinn na Lap
Corrour Shooting Lodge
Loch Ossian
Creaguaineach Lodge
Corrour Forest
Sgor Gaibhre 3124
Carn Dearg 3080
Rannoch Forest
Stob an Aonaich Mhòir 2805
Talla Bheith Forest
Beinn Mholach 2759
Loch Errochty
Trinafour
Glen Errochty
B847
Errochty Water
Tummel Forest
Craigour Forest
Loch na Caillich
Beinn a' Chuallaich 2927
Sròn Bheag 1631
Loch Mheugaidh
Leum Uilleim 2971
Loch Eilde Mòr
Loch Eilde Beag
Binnein Mòr 3700
Blackwater Reservoir
Black Water
Lochan Sròn Smeur
Lochan Loin nan Donnlaich
River Ericht
Craiganour Lodge
B846
Killichonan
Bridge of Ericht
Loch Rannoch
Kinloch Rannoch
Tempar
Dunalastair Water
Dunalastair Reservoir
Tummel Bridge
Rannoch Station
Bridge of Gaur
Finnart
Loch Finnart
Carie
Camghouran
Dall House
TAY FOREST PARK
Schiehallion 3554
White Bridge
Loch Kinardochy
Altnafeadh
Kingshouse
A82
Black Corries
A' CHRUACH
Stob na Cruaiche 2423
Meall nan Ruadhag 2120
Beinn a' Chrùlaiste 2811
White Corries
Lochan Gaineamhach
Loch Laidon
Lochan Coire na Mèinne
Loch Eigheach
Gleann Chomraidh
Loch Monaghan
Meall a' Mhuic 2444
Carn Gorm 3377
Carn Mairg 3419
Keltneyburn
APPIN
Clach Leathad 3602
Loch Ba
Lochan na h-Achlaise
BLACK MOUNT
Water of Tulla
Meall Buidhe 3054
Carn Chreag 2823
Meall Cruinn 2717
Bridge of Balgie
Innerwick
Camusvrachan
Invervar
Cambane Castle
Fortingall
Bridge of Lyon
Kenmore
Fearnan
A827
Achallader
Beinn a' Chreachain 3540
Beinn Achaladair 3404
Black Mount
Loch Tulla
Loch an Daimh
Stuchd an Lochain 3144
Gallin
Glen Lyon
Meall Luaidhe 2558
Meall Garbh 3661
Lochan nan Cat
BEN LAWERS 3984
Lawers
Acharn
Falls of Acharn
Scottish Crannog Centre
Victoria Bri.
Beinn Mhanach 3125
Beinn an Dòthaidh 3267
Cashlie
Stronuich Reservoir
Meall Ghaordie 3410
Meall nan Tarmachan 3421
Lochan na Lairige
Meall Odhar
Ardtalnaig
Bridge of Orchy
Beinn Dorain 3524
Beinn Inverveigh 2087
Beinn Heasgarnich 3530
Sgiath Bhuidhe
Meall Taurnie
Kenknock
Glen Lochay
Carie
Loch Tay
Morenish
Milton Morenish
Ardeonaig
Tullich Hill
Creag Mhor 3387
Forest of Mamlorn
River Lochay
Moirlanich Longhouse
Falls of Lochay
Creag Mhor 2359
Beinn Odhar 2948
Beinn Udlaidh 2759
Beinn Bhreac-liath 2633
B8074
Glen Orchy
A85
Clifton
Tyndrum
Ben Challum 3354
Beinn Cheathaich 3076
Meall a' Churain 3007
Beinn nan Imirean 2769
Killin
Finlarig Castle
Breadalbane Folklore
Falls of Dochart
Creag Gharbh 2090
Lochan Breaclaich
Creag Uchdag 2883
Loch Lednock Reservoir
Ben Chonzie 3048
Glen Lochy
Achnafalnich
Beinn na Sròine
Lochdochart House
Glen Dochart
Luib
Ardchyle
Beinn Leabhain 2312
Glen Ogle
Creag Each 2205
Spout Rolla
Invergeldie
Loch Boltachan
Ben Lui 3708
Beinn Dubhchraig 3204
Fiarach 2132
Loch Lubhair
Loch Dochart
Crianlarich
BEN MORE 3852
Stob Binnein 3821
Meall an t-Seallaidh 2794
Meall a' Mhadaidh
Lochearnhead
Loch Earn
St Fillans
Dunira
Melville Monument
Comrie
Dalginross
Meall nan Tighearn 2423
Glen Falloch
Falls of Falloch
River Falloch
Ardvorlich
Falls of Edinample
Rob Roy's Grave
Balquhidder
Auchtubh
Kingshouse
A84
Meall Reamhar 2225
Ben Halton 2033
Cultybraggan Camp
Troisgeach 2407
Inverarnan
Ben Glas
Beinn Tulaichean 3099
Monachyle
Braes of Balquhidder
Loch Voil
STRATHYRE
BEN VORLICH 3231
FOREST OF GLENARTNEY
Auchingarrich
Cultoch
Reservoir
Beinn Chroin 3084
Inverlochlarig
Loch Doine
Ballimore
Strathyre
Lochan a' Chroin
Dalchruin
Maol Breac 2115
Stob a' Choin 2839
QUEEN ELIZABETH FOREST PARK
Beinn Each 2660
Meall Odhar 2066
DANGER AREA
Glenfyne Lodge
Eagle's Fall
Ardlui
BEN VORLICH 3093
Loch Sloy
Cruinn Bheinn 1787
Beinn Bhreac 2295
Meall Cala 2212
Benvane 2685
Ardchullarie
Creag Beinn nan Eun 2072
Uamh Bheag 2181
Binnein an Fhidhleir
Ben Vane 3004
Inveruglas
Rob Roy's Cave
Inversnaid
Inversnaid Waterfall
Loch Arklet
Stronachlachar
Loch Katrine
Glen Finglas
Meall Gainmheich 1851
BEN LEDI 2882
Glen Finglas Reservoir
Hamilton Toy Collection
Bracklinn Falls
Callander
Kilmahog
Falls of Leny
BEINN IME 3318
Beinn an Lochain
Rest and be thankful
Cruach Tairbeirt 1362
Cruachan 1762
Loch Ard Forest
BEN VENUE 2386
Ben A'n
Brig o' Turk
Lendrick
Loch Venachar
A821
A81
Loch Mahaick
Braes of Doune
Ben Arthur 2891
Ben Donich 2777
Glen Croe Forest
Succoth
Arrochar
Tarbet
A83
A814
B828
B838
Ardgartan
Ardmay
The Brack
LOCH LOMOND
Cruinn a' Bheinn 2077
Beinn Dubh 1675
Frenich
Loch Chon
Loch Tinker
Achray Forest Drive
Loch Achray
Loch Drunkie
ACHRAY FOREST
Lochan Balloch
Menteith Hills
Torrie Forest
Drumvaich
Burn of Cambus
Buchany
Argaty Red Kites
Ashfield
Cnoc Coinnich 2497
BEN LOMOND 3194
Kinlochard
Loch Ard
B829
Milton
Aberfoyle
The Lodge
Port of Menteith
Loch Rusky
Ruskie
B822
B8032
Deanston
Doune
Kilmadock Heritage Centre
A820
Dunblane
A873
Thornhill
B826
Lochan Watston
Blair Drummond
Blair Drummond Safari & Adventure Park
Beinn Bhreac 2233
Trossachs Discovery Centre
Braeval
Inchmahome Priory
Lake of Menteith
Goodie Water
Flanders Moss
QUEEN ELIZABETH FOREST PARK
Beinn Uird 1957
Scottish Wool Centre
Cunninghame Graham Memorial
Gartmore
Dykehead
Bridge of Allan
The Saddle 1704
Doune Hill 2408
Douglas Water
Inverbeg
Rowardennan
Ben Lomond National Memorial Park
Rowardennan Forest
LOCH ARD FOREST
Drum of Clashmore 560
Kelty Water
B8034
River Forth
Blairdrummond Moss
Drip Moss
Clach Beinn 1435
Beinn a' Mhanaich 2328
Beinn Eich 2302
Edentaggart
Glen Luss
Inchlonaig
Gualann 1514
Moor Park
Muir Park Resr.
B835
Arnprior
B8037
Kippen
Cauldhame
Gargunnock
Gargunnock House
A811
M9
Buchlyvie
Cambusbarron
Portincaple
Beinn Chaorach 2339
Beinn Ruisg 1946
Luss
Conic Hill 1175
National Park
Loch Laggan
Mill Dam
Carleatheran 1592
Touch Hills
Gargunnock Hills
Gillies Hill
Garelochhead
Greenfield
DANGER AREA
Aldochlay
Inchfad
Balmaha
Milton
Garadhban Forest
B837
A875
Strone End 1678
Earlsburn Resrs.
Bannockburn 1314
Cnoc na h-Airighe
Auchenvennel
Inchcailloch
Drymen
Endrick Bridge
Balfron
Earl's Hill 1442
Cringate Law 1301
North Third Resr.
STIRLING
Glen Fruin
Inchmurrin
Boquhan
B818
Fintry Hills
Loup of Fintry
Drymen Bridge
Coulport
Lochan Ghlas Laoigh
Milnholm

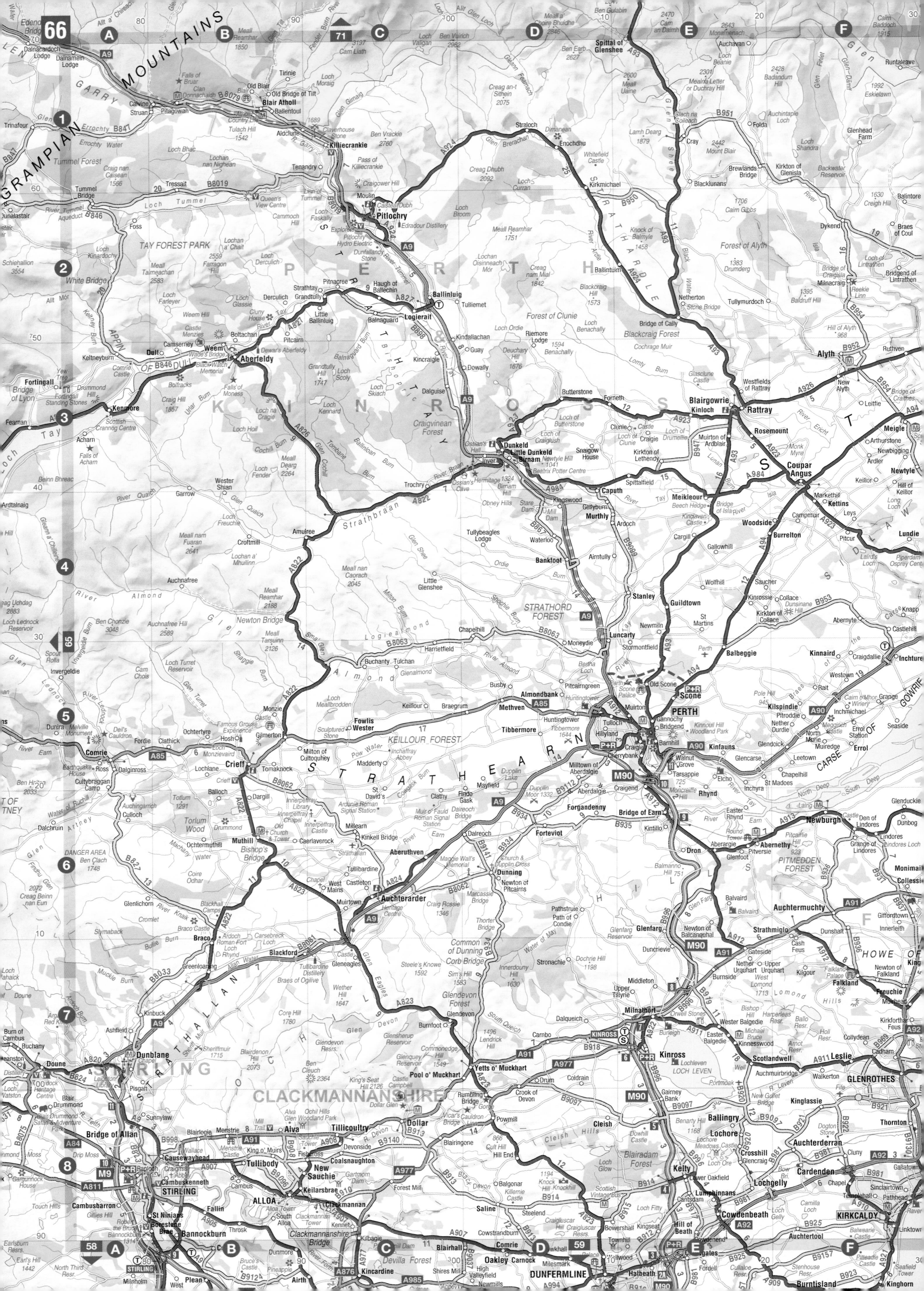
GRAMPIAN MOUNTAINS
Blair Atholl
Killiecrankie
Pitlochry
Loch Tummel
TAY FOREST PARK
Schiehallion 3554
Aberfeldy
Kenmore
Fortingall
Loch Tay
Ballinluig
Logierait
Dunkeld
Birnam
Blairgowrie
Rattray
Coupar Angus
Alyth
Kirkmichael
Spittal of Glenshee
Bridge of Cally
Forest of Alyth
Meigle
Amulree
Crieff
Comrie
Gilmerton
Methven
Almondbank
PERTH
Scone
Stanley
Luncarty
Bankfoot
Murthly
Caputh
Meikleour
Burrelton
Balbeggie
Errol
CARSE OF GOWRIE
Bridge of Earn
Abernethy
Newburgh
Auchterarder
Dunning
Forteviot
Muthill
Braco
Blackford
Gleneagles
Dunblane
Doune
Bridge of Allan
STIRLING
Cambusbarron
Bannockburn
Tullibody
ALLOA
Alva
Tillicoultry
Dollar
CLACKMANNANSHIRE
Clackmannan
Kincardine
Yetts o' Muckhart
Milnathort
Kinross
LOCH LEVEN
Glenfarg
Auchtermuchty
Strathmiglo
Falkland
Leslie
GLENROTHES
Kinglassie
Thornton
Lochgelly
Cardenden
Cowdenbeath
Kelty
Lochore
Ballingry
KIRKCALDY
Burntisland
Kinghorn
Aberdour
DUNFERMLINE
Oakley
Saline
Carnock
STRATHEARN
STRATHALLAN
STIRLING
PERTH AND KINROSS
A9
A93
A94
A90
A91
A92
A822
A827
A923
A984
A85
A912
A977
M90
M9
58
59
65
71

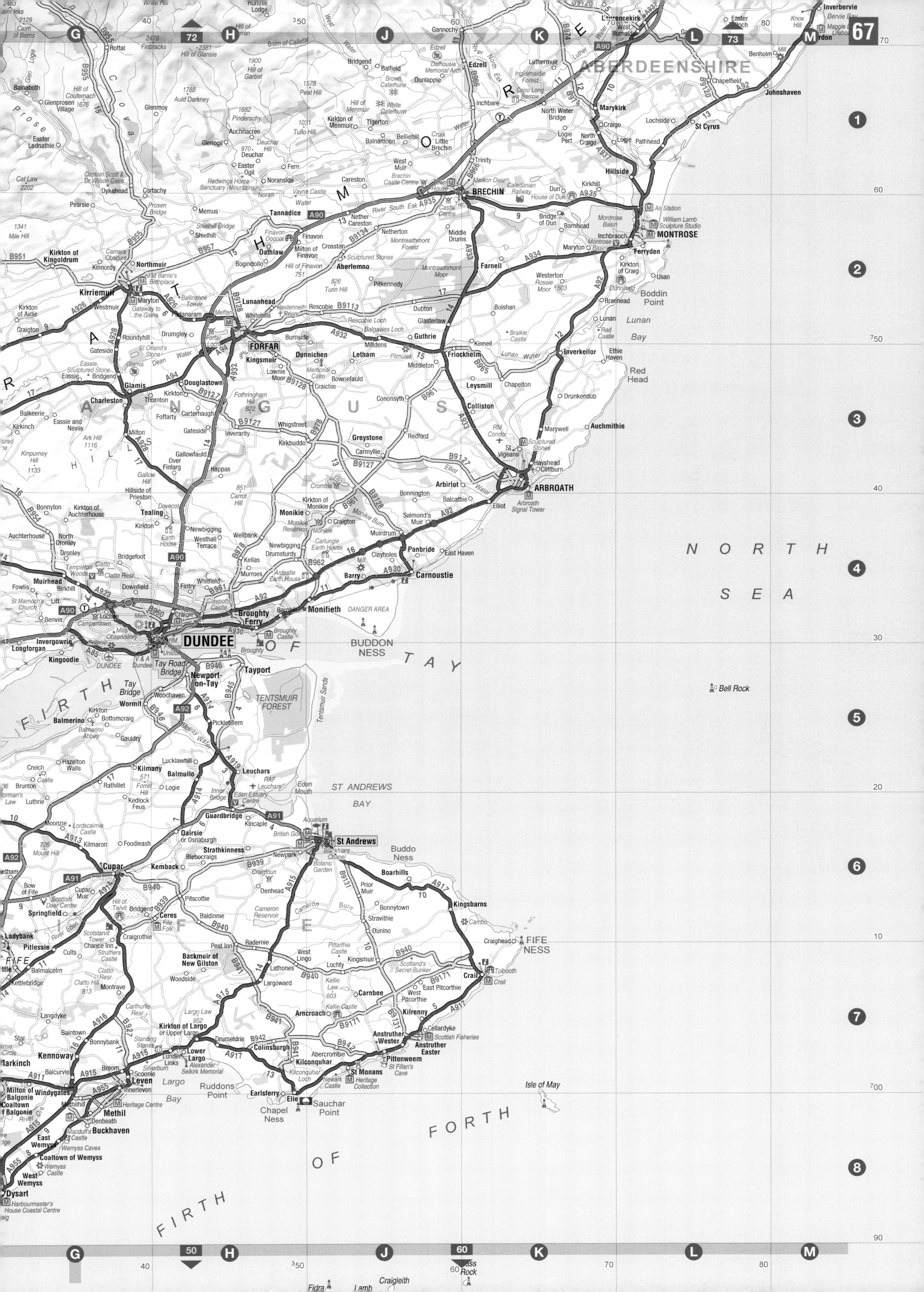

67
G
H
J
K
L
M
72
73
50
60
ABERDEENSHIRE
ANGUS
FIFE
NORTH SEA
FIRTH OF TAY
FIRTH OF FORTH
ST ANDREWS BAY
Inverbervie
Johnshaven
St Cyrus
Hillside
MONTROSE
Montrose Basin
Ferryden
Marykirk
Luthermuir
Edzell
Gannochy
Laurencekirk
Benholm
Lochside
Pathhead
Craigo
Logie
Kirkhill
Dun
House of Dun
Bridge of Dun
Barnhead
Inchbraoch
Maryton
Kirkton of Craig
Usan
Boddin Point
Lunan
Lunan Bay
Ethie Haven
Red Head
Inverkeilor
Chapelton
Drunkendub
Auchmithie
Marywell
St Vigeans
Hayshead
Cliffburn
ARBROATH
Arbroath Signal Tower
BRECHIN
Brechin Castle Centre
Trinity
Little Brechin
Caledonian Railway
Farnell
Montreathmont Moor
Montreathmont Forest
Middle Drums
Netherton
Aberlemno
Pitkennedy
Finavon
Tannadice
Oathlaw
Memus
Shielhill
Noranside
Fern
Careston
Nether Careston
Bolshan
Glasterlaw
Guthrie
Friockheim
Kinnell
Leysmill
Colliston
Letham
Dunnichen
Burnside
Milldens
Middleton
Redford
Greystone
Carmyllie
Arbirlot
Bonnington
Balcathie
Elliot
Salmond's Muir
Muirdrum
Panbride
East Haven
Carnoustie
Barry
Clayholes
Monifieth
BUDDON NESS
Bell Rock
Monikie
Kirkton of Monikie
Craigton
Newbigging
Wellbank
Kellas
Murroes
Whitfield
Fintry
Broughty Ferry
Broughty Castle
DUNDEE
Tay Road Bridge
Tay Bridge
Newport-on-Tay
Tayport
Wormit
Woodhaven
TENTSMUIR FOREST
Tentsmuir Sands
Pickletillem
Leuchars
RAF Leuchars
Eden Mouth
Guardbridge
St Andrews
Buddo Ness
Boarhills
Kingsbarns
Cambo
Craighead
FIFE NESS
Crail
Balcomie
Kilrenny
Cellardyke
Anstruther Wester
Anstruther Easter
Pittenweem
St Monans
Elie
Earlsferry
Chapel Ness
Saucharl Point
Colinsburgh
Kilconquhar
Lower Largo
Largo Bay
Ruddons Point
Leven
Methil
Buckhaven
East Wemyss
West Wemyss
Coaltown of Wemyss
Dysart
Windygates
Kennoway
Isle of May
Cupar
Ceres
Kemback
Dairsie or Osnaburgh
Strathkinness
Kilmany
Balmullo
Balmerino
Springfield
Pitlessie
Ladybank
Craigrothie
Peat Inn
Radernie
Largoward
Lathones
Backmuir of New Gilston
Kirkton of Largo or Upper Largo
Arncroach
Carnbee
Kellie Castle
Dunino
Stravithie
Kirkton of Auchterhouse
Muirhead
Birkhill
Invergowrie
Longforgan
Kingoodie
Tealing
Kirriemuir
Northmuir
Kinnordy
Kirkton of Kingoldrum
Forfar
Kingsmuir
Lunanhead
Glamis
Charleston
Douglastown
Kirkton
Thornton
Inverarity
Gateside
Roundyhill
Padanaram
Westmuir
Cortachy
Dykehead
Pearsie
Rottal
Balnaboth
Glenprosen Village
Glenmoy
Auchnacree
Glenogil
Kirkton of Menmuir
Tigerton
Balnamoon
Bridgend
Balfield
Dunlappie
Inchbare
North Water Bridge
Logie Pert
North Craigo
Chapelfield
Rescobie
Restenneth Priory
Dubton
Mill of Finavon
Crosston
Bogindollo
Happas
Gallowfauld
Carterhaugh
Letham
Bowriefauld
Craichie
Whigstreet
Kirkbuddo
Cononsyth
Balkeerie
Eassie
Kirkinch
Milton
Foffarty
Auchterhouse
North Dronley
Dronley
Bridgefoot
Downfield
Lochee
Benvie
Fowlis
Craigie
Barnhill
Balgove

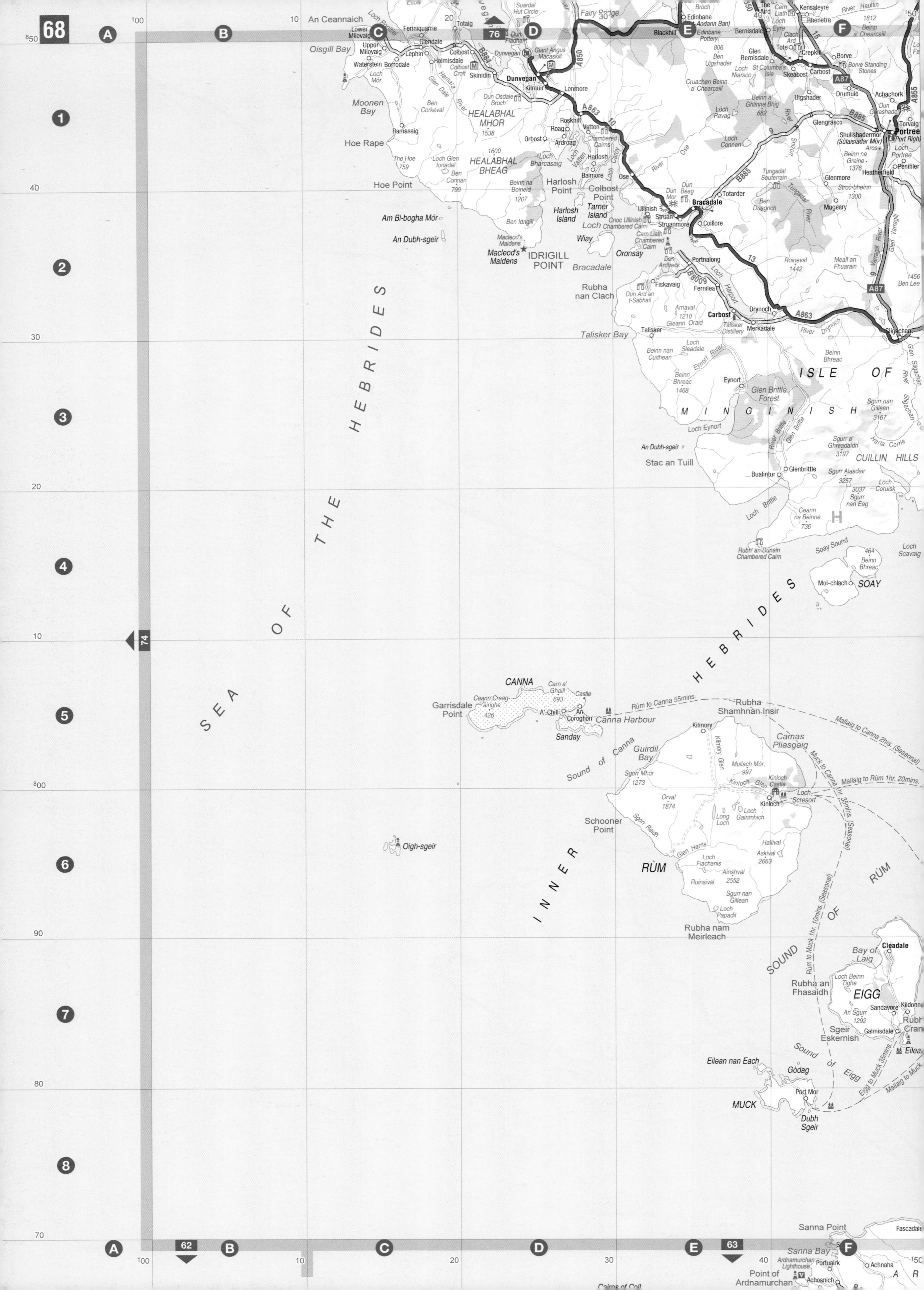
A
B
C
D
E
F
1
2
3
4
5
6
7
8
76
74
62
63
An Ceannaich
Oisgill Bay
Lower Milovaig
Upper Milovaig
Waterstein
Borrodale
Loch Mòr
Glendale
Lephin
Feriniquarrie
Colbost
Holmisdale
Totaig
Skinidin
Dunvegan
Kilmuir
Lonmore
Moonen Bay
Ramasaig
Hoe Rape
Hoe Point
HEALABHAL MHOR
1538
HEALABHAL BHEAG
1600
Orbost
Roskhill
Roag
Ardroag
Vatten
Harlosh
Balmore
Harlosh Point
Harlosh Island
Colbost Point
Tarner Island
Loch
Wiay
Oronsay
Am Bi-bogha Mór
An Dubh-sgeir
Macleod's Maidens
IDRIGILL POINT
Bracadale
Rubha nan Clach
Ullinish
Struan
Bracadale
Totardor
Coillore
Portnalong
Fiskavaig
Fernilea
Carbost
Drynoch
Merkadale
Talisker
Talisker Bay
Blackhill
Edinbane
Bernisdale
Kensaleyre
Rhenetra
Borve
Skeabost
Carbost
Drumuie
Achachork
Portree
Glengrasco
Heatherfield
Penifiler
Glenmore
Mugeary
Sligachan
A87
A850
A863
A855
B884
B885
B8009
Eynort
ISLE OF
M I N G I N I S H
Glen Brittle Forest
Loch Eynort
An Dubh-sgeir
Stac an Tuill
Bualintur
Glenbrittle
CUILLIN HILLS
Loch Brittle
Soay Sound
SOAY
Mol-chlach
Loch Scavaig
S E A   O F   T H E   H E B R I D E S
I N N E R   H E B R I D E S
CANNA
Garrisdale Point
Sanday
Canna Harbour
Rùm to Canna 55mins.
Rubha Shamhnan Insir
Kilmory
Camas Pliasgaig
Guirdil Bay
Sound of Canna
Kinloch
Loch Scresort
Schooner Point
Oigh-sgeir
RÙM
Rubha nam Meirleach
SOUND OF RÙM
Mallaig to Canna 2hrs. (Seasonal)
Mallaig to Rùm 1hr. 20mins.
Cleadale
Bay of Laig
Rubha an Fhasaidh
EIGG
Sgeir Eskernish
Galmisdale
Sound of Eigg
Eilean nan Each
Gòdag
MUCK
Port Mor
Dubh Sgeir
Sanna Point
Sanna Bay
Fascadale
Point of Ardnamurchan
Achosnich
Achnaha

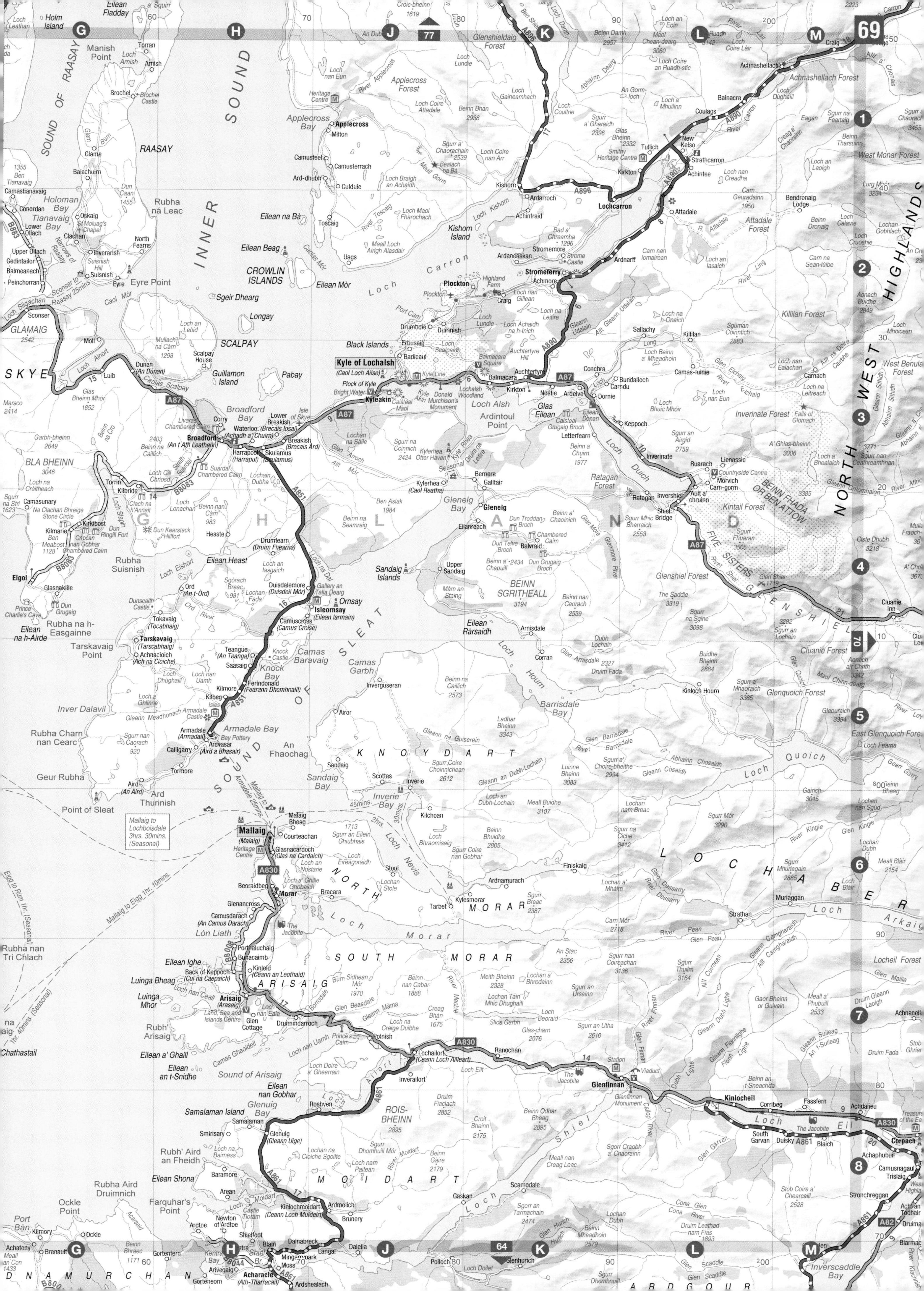
69
77
64
70
G
H
J
K
L
M
1
2
3
4
5
6
7
8
SOUND OF RAASAY
RAASAY
INNER SOUND
SKYE
GLAMAIG
2542
BLA BHEINN
3046
CROWLIN ISLANDS
Scalpay
SCALPAY
Pabay
Longay
Guillamon Island
Holm Island
Eilean Fladday
Manish Point
Torran
Arnish
Loch Arnish
Brochel
Brochel Castle
Glame
Balachuirn
Holoman Bay
Tianavaig Bay
Conordan
Lower Ollach
Upper Ollach
Gedintailor
Balmeanach
Peinchorran
Clachan
Inverarish
Suisnish
Eyre
Eyre Point
North Fearns
Rubha na Leac
Sconser
Loch Sligachan
Sconser to Raasay 25mins
Caol Mòr
Moll
Luib
Loch Ainort
Dunan
(An Dùnan)
Broadford
(An t Ath Leathann)
Broadford Bay
Corry
Waterloo
Lower Breakish
Breakish
Harrapool
Skulamus
Torrin
Kilbride
Loch Slapin
Camasunary
Kilmarie
Kirkibost
Elgol
Glasnakille
Rubha Suisnish
Eilean Heast
Heaste
Ord
Tokavaig
Tarskavaig
Tarskavaig Point
Teangue
Saasaig
Kilmore
Ferindonald
Kilbeg
Inver Dalavil
Rubha Chairn nan Cearc
Armadale
Armadale Bay
Ardvasar
Calligarry
Tormore
Aird
Point of Sleat
Ard Thurinish
Geur Rubha
Isleornsay
Ornsay
Duisdalemore
Drumfearn
Knock Bay
Camas Baravaig
SOUND OF SLEAT
Kyle of Lochalsh
Kyleakin
Plockton
Stromeferry
Lochcarron
Kishorn
Applecross
Applecross Bay
Applecross Forest
Milton
Camusteel
Camusterrach
Ard-dhubh
Culduie
Toscaig
Uags
Eilean na Bà
Eilean Beag
Eilean Mòr
Loch Carron
Kishorn Island
Ardarroch
Achintraid
Ardaneaskan
Stromemore
Strathcarron
Achintee
New Kelso
Tullich
Kirkton
Coulags
Balnacra
Achnashellach
Achnashellach Forest
Glenshieldaig Forest
Attadale
Attadale Forest
Ardnarff
Achmore
Craig
Duirinish
Drumbuie
Erbusaig
Badicaul
Black Islands
Plock of Kyle
Balmacara
Kirkton
Nostie
Auchtertyre
Ardelve
Dornie
Eilean Donan
Loch Alsh
Ardintoul Point
Glas Eilean
Keppoch
Letterfearn
Inverinate
Loch Duich
Ratagan
Ratagan Forest
Invershiel
Shiel Bridge
Morvich
Ruarach
Lienassie
Kintail Forest
FIVE SISTERS
BEINN FHADA OR BEN ATTOW
Inverinate Forest
Killilan Forest
Killilan
Sallachy
Camas-luinie
Conchra
Glenshiel Forest
Cluanie Inn
Cluanie Forest
Glenquoich Forest
Kylerhea
Glenelg
Glenelg Bay
Bernera
Galltair
Eilanreach
Balvraid
Sandaig Islands
Upper Sandaig
BEINN SGRITHEALL
Eilean Rarsaidh
Arnisdale
Corran
Loch Hourn
Kinloch Hourn
Barrisdale Bay
KNOYDART
Inverie
Inverie Bay
Scottas
Sandaig
Sandaig Bay
Airor
Inverguseran
Camas Garbh
An Fhaochag
Mallaig
Mallaig Bheag
Courteachan
Glasnacardoch
Mallaig to Lochboisdale 3hrs. 30mins. (Seasonal)
Mallaig to Armadale 25mins
Mallaig to Eigg 1hr. 10mins.
Mallaig to Rum 1hr. (Seasonal)
Loch Nevis
Kylesmorar
Tarbet
Stoul
NORTH MORAR
Morar
Bracara
Beoraidbeg
Glenancross
Camusdarach
Lòn Liath
Loch Morar
SOUTH MORAR
Portnaluchaig
Bunacaimb
Kinloid
Back of Keppoch
Arisaig
ARISAIG
Eilean Ighe
Luinga Bheag
Luinga Mhor
Rubh' Arisaig
Eilean a' Ghaill
Eilean an t-Snidhe
Sound of Arisaig
Eilean nan Gobhar
Camas Ghaoideil
Druimindarroch
Polnish
Lochailort
Inverailort
Roshven
Glenuig
Glenuig Bay
Samalaman Island
Samalaman
Smirisary
Rubh' Aird an Fheidh
Rubha Aird Druimnich
Eilean Shona
Ockle Point
Farquhar's Point
Port Bàn
Kilmory
Ockle
Achateny
Branault
Gortenfern
Arivegaig
Gorteneorn
Acharacle
Shielfoot
Blain
Mingarrypark
Moss
Langal
Dalnabreck
Ardshealach
Kentra Bay
Newton of Ardtoe
Ardtoe
Arean
Baramore
Kinlochmoidart
Ardmolich
Brunery
MOIDART
ROIS-BHEINN
Dalelia
Polloch
Gaskan
Scamodale
Loch Shiel
Glenhurich
Ranochan
Glenfinnan
Kinlocheil
Corribeg
Fassfern
Achdalieu
Corpach
Achaphubuil
Camusnagaul
Trislaig
Stronchreggan
Inverscaddle Bay
South Garvan
Duisky
Blaich
Loch Eil
Locheil Forest
Loch Arkaig
Strathan
Murlaggan
Finiskaig
Ardnamurach
LOCHABER
Loch Quoich
NORTH WEST HIGHLANDS
West Monar Forest
West Benula Forest
Loch Long
A87
A890
A896
A851
A830
A861
A82
B8083
B883
B8008
B8044
B8007

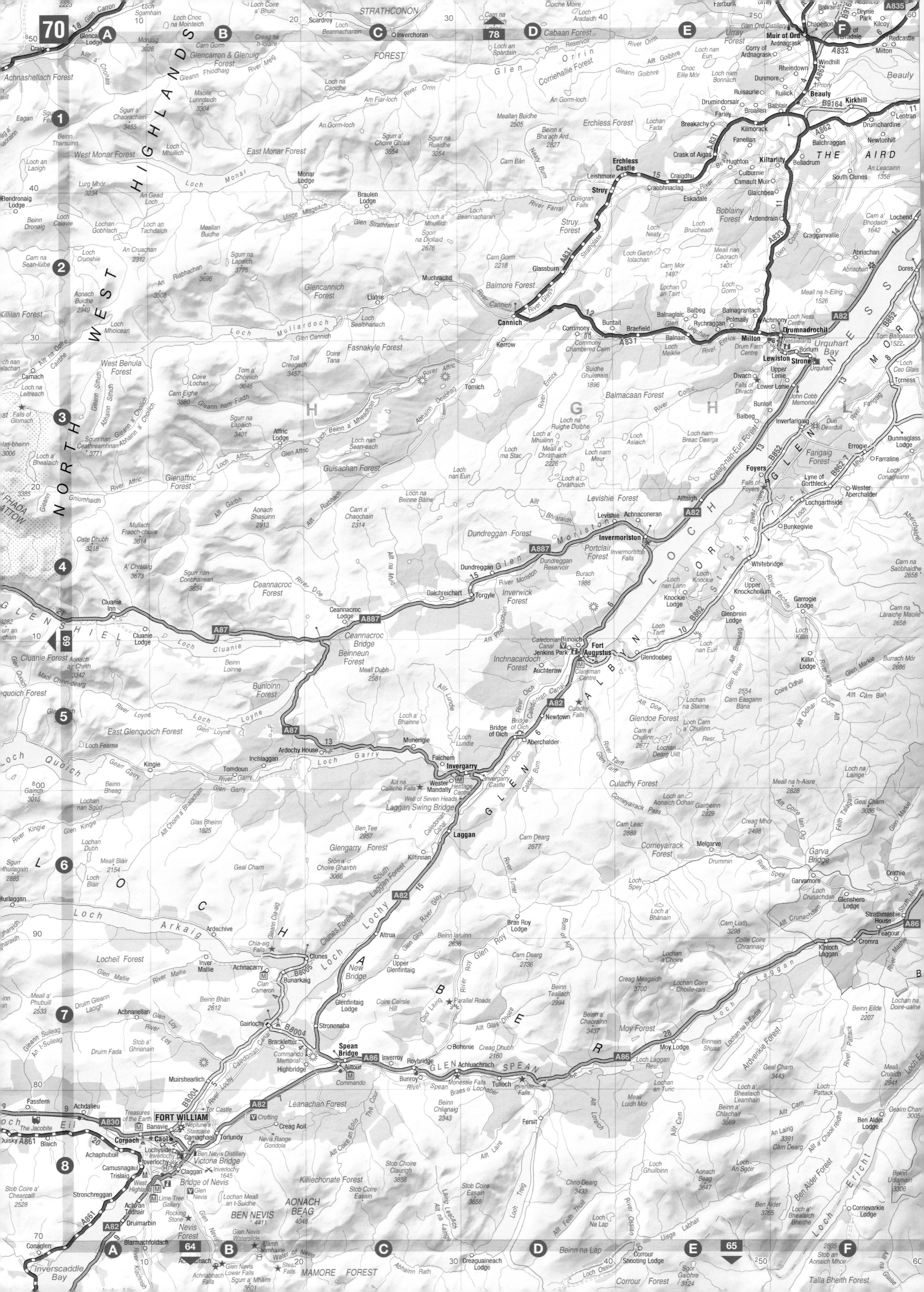
STRATHCONON
FOREST
78
Cabaan Forest
Muir of Ord
Beauly
Kirkhill
THE AIRD
Kiltarlity
Erchless Castle
Struy
Achnashellach Forest
Glencarron & Glenuig Forest
West Monar Forest
East Monar Forest
Loch Monar
NORTH WEST HIGHLANDS
Monar Lodge
Braulen Lodge
Glen Strathfarrar
Erchless Forest
Struy Forest
Glassburn
Glencannich Forest
Balmore Forest
Cannich
Loch Mullardoch
Fasnakyle Forest
Drumnadrochit
Milton
Lewiston
Strone
Urquhart Bay
Balmacaan Forest
West Benula Forest
Guisachan Forest
Glenaffric Forest
Loch Affric
Affric Lodge
Tomich
Invermoriston
Dundreggan Forest
Portclair Forest
Levishie Forest
Foyers
Farigaig Forest
Inverfarigaig
Ceannacroc Forest
Cluanie Inn
A87
A887
Loch Cluanie
GLEN SHIEL
69
Cluanie Forest
Ceannacroc Bridge
Beinneun Forest
Inchnacardoch Forest
Fort Augustus
Bunloinn Forest
East Glenquoich Forest
Loch Quoich
Loch Loyne
Loch Garry
Invergarry
Tomdoun
Inchlaggan
Aberchalder
Glendoe Forest
Culachy Forest
Laggan Swing Bridge
Laggan
Glengarry Forest
South Laggan Forest
Corrieyairack Forest
Corrieyairack Pass
Garva Bridge
Loch Arkaig
Locheil Forest
Clunes Forest
Loch Lochy
Achnacarry
Glen Roy
Parallel Roads
Kinloch Laggan
Loch Laggan
Moy Forest
Ardverikie Forest
Spean Bridge
Glen Spean
Roybridge
Tulloch
Leanachan Forest
FORT WILLIAM
Corpach
Caol
Banavie
Loch Eil
Killiechonate Forest
AONACH BEAG
BEN NEVIS 4411
Nevis Forest
Glen Nevis
Ben Alder Forest
Ben Alder 3765
Loch Ericht
Loch Treig
Chno Dearg 3433
Corrour Shooting Lodge
Corrour Forest
MAMORE FOREST
Talla Bheith Forest
Inverscaddle Bay
64
65
GLEN MOR
LOCH NESS
LOCH OICH
GREAT GLEN
A82
A86
A831
A830
A861
B852
B862

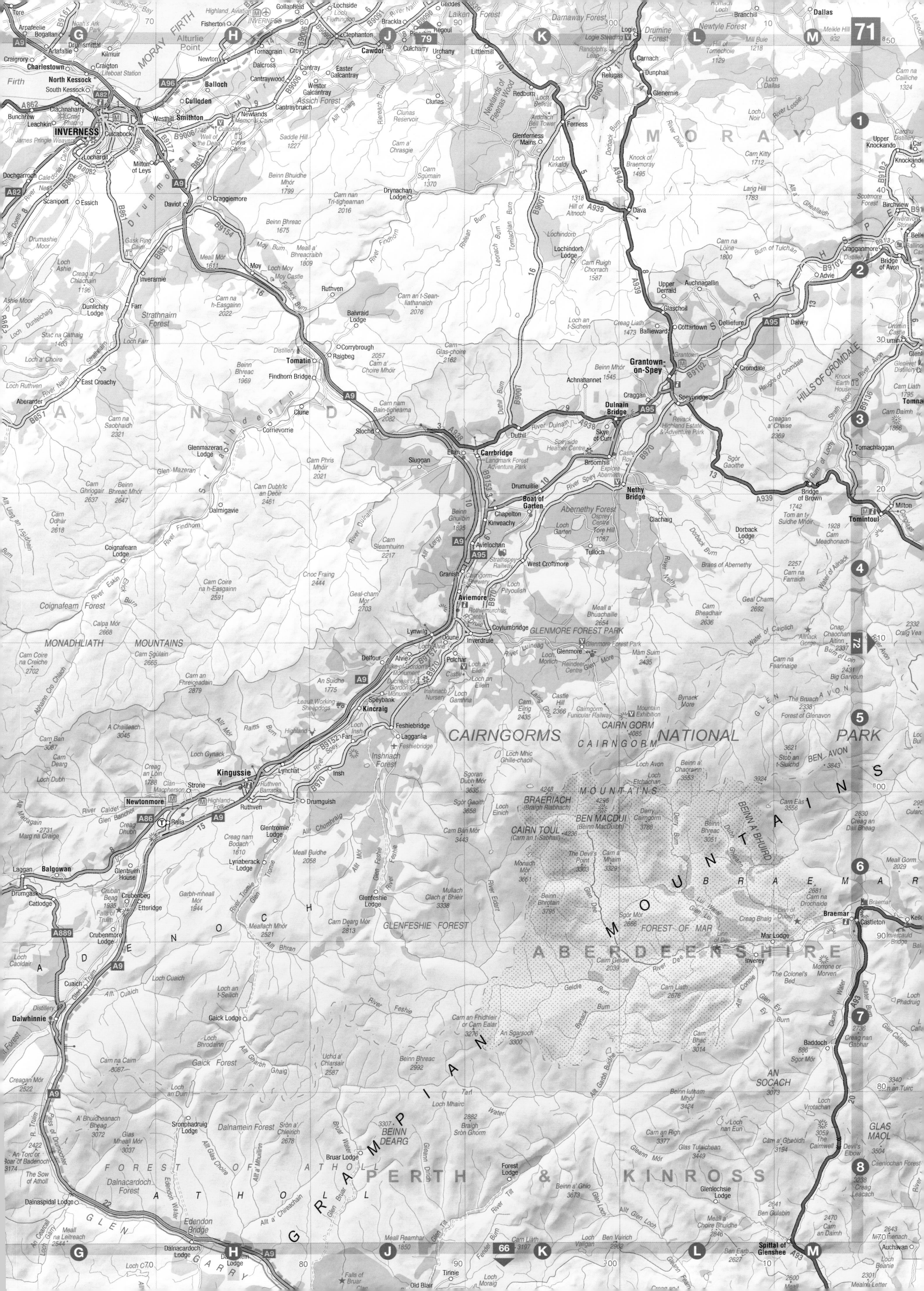

71
MORAY FIRTH
INVERNESS
North Kessock
Charlestown
Culloden
Smithton
Balloch
Cawdor
Croy
Clephanton
Ardersier
Dalcross
Cantraywood
Drumnadrochit
Daviot
Craggiemore
Moy
Inverarnie
Farr
Tomatin
Findhorn Bridge
Corrybrough
Raigbeg
East Croachy
Aberarder
Slochd
Carrbridge
Sluggan
Duthil
Dulnain Bridge
Skye of Curr
Grantown-on-Spey
Speybridge
Cromdale
Dava
Ferness
Glenferness Mains
Logie
Relugas
Dunphail
Glenernie
Lochindorb Lodge
Boat of Garten
Nethy Bridge
Broomhill
Drumuillie
Kinveachy
Avielochan
Granish
Aviemore
Coylumbridge
Inverdruie
Glenmore
Lynwilg
Alvie
Kincraig
Feshiebridge
Insh
Kingussie
Newtonmore
Ralia
Drumguish
Ruthven
Balgowan
Laggan
Catlodge
Etteridge
Crubenmore Lodge
Dalwhinnie
Cuaich
Gaick Lodge
Dalnaspidal Lodge
Dalnacardoch Lodge
Edendon Bridge
Bruar Lodge
Forest Lodge
Glenlochsie Lodge
Spittal of Glenshee
Braemar
Mar Lodge
Inverey
Tomintoul
Bridge of Brown
Tomachlaggan
Dallas
MORAY
HILLS OF CROMDALE
MONADHLIATH MOUNTAINS
CAIRNGORMS NATIONAL PARK
CAIRNGORM MOUNTAINS
GLENMORE FOREST PARK
ABERDEENSHIRE
BRAEMAR
MOUNTAINS
PERTH & KINROSS
GRAMPIAN
FOREST OF ATHOLL
GLENFESHIE FOREST
FOREST OF MAR
BEN MACDUI
CAIRN TOUL
BRAERIACH
CAIRN GORM
BEN AVON
BEINN A' BHUIRD
BEINN DEARG
GLAS MAOL
AN SOCACH
Abernethy Forest
Inshriach Forest
Gaick Forest
Dalnamein Forest
Strathnairn Forest
Coignafearn Forest
A9
A95
A939
A938
A86
A889
A93
A96
B9006
B851
B861
B970
B9152
B9153
B9007
B9102
79
66
72

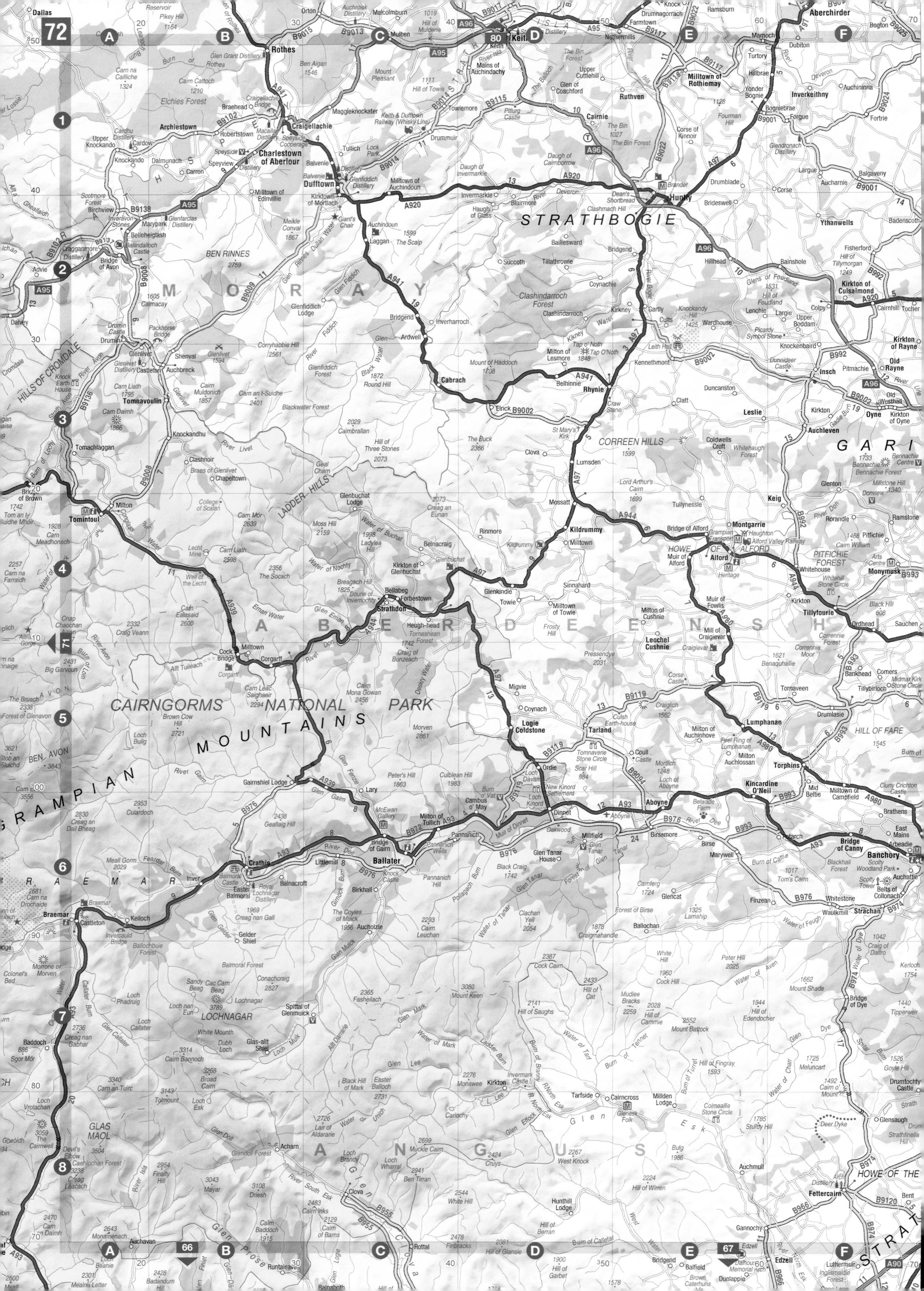

72
A
B
C
D
E
F
1
2
3
4
5
6
7
8
80
71
66
67
Dallas
Rothes
Glen Grant Distillery
Orton
Mulben
Keith
Aberchirder
Elchies Forest
Archiestown
Craigellachie
Charlestown of Aberlour
Dufftown
Huntly
STRATHBOGIE
Milltown of Rothiemay
Inverkeithny
Cairnie
Ruthven
MORAY
Glenlivet
Tomnavoulin
Tomintoul
Clashindarroch Forest
Cabrach
Rhynie
Kildrummy
Lumsden
Mossatt
CORREEN HILLS
Insch
Oyne
Auchleven
Keig
Montgarrie
Alford
HOWE OF ALFORD
Monymusk
PITFICHIE FOREST
Tillyfourie
LADDER HILLS
Glenbuchat Lodge
Bellabeg
Strathdon
Corgarff
Cock Bridge
CAIRNGORMS NATIONAL PARK
MOUNTAINS
GRAMPIAN
ABERDEENSHIRE
Leochel Cushnie
Tarland
Logie Coldstone
Lumphanan
Torphins
Kincardine O'Neil
Aboyne
Dinnet
Ballater
Crathie
Braemar
Banchory
Strachan
BRAEMAR
LOCHNAGAR
GLAS MAOL
ANGUS
Clova
Tarfside
Edzell
Fettercairn
HOWE OF THE
Glen Esk
A95
A96
A97
A920
A941
A939
A944
A980
A93
B976
A90

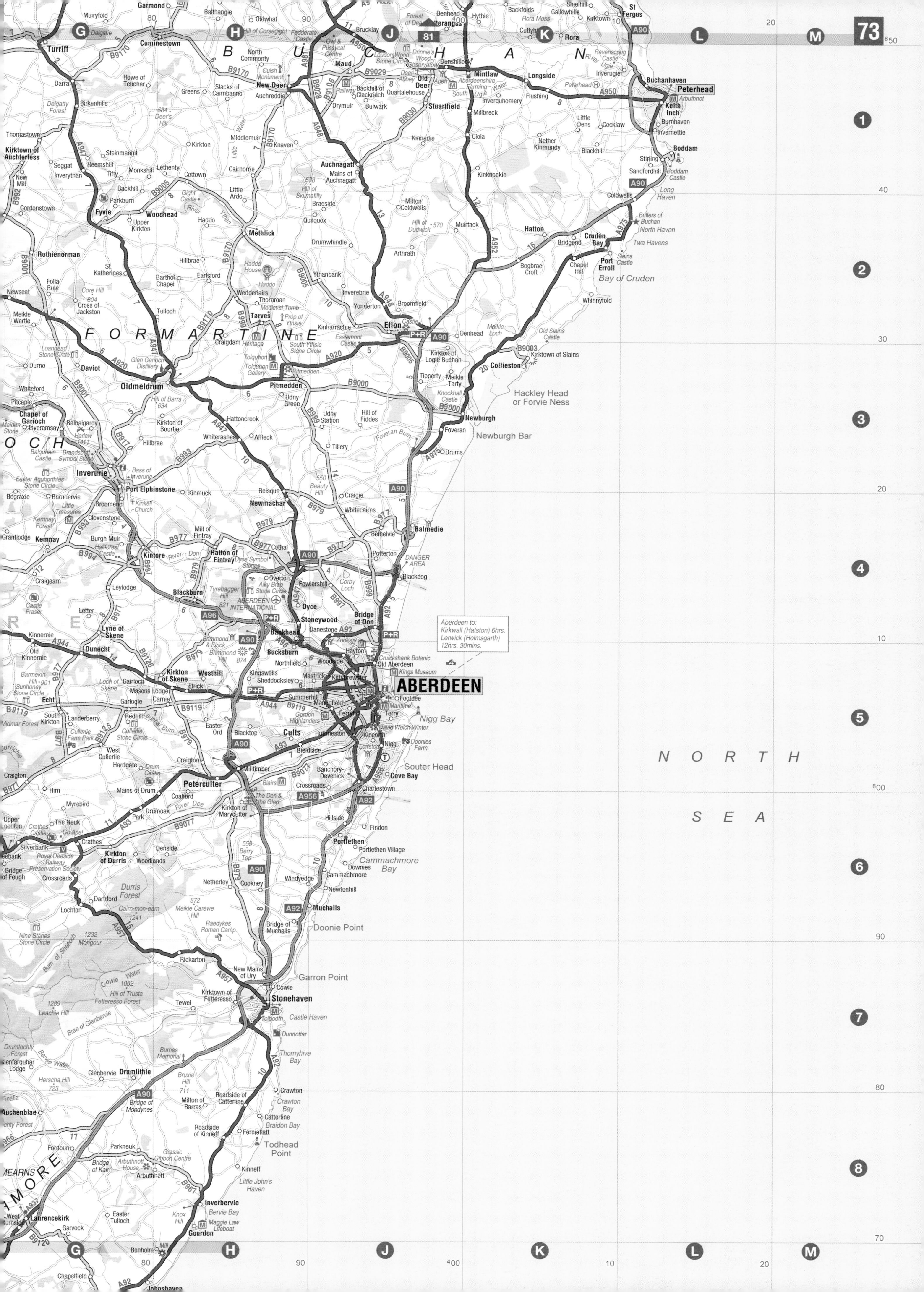
G
H
J
K
L
M
BUCHAN
FORMARTINE
NORTH SEA
ABERDEEN
Aberdeen to:
Kirkwall (Hatston) 6hrs.
Lerwick (Holmsgarth) 12hrs. 30mins.
Turriff
Cuminestown
Garmond
Muiryfold
Balthangie
Oldwhat
Hill of Corsegight
Fedderate Castle
Brucklay
Forest of Deer
Denhead
Mintlaw
Hythie
Backfolds
Gallowhills
Shielhill
St Fergus
Rora Moss
Kirktown
Cuttyhill
Rora
Ravenscraig Castle
River Ugie
Inverugie
Buchanhaven
Peterhead
Keith Inch
Arbuthnot
Burnhaven
Invernettie
Boddam
Boddam Castle
Stirling
Sandfordhill
Long Haven
Coldwells
Bullers of Buchan
North Haven
Twa Havens
Slains Castle
Port Erroll
Cruden Bay
Bay of Cruden
Bridgend
Hatton
Chapel Hill
Whinnyfold
Bogbrae Croft
Longside
Flushing
Little Dens
Cocklaw
Nether Kinmundy
Blackhill
Inverquhomery
Millbreck
Clola
Kinknockie
Muirtack
Stuartfield
Kinnadie
Dunshillock
Old Deer
Aden
Aberdeenshire Farming Museum
South Ugie Water
Maud
Owl & Pussycat Centre
Loudon Wood Stone Circle
Drinnie's Wood Observatory
Deer Abbey
Backhill of Clackriach
Quartalehouse
Drymuir
Bulwark
New Deer
Auchreddie
North Commonty
Culsh Monument
Howe of Teuchar
Slacks of Cairnbanno
Greens
Darra
Delgatty Forest
Birkenhills
Deer's Hill
Thomastown
Kirktown of Auchterless
Steinmanhill
Seggat
Reemshill
Inverythan
Tifty
Monkshill
Lethenty
Cottown
Gight Castle
River Ythan
Backhill
Parkburn
Fyvie
Woodhead
Upper Kirkton
Gordonstown
New Mill
Middlemuir
Knaven
Kirkton
Cairnorrie
Little Ardo
Haddo
Methlick
Auchnagatt
Mains of Auchnagatt
Hill of Skilmafilly
Braeside
Quilquox
Milton of Coldwells
Hill of Dudwick
Drumwhindle
Arthrath
Rothienorman
St Katherines
Hillbrae
Barthol Chapel
Earlsford
Haddo House
Ythanbank
Inverebrie
Yonderton
Broomfield
Folla Rule
Newseat
Core Hill
Cross of Jackston
Meikle Wartle
Tulloch
Wedderlairs
Thornroan
Medieval Tomb
Prop of Ythsie
Tarves
Kinharrachie
Ellon
Castle
Denhead
Meikle Loch
Old Slains Castle
Kirktown of Slains
Collieston
Craigdam
Heritage
Esslemont Castle
South Ythsie Stone Circle
Loanhead Stone Circle
Durno
Daviot
Glen Garioch Distillery
Oldmeldrum
Tolquhon
Tolquhon Gallery
Pitmedden
Udny Green
Kirkton of Logie Buchan
Tipperty
Meikle Tarty
Knockhall Castle
Hackley Head or Forvie Ness
Whiteford
Pitcaple
Chapel of Garioch
Maiden Stone
Inveramsay
Balhalgardy
Harlaw
Hill of Barra
Kirkton of Bourtie
Hillbrae
Hattoncrook
Whiterashes
Affleck
Udny Station
Hill of Fiddes
Foveran Burn
Newburgh
Foveran
Newburgh Bar
Tillery
Drums
Balquhain Castle
Brandsbutt Symbol Stone
Inverurie
Bass of Inverurie
Easter Aquhorthies Stone Circle
Port Elphinstone
Kinmuck
Beauty Hill
Craigie
Reisque
Newmachar
Whitecairns
Bograxie
Burnhervie
Little Treasures
Broomend
Kinkell Church
Kemnay Forest
Clovenstone
Grantlodge
Kemnay
Burgh Muir
Hallforest Castle
Mill of Fintray
Hatton of Fintray
Cothal
Belhelvie
Balmedie
Potterton
DANGER AREA
Kintore
River Don
Dyce Symbol Stones
Corby Loch
Blackdog
Craigearn
Leyiodge
Overton
Aiky Brae Stone Circle
Fowlershill
Tyrebagger Hill
ABERDEEN INTERNATIONAL
Dyce
Castle Fraser
Letter
Blackburn
Stoneywood
Bridge of Don
Lyne of Skene
Bankhead
Danestone
Kinnernie
Old Kinnernie
Dunecht
Brimmond & Elrick
Brimmond Hill
Bucksburn
Hayton
Zoology
Northfield
Woodside
Cruickshank Botanic
Old Aberdeen
Kings Museum
Barmekin Hill
Sunhoney Stone Circle
Echt
Loch of Skene
Gairloch
Kirkton of Skene
Westhill
Elrick
Kingswells
Sheddocksley
Mastrick
Kittybrewster
Masons Lodge
Carnie
Garlogie
Summerhill
Mannofield
Footdee
Maritime
Torry
Gordon Highlanders
Ferryhill
Nigg Bay
Midmar Forest
South Kirkton
Landerberry
Redhill
Leuchar Burn
Easter Ord
Blacktop
Cults
Ruthieston
David Welch Winter
Kincorth
Loirston
Nigg
Doonies Farm
Cullerlie Farm Park
Cullerlie Stone Circle
West Cullerlie
Bieldside
Hardgate
Drum Castle
Craigton
Milltimber
Souter Head
Cove Bay
Banchory-Devenick
Blairs
Crossroads
Charlestown
Hirn
Mains of Drum
Peterculter
Coalford
Drumoak
River Dee
The Den & the Glen
Kirkton of Maryculter
Myrebird
Park
The Neuk
Upper Lochton
Crathes Castle
Go Ape!
Crathes
Silverbank
Hillside
Findon
Portlethen
Portlethen Village
Royal Deeside Railway Preservation Society
Banchory
Bridge of Feugh
Kirkton of Durris
Woodlands
Denside
Berry Top
Downies
Cammachmore
Cammachmore Bay
Crossroads
Netherley
Cookney
Windyedge
Newtonhill
Durris Forest
Damford
Lochton
Meikle Carewe Hill
Cairn-mon-earn
Raedykes Roman Camp
Muchalls
Bridge of Muchalls
Doonie Point
Nine Stanes Stone Circle
Mongour
Burn of Sheeoch
Rickarton
New Mains of Ury
Garron Point
Cowie Water
Cowie
Hill of Trusta
Fetteresso Forest
Kirktown of Fetteresso
Tewel
Stonehaven
Castle Haven
Tolbooth
Dunnottar
Leachie Hill
Brae of Glenbervie
Burnes Memorial
Thornyhive Bay
Drumtochty Forest
Bervie Water
Glenfarquhar Lodge
Glenbervie
Drumlithie
Herscha Hill
Bruxie Hill
Crawton
Crawton Bay
Finalla
Bridge of Mondynes
Milton of Barras
Roadside of Catterline
Catterline
Braidon Bay
Auchenblae
Roadside of Kinneff
Fernieflatt
Todhead Point
Fordoun
Parkneuk
Grassic Gibbon Centre
Bridge of Kair
Arbuthnott House
Arbuthnott
Kinneff
Little John's Haven
MEARNS
HOWE O' THE MEARNS
Inverbervie
Bervie Bay
Knox Hill
Maggie Law Lifeboat
Gourdon
Easter Tulloch
West Burnside
Laurencekirk
Garvock
Benholm
Mill
Chapelfield
Johnshaven
A90
A92
A93
A96
A947
A948
A950
A952
A956
A957
A975
A920
A944
A981
B9170
B9005
B9029
B9030
B9106
B9028
B9001
B9000
B9003
B993
B999
B979
B977
B994
B987
B997
B9119
B9126
B9077
B9120
B967
P+R
81
1
2
3
4
5
6
7
8
850
40
30
20
10
800
90
80
70
400

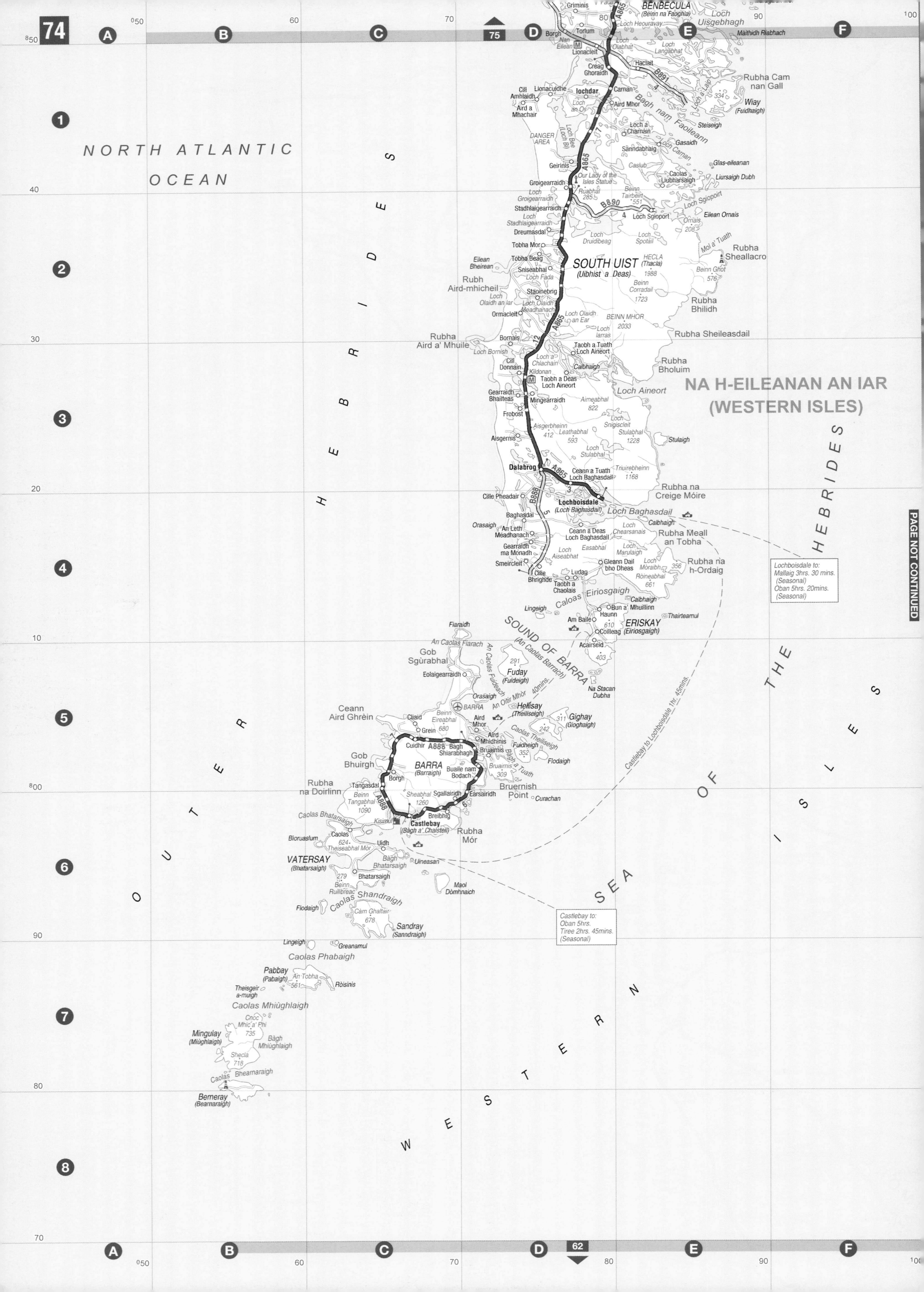
NORTH ATLANTIC OCEAN
OUTER HEBRIDES
SEA OF THE HEBRIDES
WESTERN ISLES
NA H-EILEANAN AN IAR (WESTERN ISLES)
BENBECULA (Beinn na Faoghla)
SOUTH UIST (Uibhist a Deas)
Iochdar
Lochboisdale (Loch Baghasdail)
Loch Baghasdail
Dalabrog
ERISKAY (Eiriosgaigh)
SOUND OF BARRA (An Caolas Barrach)
BARRA (Barraigh)
Castlebay (Bàgh a' Chaisteil)
VATERSAY (Bhatarsaigh)
Sandray (Sanndraigh)
Pabbay (Pabaigh)
Mingulay (Miùghlaigh)
Berneray (Bearnaraigh)
Lochboisdale to: Mallaig 3hrs. 30 mins. (Seasonal) Oban 5hrs. 20mins. (Seasonal)
Castlebay to: Oban 5hrs. Tiree 2hrs. 45mins. (Seasonal)
Castlebay to Lochboisdale 1hr. 45mins.
PAGE NOT CONTINUED
75
62

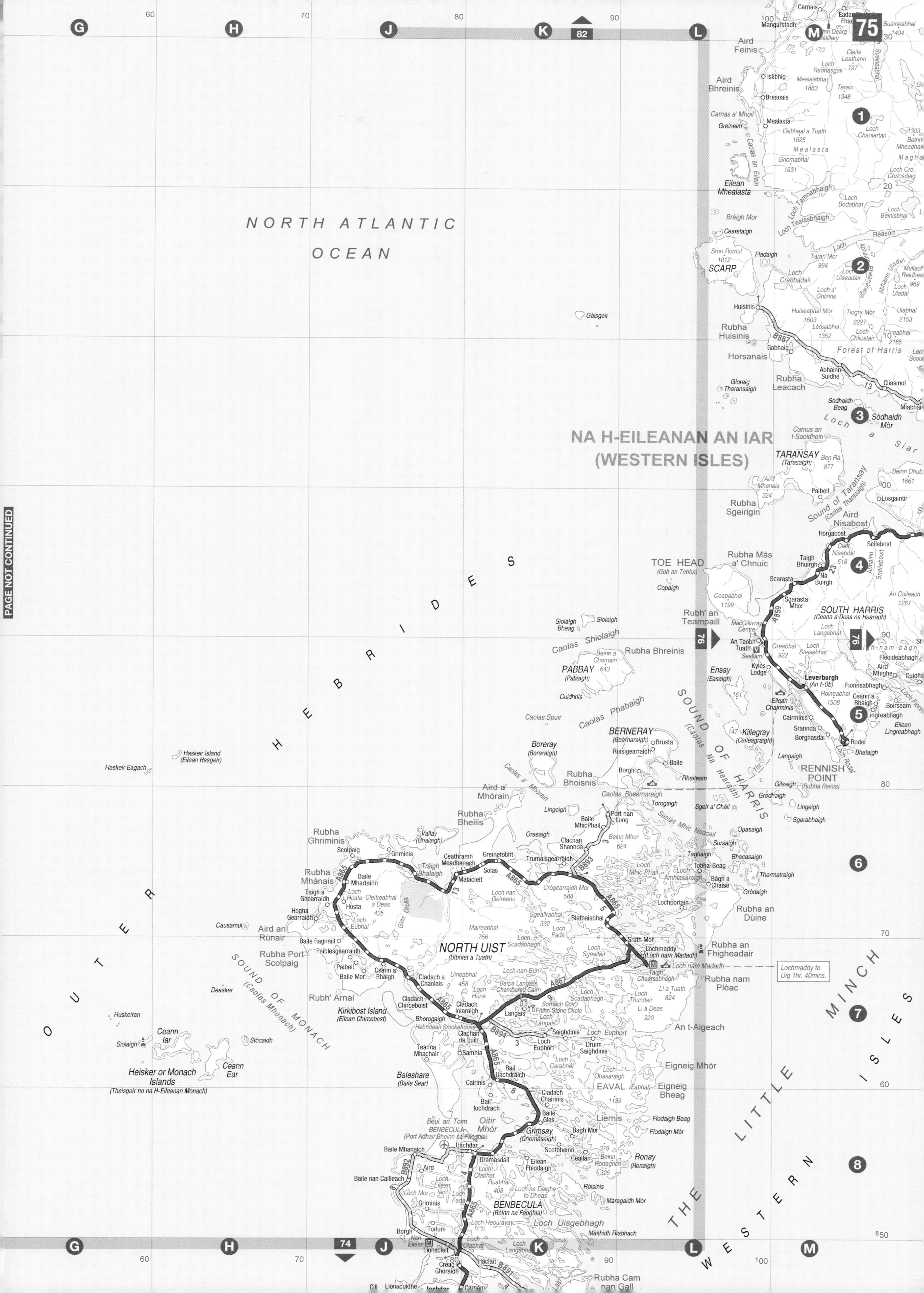
NORTH ATLANTIC
OCEAN
OUTER HEBRIDES
NA H-EILEANAN AN IAR
(WESTERN ISLES)
PAGE NOT CONTINUED
82
74
76
SOUND OF HARRIS
SOUND OF MONACH
(Caolas Mhonach)
THE LITTLE MINCH
WESTERN ISLES
Mangurstadh
Aird Feinis
Islibhig
Aird Bhreinis
Breanais
Mealasta
Mealaisbha 1883
Tarain 1348
Loch Chaolartan
Eilean Mhealasta
Caolas an Eilein
Bràigh Mor
Cearstaigh
Sron Romul 1012
SCARP
Fladaigh
Loch Tealasbhaigh
Rèasort
Huisinis
Rubha Huisinis
B887
Gobhaig
Horsanais
Forest of Harris
Abhainn Suidhe
Cliasmol
Gloraig Tharansaigh
Rubha Leacach
Sòdhaidh Beag
Sòdhaidh Mòr
Loch a Siar
Gàisgeir
TARANSAY
(Tarasaigh)
Ben Ra 877
Paibeil
Sound of Taransay
(Caolas Tharasaigh)
Rubha Sgeirigin
Aird Nisabost
Horgabost
Seilebost
Losgaintir
TOE HEAD
(Gob an Tobha)
Rubha Màs a' Chnuic
Taigh Bhuirgh
Na Buirgh
Scarasta
Ceapabhal 1199
Sgarasta Mhor
SOUTH HARRIS
(Ceann a Deas na Hearadh)
Rubh' an Teampaill
MacGillivray Centre
An Taobh Tuath
Seallam!
Kyles Lodge
Leverburgh
(An t-Ob)
Fionnsabhagh
Roineabhal 1508
Ensay
(Easaigh)
Killegray
(Ceileagraigh)
Eilean Chaluim Chille
Srannda
Borghasdal
Rodel
Bhalaigh
Langaigh
RENNISH POINT
(Rubha Reinis)
Gilsaigh
Grodhaigh
Lingeigh
Sgarabhaigh
Siolaigh Bheag
Siolaigh
Caolas Shiolaigh
PABBAY
(Pabaigh)
Rubha Bhreinis
Cuidhnis
Caolas Spuir
Caolas Phabaigh
Boreray
(Boraraigh)
BERNERAY
(Bearnaraigh)
Brusta
Ruisigearraidh
Baile
Borgh
Rhaiteam
Rubha Bhoisnis
Caolas Bhearnaraigh
Torogaigh
Sgeir a' Chàil
Caolas a' Mhòrain
Aird a' Mhòrain
Rubha Bheilis
Lingeigh
Port nan Long
Baile MhicPhail
Vallay
(Bhalaigh)
Orasaigh
Clachan Shannda
Beinn Mhor 624
Opasaigh
Sursaigh
Rubha Ghriminis
Scolpaig
Griminis
Ceathramh Meadhanach
Greinetobht
Trumaisgearraidh
Taghaigh
Tobha-Beag
Bhacasaigh
Rubha Mhànais
Baile Mhartainn
Tràigh Bhalaigh
Solas
Malacleit
Loch Hosta
Hosta
Cleitreabhal a Deas 435
Taigh a Ghearraidh
Hogha Gearraidh
Loch Eubhal
Glen Drolla
Crògearraidh Mor 588
Blathaisbhal
Lochportain
Thermatraigh
Grodaigh
Rubha an Dùine
Causamul
Aird an Rùnair
Baile Raghaill
Paiblesgearraidh
Rubha Port Scolpaig
Maireabhal 756
NORTH UIST
(Uibhist a Tuath)
Sruth Mor
Lochmaddy
(Loch nam Madadh)
Rubha an Fhigheadair
Loch nam Madadh
Lochmaddy to Uig 1hr. 40mins.
Paibeil
Baile Mor
Ceann a Bhaigh
Cladach a Chaolais
Uineabhal 458
Barpa Langass Chambered Cairn
A867
Rubha nam Plèac
Li a Tuath 824
Li a Deas 920
Deasker
Rubh' Arnal
Cladach Chirceboist
Cladach Iolaraigh
Langais
Sornach Coir Fhinn Stone Circle
Kirkibost Island
(Eilean Chirceboist)
Bhorogaigh
Hebridean Smokehouse
Clachan na Luib
A865
B894
Saighdinis
Loch Euphort
Druim Saighdinis
An t-Aigeach
Huskeiran
Ceann Iar
Siolaigh
Stòcaidh
Ceann Ear
Heisker or Monach Islands
(Theisgeir no na H-Eileanan Monach)
Haskeir Island
(Eilean Hasgeir)
Haskeir Eagach
Teanna Mhachair
Samhla
Baleshare
(Baile Sear)
Bail Uachdrach
Cairinis
Eigneig Mhòr
Eigneig Bheag
EAVAL
(Eabhal)
1139
Cladach Chairinis
Bail' Iochdrach
Baile Glas
Liernis
Flodaigh Beag
Flodaigh Mòr
Beul an Toim
BENBECULA
(Port Adhair Bheinn na Faoghla)
Oitir Mhòr
Grimsay
(Griomasaigh)
Bagh Mor
Uachdar
Scotbheinn
Ceallan
Ronay
(Ronaigh)
Baile Mhanaich
Gramasdail
Eilean Fhlodaigh
Aird
B892
Baile nan Cailleach
Loch Olabhat
Ruabhal 408
Rosinis
Loch Mor
Griminis
BENBECULA
(Beinn na Faoghla)
Maragaidh Mòr
Torlum
Loch Heouravay
Loch Uisgebhagh
Borgh
Nan Eilean
Lionacleit
Maithidh Riabhach
Creag Ghoraidh
Haclait
B891
Rubha Cam nan Gall
Lionacuidhe
Iochdar
Carnan
G
H
J
K
L
M
1
2
3
4
5
6
7
8
60
70
80
90
100

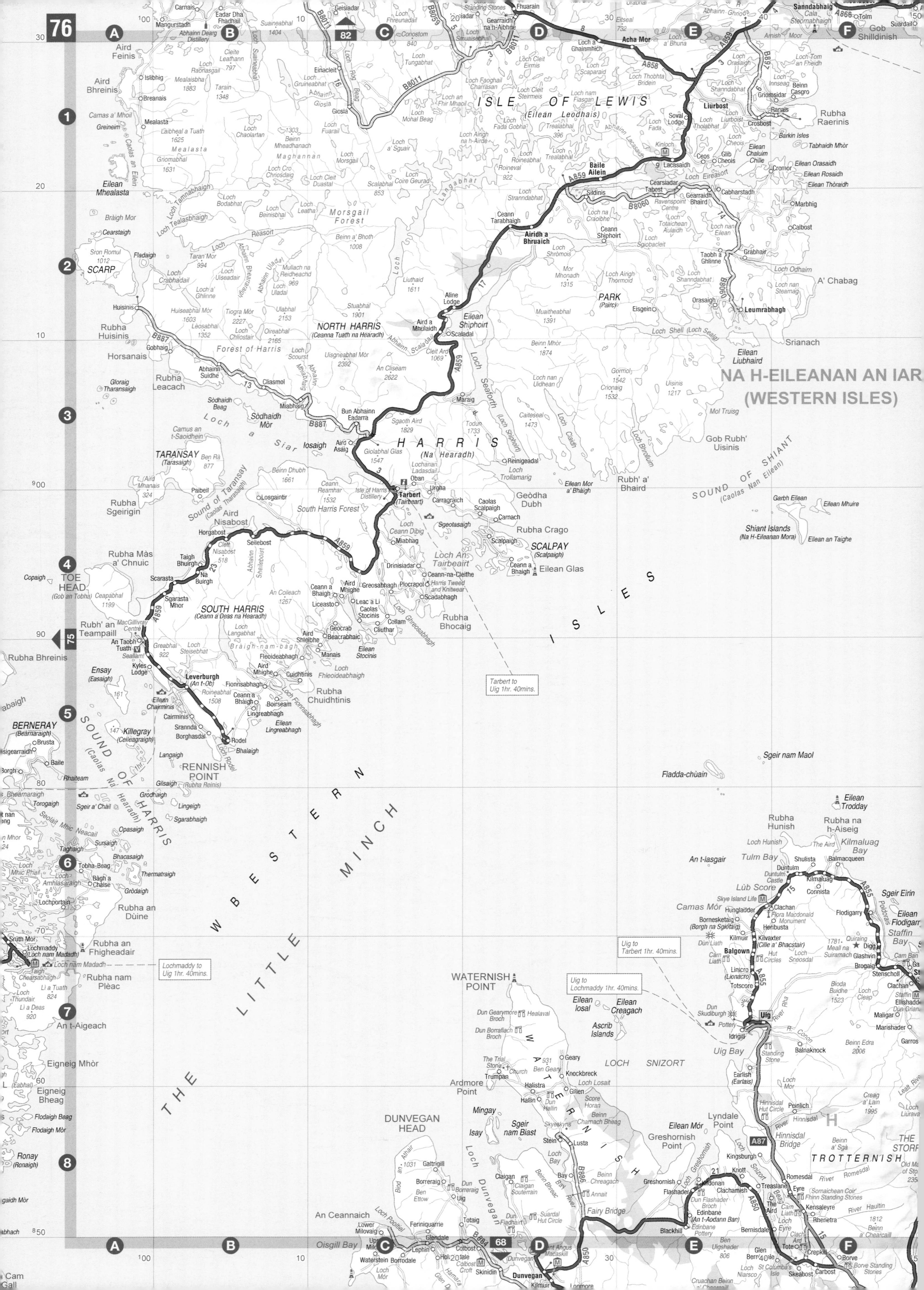

ISLE OF LEWIS
(Eilean Leodhais)
NA H-EILEANAN AN IAR
(WESTERN ISLES)
NORTH HARRIS
(Ceanna Tuath na Hearadh)
HARRIS
(Na Hearadh)
SOUTH HARRIS
(Ceann a Deas na Hearadh)
PARK
(Pairc)
Morsgail Forest
Forest of Harris
South Harris Forest
SOUND OF SHIANT
(Caolas Nan Eilean)
Shiant Islands
(Na H-Eileanan Mora)
Garbh Eilean
Eilean Mhuire
Eilean an Taighe
SOUND OF HARRIS
(Caolas Na Hearadh)
THE LITTLE MINCH
WESTERN ISLES
SCARP
TARANSAY
(Tarasaigh)
SCALPAY
(Scalpaigh)
Eilean Glas
BERNERAY
(Bearnaraigh)
Killegray
(Ceileagraigh)
Ensay
(Easaigh)
TOE HEAD
(Gob an Tobha)
RENNISH POINT
(Rubha Reinis)
Tarbert
(Tairbeart)
Leverburgh
(An t-Ob)
Rodel
Liurbost
Leumrabhagh
Baile Ailein
Acha Mor
Airidh a Bhruaich
Balgownie
Uig
Dunvegan
Isle of Harris Distillery
Harris Tweed and Knitwear
Tarbert to Uig 1hr. 40mins.
Uig to Tarbert 1hr. 40mins.
Uig to Lochmaddy 1hr. 40mins.
Lochmaddy to Uig 1hr. 40mins.
Lochmaddy
(Loch nam Madadh)
WATERNISH POINT
WATERNISH
LOCH SNIZORT
DUNVEGAN HEAD
Loch Dunvegan
TROTTERNISH
Uig Bay
Camas Mòr
Tulm Bay
Kilmaluag Bay
Staffin Bay
Fladda-chùain
Sgeir nam Maol
Eilean Trodday
Rubha Hunish
Rubha na h-Aiseig
Ascrib Islands
Eilean Mór
Greshornish Point
Lyndale Point
Fairy Bridge
Skye Island Life
Flora Macdonald Monument
Ardmore Point
Mingay
Isay
Oisgill Bay
A859
A858
B8060
B887
A855
A850
A87
B886
B884
82
68
75

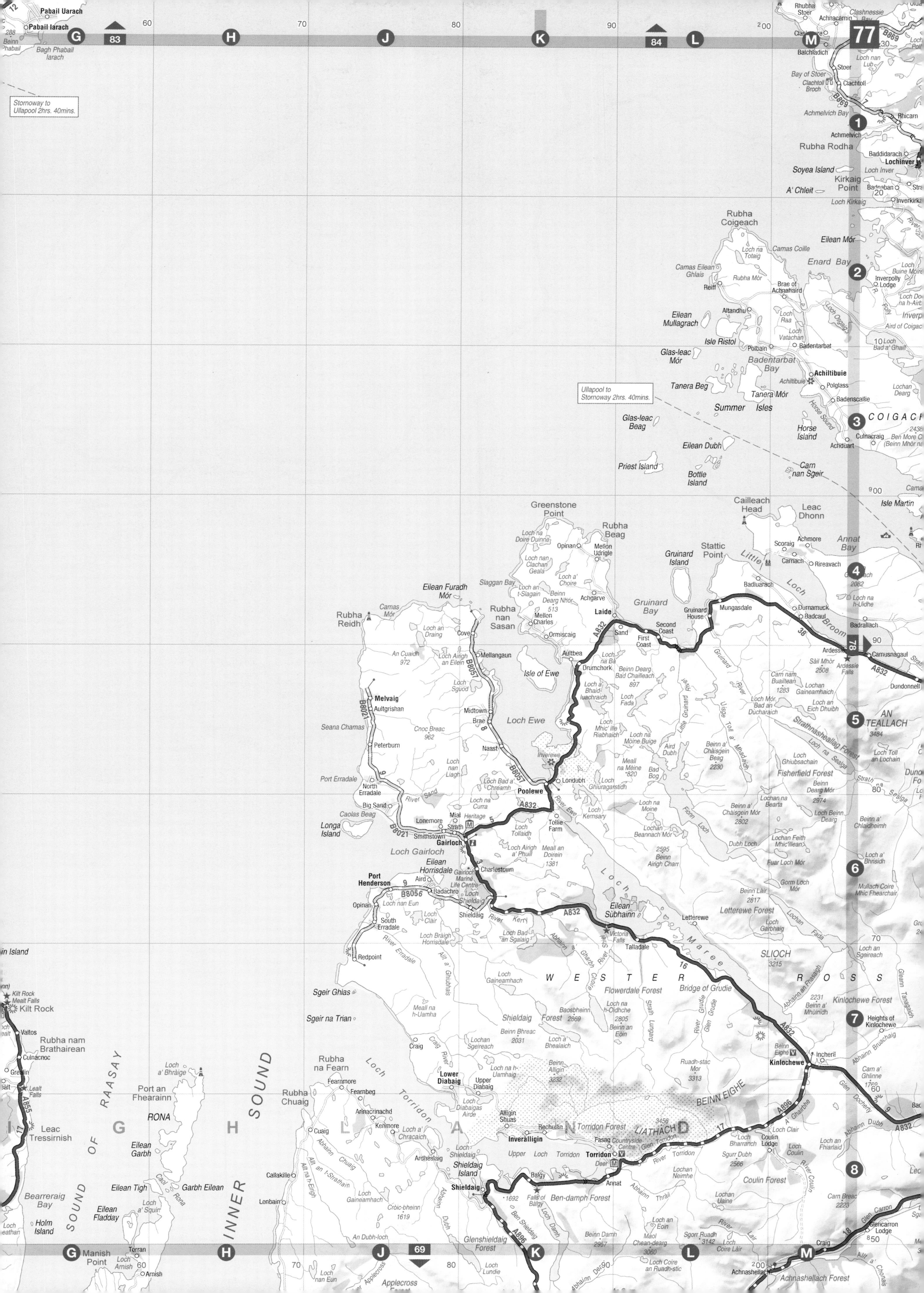

77
Pabail Uarach
Pabail Iarach
Bagh Phabail Iarach
83
84
60
70
80
90
200
Stornoway to Ullapool 2hrs. 40mins.
Ullapool to Stornoway 2hrs. 40mins.
Rhubha Stoer
Achnacarnin
Clashnessie Bay
Balchladich
Loch nan Lub
Bay of Stoer
Stoer
Clachtoll Broch
Clachtoll
B869
Achmelvich Bay
Rhicarn
Achmelvich
Rubha Rodha
Baddidarach
Lochinver
Soyea Island
Loch Inver
Kirkaig Point
A' Chleit
Badnaban
Strathan
Loch Kirkaig
Inverkirkaig
Rubha Coigeach
Loch na Totaig
Camas Coille
Eilean Mór
Enard Bay
Camas Eilean Ghlais
Rubha Mór
Brae of Achnahaird
Reiff
Loch Buine Moire
Inverpolly Lodge
Altandhu
Loch Raa
Eilean Mullagrach
Loch Vatachan
Isle Ristol
Polbain
Badentarbat
Aird of Coigach
Glas-leac Mór
Badentarbat Bay
Achiltibuie
Tanera Beg
Polglass
Tanera Mór
Summer Isles
Badenscallie
Lochan Dearg
Horse Sound
Glas-leac Beag
COIGACH
Horse Island
Culnacraig
Ben More Coigach
Eilean Dubh
Achduart
Priest Island
Bottle Island
Carn nan Sgeir
Cailleach Head
Isle Martin
Greenstone Point
Leac Dhonn
Rubha Beag
Loch na Doire Duinne
Opinan
Mellon Udrigle
Scoraig
Achmore
Annat Bay
Loch nan Clachan Geala
Gruinard Island
Stattic Point
Carnach
Rireavach
Little Loch Broom
Slaggan Bay
Loch a' Choire
Badluarach
Eilean Furadh Mór
Loch an t-Slagain
Beinn Dearg Mhór 513
Achgarve
Gruinard Bay
Camas Mór
Rubha nan Sasan
Mellon Charles
Laide
Mungasdale
Durnamuck
Badcaul
Rubha Reidh
Gruinard House
Second Coast
Badrallach
Loch an Draing
Cove
Ormiscaig
Sand
First Coast
Ardessie
Camusnagaul
An Cuaidh 972
Loch Airigh an Eilein
Mellangaun
Aultbea
Loch na Ba
Drumchork
Beinn Dearg Bad Chailleach 897
Sàil Mhór 2508
Ardessie Falls
A832
Dundonnell
B8057
Isle of Ewe
Loch Sguod
Loch a' Bhaid-luachraich
Loch Fada
Carn nam Buailtean 1283
Lochan Gaineamhaich
Melvaig
Aultgrishan
B8021
Midtown
Loch Mór Bad an Ducharaich
Loch an Eich Dhuibh
Brae
Loch Ewe
AN TEALLACH 3484
Seana Chamas
Cnoc Breac 962
Loch Mhic' ille Riabhaich
Loch na Móine Buige
Strathnasheallag Forest
Peterburn
Naast
Aird Dubh
Little Gruinard River
Loch na Sealga
Beinn a' Chàisgein Beag 2230
Loch Toll an Lochain
Loch nan Liagh
Inverewe
Meall na Mèine 820
Bad Bog
Loch Ghiubsachain
Port Erradale
Loch Bad a' Chreamh
Londubh
Loch Ghiuragarstidh
Fisherfield Forest
North Erradale
Poolewe
Beinn Dearg Mór 2974
Big Sand
River Sand
Loch na Curra
A832
Loch na Moine
Lochan na Bearta
Caolas Beag
Loch Kernsary
Beinn a' Chàisgein Mór 2802
Beinn a' Chlaidheimh
Longa Island
Lonemore
Mial
Heritage
Strath
Tollie Farm
Lochan Beannach Mór
Loch Beinn Dearg
Smithstown
Gairloch
Loch Tollaidh
Loch Airigh a' Phuill
Meall an Doirein 1381
2595 Beinn Airigh Charr
Dubh Loch
Lochan Feith Mhic'illean
Loch Gairloch
Eilean Horrisdale
Charlestown
Fuar Loch Mór
Loch a' Bhrisidh
Port Henderson
Gairloch Marine Life Centre
Aird
Gorm Loch Mór
Mullach Coire Mhic Fhearchair
B8056
Badachro
Loch Shieldaig
Beinn Lair 2817
Opinan
Loch nan Eun
Letterewe
Letterewe Forest
Loch Garbhaig
South Erradale
Loch Clair
Shieldaig
River Kerry
A832
Eilean Subhainn
Loch Braigh Horrisdale
Loch Bad an Sgalaig
Victoria Falls
Talladale
SLIOCH 3215
Loch an Sgeireach
Redpoint
River Erradale
Allt a' Ghiubhais
Abhainn a' Gharbh Choire
Loch Maree
Loch Gaineamhach
W E S T E R R O S S
Bridge of Grudie
Flowerdale Forest
Abhainn an Fhasaigh
Kinlochewe Forest
Sgeir Ghias
Meall na h-Uamha
Loch na h-Oidhche
2231 Beinn a' Mhùinidh
Strath Lungard
Baosbheinn 2869
Heights of Kinlochewe
Sgeir na Trian
Shieldaig Forest
2805 Beinn an Eoin
River Grudie
Glen Grudie
Beinn Bhreac 2031
Loch a' Bhealaich
Craig
Lochan Sgeireach
Beinn Eighe
Incheril
Kinlochewe
Rubha na Fearn
Loch na h-Uamhaig
Beinn Alligin 3232
Ruadh-stac Mor 3313
Carn a' Ghlinne 1769
Fearnmore
Lower Diabaig
Upper Diabaig
Fearnbeg
Loch Diabaigas Airde
BEINN EIGHE
Rubha Chuaig
Arinacrinachd
Loch Torridon
Alligin Shuas
A896
Kenmore
Loch a' Chracaich
Rechullin
Torridon Forest
LIATHACH 3456
Glen Docherty
Cuaig
Inveralligin
Fasag
Countryside Centre
Glen Torridon
Loch Clair
Coulin Lodge
Loch Bharranch
Loch Coulin
Loch an Fhiarlaid
Ardheslaig
Upper Loch Torridon
Torridon
Deer
River Torridon
Sgurr Dubh 2566
Loch Shieldaig
Shieldaig Island
Callakille
Balgy
Annat
Loch Neimhe
Coulin Forest
Shieldaig
Falls of Balgy
Ben-damph Forest
Lonbain
Loch Gaineamhach
Cròic-bheinn 1619
Ben Shieldaig
Loch Damh
Lochan Uaine
Carn Breac 2223
Glencarron Lodge
Loch an Eoin
Beinn Damh 2957
Maol Chean-dearg 3060
Sgorr Ruadh 3142
Loch Coire Làir
Glen Carron
An Dubh-loch
Glenshieldaig Forest
Craig
Achnashellach
Loch Coire an Ruadh-stac
Achnashellach Forest
Loch nan Eun
Applecross
Loch Lundie
69
Kilt Rock
Mealt Falls
Valtos
Rubha nam Brathairean
Culnacnoc
Loch a' Bhràige
Port an Fhearainn
RONA
A855
Leac Tressirnish
Eilean Garbh
SOUND OF RAASAY
INNER SOUND
Eilean Tigh
Garbh Eilean
Bearreraig Bay
Eilean Fladday
Loch a' Squir
Holm Island
Manish Point
Torran
Loch Arnish
Arnish
H I G H L A N D

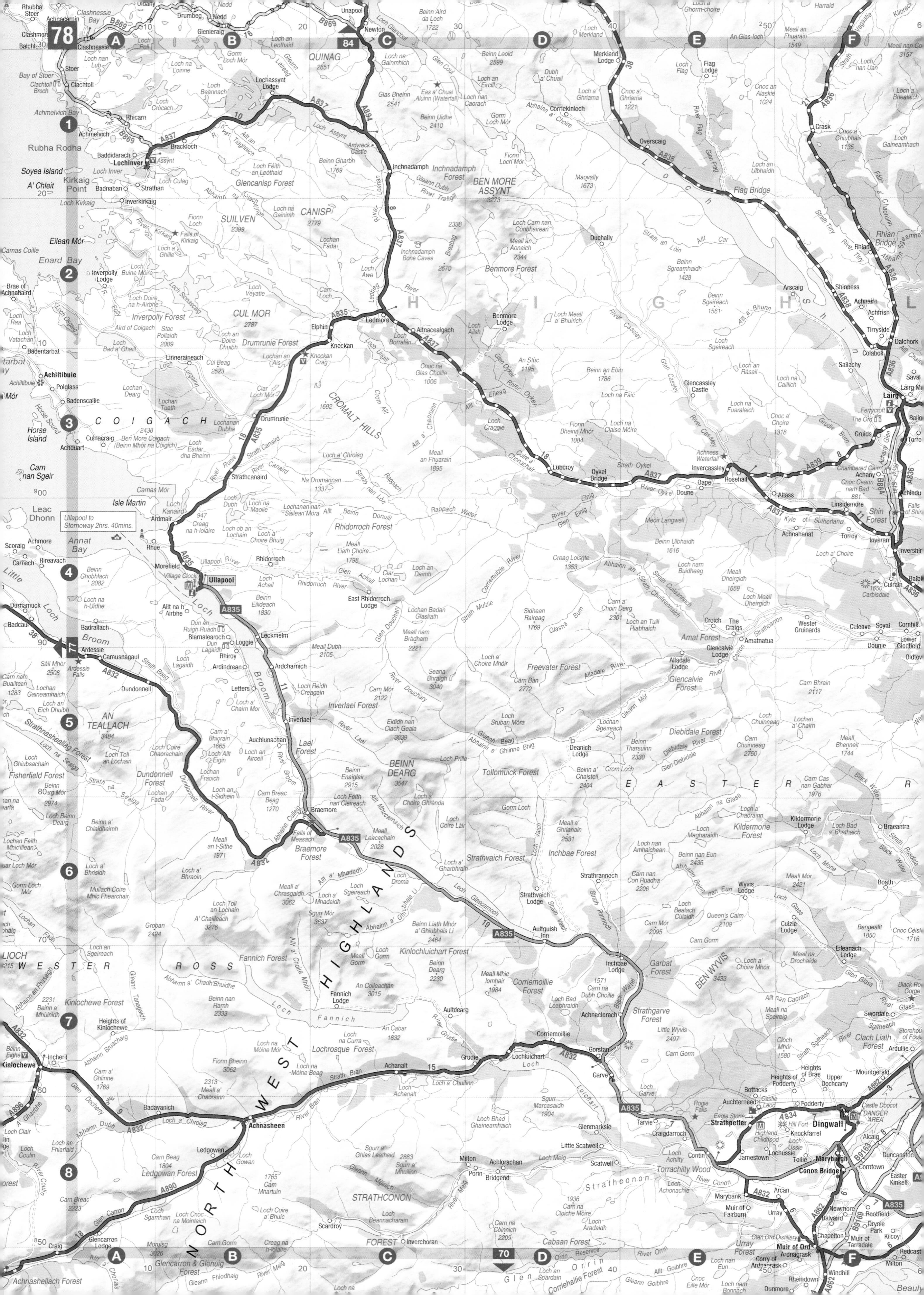

78
84
77
70
A
B
C
D
E
F
1
2
3
4
5
6
7
8
Clashnessie
Clashnessie Bay
Achnacarnin
Drumbeg
Nedd
Glenleraig
Unapool
Newton
Loch Glencoul
Beinn Aird da Loch 1722
Loch Merkland
Merkland Lodge
Harrald
Loch Poll
Loch an Leothaid
An Glas-loch
Meall an Fhuarain 1549
Meall nan Con 3157
Stoer
Clachtoll
Bay of Stoer
Loch nan Lub
Gorm Loch Mór
QUINAG 2651
Loch na Gainmhich
Glen Coul
Beinn Leoid 2599
Dubh Loch
Flag Lodge
Loch Flag
Lochassynt Lodge
Glas Bheinn 2541
Eas a' Chual Aluinn (Waterfall)
Loch an Eircill
Cnoc a' Ghriama 1221
Cnoc an Alaskie 1024
Achmelvich Bay
Achmelvich
Rhicarn
Loch Assynt
Ardvreck Castle
Beinn Uidhe 2410
Gorm Loch Mór
Corriekinloch
Overscaig
Crask
Rubha Rodha
Baddidarach
Lochinver
Brackloch
Soyea Island
Kirkaig Point
A' Chleit
Badnaban
Strathan
Inverkirkaig
Loch Kirkaig
Glencanisp Forest
Beinn Gharbh 1769
Inchnadamph
Inchnadamph Forest
BEN MORE ASSYNT 3273
Maovally 1673
Flag Bridge
Loch Shin
SUILVEN 2399
CANISP 2779
Falls of Kirkaig
Eilean Mór
Camas Coille
Enard Bay
Inverpolly Lodge
Loch Buine Mòire
Inchnadamph Bone Caves
Benmore Forest
Duchally
Strath an Lòin
Rhian Bridge
Brae of Achnahaird
Inverpolly Forest
CUL MOR 2787
Ledmore
Elphin
Altnacealgach
Benmore Lodge
Shinness
Achnairn
Achfrish
Tirryside
Dalchork
Colaboll
Badentarbat
Achiltibuie
Polglass
Badenscallie
Knockan
Knockan Crag
Drumrunie Forest
Linneraineach
Cùl Beag 2523
Glen Oykel
An Stùc 1195
Beinn an Eòin 1786
Glencassley Castle
Sallachy
Lairg
Horse Sound
Horse Island
COIGACH
Culnacraig
Achduart
Ben More Coigach (Beinn Mhòr na Coigich) 2438
Drumrunie
CROMALT HILLS
Loch Craggie
Fionn Bheinn Mhòr 1084
Achness Waterfall
Invercassley
Rosehall
Gruids
Carn nan Sgeir
Strathcanaird
Lubcroy
Oykel Bridge
Strath Oykel
Oape
Doune
Altass
Linsidemore
Shin Forest
Isle Martin
Leac Dhonn
Ardmair
Ullapool to Stornoway 2hrs. 40mins.
Rhidorroch Forest
Achnahanat
Inveran
Torroy
Scoraig
Achmore
Annat Bay
Carnach
Rireavach
Rhue
Morefield
Ullapool
Rhidorroch
Creag Loisgte 1353
Little Loch Broom
East Rhidorroch Lodge
Carbisdale
Culrain
Dundonnell
Badcaul
Badrallach
Ardessie
Camusnagaul
Leckmelm
Loggie
Rhiroy
Ardindrean
Ardcharnich
Strath Mulzie
Amat Forest
The Craigs
Amatnatua
Western Gruinards
Culeave
Soyal
Dounie
Alladale Lodge
Glencalvie Lodge
Glencalvie Forest
Freevater Forest
AN TEALLACH 3484
Strathnasheallag Forest
Fisherfield Forest
Dundonnell Forest
Inverlael
Inverlael Forest
Lael Forest
Auchlunachan
Deanich Lodge
Diebidale Forest
BEINN DEARG 3547
Tollomuick Forest
EASTER ROSS
Braemore
Braemore Forest
Falls of Measach
Gorm Loch
Kildermorie Lodge
Kildermorie Forest
Braeantra
Inchbae Forest
Strathvaich Forest
Strathrannoch
Strathvaich Lodge
Wyvis Lodge
Boath
Aultguish Inn
Loch Glascarnoch
NORTH WEST HIGHLANDS
Fannich Forest
Kinlochluichart Forest
Inchbae Lodge
Garbat Forest
BEN WYVIS 3433
Eileanach Lodge
Fannich Lodge
Corriemoillie Forest
WESTER ROSS
Kinlochewe Forest
Heights of Kinlochewe
Loch Fannich
Aultdearg
Achnaclerach
Strathgarve Forest
Swordale
Clach Liath Forest
Ardullie
Kinlochewe
Incheril
Lochrosque Forest
Grudie
Lochluichart
Corriemoillie
Gorstan
Garve
Mountgerald
Achanalt
Strath Bran
Badavanich
Achnasheen
Loch a' Chroisg
Strathpeffer
Dingwall
Auchterneed
Fodderty
Castle Leod
Eagle Stone
Knockfarrel
Jamestown
Contin
Tarvie
Craigdarroch
Glenmarksie
Little Scatwell
Scatwell
Ledgowan
Ledgowan Forest
Milton
Porin
Achlorachan
Bridgend
Torrachilty Wood
Maryburgh
Conon Bridge
Strathconon
STRATHCONON
Marybank
Muir of Fairburn
Arcan
Urray
Muir of Ord
Glencarron Lodge
Craig
Glen Carron
Achnashellach Forest
Glencarron & Glenuig Forest
FOREST
Inverchoran
Cabaan Forest
Urray Forest
Corrieshalloch Forest
Glen Orrin
Orrin Reservoir
Windhill
Rheindown
Dunmore
Beauly

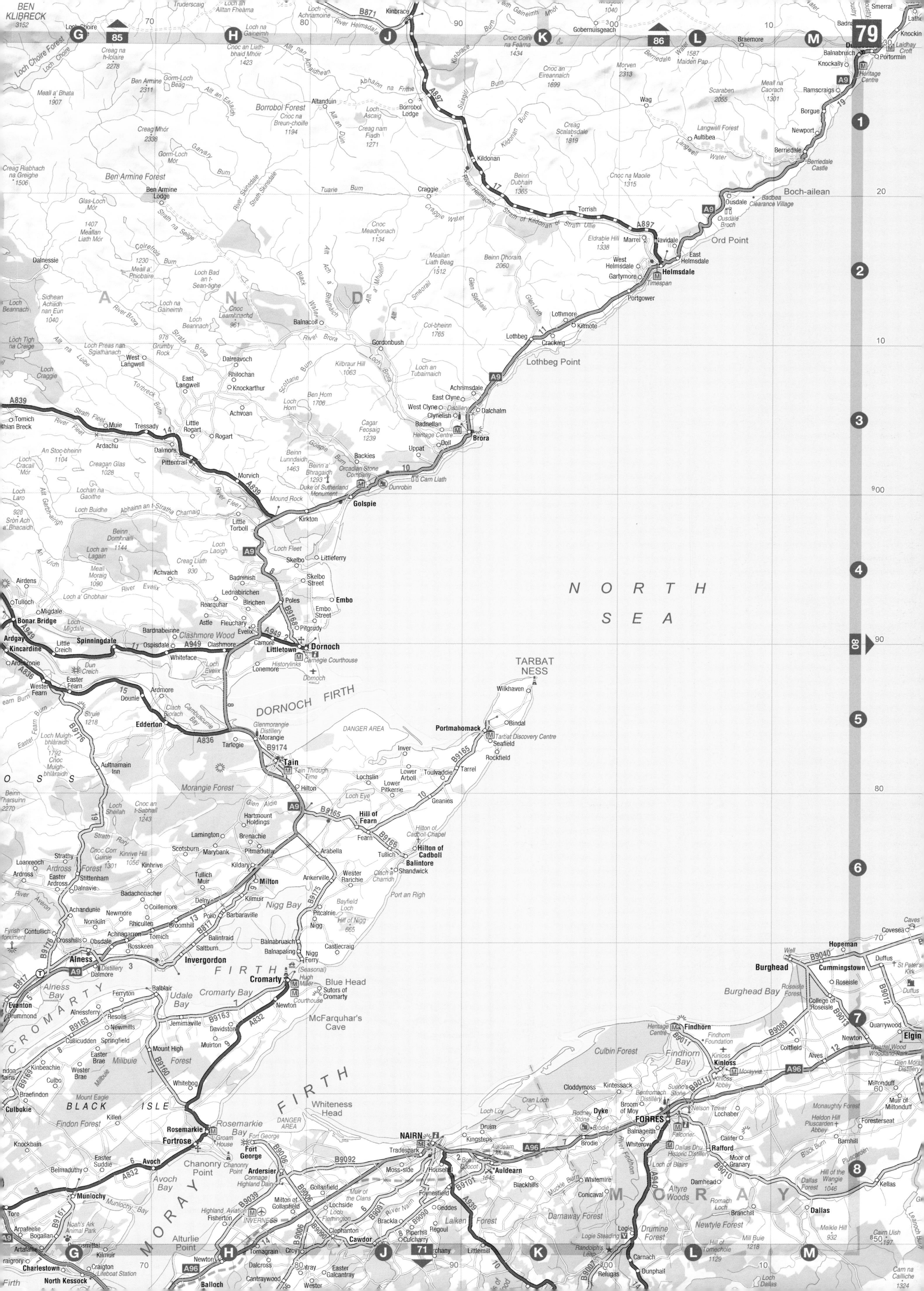

79
85
86
80
71
G
H
J
K
L
M
1
2
3
4
5
6
7
8
BEN KLIBRECK 3152
Loch Choire
Loch Choire Forest
Creag na h-Iolaire 2278
Loch na Gaineimh
Cnoc an Liath-bhaid Mhóir 1423
Kinbrace
B871
River Helmsdale
Gobernuisgeach
Cnoc Coire na Fearna 1434
Braemore
Dunbeath
Balnabruich
Portormin
Knockally
Laidhay Croft
Heritage Centre
Ramscraigs
Borgue
Newport
Berriedale
Berriedale Castle
Boch-ailean
Badbea Clearance Village
Ousdale
Ousdale Broch
Ord Point
Meall a' Bhata 1907
Ben Armine 2311
Gorm-Loch Beag
Allt an Ealaidh
Borrobol Forest
Cnoc na Breun-choille 1194
Altanduin
Borrobol Lodge
Loch Ascaig
Creag nam Fiadh 1271
Abhainn na Frithe
A897
Suisgill
Kinbrace Burn
Kildonan
Cnoc an Eireannaich 1699
Morven 2313
1587 Maiden Pap
Berriedale Water
Wag
Scaraben 2055
Meall na Caorach 1301
Creag Scalabsdale 1819
Langwell Forest
Aultibea
Langwell Water
Creag Mhór 2338
Gorm-Loch Mór
Garvary
Creag Riabhach na Greighe 1506
Ben Armine Forest
Ben Armine Lodge
Glas-Loch Mór
1407 Meallan Liath Mór
River Skinsdale
Strath Skinsdale
Strath na Seilge
Tuarie
Craggie
Craggie Water
River Helmsdale
Beinn Dubhain 1365
Cnoc na Maoile 1315
Strath of Kildonan or Strath Ullie
Torrish
A897
Eldrable Hill 1338
Marrel
Navidale
East Helmsdale
Helmsdale
West Helmsdale
Gartymore
Timespan
Portgower
Cnoc Meadhonach 1134
Meallan Liath Beag 1512
Beinn Dhorain 2060
Glen Sletdale
Glen Loth
Lothmore
Kilmote
Dalnessie
Coirefrois
1230 Meall a' Phiobaire
Loch Bad an t-Sean-tighe
Loch Beannach
Sidhean Achadh nan Eun 1040
Loch na Gaineimh
Cnoc Leamhnachd 961
Loch Beannach
River Brora
Black Water
Balnacoil
Smeorail
Col-bheinn 1765
Lothbeg
Crackaig
Lothbeg Point
A9
Loch Tigh na Creige
978 Grumby Rock
Strath Brora
Loch Preas nan Sgiathanach
West Langwell
Dalreavoch
Rhilochan
Knockarthur
East Langwell
Gordonbush
Kilbraur Hill 1063
Loch an Tubairnaich
Loch Brora
Achrimsdale
East Clyne
West Clyne
Clynelish
Distillery
Dalchalm
Badnellan
Heritage Centre
Brora
Doll
Uppat
Loch Craggie
Torbreck Burn
Scottarie Burn
Ben Horn 1706
Loch Horn
Cagar Feosaig 1239
Achvoan
A839
Tomich
Strath Fleet
River Fleet
Muie
Tressady
Ardachu
Little Rogart
Rogart
Dalmore
Pittentrail
An Stoc-bheinn 1104
Creagan Glas 1028
Loch Cracail Mór
Morvich
Beinn Lunndaidh 1463
Beinn a' Bhragaidh 1293
Backies
Orcadian Stone Company
Duke of Sutherland Monument
Dunrobin
Carn Liath
Golspie
Mound Rock
Kirkton
Lochan na Gaoithe
Loch Buidhe
Abhainn an t-Stratha Charnaig
Loch Laro
928 Sròn Ach a' Bhacaidh
Little Torboll
Beinn Domhnaill 1144
Loch an Lagain
Loch Laoigh
Loch Fleet
Creag Liath 930
Meall Moraig 1090
Littleferry
Skelbo
Skelbo Street
Airdens
Achvaich
Badninish
Lednabirichen
Rearquhar
Birichen
Poles
Embo
Embo Street
Pitgrudy
River Evelix
Loch a' Ghobhair
Tulloch
Migdale
Loch Migdale
Bonar Bridge
Astle
Fleuchary
Evelix
Bardnabeinne
Clashmore Wood
Ardgay
Kincardine
Little Creich
Spinningdale
Ospisdale
A949
Clashmore
Camore
Littletown
Dornoch
Carnegie Courthouse
Historylinks
Lonemore
Whiteface
Loch Evelix
Ardchronie
Dun Creich
Easter Fearn
Wester Fearn
Dounie
Ardmore
A836
Struie 1218
B9176
Edderton
Clach Biorach
Cambuscurrie Bay
DORNOCH FIRTH
Glenmorangie Distillery
Morangie
B9174
Tarlogie
DANGER AREA
TARBAT NESS
Wilkhaven
Portmahomack
Bindal
Tarbat Discovery Centre
Seafield
Rockfield
Inver
B9165
Tarrel
Toulvaddie
Lower Arboll
Lower Pitkerrie
Lochslin
Loch Eye
Tain
Tain Through Time
Hilton
Geanies
Loch Mugh-bhlàraidh
1792 Cnoc Mugh-bhlàraidh
Aultnamain Inn
Morangie Forest
Beinn Tharsuinn 2270
Loch Sheilah
Cnoc an t-Sabhail 1243
Glen Aldie
Hartmount Holdings
Hill of Fearn
Fearn
B9166
Hilton of Cadboll Chapel
Hilton of Cadboll
Balintore
Shandwick
Tullich
Lamington
Brenachie
Pitmaduthy
Marybank
Scotsburn
Strath Rory
Cnoc Corr Guinie 1301
Kinrive Hill 1056
Kinhrive
Strathy
Loanreoch
Ardross
Ardross Forest
Easter Ardross
Stittenham
Dalnavie
Tullich Muir
Kildary
Milton
Arabella
Ankerville
Wester Rarichie
Clach a' Charridh
Port an Righ
Badachonacher
Coillemore
Delny
Kilmuir
Nigg Bay
B9175
Bayfield Loch
Hill of Nigg 665
Pitcalnie
Nigg
River Averon
Achandunie
Newmore
Nonikiln
Rhiculen
Broomhill
Polio
Barbaraville
B817
Balintraid
Achnagarron
Tomich
Contullich
Crosshills
Obsdale
Rosskeen
Saltburn
Invergordon
Balnabruaich
Balnapaling
Nigg Ferry
Castlecraig
Alness
Distillery
Dalmore
A9
Evanton
Drummond
Alness Bay
CROMARTY FIRTH
Cromarty
Hugh Miller
Courthouse
Blue Head
Sutors of Cromarty
Cromarty Bay
Balblair
Udale Bay
Ferryton
Alnessferry
Resolis
Newmills
B9163
Jemimaville
Davidston
Newton
McFarquhar's Cave
Cullicudden
Springfield
Easter Brae
Millbuie
Wester Brae
Kinbeachie
Culbo
Mount High
Forest
B9160
Muirton
A832
Whitebog
Braefindon
Mount Eagle
Culbokie
BLACK ISLE
Findon Forest
Killen
MORAY FIRTH
Whiteness Head
DANGER AREA
Rosemarkie
Rosemarkie Bay
Fortrose
Groam House
Fort George
Chanonry Point
Knockbain
Easter Suddie
Avoch
Avoch Bay
Belmaduthy
Munlochy
Munlochy Bay
Tore
Arpafeelie
Bogallan
Noah's Ark Animal Park
Artafallie
Charlestown
North Kessock
Kilmuir
Craigton
Lifeboat Station
Alturlie Point
Ardersier
Connage Highland Dairy
B9006
B9092
Tradespark
NAIRN
Moss-side
Househill
Boath Doocot
Auldearn
Kingsteps
Golanfield
Milton of Gollanfield
Muir of the Clans
Lochside
Loch Flemington
B9091
River Nairn
Brackla
B9090
Geddes
B9101
A939
Clephanton
Cawdor
Piperhill
Culcharry
Highland Aviation
Fisherton
INVERNESS
B9039
Newton
Tornagrain
Croy
Dalcross
Cantraywood
Easter Galcantray
Wester
Balloch
A96
Regoul
Lethen
Laiken Forest
Littlemill
Blackhills
Whitemire
Conicaval
Darnaway Forest
Logie Steading
Randolph's Leap
Relugas
Dunphail
Carnach
Drumine Forest
Culbin Forest
Cloddymoss
Kintessack
Cran Loch
Loch Loy
Drum
Dyke
Rodney Stone
Brodie
Broom of Moy
Benromach Distillery
Sueno's Stone
Nelson Tower
FORRES
Balnageith
Whiterow
Falconer
Dallas Dhu Historic Distillery
Loch of Blairs
A940
Rafford
Calder
Lochaber
Moor of Granary
B9010
Damhead
Altyre Woods
Romach Loch
Branchill
Newtyle Forest
Hill of Tomechole 1129
Mill Buie 1218
MORAY
Findhorn
Heritage Centre
Findhorn Foundation
Findhorn Bay
Kinloss
Kinloss Abbey
Burghead
Burghead Bay
Hopeman
B9040
Cummingstown
Roseisle
Roseisle Forest
College of Roseisle
Duffus
St Peter's Kirk
B9012
B9013
Covesea
Caves
B9089
Coltfield
Alves
Newton
Quarrywood
Elgin
Quarrel Wood Woodland Park
Glen Moray Distillery
A96
Miltonduff
Muir of Miltonduff
Monaughty Forest
Heldon Hill
Pluscarden Abbey
Foresterseat
Barnhill
Black Burn
Pluscarden
Hill of the Wangie 1046
Dallas Forest
Kellas
Dallas
Meikle Hill 932
Cairn Uish 1197
Cam na Cailliche 1324
Lochindorb
Loch Dallas
NORTH SEA
SUTHERLAND
ROSS
Smerral
Lathe
Knockin
Badnabay

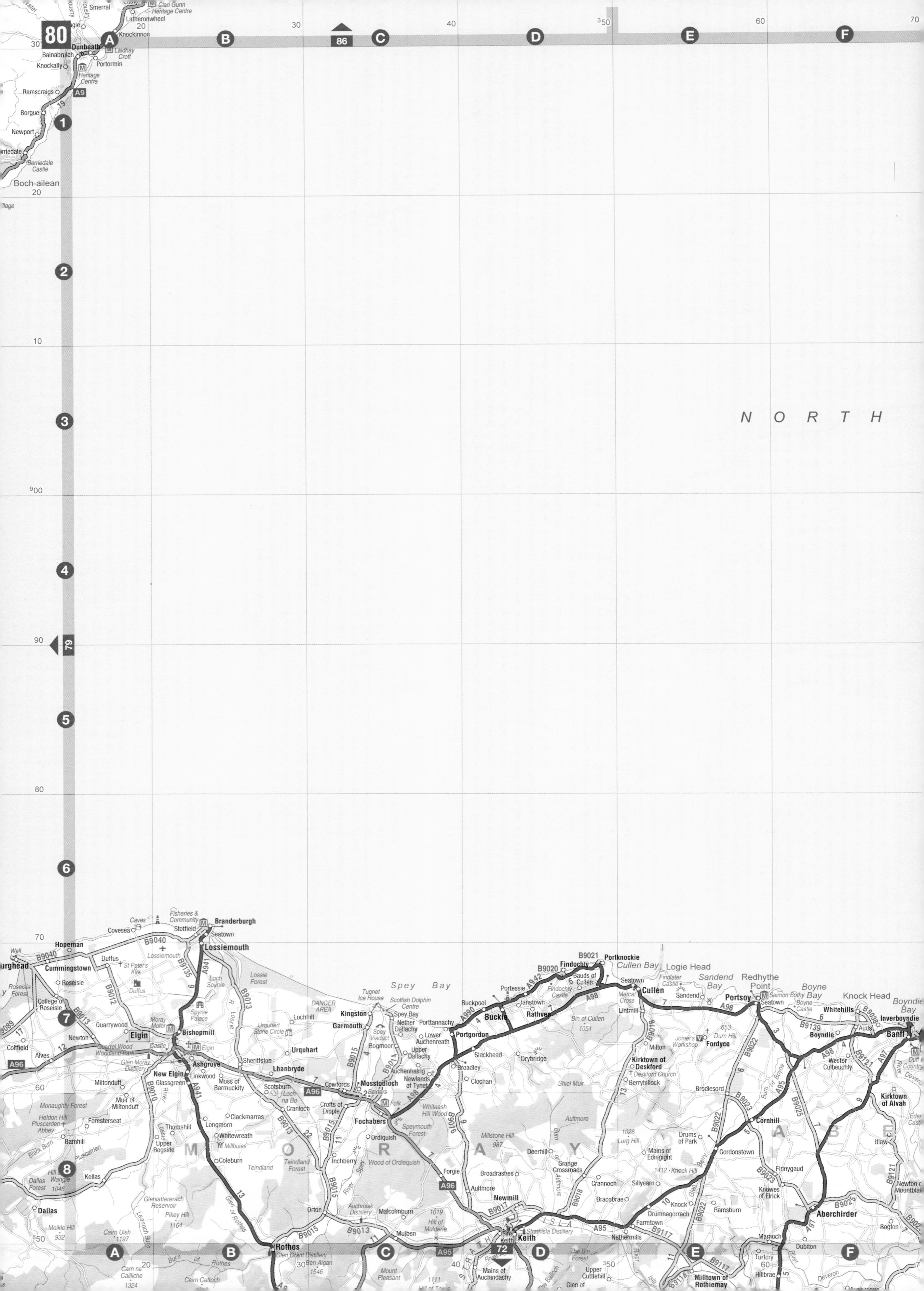

80
A
B
C
D
E
F
86
79
72
1
2
3
4
5
6
7
8
N O R T H
Smerral
Clan Gunn Heritage Centre
Latheronwheel
Knockinnon
Dunbeath
Balnabruich
Laidhay Croft
Portormin
Knockally
Heritage Centre
Ramscraigs
A9
Borgue
Newport
Berriedale Castle
Boch-ailean
Caves
Fisheries & Community
Branderburgh
Covesea
Stotfield
Seatown
Hopeman
Lossiemouth
Cummingstown
Duffus
St Peter's Kirk
Roseisle
College of Roseisle
Spynie Palace
Lossie Forest
Quarrywood
Elgin
Bishopmill
Newton
Alves
Coltfield
A96
Ashgrove
New Elgin
Glassgreen
Linkwood
Sheriffston
Lhanbryde
Urquhart
Lochhill
Spey Bay
Tugnet Ice House
Scottish Dolphin Centre
Kingston
Garmouth
Nether Dallachy
Porttannachy
Lower Auchenreath
Upper Dallachy
Bogmoor
Auchenhalrig
Newlands of Tynet
Cowfords
Mosstodloch
Fochabers
Ordiquish
Inchberry
Wood of Ordiequish
Speymouth Forest
Whiteash Hill Wood
Buckpool
Buckie
Portgordon
Portessie
Ianstown
Rathven
Findochty
Findochty Castle
Bauds of Cullen
Portknockie
Cullen Bay
Logie Head
Cullen
Seatown
Mercat Cross
Lintmill
Bin of Cullen
1051
Slackhead
Drybridge
Broadley
Clochan
Sandend Bay
Sandend
Findlater Castle
Redhythe Point
Portsoy
Salmon Bothy
Boyne Bay
Boyne Castle
Knock Head
Whitehills
Boyndie Bay
Inverboyndie
Boyndie
Banff
Fordyce
Joiner's Workshop
Durn Hill
653
Milton
Kirktown of Deskford
Deskford Church
Berryhillock
Shiel Muir
Brodiesord
Cornhill
Kirktown of Alvah
Wester Culbeuchly
Aultmore
Millstone Hill
987
Lurg Hill
1028
Drums of Park
Mains of Edingight
Gordonstown
Deerhill
Grange Crossroads
Knock Hill
1412
Crannoch
Sillyearn
Bracobrae
Knock
Drumnagorrach
Farmtown
Ramsburn
Finnygaud
Knowes of Elrick
Aberchirder
Itlaw
Begton
Newmill
Broadrashes
Aultmore
Forgie
A96
Keith
Strathisla Distillery
Netherhills
A95
Marnoch
Dubiton
Turtory
Hillbrae
Milltown of Rothiemay
Upper Cuttlehill
The Bin Forest
Mains of Auchindachy
Mulben
Malcolmburn
Hill of Mulderie
1019
Auchroisk Distillery
Orton
Rothes
Glen Grant Distillery
Ben Aigan
1546
Mount Pleasant
Crofts of Dipple
Teindland Forest
Teindland
Coleburn
Whitewreath
Longmorn
Clackmarras
Thornhill
Upper Bogside
Barmuckity
Moss of Barmuckity
Scotsburn
Cranloch
Miltonduff
Muir of Miltonduff
Monaughty Forest
Heldon Hill
Pluscarden Abbey
Foresterseat
Barnhill
Kellas
Dallas
Dallas Forest
Hill of Wangie
1046
Meikle Hill
932
Cairn Uish
1197
Carn na Cailliche
1324
Cairn Cattoch
Glenlatterach Reservoir
Pikey Hill
1164
Glen of Rothes
MORAY
B9040
B9012
B9013
B9135
A941
B9010
A98
B9015
B9016
B9017
B9018
B9020
B9021
B9022
B9023
B9025
B9117
B9139
B9121
A97
A942
A990

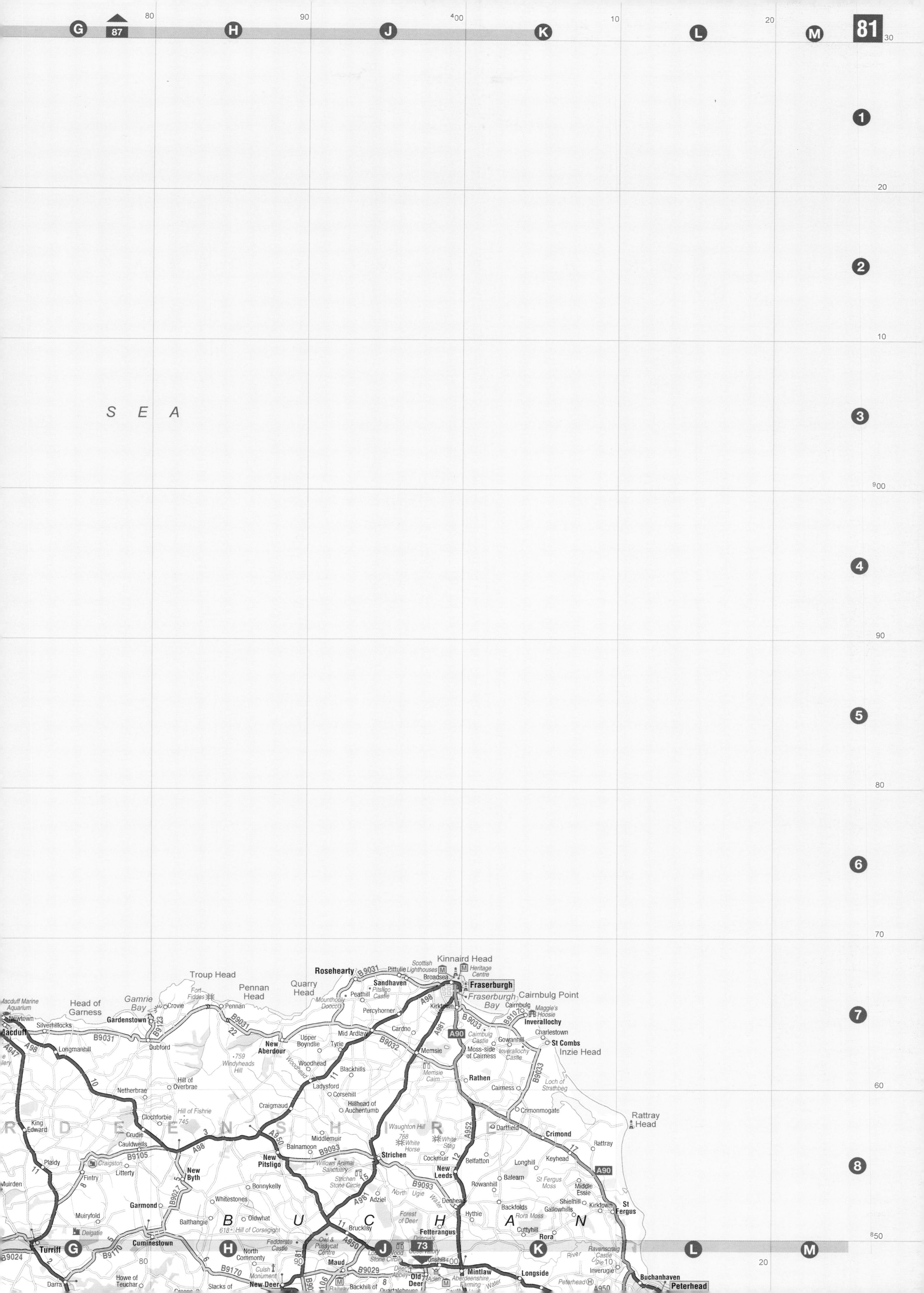

1

20

2

10

S E A

3

⁹00

4

90

5

80

6

70

Troup Head   Kinnaird Head

Rosehearty   B9031   Pittulie   *Scottish*   *Lighthouses*   *Heritage*   *Centre*

Pennan   Quarry   **Sandhaven**   Broadsea

Macduff Marine   Head   Head   *Gamrie*   Fort   *Pitsligo*   **Fraserburgh**

Aquarium   Head of   *Bay*   Fiddes   Crovie   Pennan   Peathill   *Pitsligo*   *Castle*   *Fraserburgh*   Cairnbulg Point

Newtown   Garness   **Gardenstown**   Mountholly   Percyhorner   Kirktown   *Bay*   Cairnbulg   Maggie's

Silverhillocks   B9031   Dubford   Doocot   Mid Ardlaw   Cardno   A98   B9033   B910   *Hoosie*   **7**

Macduff   B9031   22   Upper   **New**   B9032   A981   A90   Gowanhill   **Inverallochy**

Longmanhill   **Aberdour**   Boyndlie   Tyrie   Memsie   Cairnbulg   Charlestown

A947   ·759   Woodhead   Castle   Moss-side   **St Combs**

A98   *Windyheads*   Blackhills   of Cairness   Inverallochy   Inzie Head

King   Netherbrae   *Hill*   Ladysford   Memsie   Castle

Edward   Clochforbie   Corsehill   Cairn   **Rathen**   Loch of

Crudie   *Hill of Fishrie*   Hillhead of   Cairness   Strathbeg

Plaidy   Cauldwells   745   Craigmaud   Auchentumb   Crimonmogate   Rattray   60

Craigston   A98   B9024   Middlemuir   Dartfield   Head

Fintry   Litterty   A950   768   *White*   A952   **Crimond**

B9105   **New**   Balmoor   *White Horse*   *Stag*   Rattray   17   **8**

Muirfold   **Pitsligo**   B9093   **Strichen**   Cockmuir   Belfatton   Longhill   Keyhead   A90

Garmond   *Willows Animal*   *Strichen*   12   Balearn   *St Fergus*

New   *Sanctuary*   *Stone Circle*   **New**   Rowanhill   *Moss*

Whitestones   **Byth**   B9093   **Leeds**   Middle

Muiryfold   Bonnykelly   A981   Adziel   *North*   Essie   Kirktown   **St**

Balthangie   *Ugie*   Hythie   Backfolds   Shielhill   **Fergus**

Turriff   Delgatie   618   *Hill of Corsegight*   *Forest*   Denhead   *Water*   Gallowhills

G   Oldwhat   **B**   U   *of Deer*   C   H   A   Cuttyhill   **L**   **M**

B9024   **Cuminestown**   Fedderate   Bruckley   **Fetterangus**   **Rora**   *River*

Darra   North   *Castle*   *Owl &*   *Old Deer*   *Ravenscraig*   20

B9170   Commonty   *Pussycat*   *Priory*   *Aberdeenshire*   *Castle*   **Buchanhaven**

Howe of   *Centre*   **Maud**   Deer   **Old**   *Farming*   Inverugie

Teuchar   *Culsh*   *Monument*   *Railway*   **Deer**   Aden   *South*   *Water*   *Peterhead*   **Peterhead**

Slacks of   **New Deer**   B9029   Backhill of   **Mintlaw**   **Longside**   A950

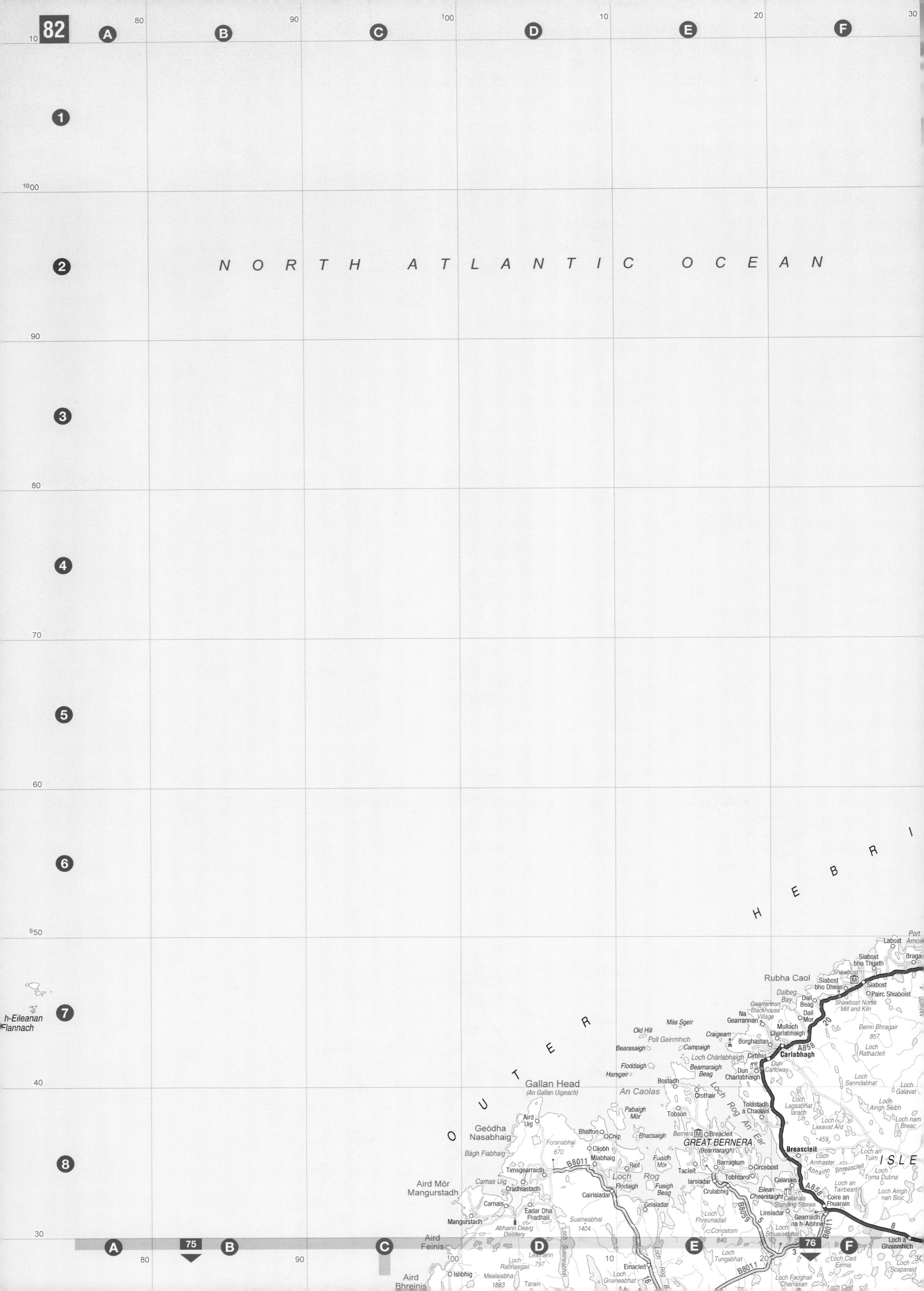
N O R T H   A T L A N T I C   O C E A N
O U T E R   H E B R I
ISLE
h-Eileanan
Flannach
Gallan Head
(An Gallan Uigeach)
An Caolas
Geòdha
Nasabhaig
Bàgh Fiabhaig
Aird Mòr
Mangurstadh
Aird
Feinis
Aird
Bhreinis
Rubha Caol
Dalbeg
Bay
Labost
Port
Arnol
Siabost
bho Thuath
Bragar
Siabost
bho Dheas
Siabost
Pairc Shiaboist
Shawbost Norse
Mill and Kiln
Dail
Beag
Dail
Mòr
Gearrannan
Blackhouse
Village
Na
Gearrannan
Mullach
Charlabhaigh
Màs Sgeir
Old Hill
Poll Gainmhich
Craigeam
Campaigh
Bearasaigh
Borghastan
Carlabhagh
Cirbhig
Loch Chàrlabhaigh
Dun
Carloway
Dun
Charlabhaigh
Floddaigh
Harsgeir
Beàrnaraigh
Beag
Bostadh
Crothair
Loch Rog an Ear
Tolastadh
a Chaolais
Tobson
Pabaigh
Mòr
Aird
Uig
Bhaltos
Cnip
Bhacsaigh
Breacleit
GREAT BERNERA
(Bearnaraigh)
Breascleit
Forsnabhal
670
B8011
Cliobh
Miabhaig
Riof
Fuaidh
Mòr
Barraglom
Circebost
Timsgearraidh
Loch Rog
Fuaigh
Beag
Tacleit
Camas Uig
Cradhlastadh
Flodaigh
Iarsiadar
Tobhtarol
Calanais
Carnais
Cairisiadar
Geisiadar
Crulabhig
Eilean
Chearstaigh
Calanais
Standing Stones
Coire an
Fhuarain
Eadar Dha
Fhadhail
B8059
Linsiadar
Gearraidh
na h-Aibhne
Mangurstadh
Abhainn Dearg
Distillery
Suaineabhal
1404
Loch
Fhreunadail
Conostom
840
Loch
Smuaisebhal
B8011
Loch a
Ghainmhich
Beinn Bhragair
857
Loch
Rathacleit
Loch
Sanndabhat
Loch
Galavat
Loch
Lagsabhat
Iarach
Loch
Airigh Seibh
Loch nam
Breac
Loch
Laxavat Ard
459
Loch an
Tuim
Loch
Amhaster
Abhainn Bhreascleit
Loch
Toma Dubha
Loch an
Tairbeart
Loch Airigh
nan Sloc
A858
Loch
Raonasgail
Leathann
797
Mealaisbha
1883
Tarain
Islibhig
Einacleit
Loch
Gruineabhat
Loch
Tungabhat
Loch Faoghail
Charrasan
Loch Cleit
Eirmis
Loch
Scaparaid
Loch Suaineabhal
75
76

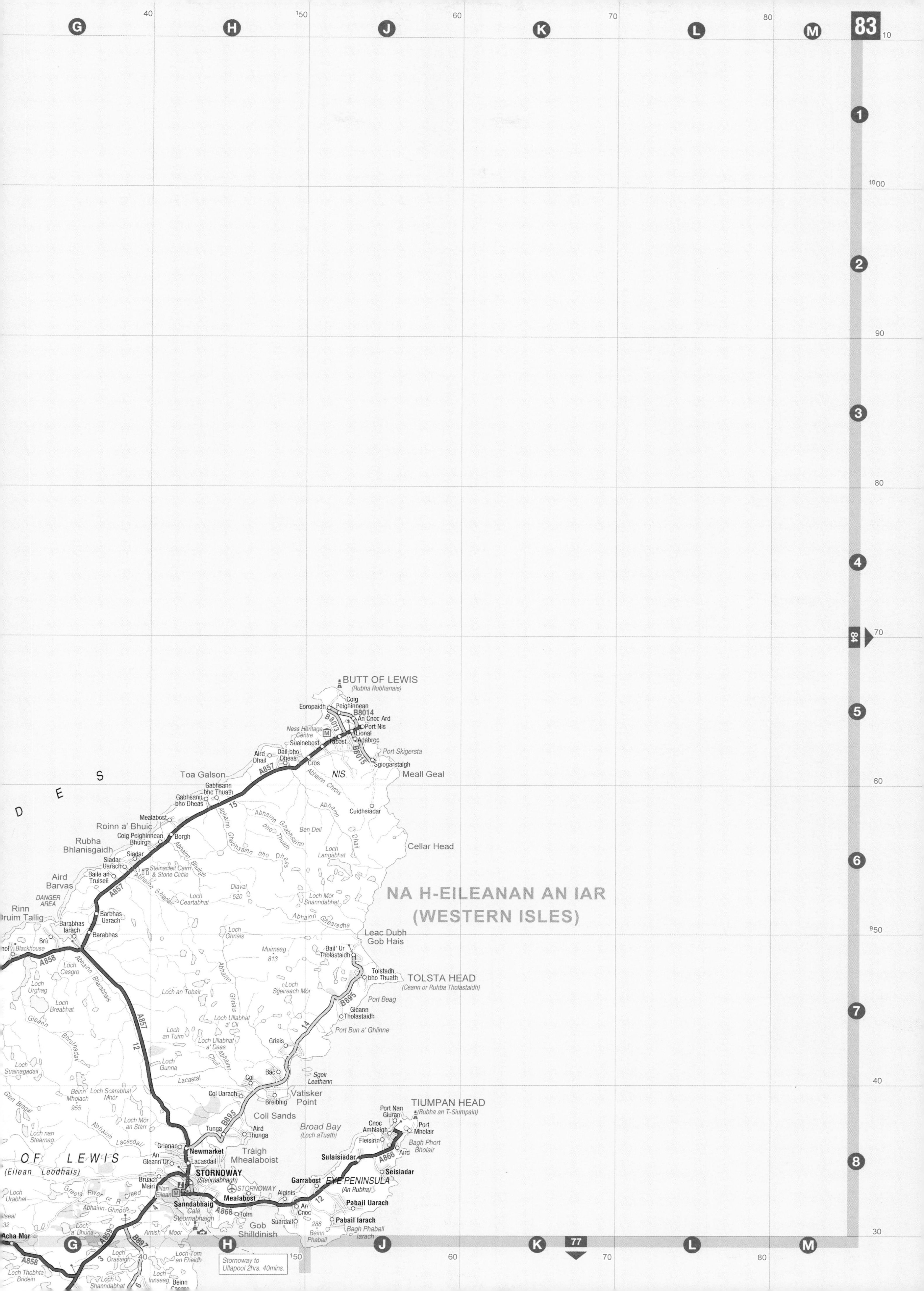

1

10
00

2

90

3

80

4

84 ▶ 70

5

60

BUTT OF LEWIS
(Rubha Robhanais)

Coig
Peighinnean
Eoropaidh B8014
An Cnoc Ard
Port Nis
Ness Heritage
Centre
Lional
Suainebost Tabost
Adabroc
Aird
Dhail
Dail bho
Dheas
Port Skigersta
Cros
Sgiogarstaigh
NIS
Toa Galson
A857
Meall Geal
Gabhsann
bho Thuath
Abhainn Chrois
Gabhsann
bho Dheas
Mealabost
15
Abhainn Ghabhsainn
Abhainn
Cuidhsiadar
Roinn a' Bhuic
bho Thuath
bho Dheas
Coig Peighinnean
Borgh
Rubha
Bhuirgh
Ben Dell
Cellar Head
Bhlanisgaidh
Siadar
Abhainn Bhuirgh
Loch
Langabhat
Dhail
Aird
Baile an
Truiseil
Steinacleit Cairn
& Stone Circle
6
Barvas
Diaval
520
Loch Mòr
Shanndabhat
Rinn
Abhainn S'hadar
Loch
Ceartabhat
Druim Tallig
DANGER
AREA
Barbhas
Uarach
Loch
Ghriais
NA H-EILEANAN AN IAR
Barbhas
Iarach
Abhainn
Ghearadha
(WESTERN ISLES)
nof Blackhouse
Brù
Barabhas
Muirneag
813
Leac Dubh
Gob Hais
950
A858
Loch
Casgro
Bail' Ur
Tholastaidh
Loch
Urghag
Tolstadh
bho Thuath
TOLSTA HEAD
Abhainn Bharabhas
Loch
Breabhat
Loch
Sgeireach Mòr
Port Beag
(Ceann or Ruhba Tholastaidh)
Gleann
A857
Gléann
Tholastaidh
7
Loch
Suainagadail
12
Loch
an Tobair
B895
Port Bun a' Ghlinne
40
Glen Bragar
Abhainn
Ghrais
Loch
an Turn
Loch Ullabhat
a' Cii
14
Loch nan
Stearnag
Loch
Gunna
Loch Ullabhat
a' Deas
Griais
Bhrtadai
Lacastal
Sgeir
Leathann
Loch
Scarabhat
Mhòr
Cal
Bac
TIUMPAN HEAD
OF LEWIS
Beinn
Mholach
955
Vatisker
Point
Port Nan
Giuran
(Rubha an T-Siumpain)
B895
Breibhig
Cnoc
Amhlaigh
Port
Abhainn Lacasdai
Coll Sands
Mholair
Tunga
Aird
Thunga
Broad Bay
Fleisirin
Bagh Phort
Bholair
8
Grianan
An
(Loch aTuath)
A866
Aird
OF LEWIS
Gleann Ur
Lacasdail
Newmarket
Tràigh
Mhealaboist
Sulaisiadar
30
(Eilean Leodhais)
Bruach
Mairi
STORNOWAY
(Steornabhagh)
Mealabost
Garrabost
EYE PENINSULA
Seisiadar
STORNOWAY
Aiginis
(An Rubha)
Loch
Urabhal
Sanndabhaig
An
Cnoc
Pabail Uarach
A866
Tolm
Suardail
itseal
32
Greeta River or R Creed
Amish
Moor
Abhainn Ghnot
288
Pabail Iarach
Acha Mor
Loch
a' Bhuna
B897
Gob
Shilldinish
Beinn
Phabail
Bagh Phabail
Iarach
A858
Loch
Orasaigh
Loch Tom
an Fheidh
Loch
Innseag
Beinn

Stornoway to
Ullapool 2hrs. 40mins.

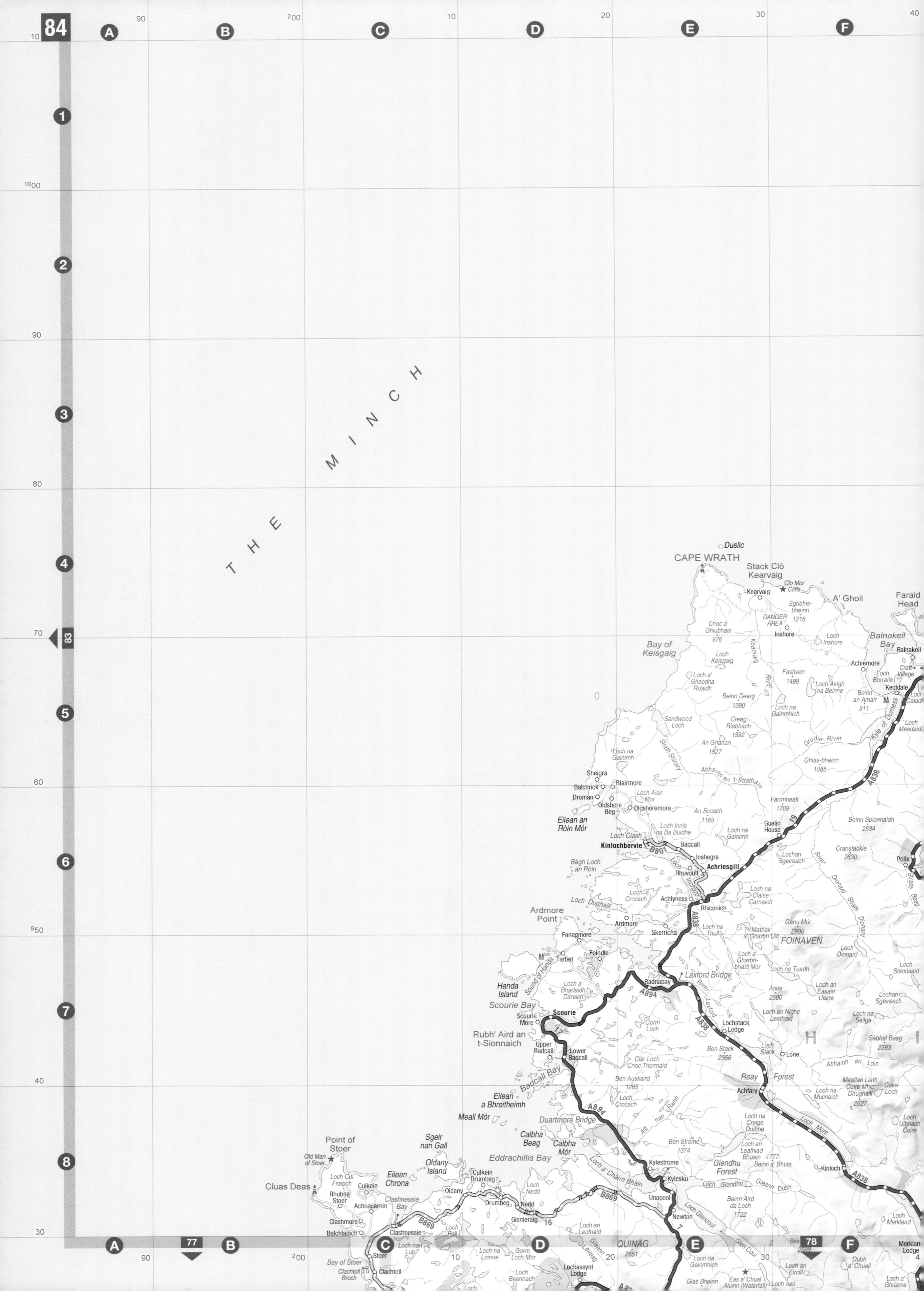

A 90 B 200 C 10 D 20 E 30 F 40

1

1000

2

90

3

80

T H E   M I N C H

4

70 83

5

60

6

950

7

40

8

30

A 77 B 200 C 10 D 20 E 30 F 40
90

Duslic
CAPE WRATH
Stack Clò
Kearvaig
Clo Mór
Cliffs
Kearvaig
A' Ghoil
Faraid
Head
Sgribhis-
bheinn
1216
Cnoc a'
Ghiubhais
976
DANGER
AREA
Inshore
Loch
Inshore
Balnakeil
Bay
Balnakeil
Achiemore
Loch
Borralie
Craft
Village
Keoldale
Beinn
an Amair
911
Loch
Calad
Loch
Meadaid
Bay of
Keisgaig
Loch a'
Gheodha
Ruaidh
Loch
Keisgaig
Fashven
1498
Loch Airigh
na Beinne
Sandwood
Loch
Beinn Dearg
1390
Loch na
Gainmhich
Creag
Riabhach
1592
An Grianan
1527
Ghlas-bheinn
1085
Loch na
Gainimh
Stair Shinary
Abhainn an t-Strath-áin
Grudie River
Sheigra
Balchrick
Blairmore
Loch Aisir
Mòr
Farrmheall
1709
Beinn Spionnaidh
2534
Droman
Oldshore
Beg
Oldshoremore
An Socach
1165
Loch na
Gainimh
Gualin
House
Cranstackie
2630
Polla
Eilean an
Ròin Mór
Loch Innis
na Ba Buidhe
Loch Clash
Kinlochbervie
B801
Badcall
Inshegra
Lochan
Sgeireach
River
Strath Beag
Achriesgill
Rhuvoult
Loch na
Claise
Carnaich
Dìonard
Loch
Dìonard
Bàgh Loch
an Ròin
Achlyness
Rhiconich
Loch na
Thuil
Ganu Mòr
2980
FOINAVEN
Ardmore
Point
Loch
Crocach
Loch
Dughaill
Ardmore
Skerricha
Mathair
a' Gharbh Uillt
Loch a'
Gharbh-
bhaid Mòr
Loch na Tuadh
Fanagmore
A838
Loch
Staonsaid
Tarbet
Sound of Handa
Loch a'
Bhadaidh
Daraich
Foindle
Laxford Bridge
River Laxford
Arkle
2580
Loch an
Easain
Uaine
Lochan
Sgeireach
Handa
Island
Badnabay
A894
Loch na
Seilge
Scourie Bay
Scourie
More
Scourie
Gorm
Loch
Lochstack
Lodge
Loch an Nighe
Leathaid
Sàbhal Beag
2393
H
Rubh' Aird an
t-Sionnaich
Upper
Badcall
Ben Stack
2356
Loch
Stack
A838
Lòne
Abhainn an Loin
Lower
Badcall
Ben Auskaird
1265
Clàr Loch
Cnoc Thormaid
Reay
Forest
Meallan Liath
Coire Mhic
Dhùghaill
2627
Loch
Ulbhach
Coire
Badcall Bay
Eilean
a Bhreitheimh
Duartmore
Bridge
A894
Loch
Crocach
Achfary
Loch na
Mucnaich
Meall Mór
Calbha
Beag
Calbha
Mór
Alt nan Ramh
Ben Strome
1374
Loch an
Leathaid
Bhuain
1777
Loch
More
Loch na
Creige
Duibhe
Point of
Stoer
Old Man
of Stoer
Sgeir
nan Gall
Eddrachillis Bay
Loch a' Chàirn Bhàin
Kylestrome
Glendhu
Forest
Beinn a' Bhuta
Beinn Aird
da Loch
1722
Kinloch
A838
Cluas Deas
Loch Cùl
Fraioch
Eilean
Chrona
Oldany
Island
Culkein
Drumbeg
Kyleskù
Loch Glendhu
Loch
Merkland
Rhubha
Stoer
Culkein
Loch
Nedd
Gleann Dubh
QUINAG
2651
Clashnessie
Bay
Oldany
Drumbeg
Nedd
Gienleraig
16
Loch an
Leothaid
Unapool
Loch Glencoul
Newton
Loch na
Gainmhich
Beinn
78
Merklan
Lodge
Clashmore
B869
Loch
Poll
Stoer
Bay of Stoer
Clachtoll
Broch
Clachtoll
Loch nan
Lub
Loch na
Loinne
Gorm
Loch Mór
10
200
20
QUINAG
Lochassynt
Lodge
Glas Bheinn
Eas a' Chual
Aluinn (Waterfall)
Loch na
Eircill
30
Dubh
a' Chuail
Loch nan
Ghriama
Balchladich

Loch Beannach

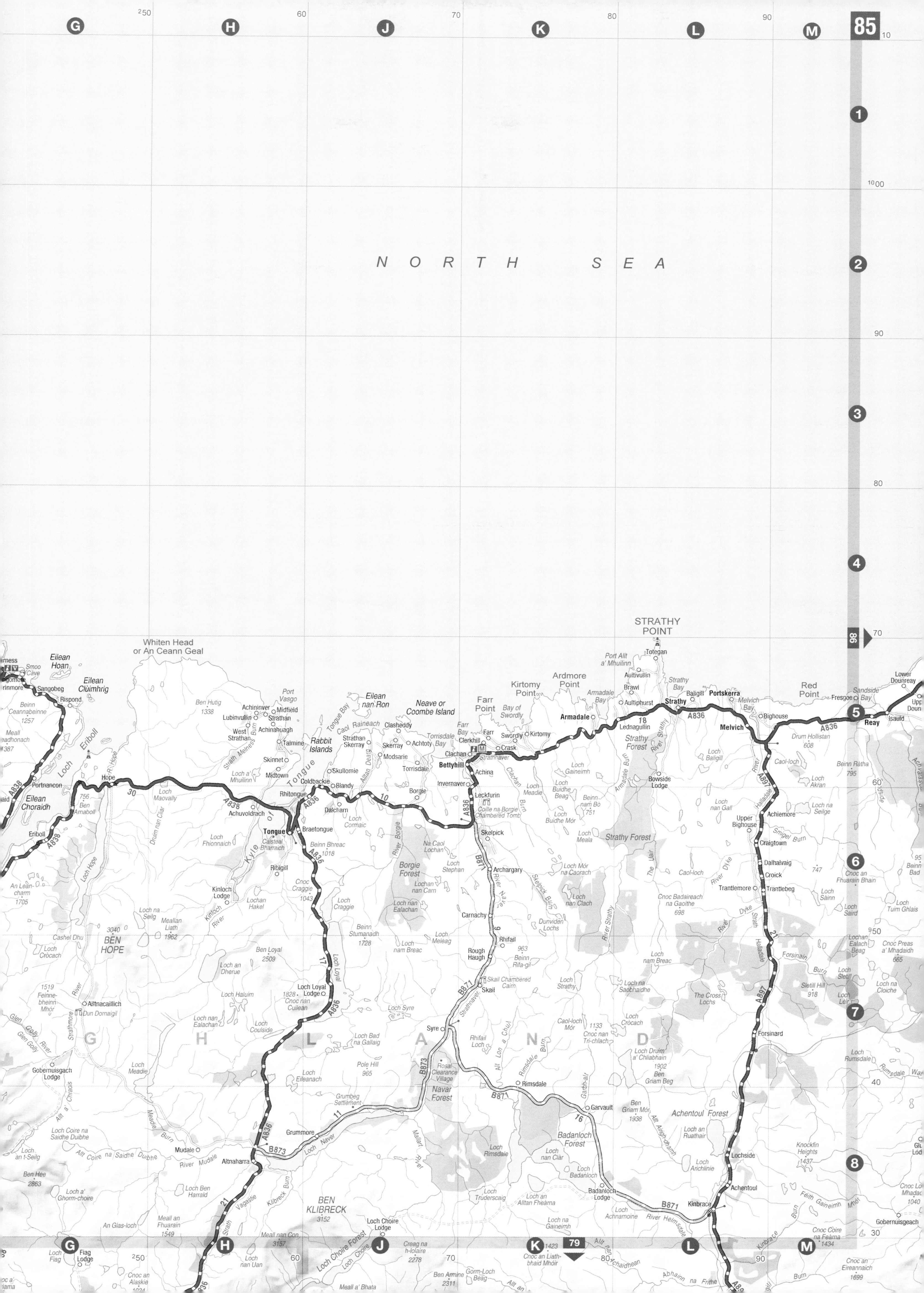
NORTH SEA
STRATHY POINT
Whiten Head or An Ceann Geal
Eilean Hoan
Eilean Cluimhrig
Smoo Cave
Sangobeg
Rispond
Loch Eriboll
Portnancon
Eilean Choraidh
Eriboll
Hope
Ben Hope
Ben Hutig
Achininver
Lubinvullin
Midfield
Strathan
West Strathan
Achinahuagh
Talmine
Rabbit Islands
Skinnet
Midtown
Kyle of Tongue
Rhitongue
Coldbackie
Tongue
Braetongue
Achuvoldrach
Ribigill
Kinloch Lodge
Ben Loyal
Loch Loyal
Loch Loyal Lodge
Eilean nan Ron
Neave or Coombe Island
Tongue Bay
Strathan Skerray
Clashaddy
Skerray
Achtoty
Modsarie
Torrisdale Bay
Torrisdale
Skullomie
Blandy
Dalcharn
Borgie
Borgie Forest
River Borgie
Farr Point
Farr Bay
Farr
Clerkhill
Clachan
Bettyhill
Invernaver
Achina
Leckfurin
Skelpick
Swordly
Bay of Swordly
Crask
Kirtomy
Kirtomy Point
Ardmore Point
Armadale
Armadale Bay
Port Allt a' Mhuilinn
Totegan
Aultivullin
Brawl
Aultiphurst
Lednagullin
Strathy
Strathy Bay
Strathy Forest
Baligill
Portskerra
Melvich
Melvich Bay
Bighouse
Red Point
Fresgoe
Sandside Bay
Reay
Isauld
Lower Dounreay
Bowside Lodge
Upper Bighouse
Achiemore
Craigtown
Dalhalvaig
Croick
Trantlemore
Trantlebeg
Halladale
Archargary
Carnachy
Rhifail
Rough Haugh
Skail
Syre
Strathnaver
River Naver
Rosal Clearance Village
Navar Forest
Loch Naver
Grummore
Mudale
Altnaharra
Rimsdale
Garvault
Badanloch Forest
Badanloch Lodge
Achentoul Forest
Achentoul
Lochside
Kinbrace
Forsinard
Forsinain
River Helmsdale
Ben Klibreck
Loch Choire Forest
Loch Choire Lodge
Flag Lodge
Gobernuisgach Lodge
Alltnacaillich
Dun Dornaigil
Strathmore
Ben Hee
Meall nan Con
Ben Armine
A836
A838
A897
B871
B873

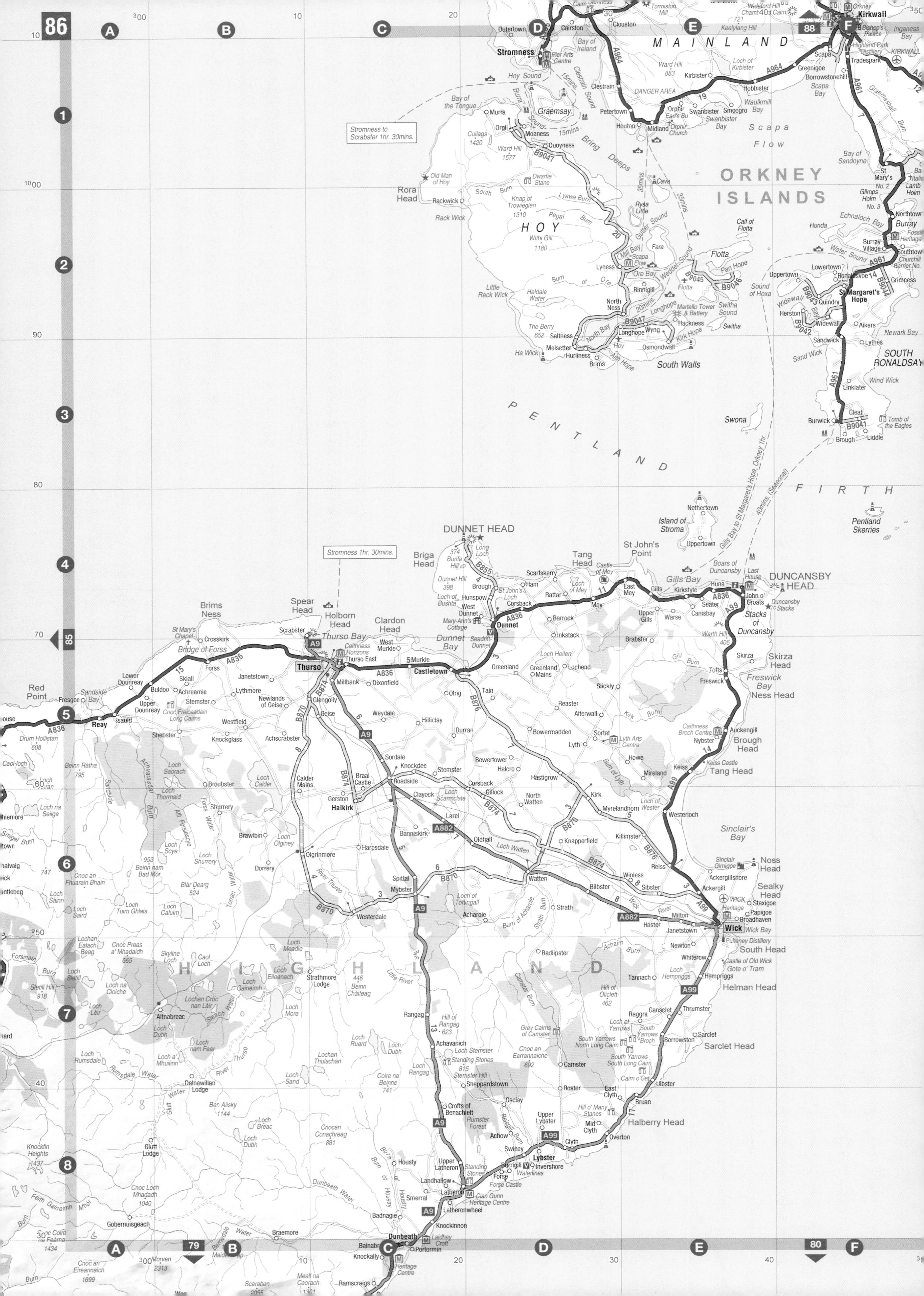

86
A
B
C
D
E
F
88
MAINLAND
Kirkwall
KIRKWALL
Stromness
Pier Arts Centre
Outertown
Cairston
Bay of Ireland
Clouston
Keelylang Hill
Tormiston Mill
Widefold Hill
Chamt
Cairn
Bishop's Palace
Inganess Bay
Highland Park Distillery
Scapa
Tradespark
Ward Hill
883
Kirbister
Loch of Kirbister
Greenigoe
Borrowstonehill
A964
A961
Clestrain
DANGER AREA
Hobbister
Waulkmill Bay
Scapa Bay
Hoy Sound
15mins
Clestrain Sound
Bay of the Tongue
Murra
Graemsay
Petertown
Orphir
Earl's Bu
Swanbister
Smoogro
Swanbister Bay
Orphir Church
Houton
Midland
Scapa Flow
Stromness to Scrabster 1hr. 30mins.
Orgil
Moaness
Cuilags
1420
Ward Hill
1577
B9047
Quoyness
Bring Deeps
35mins.
Bay of Sandoyne
St Mary's
Lamb Holm
Glimps Holm
Northtown
ORKNEY ISLANDS
Old Man of Hoy
Dwarfie Stane
Knap of Trowieglen
1310
Rora Head
Rackwick
South Burn
Lyawa Burn
Cava
Rysa Little
Gutter Sound
Rack Wick
HOY
Pegal Burn
Withi Gill
1180
Calf of Flotta
Hunda
Echnaloch Bay
Burray
Burray Village
Southtown
Churchill Barrier No.
Fara
Mill Bay
Lyness
Flotta
Pan Hope
Water Sound
Uppertown
Lowertown
Roniadsvoe
A961
B9044
Grimness
St Margaret's Hope
Sound of Hoxa
Widewall
B9043
Quindry
Herston
Widewall
Aikers
Newark Bay
Heldale Water
Little Rack Wick
Rinnigill
North Ness
B9045
B9046
Martello Tower & Battery
Switha Sound
Hackness
Switha
Longhope
The Berry
652
Saltness
North Bay
B9047
Longhope
Wyng
Kirk Hope
Melsetter
Hurliness
Hoy
Osmondwall
Ha Wick
Brims
Aith Hope
South Walls
Sandwick
B9042
Lythes
Sand Wick
SOUTH RONALDSAY
Wind Wick
A961
Linklater
Swona
Cleat
Burwick
B9041
Tomb of the Eagles
Brough
Liddle
PENTLAND FIRTH
Gills Bay to St Margaret's Hope, Orkney 1hr.
40mins. (Seasonal)
Nethertown
Island of Stroma
Uppertown
Pentland Skerries
DUNNET HEAD
Long Loch
Burifa Hill
374
Briga Head
Stromness 1hr. 30mins.
B855
Tang Head
Castle of Mey
St John's Point
Scarfskerry
Ham
Loch of Mey
Boars of Duncansby
Last House
DUNCANSBY HEAD
Gills Bay
Gills
Huna
Kirkstyle
John o' Groats
Duncansby Stacks
Dunnet Hill
398
Brough
St John's Loch
Hunspow
Corsback
Rattar
East Mey
Mey
A836
Seater
Canisbay
Loch of Bushta
West Dunnet
Mary-Ann's Cottage
Dunnet
Barrock
Upper Gills
Warse
A99
Stacks of Duncansby
Brims Ness
Spear Head
Holborn Head
Clardon Head
Scrabster
Thurso Bay
Caithness Horizons
Thurso East
West Murkle
Dunnet Bay
Seadrift Dunnet
Inkstack
Warth Hill
406
Brabster
St Mary's Chapel
Crosskirk
Bridge of Forss
A836
Thurso
Murkle
Castletown
Greenland
Loch Heilen
Greenland Mains
Lochend
Gill Burn
Skirza
Skirza Head
Tofts
Freswick
Freswick Bay
Ness Head
Red Point
Sandside Bay
Fresgoe
Lower Dounreay
Buldoo
Forss
Skiall
Achreamie
Janetstown
Lythmore
Millbank
Dixonfield
Olrig
Tain
B876
Slickly
Reay
Isauld
Upper Dounreay
Stemster
Cnoc Freiceadain Long Cairns
Newlands of Geise
Glengolly
Geise
B874
B870
Weydale
Hilliclay
Reaster
Alterwall
Kirk
Caithness Broch Centre
Auckengill
Nybster
Drum Hollistan
608
Westfield
Knockglass
Achscrabster
Shebster
Durran
Bowermadden
Sortat
Lyth Arts Centre
Lyth
Brough Head
Caol-loch
Beinn Ratha
795
Sandside
Achvarasdal Burn
Loch Saorach
Loch Thormaid
Loch Calder
Calder Mains
Braal Castle
Sordale
Knockdee
Stemster
Bowertower
Halcro
Hastigrow
Burn of Lyth
Howe
Mireland
Keiss
Keiss Castle
Tang Head
Loch na Seilge
Allt Forsiescye
Broubster
Forss Water
Shurrery
Gerston
Halkirk
Roadside
Clayock
Loch Scarmclate
Corsback
Gillock
North Watten
B874
Myrelandhorn
Loch of Wester
Westerloch
Sinclair's Bay
Brawlbin
Loch Olginey
Loch Scye
Loch Shurrery
Harpsdale
Banniskirk
Larel
A882
Oldhall
Loch Watten
B870
Knapperfield
Killimster
B876
953
Beinn nam Bad Mòr
747
Cnoc an Fhuarain Bhain
Blàr Dearg
524
Torran Water
Dorrery
Olgrinmore
River Thurso
Spittal
Mybster
B870
Watten
Bilbster
B874
Winless
Sibster
Reiss
Sinclair Girnigoe
Noss Head
Ackergillshore
Ackergill
Sealky Head
WICK
Staxigoe
Papigoe
Broadhaven
Loch Sàinn
Loch Saird
Loch Tuim Ghlais
Loch Caluim
B870
Westerdale
A9
Loch of Toftingall
Acharole
Burn of Acharole
Strath Burn
Strath
A882
Wick River
Milton
Haster
Janetstown
Wick
Wick Bay
Pulteney Distillery
South Head
Lochan Ealach Beag
Cnoc Preas a' Mhadaidh
665
Skyline Loch
Caol Loch
Loch Meadie
Badlipster
Achairn Burn
Newton
Whiterow
Castle of Old Wick
Gote o' Trams
Forsinain
Loch Sletill
Sletill Hill
918
Loch na Cloiche
HIGHLAND
Strathmore Lodge
Loch Eileanach
Loch Gaineimh
446
Beinn Châiteag
Little River
Camster Burn
Hill of Oliclett
462
Loch Hempriggs
Tannach
Hempriggs
A99
Helman Head
Loch Leir
Lochan Croc nan Lair
Altnabreac
Sleach Water
Loch More
Rangag
Hill of Rangag
623
Grey Cairns of Camster
Raggra
Gansclet
Thrumster
Loch Dubh
Loch nam Fear
Loch Ruard
Loch Dubh
Lochan Thulachan
Achavanich
Loch Stemster
Standing Stones
815
Stemster Hill
Cnoc an Earrannaiche
692
South Yarrows North Long Cairn
South Yarrows Broch
South Yarrows South Long Cairn
Cairn o'Get
Camster
Borrowston
Sarclet
Sarclet Head
Loch Rumsdale
Loch a' Mhuilinn
River Thurso
Rumsdale Water
Loch Rangag
Loch Sand
Coire na Beinne
741
Sheppardstown
Roster
East Clyth
Ulbster
Dalnawillan Lodge
Glutt Water
Ben Alisky
1144
Loch Breac
Loch Dubh
Cnocan Conachreag
881
Crofts of Benachielt
A9
Rumster Forest
Oselay
Upper Lybster
Achow
Hill o' Many Stanes
Mid Clyth
Bruan
Halberry Head
A99
Clyth
Overton
Knockfin Heights
1437
Glutt Lodge
Burn of Houstry
Houstry
Upper Latheron
Swiney
Lybster
Burrigill
Inveroshore
Waterlines
Standing Stones
Forse
Forse Castle
Landhallow
Latheron
Clan Gunn Heritage Centre
Smerral
Dunbeath Water
Latheronwheel
Cnoc Loch Mhadaidh
1040
Féith Gaineimh Mhòr
A9
Badnagie
Knockinnon
Gobernuisgeach
Braemore
Water
Dunbeath
Laidhay Croft
Balnabruich
Knockally
Portormin
Heritage Centre
Morven
2313
Maiden Pap
Beinn Coire na Feàrna
1434
Cnoc an Eireannaich
1699
Scaraben
2055
Meall na Caorach
1301
Ramscraigs
79
80
85
1
2
3
4
5
6
7
8
10
20
30
40
300
90
80
70
60
950
40
1000

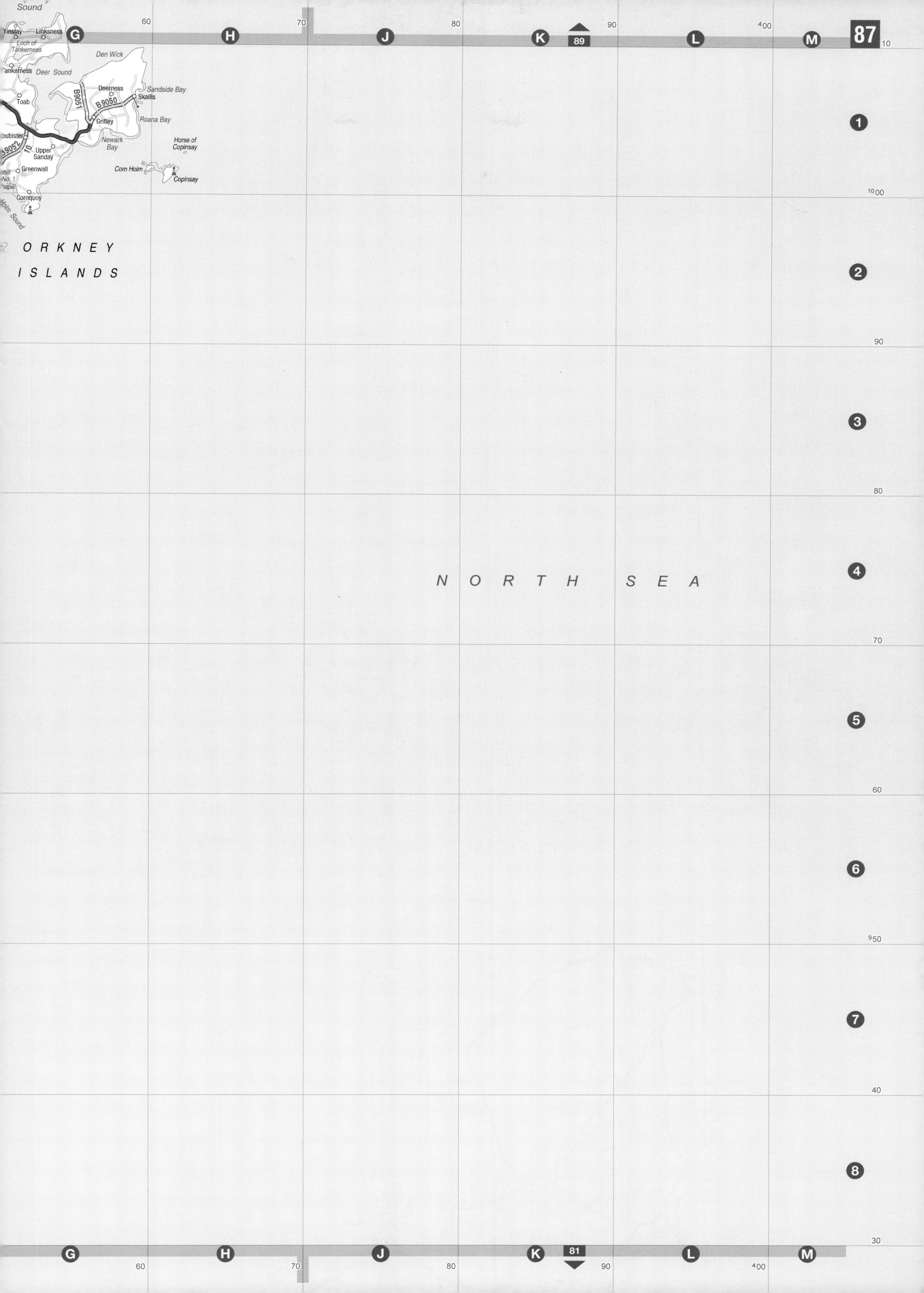

Sound

Yinstay   Linksness

Loch of
Tankerness

Tankerness   *Deer Sound*

Toab

Den Wick

Deerness

B9905   B 9050

Gritley

Sandside Bay
Skaills

Roana Bay

oubister

B905₁   10

Upper
Sanday

Newark
Bay

Horse of
Copinsay

Greenwall

Corn Hoim

Copinsay

No. 1
napel

Corniquoy

Holm Sound

O R K N E Y

I S L A N D S

N O R T H   S E A

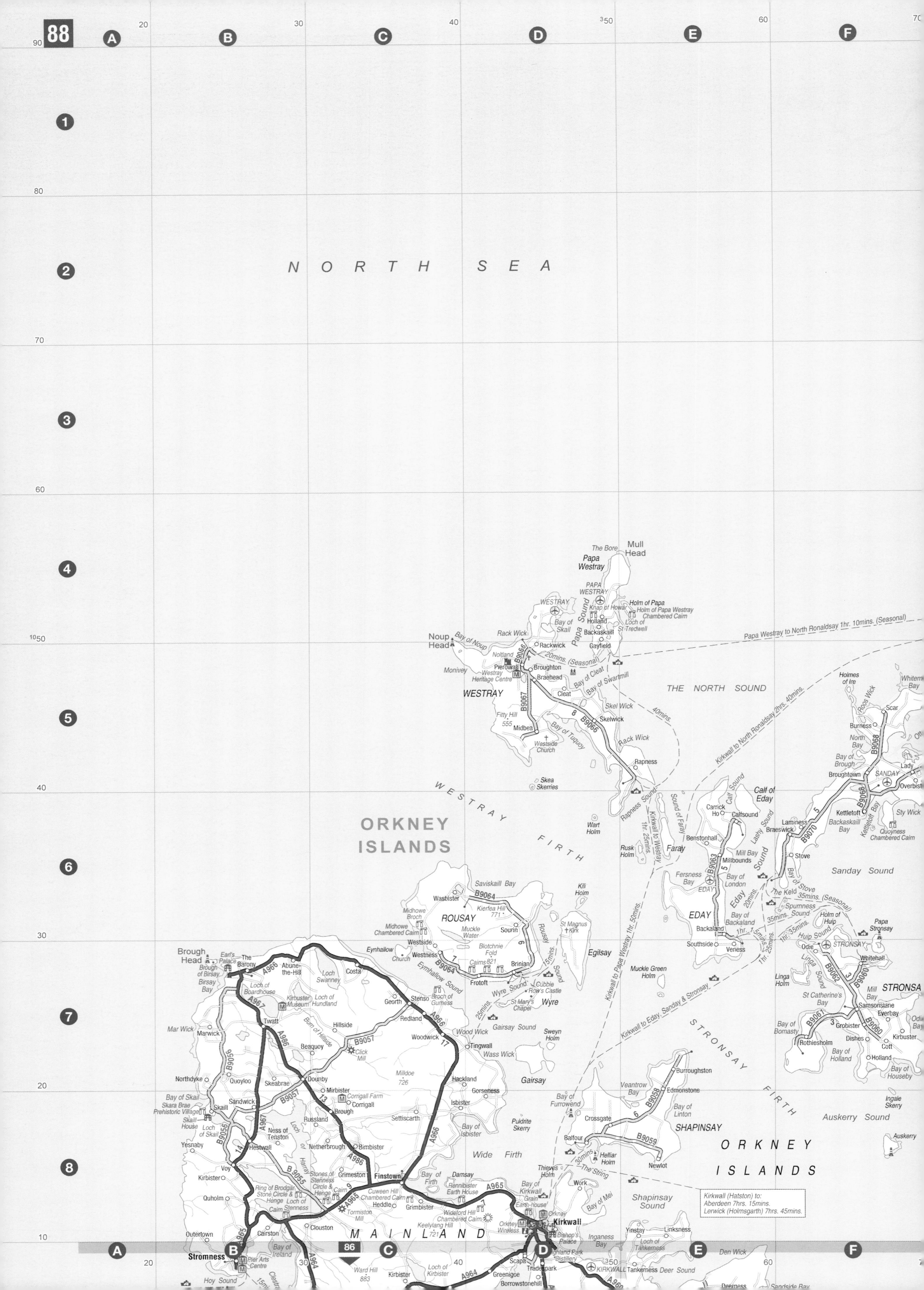

NORTH SEA

ORKNEY
ISLANDS

WESTRAY FIRTH

The Bore   Mull
Papa   Head
Westray

PAPA
WESTRAY
WESTRAY   Knap of Howar   Holm of Papa
Bay of   Holland   Holm of Papa Westray
Skail   Chambered Cairn
Backaskaill   Loch of
Gayfield   St Tredwell

Papa Westray to North Ronaldsay 1hr. 10mins. (Seasonal)

Noup   Bay of Noup   Rack Wick
Head   Rackwick
Monivey   Noltland   Broughton   20mins. (Seasonal)
Pierowall   Westray   Braehead   Bay of Cleat
Heritage Centre   Bay of Swartmill

THE NORTH SOUND   Holmes
of Ire   Whitemill
Bay
Roos Wick   Scar
Burness
Nouth
Bay   B9068
Lady
Bay of
Brough   Overbist
Broughtown   SANDAY

WESTRAY   Cleat   Skel Wick
Skelwick
Fitty Hill   40mins.
555   Midbea   Rack Wick
Westside   Bay of Tuquoy
Church   Rapness

Skea
Skerries   Wart
Holm   Rusk Holm

Kirkwall to North Ronaldsay 2hrs. 40mins.

Calf Sound   Calf of
Eday
Carrick   Calfsound   Kettletoft   Sty Wick
Ho   Lamiess   Backaskaill
Benstonhall   Braeswick   Bay
Mill Bay   Stove   Quoyness
Millbounds   Chambered Cairn
Bay of
London   Sanday Sound
Fersness
Bay   The Keld 35mins. (Seasonal)
EDAY   Spurness
Sound   35mins. Sound   Holm of
Huip
Backaland   Huip Sound   Papa
Southside   Stronsay
Veness   Odie   STRONSAY
Whitehall

Saviskaill Bay   Kili
Holm
Wasbister   B9064
Kierfea Hill
771   St Magnus
ROUSAY   Kirk
Muckle   Sourin
Water
Westside   Blotchnie
Westness   Fold   Rousay   Egilsay
Church   Cairns 821
Eynhallow   Brinian   Muckle Green
Midhowe   Frotoft   Holm
Broch   Cubbie
Midhowe   Row's Castle   Linga
Chambered Cairn   Wyre Sound   Holm   Linga
St Mary's   Sound
Chapel   Wyre   St Catherine's   Mill
Bay   Bay   STRONSAY

Brough   Earl's   The
Head   Palace   Barony
Brough   A966   Abune-   Loch
of Birsay   the-Hill   Swanney   Costa
Birsay   A967   Kirbuster   Georth
Bay   Loch of   Museum   Stenso   Bay of   Samsonslane   Everbay
Boardhouse   Hundland   Redland   Wood Wick   Bomasty   Grobister
Twatt   A966   Woodwick   Gairsay Sound   B9061   Dishes   Cott
Mar Wick   Hillside   Tingwall   Rothiesholm   Bay of
Marwick   Beaquoy   B9057   Wass Wick   Holland
B9055   Click   Gairsay   Bay of
Mill   Milldoe   Houseby
726
Northdyke   Quoyloo   Skeabrae   Dounby   Hackland   Burroughston   Ingale
Mirbister   Gorseness   Veantrow   Skerry
Bay of Skaill   Sandwick   Corrigall Farm   Isbister   Bay   Auskerry Sound
Skara Brae   Skaill   Corrigall   B9058   Edmonstone
Prehistoric Village   Brough   Puldrite   Bay of   Auskerry
Skaill   Loch of   Russland   Settiscarth   Skerry   Furrowend   Crossgate
House   Tenston   Bay of   B9059   SHAPINSAY
Yesnaby   Netherbrough   Bimbister   Isbister   Balfour   ORKNEY
Ness of   Wide   Firth   30mins.   Bay of
Tenston   Grimeston   Damsay   The 'String'   ISLANDS
Kirbister   Ring of Brodgar   Stones of   Finstown   Bay of   Helliar   Newlot
Stone Circle &   Stenness   Firth   Holm
Voy   Henge   Loch of   Circle &   Cuween Hill   Bay of   Thieves   Shapinsay
Quholm   Stenness   Cairn   Chambered Cairn   Heddle   Kirkwall   Holm   Sound
Heddle   Grimbister   Earth-house
Tormiston   Wideford Hill   Orkney
Mill   Chambered Cairn   Wireless
Outertown   Clouston   Keelylang Hill   Orkney   Kirkwall
721   Distillery

MAINLAND

Stromness   Pier Arts   Bishop's   Highland Park   Den Wick
Centre   Palace   Distillery
Ward Hill   Scapa   KIRKWALL   Tankerness   Deer Sound
883   Kirbister   Tradespark   Inganess
Loch of Kirbister   Greengate   Bay
Hoy Sound   Borrowstonehill   Deerness

Kirkwall (Hatston) to:
Aberdeen 7hrs. 15mins.
Lerwick (Holmsgarth) 7hrs. 45mins.

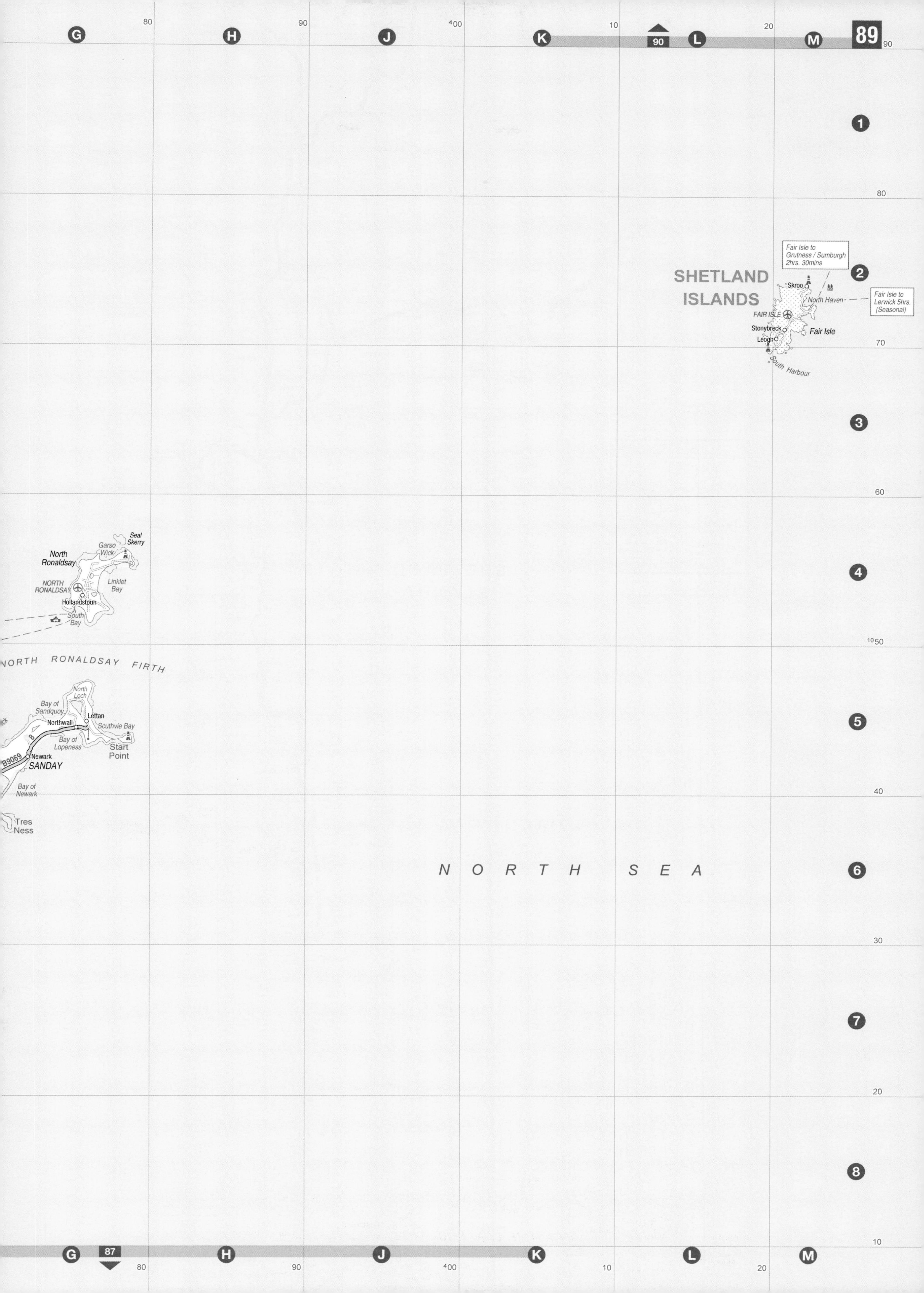

Fair Isle to Grutness / Sumburgh 2hrs. 30mins

SHETLAND ISLANDS

2

Fair Isle to Lerwick 5hrs. (Seasonal)

Skroo

North Haven

FAIR ISLE

Stonybreck   *Fair Isle*

Leogh

South Harbour

70

3

60

Seal Skerry

Garso Wick

North Ronaldsay

NORTH RONALDSAY   Linklet Bay

Hollandstoun

South Bay

4

10 50

NORTH RONALDSAY FIRTH

North Loch

Bay of Sandquoy

Northwall   Lettan   Scuthvie Bay

Bay of Lopeness

B9069   Newark   Start Point

SANDAY

Bay of Newark

5

40

Tres Ness

N O R T H   S E A

6

30

7

20

8

10

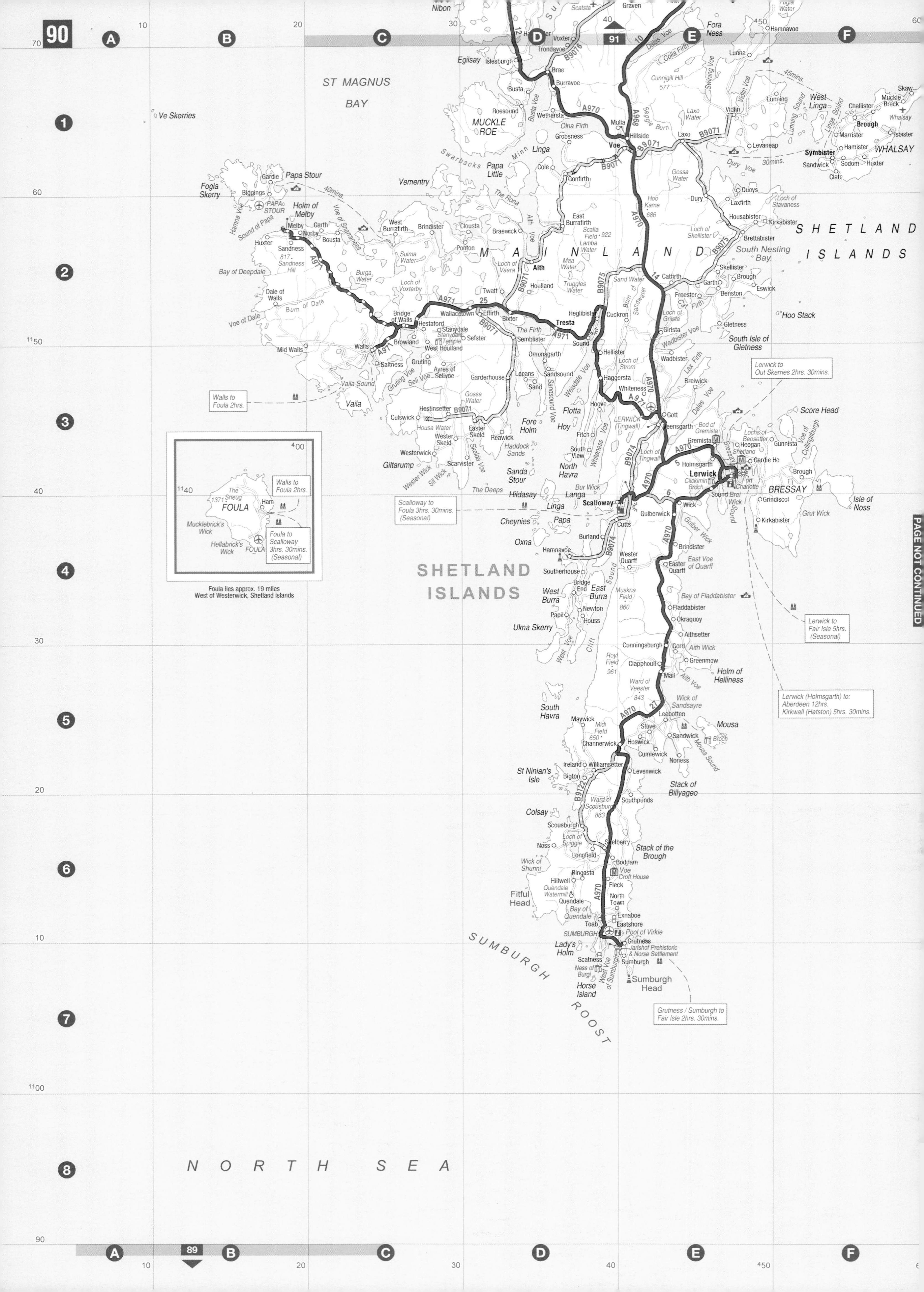

St Magnus Bay

NORTH SEA

SUMBURGH ROOST

SHETLAND ISLANDS

MAINLAND

Walls to Foula 2hrs.

Scalloway to Foula 3hrs. 30mins. (Seasonal)

Lerwick to Out Skerries 2hrs. 30mins.

Lerwick to Fair Isle 5hrs. (Seasonal)

Lerwick (Holmsgarth) to: Aberdeen 12hrs. Kirkwall (Hatston) 5hrs. 30mins.

Grutness / Sumburgh to Fair Isle 2hrs. 30mins.

Walls to Foula 2hrs.
Foula to Scalloway 3hrs. 30mins. (Seasonal)
FOULA
The Sneug 1371
Mucklebrick's Wick
Hellabrick's Wick
Ham
Foula lies approx. 19 miles West of Westerwick, Shetland Islands

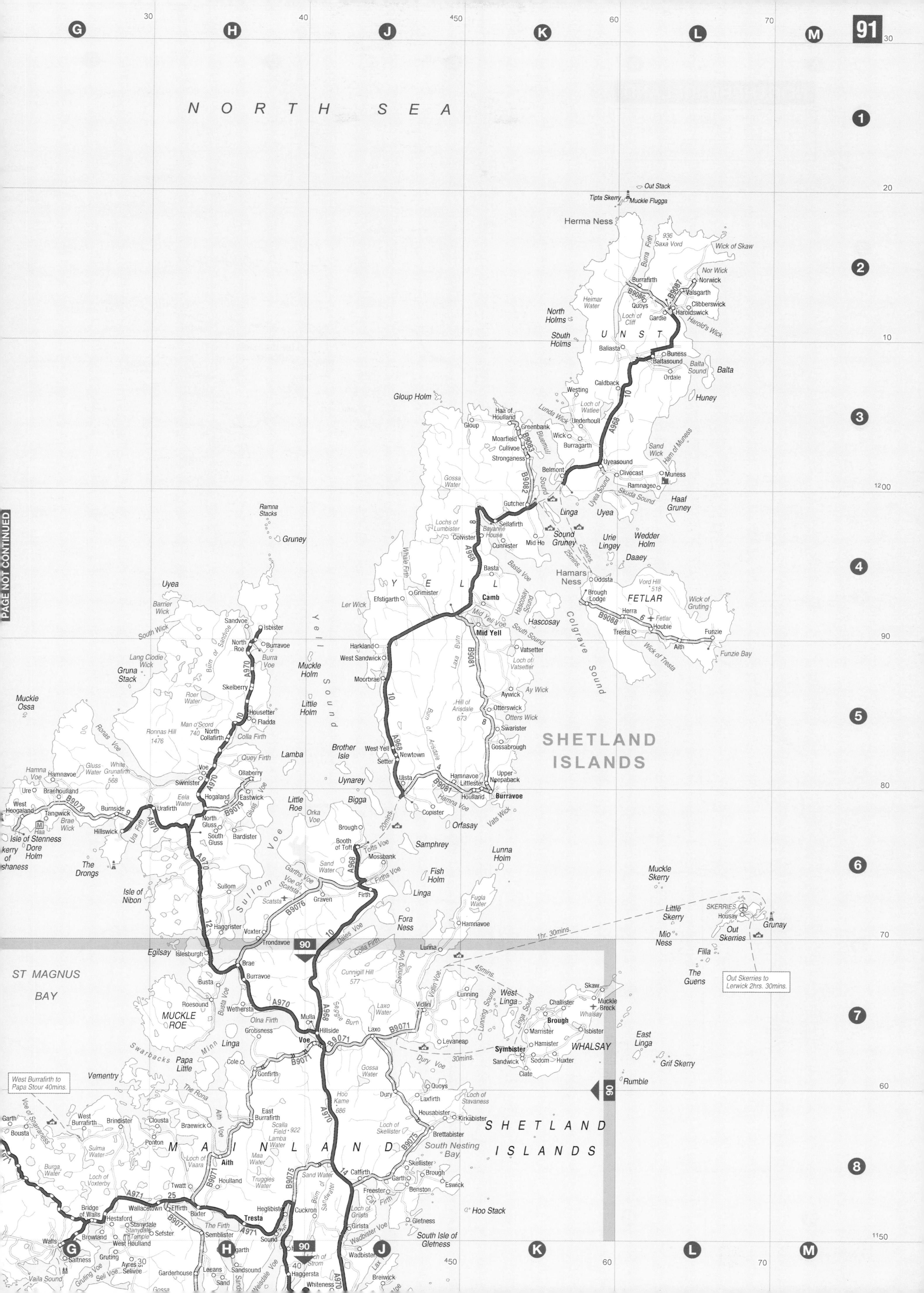

NORTH SEA
Out Stack
Tipta Skerry
Muckle Flugga
Herma Ness
Saxa Vord
Wick of Skaw
Burra Firth
Nor Wick
Norwick
Burrafirth
Valsgarth
Heimar Water
Quoys
Clibberswick
Haroldswick
Loch of Cliff
Gardie
Harold's Wick
North Holms
South Holms
UNST
Baliasta
Buness
Baltasound
Balta Sound
Balta
Ordale
Caldback
Westing
Huney
Loch of Watlee
Underhoull
Lunda Wick
Wick
Burragarth
Sand Wick
Ham of Muness
Uyeasound
Clivocast
Muness
Ramnageo
Skuda Sound
Haaf Gruney
Belmont
Uyea Sound
Linga
Uyea
Gloup Holm
Haa of Houlland
Gloup
Greenbank
Moarfield
Cullivoe
Bluemull Sound
Stronganess
Gossa Water
Gutcher
Sellafirth
Bayanne House
Lochs of Lumbister
Colvister
Cunnister
Mid Ho
Sound Gruney
Urie Lingey
Wedder Holm
Daaey
Hamars Ness
Oddsta
Brough Lodge
Vord Hill 518
FETLAR
Wick of Gruting
Herra
Fetlar
Houbie
Tresta
Funzie
Aith
Funzie Bay
Wick of Tresta
Colgrave Sound
Basta
Basta Voe
Ramna Stacks
Gruney
YELL
Whale Firth
Efstigarth
Grimister
Camb
Hascosay Sound
Hascosay
Ler Wick
Mid Yell Voe
Mid Yell
South Sound
Vatsetter
Loch of Vatsetter
Harkland
West Sandwick
Moorbrae
Laxa Burn
Burn of Arisdale
Hill of Arisdale 673
Aywick
Ay Wick
Otterswick
Otters Wick
Swarister
Gossabrough
SHETLAND ISLANDS
Yell Sound
Muckle Holm
Little Holm
Brother Isle
West Yell
Newtown
Setter
Ulsta
Hamnavoe
Upper Neepaback
Littlester
Burravoe
Houlland
Hamna Voe
Copister
Orfasay
Vats Wick
Lamba
Uynarey
Bigga
Little Roe
Orka Voe
Brough
Booth of Toft
Tofts Voe
Mossbank
Samphrey
Lunna Holm
20mins.
Uyea
Barrier Wick
Sandvoe
Isbister
South Wick
Burn of Sandvoe
North Roe
Burravoe
Burra Voe
Lang Clodie Wick
Gruna Stack
Skelberry
Roer Water
Housetter
Fladda
Man o'Scord 740
North Collafirth
Colla Firth
Ronnas Hill 1476
Quey Firth
Muckle Ossa
Ronas Voe
Gluss Water
White Grunafirth 568
Hamna Voe
Hamnavoe
Voe
Swinister
Ollaberry
Ure
Braehoulland
Eela Water
Hogaland
Eastwick
Gluss Voe
West Heogaland
Tangwick
Burnside
Urafirth
Haa
Brae Wick
Hillswick
Ura Firth
North Gluss
South Gluss
Bardister
Isle of Stenness
Dore Holm
The Drongs
Sullom Voe
Sand Water
Garths Voe
Voe of Scatsta
Firths Voe
Fish Holm
Muckle Skerry
Isle of Nibon
Sullom
Scatsta
Graven
Firth
Linga
Fugla Water
Little Skerry
SKERRIES
Housay
Grunay
Out Skerries
Haggrister
Voxter
Fora Ness
Hamnavoe
Mio Ness
Trondavoe
Dales Voe
1hr. 30mins.
Egilsay
Islesburgh
Colla Firth
Lunna
Filla
The Guens
Out Skerries to Lerwick 2hrs. 30mins.
ST MAGNUS BAY
Brae
Burravoe
Cunnigill Hill 577
Swining Voe
Vidlin Voe
45mins.
Busta
Skaw
Roesound
Busta Voe
Lunning
West Linga
Challister
Muckle Breck
MUCKLE ROE
Wethersta
A970
Laxo Water
Vidlin
Lunning Sound
Linga Sound
Brough
Whalsay
Olna Firth
Mulla
Segga Burn
East Linga
Grobsness
Hillside
Laxo
Marrister
Isbister
Linga
Minn
Voe
Levaneap
Symbister
Hamister
WHALSAY
Swarbacks Minn
Papa Little
Cole
Dury Voe
30mins.
Sandwick
Sodom
Huxter
Grif Skerry
Clate
Vementry
Gonfirth
Gossa Water
Rumble
West Burrafirth to Papa Stour 40mins.
The Rona
Hoo Kame 686
Dury
Quoys
Laxfirth
Loch of Stavaness
Housabister
Kirkabister
Garth
West Burrafirth
Brindister
Clousta
East Burrafirth
Loch of Skellister
Bousta
Braewick
Scalla Field 922
Brettabister
SHETLAND ISLANDS
Voe of Snarraness
Aith Voe
Ponton
Lamba Water
South Nesting Bay
Sulma Water
MAINLAND
Loch of Vaara
Maa Water
Aith
Sand Water
Skellister
Burga Water
Catfirth
Brough
Houlland
Truggles Water
Garth
Eswick
Loch of Voxterby
Twatt
Freester
Benston
Wallacetown
Effirth
Bixter
Heglibister
Cuckron
Burn of Sandwater
Cat Firth
Bridge of Walls
Hestaford
Tresta
Loch of Grista
Hoo Stack
Stanydale
Stanydale Temple
The Firth
Girlsta
Gletness
Browland
Sefster
Semblister
Sound
Wadbister Voe
South Isle of Gletness
Walls
West Houlland
Garth
Wadbister
Saltness
Gruting
Ayres
Selivoe
Gruting Voe
Sell Voe
Garderhouse
Leeans
Sandsound
Loch of Strom
Haggersta
Vaila Sound
Sand
Weisdale Voe
Whiteness
Breiwick
Lax Firth
Gossa
A968
A970
A971
B9078
B9079
B9076
B9071
B9075
B9081
B9082
B9083
B9084
B9086
B9087
B9088
A968 10
8
6
4
9
12
14
25
40
B9077
PAGE NOT CONTINUED
G H J K L M
1 2 3 4 5 6 7 8
30 40 450 60 70
20 10 1200 90 80 70 60 1150

90
90
90

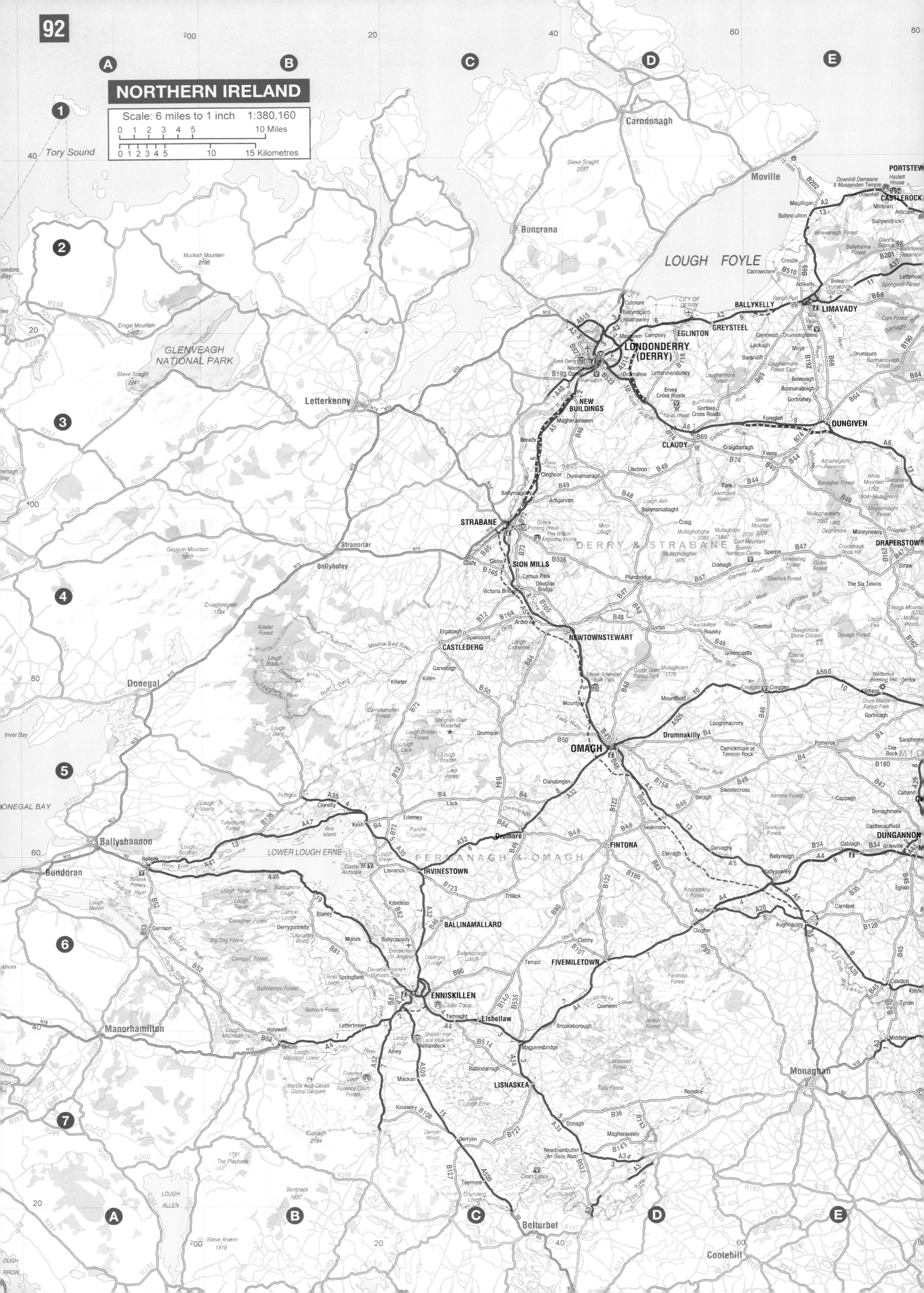
NORTHERN IRELAND
Scale: 6 miles to 1 inch 1:380,160
0 1 2 3 4 5 10 Miles
0 1 2 3 4 5 10 15 Kilometres
Tory Sound
Muckish Mountain 2198
Errigal Mountain 2467
GLENVEAGH NATIONAL PARK
Slieve Snaght 2241
Letterkenny
Buncrana
Carndonagh
Slieve Snaght 2017
Moville
LOUGH FOYLE
PORTSTEWART
CASTLEROCK
BALLYKELLY
LIMAVADY
GREYSTEEL
EGLINTON
LONDONDERRY (DERRY)
NEW BUILDINGS
CLAUDY
DUNGIVEN
STRABANE
Stranorlar
Ballybofey
Gaugum Mountain 1863
SION MILLS
DERRY & STRABANE
DRAPERSTOWN
Plumbridge
Croaghnageer 1794
CASTLEDERG
NEWTOWNSTEWART
Donegal
Inver Bay
Lough Derg
OMAGH
Drumnakilly
DONEGAL BAY
Pettigoe
Ballyshannon
Bundoran
LOWER LOUGH ERNE
IRVINESTOWN
Dromore
FINTONA
FERMANAGH & OMAGH
DUNGANNON
Ballygawley
Aughnacloy
BALLINAMALLARD
FIVEMILETOWN
ENNISKILLEN
Lisbellaw
Manorhamilton
Marble Arch Caves Global Geopark
LISNASKEA
Monaghan
Newtownbutler
Cuilcagh 2184
The Playbank 1781
LOUGH ALLEN
Benbrack 1637
Belturbet
Slieve Anierin 1919
Cootehill

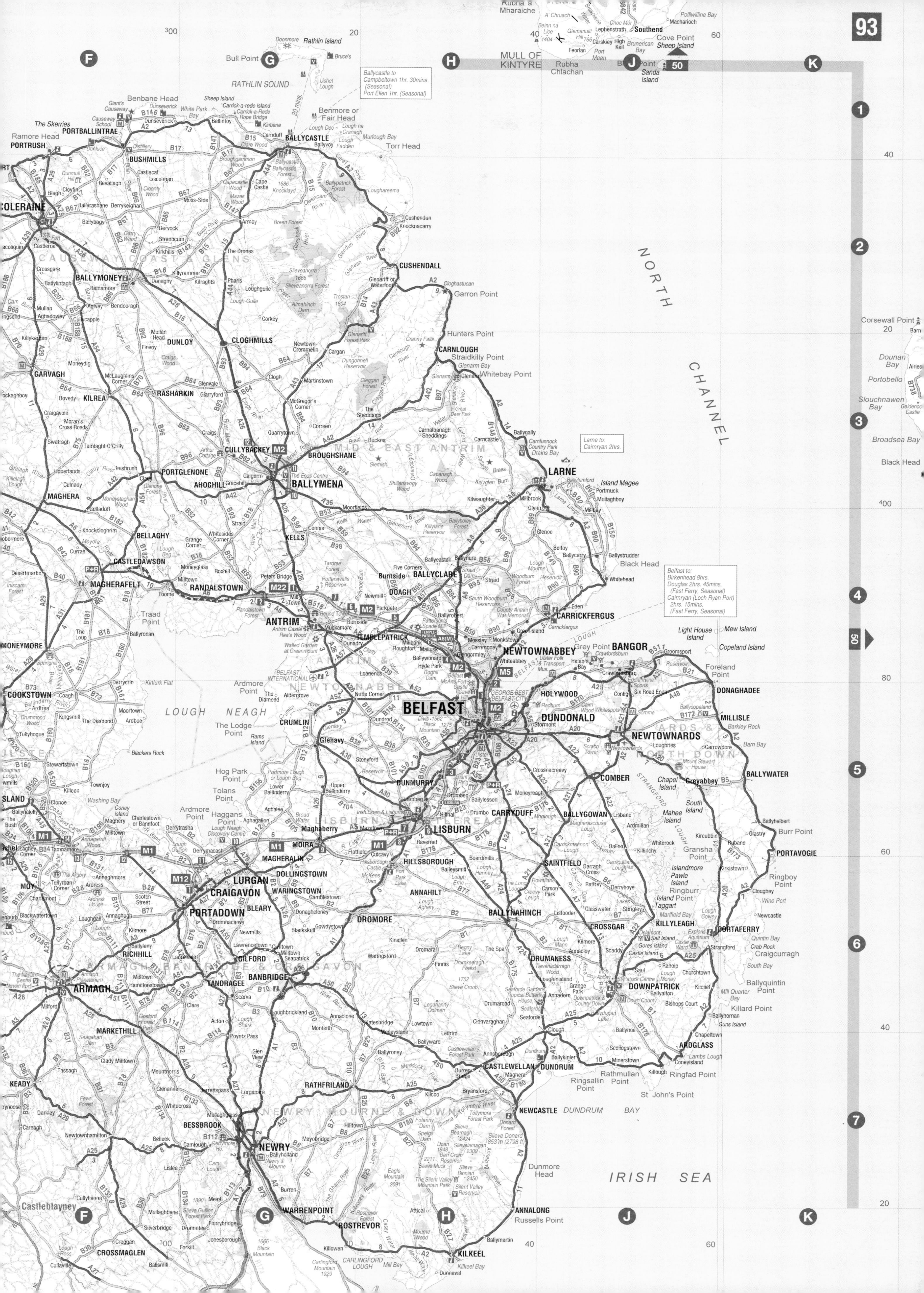
Rathlin Island
Bull Point
RATHLIN SOUND
MULL OF KINTYRE
Southend
Sanda Island
NORTH CHANNEL
The Skerries
Ramore Head
PORTRUSH
PORTBALLINTRAE
BUSHMILLS
Benbane Head
BALLYCASTLE
Benmore or Fair Head
Torr Head
COLERAINE
BALLYMONEY
CUSHENDALL
Garron Point
CLOGHMILLS
DUNLOY
GARVAGH
KILREA
RASHARKIN
CARNLOUGH
LARNE
CULLYBACKEY
BROUGHSHANE
BALLYMENA
PORTGLENONE
AHOGHILL
MAGHERA
BELLAGHY
CASTLEDAWSON
MAGHERAFELT
RANDALSTOWN
KELLS
BALLYCLARE
DOAGH
ANTRIM
TEMPLEPATRICK
CARRICKFERGUS
NEWTOWNABBEY
BANGOR
MONEYMORE
COOKSTOWN
LOUGH NEAGH
CRUMLIN
BELFAST
HOLYWOOD
DUNDONALD
DONAGHADEE
MILLISLE
NEWTOWNARDS
COMBER
BALLYWATER
DUNMURRY
LISBURN
CARRYDUFF
BALLYGOWAN
MOIRA
MAGHERALIN
HILLSBOROUGH
SAINTFIELD
PORTAVOGIE
LURGAN
CRAIGAVON
PORTADOWN
DOLLINGSTOWN
WARINGSTOWN
BLEARY
DROMORE
ANNAHILT
BALLYNAHINCH
CROSSGAR
KILLYLEAGH
PORTAFERRY
RICHHILL
GILFORD
TANDRAGEE
BANBRIDGE
ARMAGH
DRUMANESS
DOWNPATRICK
MARKETHILL
ARDGLASS
CASTLEWELLAN
DUNDRUM
KEADY
RATHFRILAND
NEWCASTLE
DUNDRUM BAY
BESSBROOK
NEWRY
IRISH SEA
Castleblayney
WARRENPOINT
ROSTREVOR
ANNALONG
CROSSMAGLEN
KILKEEL
CARLINGFORD LOUGH

INDEX TO CITIES, TOWNS, VILLAGES, HAMLETS, LOCATIONS & AIRPORTS

(1) A strict alphabetical order is used e.g. An Dùnan follows Andreas but precedes Andwell.

(2) The map reference given refers to the actual map square in which the town spot or built-up area is located and not to the place name.

(3) Major towns and destinations are shown in bold, i.e. **Aberdeen**. *Aber* 5J 73

(4) Where two or more places of the same name occur in the same County or Unitary Authority, the nearest large town is also given; e.g. Achiemore. *High* nr. Durness . . . .5F **84** indicates that Achiemore is located in square 5F on page **84** and is situated near Durness in the Unitary Authority of Highland.

(5) Only one reference is given although due to page overlaps the place may appear on more than one page.

COUNTIES and UNITARY AUTHORITIES with the abbreviations used in this index

INDEX

A

Aspenden—Biggin Hill

Aspenden. Herts 1L 21
Asperton. Linc 6K 37
Aspley Guise. C Beds 8G 29
Aspley Heath. C Beds 8G 29
Aspull. G Man 7E 40
Asselby. E Yor 5E 42
Assington. Suff 8F 30
Assington Green. Suff 6D 30
Astbury. Ches E 3G 35
Astcote. Nptn 6D 28
Asterby. Linc 2K 37
Asterley. Shrp 1B 26
Asterton. Shrp 2B 26
Asthall. Oxon 2L 19
Asthall Leigh. Oxon 2M 19
Astle. High 4H 79
Astley. G Man 7F 40
Astley. Shrp 8D 34
Astley. Warw 3M 27
Astley. Worc 5F 26
Astley Abbotts. Shrp 2F 26
Astley Bridge. G Man 6F 40
Astley Cross. Worc 5G 27
Aston. Ches E 5E 34
Aston. Ches W 2D 34
Aston. Derbs
nr. Hope 1K 35
nr. Sudbury 6K 35
Aston. Flin 3B 34
Aston. Here 5C 26
Aston. Herts 1K 21
Aston. Oxon 3M 19
Aston. Shrp
nr. Bridgnorth 2G 27
nr. Wem 7D 34
Aston. S Yor 1B 36
Aston. Staf 5F 34
Aston. Telf 1E 26
Aston. W Mid 2J 27
Aston. Wok 5E 20
Aston Abbotts. Buck 1F 20
Aston Botterell. Shrp 3E 26
Aston-by-Stone. Staf 6H 35
Aston Cantlow. Warw 6K 27
Aston Clinton. Buck 2F 20
Aston Crews. Here 1E 18
Aston Cross. Glos 8H 27
Aston End. Herts 1K 21
Aston Eyre. Shrp 2E 26
Aston Fields. Worc 5H 27
Aston Flamville. Leics 2B 28
Aston Ingham. Here 1E 18
Aston juxta Mondrum.
Ches E 4E 34
Astonlane. Shrp 2E 26
Aston le Walls. Nptn 6B 28
Aston Magna. Glos 8K 27
Aston Munslow. Shrp 3D 26
Aston on Carrant. Glos 8H 27
Aston on Clun. Shrp 3B 26
Aston-on-Trent. Derbs 7B 36
Aston Pigott. Shrp 1B 26
Aston Rogers. Shrp 1B 26
Aston Rowant. Oxon 4E 20
Aston Sandford. Buck 3E 20
Aston Somerville. Worc 8J 27
Aston Subedge. Glos 7K 27
Aston Tirrold. Oxon 5C 20
Aston Upthorpe. Oxon 5C 20
Astrop. Nptn 8C 28
Astwick. C Beds 8K 29
Astwood. Mil 7G 29
Astwood Bank. Worc 5J 27
Aswarby. Linc 6H 37
Aswardby. Linc 2L 37
Atcham. Shrp 1D 26
Atch Lench. Worc 6J 27
Athelhampton. Dors 6F 8
Athelington. Suff 4J 31
Athelney. Som 3B 8
Athelstaneford. E Lot 2C 60
Atherfield Green. IOW 8B 10
Atherington. Devn 3E 6
Atherington. W Sus 5H 11
Athersley. S Yor 7A 42
Atherstone. Warw 2M 27
Atherstone on Stour. Warw 6L 27
Atherton. G Man 7E 40
Ath-Tharracail. High 1A 64
Atlow. Derbs 5L 35
Attadale. High 2L 69
Attenborough. Notts 6C 36
Atterby. Linc 8G 43
Atterley. Shrp 2E 26
Atterton. Leics 2A 28
Attical. New M 7H 93
Attleborough. Norf 2G 31
Attleborough. Warw 2A 28
Attlebridge. Norf 8H 39
Atwick. E Yor 2J 43
Atworth. Wilts 7G 19
Auberrow. Here 7C 26
Aubourn. Linc 3G 37
Aucharnie. Abers 1F 72
Auchattie. Abers 6F 72
Auchavan. Ang 1E 66
Auchbreck. Mor 3B 72
Auchenback. E Ren 4D 58
Auchenblae. Abers 8G 73
Auchenbrack. Dum 2B 52
Auchenbreck. Arg 1K 57
Auchencairn. Dum
nr. Dalbeattie 6B 52
nr. Dumfries 3D 52
Auchencarroch. W Dun 1C 58
Auchencrow. Bord 3F 60
Auchendennan. Arg 1B 58
Auchendinny. Midl 3L 59
Auchengray. S Lan 4H 59
Auchenhalrig. Mor 7C 80
Auchenheath. S Lan 5G 59
Auchenlochan. Arg 2J 57
Auchenmade. N Ayr 5C 58
Auchenmalg. Dum 6H 51
Auchentiber. N Ayr 5B 58
Auchenvennel. Arg 1A 58
Auchindrain. Arg 7E 64
Auchininna. Abers 1F 72
Auchinleck. Dum 4K 51
Auchinleck. E Ayr 7D 58
Auchinloch. N Lan 2E 58
Auchinstarry. N Lan 2F 58
Auchleven. Abers 3F 72
Auchlochan. S Lan 6G 59
Auchlunachan. High 5B 78
Auchmillan. E Ayr 7D 58
Auchmithie. Ang 3K 67
Auchmuirbridge. Fife 7F 66
Auchmull. Ang 8E 72
Auchnacree. Ang 1H 67
Auchnafree. Per 4B 66
Auchnagallin. High 2L 71
Auchnagatt. Abers 1J 73
Aucholzie. Abers 6C 72
Auchreddie. Abers 1H 73
Auchterarder. Per 6C 66
Auchteraw. High 5D 70
Auchterderran. Fife 8F 66
Auchterhouse. Ang 4G 67
Auchtermuchty. Fife 6F 66
Auchterneed. High 8E 78
Auchtertool. Fife 8F 66
Auchtertyre. High 3K 69
Auchtubh. Stir 5K 65
Auckengill. High 5E 86
Auckley. S Yor 7D 42
Audenshaw. G Man 8H 41
Audlem. Ches E 5E 34
Audley. Staf 4F 34
Audley End. Essx 8B 30
Audmore. Staf 7G 35
Auds. Abers 7F 80
Augher. M Ulst 6D 92
Aughertree. Cumb 8G 53
Aughnacloy. M Ulst 6E 92
Aughton. E Yor 4E 42
Aughton. Lanc
nr. Lancaster 1D 40
nr. Ormskirk 7B 40
Aughton. S Yor 1B 36
Aughton. Wilts 8L 19
Aughton Park. Lanc 7C 40
Auldearn. High 8K 79
Aulden. Here 6C 26
Auldgirth. Dum 3D 52
Auldhouse. S Lan 4E 58
Ault a' chruinn. High 3L 69
Aultbea. High 5K 77
Aultdearg. High 7C 78
Aultgrishan. High 5J 77
Aultguish Inn. High 6D 78
Ault Hucknall. Derbs 3B 36
Aultibea. High 1L 79
Aultiphurst. High 5L 85
Aultivullin. High 5L 85
Aultmore. Mor 8D 80
Aultnamain Inn. High 5G 79
Aunby. Linc 8H 37
Aunsby. Linc 6H 37
Aust. S Glo 5D 18
Austerfield. S Yor 8D 42
Austin Fen. Linc 8L 43
Austrey. Warw 1L 27
Austwick. N Yor 1F 40
Authorpe. Linc 1M 37
Authorpe Row. Linc 2B 38
Avebury. Wilts 7K 19
Avebury Trusloe. Wilts 7J 19
Aveley. Thur 5B 22
Avening. Glos 4G 19
Averham. Notts 4E 36
Aveton Gifford. Devn 7J 5
Avielochan. High 4K 71
Aviemore. High 4J 71
Avington. Hants 2C 10
Avoch. High 8H 79
Avon. Hants 6K 9
Avonbridge. Falk 2H 59
Avon Dassett. Warw 6B 28
Avonmouth. Bris 6D 18
Avonwick. Devn 6K 5
Awbridge. Hants 3M 9
Awliscombe. Devn 5L 7
Awre. Glos 3F 18
Awsworth. Notts 5B 36
Axbridge. Som 8C 18
Axford. Hants 1D 10
Axford. Wilts 7L 19
Axminster. Devn 6B 8
Axmouth. Devn 6A 8
Aycliffe Village. Dur 3L 47
Aydon. Nmbd 5D 54
Aykley Heads. Dur 7F 54
Aylburton. Glos 3E 18
Aylburton Common. Glos 3E 18
Ayle. Nmbd 7M 53
Aylesbeare. Devn 6K 7
Aylesbury. Buck 2F 20
Aylesby. NE Lin 7K 43
Aylescott. Devn 4F 6
Aylesford. Kent 8D 22
Aylesham. Kent 8J 23
Aylestone. Leic 1C 28
Aylmerton. Norf 6H 39
Aylsham. Norf 7H 39
Aylton. Here 8E 26
Aylworth. Glos 1K 19
Aymestrey. Here 5C 26
Aynho. Nptn 8C 28
Ayot Green. Herts 2K 21
Ayot St Lawrence. Herts 2J 21
Ayot St Peter. Herts 2K 21
Ayr. S Ayr 7B 58
Ayres of Selivoe. Shet 3C 90
Ayreville. Torb 5L 5
Aysgarth. N Yor 7J 47
Ayshford. Devn 4K 7
Ayside. Cumb 7B 46
Ayston. Rut 1F 28
Ayton. Bord 3G 61
Aywick. Shet 5K 91
Azerley. N Yor 8L 47

B

Babbacombe. Torb 5M 5
Babbinswood. Shrp 6B 34
Babbs Green. Herts 2L 21
Babcary. Som 3D 8
Babel. Carm 1H 17
Babell. Flin 3L 33
Babingley. Norf 7C 38
Bablock Hythe. Oxon 3B 20
Babraham. Cambs 6B 30
Babworth. Notts 1D 36
Bac. W Isl 7H 83
Bachau. IOA 2D 32
Bacheldre. Powy 3M 25
Bachymbyd Fawr. Den 4K 33
Backaland. Orkn 6E 88
Backaskaill. Orkn 4D 88
Backbarrow. Cumb 7B 46
Backe. Carm 5J 15
Backfolds. Abers 8K 81
Backford. Ches W 2C 34
Backhill. Abers 2G 73
Backhill of Clackriach. Abers 1J 73
Backies. High 3J 79
Backmuir of New Gilston.
Fife 7H 67
Back of Keppoch. High 7H 69
Back Street. Suff 6D 30
Backwell. N Som 7C 18
Backworth. Tyne 4G 55
Bacon End. Essx 2C 22
Baconsthorpe. Norf 6H 39
Bacton. Here 8B 26
Bacton. Norf 6K 39
Bacton. Suff 5G 31
Bacton Green. Norf 6K 39
Bacup. Lanc 5G 41
Badachonacher. High 6G 79
Badachro. High 6J 77
Badanloch Lodge. High 8K 85
Badavanich. High 8B 78
Badbury. Swin 5K 19
Badby. Nptn 6C 28
Badcall. High 6E 84
Badcaul. High 4M 77
Baddeley Green. Stoke 4H 35
Baddesley Clinton. W Mid 4L 27
Baddesley Ensor. Warw 2L 27
Baddidarach. High 1A 78
Baddoch. Abers 7M 71
Badenscallie. High 3M 77
Badenscoth. Abers 2G 73
Badentarbat. High 2M 77
Badgall. Corn 7B 6
Badgers Mount. Kent 7A 22
Badgeworth. Glos 2H 19
Badgworth. Som 8B 18
Badicaul. High 3J 69
Badingham. Suff 5K 31
Badlesmere. Kent 8G 23
Badlipster. High 7D 86
Badluarach. High 4L 77
Badminton. S Glo 5G 19
Badnaban. High 1A 78
Badnabay. High 7E 84
Badnagie. High 8C 86
Badnellan. High 3J 79
Badninish. High 4H 79
Badrallach. High 4A 78
Badsey. Worc 7J 27
Badshot Lea. Surr 1F 10
Badsworth. W Yor 6B 42
Badwell Ash. Suff 5F 30
Bae Cinmel. Cnwy 2J 33
Bae Colwyn. Cnwy 3H 33
Bae Penrhyn. Cnwy 2H 33
Bagby. N Yor 7B 48
Bag Enderby. Linc 2L 37
Bagendon. Glos 3J 19
Bagginswood. Shrp 3E 26
Bàgh a Chàise. W Isl 6A 76
Bàgh a' Chaisteil. W Isl 6C 74
Bagham. Kent 8G 23
Baghasdal. W Isl 4D 74
Bagh Mor. W Isl 8K 75
Bagh Shiarabhagh. W Isl 5D 74
Bagillt. Flin 3M 33
Baginton. Warw 4M 27
Baglan. Neat 5G 17
Bagley. Shrp 7C 34
Bagley. Som 1C 8
Bagnall. Staf 4H 35
Bagnor. W Ber 7B 20
Bagshot. Surr 7G 21
Bagshot. Wilts 7M 19
Bagstone. S Glo 5E 18
Bagthorpe. Norf 6D 38
Bagthorpe. Notts 4B 36
Bagworth. Leics 1B 28
Bagwy Llydiart. Here 1C 18
Baildon. W Yor 4K 41
Baildon Green. W Yor 4K 41
Baile. W Isl 5L 75
Baile Ailein. W Isl 1D 76
Baile an Truiseil. W Isl 6G 83
Baile Boidheach. Arg 2G 57
Baile Glas. W Isl 8K 75
Bailemeonach. Arg 3A 64
Baile Mhanaich. W Isl 8J 75
Baile Mhartainn. W Isl 6J 75
Baile MhicPhail. W Isl 6K 75
Baile Mór. Arg 5H 63
Baile Mor. W Isl 7J 75
Baile nan Cailleach. W Isl 8J 75
Baile Raghaill. W Isl 7J 75
Bailey Green. Hants 3D 10
Baileyhead. Cumb 3K 53
Baileysmill. Lis 6H 93
Bailiesward. Abers 2D 72
Bail' Iochdrach. W Isl 8K 75
Baillieston. Glas 3E 58
Bailrigg. Lanc 2C 40
Bail Uachdraich. W Isl 7K 75
Bail' Ur Tholastaidh. W Isl 7J 83
Bainbridge. N Yor 6H 47
Bainsford. Falk 1G 59
Bainshole. Abers 2F 72
Bainton. E Yor 2G 43
Bainton. Oxon 1C 20
Bainton. Pet 1H 29
Baintown. Fife 7G 67
Baker Street. Thur 5C 22
Bakewell. Derbs 3L 35
Bala. Gwyn 7J 33
Y Bala. Gwyn 7J 33
Balachuirn. High 1G 69
Balbeg. High
nr. Cannich 2E 70
nr. Loch Ness 3E 70
Balbeggie. Per 5E 66
Balblair. High
nr. Bonar Bridge 4F 78
nr. Invergordon 7H 79
nr. Inverness 1F 70
Balby. S Yor 7C 42
Balcathie. Ang 4K 67
Balchladich. High 8C 84
Balchraggan. High 1F 70
Balchrick. High 6D 84
Balcombe. W Sus 2L 11
Balcombe Lane. W Sus 2L 11
Balcurvie. Fife 7G 67
Baldersby. N Yor 8A 48
Baldersby St James. N Yor 8A 48
Balderstone. Lanc 4E 40
Balderton. Ches W 3B 34
Balderton. Notts 4F 36
Baldinnie. Fife 6H 67
Baldock. Herts 8K 29
Baldrine. IOM 6D 44
Baldslow. E Sus 4E 12
Baldwin. IOM 6C 44
Baldwinholme. Cumb 6H 53
Baldwin's Gate. Staf 6F 34
Bale. Norf 6G 39
Balearn. Abers 8K 81
Balemartine. Arg 3E 62
Balephetrish. Arg 3F 62
Balephuil. Arg 3E 62
Balerno. Edin 3K 59
Balevullin. Arg 3E 62
Balfield. Ang 1J 67
Balfour. Orkn 8D 88
Balfron. Stir 1D 58
Balgaveny. Abers 1F 72
Balgonar. Fife 8D 66
Balgowan. High 6G 71
Balgown. High 7E 76
Balgrochan. E Dun 2E 58
Balgy. High 8K 77
Balhalgardy. Abers 3G 73
Baliasta. Shet 3L 91
Baligill. High 5L 85
Balintore. Ang 2F 66
Balintore. High 6J 79
Balintraid. High 6H 79
Balk. N Yor 7B 48
Balkeerie. Ang 3G 67
Balkholme. E Yor 5E 42
Ball. Shrp 7B 34
Ballabeg. IOM 7B 44
Ballacannell. IOM 6D 44
Ballacarnane Beg. IOM 6C 44
Ballachulish. High 2E 64
Ballagyr. IOM 6B 44
Ballajora. IOM 5D 44
Ballaleigh. IOM 6C 44
Ballamodha. IOM 7B 44
Ballantrae. S Ayr 3F 50
Ballards Gore. Essx 4F 22
Ballasalla. IOM
nr. Castletown 7B 44
nr. Kirk Michael 5C 44
Ballater. Abers 6C 72
Ballaugh. IOM 5C 44
Ballencrieff. E Lot 2B 60
Ballencrieff Toll. W Lot 2H 59
Ballentoul. Per 1B 66
Ball Hill. Hants 7B 20
Ballidon. Derbs 4L 35
Balliemore. Arg
nr. Dunoon 1K 57
nr. Oban 5C 64
Ballieward. High 2L 71
Ballig. IOM 6B 44
Ballimore. Stir 6K 65
Ballinamallard. Ferm 6C 92
Ballindarragh. Ferm 7C 92
Ballingdon. Suff 7E 30
Ballinger Common. Buck 3G 21
Ballingham. Here 8D 26
Ballingry. Fife 8E 66
Ballinluig. Per 2C 66
Ballintoy. Caus 1G 93
Ballintuim. Per 2E 66
Balliveolan. Arg 3C 64
Balloan. High 3F 78
Balloch. High 1H 71
Balloch. N Lan 2F 58
Balloch. Per 6B 66
Balloch. W Dun 1B 58
Ballochan. Abers 6E 72
Ballochgoy. Arg 3K 57
Ballochmyle. E Ayr 7D 58
Ballochroy. Arg 4G 57
Balloo. Ards 5J 93
Balls Cross. W Sus 3G 11
Ball's Green. E Sus 2A 12
Ballsmill. New M 7F 93
Ballyalton. New M 6J 93
Ballybogy. Caus 2F 93
Ballycarry. ME Ant 4J 93
Ballycassidy. Ferm 6C 92
Ballycastle. Caus 1G 93
Ballyclare. Ant 4H 93
Ballyeaston. Ant 4H 93
Ballygally. ME Ant 3H 93
Ballygawley. M Ulst 6E 92
Ballygowan. Ards 5J 93
Ballygown. Arg 3K 63
Ballygrant. Arg 3C 56
Ballyhalbert. Ards 5K 93
Ballyholland. New M 7G 93
Ballyhornan. New M 6J 93
Ballykelly. Caus 2E 92
Ballykinler. New M 7J 93
Ballylesson. Lis 5H 93
Ballymagorry. Derr 3C 92
Ballymartin. New M 7H 93
Ballymena. ME Ant 3G 93
Ballymichael. N Ayr 6J 57
Ballymoney. Caus 2F 93
Ballynagard. Derr 2D 92
Ballynahinch. New M 6H 93
Ballynakilly. M Ulst 5F 93
Ballynoe. New M 6J 93
Ballynure. Ant 4H 93
Ballyrashane. Caus 2F 93
Ballyrobert. Ant 4H 93
Ballyronan. M Ulst 4F 93
Ballyroney. Arm 7H 93
Ballyscullion. Caus 2E 92
Ballystrudder. ME Ant 4J 93
Ballyvoy. Caus 1G 93
Ballyward. New M 7H 93
Ballywonard. Ards 5K 93
Ballywater. Ant 4H 93
Balmacara. High 3K 69
Balmaclellan. Dum 4A 52
Balmacqueen. High 6F 76
Balmaha. Stir 8J 65
Balmalcolm. Fife 7G 67
Balmalloch. N Lan 2F 58
Balmeanach. High 2G 69
Balmedie. Abers 4J 73
Balmerino. Fife 5G 67
Balmerlawn. Hants 5M 9
Balmore. E Dun 2E 58
Balmore. High 1D 68
Balmullo. Fife 5H 67
Balmurrie. Dum 5H 51
Balnaboth. Ang 1G 67
Balnabruaich. High 6H 79
Balnabruich. High 1A 80
Balnacoil. High 2J 79
Balnacra. High 1L 69
Balnacroft. Abers 6B 72
Balnageith. Mor 8L 79
Balnaglaic. High 2E 70
Balnagrantach. High 2E 70
Balnaguard. Per 2C 66
Balnahard. Arg 8K 63
Balnain. High 2E 70
Balnakeil. High 5F 84
Balnaknock. High 7F 76
Balnamoon. Abers 8J 81
Balnamoon. Ang 1J 67
Balnamore. Caus 2F 93
Balnapaling. High 7H 79
Balornock. Glas 3E 58
Balquhidder. Stir 5K 65
Balsall. W Mid 4L 27
Balsall Common. W Mid 4L 27
Balscote. Oxon 7A 28
Balsham. Cambs 6B 30
Balstonia. Thur 5C 22
Baltasound. Shet 3L 91
Balterley. Staf 4F 34
Baltersan. Dum 5K 51
Balthangie. Abers 8H 81
Baltonsborough. Som 2D 8
Balvaird. High 8F 78
Balvaird. Per 6E 66
Balvenie. Mor 1C 72
Balvicar. Arg 6B 64
Balvraid. High 4K 69
Balvraid Lodge. High 2J 71
Bamber Bridge. Lanc 5D 40
Bamber's Green. Essx 1B 22
Bamburgh. Nmbd 6J 61
Bamford. Derbs 1L 35
Bamfurlong. G Man 7D 40
Bampton. Cumb 4D 46
Bampton. Devn 3J 7
Bampton. Oxon 3M 19
Bampton Grange. Cumb 4D 46
Banavie. High 8B 70
Banbridge. Arm 6G 93
Banbury. Oxon 7B 28
Bancffosfelen. Carm 5L 15
Banchory. Abers 6F 72
Banchory-Devenick. Abers 5J 73
Bancycapel. Carm 5L 15
Bancyfelin. Carm 5K 15
Banc-y-ffordd. Carm 3L 15
Banff. Abers 7F 80
Bangor. Ards 4J 93
Bangor. Gwyn 3E 32
Bangor-is-y-coed. Wrex 5B 34
Bangors. Corn 6B 6
Bangor's Green. Lanc 7B 40
Banham. Norf 3G 31
Bank, The. Ches E 4G 35
Bank. Hants 5L 9
Bank, The. Shrp 2E 26
Bankend. Dum 5E 52
Bankfoot. Per 4D 66
Bankglen. E Ayr 8E 58
Bankhead. Aber 4H 73
Bankhead. Abers 5F 72
Bankhead. S Lan 5G 59
Bankland. Som 3B 8
Bank Newton. N Yor 2H 41
Banknock. Falk 2F 58
Banks. Cumb 5K 53
Banks. Lanc 5B 40
Bankshill. Dum 3F 52
Bank Street. Worc 5E 26
Bank Top. Lanc 7D 40
Banners Gate. W Mid 2J 27
Banningham. Norf 7J 39
Banniskirk. High 6C 86
Bannister Green. Essx 1C 22
Bannockburn. Stir 8B 66
Banstead. Surr 8K 21
Bantham. Devn 7J 5
Banton. N Lan 2F 58
Banwell. N Som 8B 18
Banyard's Green. Suff 4K 31
Bapchild. Kent 7F 22
Bapton. Wilts 2H 9
Barabhas. W Isl 6G 83
Barabhas Iarach. W Isl 7G 83
Baramore. High 8H 69
Barassie. S Ayr 6B 58
Baravullin. Arg 3D 64
Barbaraville. High 6H 79
Barber Booth. Derbs 1K 35
Barber Green. Cumb 7B 46
Barbhas Uarach. W Isl 6G 83
Barbieston. S Ayr 8C 58
Barbon. Cumb 7E 46
Barbourne. Worc 6G 27
Barbridge. Ches E 4E 34
Barbrook. Devn 1G 7
Barby. Nptn 4C 28
Barby Nortoft. Nptn 4C 28
Barcaldine. Arg 3D 64
Barcheston. Warw 8L 27
Barclose. Cumb 5J 53
Barcombe. E Sus 4M 11
Barcombe Cross. E Sus 4M 11
Barden. N Yor 6K 47
Barden Scale. N Yor 2J 41
Bardfield End Green. Essx 8C 30
Bardfield Saling. Essx 1C 22
Bardister. Shet 6H 91
Bardnabeinne. High 4H 79
Bardney. Linc 3J 37
Bardon. Leics 8B 36
Bardon Mill. Nmbd 5A 54
Bardowie. E Dun 2D 58
Bardrainney. Inv 2B 58
Bardsea. Cumb 8B 46
Bardsey. W Yor 3A 42
Bardsley. G Man 7H 41
Bardwell. Suff 4F 30
Bare. Lanc 1C 40
Barelees. Nmbd 6F 60
Barewood. Here 6B 26
Barford. Hants 2F 10
Barford. Norf 1H 31
Barford. Warw 5L 27
Barford St John. Oxon 8B 28
Barford St Martin. Wilts 2J 9
Barford St Michael. Oxon 8B 28
Barfrestone. Kent 8J 23
Bargeddie. N Lan 3E 58
Bargod. Cphy 5L 17
Bargoed. Cphy 5L 17
Bargrennan. Dum 4J 51
Barham. Cambs 4J 29
Barham. Kent 8J 23
Barham. Suff 6H 31
Barharrow. Dum 6M 51
Bar Hill. Cambs 5L 29
Barholm. Linc 8H 37
Barkby. Leics 1D 28
Barkestone-le-Vale. Leics 6E 36
Barkham. Wok 7E 20
Barking. G Lon 5M 21
Barking. Suff 6G 31
Barkingside. G Lon 5A 22
Barking Tye. Suff 6G 31
Barkisland. W Yor 6J 41
Barkston. Linc 5G 37
Barkston Ash. N Yor 4B 42
Barkway. Herts 8L 29
Barlanark. Glas 3E 58
Barlaston. Staf 6G 35
Barlavington. W Sus 4G 11
Barlborough. Derbs 2B 36
Barlby. N Yor 4D 42
Barlestone. Leics 1B 28
Barley. Herts 8L 29
Barley. Lanc 3G 41
Barley Mow. Tyne 6F 54
Barleythorpe. Rut 1F 28
Barling. Essx 5F 22
Barlings. Linc 2H 37
Barlow. Derbs 2M 35
Barlow. N Yor 5D 42
Barlow. Tyne 5E 54
Barmby Moor. E Yor 3E 42
Barmby on the Marsh.
E Yor 5D 42
Barmer. Norf 6E 38
Barming. Kent 8D 22
Barming Heath. Kent 8D 22
Barmoor. Nmbd 6H 61
Barmouth. Gwyn 1F 24
Barmpton. Darl 4M 47
Barmston. E Yor 2J 43
Barmulloch. Glas 3E 58
Barnack. Pet 1H 29
Barnacle. Warw 3A 28
Barnard Castle. Dur 4J 47
Barnard Gate. Oxon 2B 20
Barnardiston. Suff 7D 30
Barnbarroch. Dum 6C 52
Barnburgh. S Yor 7B 42
Barnby. Suff 3L 31
Barnby Dun. S Yor 7D 42
Barnby in the Willows.
Notts 4F 36
Barnby Moor. Notts 1D 36
Barnes. G Lon 6K 21
Barnes Street. Kent 1C 12
Barnet. G Lon 4K 21
Barnetby le Wold. N Lin 7H 43
Barney. Norf 6F 38
Barnham. Suff 4E 30
Barnham. W Sus 5G 11
Barnham Broom. Norf 1G 31
Barnhead. Ang 2K 67
Barnhill. D'dee 4H 67
Barnhill. Mor 8M 79
Barnhill. Per 5E 66
Barnhills. Dum 4E 50
Barningham. Dur 4J 47
Barningham. Suff 4F 30
Barnoldby le Beck. NE Lin 7K 43
Barnoldswick. Lanc 3G 41
Barns Green. W Sus 3J 11
Barnsley. Glos 3J 19
Barnsley. Shrp 2F 26
Barnsley. S Yor 7M 41
Barnstaple. Devn 2E 6
Barnston. Essx 2C 22
Barnston. Mers 1A 34
Barnstone. Notts 6E 36
Barnt Green. Worc 4J 27
Barnton. Ches W 2E 34
Barnwell. Cambs 6A 30
Barnwell. Nptn 3H 29
Barnwood. Glos 2G 19
Barons Cross. Here 6C 26
Barony, The. Orkn 7B 88
Barr. Dum 1B 52
Barr. S Ayr 2H 51
Barra Airport. W Isl 5C 74
Barrachan. Dum 7J 51
Barraglom. W Isl 8E 82
Barrahormid. Arg 1G 57
Barrapol. Arg 3E 62
Barrasford. Nmbd 4C 54
Barravullin. Arg 7C 64
Barregarrow. IOM 6C 44
Barrhead. E Ren 4D 58
Barrhill. S Ayr 3H 51
Barri. V Glam 8L 17
Barrington. Cambs 7L 29
Barrington. Som 4B 8
Barripper. Corn 5K 3
Barrmill. N Ayr 4B 58
Barrock. High 4D 86
Barrow. Lanc 4F 40
Barrow. Rut 8F 36
Barrow. Shrp 1E 26
Barrow. Som 2F 8
Barrow. Suff 5D 30
Barroway Drove. Norf 1B 30
Barrow Bridge. G Man 6E 40
Barrowburn. Nmbd 8F 60
Barrowby. Linc 6F 36
Barrowcliff. N Yor 7H 49
Barrow Common. N Som 7D 18
Barrowden. Rut 1G 29
Barrowford. Lanc 4G 41
Barrow Gurney. N Som 7D 18
Barrow Haven. N Lin 5H 43
Barrow Hill. Derbs 2B 36
Barrow-in-Furness. Cumb 8M 45
Barrow Nook. Lanc 7C 40
Barrows Green. Cumb 7D 46
Barrow's Green. Hal 1D 34
Barrow Street. Wilts 2G 9
Barrow upon Humber.
N Lin 5H 43
Barrow upon Soar. Leics 8C 36
Barrow upon Trent. Derbs 7A 36
Barry. Ang 4J 67
Barry. V Glam 8L 17
Barry Island. V Glam 8L 17
Barsby. Leics 8D 36
Barsham. Suff 3K 31
Barston. W Mid 4L 27
Bartestree. Here 7D 26
Barthol Chapel. Abers 2H 73
Bartholomew Green. Essx 1D 22
Barthomley. Ches E 4F 34
Bartley. Hants 4M 9
Bartley Green. W Mid 3J 27
Bartlow. Cambs 7B 30
Barton. Cambs 6M 29
Barton. Ches W 4C 34
Barton. Cumb 3C 46
Barton. Glos 1K 19
Barton. IOW 7C 10
Barton. Lanc
nr. Ormskirk 7B 40
nr. Preston 4D 40
Barton. N Som 8B 18
Barton. N Yor 5L 47
Barton. Oxon 3C 20
Barton. Torb 5M 5
Barton. Warw 6K 27
Barton Bendish. Norf 1D 30
Barton Gate. Staf 8K 35
Barton Green. Staf 8K 35
Barton Hartsthorn. Buck 8D 28
Barton Hill. N Yor 1E 42
Barton in Fabis. Notts 6C 36
Barton in the Beans. Leics 1A 28
Barton-le-Clay. C Beds 8H 29
Barton-le-Street. N Yor 8E 48
Barton-le-Willows. N Yor 1E 42
Barton Mills. Suff 4D 30
Barton on Sea. Hants 6L 9
Barton-on-the-Heath. Warw 8L 27
Barton St David. Som 2D 8
Barton Seagrave. Nptn 4F 28
Barton Stacey. Hants 1B 10
Barton Town. Devn 1F 6
Barton Turf. Norf 7K 39
Barton-Under-Needwood.
Staf 8K 35
Barton-upon-Humber. N Lin 5H 43
Barton Waterside. N Lin 5H 43
Barugh Green. S Yor 7M 41
Barway. Cambs 4B 30
Barwell. Leics 2B 28
Barwick. Herts 2L 21
Barwick. Som 4D 8
Barwick in Elmet. W Yor 4A 42
Baschurch. Shrp 7C 34
Bascote. Warw 5B 28
Basford Green. Staf 4H 35
Bashall Eaves. Lanc 3E 40
Bashall Town. Lanc 3F 40
Bashley. Hants 6L 9
Basildon. Essx 5D 22
Basingstoke. Hants 8D 20
Baslow. Derbs 2L 35
Bason Bridge. Som 1B 8
Bassaleg. Newp 5A 18
Bassendean. Bord 5D 60
Bassenthwaite. Cumb 8G 53
Bassett. Sotn 4B 10
Bassingbourn. Cambs 7L 29
Bassingfield. Notts 6D 36
Bassingham. Linc 3G 37
Bassingthorpe. Linc 7G 37
Bassus Green. Herts 1L 21
Basta. Shet 4K 91
Baston. Linc 8J 37
Bastonford. Worc 6G 27
Bastwick. Norf 8L 39
Batchley. Worc 5J 27
Batchworth. Herts 4H 21
Batcombe. Dors 5E 8
Batcombe. Som 2E 8
Bate Heath. Ches E 2E 34
Bath. Bath 7F 18
Bathampton. Bath 7F 18
Bathealton. Som 3K 7
Batheaston. Bath 7F 18
Bathford. Bath 7F 18
Bathgate. W Lot 3H 59
Bathley. Notts 4E 36
Bathpool. Corn 8B 6
Bathpool. Som 3A 8
Bathville. W Lot 3H 59
Bathway. Som 8D 18
Batley. W Yor 5L 41
Batsford. Glos 8K 27
Batson. Devn 8K 5
Battersby. N Yor 5C 48
Battersea. G Lon 6K 21
Battisborough Cross. Devn 7J 5
Battisford. Suff 6G 31
Battisford Tye. Suff 6G 31
Battle. E Sus 4D 12
Battle. Powy 1K 17
Battleborough. Som 8B 18
Battledown. Glos 1H 19
Battlefield. Shrp 8D 34
Battlesbridge. Essx 4D 22
Battlesden. C Beds 1G 21
Battlesea Green. Suff 4J 31
Battleton. Som 3J 7
Battram. Leics 1B 28
Battramsley. Hants 6M 9
Batt's Corner. Surr 1F 10
Bauds of Cullen. Mor 7D 80
Baugh. Arg 3F 62
Baughton. Worc 7G 27
Baughurst. Hants 7C 20
Baulking. Oxon 4M 19
Baumber. Linc 2K 37
Baunton. Glos 3J 19
Baverstock. Wilts 2J 9
Bawburgh. Norf 1H 31
Bawdeswell. Norf 7G 39
Bawdrip. Som 2B 8
Bawdsey. Suff 7K 31
Bawsey. Norf 8C 38
Bawtry. S Yor 8D 42
Baxenden. Lanc 5F 40
Baxterley. Warw 2L 27
Baxter's Green. Suff 6D 30
Bay. High 8D 76
Baybridge. Hants 3C 10
Baybridge. Nmbd 6C 54
Baycliff. Cumb 8A 46
Baydon. Wilts 6L 19
Bayford. Herts 3L 21
Bayford. Som 3F 8
Bayles. Cumb 7M 53
Baylham. Suff 6H 31
Baynard's Green. Oxon 1C 20
Bayston Hill. Shrp 1C 26
Baythorne End. Essx 7D 30
Baythorpe. Linc 5K 37
Bayton. Worc 4E 26
Bayton Common. Worc 4F 26
Bayworth. Oxon 3C 20
Beach. S Glo 6F 18
Beachampton. Buck 8E 28
Beachamwell. Norf 1D 30
Beachley. Glos 4D 18
Beacon. Devn 5L 7
Beacon End. Essx 1F 22
Beacon Hill. Surr 2F 10
Beacon's Bottom. Buck 4E 20
Beaconsfield. Buck 4G 21
Beacrabhaic. W Isl 4C 76
Beadlam. N Yor 7D 48
Beadnell. Nmbd 7K 61
Beaford. Devn 4E 6
Beal. Nmbd 5H 61
Beal. N Yor 5C 42
Bealsmill. Corn 8C 6
Beam Hill. Staf 7L 35
Beamhurst. Staf 6J 35
Beaminster. Dors 5C 8
Beamish. Dur 6F 54
Beamond End. Buck 4G 21
Beamsley. N Yor 2J 41
Bean. Kent 6B 22
Beanacre. Wilts 7H 19
Beanley. Nmbd 8H 61
Beaquoy. Orkn 7C 88
Beardwood. Bkbn 5E 40
Beare Green. Surr 1J 11
Bearley. Warw 5K 27
Bearpark. Dur 7F 54
Bearsbridge. Nmbd 6A 54
Bearsden. E Dun 2D 58
Bearsted. Kent 8D 22
Bearstone. Shrp 6F 34
Bearwood. Pool 6J 9
Bearwood. W Mid 3J 27
Beattock. Dum 1E 52
Beauchamp Roding. Essx 2B 22
Beauchief. S Yor 1M 35
Beaufort. Blae 3L 17
Beaulieu. Hants 5A 10
Beauly. High 1F 70
Beaumaris. IOA 3F 32
Beaumont. Cumb 6H 53
Beaumont. Essx 1H 23
Beaumont Hill. Darl 4L 47
Beaumont Leys. Leic 1C 28
Beausale. Warw 4L 27
Beauvale. Notts 5B 36
Beauworth. Hants 3C 10
Beaworthy. Devn 6D 6
Beazley End. Essx 1D 22
Bebington. Mers 1B 34
Bebside. Nmbd 3F 54
Beccles. Suff 3L 31
Becconsall. Lanc 5C 40
Beckbury. Shrp 1F 26
Beckenham. G Lon 7L 21
Beckermet. Cumb 4K 45
Beckett End. Norf 2D 30
Beck Foot. Cumb 6E 46
Beckfoot. Cumb
nr. Broughton in Furness 6L 45
nr. Seascale 4L 45
nr. Silloth 7E 52
Beckford. Worc 8H 27
Beckhampton. Wilts 7J 19
Beck Hole. N Yor 5F 48
Beckingham. Linc 4F 36
Beckingham. Notts 8E 42
Beckington. Som 8G 19
Beckley. E Sus 3E 12
Beckley. Hants 6L 9
Beckley. Oxon 2C 20
Beck Row. Suff 4C 30
Beck Side. Cumb
nr. Cartmel 7B 46
nr. Ulverston 6M 45
Beckside. Cumb 7E 46
Beckton. G Lon 5M 21
Beckwithshaw. N Yor 2L 41
Becontree. G Lon 5A 22
Bedale. N Yor 7L 47
Bedburn. Dur 8E 54
Bedchester. Dors 4G 9
Beddau. Rhon 6K 17
Beddgelert. Gwyn 6E 32
Beddingham. E Sus 5M 11
Beddington. G Lon 7L 21
Bedfield. Suff 5J 31
Bedford. Bed 7H 29
Bedford. G Man 8E 40
Bedham. W Sus 3H 11
Bedhampton. Hants 5E 10
Bedingfield. Suff 5H 31
Bedingham Green. Norf 2J 31
Bedlam. N Yor 1L 41
Bedlar's Green. Essx 1B 22
Bedlington. Nmbd 3F 54
Bedlinog. Mer T 4K 17
Bedminster. Bris 6D 18
Bedmond. Herts 3H 21
Bednall. Staf 8H 35
Bedrule. Bord 8D 60
Bedstone. Shrp 4B 26
Bedwas. Cphy 6L 17
Bedwellty. Cphy 4L 17
Bedworth. Warw 3A 28
Beeby. Leics 1D 28
Beech. Hants 2D 10
Beech. Staf 6G 35
Beechcliffe. W Yor 3J 41
Beech Hill. W Ber 7D 20
Beechingstoke. Wilts 8J 19
Beedon. W Ber 6B 20
Beeford. E Yor 2J 43
Beeley. Derbs 3L 35
Beelsby. NE Lin 7K 43
Beenham. W Ber 7C 20
Beeny. Corn 2D 4
Beer. Devn 7M 7
Beer. Som 2C 8
Beercrocombe. Som 3B 8
Beer Hackett. Dors 4E 8
Beesands. Devn 7L 5
Beesby. Linc 1A 38
Beeson. Devn 7L 5
Beeston. C Beds 7J 29
Beeston. Ches W 4D 34
Beeston. Norf 8F 38
Beeston. Notts 6C 36
Beeston. W Yor 4L 41
Beeston Regis. Norf 5H 39
Beeswing. Dum 5C 52
Beetham. Cumb 8C 46
Beetham. Som 4A 8
Beetley. Norf 8F 38
Beffcote. Staf 8G 35
Began. Card 6M 17
Begbroke. Oxon 2B 20
Begdale. Cambs 1A 30
Begelly. Pemb 6H 15
Beggar Hill. Essx 3C 22
Beggar's Bush. Powy 5A 26
Beggearn Huish. Som 2K 7
Beguildy. Powy 5L 25
Beighton. Norf 1K 31
Beighton. S Yor 1B 36
Beighton Hill. Derbs 4L 35
Beinn Casgro. W Isl 1F 76
Beith. N Ayr 4B 58
Bekesbourne. Kent 8H 23
Belaugh. Norf 8J 39
Belbroughton. Worc 4H 27
Belchalwell. Dors 5F 8
Belchalwell Street. Dors 5F 8
Belchamp Otten. Essx 7E 30
Belchamp St Paul. Essx 7D 30
Belchamp Walter. Essx 7E 30
Belchford. Linc 2K 37
Belcoo. Ferm 7B 92
Belfast. Bel 5H 93
Belfast City George Best Airport.
Bel 5H 93
Belfast International Airport.
Ant 4G 93
Belfatton. Abers 8K 81
Belford. Nmbd 6J 61
Belgrano. Cnwy 3J 33
Belhaven. E Lot 2D 60
Belhelvie. Abers 4J 73
Belhinnie. Abers 3D 72
Bellabeg. Abers 4C 72
Belladrum. High 1F 70
Bellaghy. M Ulst 4F 93
Bellamore. S Ayr 3H 51
Bellanaleck. Ferm 7C 92
Bellanoch. Arg 8C 64
Bell Busk. N Yor 2H 41
Belleau. Linc 2M 37
Belleek. Ferm 6A 92
Belleek. New M 7F 93
Belleheiglash. Mor 2A 72
Bell End. Worc 4H 27
Bellerby. N Yor 6K 47
Bellerby Camp. N Yor 6J 47
Bellever. Devn 8F 6
Belle Vue. Cumb 8F 52
Belle Vue. Shrp 8C 34
Bellfield. S Lan 6G 59
Belliehill. Ang 1J 67
Bellingdon. Buck 3G 21
Bellingham. Nmbd 3B 54
Bellmount. Norf 7B 38
Bellochantuy. Arg 6F 56
Bellsbank. E Ayr 1K 51
Bell's Cross. Suff 6H 31
Bellshill. N Lan 4F 58
Bellshill. Nmbd 6J 61
Bellside. N Lan 4G 59
Bellspool. Bord 6K 59
Bellsquarry. W Lot 3J 59
Bells Yew Green. E Sus 2C 12
Belmaduthy. High 8G 79
Belmesthorpe. Rut 8H 37
Belmont. Bkbn 6E 40
Belmont. Shet 3K 91
Belmont. S Ayr 7B 58
Belnacraig. Abers 4C 72
Belnie. Linc 6K 37
Belowda. Corn 5B 4
Belper. Derbs 5A 36
Belper Lane End. Derbs 5M 35
Belph. Derbs 2C 36
Belsay. Nmbd 4E 54
Belsford. Devn 6K 5
Belsize. Herts 3H 21
Belstead. Suff 7H 31
Belston. S Ayr 7B 58
Belstone. Devn 6F 6
Belstone Corner. Devn 6F 6
Belthorn. Lanc 5F 40
Beltinge. Kent 7H 23
Beltoft. N Lin 7F 42
Belton. Leics 7B 36
Belton. Linc 6G 37
Belton. Norf 1L 31
Belton. N Lin 7E 42
Belton-in-Rutland. Rut 1F 28
Beltring. Kent 1C 12
Belts of Collonach. Abers 6F 72
Belvedere. G Lon 6A 22
Belvoir. Leics 6F 36
Bembridge. IOW 7D 10
Bemersyde. Bord 6C 60
Bemerton. Wilts 2K 9
Bempton. E Yor 8J 49
Benacre. Suff 3M 31
Ben Alder Lodge. High 8F 70
Ben Armine Lodge. High 2H 79
Benbecula Airport. W Isl 8J 75
Benbuie. Dum 2B 52
Benburb. M Ulst 6F 93
Benchill. G Man 1G 35
Benderloch. Arg 4D 64
Bendish. Herts 1J 21
Bendooragh. Caus 2F 93
Bendronaig Lodge. High 2M 69
Benenden. Kent 2E 12
Benfieldside. Dur 6D 54
Bengate. Norf 7K 39
Bengeworth. Worc 7J 27
Benhall Green. Suff 5K 31
Benholm. Abers 1M 67
Beningbrough. N Yor 2C 42
Benington. Herts 1K 21
Benington. Linc 5L 37
Benington Sea End. Linc 5M 37
Benllech. IOA 2E 32
Benmore Lodge. High 2D 78
Bennacott. Corn 6B 6
Bennah. Devn 7H 7
Bennecarrigan. N Ayr 7J 57
Bennethead. Cumb 3C 46
Benniworth. Linc 1K 37
Benover. Kent 1D 12
Benson. Oxon 4D 20
Benston. Shet 2E 90
Benstonhall. Orkn 6E 88
Bent. Abers 8F 72
Benthall. Shrp 1E 26
Bentham. Glos 2H 19
Bentlawnt. Shrp 1B 26
Bentley. E Yor 4H 43
Bentley. Hants 1E 10
Bentley. S Yor 7C 42
Bentley. Suff 8H 31
Bentley. Warw 2L 27
Bentley. W Mid 2H 27
Bentley Heath. Herts 4K 21
Bentley Heath. W Mid 4K 27
Bentpath. Dum 2H 53
Bents. W Lot 3H 59
Bentworth. Hants 1D 10
Benvie. D'dee 4G 67
Benville. Dors 5D 8
Benwell. Tyne 5F 54
Benwick. Cambs 2L 29
Beoley. Worc 5J 27
Beoraidbeg. High 6H 69
Bepton. W Sus 4F 10
Beragh. Ferm 5D 92
Berden. Essx 1A 22
Bere Alston. Devn 5G 5
Bere Ferrers. Devn 5G 5
Berepper. Corn 6K 3
Bere Regis. Dors 6G 9
Bergh Apton. Norf 1K 31
Berinsfield. Oxon 4C 20
Berkeley. Glos 4E 18
Berkhamsted. Herts 3G 21
Berkley. Som 1G 9
Berkswell. W Mid 4L 27
Bermondsey. G Lon 6L 21
Bernera. High 3K 69
Bernice. Arg 8F 64
Bernisdale. High 8F 76
Berrick Salome. Oxon 4D 20
Berriedale. High 1M 79
Berrier. Cumb 3B 46
Berriew. Powy 2L 25
Berrington. Nmbd 5H 61
Berrington. Shrp 1D 26
Berrington. Worc 5D 26
Berrington Green. Worc 5D 26
Berrington Law. Nmbd 5G 61
Berrow. Som 8B 18
Berrow Green. Worc 6F 26
Berry Cross. Devn 4D 6
Berry Down Cross. Devn 1E 6
Berry Hill. Glos 2D 18
Berry Hill. Pemb 2G 15
Berryhillock. Mor 7E 80
Berrynarbor. Devn 1E 6
Berry Pomeroy. Devn 5L 5
Berryscaur. Dum 2F 52
Berry's Green. G Lon 8M 21
Bersham. Wrex 5B 34
Berthengam. Flin 3L 33
Berwick. E Sus 5B 12
Berwick Bassett. Wilts 6K 19
Berwick Hill. Nmbd 4E 54
Berwick St James. Wilts 2J 9
Berwick St John. Wilts 3H 9
Berwick St Leonard. Wilts 2H 9
Berwick-upon-Tweed.
Nmbd 4G 61
Berwyn. Den 6L 33
Bescaby. Leics 7F 36
Bescar. Lanc 6B 40
Besford. Worc 7H 27
Bessacarr. S Yor 7D 42
Bessbrook. New M 7G 93
Bessels Leigh. Oxon 3B 20
Bessingby. E Yor 1J 43
Bessingham. Norf 6H 39
Best Beech Hill. E Sus 2C 12
Besthorpe. Norf 2G 31
Besthorpe. Notts 3F 36
Bestwood Village. Notts 5C 36
Beswick. E Yor 3H 43
Betchworth. Surr 8K 21
Bethania. Cdgn 6E 24
Bethania. Gwyn
nr. Blaenau Ffestiniog 6G 33
nr. Caernarfon 5F 32
Bethel. Gwyn
nr. Bala 7J 33
nr. Caernarfon 4E 32
Bethel. IOA 3C 32
Bethersden. Kent 1F 12
Bethesda. Gwyn 4F 32
Bethesda. Pemb 5G 15
Bethlehem. Carm 2F 16
Bethnal Green. G Lon 5L 21
Betley. Staf 5F 34
Betsham. Kent 6C 22
Betteshanger. Kent 8K 23
Bettiscombe. Dors 6C 8
Bettisfield. Wrex 6C 34
Betton. Shrp 6E 34
Betton Strange. Shrp 1D 26
Bettws. B'end 6J 17
Bettws. Newp 4A 18
Bettws Bledrws. Cdgn 7E 24
Bettws Cedewain. Powy 3L 25
Bettws Gwerfil Goch. Den 6K 33
Bettws Ifan. Cdgn 2K 15
Bettws Newydd. Mon 3B 18
Bettyhill. High 5K 85
Betws. Carm 3F 16
Betws Garmon. Gwyn 5E 32
Betws-y-Coed. Cnwy 5G 33
Betws-yn-Rhos. Cnwy 3J 33
Beulah. Cdgn 2J 15
Beulah. Powy 7J 25
Beul an Atha. Arg 3C 56
Bevendean. Brig 5L 11
Bevercotes. Notts 2E 36
Beverley. E Yor 4H 43
Beverston. Glos 4G 19
Bevington. Glos 4E 18
Bewaldeth. Cumb 8G 53
Bewcastle. Cumb 4K 53
Bewdley. Worc 4F 26
Bewerley. N Yor 1K 41
Bewholme. E Yor 2J 43
Bexfield. Norf 7G 39
Bexhill. E Sus 5D 12
Bexley. G Lon 6A 22
Bexleyheath. G Lon 6A 22
Bexleyhill. W Sus 3G 11
Bexwell. Norf 1C 30
Beyton. Suff 5F 30
Bhalton. W Isl 8D 82
Bhatarsaigh. W Isl 6C 74
Bibbington. Derbs 2J 35
Bibury. Glos 3K 19
Bicester. Oxon 1C 20
Bickenhall. Som 4A 8
Bickenhill. W Mid 3K 27
Bicker. Linc 6K 37
Bicker Bar. Linc 6K 37
Bicker Gauntlet. Linc 6K 37
Bickershaw. G Man 7E 40
Bickerstaffe. Lanc 7C 40
Bickerton. Ches E 4D 34
Bickerton. Nmbd 1C 54
Bickerton. N Yor 2B 42
Bickford. Staf 8G 35
Bickington. Devn
nr. Barnstaple 2E 6
nr. Newton Abbot 8G 7
Bickleigh. Devn
nr. Plymouth 5H 5
nr. Tiverton 5J 7
Bickleton. Devn 2E 6
Bickley. N Yor 6G 49
Bickley Moss. Ches W 5D 34
Bickmarsh. Worc 7K 27
Bicknacre. Essx 3D 22
Bicknoller. Som 2L 7
Bicknor. Kent 8E 22
Bickton. Hants 4K 9
Bicton. Here 5C 26
Bicton. Shrp
nr. Bishop's Castle 3A 26
nr. Shrewsbury 8C 34
Bicton Heath. Shrp 8C 34
Bidborough. Kent 1B 12
Biddenden. Kent 2E 12
Biddenden Green. Kent 1E 12
Biddenham. Bed 6H 29
Biddestone. Wilts 6G 19
Biddisham. Som 8B 18
Biddlesden. Buck 7D 28
Biddlestone. Nmbd 1C 54
Biddulph. Staf 4G 35
Biddulph Moor. Staf 4H 35
Bideford. Devn 3D 6
Bidford-on-Avon. Warw 6J 27
Bidlake. Devn 7E 6
Bidston. Mers 1A 34
Bielby. E Yor 3E 42
Bieldside. Aber 5H 73
Bierley. IOW 8C 10
Bierley. W Yor 4K 41
Bierton. Buck 2F 20
Bigbury. Devn 7J 5
Bigbury-on-Sea. Devn 7J 5
Bigby. Linc 7H 43
Biggar. Cumb 8L 45
Biggar. S Lan 6J 59
Biggin. Derbs
nr. Hartington 4K 35
nr. Hulland 5L 35
Biggin. N Yor 4C 42
Biggings. Shet 1B 90
Biggin Hill. G Lon 8M 21

Broad Hinton—Castle Park

Broad Hinton. Wilts 6K 19
Broadholme. Derbs 5A 36
Broadholme. Linc 2F 36
Broadlay. Carm 6K 15
Broad Laying. Hants 7B 20
Broadley. Lanc 6G 41
Broadley. Mor 7C 80
Broadley Common. Essx 3M 21
Broad Marston. Worc 7K 27
Broadmayne. Dors 7F 8
Broadmere. Hants 1D 10
Broadmoor. Pemb 6G 15
Broad Oak. Carm 2E 16
Broad Oak. Cumb 5L 45
Broad Oak. Devn 6K 7
Broad Oak. Dors 4F 8
Broadoak. Dors 6C 8
Broad Oak. E Sus
nr. Hastings 4E 12
nr. Heathfield 3C 12
Broadoak. Glos 2E 18
Broadoak. Hants 4C 10
Broad Oak. Here 1C 18
Broad Oak. Kent 7H 23
Broadrashes. Mor 8D 80
Broadsea. Abers 7J 81
Broad's Green. Essx 2C 22
Broadshard. Som 4C 8
Broadstairs. Kent 7K 23
Broadstone. Pool 6J 9
Broadstone. Shrp 3D 26
Broad Street. E Sus 4E 12
Broad Street. Kent
nr. Ashford 1H 13
nr. Maidstone 8E 22
Broad Street Green. Essx 3E 22
Broad Town. Wilts 6J 19
Broadwas. Worc 6F 26
Broadwath. Cumb 6J 53
Broadway. Carm
nr. Kidwelly 6K 15
nr. Laugharne 6J 15
Broadway. Pemb 5E 14
Broadway. Som 4B 8
Broadway. Suff 4K 31
Broadway. Worc 8J 27
Broadwell. Glos
nr. Cinderford 2D 18
nr. Stow-on-the-Wold 1L 19
Broadwell. Oxon 3L 19
Broadwell. Warw 5B 28
Broadwell House. Nmbd 6C 54
Broadwey. Dors 7E 8
Broadwindsor. Dors 5C 8
Broadwoodkelly. Devn 5F 6
Broadwoodwidger. Devn 7D 6
Broallan. High 1E 70
Brobury. Here 7B 26
Brochel. High 1G 69
Brockaghboy. Caus 3F 93
Brockamin. Worc 6F 26
Brockbridge. Hants 4D 10
Brockdish. Norf 4J 31
Brockencote. Worc 4G 27
Brockenhurst. Hants 5L 9
Brocketsbrae. S Lan 6G 59
Brockford Street. Suff 5H 31
Brockhall. Nptn 5D 28
Brockham. Surr 1J 11
Brockhampton. Glos
nr. Bishop's Cleeve 1H 19
nr. Sevenhampton 1J 19
Brockhampton. Here 8D 26
Brockhill. Bord 7A 60
Brockholes. W Yor 6K 41
Brockhurst. Hants 5C 10
Brocklesby. Linc 6J 43
Brockley. N Som 7C 18
Brockley Corner. Suff 4E 30
Brockley Green. Suff
nr. Bury St Edmunds 7D 30
nr. Haverhill 6E 30
Brockleymoor. Cumb 8J 53
Brockmoor. W Mid 3H 27
Brockton. Shrp
nr. Bishop's Castle 3B 26
nr. Madeley 1F 26
nr. Much Wenlock 2D 26
nr. Pontesbury 1B 26
Brockton. Staf 6G 35
Brockton. Telf 8F 34
Brockweir. Glos 3D 18
Brockworth. Glos 2G 19
Brocton. Staf 8H 35
Brodick. N Ayr 6K 57
Brodie. Mor 8K 79
Brodiesord. Abers 8E 80
Brodsworth. S Yor 7C 42
Brogaig. High 7F 78
Brogborough. C Beds 8G 29
Brokenborough. Wilts 5H 19
Broken Cross. Ches E 2G 35
Bromborough. Mers 1B 34
Bromdon. Shrp 3E 26
Brome. Suff 4H 31
Brome Street. Suff 4H 31
Bromeswell. Suff 6K 31
Bromfield. Cumb 7F 52
Bromfield. Shrp 4C 26
Bromford. W Mid 2K 27
Bromham. Bed 6H 29
Bromham. Wilts 7H 19
Bromley. G Lon 7M 21
Bromley. Herts 1M 21
Bromley. Shrp 2F 26
Bromley Cross. G Man 6F 40
Bromley Green. Kent 2F 12
Bromley Wood. Staf 7K 35
Brompton. Medw 7D 22
Brompton. N Yor
nr. Northallerton 6A 48
nr. Scarborough 7G 49
Brompton. Shrp 1D 26
Brompton-on-Swale. N Yor 6L 47
Brompton Ralph. Som 2K 7
Brompton Regis. Som 2J 7
Bromsash. Here 1E 18
Bromsberrow. Glos 8F 26
Bromsberrow Heath. Glos 8F 26
Bromsgrove. Worc 4H 27
Bromstead Heath. Staf 8F 34
Bromyard. Here 6E 26
Bromyard Downs. Here 6E 26
Bronaber. Gwyn 7G 33
Broncroft. Shrp 3D 26
Brongest. Cdgn 2K 15
Brongwyn. Cdgn 2J 15
Bronington. Wrex 6C 34
Bronllys. Powy 1L 17
Bronnant. Cdgn 6F 24
Bronwydd Arms. Carm 4L 15
Bronydd. Powy 8M 25
Bronygarth. Shrp 6A 34
Brook. Carm 6J 15
Brook. Hants
nr. Cadnam 4L 9
nr. Romsey 3M 9
Brook. IOW 7A 10
Brook. Kent 1G 13
Brook. Surr
nr. Guildford 1H 11
nr. Haslemere 2G 11
Brooke. Norf 2J 31
Brooke. Rut 1F 28
Brookeborough. Ferm 6C 92
Brookenby. Linc 8K 43
Brookend. Glos 3E 18
Brook End. Worc 7G 27
Brookfield. Lanc 4D 40
Brookfield. Ren 3C 58
Brookhouse. Lanc 1D 40
Brookhouse. S Yor 1C 36
Brookhouse Green. Ches E 3G 35
Brookhouses. Staf 5H 35
Brookhurst. Mers 1B 34
Brookland. Kent 3F 12
Brooklands. G Man 8F 40
Brooklands. Shrp 5D 34
Brookmans Park. Herts 3K 21
Brooks. Powy 3L 25
Brooksby. Leics 8D 36
Brooks Green. W Sus 3J 11
Brook Street. Essx 4B 22
Brook Street. Kent 2F 12
Brook Street. W Sus 3L 11
Brookthorpe. Glos 2G 19
Brookville. Norf 2D 30
Brookwood. Surr 8G 21
Broom. C Beds 7J 29
Broom. Fife 7G 67
Broom. Warw 6J 27
Broome. Norf 2K 31
Broome. Shrp
nr. Cardington 2D 26
nr. Craven Arms 3C 26
Broome. Worc 4H 27
Broomedge. Warr 1F 34
Broomend. Abers 4G 73
Broomer's Corner. W Sus 3J 11
Broomfield. Abers 2J 73
Broomfield. Essx 2D 22
Broomfield. Kent
nr. Herne Bay 7H 23
nr. Maidstone 8E 22
Broomfield. Som 2M 7
Broomfleet. E Yor 5F 42
Broom Green. Norf 7F 38
Broomhall. Ches E 5E 34
Broomhall. Wind 7G 21
Broomhaugh. Nmbd 5D 54
Broom Hill. Dors 5J 9
Broomhill. High
nr. Grantown-on-Spey 3K 71
nr. Invergordon 6H 79
Broomhill. Norf 1C 30
Broomhill. S Yor 7B 42
Broom Hill. Worc 4H 27
Broomhillbank. Dum 2F 52
Broomholm. Norf 6K 39
Broomlands. Dum 1E 52
Broomley. Nmbd 5D 54
Broom of Moy. Mor 8L 79
Broompark. Dur 7F 54
Broom's Green. Glos 8F 26
Brora. High 3K 79
Broseley. Shrp 1E 26
Brotherhouse Bar. Linc 8K 37
Brotheridge Green. Worc 7G 27
Brotherlee. Dur 8C 54
Brothertoft. Linc 5K 37
Brotherton. N Yor 5B 42
Brotton. Red C 4D 48
Broubster. High 5B 86
Brough. Cumb 4F 46
Brough. Derbs 1K 35
Brough. E Yor 5G 43
Brough. High 4D 86
Brough. Notts 4F 36
Brough. Orkn
nr. Finstown 8C 88
nr. St Margaret's Hope 3F 86
Brough. Shet
nr. Benston 2E 90
nr. Booth of Toft 6J 91
on Bressay 3F 90
on Whalsay 1F 90
Broughall. Shrp 5D 34
Brougham. Cumb 3D 46
Brough Lodge. Shet 4K 91
Broughshane. ME Ant 3G 93
Brough Sowerby. Cumb 4F 46
Broughton. Cambs 4K 29
Broughton. Flin 3B 34
Broughton. Hants 2M 9
Broughton. Lanc 4D 40
Broughton. Mil 8F 28
Broughton. Nptn 4F 28
Broughton. N Lin 7G 43
Broughton. N Yor
nr. Malton 8E 48
nr. Skipton 2H 41
Broughton. Orkn 5D 88
Broughton. Oxon 8B 28
Broughton. Bord 6K 59
Broughton. Staf 6F 34
Broughton. V Glam 7J 17
Broughton Astley. Leics 2C 28
Broughton Beck. Cumb 7A 46
Broughton Cross. Cumb 8E 52
Broughton Gifford. Wilts 7G 19
Broughton Green. Worc 5H 27
Broughton Hackett. Worc 6H 27
Broughton in Furness. Cumb 6M 45
Broughton Mills. Cumb 5M 45
Broughton Moor. Cumb 8E 52
Broughton Park. G Man 7G 41
Broughton Poggs. Oxon 3L 19
Broughtown. Orkn 5F 88
Broughty Ferry. D'dee 4H 67
Browland. Shet 2C 90
Brownbread Street. E Sus 4C 12
Brown Candover. Hants 2C 10
Brown Edge. Lanc 6B 40
Brown Edge. Staf 4H 35
Brownhill. Bkbn 4E 40
Brownhill. Shrp 7C 34
Brownhills. Shrp 6E 34
Brownhills. W Mid 1J 27
Brown Knowl. Ches W 4C 34
Brownlow. Ches E 3G 35
Brownlow Heath. Ches E 3G 35
Brown's Green. W Mid 2J 27
Brownshill. Glos 3G 19
Brownston. Devn 6J 5
Brownstone. Devn 5G 7
Browston Green. Norf 1L 31
Broxa. N Yor 6G 49
Broxbourne. Herts 3L 21
Broxburn. E Lot 2D 60
Broxburn. W Lot 2J 59
Broxholme. Linc 2G 37
Broxted. Essx 1B 22
Broxton. Ches W 4C 34
Broxwood. Here 6B 26
Broyle Side. E Sus 4A 12
Brù. W Isl 7G 83
Bruach Mairi. W Isl 8H 83
Bruairnis. W Isl 5D 74
Bruan. High 8E 86
Bruar Lodge. Per 8J 71
Brucehill. W Dun 2B 58
Brucklay. Abers 8J 81
Bruera. Ches W 3C 34
Bruern Abbey. Oxon 1L 19
Bruichladdich. Arg 3B 56
Bruisyard. Suff 5K 31
Bruisyard Street. Suff 5K 31
Brund. Staf 3K 35
Brundall. Norf 1K 31
Brundish. Norf 2K 31
Brundish. Suff 5J 31
Brundish Street. Suff 4J 31
Brunery. High 8J 69
Brunswick Village. Tyne 4F 54
Brunthwaite. W Yor 3J 41
Bruntingthorpe. Leics 2D 28
Brunton. Fife 5G 67
Brunton. Nmbd 7K 61
Brunton. Wilts 8L 19
Brushford. Devn 5F 6
Brushford. Som 3J 7
Brusta. W Isl 5L 75
Bruton. Som 2E 8
Bryansford. New M 7H 93
Bryanston. Dors 5G 9
Bryant's Bottom. Buck 4F 20
Brydekirk. Dum 4F 52
Brymbo. Cnwy 3H 33
Brymbo. Wrex 4A 34
Brympton D'Evercy. Som 4D 8
Bryn. Carm 6M 15
Bryn. G Man 7D 40
Bryn. Neat 5H 17
Bryn. Shrp 3A 26
Brynamman. Carm 3G 17
Brynberian. Pemb 3H 15
Brynbryddan. Neat 5G 17
Bryncae. Rhon 6J 17
Bryncethin. B'end 6J 17
Bryncir. Gwyn 6D 32
Bryncoch. Neat 5G 17
Bryncroes. Gwyn 7B 32
Bryncrug. Gwyn 2F 24
Bryn Du. IOA 3C 32
Bryn Eden. Gwyn 8G 33
Bryneglwys. Den 6L 33
Bryn Eglwys. Gwyn 4F 32
Bryngates. G Man 7D 40
Bryn Golau. Rhon 6K 17
Bryngwran. IOA 3C 32
Bryngwyn. Mon 3B 18
Bryngwyn. Powy 8L 25
Bryn-henllan. Pemb 3G 15
Brynhoffnant. Cdgn 1K 15
Bryn-llwyn. Den 2K 33
Brynllywarch. Powy 4L 25
Brynmawr. Blae 3L 17
Bryn-mawr. Gwyn 7B 32
Brynmenyn. B'end 6J 17
Brynmill. Swan 5F 16
Brynna. Rhon 6J 17
Brynrefail. Gwyn 4E 32
Brynrefail. IOA 2D 32
Brynsadler. Rhon 6K 17
Bryn-Saith Marchog. Den 5K 33
Brynsiencyn. IOA 4D 32
Brynteg. IOA 2D 32
Brynteg. Wrex 4B 34
Brynygwenyn. Mon 2B 18
Bryn-y-maen. Cnwy 3H 33
Buaile nam Bodach. W Isl 5D 74
Bualintur. High 3F 68
Bubbenhall. Warw 4A 28
Bubwith. E Yor 4E 42
Buccleuch. Bord 8M 59
Buchanan Smithy. Stir 1C 58
Buchanhaven. Abers 1L 73
Buchanty. Per 5C 66
Buchany. Stir 7M 65
Buchley. E Dun 2D 58
Buchlyvie. Stir 8K 65
Buckabank. Cumb 7H 53
Buckden. Cambs 5J 29
Buckden. N Yor 8H 47
Buckenham. Norf 1K 31
Buckerell. Devn 5L 7
Buckfast. Devn 5K 5
Buckfastleigh. Devn 5K 5
Buckhaven. Fife 8G 67
Buckholm. Bord 6B 60
Buckholt. Here 2D 18
Buckhorn Weston. Dors 3F 8
Buckhurst Hill. Essx 4M 21
Buckie. Mor 7D 80
Buckingham. Buck 8D 28
Buckland. Buck 2F 20
Buckland. Glos 8J 27
Buckland. Here 6D 26
Buckland. Herts 8L 29
Buckland. Kent 1K 13
Buckland. Oxon 4M 19
Buckland. Surr 8K 21
Buckland Brewer. Devn 3D 6
Buckland Common. Buck 3G 21
Buckland Dinham. Som 8F 18
Buckland Filleigh. Devn 5D 6
Buckland in the Moor. Devn 8G 7
Buckland Monachorum. Devn 5G 5
Buckland Newton. Dors 5E 8
Buckland Ripers. Dors 7E 8
Buckland St Mary. Som 4A 8
Buckland-tout-Saints. Devn 7K 5
Bucklebury. W Ber 6C 20
Bucklegate. Linc 6L 37
Buckleigh. Devn 3D 6
Buckler's Hard. Hants 6B 10
Bucklesham. Suff 7J 31
Buckley. Flin 3A 34
Buckley Green. Warw 5K 27
Buckley Hill. Mers 8B 40
Bucklow Hill. Ches E 1F 34
Buckminster. Leics 7F 36
Bucknall. Linc 3J 37
Bucknall. Stoke 5H 35
Bucknell. Oxon 1C 20
Bucknell. Shrp 4B 26
Buckpool. Mor 7D 80
Bucksburn. Aber 5H 73
Buck's Cross. Devn 3C 6
Bucks Green. W Sus 2H 11
Buckshaw Village. Lanc 5D 40
Bucks Hill. Herts 3H 21
Bucks Horn Oak. Hants 1F 10
Buck's Mills. Devn 3C 6
Buckton. E Yor 8J 49
Buckton. Here 4B 26
Buckton. Nmbd 6H 61
Buckton Vale. G Man 7H 41
Buckworth. Cambs 4J 29
Budby. Notts 3D 36
Bude. Corn 5B 6
Budge's Shop. Corn 6F 4
Budlake. Devn 5J 7
Budle. Nmbd 6J 61
Budleigh Salterton. Devn 7K 7
Budock Water. Corn 5L 3
Buerton. Ches E 5E 34
Buffler's Holt. Buck 8D 28
Bugbrooke. Nptn 6D 28
Buglawton. Ches E 3G 35
Bugle. Corn 6C 4
Bugthorpe. E Yor 2E 42
Buildwas. Shrp 1E 26
Builth Road. Powy 7K 25
Builth Wells. Powy 7K 25
Bulbourne. Herts 2G 21
Bulby. Linc 7H 37
Bulcote. Notts 5D 36
Buldoo. High 5A 86
Bulford. Wilts 1K 9
Bulford Camp. Wilts 1K 9
Bulkeley. Ches E 4D 34
Bulkington. Warw 3A 28
Bulkington. Wilts 8H 19
Bulkworthy. Devn 4C 6
Bullamoor. N Yor 6A 48
Bull Bay. IOA 1D 32
Bullbridge. Derbs 4A 36
Bullgill. Cumb 8E 52
Bull Hill. Hants 6M 9
Bullinghope. Here 8D 26
Bull's Green. Herts 2K 21
Bullwood. Arg 2L 57
Bulmer. Essx 7E 30
Bulmer. N Yor 1D 42
Bulmer Tye. Essx 8E 30
Bulphan. Thur 5C 22
Bulverhythe. E Sus 5D 12
Bulwark. Abers 1J 73
Bulwell. Nott 5C 36
Bulwick. Nptn 2G 29
Bumble's Green. Essx 3M 21
Bun Abhainn Eadarra. W Isl 3C 76
Bunacaimb. High 7H 69
Bun a' Mhuillinn. W Isl 4D 74
Bunarkaig. High 7B 70
Bunbury. Ches E 4D 34
Bunchrew. High 1G 71
Bundalloch. High 3K 69
Buness. Shet 3L 91
Bunessan. Arg 5J 63
Bungay. Suff 3K 31
Bunkegivie. High 4F 70
Bunker's Hill. Cambs 1M 29
Bunkers Hill. Linc 4K 37
Bunker's Hill. Suff 1M 31
Bunloit. High 3F 70
Bunnahabhain. Arg 2D 56
Bunny. Notts 7C 36
Bunoich. High 5D 70
Bunree. High 1E 64
Bunroy. High 7C 70
Buntait. High 2E 70
Buntingford. Herts 1L 21
Bunting's Green. Essx 8E 30
Bunwell. Norf 2H 31
Burbage. Derbs 2J 35
Burbage. Leics 2B 28
Burbage. Wilts 7L 19
Burcher. Here 5B 26
Burchett's Green. Wind 5F 20
Burcombe. Wilts 2J 9
Burcot. Oxon 4C 20
Burcot. Worc 4H 27
Burcote. Shrp 2F 26
Burcott. Buck 1F 20
Burcott. Som 1D 8
Burdale. N Yor 1F 42
Burdrop. Oxon 8A 28
Bures. Suff 8F 30
Burf, The. Worc 5G 27
Burford. Oxon 2L 19
Burford. Shrp 5D 26
Burg. Arg 3J 63
Burgate Great Green. Suff 4G 31
Burgate Little Green. Suff 4G 31
Burgess Hill. W Sus 4L 11
Burgh. Suff 6J 31
Burgh by Sands. Cumb 6H 53
Burgh Castle. Norf 1L 31
Burghclere. Hants 7B 20
Burghead. Mor 7M 79
Burghfield. W Ber 7D 20
Burghfield Common. W Ber 7D 20
Burghfield Hill. W Ber 7D 20
Burgh Heath. Surr 8K 21
Burghill. Here 7C 26
Burgh le Marsh. Linc 3B 38
Burgh Muir. Abers 4G 73
Burgh next Aylsham. Norf 7J 39
Burgh on Bain. Linc 1K 37
Burgh St Margaret. Norf 8L 39
Burgh St Peter. Norf 2L 31
Burghwallis. S Yor 6C 42
Burham. Kent 7D 22
Buriton. Hants 3E 10
Burland. Ches E 4E 34
Burland. Shet 4D 90
Burlawn. Corn 5B 4
Burleigh. Glos 3G 19
Burleigh. Wind 6F 20
Burlescombe. Devn 4K 7
Burleston. Dors 6F 8
Burlestone. Devn 7L 5
Burley. Hants 5L 9
Burley. Rut 8F 36
Burley. W Yor 4L 41
Burleydam. Ches E 5E 34
Burley Gate. Here 7D 26
Burley in Wharfedale. W Yor 3K 41
Burley Street. Hants 5L 9
Burley Woodhead. W Yor 3K 41
Burlingjobb. Powy 6A 26
Burlington. Shrp 8F 34
Burlton. Shrp 7C 34
Burmantofts. W Yor 4M 41
Burmarsh. Kent 2H 13
Burmington. Warw 8L 27
Burn. N Yor 5C 42
Burnage. G Man 8G 41
Burnaston. Derbs 6L 35
Burnbanks. Cumb 4D 46
Burnby. E Yor 3F 42
Burncross. S Yor 8M 41
Burneside. Cumb 6D 46
Burness. Orkn 5F 88
Burneston. N Yor 7M 47
Burnett. Bath 7E 18
Burnfoot. E Ayr 1K 51
Burnfoot. Per 7C 66
Burnfoot. Bord
nr. Hawick 8C 60
nr. Roberton 8B 60
Burngreave. S Yor 1A 36
Burnham. Buck 5G 21
Burnham. N Lin 6H 43
Burnham Deepdale. Norf 5E 38
Burnham Green. Herts 2K 21
Burnham Market. Norf 5E 38
Burnham Norton. Norf 5E 38
Burnham-on-Crouch. Essx 4F 22
Burnham-on-Sea. Som 1B 8
Burnham Overy Staithe. Norf 5E 38
Burnham Overy Town. Norf 5E 38
Burnham Thorpe. Norf 5E 38
Burnhaven. Abers 1L 73
Burnhead. Dum 2C 52
Burnhervie. Abers 4G 73
Burnhill Green. Staf 1F 26
Burnhope. Dur 7E 54
Burnhouse. N Ayr 4B 58
Burniston. N Yor 6H 49
Burnlee. W Yor 7K 41
Burnley. Lanc 4G 41
Burnmouth. Bord 3G 61
Burn Naze. Lanc 3B 40
Burn of Cambus. Stir 7M 65
Burnopfield. Dur 6E 54
Burnsall. N Yor 1J 41
Burnside. Ang 2J 67
Burnside. Ant
nr. Antrim 4G 93
nr. Ballyclare 4H 93
Burnside. E Ayr 8D 58
Burnside. Per 7E 66
Burnside. Shet 6G 91
Burnside. S Lan 4E 58
Burnside. W Lot
nr. Broxburn 2J 59
nr. Winchburgh 2J 59
Burntcommon. Surr 8H 21
Burntheath. Derbs 6L 35
Burnt Heath. Essx 1G 23
Burnt Hill. W Ber 6C 20
Burnt Houses. Dur 3K 47
Burntisland. Fife 1L 59
Burnt Oak. G Lon 4K 21
Burnton. E Ayr 1K 51
Burntstalk. Norf 6D 38
Burntwood. Staf 1J 27
Burntwood Green. Staf 1J 27
Burnt Yates. N Yor 1L 41
Burnwynd. Edin 3K 59
Burpham. Surr 8H 21
Burpham. W Sus 5H 11
Burradon. Nmbd 1C 54
Burradon. Tyne 4F 54
Burrafirth. Shet 2L 91
Burragarth. Shet 3K 91
Burras. Corn 5K 3
Burraton. Corn 6G 5
Burravoe. Shet
nr. North Roe 5H 91
on Mainland 1D 90
on Yell 6K 91
Burray Village. Orkn 2F 86
Burrells. Cumb 4E 46
Burrelton. Per 4E 66
Burren. New M 7G 93
Burren Bridge. New M 7H 93
Burridge. Hants 4C 10
Burridge. Som 5B 8
Burrigill. High 8D 86
Burrill. N Yor 7L 47
Burringham. N Lin 7F 42
Burrington. Devn 4F 6
Burrington. Here 4C 26
Burrington. N Som 8C 18
Burrough End. Cambs 6C 30
Burrough Green. Cambs 6C 30
Burrough on the Hill. Leics 8E 36
Burroughston. Orkn 7E 88
Burrow. Devn 7K 7
Burrow. Som 1J 7
Burrowbridge. Som 3B 8
Burrowhill. Surr 7G 21
Burry. Swan 7L 15
Burry Green. Swan 7L 15
Burry Port. Carm 6L 15
Burscough. Lanc 6C 40
Burscough Bridge. Lanc 6C 40
Bursea. E Yor 4F 42
Burshill. E Yor 3H 43
Bursledon. Hants 5B 10
Burslem. Stoke 5G 35
Burstall. Suff 7G 31
Burstock. Dors 5C 8
Burston. Devn 5G 7
Burston. Norf 3H 31
Burston. Staf 6H 35
Burstow. Surr 1L 11
Burstwick. E Yor 5K 43
Burtersett. N Yor 7G 47
Burtholme. Cumb 5K 53
Burthorpe. Suff 5D 30
Burthwaite. Cumb 7J 53
Burtle. Som 1C 8
Burtoft. Linc 6K 37
Burton. Ches W
nr. Kelsall 3D 34
nr. Neston 2B 34
Burton. Dors
nr. Christchurch 6K 9
nr. Dorchester 6E 8
Burton. Nmbd 6J 61
Burton. Pemb 6F 14
Burton. Som 1L 7
Burton. Wilts
nr. Chippenham 6G 19
nr. Warminster 2G 9
Burton. Wrex 4B 34
Burton Agnes. E Yor 1J 43
Burton Bradstock. Dors 7C 8
Burton-by-Lincoln. Linc 2G 37
Burton Coggles. Linc 7G 37
Burton Constable. E Yor 4J 43
Burton Corner. Linc 5L 37
Burton End. Cambs 7C 30
Burton End. Essx 1B 22
Burton Fleming. E Yor 8H 49
Burton Green. Warw 4L 27
Burton Green. Wrex 4B 34
Burton Hastings. Warw 3B 28
Burton-in-Kendal. Cumb 8D 46
Burton in Lonsdale. N Yor 8E 46
Burton Joyce. Notts 5D 36
Burton Latimer. Nptn 4G 29
Burton Lazars. Leics 8E 36
Burton Leonard. N Yor 1M 41
Burton on the Wolds. Leics 7C 36
Burton Overy. Leics 2D 28
Burton Pedwardine. Linc 5J 37
Burton Pidsea. E Yor 4K 43
Burton Salmon. N Yor 5B 42
Burton's Green. Essx 1E 22
Burton Stather. N Lin 6F 42
Burton upon Stather. N Lin 6F 42
Burton upon Trent. Staf 7L 35
Burton Wolds. Leics 7D 36
Burtonwood. Warr 8D 40
Burwardsley. Ches W 4D 34
Burwarton. Shrp 3E 26
Burwash. E Sus 3C 12
Burwash Common. E Sus 3C 12
Burwash Weald. E Sus 3C 12
Burwell. Cambs 5B 30
Burwell. Linc 2L 37
Burwen. IOA 1D 32
Burwick. Orkn 3F 86
Bury. Cambs 3K 29
Bury. G Man 6G 41
Bury. Som 3J 7
Bury. W Sus 4H 11
Burybank. Staf 6G 35
Bury End. Worc 8J 27
Bury Green. Herts 1A 22
Bury St Edmunds. Suff 5E 30
Burythorpe. N Yor 1E 42
Busbridge. Surr 1G 11
Busby. E Ren 4D 58
Busby. Per 5D 66
Buscot. Oxon 4L 19
Bush. Corn 5B 6
Bush, The. M Ulst 5F 93
Bush Bank. Here 6C 26
Bushbury. W Mid 1H 27
Bushby. Leics 1D 28
Bushey. Dors 7H 9
Bushey. Herts 4J 21
Bushey Heath. Herts 4J 21
Bush Green. Norf
nr. Attleborough 2G 31
nr. Harleston 3J 31
Bush Green. Suff 6F 30
Bushley. Worc 8G 27
Bushley Green. Worc 8G 27
Bushmead. Bed 5J 29
Bushmills. Caus 1F 93
Bushmoor. Shrp 3C 26
Bushton. Wilts 6J 19
Bushy Common. Norf 8F 38
Busk. Cumb 7L 53
Buslingthorpe. Linc 1H 37
Bussage. Glos 3G 19
Bussex. Som 2B 8
Busta. Shet 1D 90
Butcher's Cross. E Sus 3B 12
Butcombe. N Som 7D 18
Bute Town. Cphy 4L 17
Butleigh. Som 2D 8
Butleigh Wootton. Som 2D 8
Butlers Marston. Warw 7M 27
Butley. Suff 6K 31
Butley High Corner. Suff 7K 31
Butlocks Heath. Hants 5B 10
Butterburn. Cumb 4L 53
Buttercrambe. N Yor 2E 42
Butterknowle. Dur 3K 47
Butterleigh. Devn 5J 7
Buttermere. Cumb 3L 45
Buttermere. Wilts 7M 19
Buttershaw. W Yor 5K 41
Butterstone. Per 3D 66
Butterton. Staf
nr. Leek 4J 35
nr. Stoke-on-Trent 5G 35
Butterwick. Dur 3A 48
Butterwick. Linc 5L 37
Butterwick. N Yor
nr. Malton 8E 48
nr. Weaverthorpe 8G 49
Butteryhaugh. Nmbd 2L 53
Butt Green. Ches E 4E 34
Buttington. Powy 1A 26
Buttonbridge. Shrp 4F 26
Buttonoak. Shrp 4F 26
Buttsash. Hants 5B 10
Butt's Green. Essx 3D 22
Butt Yeats. Lanc 1D 40
Buxhall. Suff 6G 31
Buxted. E Sus 3A 12
Buxton. Derbs 2J 35
Buxton. Norf 7J 39
Buxworth. Derbs 1J 35
Bwcle. Flin 3A 34
Bwlch. Powy 2L 17
Bwlchderwin. Gwyn 6D 32
Bwlchgwyn. Wrex 4A 34
Bwlch-Llan. Cdgn 7E 24
Bwlchnewydd. Carm 4K 15
Bwlchtocyn. Gwyn 8C 32
Bwlch-y-cibau. Powy 1L 25
Bwlchyddar. Powy 8L 33
Bwlch-y-fadfa. Cdgn 2L 15
Bwlch-y-ffridd. Powy 3K 25
Bwlch y Garreg. Powy 3K 25
Bwlch-y-groes. Pemb 3J 15
Bwlch-y-sarnau. Powy 5K 25
Bybrook. Kent 1G 13
Byermoor. Tyne 6E 54
Byers Garth. Dur 7G 55
Byers Green. Dur 8F 54
Byfield. Nptn 6C 28
Byfleet. Surr 7H 21
Byford. Here 7B 26
Bygrave. Herts 8K 29
Byker. Tyne 5F 54
Byland Abbey. N Yor 8C 48
Bylchau. Cnwy 4J 33
Byley. Ches W 3F 34
Bynea. Carm 7M 15
Byram. N Yor 5B 42
Byrness. Nmbd 1A 54
Bystock. Devn 7K 7
Bythorn. Cambs 4H 29
Byton. Here 5B 26
Bywell. Nmbd 5D 54
Byworth. W Sus 3G 11

C

Cabharstadh. W Isl 2E 76
Cabourne. Linc 7J 43
Cabrach. Arg 3D 56
Cabrach. Mor 3C 72
Cabragh. M Ulst 5E 92
Cabus. Lanc 3C 40
Cadbury. Devn 5J 7
Cadder. E Dun 2E 58
Caddington. C Beds 2H 21
Caddonfoot. Bord 6B 60
Cadeby. Leics 1B 28
Cadeby. S Yor 7C 42
Cadeleigh. Devn 5J 7
Cade Street. E Sus 3C 12
Cadgwith. Corn 7L 3
Cadham. Fife 7F 66
Cadishead. G Man 8F 40
Cadle. Swan 5F 16
Cadley. Lanc 4D 40
Cadley. Wilts
nr. Ludgershall 8L 19
nr. Marlborough 7L 19
Cadmore End. Buck 4E 20
Cadnam. Hants 4L 9
Cadney. N Lin 7H 43
Cadole. Flin 4M 33
Cadoxton-juxta-Neath. Neat 5G 17
Cadwell. Herts 8J 29
Cadwst. Den 7K 33
Caeathro. Gwyn 4E 32
Caehopkin. Powy 3H 17
Caenby. Linc 1H 37
Caerau. B'end 5H 17
Caerau. Card 7L 17
Cae'r-bont. Powy 3H 17
Cae'r-bryn. Carm 3E 16
Caerdeon. Gwyn 1F 24
Caerdydd. Card 7L 17
Caerfarchell. Pemb 4D 14
Caerffili. Cphy 6L 17
Caerfyrddin. Carm 5L 15
Caergeiliog. IOA 3C 32
Caergwrle. Flin 4B 34
Caergybi. IOA 2B 32
Caerlaverock. Per 6B 66
Caerleon. Newp 4B 18
Caerlleon. Carm 4J 15
Caerllion. Newp 4B 18
Caernarfon. Gwyn 4D 32
Caerphilly. Cphy 6L 17
Caersws. Powy 3K 25
Caerwedros. Cdgn 1K 15
Caerwent. Mon 4C 18
Caerwys. Flin 3L 33
Caim. IOA 2F 32
Caio. Carm 1F 16
Cairinis. W Isl 7K 75
Cairisiadar. W Isl 8D 82
Cairminis. W Isl 5B 76
Cairnbaan. Arg 8C 64
Cairnbulg. Abers 7K 81
Cairncross. Ang 8D 72
Cairndow. Arg 6F 64
Cairness. Abers 7K 81
Cairneyhill. Fife 1J 59
Cairngarroch. Dum 7F 50
Cairnhill. Abers 2F 72
Cairnie. Abers 1D 72
Cairnorrie. Abers 1H 73
Cairnryan. Dum 5F 50
Cairston. Orkn 8B 88
Caister-on-Sea. Norf 8M 39
Caistor. Linc 7J 43
Caistor St Edmund. Norf 1J 31
Caistron. Nmbd 1C 54
Cakebole. Worc 4G 27
Calais Street. Suff 7F 30
Calanais. W Isl 8F 82
Calbost. W Isl 2F 76
Calbourne. IOW 7B 10
Calceby. Linc 2L 37
Calcot. Glos 2J 19
Calcot Row. W Ber 6D 20
Calcott. Kent 7H 23
Calcott. Shrp 8C 34
Caldback. Shet 3L 91
Caldbeck. Cumb 8H 53
Caldbergh. N Yor 7J 47
Caldecote. Cambs
nr. Cambridge 6L 29
nr. Peterborough 3J 29
Caldecote. Herts 8K 29
Caldecote. Nptn 6D 28
Caldecote. Warw 2A 28
Caldecott. Nptn 5G 29
Caldecott. Oxon 4B 20
Caldecott. Rut 2F 28
Calderbank. N Lan 3F 58
Calder Bridge. Cumb 4K 45
Calderbrook. G Man 6H 41
Caldercruix. N Lan 3G 59
Calder Grove. W Yor 6M 41
Calder Mains. High 6B 86
Caldermill. S Lan 5E 58
Calder Vale. Lanc 3D 40
Calderwood. S Lan 4E 58
Caldicot. Mon 5C 18
Caldwell. Derbs 8L 35
Caldwell. N Yor 4K 47
Caldy. Mers 2M 33
Calebrack. Cumb 8H 53
Caledon. M Ulst 6E 92
Calf Heath. Staf 1H 27
Calford Green. Suff 7C 30
Calfsound. Orkn 6E 88
Calgary. Arg 2J 63
Califer. Mor 8L 79
California. Cambs 3B 30
California. Falk 2H 59
California. Norf 8M 39
California. Suff 7H 31
Calke. Derbs 7A 36
Callakille. High 8H 77
Callaly. Nmbd 1D 54
Callander. Stir 7L 65
Callaughton. Shrp 2E 26
Callendoun. Arg 1B 58
Callestick. Corn 3L 3
Calligarry. High 5H 69
Callington. Corn 5F 4
Callingwood. Staf 7K 35
Callow. Here 8C 26
Callowell. Glos 3G 19
Callow End. Worc 7G 27
Callow Hill. Wilts 5J 19
Callow Hill. Worc
nr. Bewdley 4F 26
nr. Redditch 5J 27
Calmore. Hants 4M 9
Calmsden. Glos 3J 19
Calne. Wilts 6H 19
Calow. Derbs 2B 36
Calshot. Hants 5B 10
Calstock. Corn 5G 5
Calstone Wellington. Wilts 7J 19
Calthorpe. Norf 6H 39
Calthorpe Street. Norf 7L 39
Calthwaite. Cumb 7J 53
Calton. N Yor 2H 41
Calton. Staf 4K 35
Calveley. Ches E 4D 34
Calver. Derbs 2L 35
Calverhall. Shrp 6E 34
Calverleigh. Devn 4J 7
Calverley. W Yor 4L 41
Calvert. Buck 1D 20
Calverton. Mil 8E 28
Calverton. Notts 5D 36
Calvine. Per 1B 66
Calvo. Cumb 6F 52
Cam. Glos 4F 18
Camaghael. High 8B 70
Camas-luinie. High 3L 69
Camasnacroise. High 2C 64
Camastianavaig. High 2G 69
Camasunary. High 4G 69
Camault Muir. High 1F 70
Camb. Shet 4K 91
Camber. E Sus 4F 12
Camberley. Surr 7F 20
Camberwell. G Lon 6L 21
Camblesforth. N Yor 5D 42
Cambo. Nmbd 3D 54
Cambois. Nmbd 3G 55
Camborne. Corn 5K 3
Cambourne. Cambs 6L 29
Cambridge. Cambs 6A 30
Cambridge. Glos 3F 18
Cambrose. Corn 4K 3
Cambus. Clac 8B 66
Cambusbarron. Stir 8A 66
Cambuskenneth. Stir 8B 66
Cambuslang. S Lan 3E 58
Cambusnethan. N Lan 4G 59
Cambus o' May. Abers 6D 72
Camden Town. G Lon 5K 21
Cameley. Bath 8E 18
Camelford. Corn 3D 4
Camelon. Falk 1G 59
Camelsdale. W Sus 2F 10
Camer's Green. Worc 8F 26
Camerton. Bath 8E 18
Camerton. Cumb 8E 52
Camerton. E Yor 5K 43
Camghouran. Per 2K 65
Camlough. New M 7G 93
Cammachmore. Abers 6J 73
Cammeringham. Linc 1G 37
Camore. High 4H 79
Camp, The. Glos 3H 19
Campbelton. N Ayr 4L 57
Campbeltown. Arg 7G 57
Campbeltown Airport. Arg 7F 56
Cample. Dum 2C 52
Campmuir. Per 4F 66
Campsall. S Yor 6C 42
Campsea Ashe. Suff 6K 31
Camps End. Cambs 7C 30
Campsey. Derr 2D 92
Campton. C Beds 8J 29
Camptoun. E Lot 2C 60
Camptown. Bord 8D 60
Camrose. Pemb 4F 14
Camserney. Per 3B 66
Camster. High 7D 86
Camus Croise. High 4H 69
Camuscross. High 4H 69
Camusdarach. High 6H 69
Camusnagaul. High
nr. Fort William 8A 70
nr. Little Loch Broom 5A 78
Camus Park. Derr 4C 92
Camusteel. High 1J 69
Camusterrach. High 1J 69
Camusvrachan. Per 3L 65
Canada. Hants 4L 9
Canadia. E Sus 4D 12
Canaston Bridge. Pemb 5G 15
Candlesby. Linc 3A 38
Candle Street. Suff 4G 31
Candy Mill. S Lan 5J 59
Cane End. Oxon 6D 20
Canewdon. Essx 4F 22
Canford Cliffs. Pool 7J 9
Canford Heath. Pool 6J 9
Canford Magna. Pool 6J 9
Cangate. Norf 8K 39
Canham's Green. Suff 5G 31
Canholes. Derbs 2J 35
Canisbay. High 4E 86
Canley. W Mid 4M 27
Cann. Dors 3G 9
Cann Common. Dors 3G 9
Cannich. High 2D 70
Cannington. Som 2A 8
Cannock. Staf 8H 35
Cannock Wood. Staf 8J 35
Canonbie. Dum 4H 53
Canon Bridge. Here 7C 26
Canon Frome. Here 7E 26
Canon Pyon. Here 7C 26
Canons Ashby. Nptn 6C 28
Canonstown. Corn 5J 3
Canterbury. Kent 8H 23
Cantley. Norf 1K 31
Cantley. S Yor 7D 42
Cantlop. Shrp 1D 26
Canton. Card 7L 17
Cantray. High 1H 71
Cantraybruich. High 1H 71
Cantraywood. High 1H 71
Cantsdam. Fife 8E 66
Cantsfield. Lanc 8E 46
Canvey Island. Essx 5D 22
Canwick. Linc 3G 37
Canworthy Water. Corn 6B 6
Caol. High 8B 70
Caolas. Arg 3F 62
Caolas. W Isl 6C 74
Caolas Liubharsaigh. W Isl 1E 74
Caolas Scalpaigh. W Isl 4D 76
Caolas Stocinis. W Isl 4C 76
Caol Ila. Arg 2D 56
Caol Loch Ailse. High 3J 69
Caol Reatha. High 3J 69
Capel. Kent 1C 12
Capel. Surr 1J 11
Capel Bangor. Cdgn 4F 24
Capel Betws Lleucu. Cdgn 7F 24
Capel Coch. IOA 2D 32
Capel Curig. Cnwy 5G 33
Capel Cynon. Cdgn 2K 15
Capel Dewi. Carm 4L 15
Capel Dewi. Cdgn
nr. Aberystwyth 4F 24
nr. Llandysul 2L 15
Capel Garmon. Cnwy 5H 33
Capel Green. Suff 7K 31
Capel Gwyn. IOA 3C 32
Capel Gwynfe. Carm 2G 17
Capel Hendre. Carm 3E 16
Capel Isaac. Carm 2E 16
Capel Iwan. Carm 3J 15
Capel-le-Ferne. Kent 2J 13
Capel Llanilltern. Card 7K 17
Capel Mawr. IOA 3D 32
Capel Newydd. Pemb 3J 15
Capel St Andrew. Suff 7K 31
Capel St Mary. Suff 8G 31
Capel Seion. Carm 5M 15
Capel Seion. Cdgn 5F 24
Capel Uchaf. Gwyn 6D 32
Capel-y-ffin. Powy 8A 26
Capenhurst. Ches W 2B 34
Capernwray. Lanc 8D 46
Capheaton. Nmbd 3D 54
Cappagh. M Ulst 5E 92
Cappercleuch. Bord 7L 59
Capplegill. Dum 1F 52
Capton. Devn 6L 5
Capton. Som 2K 7
Caputh. Per 4D 66
Caradon Town. Corn 8B 6
Carbis Bay. Corn 5J 3
Carbost. High
nr. Loch Harport 2E 68
nr. Portree 1F 68
Carbrook. S Yor 1A 36
Carbrooke. Norf 1F 30
Carburton. Notts 2D 36
Carcluie. S Ayr 8B 58
Car Colston. Notts 5E 36
Carcroft. S Yor 7C 42
Cardenden. Fife 8F 66
Cardeston. Shrp 8B 34
Cardewlees. Cumb 6H 53
Cardiff. Card 7L 17
Cardiff Airport. V Glam 8K 17
Cardigan. Cdgn 2H 15
Cardinal's Green. Cambs 7C 30
Cardington. Bed 7H 29
Cardington. Shrp 2D 26
Cardinham. Corn 5D 4
Cardno. Abers 7J 81
Cardow. Mor 1A 72
Cardross. Arg 2B 58
Cardurnock. Cumb 6F 52
Careby. Linc 8H 37
Careston. Ang 1J 67
Carew. Pemb 6G 15
Carew Cheriton. Pemb 6G 15
Carew Newton. Pemb 6G 15
Carey. Here 8D 26
Carfin. N Lan 4F 58
Carfrae. Bord 4C 60
Cargan. ME Ant 3G 93
Cargate Green. Norf 8K 39
Cargenbridge. Dum 4D 52
Cargill. Per 4E 66
Cargo. Cumb 6H 53
Cargreen. Corn 5G 5
Carham. Nmbd 6F 60
Carhampton. Som 1K 7
Carharrack. Corn 4L 3
Carie. Per
nr. Loch Rannah 2L 65
nr. Loch Tay 4L 65
Carisbrooke. IOW 7B 10
Cark. Cumb 8B 46
Carkeel. Corn 5G 5
Carlabhagh. W Isl 7F 82
Carland Cross. Corn 3M 3
Carlbury. Darl 4L 47
Carlby. Linc 8H 37
Carlecotes. S Yor 7K 41
Carleen. Corn 6K 3
Carlesmoor. N Yor 8K 47
Carleton. Cumb
nr. Carlisle 6J 53
nr. Egremont 4K 45
nr. Penrith 3D 46
Carleton. Lanc 3B 40
Carleton. N Yor 3H 41
Carleton. W Yor 5B 42
Carleton Forehoe. Norf 1G 31
Carleton Rode. Norf 2H 31
Carleton St Peter. Norf 1K 31
Carlidnack. Corn 6L 3
Carlingcott. Bath 8E 18
Carlin How. Red C 4E 48
Carlisle. Cumb 6J 53
Carloonan. Arg 6E 64
Carlops. Bord 4K 59
Carlton. Bed 6G 29
Carlton. Cambs 6C 30
Carlton. Leics 1A 28
Carlton. N Yor
nr. Helmsley 7D 48
nr. Middleham 7J 47
nr. Selby 5D 42
Carlton. Notts 5D 36
Carlton. S Yor 6A 42
Carlton. Stoc T 3A 48
Carlton. Suff 5K 31
Carlton. W Yor 5M 41
Carlton Colville. Suff 2M 31
Carlton Curlieu. Leics 2D 28
Carlton Husthwaite. N Yor 8B 48
Carlton in Cleveland. N Yor 5C 48
Carlton in Lindrick. Notts 1C 36
Carlton-le-Moorland. Linc 4G 37
Carlton Miniott. N Yor 7A 48
Carlton-on-Trent. Notts 3F 36
Carlton Scroop. Linc 5G 37
Carluke. S Lan 4G 59
Carlyon Bay. Corn 6C 4
Carmarthen. Carm 5L 15
Carmel. Carm 3E 16
Carmel. Flin 3L 33
Carmel. Gwyn 5D 32
Carmel. IOA 2C 32
Carmichael. S Lan 6H 59
Carmunnock. Glas 4E 58
Carmyle. Glas 3E 58
Carmyllie. Ang 3J 67
Carnaby. E Yor 1J 43
Carnach. High
nr. Lochcarron 3M 69
nr. Ullapool 4M 77
Carnach. Mor 1L 71
Carnach. W Isl 4D 76
Carnachy. High 6K 85
Carnain. Arg 3C 56
Carnais. W Isl 8D 82
Carnan. Arg 3F 62
Carnan. W Isl 1D 74
Carnbee. Fife 7J 67
Carnbo. Per 7D 66
Carn Brea Village. Corn 4K 3
Carndu. High 3K 69
Carnduff. Caus 1G 93
Carne. Corn 8B 4
Carnell. S Ayr 6C 58
Carnforth. Lanc 8D 46
Carn-gorm. High 3L 69
Carnhedryn. Pemb 4E 14
Carnhell Green. Corn 5K 3
Carnie. Abers 5H 73
Carnkie. Corn
nr. Falmouth 5L 3
nr. Redruth 5K 3
Carnkief. Corn 3L 3
Carnlough. ME Ant 3H 93
Carnmoney. Ant 4H 93
Carno. Powy 3J 25
Carnock. Fife 1J 59
Carnon Downs. Corn 4L 3
Carnoustie. Ang 4J 67
Carnteel. M Ulst 6E 92
Carntyne. Glas 3E 58
Carnwath. S Lan 5H 59
Carnyorth. Corn 5G 3
Carol Green. W Mid 4L 27
Carpalla. Corn 6B 4
Carperby. N Yor 7J 47
Carradale. Arg 6H 57
Carragraich. W Isl 4C 76
Carrbridge. High 3K 71
Carr Cross. Lanc 6B 40
Carreglefn. IOA 2C 32
Carrhouse. N Lin 7E 42
Carrick Castle. Arg 8F 64
Carrickfergus. ME Ant 4J 93
Carrick Ho. Orkn 6E 88
Carrickmore. Ferm 5E 92
Carriden. Falk 1J 59
Carrington. G Man 8F 40
Carrington. Linc 4L 37
Carrington. Midl 3M 59
Carrog. Cnwy 6G 33
Carrog. Den 6L 33
Carron. Falk 1G 59
Carron. Mor 1B 72
Carronbridge. Dum 2C 52
Carronshore. Falk 1G 59
Carrowclare. Caus 2E 92
Carrowdore. Ards 5J 93
Carrow Hill. Mon 4C 18
Carr Shield. Nmbd 7B 54
Carrutherstown. Dum 4F 52
Carr Vale. Derbs 3B 36
Carrville. Dur 7G 55
Carryduff. Lis 5H 93
Carsaig. Arg 5L 63
Carscreugh. Dum 5H 51
Carsegowan. Dum 6K 51
Carse House. Arg 3G 57
Carseriggan. Dum 5J 51
Carsethorn. Dum 6D 52
Carshalton. G Lon 7K 21
Carsington. Derbs 4L 35
Carskiey. Arg 1B 50
Carsluith. Dum 6K 51
Carson Park. New M 6J 93
Carsphairn. Dum 2L 51
Carstairs. S Lan 5H 59
Carstairs Junction. S Lan 5H 59
Cartbridge. Surr 8H 21
Carterhaugh. Ang 3H 67
Carter's Clay. Hants 3M 9
Carterton. Oxon 3L 19
Carterway Heads. Nmbd 6D 54
Carthew. Corn 6C 4
Carthorpe. N Yor 7M 47
Cartington. Nmbd 1D 54
Cartland. S Lan 5G 59
Cartmel. Cumb 8B 46
Cartmel Fell. Cumb 7C 46
Cartworth. W Yor 7K 41
Carwath. Cumb 7H 53
Carway. Carm 6L 15
Carwinley. Cumb 4J 53
Cascob. Powy 6M 25
Cas-gwent. Mon 4D 18
Cash Feus. Fife 7F 66
Cashlie. Per 3J 65
Cashmoor. Dors 4H 9
Cas-Mael. Pemb 4G 15
Casnewydd. Newp 5B 18
Cassington. Oxon 2B 20
Cassop. Dur 8G 55
Castell. Cnwy 4G 33
Castell. Den 4L 33
Castell Hendre. Pemb 4G 15
Castell-Nedd. Neat 5G 17
Castell Newydd Emlyn. Carm 2K 15
Castell-y-bwch. Torf 4A 18
Casterton. Cumb 8E 46
Castle. Som 1D 8
Castle Acre. Norf 8E 38
Castle Ashby. Nptn 6F 28
Castlebay. W Isl 6C 74
Castle Bolton. N Yor 6J 47
Castle Bromwich. W Mid 3K 27
Castle Bytham. Linc 8G 37
Castlebythe. Pemb 4G 15
Castle Caereinion. Powy 2L 25
Castle Camps. Cambs 7C 30
Castle Carrock. Cumb 6K 53
Castlecary. N Lan 2F 58
Castle Cary. Som 2E 8
Castlecaulfield. M Ulst 5E 92
Castle Combe. Wilts 6G 19
Castlecraig. High 7J 79
Castledawson. M Ulst 4F 93
Castlederg. Derr 4C 92
Castle Donington. Leics 7B 36
Castle Douglas. Dum 5B 52
Castle Eaton. Swin 4K 19
Castle Eden. Dur 8H 55
Castleford. W Yor 5B 42
Castle Frome. Here 7E 26
Castle Green. Surr 7G 21
Castle Green. Warw 4L 27
Castle Gresley. Derbs 8L 35
Castle Heaton. Nmbd 5G 61
Castle Hedingham. Essx 8D 30
Castle Hill. Kent 1C 12
Castlehill. Per 4F 66
Castlehill. S Lan 4G 59
Castle Hill. Suff 7H 31
Castlehill. W Dun 2B 58
Castle Kennedy. Dum 6G 51
Castle Lachlan. Arg 8E 64
Castlemartin. Pemb 7F 14
Castlemilk. Glas 4E 58
Castlemorris. Pemb 3F 14
Castlemorton. Worc 8F 26
Castle O'er. Dum 2G 53
Castle Park. N Yor 4F 48

Deans—Edmondsley

Deans. *W Lot* 3J 59
Deanscales. *Cumb* 2K 45
Deanshanger. *Nptn* 7E 28
Deanston. *Stir* 7M 65
Dearham. *Cumb* 8E 52
Dearne Valley. *S Yor* 7A 42
Debach. *Suff* 6J 31
Debden. *Essx* 8B 30
Debden Green. *Essx*
nr. Loughton 4M 21
nr. Saffron Walden 8B 30
Debenham. *Suff* 5H 31
Dechmont. *W Lot* 2J 59
Deddington. *Oxon* 8B 28
Dedham. *Essx* 8G 31
Dedham Heath. *Essx* 8G 31
Deebank. *Abers* 6F 72
Deene. *Nptn* 2G 29
Deenethorpe. *Nptn* 2G 29
Deepcar. *S Yor* 8L 41
Deepcut. *Surr* 8G 21
Deepdale. *Cumb* 7F 46
Deepdale. *N Lin* 6H 43
Deepdale. *N Yor* 8G 47
Deeping Gate. *Pet* 1J 29
Deeping St James. *Linc* 8J 37
Deeping St Nicholas. *Linc* 8K 37
Deerhill. *Mor* 8D 80
Deerhurst. *Glos* 1G 19
Deerhurst Walton. *Glos* 1G 19
Deerness. *Orkn* 1G 87
Defford. *Worc* 7H 27
Defynnog. *Powy* 2J 17
Deganwy. *Cnwy* 3G 33
Deighton. *N Yor* 5A 48
Deighton. *W Yor* 6K 41
Deighton. *York* 3D 42
Deiniolen. *Gwyn* 4E 32
Delabole. *Corn* 3C 4
Delamere. *Ches W* 3D 34
Delfour. *High* 5J 71
Dell, The. *Suff* 2L 31
Delliefure. *High* 2L 71
Delly End. *Oxon* 2A 20
Delny. *High* 6H 79
Delph. *G Man* 7H 41
Delves. *Dur* 7E 54
Delves, The. *W Mid* 2J 27
Delvin End. *Essx* 8D 30
Dembleby. *Linc* 6H 37
Demelza. *Corn* 5B 4
Den, The. *N Ayr* 4B 58
Denaby Main. *S Yor* 8B 42
Denbeath. *Fife* 8G 67
Denbigh. *Den* 4K 33
Denbury. *Devn* 5L 5
Denby. *Derbs* 5A 36
Denby Common. *Derbs* 5B 36
Denby Dale. *W Yor* 7L 41
Denchworth. *Oxon* 4A 20
Dendron. *Cumb* 7M 45
Deneside. *Dur* 7H 55
Denford. *Nptn* 4G 29
Dengie. *Essx* 3F 22
Denham. *Buck* 5H 21
Denham. *Suff*
nr. Bury St Edmunds 5D 30
nr. Eye 4H 31
Denham Green. *Buck* 5H 21
Denham Street. *Suff* 4H 31
Denhead. *Abers*
nr. Ellon 2J 73
nr. Strichen 8J 81
Denhead. *Fife* 6H 67
Denholm. *Bord* 8C 60
Denholme. *W Yor* 4J 41
Denholme Clough. *W Yor* 4J 41
Denholme Gate. *W Yor* 4J 41
Denio. *Gwyn* 7C 32
Denmead. *Hants* 4D 10
Dennington. *Suff* 5J 31
Denny. *Falk* 1G 59
Denny End. *Cambs* 5A 30
Dennyloanhead. *Falk* 1G 59
Den of Lindores. *Fife* 6F 66
Denshaw. *G Man* 6H 41
Denside. *Abers* 6H 73
Densole. *Kent* 1J 13
Denston. *Suff* 6D 30
Denstone. *Staf* 5K 35
Denstroude. *Kent* 7H 23
Dent. *Cumb* 7F 46
Denton. *Cambs* 3J 29
Denton. *Darl* 4L 47
Denton. *E Sus* 5A 12
Denton. *G Man* 8H 41
Denton. *Kent* 1J 13
Denton. *Linc* 6F 36
Denton. *Norf* 3J 31
Denton. *Nptn* 6F 28
Denton. *N Yor* 3K 41
Denton. *Oxon* 3C 20
Denver. *Norf* 1C 30
Denwick. *Nmbd* 8K 61
Deopham. *Norf* 1G 31
Deopham Green. *Norf* 2G 31
Depden. *Suff* 6D 30
Depden Green. *Suff* 6D 30
Deptford. *G Lon* 6L 21
Deptford. *Wilts* 2J 9
Derby. *Derb* 6A 36
Derbyhaven. *IOM* 8B 44
Derculich. *Per* 2B 66
Dereham. *Norf* 8F 38
Deri. *Cphy* 4L 17
Derril. *Devn* 5C 6
Derringstone. *Kent* 1J 13
Derrington. *Shrp* 2E 26
Derrington. *Staf* 7G 35
Derriton. *Devn* 5C 6
Derry. *Derr* 3D 92
Derryboye. *New M* 6J 93
Derrycrin. *M Ulst* 5F 93
Derrygonnelly. *Ferm* 6B 92
Derryguaig. *Arg* 4K 63
Derry Hill. *Wilts* 6H 19
Derrykeighan. *Caus* 2F 93
Derrylin. *Ferm* 7C 92
Derrymacash. *Arm* 6G 93
Derrythorpe. *N Lin* 7F 42
Derrytrasna. *Arm* 5F 93
Dersingham. *Norf* 6C 38
Dervaig. *Arg* 2K 63
Dervock. *Caus* 2F 93
Derwen. *Den* 5K 33
Derwen Gam. *Cdgn* 1L 15
Derwenlas. *Powy* 3G 25
Desborough. *Nptn* 3F 28
Desertmartin. *M Ulst* 4F 93
Desford. *Leics* 1B 28
Detchant. *Nmbd* 6H 61
Dethick. *Derbs* 4M 35
Detling. *Kent* 8D 22
Deuchar. *Ang* 1H 67
Deuddwr. *Powy* 1M 25
Devauden. *Mon* 4C 18
Devil's Bridge. *Cdgn* 5G 25
Devitts Green. *Warw* 2L 27
Devizes. *Wilts* 7J 19
Devonport. *Plym* 6G 5
Devonside. *Clac* 8C 66
Devoran. *Corn* 5L 3
Dewartown. *Midl* 3A 60
Dewlish. *Dors* 6F 8
Dewsall Court. *Here* 8C 26
Dewsbury. *W Yor* 5L 41
Dexbeer. *Devn* 5B 6
Dhoon. *IOM* 6D 44
Dhoor. *IOM* 5D 44
Dhowin. *IOM* 4D 44
Dial Green. *W Sus* 3G 11
Dial Post. *W Sus* 4J 11
Diamond, The. *M Ulst* 5F 93
Dibberford. *Dors* 5C 8
Dibden. *Hants* 5B 10
Dibden Purlieu. *Hants* 5B 10
Dickleburgh. *Norf* 3H 31
Didbrook. *Glos* 8J 27
Didcot. *Oxon* 4C 20
Diddington. *Cambs* 5J 29
Diddlebury. *Shrp* 3D 26
Didley. *Here* 8C 26
Didling. *W Sus* 4F 10
Didmarton. *Glos* 5G 19
Didsbury. *G Man* 8G 41
Didworthy. *Devn* 5J 5
Digby. *Linc* 4H 37
Digg. *High* 7F 76
Diggle. *G Man* 7J 41
Digmoor. *Lanc* 7C 40
Digswell. *Herts* 2K 21
Dihewyd. *Cdgn* 1L 15
Dilham. *Norf* 7K 39
Dilhorne. *Staf* 5H 35
Dillarburn. *S Lan* 5G 59
Dillington. *Cambs* 5J 29
Dilston. *Nmbd* 5C 54
Dilston Marsh. *Wilts* 1G 9
Dilwyn. *Here* 6C 26
Dimmer. *Som* 2E 8
Dimple. *G Man* 6F 40
Dinas. *Carm* 3J 15
Dinas. *Gwyn*
nr. Caernarfon 5D 32
nr. Tudweiliog 7B 32
Dinas Cross. *Pemb* 3G 15
Dinas Dinlle. *Gwyn* 5D 32
Dinas Mawddwy. *Gwyn* 1H 25
Dinas Powys. *V Glam* 7L 17
Dinbych. *Den* 4K 33
Dinbych-y-Pysgod. *Pemb* 6H 15
Dinckley. *Lanc* 4E 40
Dinder. *Som* 1D 8
Dinedor. *Here* 8D 26
Dinedor Cross. *Here* 8D 26
Dingestow. *Mon* 2C 18
Dingle. *Mers* 1B 34
Dingleden. *Kent* 2E 12
Dingleton. *Bord* 6C 60
Dingley. *Nptn* 3E 28
Dingwall. *High* 8F 78
Dinmael. *Cnwy* 6K 33
Dinnet. *Abers* 6D 72
Dinnington. *Som* 4C 8
Dinnington. *S Yor* 1C 36
Dinnington. *Tyne* 4F 54
Dinorwig. *Gwyn* 4E 32
Dinton. *Buck* 2E 20
Dinton. *Wilts* 2J 9
Dinworthy. *Devn* 4C 6
Dipley. *Hants* 8E 20
Dippen. *Arg* 6G 57
Dippenhall. *Surr* 1F 10
Dippertown. *Devn* 7D 6
Dippin. *N Ayr* 7K 57
Dipple. *S Ayr* 1H 51
Diptford. *Devn* 6K 5
Dipton. *Dur* 6E 54
Dirleton. *E Lot* 1C 60
Dirt Pot. *Nmbd* 7B 54
Discoed. *Powy* 5A 26
Diseworth. *Leics* 7B 36
Dishes. *Orkn* 7F 88
Dishforth. *N Yor* 8A 48
Disley. *Ches E* 1H 35
Diss. *Norf* 4H 31
Disserth. *Powy* 7K 25
Distington. *Cumb* 2K 45
Ditchampton. *Wilts* 2J 9
Ditcheat. *Som* 2E 8
Ditchingham. *Norf* 2K 31
Ditchling. *E Sus* 4L 11
Ditteridge. *Wilts* 7G 19
Dittisham. *Devn* 6L 5
Ditton. *Hal* 1C 34
Ditton. *Kent* 8D 22
Ditton Green. *Cambs* 6C 30
Ditton Priors. *Shrp* 3E 26
Divach. *High* 3E 70
Dixonfield. *High* 5C 86
Dixton. *Glos* 8H 27
Dixton. *Mon* 2D 18
Dizzard. *Corn* 6A 6
Doagh. *Ant* 4H 93
Dobcross. *G Man* 7H 41
Dobs Hill. *Flin* 3B 34
Dobson's Bridge. *Shrp* 6C 34
Dobwalls. *Corn* 5E 4
Doccombe. *Devn* 7G 7
Dochgarroch. *High* 1G 71
Docking. *Norf* 6D 38
Docklow. *Here* 6D 26
Dockray. *Cumb* 3B 46
Doc Penfro. *Pemb* 6F 14
Dodbrooke. *Devn* 7K 5
Doddenham. *Worc* 6F 26
Doddinghurst. *Essx* 4B 22
Doddington. *Cambs* 2L 29
Doddington. *Kent* 8F 22
Doddington. *Linc* 2G 37
Doddington. *Nmbd* 6G 61
Doddington. *Shrp* 4E 26
Doddiscombsleigh. *Devn* 7H 7
Doddshill. *Norf* 6D 38
Dodford. *Nptn* 5D 28
Dodford. *Worc* 4H 27
Dodington. *Som* 1L 7
Dodington. *S Glo* 5F 18
Dodleston. *Ches W* 3B 34
Dods Leigh. *Staf* 6J 35
Dodworth. *S Yor* 7M 41
Doe Lea. *Derbs* 3B 36
Dogdyke. *Linc* 4K 37
Dogmersfield. *Hants* 8E 20
Dogsthorpe. *Pet* 1K 29
Dog Village. *Devn* 6J 7
Dolanog. *Powy* 1K 25
Dolau. *Powy* 6L 25
Dolau. *Rhon* 6K 17
Dolbenmaen. *Gwyn* 6E 32
Doley. *Staf* 7F 34
Dol-fâch. *Powy* 2J 25
Dolfach. *Powy* 5J 25
Dolfor. *Powy* 4L 25
Dolgarrog. *Cnwy* 4G 33
Dolgellau. *Gwyn* 1G 25
Dolgoch. *Gwyn* 2F 24
Dol-gran. *Carm* 3L 15
Dolhelfa. *Powy* 5J 25
Doll. *High* 3J 79
Dollar. *Clac* 8C 66
Dolley Green. *Powy* 6A 26
Dollingstown. *Arm* 6G 93
Dollwen. *Cdgn* 4F 24
Dolphin. *Flin* 3L 33
Dolphinholme. *Lanc* 2D 40
Dolphinton. *S Lan* 5K 59
Dolton. *Devn* 4E 6
Dolwen. *Cnwy* 3H 33
Dolwyddelan. *Cnwy* 5G 33
Dol-y-Bont. *Cdgn* 4F 24
Dolyhir. *Powy* 7M 25
Domgay. *Powy* 8A 34
Donagh. *Ferm* 7C 92
Donaghadee. *Ards* 5J 93
Donaghcloney. *Arm* 6G 93
Donaghmore. *M Ulst* 5E 92
Doncaster. *S Yor* 7C 42
Doncaster Sheffield Airport.
S Yor 8D 42
Donhead St Andrew. *Wilts* 3H 9
Donhead St Mary. *Wilts* 3H 9
Doniford. *Som* 1K 7
Donington. *Linc* 6K 37
Donington. *Shrp* 1G 27
Donington Eaudike. *Linc* 6K 37
Donington le Heath. *Leics* 8B 36
Donington on Bain. *Linc* 1K 37
Donington South Ing. *Linc* 6K 37
Donisthorpe. *Leics* 8M 35
Donkey Street. *Kent* 2H 13
Donkey Town. *Surr* 7G 21
Donna Nook. *Linc* 8M 43
Donnington. *Glos* 1K 19
Donnington. *Here* 8F 26
Donnington. *Shrp* 1D 26
Donnington. *Telf* 8F 34
Donnington. *W Ber* 7B 20
Donnington. *W Sus* 5F 10
Donyatt. *Som* 4B 8
Doomsday Green. *W Sus* 3J 11
Doonfoot. *S Ayr* 8B 58
Doonholm. *S Ayr* 8B 58
Dorback Lodge. *High* 4L 71
Dorchester. *Dors* 6E 8
Dorchester on Thames.
Oxon 4C 20
Dordon. *Warw* 1L 27
Dore. *S Yor* 1M 35
Dores. *High* 2F 70
Dorking. *Surr* 1J 11
Dorking Tye. *Suff* 8F 30
Dormansland. *Surr* 1M 11
Dormans Park. *Surr* 1L 11
Dormanstown. *Red C* 3C 48
Dormington. *Here* 7D 26
Dormston. *Worc* 6H 27
Dorn. *Glos* 8L 27
Dorney. *Buck* 6G 21
Dornie. *High* 3K 69
Dornoch. *High* 5H 79
Dornock. *Dum* 5G 53
Dorrery. *High* 6B 86
Dorridge. *W Mid* 4K 27
Dorrington. *Linc* 4H 37
Dorrington. *Shrp* 1C 26
Dorsington. *Warw* 7K 27
Dorstone. *Here* 7B 26
Dorton. *Buck* 2D 20
Dosthill. *Staf* 1L 27
Dotham. *IOA* 3C 32
Dottery. *Dors* 6C 8
Doublebois. *Corn* 5D 4
Dougarie. *N Ayr* 6H 57
Doughton. *Glos* 4G 19
Douglas. *IOM* 7C 44
Douglas. *S Lan* 6G 59
Douglas Bridge. *Derr* 4C 92
Douglastown. *Ang* 3H 67
Douglas Water. *S Lan* 6G 59
Doulting. *Som* 1E 8
Dounby. *Orkn* 7B 88
Doune. *High*
nr. Kingussie 4J 71
nr. Lairg 3E 78
Doune. *Stir* 7M 65
Doune. *High*
nr. Bonar Bridge 4F 78
nr. Tain 5G 79
Dounreay, Upper & Lower.
High 5A 86
Doura. *N Ayr* 5B 58
Dousland. *Devn* 5H 5
Dovaston. *Shrp* 7B 34
Dove Holes. *Derbs* 2J 35
Dovenby. *Cumb* 8E 52
Dover. *Kent* 1K 13
Dovercourt. *Essx* 8J 31
Doverdale. *Worc* 5G 27
Doveridge. *Derbs* 6K 35
Doversgreen. *Surr* 1K 11
Dowally. *Per* 3D 66
Dowbridge. *Lanc* 4C 40
Dowdeswell. *Glos* 2J 19
Dowlais. *Mer T* 4K 17
Dowland. *Devn* 4E 6
Dowlands. *Devn* 6A 8
Dowles. *Worc* 4F 26
Dowlesgreen. *Wok* 7F 20
Dowlish Wake. *Som* 4B 8
Down, The. *Shrp* 2E 26
Downall Green. *Mers* 7D 40
Down Ampney. *Glos* 4K 19
Downderry. *Corn*
nr. Looe 6F 4
nr. St Austell 6B 4
Downe. *G Lon* 7M 21
Downend. *IOW* 7C 10
Downend. *S Glo* 6E 18
Downend. *W Ber* 6B 20
Down Field. *Cambs* 4C 30
Downfield. *D'dee* 4G 67
Downgate. *Corn*
nr. Kelly Bray 8C 6
nr. Upton Cross 8B 6
Downham. *Essx* 4D 22
Downham. *Lanc* 3F 40
Downham. *Nmbd* 6F 60
Downham Market. *Norf* 1C 30
Down Hatherley. *Glos* 1G 19
Downhead. *Som*
nr. Frome 1E 8
nr. Yeovil 3D 8
Downhill. *Caus* 2E 92
Downholland Cross. *Lanc* 7B 40
Downholme. *N Yor* 6K 47
Downies. *Abers* 6J 73
Downley. *Buck* 4F 20
Downpatrick. *New M* 6J 93
Down St Mary. *Devn* 5G 7
Downside. *Som*
nr. Chilcompton 8E 18
nr. Shepton Mallet 1E 8
Downside. *Surr* 8J 21
Down Thomas. *Devn* 6H 5
Downton. *Hants* 6L 9
Downton. *Wilts* 3K 9
Downton on the Rock. *Here* 4C 26
Dowsby. *Linc* 7J 37
Dowsdale. *Linc* 8K 37
Dowthwaitehead. *Cumb* 3B 46
Doxey. *Staf* 7H 35
Doxford. *Nmbd* 7J 61
Doynton. *S Glo* 6F 18
Drabblegate. *Norf* 7J 39
Draethen. *Cphy* 6M 17
Draffan. *S Lan* 5F 58
Dragonby. *N Lin* 6G 43
Dragon's Green. *W Sus* 3J 11
Drakelow. *Worc* 3G 27
Drakemyre. *N Ayr* 4A 58
Drakes Broughton. *Worc* 7H 27
Drakes Cross. *Worc* 4J 27
Drakewalls. *Corn* 8D 6
Draperstown. *M Ulst* 4E 92
Draughton. *Nptn* 4E 28
Draughton. *N Yor* 2J 41
Drax. *N Yor* 5D 42
Draycot. *Oxon* 3D 20
Draycote. *Warw* 4B 28
Draycot Foliat. *Swin* 6K 19
Draycott. *Derbs* 6B 36
Draycott. *Glos* 8K 27
Draycott. *Shrp* 2G 27
Draycott. *Som*
nr. Cheddar 8C 18
nr. Yeovil 3D 8
Draycott. *Worc* 7G 27
Draycott in the Clay. *Staf* 7K 35
Draycott in the Moors. *Staf* 5H 35
Drayford. *Devn* 4G 7
Drayton. *Leics* 2F 28
Drayton. *Linc* 6K 37
Drayton. *Norf* 8H 39
Drayton. *Nptn* 5C 28
Drayton. *Oxon*
nr. Abingdon 4B 20
nr. Banbury 7B 28
Drayton. *Port* 5D 10
Drayton. *Som* 3C 8
Drayton. *Warw* 6K 27
Drayton. *Worc* 4H 27
Drayton Bassett. *Staf* 1K 27
Drayton Beauchamp. *Buck* 2G 21
Drayton Parslow. *Buck* 1F 20
Drayton St Leonard. *Oxon* 4C 20
Drebley. *N Yor* 2J 41
Dreenhill. *Pemb* 5F 14
Y Dref. *Gwyn* 7D 32
Drefach. *Carm*
nr. Meidrim 5M 15
nr. Newcastle Emlyn 3K 15
nr. Tumble 4J 15
Drefach. *Cdgn* 2L 15
Dreghorn. *N Ayr* 6B 58
Drellingore. *Kent* 1J 13
Drem. *E Lot* 2C 60
Y Drenewydd. *Powy* 3L 25
Dreumasdal. *W Isl* 2D 74
Drewsteignton. *Devn* 6G 7
Driby. *Linc* 2L 37
Driffield. *E Yor* 2H 43
Driffield. *Glos* 4J 19
Drift. *Corn* 6H 3
Drigg. *Cumb* 5K 45
Drighlington. *W Yor* 5L 41
Drimnin. *High* 2L 63
Drimpton. *Dors* 5C 8
Dringhoe. *E Yor* 2J 43
Drinisiadar. *W Isl* 4C 76
Drinkstone. *Suff* 5F 30
Drinkstone Green. *Suff* 5F 30
Drointon. *Staf* 7J 35
Droitwich Spa. *Worc* 5G 27
Droman. *High* 6D 84
Dromara. *Lis* 6H 93
Dromore. *Arm* 6H 93
Dromore. *Ferm* 5C 92
Dron. *Per* 6E 66
Dronfield. *Derbs* 2A 36
Dronfield Woodhouse.
Derbs 2M 35
Drongan. *E Ayr* 8C 58
Dronley. *Ang* 4G 67
Droop. *Dors* 5F 8
Drope. *V Glam* 7L 17
Droxford. *Hants* 4D 10
Droylsden. *G Man* 8G 41
Druggers End. *Worc* 8F 26
Druid. *Den* 6K 33
Druid's Heath. *W Mid* 1J 27
Druidston. *Pemb* 5E 14
Druim. *High* 8K 79
Druimarbin. *High* 8A 70
Druim Fhearna. *High* 4H 69
Druimindarroch. *High* 7H 69
Druim Saighdinis. *W Isl* 7K 75
Drum. *Per* 7D 66
Drumaness. *New M* 6H 93
Drumaroad. *New M* 6H 93
Drumbeg. *High* 8D 84
Drumblade. *Abers* 1E 72
Drumbo. *Lis* 5H 93
Drumbuie. *Dum* 3L 51
Drumbuie. *High* 2J 69
Drumburgh. *Cumb* 6G 53
Drumburn. *Dum* 5D 52
Drumchapel. *Glas* 2D 58
Drumchardine. *High* 1F 70
Drumchork. *High* 5K 77
Drumclog. *S Lan* 6E 58
Drumeldrie. *Fife* 7H 67
Drumelzier. *Bord* 6K 59
Drumfearn. *High* 4H 69
Drumgask. *High* 6G 71
Drumgelloch. *N Lan* 3F 58
Drumgley. *Ang* 2H 67
Drumguish. *High* 6H 71
Drumin. *Mor* 2A 72
Drumindorsair. *High* 1E 70
Drumintee. *New M* 7G 93
Drumlamford House. *S Ayr* 4H 51
Drumlasie. *Abers* 5F 72
Drumlemble. *Arg* 8F 56
Drumlithie. *Abers* 7G 73
Drummoddie. *Dum* 7J 51
Drummond. *High* 7G 79
Drummore. *Dum* 8G 51
Drummuir. *Mor* 1C 72
Drumnacanvy. *Arm* 6G 93
Drumnadrochit. *High* 2F 70
Drumnagorrach. *Mor* 8E 80
Drumnakilly. *Ferm* 5D 92
Drumoak. *Abers* 6G 73
Drumquin. *Ferm* 5C 92
Drumraighland. *Caus* 2E 92
Drumrunie. *High* 3B 78
Drumry. *W Dun* 2D 58
Drums. *Abers* 3J 73
Drumsleet. *Dum* 4D 52
Drumsmittal. *High* 1G 71
Drums of Park. *Abers* 8E 80
Drumsturdy. *Ang* 4H 67
Drumsurn. *Caus* 3E 92
Drumtochty Castle. *Abers* 7F 72
Drumuie. *High* 1F 68
Drumuillie. *High* 3K 71
Drumvaich. *Stir* 7L 65
Drumwhindle. *Abers* 2J 73
Drunkendub. *Ang* 3K 67
Drury. *Flin* 3A 34
Drury Square. *Norf* 8F 38
Drybeck. *Cumb* 4E 46
Drybridge. *Mor* 7D 80
Drybridge. *N Ayr* 6B 58
Drybrook. *Glos* 2E 18
Drybrook. *Here* 2D 18
Dryburgh. *Bord* 6C 60
Dry Doddington. *Linc* 5F 36
Dry Drayton. *Cambs* 5L 29
Drym. *Corn* 5K 3
Drymen. *Stir* 1C 58
Drymuir. *Abers* 1J 73
Drynachan Lodge. *High* 2J 71
Drynie Park. *High* 8F 78
Drynoch. *High* 2F 68
Dry Sandford. *Oxon* 3B 20
Dryslwyn. *Carm* 2E 16
Dry Street. *Essx* 5C 22
Dryton. *Shrp* 1D 26
Dubford. *Abers* 7G 81
Dubiton. *Abers* 8F 80
Dubton. *Ang* 2J 67
Duchally. *High* 2D 78
Duck End. *Essx* 1C 22
Duckington. *Ches W* 4C 34
Ducklington. *Oxon* 3A 20
Duckmanton. *Derbs* 2B 36
Duck Street. *Hants* 1M 9
Dudbridge. *Glos* 3G 19
Duddenhoe End. *Essx* 8A 30
Duddingston. *Edin* 2L 59
Duddington. *Nptn* 1G 29
Duddleswell. *E Sus* 3A 12
Duddo. *Nmbd* 5G 61
Duddon. *Ches W* 3D 34
Duddon Bridge. *Cumb* 6L 45
Dudleston. *Shrp* 6B 34
Dudleston Heath. *Shrp* 6B 34
Dudley. *Tyne* 4F 54
Dudley. *W Mid* 3H 27
Dudston. *Shrp* 3M 25
Dudwells. *Pemb* 4F 14
Duffield. *Derbs* 5M 35
Duffryn. *Neat* 5H 17
Dufftown. *Mor* 1C 72
Duffus. *Mor* 7A 80
Dufton. *Cumb* 3E 46
Duggleby. *N Yor* 1F 42
Duirinish. *High* 2J 69
Duisdalemore. *High* 4H 69
Duisdeil Mòr. *High* 4H 69
Duisky. *High* 8M 69
Dukesfield. *Nmbd* 6C 54
Dukestown. *Blae* 4L 17
Dukinfield. *G Man* 8H 41
Dulas. *IOA* 2D 32
Dulcote. *Som* 1D 8
Dulford. *Devn* 5K 7
Dull. *Per* 3B 66
Dullatur. *N Lan* 2F 58
Dullingham. *Cambs* 6C 30
Dullingham Ley. *Cambs* 6C 30
Dulnain Bridge. *High* 3K 71
Duloe. *Bed* 5J 29
Duloe. *Corn* 6E 4
Dulverton. *Som* 3J 7
Dulwich. *G Lon* 6L 21
Dumbarton. *W Dun* 2C 58
Dumbleton. *Glos* 8J 27
Dumfin. *Arg* 1B 58
Dumfries. *Dum* 4D 52
Dumgoyne. *Stir* 1D 58
Dummer. *Hants* 1C 10
Dumpford. *W Sus* 3F 10
Dun. *Ang* 1K 67
Dunadry. *Ant* 4G 93
Dunaghy. *Caus* 2F 93
Dunagoil. *Arg* 4K 57
Dunalastair. *Per* 2M 65
Dunan. *High* 3G 69
Dunball. *Som* 1B 8
Dunbar. *E Lot* 2D 60
Dunbeath. *High* 1A 80
Dunbeg. *Arg* 4C 64
Dunblane. *Stir* 7A 66
Dunbog. *Fife* 6F 66
Dunbridge. *Hants* 3M 9
Duncanston. *Abers* 3E 72
Duncanston. *High* 8F 78
Dun Charlabhaigh. *W Isl* 7E 82
Dunchideock. *Devn* 7H 7
Dunchurch. *Warw* 4B 28
Duncote. *Nptn* 6D 28
Duncow. *Dum* 3D 52
Duncrievie. *Per* 7E 66
Duncton. *W Sus* 4G 11
Dundee. *D'dee* 4H 67
Dundee Airport. *D'dee* 5G 67
Dundon. *Som* 2C 8
Dundonald. *Lis* 5J 93
Dundonald. *S Ayr* 6B 58
Dundonnell. *High* 5A 78
Dundraw. *Cumb* 7G 53
Dundreggan. *High* 4D 70
Dundrennan. *Dum* 7B 52
Dundridge. *Hants* 4C 10
Dundrod. *Lis* 5H 93
Dundrum. *New M* 7J 93
Dundry. *N Som* 7D 18
Dunecht. *Abers* 5G 73
Dunfermline. *Fife* 1J 59
Dunford Bridge. *S Yor* 7K 41
Dungannon. *M Ulst* 5E 92
Dungate. *Kent* 8F 22
Dunge. *Wilts* 8G 19
Dungeness. *Kent* 4G 13
Dungiven. *Caus* 3E 92
Dungworth. *S Yor* 1L 35
Dunham-on-the-Hill.
Ches W 2C 34
Dunham-on-Trent. *Notts* 2F 36
Dunhampton. *Worc* 5G 27
Dunham Town. *G Man* 1F 34
Dunham Woodhouses.
G Man 1F 34
Dunholme. *Linc* 2H 37
Dunino. *Fife* 6J 67
Dunipace. *Falk* 1G 59
Dunira. *Per* 5M 65
Dunkeld. *Per* 3D 66
Dunkerton. *Bath* 8F 18
Dunkeswell. *Devn* 5L 7
Dunkeswick. *N Yor* 3M 41
Dunkirk. *Kent* 8G 23
Dunkirk. *S Glo* 5F 18
Dunkirk. *Staf* 4G 35
Dunkirk. *Wilts* 7H 19
Dunk's Green. *Kent* 8C 22
Dunlappie. *Ang* 1J 67
Dunley. *Hants* 8B 20
Dunley. *Worc* 5F 26
Dunlichity Lodge. *High* 2G 71
Dunlop. *E Ayr* 5C 58
Dunloy. *Caus* 3G 93
Dunmaglass Lodge. *High* 3F 70
Dunmore. *Arg* 3G 57
Dunmore. *Falk* 1G 59
Dunmore. *High* 1F 70
Dunmurry. *Bel* 5H 93
Dunnamanagh. *Derr* 3D 92
Dunnaval. *New M* 7H 93
Dunnet. *High* 4D 86
Dunnichen. *Ang* 3J 67
Dunning. *Per* 6D 66
Dunnington. *E Yor* 2J 43
Dunnington. *Warw* 6J 27
Dunnington. *York* 2D 42
Dunningwell. *Cumb* 6L 45
Dunnockshaw. *Lanc* 5G 41
Dunoon. *Arg* 2L 57
Dunphail. *Mor* 1L 71
Dunragit. *Dum* 6G 51
Dunrostan. *Arg* 1G 57
Duns. *Bord* 4E 60
Dunsby. *Linc* 7J 37
Dunscar. *G Man* 6F 40
Dunscore. *Dum* 3C 52
Dunscroft. *S Yor* 7D 42
Dunsdale. *Red C* 4D 48
Dunsden Green. *Oxon* 6E 20
Dunsfold. *Surr* 2H 11
Dunsford. *Devn* 7H 7
Dunshalt. *Fife* 6F 66
Dunshillock. *Abers* 1J 73
Dunsley. *N Yor* 4F 48
Dunsley. *Staf* 3G 27
Dunsmore. *Buck* 3F 20
Dunsop Bridge. *Lanc* 2E 40
Dunstable. *C Beds* 1H 21
Dunstal. *Staf* 7J 35
Dunstall. *Staf* 7K 35
Dunstall Green. *Suff* 5D 30
Dunstall Hill. *W Mid* 1H 27
Dunstan. *Nmbd* 8K 61
Dunster. *Som* 1J 7
Duns Tew. *Oxon* 1B 20
Dunston. *Linc* 3H 37
Dunston. *Norf* 1J 31
Dunston. *Staf* 8H 35
Dunston. *Tyne* 5F 54
Dunstone. *Devn* 6H 5
Dunston Heath. *Staf* 8H 35
Dunsville. *S Yor* 7D 42
Dunswell. *E Yor* 4H 43
Dunsyre. *S Lan* 5J 59
Dunterton. *Devn* 8C 6
Duntisbourne Abbots. *Glos* 3H 19
Duntisbourne Leer. *Glos* 3H 19
Duntisbourne Rouse. *Glos* 3H 19
Duntish. *Dors* 5E 8
Duntocher. *W Dun* 2C 58
Dunton. *Buck* 1F 20
Dunton. *C Beds* 7K 29
Dunton. *Norf* 6E 38
Dunton Bassett. *Leics* 2C 28
Dunton Green. *Kent* 8B 22
Dunton Patch. *Norf* 6E 38
Duntulm. *High* 6F 76
Dunure. *S Ayr* 8A 58
Dunvant. *Swan* 5E 16
Dunvegan. *High* 1D 68
Dunwich. *Suff* 4L 31
Dunwood. *Staf* 4H 35
Durdar. *Cumb* 6J 53
Durgates. *E Sus* 2C 12
Durham. *Dur* 7F 54
Durham Tees Valley Airport.
Darl 4A 48
Durisdeer. *Dum* 1C 52
Durisdeermill. *Dum* 1C 52
Durkar. *W Yor* 6M 41
Durleigh. *Som* 2A 8
Durley. *Hants* 4C 10
Durley. *Wilts* 7L 19
Durley Street. *Hants* 4C 10
Durlow Common. *Here* 8E 26
Durnamuck. *High* 4M 77
Durness. *High* 5G 85
Durno. *Abers* 3G 73
Durns Town. *Hants* 6L 9
Duror. *High* 2D 64
Durran. *Arg* 7D 64
Durran. *High* 5C 86
Durrant Green. *Kent* 2E 12
Durrants. *Hants* 4E 10
Durrington. *W Sus* 5J 11
Durrington. *Wilts* 1K 9
Dursley. *Glos* 4F 18
Dursley Cross. *Glos* 2E 18
Durston. *Som* 3A 8
Durweston. *Dors* 5G 9
Dury. *Shet* 2E 90
Duston. *Nptn* 5E 28
Duthil. *High* 3K 71
Dutlas. *Powy* 5M 25
Duton Hill. *Essx* 1C 22
Dutson. *Corn* 7C 6
Dutton. *Ches W* 2D 34
Duxford. *Cambs* 7A 30
Duxford. *Oxon* 4A 20
Dwygyfylchi. *Cnwy* 3G 33
Dwyran. *IOA* 4D 32
Dyce. *Aber* 4H 73
Dyffryn. *B'end* 5H 17
Dyffryn. *Carm* 4K 15
Dyffryn. *Pemb* 3F 14
Dyffryn. *V Glam* 7K 17
Dyffryn Ardudwy. *Gwyn* 8E 32
Dyffryn Castell. *Cdgn* 4G 25
Dyffryn Ceidrych. *Carm* 2G 17
Dyffryn Cellwen. *Neat* 4H 17
Dyke. *Linc* 7J 37
Dyke. *Mor* 8K 79
Dykehead. *Ang* 1G 67
Dykehead. *N Lan* 3G 59
Dykehead. *Stir* 8K 65
Dykend. *Ang* 2F 66
Dykesfield. *Cumb* 6H 53
Dylife. *Powy* 3H 25
Dymchurch. *Kent* 3H 13
Dymock. *Glos* 8F 26
Dyrham. *S Glo* 6F 18
Dysart. *Fife* 8G 67
Dyserth. *Den* 3K 33

E

Eachwick. *Nmbd* 4E 54
Eadar Dha Fhadhail. *W Isl* 8D 82
Eagland Hill. *Lanc* 3C 40
Eagle. *Linc* 3F 36
Eagle Barnsdale. *Linc* 3F 36
Eagle Moor. *Linc* 3F 36
Eaglescliffe. *Stoc T* 4B 48
Eaglesfield. *Cumb* 2K 45
Eaglesfield. *Dum* 4G 53
Eaglesham. *E Ren* 4D 58
Eaglethorpe. *Nptn* 2H 29
Eagley. *G Man* 6F 40
Eairy. *IOM* 7B 44
Eakley Lanes. *Mil* 6F 28
Eakring. *Notts* 3D 36
Ealand. *N Lin* 6E 42
Ealing. *G Lon* 5J 21
Eallabus. *Arg* 3C 56
Eals. *Nmbd* 6L 53
Eamont Bridge. *Cumb* 3D 46
Earby. *Lanc* 3H 41
Earcroft. *Bkbn* 5E 40
Eardington. *Shrp* 2F 26
Eardisland. *Here* 6C 26
Eardisley. *Here* 7B 26
Eardiston. *Shrp* 7B 34
Eardiston. *Worc* 5E 26
Earith. *Cambs* 4L 29
Earlais. *High* 7E 76
Earle. *Nmbd* 7G 61
Earlesfield. *Linc* 6G 37
Earlestown. *Mers* 8D 40
Earley. *Wok* 6E 20
Earlham. *Norf* 1H 31
Earlish. *High* 7E 76
Earls Barton. *Nptn* 5F 28
Earls Colne. *Essx* 1E 22
Earls Common. *Worc* 6H 27
Earl's Croome. *Worc* 7G 27
Earlsdon. *W Mid* 4M 27
Earlsferry. *Fife* 7H 67
Earlsford. *Abers* 2H 73
Earl's Green. *Suff* 5G 31
Earlsheaton. *W Yor* 5L 41
Earl Shilton. *Leics* 2B 28
Earl Soham. *Suff* 5J 31
Earl Sterndale. *Derbs* 3J 35
Earlston. *E Ayr* 6C 58
Earlston. *Bord* 6C 60
Earl Stonham. *Suff* 6H 31
Earlstoun. *Dum* 3M 51
Earlswood. *Mon* 4C 18
Earlswood. *Warw* 4K 27
Earlyvale. *Bord* 4L 59
Earnley. *W Sus* 6F 10
Earsairidh. *W Isl* 6D 74
Earsdon. *Tyne* 4G 55
Earsham. *Norf* 3K 31
Earsham Street. *Suff* 4J 31
Earswick. *York* 2D 42
Eartham. *W Sus* 5G 11
Earthcott Green. *S Glo* 5E 18
Easby. *N Yor*
nr. Great Ayton 5C 48
nr. Richmond 5K 47
Easdale. *Arg* 6B 64
Easebourne. *W Sus* 3F 10
Easenhall. *Warw* 4B 28
Eashing. *Surr* 1G 11
Easington. *Buck* 2D 20
Easington. *Dur* 7H 55
Easington. *E Yor* 6L 43
Easington. *Nmbd* 6J 61
Easington. *Oxon*
nr. Banbury 8B 28
nr. Watlington 4D 20
Easington. *Red C* 4E 48
Easington Colliery. *Dur* 7H 55
Easington Lane. *Tyne* 7G 55
Easingwold. *N Yor* 8C 48
Eassie. *Ang* 3G 67
Eassie and Nevay. *Ang* 3G 67
East Aberthaw. *V Glam* 8K 17
Eastacombe. *Devn* 3E 6
Eastacott. *Devn* 3F 6
East Allington. *Devn* 7K 5
East Anstey. *Devn* 3H 7
East Anton. *Hants* 1A 10
East Appleton. *N Yor* 6L 47
East Ardsley. *W Yor* 5M 41
East Ashley. *Devn* 4F 6
East Ashling. *W Sus* 5F 10
East Aston. *Hants* 1B 10
East Ayton. *N Yor* 7G 49
East Barkwith. *Linc* 1J 37
East Barnby. *N Yor* 4F 48
East Barnet. *G Lon* 4K 21
East Barns. *E Lot* 2E 60
East Barsham. *Norf* 6F 38
East Beach. *W Sus* 6F 10
East Beckham. *Norf* 6H 39
East Bedfont. *G Lon* 6H 21
East Bennan. *N Ayr* 7J 57
East Bergholt. *Suff* 8G 31
East Bierley. *W Yor* 5L 41
East Bilney. *Norf* 8F 38
East Blatchington. *E Sus* 5A 12
East Bloxworth. *Dors* 6G 9
East Boldre. *Hants* 5A 10
East Bolton. *Nmbd* 8J 61
Eastbourne. *Darl* 4L 47
Eastbourne. *E Sus* 6C 12
East Brent. *Som* 8B 18
East Bridge. *Suff* 5L 31
East Bridgford. *Notts* 5D 36
East Briscoe. *Dur* 4H 47
East Buckland. *Devn*
nr. Barnstaple 2F 6
nr. Thurlestone 7J 5
East Budleigh. *Devn* 7K 7
Eastburn. *W Yor* 3J 41
East Burnham. *Buck* 5G 21
East Burrafirth. *Shet* 2D 90
East Burton. *Dors* 7G 9
Eastbury. *Herts* 4H 21
Eastbury. *W Ber* 6M 19
East Butsfield. *Dur* 7E 54
East Butterleigh. *Devn* 5J 7
East Butterwick. *N Lin* 7F 42
Eastby. *N Yor* 2J 41
East Calder. *W Lot* 3J 59
East Carleton. *Norf* 1H 31
East Carlton. *Nptn* 3F 28
East Carlton. *W Yor* 3L 41
East Chaldon. *Dors* 7F 8
East Challow. *Oxon* 5A 20
East Charleton. *Devn* 7K 5
East Chelborough. *Dors* 5D 8
East Chiltington. *E Sus* 4L 11
East Chinnock. *Som* 4C 8
East Chisenbury. *Wilts* 8K 19
Eastchurch. *Kent* 6F 22
East Clandon. *Surr* 8H 21
East Claydon. *Buck* 1E 20
East Clevedon. *N Som* 6C 18
East Clyne. *High* 3J 79
East Clyth. *High* 8D 86
East Coker. *Som* 4D 8
Eastcombe. *Glos* 3G 19
East Combe. *Som* 2L 7
East Common. *N Yor* 4D 42
East Compton. *Som* 1E 8
East Cornworthy. *Devn* 6L 5
Eastcote. *G Lon* 5J 21
Eastcote. *Nptn* 6D 28
Eastcote. *W Mid* 4K 27
Eastcott. *Corn* 4B 6
Eastcott. *Wilts* 8J 19
East Cottingwith. *E Yor* 3E 42
Eastcourt. *Wilts*
nr. Pewsey 7L 19
nr. Tetbury 4H 19
East Cowes. *IOW* 6C 10
East Cowick. *E Yor* 5D 42
East Cowton. *N Yor* 5M 47
East Cramlington. *Nmbd* 4F 54
East Cranmore. *Som* 1E 8
East Creech. *Dors* 7H 9
East Croachy. *High* 3G 71
East Dean. *E Sus* 6B 12
East Dean. *Glos* 1E 18
East Dean. *Hants* 3L 9
East Dean. *W Sus* 4G 11
East Down. *Devn* 1F 6
East Drayton. *Notts* 2E 36
East Dundry. *N Som* 7D 18
East Ella. *Hull* 5H 43
East End. *Cambs* 4L 29
East End. *Dors* 6H 9
East End. *E Yor*
nr. Ulrome 2J 43
nr. Withernsea 5K 43
East End. *Hants*
nr. Lymington 6A 10
nr. Newbury 7B 20
East End. *Herts* 1A 22
East End. *Kent*
nr. Minster 6F 22
nr. Tenterden 2E 12
East End. *N Som* 6C 18
East End. *Oxon* 2A 20
East End. *Som* 8D 18
East End. *Suff* 8H 31
Easter Ardross. *High* 6G 79
Easter Balgedie. *Per* 7E 66
Easter Balmoral. *Abers* 6B 72
Easter Brae. *High* 7G 79
Easter Buckieburn. *Stir* 1F 58
Easter Compton. *S Glo* 5D 18
Easter Fearn. *High* 5G 79
Easter Galcantray. *High* 1J 71
Eastergate. *W Sus* 5G 11
Easterhouse. *Glas* 3E 58
Easter Howgate. *Midl* 3L 59
Easter Kinkell. *High* 8F 78
Easter Lednathie. *Ang* 1G 67
Easter Ogil. *Ang* 1H 67
Easter Ord. *Abers* 5H 73
Easter Quarff. *Shet* 4E 90
Easter Rhynd. *Per* 6E 66
Easter Skeld. *Shet* 3D 90
Easter Suddie. *High* 8G 79
Easterton. *Wilts* 8J 19
Eastertown. *Som* 8B 18
Easter Tulloch. *Abers* 8G 73
East Everleigh. *Wilts* 8L 19
East Farleigh. *Kent* 8D 22
East Farndon. *Nptn* 3E 28
East Ferry. *Linc* 8F 42
Eastfield. *N Lan*
nr. Caldercruix 3G 59
nr. Harthill 3G 59
Eastfield. *N Yor* 7H 49
Eastfield. *S Lan* 3E 58
Eastfield Hall. *Nmbd* 1F 54
East Fortune. *E Lot* 2C 60
East Garforth. *W Yor* 4B 42
East Garston. *W Ber* 6A 20
Eastgate. *Dur* 8C 54
Eastgate. *Norf* 7H 39
East Ginge. *Oxon* 5B 20
East Gores. *Essx* 1E 22
East Goscote. *Leics* 8D 36
East Grafton. *Wilts* 7L 19
East Green. *Suff* 6C 30
East Grimstead. *Wilts* 3L 9
East Grinstead. *W Sus* 2L 11
East Guldeford. *E Sus* 3F 12
East Haddon. *Nptn* 5D 28
East Hagbourne. *Oxon* 5C 20
East Halton. *N Lin* 5J 43
East Ham. *G Lon* 5M 21
Eastham. *Mers* 1B 34
Eastham. *Worc* 5E 26
Eastham Ferry. *Mers* 1B 34
Easthampstead. *Brac* 7F 20
Easthampton. *Here* 5C 26
East Hanney. *Oxon* 4B 20
East Hanningfield. *Essx* 3D 22
East Hardwick. *W Yor* 6B 42
East Harling. *Norf* 3F 30
East Harlsey. *N Yor* 6B 48
East Harptree. *Bath* 8D 18
East Hartford. *Nmbd* 4F 54
East Harting. *W Sus* 4E 10
East Hatch. *Wilts* 3H 9
East Hatley. *Cambs* 6K 29
Easthaugh. *Norf* 8G 39
East Hauxwell. *N Yor* 6K 47
East Haven. *Ang* 4J 67
Eastheath. *Wok* 7F 20
East Heckington. *Linc* 5J 37
East Hedleyhope. *Dur* 7E 54
East Helmsdale. *High* 2L 79
East Hendred. *Oxon* 5B 20
East Heslerton. *N Yor* 8G 49
East Hoathly. *E Sus* 4B 12
East Holme. *Dors* 7G 9
Easthope. *Shrp* 2D 26
Easthorpe. *Essx* 1F 22
Easthorpe. *Leics* 6F 36
East Horrington. *Som* 1D 8
East Horsley. *Surr* 8H 21
East Horton. *Nmbd* 6H 61
Easthouses. *Midl* 3M 59
East Howe. *Bour* 6J 9
East Huntspill. *Som* 1B 8
East Hyde. *C Beds* 2J 21
East Ilsley. *W Ber* 5B 20
Eastington. *Devn* 5G 7
Eastington. *Glos*
nr. Northleach 2K 19
nr. Stonehouse 3F 18
East Keal. *Linc* 3L 37
East Kennett. *Wilts* 7K 19
East Keswick. *W Yor* 3A 42
East Kilbride. *S Lan* 4E 58
East Kirkby. *Linc* 3L 37
East Knapton. *N Yor* 8F 48
East Knighton. *Dors* 7G 9
East Knowstone. *Devn* 3H 7
East Knoyle. *Wilts* 2G 9
East Kyloe. *Nmbd* 6H 61
East Lambrook. *Som* 4C 8
East Langdon. *Kent* 1K 13
East Langton. *Leics* 2E 28
East Langwell. *High* 3H 79
East Lavant. *W Sus* 5F 10
East Lavington. *W Sus* 4G 11
East Layton. *N Yor* 5K 47
Eastleach Martin. *Glos* 3L 19
Eastleach Turville. *Glos* 3K 19
East Leake. *Notts* 7C 36
East Learmouth. *Nmbd* 6F 60
East Leigh. *Devn*
nr. Crediton 5F 6
nr. Modbury 6J 5
Eastleigh. *Devn* 3D 6
Eastleigh. *Hants* 4B 10
East Lexham. *Norf* 8E 38
East Lilburn. *Nmbd* 7H 61
Eastling. *Kent* 8F 22
East Linton. *E Lot* 2C 60
East Liss. *Hants* 3E 10
East Lockinge. *Oxon* 5B 20
East Looe. *Corn* 6E 4
East Lound. *N Lin* 8E 42
East Lulworth. *Dors* 7G 9
East Lutton. *N Yor* 1G 43
East Lydford. *Som* 2D 8
East Lyng. *Som* 3B 8
East Mains. *Abers* 6F 72
East Malling. *Kent* 8D 22
East Marden. *W Sus* 4F 10
East Markham. *Notts* 2E 36
East Marton. *N Yor* 2H 41
East Meon. *Hants* 3D 10
East Mersea. *Essx* 2G 23
East Mey. *High* 4E 86
East Midlands Airport.
Leics 7B 36
East Molesey. *Surr* 7J 21
Eastmoor. *Norf* 1D 30
East Morden. *Dors* 6H 9
East Morton. *W Yor* 3K 41
East Ness. *N Yor* 8D 48
East Newton. *E Yor* 4K 43
East Newton. *N Yor* 8D 48
Eastney. *Port* 6D 10
Eastnor. *Here* 8F 26
East Norton. *Leics* 1E 28
East Nynehead. *Som* 3L 7
East Oakley. *Hants* 8C 20
Eastoft. *N Lin* 6F 42
East Ogwell. *Devn* 8H 7
Easton. *Cambs* 4J 29
Easton. *Cumb*
nr. Burgh by Sands 6G 53
nr. Longtown 4J 53
Easton. *Devn* 7G 7
Easton. *Dors* 8E 8
Easton. *Hants* 2C 10
Easton. *Linc* 7G 37
Easton. *Norf* 8H 39
Easton. *Som* 1D 8
Easton. *Suff* 6J 31
Easton. *Wilts* 6G 19
Easton Grey. *Wilts* 5G 19
Easton-in-Gordano. *N Som* 6D 18
Easton Maudit. *Nptn* 6F 28
Easton on the Hill. *Nptn* 1H 29
Easton Royal. *Wilts* 7L 19
East Orchard. *Dors* 4G 9
East Ord. *Nmbd* 4G 61
East Panson. *Devn* 6C 6
East Peckham. *Kent* 1C 12
East Pennard. *Som* 2D 8
East Perry. *Cambs* 5J 29
East Pitcorthie. *Fife* 7J 67
East Portlemouth. *Devn* 8K 5
East Prawle. *Devn* 8K 5
East Preston. *W Sus* 5H 11
East Putford. *Devn* 4C 6
East Quantoxhead. *Som* 1L 7
East Rainton. *Tyne* 7G 55
East Ravendale. *NE Lin* 8K 43
East Raynham. *Norf* 7E 38
Eastrea. *Cambs* 2K 29
East Rhidorroch Lodge.
High 4C 78
Eastriggs. *Dum* 5G 53
East Rigton. *W Yor* 3A 42
Eastrington. *E Yor* 5E 42
East Rounton. *N Yor* 5B 48
East Row. *N Yor* 4F 48
East Rudham. *Norf* 7E 38
East Runton. *Norf* 5H 39
East Ruston. *Norf* 7K 39
Eastry. *Kent* 8K 23
East Saltoun. *E Lot* 3B 60
East Shaws. *Dur* 4J 47
East Shefford. *W Ber* 6A 20
Eastshore. *Shet* 6D 90
East Sleekburn. *Nmbd* 3F 54
East Somerton. *Norf* 8L 39
East Stockwith. *Linc* 8E 42
East Stoke. *Dors* 7G 9
East Stoke. *Notts* 5E 36
East Stoke. *Som* 4C 8
East Stour. *Dors* 3G 9
East Stourmouth. *Kent* 7J 23
East Stowford. *Devn* 3F 6
East Stratton. *Hants* 1C 10
East Studdal. *Kent* 1K 13
East Taphouse. *Corn* 5D 4
East-the-Water. *Devn* 3D 6
East Thirston. *Nmbd* 2E 54
East Tilbury. *Thur* 6C 22
East Tisted. *Hants* 2E 10
East Torrington. *Linc* 1J 37
East Tuddenham. *Norf* 8G 39
East Tytherley. *Hants* 3L 9
East Tytherton. *Wilts* 6H 19
East Village. *Devn* 5H 7
Eastville. *Linc* 4M 37
East Wall. *Shrp* 2D 26
East Walton. *Norf* 8D 38
East Week. *Devn* 6F 6
Eastwell. *Leics* 7E 36
East Wellow. *Hants* 3M 9
East Wemyss. *Fife* 8G 67
East Whitburn. *W Lot* 3H 59
Eastwick. *Herts* 2M 21
Eastwick. *Shet* 6H 91
East Williamston. *Pemb* 6G 15
East Winch. *Norf* 8C 38
East Winterslow. *Wilts* 2L 9
East Wittering. *W Sus* 6E 10
East Witton. *N Yor* 7K 47
Eastwood. *Notts* 5B 36
Eastwood. *S'end* 5E 22
East Woodburn. *Nmbd* 3C 54
Eastwood End. *Cambs* 2M 29
East Woodhay. *Hants* 7B 20
East Woodlands. *Som* 1F 8
East Worldham. *Hants* 2E 10
East Worlington. *Devn* 4G 7
East Wretham. *Norf* 2F 30
East Youlstone. *Devn* 4B 6
Eathorpe. *Warw* 5A 28
Eaton. *Ches E* 3G 35
Eaton. *Ches W* 3D 34
Eaton. *Leics* 7E 36
Eaton. *Norf*
nr. Heacham 6C 38
nr. Norwich 1J 31
Eaton. *Notts* 2E 36
Eaton. *Oxon* 3B 20
Eaton. *Shrp*
nr. Bishop's Castle 3B 26
nr. Church Stretton 3D 26
Eaton Bishop. *Here* 8C 26
Eaton Bray. *C Beds* 1G 21
Eaton Constantine. *Shrp* 1D 26
Eaton Hastings. *Oxon* 4L 19
Eaton Socon. *Cambs* 6J 29
Eaton upon Tern. *Shrp* 7E 34
Eau Brink. *Norf* 8B 38
Eaves Green. *W Mid* 3L 27
Ebberley Hill. *Devn* 4E 6
Ebberston. *N Yor* 7F 48
Ebbesbourne Wake. *Wilts* 3H 9
Ebblake. *Dors* 5K 9
Ebbsfleet. *Kent* 6C 22
Ebbw Vale. *Blae* 4L 17
Ebchester. *Dur* 6E 54
Ebernoe. *W Sus* 3G 11
Ebford. *Devn* 7J 7
Ebley. *Glos* 3G 19
Ebnal. *Ches W* 5C 34
Ebrington. *Glos* 7K 27
Ecchinswell. *Hants* 8C 20
Ecclefechan. *Dum* 4F 52
Eccles. *G Man* 8F 40
Eccles. *Kent* 7D 22
Eccles. *Bord* 5E 60
Ecclesall. *S Yor* 1M 35
Ecclesfield. *S Yor* 8A 42
Eccles Green. *Here* 7B 26
Eccleshall. *Staf* 7G 35
Eccleshill. *W Yor* 4K 41
Ecclesmachan. *W Lot* 2J 59
Eccles on Sea. *Norf* 7L 39
Eccles Road. *Norf* 2G 31
Eccleston. *Ches W* 3C 34
Eccleston. *Lanc* 6D 40
Eccleston. *Mers* 8C 40
Eccup. *W Yor* 3L 41
Echt. *Abers* 5G 73
Eckford. *Bord* 7E 60
Eckington. *Derbs* 2B 36
Eckington. *Worc* 7H 27
Ecton. *Nptn* 5F 28
Edale. *Derbs* 1K 35
Eday Airport. *Orkn* 6E 88
Edburton. *W Sus* 4K 11
Edderside. *Cumb* 7F 52
Edderton. *High* 5H 79
Eddington. *Kent* 7H 23
Eddington. *W Ber* 7M 19
Eddleston. *Bord* 5L 59
Eddlewood. *S Lan* 4F 58
Edenbridge. *Kent* 1M 11
Edendonich. *Arg* 5F 64
Edenfield. *Lanc* 6F 40
Edenhall. *Cumb* 8K 53
Edenham. *Linc* 7H 37
Edensor. *Derbs* 2L 35
Edentaggart. *Arg* 8H 65
Edenthorpe. *S Yor* 7D 42
Eden Vale. *Dur* 8H 55
Edern. *Gwyn* 7B 32
Ederney. *Ferm* 5C 92
Edgarley. *Som* 2D 8
Edgbaston. *W Mid* 3J 27
Edgcott. *Buck* 1D 20
Edgcott. *Som* 2H 7
Edge. *Glos* 3G 19
Edge. *Shrp* 1B 26
Edgebolton. *Shrp* 7D 34
Edge End. *Glos* 2D 18
Edgefield. *Norf* 6G 39
Edgefield Street. *Norf* 6G 39
Edge Green. *Ches W* 4C 34
Edgehead. *Midl* 3A 60
Edgeley. *Shrp* 5D 34
Edgeside. *Lanc* 5G 41
Edgeworth. *Glos* 3H 19
Edgiock. *Worc* 5J 27
Edgmond. *Telf* 8F 34
Edgmond Marsh. *Telf* 7F 34
Edgton. *Shrp* 3B 26
Edgware. *G Lon* 4J 21
Edgworth. *Bkbn* 6F 40
Edinbane. *High* 8E 76
Edinburgh. *Edin* 2L 59
Edinburgh Airport. *Edin* 2K 59
Edingale. *Staf* 8L 35
Edingley. *Notts* 4D 36
Edingthorpe. *Norf* 6K 39
Edington. *Som* 2B 8
Edington. *Wilts* 8H 19
Edingworth. *Som* 8B 18
Edistone. *Devn* 3B 6
Edithmead. *Som* 1B 8
Edith Weston. *Rut* 1G 29
Edlaston. *Derbs* 5K 35
Edlesborough. *Buck* 2G 21
Edlingham. *Nmbd* 1E 54
Edlington. *Linc* 2K 37
Edmondsham. *Dors* 4J 9
Edmondsley. *Dur* 7F 54

Edmondthorpe—Fundenhall

Edmondthorpe. *Leics* 8F 36
Edmonstone. *Orkn* 7E 88
Edmonton. *Corn* 4B 4
Edmonton. *G Lon* 4L 21
Edmundbyers. *Dur* 6D 54
Ednam. *Bord* 6E 60
Ednaston. *Derbs* 5L 35
Edney Common. *Essx* 3C 22
Edrom. *Bord* 4F 60
Edstaston. *Shrp* 6D 34
Edstone. *Warw* 5K 27
Edwalton. *Notts* 6C 36
Edwardstone. *Suff* 7F 30
Edwardsville. *Mer T* 5K 17
Edwinsford. *Carm* 1F 16
Edwinstowe. *Notts* 3D 36
Edworth. *C Beds* 7K 29
Edwyn Ralph. *Here* 6E 26
Edzell. *Ang* 1K 67
Efail-fach. *Neat* 5G 17
Efail Isaf. *Rhon* 6K 17
Efailnewydd. *Gwyn* 7C 32
Efail-rhyd. *Powy* 8L 33
Efailwen. *Carm* 4H 15
Efenechtyd. *Den* 5L 33
Effingham. *Surr* 8J 21
Effingham Common. *Surr* 8J 21
Effirth. *Shet* 2D 90
Efflinch. *Staf* 8K 35
Efford. *Devn* 5H 7
Efstigarth. *Shet* 4J 91
Egbury. *Hants* 8B 20
Egdon. *Worc* 6H 27
Egerton. *G Man* 6F 40
Egerton. *Kent* 1F 12
Egerton Forstal. *Kent* 1E 12
Eggborough. *N Yor* 5C 42
Eggbuckland. *Plym* 6G 5
Eggesford. *Devn* 4F 6
Eggington. *C Beds* 1G 21
Egginton. *Derbs* 7L 35
Egglescliffe. *Stoc T* 4B 48
Eggleston. *Dur* 3H 47
Egham. *Surr* 6H 21
Egham Hythe. *Surr* 6H 21
Egleton. *Rut* 1F 28
Eglingham. *Nmbd* 8J 61
Eglinton. *Derr* 2D 92
Eglish. *M Ulst* 6E 92
Egloshayle. *Corn* 4C 4
Egloskerry. *Corn* 7B 6
Eglwysbach. *Cnwy* 3H 33
Eglwys-Brewis. *V Glam* 8K 17
Eglwys Fach. *Cdgn* 3F 24
Eglwyswrw. *Pemb* 3H 15
Egmanton. *Notts* 3E 36
Egmere. *Norf* 6F 38
Egremont. *Cumb* 3K 45
Egremont. *Mers* 8B 40
Egton. *N Yor* 5F 48
Egton Bridge. *N Yor* 5F 48
Egypt. *Buck* 5G 21
Egypt. *Hants* 1B 10
Eight Ash Green. *Essx* 1F 22
Eight Mile Burn. *Midl* 4K 59
Eignaig. *High* 3B 64
Eilanreach. *High* 4K 69
Eildon. *Bord* 6C 60
Eileanach Lodge. *High* 7F 78
Eilean Fhlodaigh. *W Isl* 8K 75
Eilean Iarmain. *High* 4J 69
Einacleit. *W Isl* 1C 76
Eisgein. *W Isl* 2E 76
Eisingrug. *Gwyn* 7F 32
Elan Village. *Powy* 6J 25
Elberton. *S Glo* 5E 18
Elbridge. *W Sus* 5G 11
Elburton. *Plym* 6H 5
Elcho. *Per* 5E 66
Elcombe. *Swin* 5K 19
Elcot. *W Ber* 7A 20
Eldernell. *Cambs* 2L 29
Eldersfield. *Worc* 8G 27
Elderslie. *Ren* 3C 58
Elder Street. *Essx* 8B 30
Eldon. *Dur* 3L 47
Eldroth. *N Yor* 1F 40
Eldwick. *W Yor* 3K 41
Elfhowe. *Cumb* 6C 46
Elford. *Nmbd* 6J 61
Elford. *Staf* 8K 35
Elford Closes. *Cambs* 4A 30
Elgin. *Mor* 7B 80
Elgol. *High* 4G 69
Elham. *Kent* 1H 13
Elie. *Fife* 7H 67
Eling. *Hants* 4A 10
Eling. *W Ber* 6C 20
Elishaw. *Nmbd* 2B 54
Elizafield. *Dum* 4E 52
Elkesley. *Notts* 2D 36
Elkington. *Nptn* 4D 28
Elkins Green. *Essx* 3C 22
Elkstone. *Glos* 2H 19
Ellan. *High* 3J 71
Elland. *W Yor* 5K 41
Ellary. *Arg* 2G 57
Ellastone. *Staf* 5K 35
Ellbridge. *Corn* 5G 5
Ellel. *Lanc* 2C 40
Ellemford. *Bord* 3E 60
Ellenabeich. *Arg* 6B 64
Ellenborough. *Cumb* 8E 52
Ellenbrook. *Herts* 3K 21
Ellenhall. *Staf* 7G 35
Ellen's Green. *Surr* 2H 11
Ellerbeck. *N Yor* 6B 48
Ellerburn. *N Yor* 7F 48
Ellerby. *N Yor* 4E 48
Ellerdine. *Telf* 7E 34
Ellerdine Heath. *Telf* 7E 34
Ellerhayes. *Devn* 5J 7
Elleric. *Arg* 3E 64
Ellerker. *E Yor* 5G 43
Ellerton. *E Yor* 4E 42
Ellerton. *Shrp* 7F 34
Ellerton-on-Swale. *N Yor* 6L 47
Ellesborough. *Buck* 3F 20
Ellesmere. *Shrp* 6C 34
Ellesmere Port. *Ches W* 2C 34
Ellingham. *Hants* 5K 9
Ellingham. *Norf* 2K 31
Ellingham. *Nmbd* 7J 61
Ellingstring. *N Yor* 7K 47
Ellington. *Cambs* 4J 29
Ellington. *Nmbd* 2F 54
Ellington Thorpe. *Cambs* 4J 29
Elliot. *Ang* 4K 67
Ellisfield. *Hants* 1D 10
Ellishadder. *High* 7G 77
Ellistown. *Leics* 8B 36
Ellon. *Abers* 2J 73
Ellonby. *Cumb* 8J 53
Ellough. *Suff* 3L 31
Elloughton. *E Yor* 5G 43
Ellwood. *Glos* 3D 18
Elm. *Cambs* 1A 30
Elmbridge. *Glos* 2G 19
Elmbridge. *Worc* 5H 27
Elmdon. *Essx* 8A 30
Elmdon. *W Mid* 3K 27
Elmdon Heath. *W Mid* 3K 27
Elmesthorpe. *Leics* 2B 28
Elmfield. *IOW* 6D 10
Elm Hill. *Dors* 3G 9
Elmhurst. *Staf* 8K 35
Elmley Castle. *Worc* 7H 27
Elmley Lovett. *Worc* 5G 27
Elmore. *Glos* 2F 18
Elmore Back. *Glos* 2F 18
Elm Park. *G Lon* 5B 22
Elmscott. *Devn* 3B 6
Elmsett. *Suff* 7G 31
Elmstead. *Essx* 1G 23
Elmstead Heath. *Essx* 1G 23
Elmstead Market. *Essx* 1G 23
Elmsted. *Kent* 1H 13
Elmstone. *Kent* 7J 23
Elmstone Hardwicke. *Glos* 1H 19
Elmswell. *E Yor* 2G 43
Elmswell. *Suff* 5F 30
Elmton. *Derbs* 2C 36
Elphin. *High* 2C 78
Elphinstone. *E Lot* 2A 60
Elrick. *Abers* 5H 73
Elrick. *Mor* 3D 72
Elrig. *Dum* 7J 51
Elsdon. *Nmbd* 2C 54
Elsecar. *S Yor* 8A 42
Elsenham. *Essx* 1B 22
Elsfield. *Oxon* 2C 20
Elsham. *N Lin* 6H 43
Elsing. *Norf* 8G 39
Elslack. *N Yor* 3H 41
Elsrickle. *S Lan* 5J 59
Elstead. *Surr* 1G 11
Elsted. *W Sus* 4F 10
Elsted Marsh. *W Sus* 3F 10
Elsthorpe. *Linc* 7H 37
Elstob. *Dur* 3M 47
Elston. *Devn* 5G 7
Elston. *Lanc* 4E 40
Elston. *Notts* 5E 36
Elston. *Wilts* 1J 9
Elstone. *Devn* 4F 6
Elstow. *Bed* 7H 29
Elstree. *Herts* 4J 21
Elstronwick. *E Yor* 4K 43
Elswick. *Lanc* 4C 40
Elswick. *Tyne* 5F 54
Elsworth. *Cambs* 5L 29
Elterwater. *Cumb* 5B 46
Eltham. *G Lon* 6M 21
Eltisley. *Cambs* 6K 29
Elton. *Cambs* 2H 29
Elton. *Ches W* 2C 34
Elton. *Derbs* 3L 35
Elton. *Glos* 2F 18
Elton. *G Man* 6F 40
Elton. *Here* 4C 26
Elton. *Notts* 6E 36
Elton. *Stoc T* 4B 48
Elton Green. *Ches W* 2C 34
Eltringham. *Nmbd* 5D 54
Elvanfoot. *S Lan* 8H 59
Elvaston. *Derbs* 6B 36
Elveden. *Suff* 4E 30
Elvetham Heath. *Hants* 8E 20
Elvingston. *E Lot* 2B 60
Elvington. *Kent* 8J 23
Elvington. *York* 3E 42
Elwick. *Hart* 8H 55
Elwick. *Nmbd* 6J 61
Elworth. *Ches E* 3F 34
Elworth. *Dors* 7D 8
Elworthy. *Som* 2K 7
Ely. *Cambs* 3B 30
Ely. *Card* 7L 17
Emberton. *Mil* 7F 28
Embleton. *Cumb* 8F 52
Embleton. *Hart* 3B 48
Embleton. *Nmbd* 7K 61
Embo. *High* 4J 79
Emborough. *Som* 8E 18
Embo Street. *High* 4J 79
Embsay. *N Yor* 2J 41
Emery Down. *Hants* 5L 9
Emley. *W Yor* 6L 41
Emmbrook. *Wok* 7E 20
Emmer Green. *Read* 6E 20
Emmington. *Oxon* 3E 20
Emneth. *Norf* 1A 30
Emneth Hungate. *Norf* 1B 30
Empingham. *Rut* 1G 29
Empshott. *Hants* 2E 10
Emsworth. *Hants* 5E 10
Enborne. *W Ber* 7B 20
Enborne Row. *W Ber* 7B 20
Enchmarsh. *Shrp* 2D 26
Enderby. *Leics* 2C 28
Endmoor. *Cumb* 7D 46
Endon. *Staf* 4H 35
Endon Bank. *Staf* 4H 35
Enfield. *G Lon* 4L 21
Enfield Wash. *G Lon* 4L 21
Enford. *Wilts* 8K 19
Engine Common. *S Glo* 5E 18
Englefield. *W Ber* 6D 20
Englefield Green. *Surr* 6G 21
Englesea-brook. *Ches E* 4F 34
English Bicknor. *Glos* 2D 18
Englishcombe. *Bath* 7F 18
English Frankton. *Shrp* 7C 34
Enham Alamein. *Hants* 1A 10
Enmore. *Som* 2M 7
Ennerdale Bridge. *Cumb* 3K 45
Enniscaven. *Corn* 6B 4
Enniskillen. *Ferm* 6C 92
Enoch. *Dum* 1C 52
Enochdhu. *Per* 1D 66
Ensay. *Arg* 3J 63
Ensbury. *Bour* 6J 9
Ensdon. *Shrp* 8C 34
Ensis. *Devn* 3E 6
Enson. *Staf* 7H 35
Enstone. *Oxon* 1A 20
Enterkinfoot. *Dum* 1C 52
Enville. *Staf* 3G 27
Eolaigearraidh. *W Isl* 5D 74
Eorabus. *Arg* 5J 63
Eoropaidh. *W Isl* 5J 83
Epney. *Glos* 2F 18
Epperstone. *Notts* 5D 36
Epping. *Essx* 3A 22
Epping Green. *Essx* 3M 21
Epping Green. *Herts* 3K 21
Epping Upland. *Essx* 3M 21
Eppleby. *N Yor* 4K 47
Eppleworth. *E Yor* 4H 43
Epsom. *Surr* 7K 21
Epwell. *Oxon* 7A 28
Epworth. *N Lin* 7E 42
Epworth Turbary. *N Lin* 7E 42
Erbistock. *Wrex* 5B 34
Erbusaig. *High* 3J 69
Erchless Castle. *High* 1E 70
Erdington. *W Mid* 2K 27
Eredine. *Arg* 7D 64
Erganagh. *Derr* 4C 92
Eriboll. *High* 6G 85
Ericstane. *Dum* 8J 59
Eridge Green. *E Sus* 2B 12
Erines. *Arg* 2H 57
Eriswell. *Suff* 4D 30
Erith. *G Lon* 6B 22
Erlestoke. *Wilts* 8H 19
Ermine. *Linc* 2G 37
Ermington. *Devn* 6J 5
Ernesettle. *Plym* 6G 5
Erpingham. *Norf* 6H 39
Erriott Wood. *Kent* 8F 22
Errogie. *High* 3F 70
Errol. *Per* 5F 66
Errol Station. *Per* 5F 66
Erskine. *Ren* 2C 58
Erskine Bridge. *Ren* 2C 58
Ervie. *Dum* 5F 50
Erwarton. *Suff* 8J 31
Erwood. *Powy* 8K 25
Eryholme. *N Yor* 5M 47
Eryrys. *Den* 5M 33
Escalls. *Corn* 6G 3
Escomb. *Dur* 8E 54
Escrick. *N Yor* 3D 42
Esgair. *Carm*
nr. Carmarthen 4K 15
nr. St Clears 5J 15
Esgairgeiliog. *Powy* 2G 25
Esh. *Dur* 7E 54
Esher. *Surr* 7J 21
Esholt. *W Yor* 3K 41
Eshott. *Nmbd* 2F 54
Eshton. *N Yor* 2H 41
Esh Winning. *Dur* 7E 54
Eskadale. *High* 2E 70
Eskbank. *Midl* 3M 59
Eskdale Green. *Cumb* 4L 45
Eskdalemuir. *Dum* 2G 53
Eskham. *Linc* 8L 43
Esknish. *Arg* 3C 56
Esk Valley. *N Yor* 5F 48
Eslington Hall. *Nmbd* 8H 61
Esprick. *Lanc* 4C 40
Essendine. *Rut* 8H 37
Essendon. *Herts* 3K 21
Essich. *High* 2G 71
Essington. *Staf* 1H 27
Eston. *Red C* 4C 48
Estover. *Plym* 6H 5
Eswick. *Shet* 2E 90
Etal. *Nmbd* 6G 61
Etchilhampton. *Wilts* 7J 19
Etchingham. *E Sus* 3D 12
Etchinghill. *Kent* 2H 13
Etchinghill. *Staf* 8J 35
Etherley Dene. *Dur* 3K 47
Ethie Haven. *Ang* 3K 67
Etling Green. *Norf* 8G 39
Etloe. *Glos* 3E 18
Eton. *Wind* 6G 21
Eton Wick. *Wind* 6G 21
Etteridge. *High* 6G 71
Ettersgill. *Dur* 3G 47
Ettiley Heath. *Ches E* 3F 34
Ettington. *Warw* 7L 27
Etton. *E Yor* 3G 43
Etton. *Pet* 1J 29
Ettrick. *Bord* 8L 59
Ettrickbridge. *Bord* 7A 60
Etwall. *Derbs* 6L 35
Eudon Burnell. *Shrp* 3F 26
Eudon George. *Shrp* 3E 26
Euston. *Suff* 4E 30
Euxton. *Lanc* 6D 40
Evanstown. *B'end* 6J 17
Evanton. *High* 7G 79
Evedon. *Linc* 5H 37
Evelix. *High* 4H 79
Evendine. *Here* 7F 26
Evenjobb. *Powy* 5A 26
Evenley. *Nptn* 8C 28
Evenlode. *Glos* 1L 19
Even Swindon. *Swin* 5K 19
Evenwood. *Dur* 3K 47
Evenwood Gate. *Dur* 3K 47
Everbay. *Orkn* 7F 88
Evercreech. *Som* 2E 8
Everdon. *Nptn* 6C 28
Everingham. *E Yor* 3F 42
Everleigh. *Wilts* 8L 19
Everley. *N Yor* 7G 49
Eversholt. *C Beds* 8G 29
Evershot. *Dors* 5D 8
Eversley. *Hants* 7E 20
Eversley Centre. *Hants* 7E 20
Eversley Cross. *Hants* 7E 20
Everthorpe. *E Yor* 4G 43
Everton. *C Beds* 6K 29
Everton. *Hants* 6L 9
Everton. *Mers* 8B 40
Everton. *Notts* 8D 42
Evertown. *Dum* 4H 53
Evesbatch. *Here* 7E 26
Evesham. *Worc* 7J 27
Evington. *Leic* 1D 28
Ewden Village. *S Yor* 8L 41
Ewdness. *Shrp* 2F 26
Ewell. *Surr* 7K 21
Ewell Minnis. *Kent* 1J 13
Ewelme. *Oxon* 4D 20
Ewen. *Glos* 4J 19
Ewenny. *V Glam* 7J 17
Ewerby. *Linc* 5J 37
Ewes. *Dum* 2H 53
Ewesley. *Nmbd* 2D 54
Ewhurst. *Surr* 1H 11
Ewhurst Green. *E Sus* 3D 12
Ewhurst Green. *Surr* 2H 11
Ewlo. *Flin* 3A 34
Ewloe. *Flin* 3A 34
Ewood Bridge. *Lanc* 5F 40
Eworthy. *Devn* 6D 6
Ewshot. *Hants* 8F 20
Ewyas Harold. *Here* 1B 18
Exbourne. *Devn* 5F 6
Exbury. *Hants* 5B 10
Exceat. *E Sus* 6B 12
Exebridge. *Som* 3J 7
Exelby. *N Yor* 7L 47
Exeter. *Devn* 6J 7
Exeter Airport. *Devn* 6K 7
Exford. *Som* 2H 7
Exfords Green. *Shrp* 1C 26
Exhall. *Warw* 6K 27
Exlade Street. *Oxon* 5D 20
Exminster. *Devn* 7J 7
Exmouth. *Devn* 7K 7
Exnaboe. *Shet* 6D 90
Exning. *Suff* 5C 30
Exton. *Devn* 7J 7
Exton. *Hants* 3D 10
Exton. *Rut* 8G 37
Exton. *Som* 2J 7
Exwick. *Devn* 6J 7
Eyam. *Derbs* 2L 35
Eydon. *Nptn* 6C 28
Eye. *Here* 5C 26
Eye. *Pet* 1K 29
Eye. *Suff* 4H 31
Eye Green. *Pet* 1K 29
Eyemouth. *Bord* 3G 61
Eyeworth. *C Beds* 7K 29
Eyhorne Street. *Kent* 8E 22
Eyke. *Suff* 6K 31
Eynesbury. *Cambs* 6J 29
Eynort. *High* 3E 68
Eynsford. *Kent* 7B 22
Eynsham. *Oxon* 3B 20
Eyre. *High*
on Isle of Skye 8F 76
on Raasay 2G 69
Eythorne. *Kent* 1J 13
Eyton. *Here* 5C 26
Eyton. *Shrp*
nr. Bishop's Castle 3B 26
nr. Shrewsbury 8B 34
Eyton. *Wrex* 5B 34
Eyton on Severn. *Shrp* 1D 26
Eyton upon the Weald Moors. *Telf* 8E 34

F

Faccombe. *Hants* 8A 20
Faceby. *N Yor* 5B 48
Faddiley. *Ches E* 4D 34
Fadmoor. *N Yor* 7D 48
Fagwyr. *Swan* 4F 16
Faichem. *High* 5C 70
Faifley. *W Dun* 2D 58
Fail. *S Ayr* 7C 58
Failand. *N Som* 6D 18
Failford. *S Ayr* 7C 58
Failsworth. *G Man* 7H 41
Fairbourne. *Gwyn* 1F 24
Fairbourne Heath. *Kent* 8E 22
Fairburn. *N Yor* 5B 42
Fairfield. *Derbs* 2J 35
Fairfield. *Kent* 3F 12
Fairfield. *Worc*
nr. Bromsgrove 4H 27
nr. Evesham 7J 27
Fairford. *Glos* 3K 19
Fair Green. *Norf* 8C 38
Fair Hill. *Cumb* 8K 53
Fairhill. *S Lan* 4F 58
Fair Isle Airport. *Shet* 2M 89
Fairlands. *Surr* 8G 21
Fairlie. *N Ayr* 4M 57
Fairlight. *E Sus* 4E 12
Fairlight Cove. *E Sus* 4E 12
Fairmile. *Devn* 6K 7
Fairmile. *Surr* 7J 21
Fairmilehead. *Edin* 3L 59
Fair Oak. *Devn* 4K 7
Fair Oak. *Hants*
nr. Eastleigh 4B 10
nr. Kingsclere 7C 20
Fairoak. *Staf* 6F 34
Fair Oak Green. *Hants* 7D 20
Fairseat. *Kent* 7C 22
Fairstead. *Essx* 2D 22
Fairstead. *Norf* 8C 38
Fairwarp. *E Sus* 3A 12
Fairwater. *Card* 7L 17
Fairy Cross. *Devn* 3D 6
Fakenham. *Norf* 6F 38
Fakenham Magna. *Suff* 4F 30
Fala. *Midl* 3B 60
Fala Dam. *Midl* 3B 60
Falcon. *Here* 8E 26
Faldingworth. *Linc* 1H 37
Falfield. *S Glo* 4E 18
Y Fali. *IOA* 3B 32
Falkenham. *Suff* 8J 31
Falkirk. *Falk* 1G 59
Falkland. *Fife* 7F 66
Fallin. *Stir* 8B 66
Fallowfield. *G Man* 8G 41
Falmer. *E Sus* 5L 11
Falmouth. *Corn* 5M 3
Falsgrave. *N Yor* 7H 49
Falstone. *Nmbd* 3M 53
Fanagmore. *High* 7D 84
Fancott. *C Beds* 1H 21
Fanellan. *High* 1E 70
Fangdale Beck. *N Yor* 6C 48
Fangfoss. *E Yor* 2E 42
Fankerton. *Falk* 1F 58
Fanmore. *Arg* 3K 63
Fanner's Green. *Essx* 2C 22
Fannich Lodge. *High* 7C 78
Fans. *Bord* 5D 60
Farcet. *Cambs* 2K 29
Far Cotton. *Nptn* 6E 28
Fareham. *Hants* 5C 10
Farewell. *Staf* 8J 35
Far Forest. *Worc* 4F 26
Farforth. *Linc* 2L 37
Far Green. *Glos* 3F 18
Far Hoarcross. *Staf* 7K 35
Faringdon. *Oxon* 4L 19
Farington. *Lanc* 5D 40
Farlam. *Cumb* 6K 53
Farleigh. *N Som* 7C 18
Farleigh. *Surr* 7L 21
Farleigh Hungerford. *Som* 8G 19
Farleigh Wallop. *Hants* 1D 10
Farleigh Wick. *Wilts* 7G 19
Farlesthorpe. *Linc* 2A 38
Farleton. *Cumb* 7D 46
Farleton. *Lanc* 1D 40
Farley. *High* 1E 70
Farley. *Shrp*
nr. Shrewsbury 1B 26
nr. Telford 1E 26
Farley. *Staf* 5J 35
Farley. *Wilts* 3L 9
Farley Green. *Suff* 6D 30
Farley Green. *Surr* 1H 11
Farley Hill. *Wok* 7E 20
Farley's End. *Glos* 2F 18
Farlington. *N Yor* 1D 42
Farlington. *Port* 5D 10
Farlow. *Shrp* 3E 26
Farmborough. *Bath* 7E 18
Farmcote. *Glos* 1J 19
Farmcote. *Shrp* 2F 26
Farmington. *Glos* 2K 19
Far Moor. *G Man* 7D 40
Farmoor. *Oxon* 3B 20
Farmtown. *Mor* 8E 80
Farnah Green. *Derbs* 5M 35
Farnborough. *G Lon* 7M 21
Farnborough. *Hants* 8F 20
Farnborough. *Warw* 7B 28
Farnborough. *W Ber* 5B 20
Farncombe. *Surr* 1G 11
Farndish. *Bed* 5G 29
Farndon. *Ches W* 4C 34
Farndon. *Notts* 4E 36
Farnell. *Ang* 2K 67
Farnham. *Dors* 4H 9
Farnham. *Essx* 1A 22
Farnham. *N Yor* 1A 42
Farnham. *Suff* 5K 31
Farnham. *Surr* 1F 10
Farnham Common. *Buck* 5G 21
Farnham Green. *Essx* 1A 22
Farnham Royal. *Buck* 5G 21
Farnhill. *N Yor* 3J 41
Farningham. *Kent* 7B 22
Farnley. *N Yor* 3L 41
Farnley Tyas. *W Yor* 6K 41
Farnsfield. *Notts* 4D 36
Farnworth. *G Man* 7F 40
Farnworth. *Hal* 1D 34
Far Oakridge. *Glos* 3H 19
Farr. *High*
nr. Bettyhill 5K 85
nr. Inverness 2G 71
nr. Kingussie 5J 71
Farraline. *High* 3F 70
Farringdon. *Devn* 6K 7
Farrington. *Dors* 4G 9
Farrington Gurney. *Bath* 8E 18
Far Sawrey. *Cumb* 6B 46
Farsley. *W Yor* 4L 41
Farthinghoe. *Nptn* 8C 28
Farthingstone. *Nptn* 6D 28
Farthorpe. *Linc* 2K 37
Fartown. *W Yor* 6K 41
Farway. *Devn* 6L 7
Fasag. *High* 8K 77
Fascadale. *High* 8G 69
Fasnacloich. *Arg* 3E 64
Fassfern. *High* 8M 69
Fatfield. *Tyne* 6G 55
Faugh. *Cumb* 6K 53
Fauld. *Staf* 7K 35
Fauldhouse. *W Lot* 3H 59
Faulkbourne. *Essx* 2D 22
Faulkland. *Som* 8F 18
Fauls. *Shrp* 6D 34
Faverdale. *Darl* 4L 47
Faversham. *Kent* 7G 23
Fawdington. *N Yor* 8B 48
Fawfieldhead. *Staf* 3J 35
Fawkham Green. *Kent* 7B 22
Fawler. *Oxon* 2A 20
Fawley. *Buck* 5E 20
Fawley. *Hants* 5B 10
Fawley. *W Ber* 5A 20
Fawley Chapel. *Here* 1D 18
Fawton. *Corn* 5D 4
Faxfleet. *E Yor* 5F 42
Faygate. *W Sus* 2K 11
Fazakerley. *Mers* 8B 40
Fazeley. *Staf* 1K 27
Feagour. *High* 6F 70
Fearann Dhomhnaill. *High* 5H 69
Fearby. *N Yor* 7K 47
Fearn. *High* 6J 79
Fearnan. *Per* 3M 65
Fearnbeg. *High* 8J 77
Fearnhead. *Warr* 8E 40
Fearnmore. *High* 7J 77
Featherstone. *Staf* 1H 27
Featherstone. *W Yor* 5B 42
Featherstone Castle. *Nmbd* 5L 53
Feckenham. *Worc* 5J 27
Feeny. *Caus* 3E 92
Feering. *Essx* 1E 22
Feetham. *N Yor* 6H 47
Feizor. *N Yor* 1F 40
Felbridge. *Surr* 2L 11
Felbrigg. *Norf* 6J 39
Felcourt. *Surr* 1L 11
Felden. *Herts* 3H 21
Felhampton. *Shrp* 3C 26
Felindre. *Carm*
nr. Llandeilo 2E 16
nr. Llandovery 1F 16
nr. Newcastle Emlyn 3K 15
Felindre. *Powy* 4L 25
Felindre. *Swan* 4F 16
Felindre Farchog. *Pemb* 3H 15
Felinfach. *Cdgn* 1M 15
Felinfach. *Powy* 1K 17
Felinfoel. *Carm* 6M 15
Felingwmisaf. *Carm* 4M 15
Felingwmuchaf. *Carm* 4M 15
Y Felinheli. *Gwyn* 4E 32
Felin Newydd. *Powy*
nr. Newtown 2K 25
nr. Oswestry 8M 33
Felin Wnda. *Cdgn* 2K 15
Felinwynt. *Cdgn* 1J 15
Felixkirk. *N Yor* 7B 48
Felixstowe. *Suff* 8J 31
Felixstowe Ferry. *Suff* 8K 31
Felkington. *Nmbd* 5G 61
Fell End. *Cumb* 6F 46
Felling. *Tyne* 5F 54
Fell Side. *Cumb* 8H 53
Felmersham. *Bed* 6G 29
Felmingham. *Norf* 7J 39
Felpham. *W Sus* 6G 11
Felsham. *Suff* 6F 30
Felsted. *Essx* 1C 22
Feltham. *G Lon* 6J 21
Felthamhill. *Surr* 6H 21
Felthorpe. *Norf* 8H 39
Felton. *Here* 7D 26
Felton. *N Som* 7D 18
Felton. *Nmbd* 1E 54
Felton Butler. *Shrp* 8B 34
Feltwell. *Norf* 2D 30
Fenay Bridge. *W Yor* 6K 41
Fence. *Lanc* 4G 41
Fence Houses. *Tyne* 6G 55
Fencott. *Oxon* 2C 20
Fen Ditton. *Cambs* 5A 30
Fen Drayton. *Cambs* 5L 29
Fen End. *Linc* 7K 37
Fen End. *W Mid* 4L 27
Fenham. *Nmbd* 5H 61
Fenham. *Tyne* 5F 54
Fenhouses. *Linc* 5K 37
Feniscowles. *Bkbn* 5E 40
Feniton. *Devn* 6K 7
Fenn Green. *Shrp* 3F 26
Y Fenni. *Mon* 2B 18
Fenn's Bank. *Wrex* 6D 34
Fenn Street. *Medw* 6D 22
Fenny Bentley. *Derbs* 4K 35
Fenny Bridges. *Devn* 6L 7
Fenny Compton. *Warw* 6B 28
Fenny Drayton. *Leics* 2M 27
Fenny Stratford. *Mil* 8F 28
Fenrother. *Nmbd* 2E 54
Fenstanton. *Cambs* 5L 29
Fen Street. *Norf* 2G 31
Fenton. *Cambs* 4L 29
Fenton. *Cumb* 6K 53
Fenton. *Linc*
nr. Caythorpe 4F 36
nr. Saxilby 2F 36
Fenton. *Nmbd* 6G 61
Fenton. *Notts* 1E 36
Fenton. *Stoke* 5G 35
Fentonadle. *Corn* 4C 4
Fenton Barns. *E Lot* 1C 60
Fenwick. *E Ayr* 5C 58
Fenwick. *Nmbd*
nr. Berwick-upon-Tweed 5H 61
nr. Hexham 4D 54
Fenwick. *S Yor* 6C 42
Feochaig. *Arg* 8G 57
Feock. *Corn* 5M 3
Feolin Ferry. *Arg* 3D 56
Feorlan. *Arg* 1B 50
Ferindonald. *High* 5H 69
Feriniquarrie. *High* 8C 76
Fern. *Ang* 1H 67
Ferndale. *Rhon* 5J 17
Ferndown. *Dors* 5J 9
Ferness. *High* 1K 71
Fernham. *Oxon* 4L 19
Fernhill. *W Sus* 1L 11
Fernhill Heath. *Worc* 6G 27
Fernhurst. *W Sus* 3F 10
Fernieflatt. *Abers* 8H 73
Ferniegair. *S Lan* 4F 58
Fernilea. *High* 2E 68
Fernilee. *Derbs* 2J 35
Ferrensby. *N Yor* 1A 42
Ferriby Sluice. *N Lin* 5G 43
Ferring. *W Sus* 5H 11
Ferrybridge. *W Yor* 5B 42
Ferryden. *Ang* 2L 67
Ferryhill. *Aber* 5J 73
Ferry Hill. *Cambs* 3L 29
Ferryhill. *Dur* 8F 54
Ferryhill Station. *Dur* 8G 55
Ferryside. *Carm* 5K 15
Ferryton. *High* 7G 79
Fersfield. *Norf* 3G 31
Fersit. *High* 8D 70
Y Ferwig. *Cdgn* 2H 15
Feshiebridge. *High* 5J 71
Fetcham. *Surr* 8J 21
Fetterangus. *Abers* 8J 81
Fettercairn. *Abers* 8F 72
Fewcott. *Oxon* 1C 20
Fewston. *N Yor* 2K 41
Ffairfach. *Carm* 2F 16
Ffair Rhos. *Cdgn* 6G 25
Ffaldybrenin. *Carm* 8F 24
Ffarmers. *Carm* 8F 24
Ffawyddog. *Powy* 3M 17
Y Fflint. *Flin* 3M 33
Ffodun. *Powy* 2M 25
Ffont-y-gari. *V Glam* 8K 17
Y Ffor. *Gwyn* 7C 32
Fforest. *Carm* 4E 16
Fforest-fach. *Swan* 5F 16
Fforest Goch. *Neat* 4G 17
Ffostrasol. *Cdgn* 2K 15
Ffos-y-ffin. *Cdgn* 6D 24
Ffrith. *Flin* 4A 34
Ffwl-y-mwn. *V Glam* 8K 17
Ffynnon-ddrain. *Carm* 4L 15
Ffynnongroyw. *Flin* 2L 33
Ffynnon Gynydd. *Powy* 8L 25
Ffynnon-oer. *Cdgn* 1M 15
Fiag Lodge. *High* 1E 78
Fidden. *Arg* 5J 63
Fiddington. *Glos* 8H 27
Fiddington. *Som* 1M 7
Fiddleford. *Dors* 4G 9
Fiddlers Hamlet. *Essx* 3A 22
Field. *Staf* 6J 35
Field Assarts. *Oxon* 2M 19
Field Broughton. *Cumb* 7B 46
Field Dalling. *Norf* 6G 39
Fieldhead. *Cumb* 8J 53
Field Head. *Leics* 1B 28
Fifehead Magdalen. *Dors* 3F 8
Fifehead Neville. *Dors* 4F 8
Fifehead St Quintin. *Dors* 4F 8
Fife Keith. *Mor* 8D 80
Fifield. *Oxon* 2L 19
Fifield. *Wilts* 8K 19
Fifield. *Wind* 6G 21
Fifield Bavant. *Wilts* 3J 9
Figheldean. *Wilts* 1K 9
Filby. *Norf* 8L 39
Filey. *N Yor* 7J 49
Filford. *Dors* 6C 8
Filgrave. *Mil* 7F 28
Filkins. *Oxon* 3L 19
Filleigh. *Devn*
nr. Crediton 4G 7
nr. South Molton 3F 6
Fillingham. *Linc* 1G 37
Fillongley. *Warw* 3L 27
Filton. *S Glo* 6E 18
Fimber. *E Yor* 1F 42
Finavon. *Ang* 2H 67
Fincham. *Norf* 1C 30
Finchampstead. *Wok* 7E 20
Fincharn. *Arg* 7D 64
Finchdean. *Hants* 4E 10
Finchingfield. *Essx* 8C 30
Finchley. *G Lon* 4K 21
Findern. *Derbs* 6M 35
Findhorn. *Mor* 7L 79
Findhorn Bridge. *High* 3J 71
Findochty. *Mor* 7D 80
Findo Gask. *Per* 5D 66
Findon. *Abers* 6J 73
Findon. *W Sus* 5J 11
Findon Mains. *High* 7G 79
Findon Valley. *W Sus* 5J 11
Finedon. *Nptn* 4G 29
Fingal Street. *Suff* 4J 31
Fingest. *Buck* 4E 20
Finghall. *N Yor* 7K 47
Fingland. *Cumb* 6G 53
Fingland. *Dum* 8F 58
Finglesham. *Kent* 8K 23
Fingringhoe. *Essx* 1G 23
Finiskaig. *High* 6K 69
Finmere. *Oxon* 8D 28
Finnart. *Per* 2K 65
Finningham. *Suff* 5G 31
Finningley. *S Yor* 8D 42
Finnygaud. *Abers* 8F 80
Finsbury. *G Lon* 5L 21
Finstall. *Worc* 5H 27
Finsthwaite. *Cumb* 7B 46
Finstock. *Oxon* 2A 20
Finstown. *Orkn* 8C 88
Fintona. *Ferm* 5D 92
Fintry. *Abers* 8G 81
Fintry. *D'dee* 4H 67
Fintry. *Stir* 1E 58
Finvoy. *Caus* 3F 93
Finwood. *Warw* 5K 27
Finzean. *Abers* 6F 72
Fionnphort. *Arg* 5J 63
Fionnsabhagh. *W Isl* 5B 76
Firbeck. *S Yor* 1C 36
Firby. *N Yor*
nr. Bedale 7L 47
nr. Malton 1E 42
Firgrove. *G Man* 6H 41
Firle. *E Sus* 5A 12
Firsby. *Linc* 3A 38
Firsdown. *Wilts* 2L 9
First Coast. *High* 4L 77
Firth. *Shet* 6J 91
Fir Tree. *Dur* 8E 54
Fishbourne. *IOW* 6C 10
Fishbourne. *W Sus* 5F 10
Fishburn. *Dur* 8G 55
Fishcross. *Clac* 8B 66
Fisherford. *Abers* 2F 72
Fisherrow. *E Lot* 2M 59
Fisher's Pond. *Hants* 3B 10
Fisher's Row. *Lanc* 3C 40
Fisherstreet. *W Sus* 2G 11
Fisherton. *High* 8H 79
Fisherton. *S Ayr* 8A 58
Fisherton de la Mere. *Wilts* 2H 9
Fishguard. *Pemb* 3F 14
Fishlake. *S Yor* 6D 42
Fishley. *Norf* 8L 39
Fishnish. *Arg* 3A 64
Fishpond Bottom. *Dors* 6B 8
Fishponds. *Bris* 6E 18
Fishpool. *Glos* 1E 18
Fishpool. *G Man* 6G 41
Fishpools. *Powy* 6L 25
Fishtoft. *Linc* 5L 37
Fishtoft Drove. *Linc* 5L 37
Fishwick. *Bord* 4G 61
Fiskavaig. *High* 2E 68
Fiskerton. *Linc* 2H 37
Fiskerton. *Notts* 4E 36
Fitch. *Shet* 3D 90
Fitling. *E Yor* 4K 43
Fittleton. *Wilts* 1K 9
Fittleworth. *W Sus* 4H 11
Fitton End. *Cambs* 8M 37
Fitz. *Shrp* 8C 34
Fitzhead. *Som* 3L 7
Fitzwilliam. *W Yor* 6B 42
Fiunary. *High* 3M 63
Five Ash Down. *E Sus* 3A 12
Five Ashes. *E Sus* 3B 12
Five Bells. *Som* 1K 7
Five Bridges. *Here* 7E 26
Fivehead. *Som* 3B 8
Fivelanes. *Corn* 7B 6
Fivemiletown. *M Ulst* 6D 92
Five Oak Green. *Kent* 1C 12
Five Oaks. *W Sus* 3H 11
Five Roads. *Carm* 6L 15
Five Ways. *Warw* 4L 27
Flack's Green. *Essx* 2D 22
Flackwell Heath. *Buck* 5F 20
Fladbury. *Worc* 7H 27
Fladda. *Shet* 5H 91
Fladdabister. *Shet* 4E 90
Flagg. *Derbs* 3K 35
Flamborough. *E Yor* 8K 49
Flamstead. *Herts* 2H 21
Flansham. *W Sus* 5G 11
Flasby. *N Yor* 2H 41
Flash. *Staf* 3J 35
Flashader. *High* 8E 76
Flatt, The. *Cumb* 4K 53
Flaunden. *Herts* 3H 21
Flawborough. *Notts* 5E 36
Flawith. *N Yor* 1B 42
Flax Bourton. *N Som* 7D 18
Flaxby. *N Yor* 2A 42
Flaxholme. *Derbs* 5M 35
Flaxley. *Glos* 2E 18
Flaxley Green. *Staf* 8J 35
Flaxpool. *Som* 2L 7
Flaxton. *N Yor* 1D 42
Fleck. *Shet* 6D 90
Fleckney. *Leics* 2D 28
Flecknoe. *Warw* 5C 28
Fledborough. *Notts* 2F 36
Fleet. *Dors* 7E 8
Fleet. *Hants*
nr. Farnborough 8F 20
Fleet. *Hants*
nr. South Hayling 5E 10
Fleet. *Linc* 7L 37
Fleet Hargate. *Linc* 7L 37
Fleetville. *Herts* 3J 21
Fleetwood. *Lanc* 3B 40
Fleggburgh. *Norf* 8L 39
Fleisirin. *W Isl* 8J 83
Flemingston. *V Glam* 8K 17
Flemington. *S Lan*
nr. Glasgow 3E 58
nr. Strathaven 5F 58
Flempton. *Suff* 5E 30
Fleoideabhagh. *W Isl* 5B 76
Fletcher's Green. *Kent* 1B 12
Fletchertown. *Cumb* 7G 53
Fletching. *E Sus* 3M 11
Fleuchary. *High* 4H 79
Flexbury. *Corn* 5B 6
Flexford. *Surr* 1G 11
Flimby. *Cumb* 8E 52
Flimwell. *E Sus* 2D 12
Flint. *Flin* 3M 33
Flintham. *Notts* 5E 36
Flint Mountain. *Flin* 3M 33
Flinton. *E Yor* 4K 43
Flintsham. *Here* 6B 26
Flishinghurst. *Kent* 2D 12
Flitcham. *Norf* 7D 38
Flitton. *C Beds* 8H 29
Flitwick. *C Beds* 8H 29
Flixborough. *N Lin* 6F 42
Flixton. *G Man* 8F 40
Flixton. *N Yor* 8H 49
Flixton. *Suff* 3K 31
Flockton. *W Yor* 6L 41
Flodden. *Nmbd* 6G 61
Flodigarry. *High* 6F 76
Flood's Ferry. *Cambs* 2L 29
Flookburgh. *Cumb* 8B 46
Flordon. *Norf* 2H 31
Flore. *Nptn* 5D 28
Flotterton. *Nmbd* 1C 54
Flowton. *Suff* 7G 31
Flushing. *Abers* 1K 73
Flushing. *Corn* 5M 3
Fluxton. *Devn* 6K 7
Flyford Flavell. *Worc* 6H 27
Fobbing. *Thur* 5D 22
Fochabers. *Mor* 8C 80
Fochriw. *Cphy* 4L 17
Fockerby. *N Lin* 6F 42
Fodderty. *High* 8F 78
Foddington. *Som* 3D 8
Foel. *Powy* 1J 25
Foffarty. *Ang* 3H 67
Foggathorpe. *E Yor* 4E 42
Fogo. *Bord* 5E 60
Fogorig. *Bord* 5E 60
Foindle. *High* 7D 84
Folda. *Ang* 1E 66
Fole. *Staf* 6J 35
Foleshill. *W Mid* 3A 28
Foley Park. *Worc* 4G 27
Folke. *Dors* 4E 8
Folkestone. *Kent* 2J 13
Folkingham. *Linc* 6H 37
Folkington. *E Sus* 5B 12
Folksworth. *Cambs* 3J 29
Folkton. *N Yor* 8H 49
Folla Rule. *Abers* 2G 73
Follifoot. *N Yor* 2M 41
Folly, The. *Herts* 2J 21
Folly Cross. *Devn* 5D 6
Folly Gate. *Devn* 6E 6
Fonmon. *V Glam* 8K 17
Fonthill Bishop. *Wilts* 2H 9
Fonthill Gifford. *Wilts* 2H 9
Fontmell Magna. *Dors* 4G 9
Fontwell. *W Sus* 5G 11
Font-y-gary. *V Glam* 8K 17
Foodieash. *Fife* 6G 67
Foolow. *Derbs* 2K 35
Footdee. *Aber* 5J 73
Footherley. *Staf* 1K 27
Foots Cray. *G Lon* 6A 22
Forbestown. *Abers* 4C 72
Force Forge. *Cumb* 6B 46
Force Mills. *Cumb* 6B 46
Forcett. *N Yor* 4K 47
Ford. *Arg* 7C 64
Ford. *Buck* 3E 20
Ford. *Derbs* 1B 36
Ford. *Devn*
nr. Bideford 3D 6
nr. Holbeton 6J 5
nr. Salcombe 7K 5
Ford. *Glos* 1J 19
Ford. *Nmbd* 6G 61
Ford. *Plym* 6G 5
Ford. *Shrp* 8C 34
Ford. *Som*
nr. Wells 8D 18
nr. Wiveliscombe 3K 7
Ford. *Staf* 4J 35
Ford. *W Sus* 5H 11
Ford. *Wilts*
nr. Chippenham 6G 19
nr. Salisbury 2K 9
Forda. *Devn* 2D 6
Ford Barton. *Devn* 4J 7
Fordcombe. *Kent* 1B 12
Fordell. *Fife* 1K 59
Forden. *Powy* 2M 25
Ford End. *Essx* 2C 22
Forder Green. *Devn* 5K 5
Ford Green. *Lanc* 3C 40
Fordham. *Cambs* 4C 30
Fordham. *Essx* 1F 22
Fordham. *Norf* 2C 30
Fordham Heath. *Essx* 1F 22
Ford Heath. *Shrp* 8C 34
Fordhouses. *W Mid* 1H 27
Fordie. *Per* 5A 66
Fordingbridge. *Hants* 4K 9
Fordington. *Linc* 2M 37
Fordon. *E Yor* 8H 49
Fordoun. *Abers* 8G 73
Ford Street. *Essx* 1F 22
Ford Street. *Som* 4L 7
Fordton. *Devn* 6H 7
Fordwells. *Oxon* 2M 19
Fordwich. *Kent* 8H 23
Fordyce. *Abers* 7E 80
Forebridge. *Staf* 7H 35
Foreglen. *Caus* 3E 92
Foremark. *Derbs* 7M 35
Forest. *N Yor* 5L 47
Forestburn Gate. *Nmbd* 2D 54
Foresterseat. *Mor* 8A 80
Forest Green. *Glos* 4G 19
Forest Green. *Surr* 1J 11
Forest Hall. *Cumb* 5D 46
Forest Head. *Cumb* 6K 53
Forest Hill. *Oxon* 3C 20
Forest-in-Teesdale. *Dur* 3G 47
Forest Lodge. *Per* 8K 71
Forest Mill. *Clac* 8C 66
Forest Row. *E Sus* 2M 11
Forestside. *W Sus* 4E 10
Forest Town. *Notts* 3C 36
Forfar. *Ang* 2H 67
Forgandenny. *Per* 6D 66
Forge, The. *Here* 6B 26
Forge. *Powy* 3G 25
Forge Side. *Torf* 4M 17
Forgewood. *N Lan* 4F 58
Forgie. *Mor* 8C 80
Forgue. *Abers* 1F 72
Forkill. *New M* 7G 93
Formby. *Mers* 7B 40
Forncett End. *Norf* 2H 31
Forncett St Mary. *Norf* 2H 31
Forncett St Peter. *Norf* 2H 31
Forneth. *Per* 3D 66
Fornham All Saints. *Suff* 5E 30
Fornham St Martin. *Suff* 5E 30
Forres. *Mor* 8L 79
Forrestfield. *N Lan* 3G 59
Forrest Lodge. *Dum* 3L 51
Forsbrook. *Staf* 5H 35
Forse. *High* 8D 86
Forsinard. *High* 7L 85
Forss. *High* 5B 86
Forstal, The. *Kent* 2G 13
Forston. *Dors* 6E 8
Fort Augustus. *High* 5D 70
Forteviot. *Per* 6D 66
Fort George. *High* 8H 79
Forth. *S Lan* 4H 59
Forthampton. *Glos* 8G 27
Forthay. *Glos* 4F 18
Fortingall. *Per* 3M 65
Fort Matilda. *Inv* 2A 58
Forton. *Hants* 1B 10
Forton. *Lanc* 2C 40
Forton. *Shrp* 8C 34
Forton. *Som* 5B 8
Forton. *Staf* 7F 34
Forton Heath. *Shrp* 8C 34
Fortrie. *Abers* 1F 72
Fortrose. *High* 8H 79
Fortuneswell. *Dors* 8E 8
Fort William. *High* 8B 70
Forty Green. *Buck* 4G 21
Forty Hill. *G Lon* 4L 21
Forward Green. *Suff* 6G 31
Fosbury. *Wilts* 8M 19
Foscot. *Oxon* 1L 19
Fosdyke. *Linc* 6L 37
Foss. *Per* 2A 66
Fossebridge. *Glos* 2J 19
Foster Street. *Essx* 3A 22
Foston. *Derbs* 6K 35
Foston. *Leics* 2D 28
Foston. *Linc* 5F 36
Foston. *N Yor* 1D 42
Foston on the Wolds. *E Yor* 2J 43
Fotherby. *Linc* 8L 43
Fothergill. *Cumb* 8E 52
Fotheringhay. *Nptn* 2H 29
Foubister. *Orkn* 1G 87
Foula Airport. *Shet* 4B 90
Foul Anchor. *Cambs* 8A 38
Foulbridge. *Cumb* 7J 53
Foulden. *Norf* 2D 30
Foulden. *Bord* 4G 61
Foul Mile. *E Sus* 4C 12
Foulridge. *Lanc* 3G 41
Foulsham. *Norf* 7G 39
Fountainhall. *Bord* 5B 60
Four Alls, The. *Shrp* 6E 34
Four Ashes. *Staf*
nr. Cannock 1H 27
nr. Kinver 3G 27
Four Ashes. *Suff* 4G 31
Four Crosses. *Powy*
nr. Llanerfyl 2K 25
nr. Llanymynech 8A 34
Four Crosses. *Staf* 1H 27
Four Elms. *Kent* 1A 12
Four Forks. *Som* 2M 7
Four Gotes. *Cambs* 8A 38
Four Lane End. *S Yor* 7L 41
Four Lane Ends. *Lanc* 2D 40
Four Lanes. *Corn* 5K 3
Fourlanes End. *Ches E* 4G 35
Four Marks. *Hants* 2D 10
Four Mile Bridge. *IOA* 3B 32
Four Oaks. *E Sus* 3E 12
Four Oaks. *Glos* 1E 18
Four Oaks. *W Mid* 3L 27
Four Roads. *Carm* 6L 15
Four Roads. *IOM* 8B 44
Fourstones. *Nmbd* 5B 54
Four Throws. *Kent* 3D 12
Fovant. *Wilts* 3J 9
Foveran. *Abers* 3J 73
Fowey. *Corn* 6D 4
Fowlershill. *Aber* 4J 73
Fowley Common. *Warr* 8E 40
Fowlis. *Ang* 4G 67
Fowlis Wester. *Per* 5C 66
Fowlmere. *Cambs* 7M 29
Fownhope. *Here* 8D 26
Fox Corner. *Surr* 8G 21
Foxcote. *Glos* 2J 19
Foxcote. *Som* 8F 18
Foxdale. *IOM* 7B 44
Foxearth. *Essx* 7E 30
Foxfield. *Cumb* 6M 45
Foxham. *Wilts* 6H 19
Fox Hatch. *Essx* 4B 22
Foxhole. *Corn* 6B 4
Foxholes. *N Yor* 8H 49
Foxhunt Green. *E Sus* 4B 12
Fox Lane. *Hants* 8F 20
Foxley. *Norf* 7G 39
Foxley. *Nptn* 6D 28
Foxley. *Wilts* 5G 19
Foxlydiate. *Worc* 5J 27
Fox Street. *Essx* 1G 23
Foxt. *Staf* 5J 35
Foxton. *Cambs* 7M 29
Foxton. *Dur* 3A 48
Foxton. *Leics* 3D 28
Foxton. *N Yor* 6B 48
Foxup. *N Yor* 8G 47
Foxwist Green. *Ches W* 3E 34
Foxwood. *Shrp* 4E 26
Foy. *Here* 1D 18
Foyers. *High* 3E 70
Foynesfield. *High* 8J 79
Fraddam. *Corn* 5J 3
Fraddon. *Corn* 6B 4
Fradley. *Staf* 8K 35
Fradley South. *Staf* 8K 35
Fradswell. *Staf* 6H 35
Fraisthorpe. *E Yor* 1J 43
Framfield. *E Sus* 3A 12
Framingham Earl. *Norf* 1J 31
Framingham Pigot. *Norf* 1J 31
Framlingham. *Suff* 5J 31
Frampton. *Dors* 6E 8
Frampton. *Linc* 6L 37
Frampton Cotterell. *S Glo* 5E 18
Frampton Mansell. *Glos* 3H 19
Frampton on Severn. *Glos* 3F 18
Frampton West End. *Linc* 5K 37
Framsden. *Suff* 6H 31
Framwellgate Moor. *Dur* 7F 54
Franche. *Worc* 4G 27
Frandley. *Ches W* 2E 34
Frankby. *Mers* 2M 33
Frankfort. *Norf* 7K 39
Frankley. *Worc* 3H 27
Frank's Bridge. *Powy* 7L 25
Frankton. *Warw* 4B 28
Frankwell. *Shrp* 8C 34
Frant. *E Sus* 2B 12
Fraserburgh. *Abers* 7J 81
Frating Green. *Essx* 1G 23
Fratton. *Port* 5D 10
Freathy. *Corn* 6G 5
Freckenham. *Suff* 4C 30
Freckleton. *Lanc* 5C 40
Freeby. *Leics* 7F 36
Freefolk Priors. *Hants* 1B 10
Freehay. *Staf* 5J 35
Freeland. *Oxon* 2B 20
Freester. *Shet* 2E 90
Freethorpe. *Norf* 1L 31
Freiston. *Linc* 5L 37
Freiston Shore. *Linc* 5L 37
Fremington. *Devn* 2E 6
Fremington. *N Yor* 6J 47
Frenchay. *S Glo* 6E 18
Frenchbeer. *Devn* 7F 6
Frenich. *Stir* 7J 65
Frensham. *Surr* 1F 10
Frenze. *Norf* 3H 31
Fresgoe. *High* 5A 86
Freshfield. *Mers* 7A 40
Freshford. *Bath* 7F 18
Freshwater. *IOW* 7M 9
Freshwater Bay. *IOW* 7M 9
Freshwater East. *Pemb* 7G 15
Fressingfield. *Suff* 4J 31
Freston. *Suff* 8H 31
Freswick. *High* 5E 86
Fretherne. *Glos* 3F 18
Frettenham. *Norf* 8J 39
Freuchie. *Fife* 7F 66
Freystrop. *Pemb* 5F 14
Friar's Gate. *E Sus* 2A 12
Friar Waddon. *Dors* 7E 8
Friday Bridge. *Cambs* 1A 30
Friday Street. *E Sus* 5C 12
Friday Street. *Surr* 1J 11
Fridaythorpe. *E Yor* 2F 42
Friden. *Derbs* 3K 35
Friern Barnet. *G Lon* 4K 21
Friesthorpe. *Linc* 1H 37
Frieston. *Linc* 5G 37
Frieth. *Buck* 4E 20
Friezeland. *Notts* 4B 36
Frilford. *Oxon* 4B 20
Frilsham. *W Ber* 6C 20
Frimley. *Surr* 8F 20
Frimley Green. *Surr* 8F 20
Frindsbury. *Medw* 7D 22
Fring. *Norf* 6D 38
Fringford. *Oxon* 1D 20
Frinsted. *Kent* 8E 22
Frinton-on-Sea. *Essx* 2J 23
Friockheim. *Ang* 3J 67
Friog. *Gwyn* 1F 24
Frisby. *Leics* 1E 28
Frisby on the Wreake. *Leics* 8D 36
Friskney. *Linc* 4A 38
Friskney Eaudyke. *Linc* 4A 38
Friston. *E Sus* 6B 12
Friston. *Suff* 5L 31
Fritchley. *Derbs* 4A 36
Fritham. *Hants* 4L 9
Frith Bank. *Linc* 5L 37
Frith Common. *Worc* 5E 26
Frithelstock. *Devn* 4D 6
Frithelstock Stone. *Devn* 4D 6
Frithsden. *Herts* 3H 21
Frithville. *Linc* 4L 37
Frittenden. *Kent* 1E 12
Frittiscombe. *Devn* 7L 5
Fritton. *Norf*
nr. Great Yarmouth 1L 31
nr. Long Stratton 2J 31
Fritwell. *Oxon* 1C 20
Frizinghall. *W Yor* 4K 41
Frizington. *Cumb* 3K 45
Frobost. *W Isl* 3D 74
Frocester. *Glos* 3F 18
Frochas. *Powy* 2L 25
Frodesley. *Shrp* 1D 26
Frodingham. *N Lin* 6G 43
Frodsham. *Ches W* 2D 34
Froggatt. *Derbs* 2L 35
Froghall. *Staf* 5J 35
Frogham. *Hants* 4K 9
Frogham. *Kent* 8J 23
Frogmore. *Devn* 7K 5
Frogmore. *Hants* 7F 20
Frogmore. *Herts* 3J 21
Frognall. *Linc* 8J 37
Frogshall. *Norf* 6J 39
Frogwell. *Corn* 5F 4
Frolesworth. *Leics* 2C 28
Frome. *Som* 1F 8
Fromefield. *Som* 1F 8
Frome St Quintin. *Dors* 5D 8
Fromes Hill. *Here* 7E 26
Fron. *Gwyn* 7C 32
Y Fron. *Gwyn* 5E 32
Fron. *Powy*
nr. Llandrindod Wells 6K 25
nr. Newtown 3L 25
nr. Welshpool 2M 25
Froncysyllte. *Wrex* 5A 34
Frongoch. *Gwyn* 7J 33
Fron Isaf. *Wrex* 5A 34
Fronoleu. *Gwyn* 7G 33
Frosterley. *Dur* 8D 54
Frotoft. *Orkn* 7D 88
Froxfield. *C Beds* 8G 29
Froxfield. *Wilts* 7L 19
Froxfield Green. *Hants* 3E 10
Fryern Hill. *Hants* 3B 10
Fryerning. *Essx* 3C 22
Fryton. *N Yor* 8D 48
Fugglestone St Peter. *Wilts* 2K 9
Fulbeck. *Linc* 4G 37
Fulbourn. *Cambs* 6B 30
Fulbrook. *Oxon* 2L 19
Fulflood. *Hants* 2B 10
Fulford. *Som* 3M 7
Fulford. *Staf* 6H 35
Fulford. *York* 3D 42
Fulham. *G Lon* 6K 21
Fulking. *W Sus* 4K 11
Fuller's Moor. *Ches W* 4C 34
Fuller Street. *Essx* 2D 22
Fullerton. *Hants* 2A 10
Fulletby. *Linc* 2K 37
Full Sutton. *E Yor* 2E 42
Fullwood. *E Ayr* 4C 58
Fulmer. *Buck* 5G 21
Fulmodestone. *Norf* 6F 38
Fulnetby. *Linc* 2H 37
Fulney. *Linc* 7K 37
Fulstow. *Linc* 8L 43
Fulthorpe. *Stoc T* 3B 48
Fulwell. *Tyne* 6G 55
Fulwood. *Lanc* 4D 40
Fulwood. *Notts* 4B 36
Fulwood. *Som* 4M 7
Fulwood. *S Yor* 1L 35
Fundenhall. *Norf* 2H 31

Funtington—Gwaenysgor

Funtington. W Sus 5F 10
Funtley. Hants 5C 10
Funzie. Shet 4L 91
Furley. Devn 5A 8
Furnace. Arg 7E 64
Furnace. Carm 6M 15
Furnace. Cdgn 3F 24
Furner's Green. E Sus 3M 11
Furness Vale. Derbs 1J 35
Furneux Pelham. Herts 1M 21
Furzebrook. Dors 7H 9
Furzehill. Devn 1G 7
Furzehill. Dors 5J 9
Furzeley Corner. Hants 4D 10
Furzey Lodge. Hants 5A 10
Furzley. Hants 4L 9
Fyfield. Essx 3B 22
Fyfield. Glos 3L 19
Fyfield. Hants 1L 9
Fyfield. Oxon 4B 20
Fyfield. Wilts 7K 19
Fylde, The. Lanc 4B 40
Fylingthorpe. N Yor 5G 49
Fyning. W Sus 3F 10
Fyvie. Abers 2G 73

G

Gabhsann bho Dheas. W Isl 6H 83
Gabhsann bho Thuath. W Isl 6H 83
Gabroc Hill. E Ayr 4C 58
Gadbrook. Surr 1K 11
Gaddesby. Leics 8D 36
Gadfa. IOA 2D 32
Gadgirth. S Ayr 7C 58
Gaer. Powy 2L 17
Gaerwen. IOA 3D 32
Gagingwell. Oxon 1B 20
Gaick Lodge. High 7H 71
Gailey. Staf 8H 35
Gainford. Dur 4K 47
Gainsborough. Linc 8F 42
Gainsborough. Suff 7H 31
Gainsford End. Essx 8D 30
Gairletter. Arg 1L 57
Gairloch. Abers 5G 73
Gairloch. High 6K 77
Gairlochy. High 7B 70
Gairney Bank. Per 8E 66
Gairnshiel Lodge. Abers 5B 72
Gaisgill. Cumb 5E 46
Gaitsgill. Cumb 7H 53
Galashiels. Bord 6B 60
Galgate. Lanc 2C 40
Galgorm. ME Ant 3G 93
Galhampton. Som 3E 8
Gallatown. Fife 8F 66
Galley Common. Warw 2M 27
Galleyend. Essx 3D 22
Galleywood. Essx 3D 22
Gallin. Per 3K 65
Gallowfauld. Ang 3H 67
Gallowhill. Per 4E 66
Gallowhill. Ren 3C 58
Gallowhills. Abers 8K 81
Gallows Green. Staf 5J 35
Gallows Green. Worc 5H 27
Gallowstree Common. Oxon 5D 20
Galltair. High 3K 69
Gallt Melyd. Den 2K 33
Galmington. Som 3M 7
Galmisdale. High 7F 68
Galmpton. Devn 7J 5
Galmpton. Torb 6L 5
Galmpton Warborough. Torb 6L 5
Galphay. N Yor 8L 47
Galston. E Ayr 6C 58
Galton. Dors 7F 8
Galtrigill. High 8C 76
Gamblesby. Cumb 8L 53
Gamblestown. Arm 6G 93
Gamelsby. Cumb 6G 53
Gamesley. Derbs 8J 41
Gamlingay. Cambs 6K 29
Gamlingay Cinques. Cambs 6K 29
Gamlingay Great Heath. Cambs 6K 29
Gammaton. Devn 3D 6
Gammersgill. N Yor 7J 47
Gamston. Notts
nr. Nottingham 6D 36
nr. Retford 2E 36
Ganarew. Here 2D 18
Ganavan. Arg 4C 64
Ganborough. Glos 1K 19
Gang. Corn 5F 4
Ganllwyd. Gwyn 8G 33
Gannochy. Ang 8E 72
Gannochy. Per 5E 66
Gansclet. High 7E 86
Ganstead. E Yor 4J 43
Ganthorpe. N Yor 8D 48
Ganton. N Yor 8G 49
Gants Hill. G Lon 5M 21
Gappah. Devn 8H 7
Garafad. High 7F 76
Garboldisham. Norf 3G 31
Garden City. Flin 3B 34
Gardeners Green. Wok 7F 20
Gardenstown. Abers 7H 81
Garden Village. S Yor 8L 41
Garden Village. Swan 5E 16
Garderhouse. Shet 3D 90
Gardham. E Yor 3G 43
Gardie. Shet
on Papa Stour 1B 90
on Unst 2L 91
Gardie Ho. Shet 3E 90
Gare Hill. Wilts 1F 8
Garelochhead. Arg 8G 65
Garford. Oxon 4B 20
Garforth. W Yor 4B 42
Gargrave. N Yor 2H 41
Gargunnock. Stir 8M 65
Garleffin. S Ayr 3F 50
Garlieston. Dum 7K 51
Garlinge Green. Kent 8H 23
Garlogie. Abers 5G 73
Garmelow. Staf 7F 34
Garmond. Abers 8H 81
Garmondsway. Dur 8G 55
Garmony. Arg 3A 64
Garmouth. Mor 7C 80
Garmston. Shrp 1E 26
Garnant. Carm 3F 16
Garndiffaith. Torf 3A 18
Garndolbenmaen. Gwyn 6D 32
Garnett Bridge. Cumb 6D 46
Garnfadryn. Gwyn 7B 32
Garnkirk. N Lan 3E 58
Garnlydan. Blae 3L 17
Garnsgate. Linc 7M 37
Garnswllt. Swan 4F 16
Garn yr Erw. Torf 3M 17
Garrabost. W Isl 8J 83
Garrallan. E Ayr 8D 58
Garras. Corn 6L 3
Garreg. Gwyn 6F 32
Garrigill. Cumb 7M 53
Garrison. Ferm 6A 92
Garriston. N Yor 6K 47
Garrogie Lodge. High 4F 70
Garros. High 7F 76
Garrow. Per 3B 66
Garsdale. Cumb 7F 46
Garsdale Head. Cumb 6F 46
Garsdon. Wilts 5H 19
Garshall Green. Staf 6H 35
Garsington. Oxon 3C 20
Garstang. Lanc 3C 40
Garston. Mers 1C 34
Garswood. Mers 8D 40
Gartcosh. N Lan 3E 58
Garth. B'end 5H 17
Garth. Cdgn 4F 24
Garth. Gwyn 7E 32
Garth. IOM 7C 44
Garth. Powy
nr. Builth Wells 8J 25
nr. Knighton 4A 26
Garth. Shet
nr. Sandness 2C 90
nr. Skellister 2E 90
Garth. Wrex 5A 34
Garthamlock. Glas 3E 58
Garthbrengy. Powy 1K 17
Gartheli. Cdgn 7E 24
Garthmyl. Powy 3L 25
Garthorpe. Leics 7F 36
Garthorpe. N Lin 6F 42
Garth Owen. Powy 3L 25
Garth Place. Cphy 6L 17
Garth Row. Cumb 6D 46
Gartly. Abers 2E 72
Gartmore. Stir 8K 65
Gartness. N Lan 3F 58
Gartness. Stir 1D 58
Gartocharn. W Dun 1C 58
Garton. E Yor 4K 43
Garton-on-the-Wolds. E Yor 2G 43
Gartsherrie. N Lan 3F 58
Gartymore. High 2L 79
Garvagh. Caus 3F 93
Garvaghy. Ferm 5D 92
Garvald. E Lot 2C 60
Garvamore. High 6F 70
Garvard. Arg 8J 63
Garvault. High 8K 85
Garve. High 7D 78
Garvestone. Norf 1G 31
Garvetagh. Derr 4C 92
Garvie. Arg 8E 64
Garvock. Abers 8G 73
Garvock. Inv 2A 58
Garway. Here 1C 18
Garway Common. Here 1C 18
Garway Hill. Here 1C 18
Garwick. Linc 5J 37
Gaskan. High 8K 69
Gasper. Wilts 2F 8
Gastard. Wilts 7G 19
Gasthorpe. Norf 3F 30
Gatcombe. IOW 7B 10
Gateacre. Mers 1C 34
Gatebeck. Cumb 7D 46
Gate Burton. Linc 1F 36
Gateforth. N Yor 5C 42
Gatehead. E Ayr 6B 58
Gate Helmsley. N Yor 2D 42
Gatehouse. Nmbd 3A 54
Gatehouse of Fleet. Dum 6M 51
Gatelawbridge. Dum 2D 52
Gateley. Norf 7F 38
Gatenby. N Yor 7M 47
Gatesgarth. Cumb 3L 45
Gateshead. Tyne 5F 54
Gatesheath. Ches W 3C 34
Gateside. Ang
nr. Forfar 3H 67
nr. Kirriemuir 3G 67
Gateside. Fife 7E 66
Gateside. N Ayr 4B 58
Gathurst. G Man 7D 40
Gatley. G Man 1G 35
Gatton. Surr 8K 21
Gattonside. Bord 6C 60
Gatwick Airport. W Sus 1K 11
Gaufron. Powy 6J 25
Gaulby. Leics 1D 28
Gauldry. Fife 5G 67
Gaultree. Norf 1A 30
Gaunt's Common. Dors 5J 9
Gaunt's Earthcott. S Glo 5E 18
Gautby. Linc 2J 37
Gavinton. Bord 4E 60
Gawber. S Yor 7M 41
Gawcott. Buck 8D 28
Gawsworth. Ches E 3G 35
Gawthorpe. W Yor 5L 41
Gawthrop. Cumb 7E 46
Gawthwaite. Cumb 7A 46
Gay Bowers. Essx 3D 22
Gaydon. Warw 6A 28
Gayfield. Orkn 4D 88
Gayhurst. Mil 7F 28
Gayle. N Yor 7G 47
Gayles. N Yor 5K 47
Gay Street. W Sus 3H 11
Gayton. Mers 1A 34
Gayton. Norf 8D 38
Gayton. Nptn 6E 28
Gayton. Staf 7H 35
Gayton le Marsh. Linc 1M 37
Gayton le Wold. Linc 1K 37
Gayton Thorpe. Norf 8D 38
Gaywood. Norf 7C 38
Gazeley. Suff 5D 30
Geanies. High 6J 79
Gearraidh Bhailteas. W Isl 3D 74
Gearraidh Bhaird. W Isl 2E 76
Gearraidh ma Monadh. W Isl 4D 74
Gearraidh na h-Aibhne. W Isl 8F 82
Geary. High 7D 76
Geddes. High 8J 79
Gedding. Suff 6F 30
Geddington. Nptn 3F 28
Gedintailor. High 2G 69
Gedling. Notts 5D 36
Gedney. Linc 7M 37
Gedney Broadgate. Linc 7M 37
Gedney Drove End. Linc 7A 38
Gedney Dyke. Linc 7M 37
Gedney Hill. Linc 8L 37
Gee Cross. G Man 8H 41
Geeston. Rut 1G 29
Geilston. Arg 2B 58
Geirinis. W Isl 1D 74
Geise. High 5C 86
Geisiadar. W Isl 8E 82
Gelder Shiel. Abers 7B 72
Geldeston. Norf 2K 31
Gell. Cnwy 4H 33
Gelli. Pemb 5G 15
Gelli. Rhon 5J 17
Gellifor. Den 4L 33
Gelligaer. Cphy 5L 17
Y Gelli Gandryll. Powy 8M 25
Gellilydan. Gwyn 7F 32
Gellinudd. Neat 4G 17
Gellyburn. Per 4D 66
Gellywen. Carm 4J 15
Gelston. Dum 6B 52
Gelston. Linc 5G 37
Gembling. E Yor 2J 43
Geneva. Cdgn 1L 15
Gentleshaw. Staf 8J 35
Geocrab. W Isl 4C 76
George Best Belfast City Airport. Bel 5H 93
George Green. Buck 5G 21
Georgeham. Devn 2D 6
George Nympton. Devn 3G 7
Georgetown. Blae 4L 17
Georgetown. Ren 3C 58
Georth. Orkn 7C 88
Gerlan. Gwyn 4F 32
Germansweek. Devn 6D 6
Germoe. Corn 6J 3
Gerrans. Corn 8A 4
Gerrard's Bromley. Staf 6F 34
Gerrards Cross. Buck 5G 21
Gerston. High 6C 86
Gestingthorpe. Essx 8E 30
Gethsemane. Pemb 2G 15
Geuffordd. Powy 1M 25
Gibraltar. Buck 2E 20
Gibraltar. Linc 4B 38
Gibraltar. Suff 6H 31
Gibsmere. Notts 5E 36
Giddeahall. Wilts 6G 19
Gidea Park. G Lon 5B 22
Gidleigh. Devn 7F 6
Giffnock. E Ren 4D 58
Gifford. E Lot 3C 60
Giffordtown. Fife 6F 66
Giggetty. Staf 2G 27
Giggleswick. N Yor 1G 41
Gignog. Pemb 4E 14
Gilberdyke. E Yor 5F 42
Gilbert's End. Worc 7G 27
Gilbert's Green. Warw 4K 27
Gilchriston. E Lot 3B 60
Gilcrux. Cumb 8F 52
Gildersome. W Yor 5L 41
Gildingwells. S Yor 1C 36
Gilesgate Moor. Dur 7F 54
Gileston. V Glam 8K 17
Gilfach. Cphy 5L 17
Gilfach Goch. Rhon 6J 17
Gilfachreda. Cdgn 1L 15
Gilford. Arm 6G 93
Gilgarran. Cumb 2K 45
Gillamoor. N Yor 6D 48
Gillan. Corn 6L 3
Gillar's Green. Mers 8C 40
Gillen. High 8D 76
Gilling East. N Yor 8D 48
Gillingham. Dors 3G 9
Gillingham. Medw 7D 22
Gillingham. Norf 2L 31
Gilling West. N Yor 5K 47
Gillock. High 6D 86
Gillow Heath. Staf 4G 35
Gills. High 4E 86
Gill's Green. Kent 2D 12
Gilmanscleuch. Bord 7M 59
Gilmerton. Edin 3L 59
Gilmerton. Per 5B 66
Gilmonby. Dur 4H 47
Gilmorton. Leics 3C 28
Gilsland. Nmbd 5L 53
Gilsland Spa. Cumb 5L 53
Gilston. Bord 4B 60
Giltbrook. Notts 5B 36
Gilwern. Mon 3M 17
Gimingham. Norf 6J 39
Giosla. W Isl 1C 76
Gipping. Suff 5G 31
Gipsey Bridge. Linc 5K 37
Gipton. W Yor 4M 41
Girdle Toll. N Ayr 5B 58
Girlsta. Shet 2E 90
Girsby. N Yor 5A 48
Girthon. Dum 6M 51
Girton. Cambs 5M 29
Girton. Notts 3F 36
Girvan. S Ayr 2G 51
Gisburn. Lanc 3G 41
Gisleham. Suff 3M 31
Gislingham. Suff 4G 31
Gissing. Norf 3H 31
Gittisham. Devn 6L 7
Gladestry. Powy 7M 25
Gladsmuir. E Lot 2B 60
Glaichbea. High 2F 70
Glais. Swan 4G 17
Glaisdale. N Yor 5E 48
Glame. High 1G 69
Glamis. Ang 3G 67
Glanaman. Carm 3F 16
Glan-Conwy. Cnwy 5H 33
Glandford. Norf 5G 39
Glan Duar. Carm 2M 15
Glandwr. Blae 4M 17
Glandwr. Pemb 4H 15
Glan-Dwyfach. Gwyn 6D 32
Glandy Cross. Carm 4H 15
Glandyfi. Cdgn 3F 24
Glangrwyney. Powy 3M 17
Glanmule. Powy 3L 25
Glanrhyd. Gwyn 7B 32
Glan-rhyd. Pemb 3H 15
Glanrhyd. Pemb 2H 15
Glan-rhyd. Powy 4G 17
Glanton. Nmbd 8H 61
Glanton Pyke. Nmbd 8H 61
Glanvilles Wootton. Dors 5E 8
Glan-y-don. Flin 3L 33
Glan-y-nant. Powy 4J 25
Glan-yr-afon. Gwyn 6K 33
Glan-yr-afon. IOA 2F 32
Glan-yr-afon. Powy 2K 25
Glan-y-wern. Gwyn 7F 32
Glapthorn. Nptn 2H 29
Glapwell. Derbs 3B 36
Glarryford. ME Ant 3G 93
Glas Aird. Arg 8J 63
Glas-allt Shiel. Abers 7B 72
Glasbury. Powy 1L 17
Glaschoil. High 2L 71
Glascoed. Den 3J 33
Glascoed. Mon 3B 18
Glascote. Staf 1L 27
Glascwm. Powy 7L 25
Glasfryn. Cnwy 5J 33
Glasgow. Glas 3D 58
Glasgow Airport. Ren 3C 58
Glasgow Prestwick Airport. S Ayr 7B 58
Glashvin. High 7F 76
Glasinfryn. Gwyn 4E 32
Glas na Cardaich. High 6H 69
Glasnacardoch. High 6H 69
Glasnakille. High 4G 69
Glaspwll. Cdgn 3G 25
Glassburn. High 2D 70
Glassenbury. Kent 2D 12
Glasserton. Dum 8K 51
Glassford. S Lan 5F 58
Glassgreen. Mor 7B 80
Glasshouse. Glos 1F 18
Glasshouses. N Yor 1K 41
Glasson. Cumb 5G 53
Glasson. Lanc 2C 40
Glassonby. Cumb 8K 53
Glasswater. New M 6J 93
Glasterlaw. Ang 2J 67
Glaston. Rut 1F 28
Glastonbury. Som 2C 8
Glatton. Cambs 3J 29
Glazebrook. Warr 8E 40
Glazebury. Warr 8E 40
Glazeley. Shrp 3F 26
Gleadless. S Yor 1A 36
Gleadsmoss. Ches E 3G 35
Gleann Dail bho Dheas. W Isl 4D 74
Gleann Tholastaidh. W Isl 7J 83
Gleann Uige. High 8H 69
Gleaston. Cumb 8A 46
Glebe. Derr 4C 92
Glecknabae. Arg 3K 57
Gledrid. Shrp 6A 34
Gleiniant. Powy 3J 25
Glemsford. Suff 7E 30
Glen. Dum 6L 51
Glenancross. High 6H 69
Glenanne. Arm 7F 93
Glenariff. Caus 2H 93
Glenarm. ME Ant 3H 93
Glen Auldyn. IOM 5D 44
Glenavy. Lis 5G 93
Glenbarr. Arg 6F 56
Glenbeg. High 1L 63
Glen Bernisdale. High 1F 68
Glenbervie. Abers 7G 73
Glenboig. N Lan 3F 58
Glenborrodale. High 1M 63
Glenbranter. Arg 8F 64
Glenbreck. Bord 7J 59
Glenbrein Lodge. High 4E 70
Glenbrittle. High 3F 68
Glenbuchat Lodge. Abers 4C 72
Glenbuck. E Ayr 7F 58
Glenburn. Ren 3C 58
Glencalvie Lodge. High 5E 78
Glencaple. Dum 5D 52
Glencarron Lodge. High 8A 78
Glencarse. Per 5E 66
Glencassley Castle. High 3E 78
Glencat. Abers 6E 72
Glencoe. High 2F 64
Glen Cottage. High 7H 69
Glencraig. Fife 8E 66
Glendale. High 1C 68
Glendevon. Per 7C 66
Glendoebeg. High 5E 70
Glendoick. Per 5F 66
Glendoune. S Ayr 2G 51
Glenduckie. Fife 6F 66
Gleneagles. Per 7C 66
Glenegedale. Arg 4C 56
Glenegedale Lots. Arg 4C 56
Glenelg. High 4K 69
Glenernie. Mor 1L 71
Glenesslin. Dum 3C 52
Glenfarg. Per 6E 66
Glenfarquhar Lodge. Abers 7G 73
Glenferness Mains. High 1K 71
Glenfeshie Lodge. High 6J 71
Glenfiddich Lodge. Mor 2C 72
Glenfield. Leics 1C 28
Glenfinnan. High 7L 69
Glenfintaig Lodge. High 7C 70
Glenfoot. Per 6E 66
Glenfyne Lodge. Arg 6G 65
Glengap. Dum 6A 52
Glengarnock. N Ayr 4B 58
Glengolly. High 5C 86
Glengorm Castle. Arg 2K 63
Glengormley. Ant 4H 93
Glengrasco. High 1F 68
Glenhead Farm. Ang 1F 66
Glenholm. Bord 6K 59
Glen House. Bord 6L 59
Glenhurich. High 1C 64
Glenkerry. Bord 8L 59
Glenkiln. Dum 4C 52
Glenkindie. Abers 4D 72
Glenkinglass Lodge. Arg 4F 64
Glenkirk. Bord 7J 59
Glenlean. Arg 1K 57
Glenlee. Dum 3M 51
Glenleraig. High 8D 84
Glenlichorn. Per 6A 66
Glenlivet. Mor 3A 72
Glenlochar. Dum 5B 52
Glenlochsie Lodge. Per 8L 71
Glenluce. Dum 6G 51
Glenmarksie. High 8D 78
Glenmassan. Arg 1L 57
Glenmavis. N Lan 3F 58
Glen Maye. IOM 7B 44
Glenmazeran Lodge. High 3H 71
Glenmidge. Dum 3C 52
Glen Mona. IOM 6D 44
Glenmore. High
nr. Glenborrodale 1L 63
nr. Kingussie 5K 71
on Isle of Skye 1F 68
Glenmoy. Ang 1H 67
Glennoe. Arg 4E 64
Glen of Coachford. Abers 1D 72
Glenogil. Ang 1H 67
Glen Parva. Leics 2C 28
Glenprosen Village. Ang 1G 67
Glenree. N Ayr 7J 57
Glenridding. Cumb 4B 46
Glenrosa. N Ayr 6K 57
Glenrothes. Fife 7F 66
Glensanda. High 3C 64
Glensaugh. Abers 8F 72
Glenshero Lodge. High 6F 70
Glensluain. Arg 8E 64
Glenstockadale. Dum 5F 50
Glenstriven. Arg 2K 57
Glen Tanar House. Abers 6D 72
Glentham. Linc 8H 43
Glenton. Abers 3F 72
Glentress. Bord 6L 59
Glentromie Lodge. High 6H 71
Glentrool Lodge. Dum 3K 51
Glentrool Village. Dum 4J 51
Glentruim House. High 6G 71
Glentworth. Linc 1G 37
Glenuig. High 8H 69
Glen View. New M 7G 93
Glen Village. Falk 2G 59
Glen Vine. IOM 7C 44
Glenwhilly. Dum 4G 51
Glenzierfoot. Dum 4H 53
Glespin. S Lan 7G 59
Gletness. Shet 2E 90
Glewstone. Here 1D 18
Glib Cheois. W Isl 1E 76
Glinton. Pet 1J 29
Glooston. Leics 2E 28
Glossop. Derbs 8J 41
Gloster Hill. Nmbd 1F 54
Gloucester. Glos 2G 19
Gloucestershire Airport. Glos 1G 19
Gloup. Shet 3K 91
Glusburn. N Yor 3J 41
Glutt Lodge. High 8A 86
Glutton Bridge. Derbs 3J 35
Gluvian. Corn 5B 4
Glympton. Oxon 1B 20
Glyn. Cnwy 3H 33
Glynarthen. Cdgn 2K 15
Glynbrochan. Powy 4J 25
Glyn Ceiriog. Wrex 7M 33
Glyncoch. Rhon 5K 17
Glyncorrwg. Neat 5H 17
Glynde. E Sus 5A 12
Glyndebourne. E Sus 4A 12
Glyndyfrdwy. Den 6L 33
Glyn Ebwy. Blae 4L 17
Glynllan. B'end 6J 17
Glynn. ME Ant 4J 93
Glyn-neath. Neat 4H 17
Glynogwr. B'end 6J 17
Glyntaff. Rhon 6K 17
Glyntawe. Powy 3H 17
Glynteg. Carm 3K 15
Gnosall. Staf 7G 35
Gnosall Heath. Staf 7G 35
Goadby. Leics 2E 28
Goadby Marwood. Leics 7E 36
Goatacre. Wilts 6J 19
Goathill. Dors 4E 8
Goathland. N Yor 5F 48
Goathurst. Som 2A 8
Goathurst Common. Kent 8A 22
Goat Lees. Kent 1G 13
Gobernuisgach Lodge. High 7G 85
Gobernuisgeach. High 8A 86
Gobhaig. W Isl 3B 76
Gobowen. Shrp 6B 34
Godalming. Surr 1G 11
Goddard's Corner. Suff 5J 31
Goddard's Green. Kent
nr. Benenden 2E 12
nr. Cranbrook 2D 12
Goddards' Green. W Sus 3K 11
Godford Cross. Devn 5L 7
Godleybrook. Staf 5H 35
Godmanchester. Cambs 4K 29
Godmanstone. Dors 6E 8
Godmersham. Kent 8G 23
Godolphin Cross. Corn 5K 3
Godre'r-graig. Neat 4G 17
Godshill. Hants 4K 9
Godshill. IOW 7C 10
Godstone. Staf 6J 35
Godstone. Surr 8L 21
Goetre. Mon 3B 18
Goff's Oak. Herts 3L 21
Gogar. Edin 2K 59
Goginan. Cdgn 4F 24
Golan. Gwyn 6E 32
Golant. Corn 6D 4
Golberdon. Corn 8C 6
Golborne. G Man 8E 40
Golcar. W Yor 6J 41
Goldcliff. Newp 5B 18
Golden Cross. E Sus 4B 12
Golden Green. Kent 1C 12
Golden Grove. Carm 3E 16
Golden Grove. N Yor 5F 48
Golden Hill. Pemb 4F 14
Goldenhill. Stoke 4G 35
Golden Pot. Hants 1E 10
Golden Valley. Glos 1H 19
Golders Green. G Lon 5K 21
Goldhanger. Essx 3F 22
Gold Hill. Norf 2B 30
Golding. Shrp 1D 26
Goldington. Bed 6H 29
Goldsborough. N Yor
nr. Harrogate 2A 42
nr. Whitby 4F 48
Goldsithney. Corn 5J 3
Goldstone. Kent 7J 23
Goldstone. Shrp 7F 34
Goldthorpe. S Yor 7B 42
Goldworthy. Devn 3C 6
Golfa. Powy 8L 33
Gollanfield. High 8J 79
Gollinglith Foot. N Yor 7K 47
Golsoncott. Som 2K 7
Golspie. High 4J 79
Gomeldon. Wilts 2K 9
Gomersal. W Yor 5L 41
Gometra House. Arg 3J 63
Gomshall. Surr 1H 11
Gonalston. Notts 5D 36
Gonerby Hill Foot. Linc 6G 37
Gonfirth. Shet 1D 90
Good Easter. Essx 2C 22
Gooderstone. Norf 1D 30
Goodleigh. Devn 2F 6
Goodmanham. E Yor 3F 42
Goodmayes. G Lon 5A 22
Goodnestone. Kent
nr. Aylesham 8J 23
nr. Faversham 7G 23
Goodrich. Here 2D 18
Goodrington. Torb 6L 5
Goodshaw. Lanc 5G 41
Goodshaw Fold. Lanc 5G 41
Goodstone. Devn 8G 7
Goodwick. Pemb 3F 14
Goodworth Clatford. Hants 1A 10
Goole. E Yor 5E 42
Goom's Hill. Worc 6J 27
Goonabarn. Corn 6B 4
Goonbell. Corn 4L 3
Goonhavern. Corn 3L 3
Goonlaze. Corn 5L 3
Goonvrea. Corn 4L 3
Goose Green. Cumb 7D 46
Goose Green. S Glo 5F 18
Gooseham. Corn 4B 6
Goosewell. Plym 6H 5
Goosey. Oxon 4A 20
Goosnargh. Lanc 4D 40
Goostrey. Ches E 2F 34
Gorcott Hill. Warw 5J 27
Gord. Shet 5E 90
Gordon. Bord 5D 60
Gordonbush. High 3J 79
Gordonstown. Abers
nr. Cornhill 8E 80
nr. Fyvie 2G 73
Gorebridge. Midl 3M 59
Gorefield. Cambs 8M 37
Gores. Wilts 8K 19
Gorgie. Edin 2L 59
Goring. Oxon 5D 20
Goring-by-Sea. W Sus 5J 11
Goring Heath. Oxon 6D 20
Gorleston-on-Sea. Norf 1M 31
Gornalwood. W Mid 2H 27
Gorran Churchtown. Corn 7B 4
Gorran Haven. Corn 7C 4
Gorran High Lanes. Corn 7B 4
Gors. Cdgn 5F 24
Gorsedd. Flin 3L 33
Gorseinon. Swan 5E 16
Gorseness. Orkn 8D 88
Gorseybank. Derbs 4L 35
Gorsgoch. Cdgn 1L 15
Gorslas. Carm 3E 16
Gorsley. Glos 1E 18
Gorsley Common. Here 1E 18
Gorstan. High 7D 78
Gorstella. Ches W 3B 34
Gorsty Common. Here 8C 26
Gorsty Hill. Staf 7K 35
Gortantaoid. Arg 2C 56
Gorteneorn. High 1M 63
Gortenfern. High 1M 63
Gortin. Ferm 4D 92
Gortnahey. Caus 3E 92
Gorton. G Man 8G 41
Gosbeck. Suff 6H 31
Gosberton. Linc 6K 37
Gosberton Cheal. Linc 7K 37
Gosberton Clough. Linc 7J 37
Goseley Dale. Derbs 7M 35
Gosfield. Essx 1D 22
Gosford. Oxon 2C 20
Gosforth. Cumb 4K 45
Gosforth. Tyne 5F 54
Gosmore. Herts 1J 21
Gospel End. Staf 2G 27
Gosport. Hants 6D 10
Gossabrough. Shet 5K 91
Gossington. Glos 3F 18
Gossops Green. W Sus 2K 11
Goswick. Nmbd 5H 61
Gotham. Notts 6C 36
Gotherington. Glos 1H 19
Gott. Arg 3F 62
Gott. Shet 3E 90
Goudhurst. Kent 2D 12
Goulceby. Linc 2K 37
Gourdon. Abers 8H 73
Gourock. Inv 2M 57
Govan. Glas 3D 58
Govanhill. Glas 3D 58
Goverton. Notts 5E 36
Goveton. Devn 7K 5
Govilon. Mon 2A 18
Gowanhill. Abers 7K 81
Gowdall. E Yor 5D 42
Gowdystown. Arm 6G 93
Gowerton. Swan 5E 16
Gowkhall. Fife 1J 59
Gowthorpe. E Yor 2E 42
Goxhill. E Yor 3J 43
Goxhill. N Lin 5J 43
Goxhill Haven. N Lin 5J 43
Goytre. Neat 6G 17
Grabhair. W Isl 2E 76
Graby. Linc 7H 37
Gracehill. ME Ant 3G 93
Graffham. W Sus 4G 11
Grafham. Cambs 5J 29
Grafham. Surr 1H 11
Grafton. Here 8C 26
Grafton. N Yor 1B 42
Grafton. Oxon 3L 19
Grafton. Shrp 8C 34
Grafton. Worc
nr. Evesham 8H 27
nr. Leominster 5D 26
Grafton Flyford. Worc 6H 27
Grafton Regis. Nptn 7E 28
Grafton Underwood. Nptn 3G 29
Grafty Green. Kent 1E 12
Graianrhyd. Den 5M 33
Graig. Carm 6L 15
Graig. Cnwy 3H 33
Graig. Den 3K 33
Graig-fechan. Den 5L 33
Graig Penllyn. V Glam 7J 17
Grain. Medw 6E 22
Grainsby. Linc 8K 43
Grainthorpe. Linc 8L 43
Grainthorpe Fen. Linc 8L 43
Graiselound. N Lin 8E 42
Gramasdail. W Isl 8K 75
Grampound. Corn 7B 4
Grampound Road. Corn 6B 4
Granborough. Buck 1E 20
Granby. Notts 6E 36
Grandborough. Warw 5B 28
Grandpont. Oxon 3C 20
Grandtully. Per 2C 66
Grange. Cumb 4A 46
Grange. E Ayr 6C 58
Grange. Here 4C 26
Grange. Mers 2M 33
Grange, The. N Yor 6C 48
Grange. Per 5F 66
Grange Corner. ME Ant 4G 93
Grange Crossroads. Mor 8D 80
Grange Hill. Essx 4M 21
Grangemill. Derbs 4L 35
Grange Moor. W Yor 6L 41
Grangemouth. Falk 1H 59
Grange of Lindores. Fife 6F 66
Grange-over-Sands. Cumb 8C 46
Grangepans. Falk 1J 59
Grange Park. New M 6J 93
Grangetown. Card 7L 17
Grangetown. Red C 3C 48
Grange Villa. Dur 6F 54
Granish. High 4J 71
Gransmoor. E Yor 2J 43
Granston. Pemb 3E 14
Grantchester. Cambs 6M 29
Grantham. Linc 6G 37
Grantley. N Yor 1L 41
Grantlodge. Abers 4G 73
Granton. Edin 2L 59
Grantown-on-Spey. High 3L 71
Grantshouse. Bord 3F 60
Grappenhall. Warr 1E 34
Grasby. Linc 7H 43
Grasmere. Cumb 5B 46
Grasscroft. G Man 7H 41
Grassendale. Mers 1B 34
Grassgarth. Cumb 7H 53
Grassholme. Dur 3H 47
Grassington. N Yor 1J 41
Grassmoor. Derbs 3B 36
Grassthorpe. Notts 3E 36
Grateley. Hants 1L 9
Gratton. Devn 4C 6
Gratton. Staf 4H 35
Gratwich. Staf 6J 35
Graveley. Cambs 5K 29
Graveley. Herts 1K 21
Gravelhill. Shrp 8C 34
Gravel Hole. G Man 7H 41
Gravelly Hill. W Mid 2K 27
Graven. Shet 6J 91
Graveney. Kent 7G 23
Gravesend. Kent 6C 22
Grayingham. Linc 8G 43
Grayrigg. Cumb 6D 46
Grays. Thur 6C 22
Grayshott. Hants 2F 10
Grayson Green. Cumb 2J 45
Grayswood. Surr 2G 11
Graythorp. Hart 3C 48
Grazeley. Wok 7D 20
Grealin. High 7G 77
Greasbrough. S Yor 8B 42
Greasby. Mers 1A 34
Great Abington. Cambs 7B 30
Great Addington. Nptn 4G 29
Great Alne. Warw 6K 27
Great Altcar. Lanc 7B 40
Great Amwell. Herts 2L 21
Great Asby. Cumb 4E 46
Great Ashfield. Suff 5F 30
Great Ayton. N Yor 4C 48
Great Baddow. Essx 3D 22
Great Bardfield. Essx 8C 30
Great Barford. Bed 6J 29
Great Barr. W Mid 2J 27
Great Barrington. Glos 2L 19
Great Barrow. Ches W 3C 34
Great Barton. Suff 5E 30
Great Barugh. N Yor 8E 48
Great Bavington. Nmbd 3C 54
Great Bealings. Suff 7J 31
Great Bedwyn. Wilts 7L 19
Great Bentley. Essx 1H 23
Great Billing. Nptn 5F 28
Great Bircham. Norf 6D 38
Great Blakenham. Suff 6H 31
Great Blencow. Cumb 8J 53
Great Bolas. Telf 7E 34
Great Bookham. Surr 8J 21
Great Bosullow. Corn 5H 3
Great Bourton. Oxon 7B 28
Great Bowden. Leics 3E 28
Great Bradley. Suff 6C 30
Great Braxted. Essx 2E 22
Great Bricett. Suff 6G 31
Great Brickhill. Buck 8G 29
Great Bridgeford. Staf 7G 35
Great Brington. Nptn 5D 28
Great Bromley. Essx 1G 23
Great Broughton. Cumb 8E 52
Great Broughton. N Yor 5C 48
Great Budworth. Ches W 2E 34
Great Burdon. Darl 4M 47
Great Burstead. Essx 4C 22
Great Busby. N Yor 5C 48
Great Canfield. Essx 2B 22
Great Carlton. Linc 1M 37
Great Casterton. Rut 1G 29
Great Chalfield. Wilts 7G 19
Great Chart. Kent 1F 12
Great Chatwell. Staf 8F 34
Great Chesterford. Essx 7B 30
Great Cheverell. Wilts 8H 19
Great Chilton. Dur 8F 54
Great Chishill. Cambs 8M 29
Great Clacton. Essx 2H 23
Great Cliff. W Yor 6M 41
Great Clifton. Cumb 2K 45
Great Coates. NE Lin 6K 43
Great Comberton. Worc 7H 27
Great Corby. Cumb 6J 53
Great Cornard. Suff 7E 30
Great Cowden. E Yor 3K 43
Great Coxwell. Oxon 4L 19
Great Crakehall. N Yor 6L 47
Great Cransley. Nptn 4F 28
Great Cressingham. Norf 1E 30
Great Crosby. Mers 7B 40
Great Cubley. Derbs 6K 35
Great Dalby. Leics 8E 36
Great Doddington. Nptn 5F 28
Great Doward. Here 2D 18
Great Dunham. Norf 8E 38
Great Dunmow. Essx 1C 22
Great Durnford. Wilts 2K 9
Great Easton. Essx 1C 22
Great Easton. Leics 2F 28
Great Eccleston. Lanc 3C 40
Great Edstone. N Yor 7E 48
Great Ellingham. Norf 2G 31
Great Elm. Som 1F 8
Great Eppleton. Tyne 7G 55
Great Eversden. Cambs 6L 29
Great Fencote. N Yor 6L 47
Great Finborough. Suff 6G 31
Greatford. Linc 8H 37
Great Fransham. Norf 8E 38
Great Gaddesden. Herts 2H 21
Great Gate. Staf 5J 35
Great Gidding. Cambs 3J 29
Great Givendale. E Yor 2F 42
Great Glemham. Suff 5K 31
Great Glen. Leics 2D 28
Great Gonerby. Linc 6F 36
Great Gransden. Cambs 6K 29
Great Green. Norf 3J 31
Great Green. Suff
nr. Lavenham 6F 30
nr. Palgrave 4H 31
Great Habton. N Yor 8E 48
Great Hale. Linc 5J 37
Great Hallingbury. Essx 2B 22
Greatham. Hants 2E 10
Greatham. Hart 3B 48
Greatham. W Sus 4H 11
Great Hampden. Buck 3F 20
Great Harrowden. Nptn 4F 28
Great Harwood. Lanc 4F 40
Great Haseley. Oxon 3D 20
Great Hatfield. E Yor 3J 43
Great Haywood. Staf 7H 35
Great Heath. W Mid 3M 27
Great Heck. N Yor 5C 42
Great Henny. Essx 8E 30
Great Hinton. Wilts 8H 19
Great Hockham. Norf 2F 30
Great Holland. Essx 2J 23
Great Horkesley. Essx 8F 30
Great Hormead. Herts 8M 29
Great Horton. W Yor 4K 41
Great Horwood. Buck 8E 28
Great Houghton. Nptn 6E 28
Great Houghton. S Yor 7B 42
Great Hucklow. Derbs 2K 35
Great Kelk. E Yor 2J 43
Great Kendale. E Yor 1H 43
Great Kimble. Buck 3F 20
Great Kingshill. Buck 4F 20
Great Langdale. Cumb 5A 46
Great Langton. N Yor 6L 47
Great Leighs. Essx 2D 22
Great Limber. Linc 7J 43
Great Linford. Mil 7F 28
Great Livermere. Suff 4E 30
Great Longstone. Derbs 2L 35
Great Lumley. Dur 7F 54
Great Lyth. Shrp 1C 26
Great Malvern. Worc 7F 26
Great Maplestead. Essx 8E 30
Great Marton. Bkpl 4B 40
Great Massingham. Norf 7D 38
Great Melton. Norf 1H 31
Great Milton. Oxon 3D 20
Great Missenden. Buck 3F 20
Great Mitton. Lanc 4F 40
Great Mongeham. Kent 8K 23
Great Moulton. Norf 2H 31
Great Munden. Herts 1L 21
Great Musgrave. Cumb 4F 46
Great Ness. Shrp 8B 34
Great Notley. Essx 1D 22
Great Oak. Mon 3B 18
Great Oakley. Essx 1H 23
Great Oakley. Nptn 3F 28
Great Offley. Herts 1J 21
Great Ormside. Cumb 4F 46
Great Orton. Cumb 6H 53
Great Ouseburn. N Yor 1B 42
Great Oxendon. Nptn 3E 28
Great Oxney Green. Essx 3C 22
Great Parndon. Essx 3M 21
Great Paxton. Cambs 5K 29
Great Plumpton. Lanc 4B 40
Great Plumstead. Norf 8K 39
Great Ponton. Linc 6G 37
Great Potheridge. Devn 4E 6
Great Preston. W Yor 5B 42
Great Raveley. Cambs 3K 29
Great Rissington. Glos 2K 19
Great Rollright. Oxon 8M 27
Great Ryburgh. Norf 7F 38
Great Ryle. Nmbd 8H 61
Great Ryton. Shrp 1C 26
Great Saling. Essx 1D 22
Great Salkeld. Cumb 8K 53
Great Sampford. Essx 8C 30
Great Sankey. Warr 1D 34
Great Saredon. Staf 1H 27
Great Saxham. Suff 5D 30
Great Shefford. W Ber 6A 20
Great Shelford. Cambs 6A 30
Great Shoddesden. Hants 1L 9
Great Smeaton. N Yor 5M 47
Great Snoring. Norf 6F 38
Great Somerford. Wilts 5H 19
Great Stainton. Darl 3M 47
Great Stambridge. Essx 4E 22
Great Staughton. Cambs 5J 29
Great Steeping. Linc 3M 37
Great Stonar. Kent 8K 23
Greatstone-on-Sea. Kent 3G 13
Great Strickland. Cumb 3D 46
Great Stukeley. Cambs 4K 29
Great Sturton. Linc 2K 37
Great Sutton. Ches W 2B 34
Great Sutton. Shrp 3D 26
Great Swinburne. Nmbd 4C 54
Great Tew. Oxon 1A 20
Great Tey. Essx 1E 22
Great Thirkleby. N Yor 8B 48
Great Thorness. IOW 6B 10
Great Thurlow. Suff 6C 30
Great Torr. Devn 7J 5
Great Torrington. Devn 4D 6
Great Tosson. Nmbd 1D 54
Great Totham North. Essx 2E 22
Great Totham South. Essx 2E 22
Great Tows. Linc 8K 43
Great Urswick. Cumb 8A 46
Great Wakering. Essx 5F 22
Great Waldingfield. Suff 7F 30
Great Walsingham. Norf 6F 38
Great Waltham. Essx 2C 22
Great Warley. Essx 4B 22
Great Washbourne. Glos 8H 27
Great Wenham. Suff 8G 31
Great Whelnetham. Suff 6E 30
Great Whittington. Nmbd 4D 54
Great Wigborough. Essx 2F 22
Great Wilbraham. Cambs 6B 30
Great Wilne. Derbs 6B 36
Great Wishford. Wilts 2J 9
Great Witchingham. Norf 7H 39
Great Witcombe. Glos 2H 19
Great Witley. Worc 5F 26
Great Wolford. Warw 8L 27
Greatworth. Nptn 7C 28
Great Wratting. Suff 7C 30
Great Wymondley. Herts 1K 21
Great Wyrley. Staf 1H 27
Great Wytheford. Shrp 8D 34
Great Yarmouth. Norf 1M 31
Great Yeldham. Essx 8D 30
Grebby. Linc 3M 37
Greeba Castle. IOM 6C 44
Green, The. Cumb 6L 45
Green, The. Wilts 2G 9
Greenbank. Shet 3K 91
Greenbottom. Corn 4L 3
Greenburn. W Lot 3H 59
Greencastle. Ferm 4D 92
Greencroft. Dur 6E 54
Greendown. Som 8D 18
Greendykes. Nmbd 7H 61
Green End. Bed
nr. Bedford 7H 29
nr. Little Staughton 5J 29
Green End. Herts
nr. Buntingford 8L 29
nr. Stevenage 1L 21
Green End. N Yor 5F 48
Green End. Warw 3L 27
Greenfield. Arg 8G 65
Greenfield. C Beds 8H 29
Greenfield. Flin 3L 33
Greenfield. G Man 7H 41
Greenfield. Oxon 4E 20
Greenfoot. N Lan 3F 58
Greenford. G Lon 5J 21
Greengairs. N Lan 2F 58
Greengate. Norf 8G 39
Greengill. Cumb 8F 52
Greenhalgh. Lanc 4C 40
Greenham. Dors 5C 8
Greenham. Som 3K 7
Greenham. W Ber 7B 20
Green Hammerton. N Yor 2B 42
Greenhaugh. Nmbd 3A 54
Greenhead. Nmbd 5L 53
Green Heath. Staf 8H 35
Greenhill. Dum 4F 52
Greenhill. Falk 2G 59
Greenhill. Kent 7H 23
Greenhill. S Yor 1M 35
Greenhill. Worc 4G 27
Greenhills. N Ayr 4B 58
Greenhithe. Kent 6B 22
Greenholm. E Ayr 6D 58
Greenhow Hill. N Yor 1K 41
Greenigoe. Orkn 1F 86
Greenisland. ME Ant 4H 93
Greenland. High 5D 86
Greenland Mains. High 5D 86
Greenlands. Worc 5J 27
Green Lane. Shrp 7E 34
Green Lane. Worc 5J 27
Greenlaw. Bord 5E 60
Greenlea. Dum 4E 52
Greenloaning. Per 7B 66
Greenmount. G Man 6F 40
Greenmow. Shet 5E 90
Greenock. Inv 2A 58
Greenock Mains. E Ayr 7E 58
Greenodd. Cumb 7B 46
Green Ore. Som 8D 18
Greenrow. Cumb 6F 52
Greens. Abers 1H 73
Greensgate. Norf 8H 39
Greenside. Tyne 5E 54
Greensidehill. Nmbd 8G 61
Greens Norton. Nptn 7D 28
Greenstead Green. Essx 1E 22
Greensted Green. Essx 3B 22
Green Street. Herts 4J 21
Green Street. Suff 4H 31
Green Street Green. G Lon 7A 22
Green Street Green. Kent 6B 22
Greenstreet Green. Suff 7G 31
Green Tye. Herts 2M 21
Greenwall. Orkn 1G 87
Greenway. Pemb 3G 15
Greenway. V Glam 7K 17
Greenwell. Cumb 6K 53
Greenwich. G Lon 6L 21
Greet. Glos 8J 27
Greete. Shrp 4D 26
Greetham. Linc 2L 37
Greetham. Rut 8G 37
Greetland. W Yor 5J 41
Gregson Lane. Lanc 5D 40
Grein. W Isl 5C 74
Greinetobht. W Isl 6K 75
Greinton. Som 2C 8
Gremista. Shet 3E 90
Grenaby. IOM 7B 44
Grendon. Nptn 5F 28
Grendon. Warw 2L 27
Grendon Common. Warw 2L 27
Grendon Green. Here 6D 26
Grendon Underwood. Buck 1D 20
Grenofen. Devn 8D 6
Grenoside. S Yor 8M 41
Greosabhagh. W Isl 4C 76
Gresford. Wrex 4B 34
Gresham. Norf 6H 39
Greshornish. High 8E 76
Gressenhall. Norf 8F 38
Gressingham. Lanc 1D 40
Greta Bridge. Dur 4J 47
Gretna. Dum 5H 53
Gretna Green. Dum 5H 53
Gretton. Glos 8J 27
Gretton. Nptn 2G 29
Gretton. Shrp 2D 26
Grewelthorpe. N Yor 8L 47
Greyabbey. Ards 5J 93
Greygarth. N Yor 8K 47
Grey Green. N Lin 7E 42
Greylake. Som 2B 8
Greysouthen. Cumb 2K 45
Greysteel. Caus 2D 92
Greystoke. Cumb 8J 53
Greystoke Gill. Cumb 3C 46
Greystone. Ang 3J 67
Greystones. S Yor 1M 35
Greywell. Hants 8E 20
Griais. W Isl 7H 83
Grianan. W Isl 8H 83
Gribthorpe. E Yor 4E 42
Gribun. Arg 4K 63
Griff. Warw 3A 28
Griffithstown. Torf 4A 18
Griffydam. Leics 8B 36
Griggs Green. Hants 2F 10
Grimbister. Orkn 8C 88
Grimeford Village. Lanc 6E 40
Grimeston. Orkn 8C 88
Grimethorpe. S Yor 7B 42
Griminis. W Isl
on Benbecula 8J 75
on North Uist 6J 75
Grimister. Shet 4J 91
Grimley. Worc 5G 27
Grimness. Orkn 2F 86
Grimoldby. Linc 1L 37
Grimpo. Shrp 7B 34
Grimsargh. Lanc 4D 40
Grimsbury. Oxon 7B 28
Grimsby. NE Lin 7K 43
Grimscote. Nptn 6D 28
Grimscott. Corn 5B 6
Grimshaw. Bkbn 5F 40
Grimshaw Green. Lanc 6C 40
Grimsthorpe. Linc 7H 37
Grimston. E Yor 4K 43
Grimston. Leics 7D 36
Grimston. Norf 7D 38
Grimston. York 2D 42
Grimstone. Dors 6E 8
Grimstone End. Suff 5F 30
Grinacombe Moor. Devn 6D 6
Grindale. E Yor 8J 49
Grindhill. Devn 6D 6
Grindiscol. Shet 4E 90
Grindle. Shrp 1F 26
Grindleford. Derbs 2L 35
Grindleton. Lanc 3F 40
Grindley. Staf 7J 35
Grindley Brook. Shrp 5D 34
Grindlow. Derbs 2K 35
Grindon. Nmbd 5G 61
Grindon. Staf 4J 35
Gringley on the Hill. Notts 8E 42
Grinsdale. Cumb 6H 53
Grinshill. Shrp 7D 34
Grinton. N Yor 6J 47
Griomsidar. W Isl 1F 76
Grishipoll. Arg 2G 63
Grisling Common. E Sus 3M 11
Gristhorpe. N Yor 7H 49
Griston. Norf 2F 30
Gritley. Orkn 1G 87
Grittenham. Wilts 5J 19
Grittleton. Wilts 5G 19
Grizebeck. Cumb 6M 45
Grizedale. Cumb 6B 46
Grobister. Orkn 7F 88
Grobsness. Shet 1D 90
Groby. Leics 1C 28
Groes. Cnwy 4K 33
Groes. Neat 6G 17
Groes-faen. Rhon 6K 17
Groesffordd. Gwyn 7B 32
Groesffordd. Powy 2K 17
Groeslon. Gwyn 5D 32
Groes-lwyd. Powy 1M 25
Groes-wen. Cphy 6L 17
Grogport. Arg 5H 57
Groigearraidh. W Isl 1D 74
Gromford. Suff 6K 31
Gronant. Flin 2K 33
Groombridge. E Sus 2B 12
Groomsport. Ards 4J 93
Grosmont. Mon 1C 18
Grosmont. N Yor 5F 48
Groton. Suff 7F 30
Grove. Dors 8E 8
Grove, The. Dum 4D 52
Grove. Kent 7J 23
Grove. Notts 2E 36
Grove. Oxon 4A 20
Grove, The. Worc 7G 27
Grovehill. E Yor 4H 43
Grove Park. G Lon 6M 21
Grovesend. Swan 4E 16
Grub Street. Staf 7F 34
Grudie. High 7D 78
Gruids. High 3F 78
Gruinard House. High 4L 77
Gruinart. Arg 3B 56
Grulinbeg. Arg 3B 56
Gruline. Arg 3L 63
Grummore. High 8J 85
Grundisburgh. Suff 6J 31
Gruting. Shet 3C 90
Grutness. Shet 7E 90
Gualachulain. High 3F 64
Gualin House. High 6F 84
Guardbridge. Fife 6H 67
Guarlford. Worc 7G 27
Guay. Per 3D 66
Gubblecote. Herts 2G 21
Guestling Green. E Sus 4E 12
Guestling Thorn. E Sus 4E 12
Guestwick. Norf 7G 39
Guestwick Green. Norf 7G 39
Guide. Bkbn 5F 40
Guide Post. Nmbd 3F 54
Guilden Down. Shrp 3B 26
Guilden Morden. Cambs 7K 29
Guilden Sutton. Ches W 3C 34
Guildford. Surr 1G 11
Guildtown. Per 4E 66
Guilsborough. Nptn 4D 28
Guilsfield. Powy 1M 25
Guineaford. Devn 2E 6
Guisborough. Red C 4D 48
Guiseley. W Yor 3K 41
Guist. Norf 7F 38
Guiting Power. Glos 1J 19
Gulberwick. Shet 4E 90
Gulladuff. M Ulst 4F 93
Gullane. E Lot 1B 60
Gulling Green. Suff 6E 30
Gulval. Corn 5H 3
Gulworthy. Devn 8D 6
Gumfreston. Pemb 6H 15
Gumley. Leics 2D 28
Gunby. E Yor 4E 42
Gunby. Linc 7G 37
Gundleton. Hants 2D 10
Gun Green. Kent 2D 12
Gun Hill. E Sus 4B 12
Gunn. Devn 2F 6
Gunnerside. N Yor 6H 47
Gunnerton. Nmbd 4C 54
Gunness. N Lin 6F 42
Gunnislake. Corn 8D 6
Gunnista. Shet 3E 90
Gunsgreenhill. Bord 3G 61
Gunstone. Staf 1G 27
Gunthorpe. Norf 6G 39
Gunthorpe. N Lin 8F 42
Gunthorpe. Notts 5D 36
Gunthorpe. Pet 1J 29
Gunville. IOW 7B 10
Gupworthy. Som 2J 7
Gurnard. IOW 6B 10
Gurney Slade. Som 1E 8
Gurnos. Powy 4G 17
Gussage All Saints. Dors 4J 9
Gussage St Andrew. Dors 4H 9
Gussage St Michael. Dors 4H 9
Guston. Kent 1K 13
Gutcher. Shet 4K 91
Guthram Gowt. Linc 7J 37
Guthrie. Ang 2J 67
Guyhirn. Cambs 1M 29
Guyhirn Gull. Cambs 1L 29
Guy's Head. Linc 7A 38
Guy's Marsh. Dors 3G 9
Guyzance. Nmbd 1F 54
Gwaelod-y-garth. Card 6L 17
Gwaenynog Bach. Den 4K 33
Gwaenysgor. Flin 2K 33

Gwalchmai—Hill Top

Gwalchmai. IOA 3C 32
Gwastad. Pemb 4G 15
Gwaun-Cae-Gurwen. Neat 3G 17
Gwbert. Cdgn 2H 15
Gweek. Corn 6L 3
Gwehelog. Mon 3B 18
Gwenddwr. Powy 8K 25
Gwennap. Corn 4L 3
Gwenter. Corn 7L 3
Gwernaffield. Flin 4M 33
Gwernesney. Mon 3C 18
Gwernogle. Carm 3M 15
Gwern-y-go. Powy 3M 25
Gwernymynydd. Flin 4M 33
Gwersyllt. Wrex 4B 34
Gwespyr. Flin 2L 33
Gwinear. Corn 5J 3
Gwithian. Corn 4J 3
Gwredog. IOA 2D 32
Gwyddelwern. Den 6K 33
Gwyddgrug. Carm 3L 15
Gwynfryn. Wrex 4A 34
Gwystre. Powy 6K 25
Gwytherin. Cnwy 4H 33
Gyfelia. Wrex 5B 34
Gyffin. Cnwy 3G 33

H

Haa of Houlland. Shet 3K 91
Habberley. Shrp 1C 26
Habblesthorpe. Notts 1E 36
Habergham. Lanc 4G 41
Habin. W Sus 3F 10
Habrough. NE Lin 6J 43
Haceby. Linc 6H 37
Hacheston. Suff 6K 31
Hackenthorpe. S Yor 1B 36
Hackford. Norf 1G 31
Hackforth. N Yor 5L 47
Hackland. Orkn 7C 88
Hackleton. Nptn 6F 28
Hackman's Gate. Worc 4G 27
Hackness. N Yor 6G 49
Hackness. Orkn 2E 86
Hackney. G Lon 5L 21
Hackthorn. Linc 1G 37
Hackthorpe. Cumb 3D 46
Haclait. W Isl 1E 74
Haconby. Linc 7J 37
Hadden. Bord 6E 60
Haddenham. Buck 3E 20
Haddenham. Cambs 4A 30
Haddenham End Field.
Cambs 4A 30
Haddington. E Lot 2C 60
Haddington. Linc 3G 37
Haddiscoe. Norf 2L 31
Haddo. Abers 2H 73
Haddon. Cambs 2J 29
Hademore. Staf 1K 27
Hadfield. Derbs 8J 41
Hadham Cross. Herts 2M 21
Hadham Ford. Herts 1M 21
Hadleigh. Essx 5E 22
Hadleigh. Suff 7G 31
Hadleigh Heath. Suff 7F 30
Hadley. Telf 8E 34
Hadley. Worc 5G 27
Hadley End. Staf 7K 35
Hadley Wood. G Lon 4K 21
Hadlow. Kent 1C 12
Hadlow Down. E Sus 3B 12
Hadnall. Shrp 7D 34
Hadstock. Essx 7B 30
Hadston. Nmbd 1F 54
Hady. Derbs 2A 36
Hadzor. Worc 5H 27
Haffenden Quarter. Kent 1E 12
Haggate. Lanc 4G 41
Haggbeck. Cumb 4J 53
Haggersta. Shet 3D 90
Haggerston. Nmbd 5H 61
Haggrister. Shet 6H 91
Hagley. Here 7D 26
Hagley. Worc 3H 27
Hagnaby. Linc 3L 37
Hagworthingham. Linc 3L 37
Haigh. G Man 7E 40
Haigh Moor. W Yor 5L 41
Haighton Green. Lanc 4D 40
Haile. Cumb 4K 45
Hailes. Glos 8J 27
Hailey. Herts 2L 21
Hailey. Oxon 2A 20
Hailsham. E Sus 5B 12
Hail Weston. Cambs 5J 29
Hainault. G Lon 4A 22
Hainford. Norf 8J 39
Hainton. Linc 1J 37
Hainworth. W Yor 4J 41
Haisthorpe. E Yor 1J 43
Hakin. Pemb 6E 14
Halam. Notts 4D 36
Halbeath. Fife 1K 59
Halberton. Devn 4K 7
Halcro. High 5D 86
Hale. Cumb 8D 46
Hale. G Man 1F 34
Hale. Hal 1C 34
Hale. Hants 4K 9
Hale. Surr 1F 10
Hale Bank. Hal 1C 34
Halebarns. G Man 1F 34
Hales. Norf 2K 31
Hales. Staf 6F 34
Halesgate. Linc 7L 37
Hales Green. Derbs 5K 35
Halesowen. W Mid 3H 27
Hale Street. Kent 1C 12
Halesworth. Suff 4K 31
Halewood. Mers 1C 34
Halford. Shrp 3C 26
Halford. Warw 7L 27
Halfpenny. Cumb 7D 46
Halfpenny Furze. Carm 5J 15
Halfpenny Green. Staf 2G 27
Halfway. Carm
nr. Llandeilo 1F 16
nr. Llandovery 1H 17
Halfway. S Yor 1B 36
Halfway. W Ber 7B 20
Halfway House. Shrp 8B 34
Halfway Houses. Kent 6F 22
Halgabron. Corn 3C 4
Halifax. W Yor 5J 41
Halistra. High 8D 76
Halket. E Ayr 4C 58
Halkirk. High 6C 86
Halkyn. Flin 3M 33
Hall. E Ren 4C 58
Hallam Fields. Derbs 5B 36
Halland. E Sus 4B 12
Hallands, The. N Lin 5H 43
Hallaton. Leics 2E 28
Hallatrow. Bath 8E 18
Hallbank. Cumb 4E 46
Hallbankgate. Cumb 6K 53
Hall Dunnerdale. Cumb 5M 45
Hallen. S Glo 5D 18
Hall End. Bed 7H 29
Hallgarth. Dur 7A 54
Hall Green. Ches E 4G 35
Hall Green. Norf 3H 31
Hall Green. W Mid 3K 27
Hall Green. W Yor 6M 41
Hall Green. Wrex 5C 34
Halliburton. Bord 5D 60
Hallin. High 8D 76
Halling. Medw 7D 22
Hallington. Linc 1L 37
Hallington. Nmbd 4C 54
Halloughton. Notts 4D 36
Hallow. Worc 6G 27
Hallow Heath. Worc 6G 27
Hallowsgate. Ches W 3D 34
Hallsands. Devn 8L 5
Hall's Green. Herts 1K 21
Hallspill. Devn 3D 6
Hallthwaites. Cumb 6L 45
Hall Waberthwaite. Cumb 5L 45
Hallwood Green. Glos 8E 26
Hallworthy. Corn 7A 6
Hallyne. Bord 5K 59
Halmer End. Staf 5F 34
Halmond's Frome. Here 7E 26
Halmore. Glos 3E 18
Halnaker. W Sus 5G 11
Halsall. Lanc 6B 40
Halse. Nptn 7C 28
Halse. Som 3L 7
Halsetown. Corn 5J 3
Halsham. E Yor 5K 43
Halsinger. Devn 2E 6
Halstead. Essx 8E 30
Halstead. Kent 7A 22
Halstead. Leics 1E 28
Halstock. Dors 5D 8
Halsway. Som 2L 7
Haltcliff Bridge. Cumb 8H 53
Haltham. Linc 3K 37
Haltoft End. Linc 5L 37
Halton. Buck 3F 20
Halton. Hal 1D 34
Halton. Lanc 1D 40
Halton. Nmbd 5C 54
Halton. W Yor 4A 42
Halton. Wrex 6B 34
Halton East. N Yor 2J 41
Halton Fenside. Linc 3M 37
Halton Gill. N Yor 8G 47
Halton Holegate. Linc 3M 37
Halton Lea Gate. Nmbd 6L 53
Halton Moor. W Yor 4M 41
Halton Shields. Nmbd 5D 54
Halton West. N Yor 2G 41
Haltwhistle. Nmbd 5M 53
Halvergate. Norf 1L 31
Halwell. Devn 6K 5
Halwill. Devn 6D 6
Halwill Junction. Devn 6D 6
Ham. Devn 5M 7
Ham. Glos 4E 18
Ham. G Lon 6J 21
Ham. High 4D 86
Ham. Kent 8K 23
Ham. Plym 6G 5
Ham. Shet 4B 90
Ham. Som
nr. Ilminster 4A 8
nr. Taunton 3A 8
nr. Wellington 3L 7
Ham. Wilts 7M 19
Hambleden. Buck 5E 20
Hambledon. Hants 4D 10
Hambledon. Surr 2G 11
Hamble-le-Rice. Hants 5B 10
Hambleton. Lanc 3B 40
Hambleton. N Yor 4C 42
Hambridge. Som 3B 8
Hambrook. S Glo 6E 18
Hambrook. W Sus 5E 10
Ham Common. Dors 3G 9
Hameringham. Linc 3L 37
Hamerton. Cambs 4J 29
Ham Green. Here 7F 26
Ham Green. Kent 7E 22
Ham Green. N Som 6D 18
Ham Green. Worc 5J 27
Ham Hill. Kent 7C 22
Hamilton. Leic 1D 28
Hamilton. S Lan 4F 58
Hamiltonsbawn. Arm 6F 93
Hamister. Shet 1F 90
Hammer. W Sus 2F 10
Hammersmith. G Lon 6K 21
Hammerwich. Staf 1J 27
Hammerwood. E Sus 2M 11
Hammill. Kent 8J 23
Hammond Street. Herts 3L 21
Hammoon. Dors 4G 9
Hamnavoe. Shet
nr. Braehoulland 5G 91
nr. Burland 4D 90
nr. Lunna 6J 91
on Yell 5J 91
Hamp. Som 2B 8
Hampden Park. E Sus 5B 12
Hampen. Glos 2J 19
Hamperden End. Essx 8B 30
Hamperley. Shrp 3C 26
Hampnett. Glos 2K 19
Hampole. S Yor 6C 42
Hampreston. Dors 6J 9
Hampstead. G Lon 5K 21
Hampstead Norreys. W Ber 6C 20
Hampsthwaite. N Yor 2L 41
Hampton. Devn 6A 8
Hampton. G Lon 6J 21
Hampton. Kent 7H 23
Hampton. Shrp 3F 26
Hampton. Swin 4K 19
Hampton. Worc 7J 27
Hampton Bishop. Here 8D 26
Hampton Fields. Glos 4G 19
Hampton Hargate. Pet 2J 29
Hampton Heath. Ches W 5C 34
Hampton in Arden. W Mid 3L 27
Hampton Loade. Shrp 3F 26
Hampton Lovett. Worc 5G 27
Hampton Lucy. Warw 6L 27
Hampton Magna. Warw 5L 27
Hampton on the Hill. Warw 5L 27
Hampton Poyle. Oxon 2C 20
Hampton Wick. G Lon 7J 21
Hamptworth. Wilts 4L 9
Hamrow. Norf 7F 38
Hamsey. E Sus 4M 11
Hamsey Green. Surr 8L 21
Hamstall Ridware. Staf 8K 35
Hamstead. IOW 6B 10
Hamstead. W Mid 2J 27
Hamstead Marshall. W Ber 7B 20
Hamsterley. Dur
nr. Consett 6E 54
nr. Wolsingham 8E 54
Hamsterley Mill. Dur 6E 54
Hamstreet. Kent 2G 13
Ham Street. Som 2D 8
Hamworthy. Pool 6H 9
Hanbury. Staf 7K 35
Hanbury. Worc 5H 27
Hanbury Woodend. Staf 7K 35
Hanby. Linc 6H 37
Hanchurch. Staf 5G 35
Hand and Pen. Devn 6K 7
Handbridge. Ches W 3C 34
Handcross. W Sus 3K 11
Handforth. Ches E 1G 35
Handley. Ches W 4C 34
Handley. Derbs 3A 36
Handsacre. Staf 8J 35
Handsworth. S Yor 1B 36
Handsworth. W Mid 2J 27
Handy Cross. Buck 4F 20
Hanford. Dors 4G 9
Hanford. Stoke 5G 35
Hangersley. Hants 5K 9
Hanging Houghton. Nptn 4E 28
Hanging Langford. Wilts 2J 9
Hangleton. Brig 5K 11
Hangleton. W Sus 5H 11
Hanham. S Glo 6E 18
Hanham Green. S Glo 6E 18
Hankelow. Ches E 5E 34
Hankerton. Wilts 4H 19
Hankham. E Sus 5B 12
Hanley. Stoke 5G 35
Hanley Castle. Worc 7G 27
Hanley Childe. Worc 5E 26
Hanley Swan. Worc 7G 27
Hanley William. Worc 5E 26
Hanlith. N Yor 1H 41
Hanmer. Wrex 6C 34
Hannaborough. Devn 5E 6
Hannaford. Devn 3F 7
Hannah. Linc 2B 38
Hannington. Hants 8C 20
Hannington. Nptn 4F 28
Hannington. Swin 4K 19
Hannington Wick. Swin 4K 19
Hanscombe End. C Beds 8J 29
Hanslope. Mil 7F 28
Hanthorpe. Linc 7H 37
Hanwell. G Lon 5J 21
Hanwell. Oxon 7B 28
Hanwood. Shrp 1C 26
Hanworth. G Lon 6J 21
Hanworth. Norf 6H 39
Happas. Ang 3H 67
Happendon. S Lan 6G 59
Happisburgh. Norf 6K 39
Happisburgh Common. Norf 7K 39
Hapsford. Ches W 2C 34
Hapton. Lanc 4F 40
Hapton. Norf 2H 31
Harberton. Devn 6K 5
Harbertonford. Devn 6K 5
Harbledown. Kent 8H 23
Harborne. W Mid 3J 27
Harborough Magna. Warw 4B 28
Harbottle. Nmbd 1C 54
Harbourneford. Devn 5K 5
Harbours Hill. Worc 5H 27
Harbridge. Hants 4K 9
Harbury. Warw 5A 28
Harby. Leics 6E 36
Harby. Notts 2F 36
Harcombe. Devn 6L 7
Harcombe Bottom. Devn 6B 8
Harcourt. Corn 5M 3
Harden. W Yor 4J 41
Hardenhuish. Wilts 6H 19
Hardgate. Abers 5G 73
Hardgate. Dum 5C 52
Hardham. W Sus 4H 11
Hardingham. Norf 1G 31
Hardingstone. Nptn 6E 28
Hardings Wood. Staf 4G 35
Hardington. Som 8F 18
Hardington Mandeville. Som 4D 8
Hardington Marsh. Som 5D 8
Hardington Moor. Som 4D 8
Hardley. Hants 5B 10
Hardley Street. Norf 1K 31
Hardmead. Mil 7G 29
Hardraw. N Yor 6G 47
Hardstoft. Derbs 3B 36
Hardway. Hants 5D 10
Hardway. Som 2F 8
Hardwick. Buck 2F 20
Hardwick. Cambs 6L 29
Hardwick. Norf 3J 31
Hardwick. Nptn 5F 28
Hardwick. Oxon
nr. Bicester 1C 20
nr. Witney 3A 20
Hardwick. Shrp 2B 26
Hardwick. S Yor 1B 36
Hardwick. Stoc T 3B 48
Hardwick. W Mid 2J 27
Hardwicke. Glos
nr. Cheltenham 1H 19
nr. Gloucester 2F 18
Hardwicke. Here 7A 26
Hardwick Village. Notts 2D 36
Hardy's Green. Essx 1F 22
Hare. Som 4A 8
Hareby. Linc 3L 37
Hareden. Lanc 2E 40
Harefield. G Lon 4H 21
Hare Green. Essx 1G 23
Hare Hatch. Wok 6F 20
Harehill. Derbs 6K 35
Harehills. W Yor 4M 41
Harehope. Nmbd 7H 61
Harelaw. Dum 4J 53
Harelaw. Dur 6E 54
Hareplain. Kent 2E 12
Haresceugh. Cumb 7L 53
Harescombe. Glos 2G 19
Haresfield. Glos 2G 19
Haresfinch. Mers 8D 40
Hareshaw. N Lan 3G 59
Hare Street. Essx 3M 21
Hare Street. Herts 1L 21
Harewood. W Yor 3M 41
Harewood End. Here 1D 18
Harford. Devn 6J 5
Hargate. Norf 2H 31
Hargatewall. Derbs 2K 35
Hargrave. Ches W 3C 34
Hargrave. Nptn 4H 29
Hargrave. Suff 6D 30
Harker. Cumb 5H 53
Harkland. Shet 5J 91
Harkstead. Suff 8H 31
Harlaston. Staf 8L 35
Harlaxton. Linc 6F 36
Harlech. Gwyn 7E 32
Harlequin. Notts 6D 36
Harlescott. Shrp 8D 34
Harleston. Devn 7K 5
Harleston. Norf 3J 31
Harleston. Suff 5G 31
Harlestone. Nptn 5E 28
Harley. Shrp 1D 26
Harley. S Yor 8A 42
Harling Road. Norf 3F 30
Harlington. C Beds 8H 29
Harlington. G Lon 6H 21
Harlington. S Yor 7B 42
Harlosh. High 1D 68
Harlow. Essx 2M 21
Harlow Hill. Nmbd 5D 54
Harlsey Castle. N Yor 6B 48
Harlthorpe. E Yor 4E 42
Harlton. Cambs 6L 29
Harlyn Bay. Corn 4A 4
Harman's Cross. Dors 7H 9
Harmby. N Yor 7K 47
Harmer Green. Herts 2K 21
Harmer Hill. Shrp 7C 34
Harmondsworth. G Lon 6H 21
Harmston. Linc 3G 37
Harnage. Shrp 1D 26
Harnham. Nmbd 3D 54
Harnham. Wilts 3K 9
Harnhill. Glos 3J 19
Harold Hill. G Lon 4B 22
Haroldston West. Pemb 5E 14
Haroldswick. Shet 2L 91
Harold Wood. G Lon 4B 22
Harome. N Yor 7D 48
Harpenden. Herts 2J 21
Harpford. Devn 6L 7
Harpham. E Yor 1H 43
Harpley. Norf 7D 38
Harpley. Worc 5E 26
Harpole. Nptn 5E 28
Harpsdale. High 6C 86
Harpsden. Oxon 5E 20
Harpswell. Linc 1G 37
Harpurhey. G Man 7G 41
Harpur Hill. Derbs 2J 35
Harraby. Cumb 6J 53
Harracott. Devn 3E 6
Harrapool. High 3H 69
Harrapul. High 3H 69
Harrietfield. Per 5C 66
Harrietsham. Kent 8E 22
Harrington. Cumb 2J 45
Harrington. Linc 2L 37
Harrington. Nptn 3E 28
Harringworth. Nptn 2G 29
Harriseahead. Staf 4G 35
Harriston. Cumb 7F 52
Harrogate. N Yor 2M 41
Harrold. Bed 6G 29
Harrop Dale. G Man 7J 41
Harrow. G Lon 5J 21
Harrowbarrow. Corn 5F 4
Harrowden. Bed 7H 29
Harrowgate Hill. Darl 4L 47
Harrow on the Hill.
G Lon 5J 21
Harrow Weald. G Lon 4J 21
Harry Stoke. S Glo 6E 18
Harston. Cambs 6M 29
Harston. Leics 6F 36
Harswell. E Yor 3F 42
Hart. Hart 8H 55
Hartburn. Nmbd 3D 54
Hartburn. Stoc T 4B 48
Hartest. Suff 6E 30
Hartfield. E Sus 2A 12
Hartford. Cambs 4K 29
Hartford. Ches W 2E 34
Hartford. Som 3J 7
Hartford Bridge. Hants 8E 20
Hartford End. Essx 2C 22
Harthill. Ches W 4D 34
Harthill. N Lan 3H 59
Harthill. S Yor 1B 36
Hartington. Derbs 3K 35
Hartland. Devn 3B 6
Hartland Quay. Devn 3B 6
Hartle. Worc 4H 27
Hartlebury. Worc 4G 27
Hartlepool. Hart 8J 55
Hartley. Cumb 5F 46
Hartley. Kent
nr. Cranbrook 2D 12
nr. Dartford 7C 22
Hartley. Nmbd 4G 55
Hartley Green. Staf 7H 35
Hartley Mauditt. Hants 2E 10
Hartley Wespall. Hants 8D 20
Hartley Wintney. Hants 8E 20
Hartlip. Kent 7E 22
Hartmount Holdings. High 6H 79
Hartoft End. N Yor 6E 48
Harton. N Yor 1E 42
Harton. Shrp 3C 26
Harton. Tyne 5G 55
Hartpury. Glos 1G 19
Hartshead. W Yor 5K 41
Hartshill. Warw 2M 27
Hartshorne. Derbs 7M 35
Hartsop. Cumb 4C 46
Hart Station. Hart 8H 55
Hartswell. Som 3K 7
Hartwell. Nptn 6E 28
Hartwood. Lanc 6D 40
Hartwood. N Lan 4G 59
Harvel. Kent 7C 22
Harvington. Worc
nr. Evesham 7J 27
nr. Kidderminster 4G 27
Harwell. Oxon 5B 20
Harwich. Essx 8J 31
Harwood. Dur 8B 54
Harwood. G Man 6F 40
Harwood Dale. N Yor 6H 49
Harworth. Notts 8D 42
Hascombe. Surr 2G 11
Haselbech. Nptn 4E 28
Haselbury Plucknett. Som 4C 8
Haseley. Warw 5L 27
Hasfield. Glos 1G 19
Hasguard. Pemb 6E 14
Haskayne. Lanc 7B 40
Hasketon. Suff 6J 31
Hasland. Derbs 3A 36
Haslemere. Surr 2G 11
Haslingden. Lanc 5F 40
Haslingfield. Cambs 6M 29
Haslington. Ches E 4F 34
Hassall. Ches E 4F 34
Hassall Green. Ches E 4F 34
Hassell Street. Kent 1G 13
Hassendean. Bord 7C 60
Hassingham. Norf 1K 31
Hassness. Cumb 3L 45
Hassocks. W Sus 4L 11
Hassop. Derbs 2L 35
Haster. High 6E 86
Hasthorpe. Linc 3A 38
Hastigrow. High 5D 86
Hastingleigh. Kent 1G 13
Hastings. E Sus 5E 12
Hastingwood. Essx 3A 22
Hastoe. Herts 3G 21
Haston. Shrp 7D 34
Haswell. Dur 7G 55
Haswell Plough. Dur 7G 55
Hatch. C Beds 7J 29
Hatch Beauchamp. Som 3B 8
Hatch End. G Lon 4J 21
Hatch Green. Som 4B 8
Hatching Green. Herts 2J 21
Hatchmere. Ches W 2D 34
Hatch Warren. Hants 1D 10
Hatcliffe. NE Lin 7K 43
Hatfield. Here 6D 26
Hatfield. Herts 3K 21
Hatfield. S Yor 7D 42
Hatfield. Worc 6G 27
Hatfield Broad Oak. Essx 2B 22
Hatfield Garden Village.
Herts 3K 21
Hatfield Heath. Essx 2B 22
Hatfield Hyde. Herts 2K 21
Hatfield Peverel. Essx 2D 22
Hatfield Woodhouse. S Yor 7D 42
Hatford. Oxon 4M 19
Hatherden. Hants 8M 19
Hatherleigh. Devn 5E 6
Hathern. Leics 7B 36
Hatherop. Glos 3K 19
Hathersage. Derbs 1L 35
Hathersage Booths. Derbs 1L 35
Hatherton. Ches E 5E 34
Hatherton. Staf 8H 35
Hatley St George. Cambs 6K 29
Hatt. Corn 5F 4
Hattersley. G Man 8H 41
Hattingley. Hants 2D 10
Hatton. Abers 2K 73
Hatton. Derbs 6L 35
Hatton. G Lon 6H 21
Hatton. Linc 2J 37
Hatton. Shrp 2C 26
Hatton. Warr 1D 34
Hatton. Warw 5L 27
Hattoncrook. Abers 3H 73
Hatton Heath. Ches W 3C 34
Hatton of Fintray. Abers 4H 73
Haugh. E Ayr 7C 58
Haugh. Linc 2M 37
Haugham. Linc 1L 37
Haugh Head. Nmbd 7H 61
Haughley. Suff 5G 31
Haughley Green. Suff 5G 31
Haugh of Ballechin. Per 2C 66
Haugh of Glass. Mor 2D 72
Haugh of Urr. Dum 5C 52
Haughton. Ches E 4D 34
Haughton. Notts 2D 36
Haughton. Shrp
nr. Bridgnorth 2E 26
nr. Oswestry 7B 34
nr. Shifnal 1F 26
nr. Shrewsbury 8D 34
Haughton. Staf 7G 35
Haughton Green. G Man 8H 41
Haughton le Skerne. Darl 4M 47
Haultwick. Herts 1L 21
Haunn. Arg 3J 63
Haunn. W Isl 4D 74
Haunton. Staf 8L 35
Hauxton. Cambs 6M 29
Havannah. Ches E 3G 35
Havant. Hants 5E 10
Haven. Here 6C 26
Haven, The. W Sus 2H 11
Haven Bank. Linc 4K 37
Havenstreet. IOW 6C 10
Havercroft. W Yor 6A 42
Haverfordwest. Pemb 5F 14
Haverhill. Suff 7C 30
Haverigg. Cumb 7L 45
Havering-Atte-Bower.
G Lon 4B 22
Havering's Grove. Essx 4C 22
Haversham. Mil 7F 28
Haverthwaite. Cumb 7B 46
Haverton Hill. Stoc T 3B 48
Havyatt. Som 2D 8
Hawarden. Flin 3B 34
Hawbridge. Worc 7H 27
Hawcoat. Cumb 8M 45
Hawcross. Glos 8F 26
Hawen. Cdgn 2K 15
Hawes. N Yor 7G 47
Hawes Green. Norf 2J 31
Hawick. Bord 8C 60
Hawkchurch. Devn 5B 8
Hawkedon. Suff 6D 30
Hawkenbury. Kent 1E 12
Hawkeridge. Wilts 8G 19
Hawkerland. Devn 7L 7
Hawkesbury. S Glo 5F 18
Hawkesbury. Warw 3A 28
Hawkesbury Upton. S Glo 5F 18
Hawkes End. W Mid 3M 27
Hawk Green. G Man 1H 35
Hawkhurst. Kent 2D 12
Hawkhurst Common. E Sus 4B 12
Hawkinge. Kent 1J 13
Hawkley. Hants 3E 10
Hawkridge. Som 2H 7
Hawksdale. Cumb 7H 53
Hawkshaw. G Man 6F 40
Hawkshead. Cumb 6B 46
Hawkshead Hill. Cumb 6B 46
Hawkswick. N Yor 8H 47
Hawksworth. Notts 5E 36
Hawksworth. W Yor 3K 41
Hawkwell. Essx 4E 22
Hawley. Hants 8F 20
Hawley. Kent 6B 22
Hawling. Glos 1J 19
Hawnby. N Yor 7C 48
Haworth. W Yor 4J 41
Hawstead. Suff 6E 30
Hawthorn. Dur 7H 55
Hawthorn Hill. Brac 6F 20
Hawthorn Hill. Linc 4K 37
Hawthorpe. Linc 7H 37
Hawton. Notts 4E 36
Haxby. York 2D 42
Haxey. N Lin 8E 42
Haybridge. Shrp 4E 26
Haybridge. Som 1D 8
Haydock. Mers 8D 40
Haydon. Bath 8E 18
Haydon. Dors 4E 8
Haydon. Som 3A 8
Haydon Bridge. Nmbd 5B 54
Haydon Wick. Swin 5K 19
Haye. Corn 5F 4
Hayes. G Lon
nr. Bromley 7M 21
nr. Uxbridge 5H 21
Hayfield. Derbs 1J 35
Hay Green. Norf 8B 38
Hayhill. E Ayr 8C 58
Haylands. IOW 6C 10
Hayle. Corn 5J 3
Hayley Green. W Mid 3H 27
Hayling Island. Hants 6E 10
Hayne. Devn 5H 7
Haynes. C Beds 7H 29
Haynes West End. C Beds 7H 29
Hay-on-Wye. Powy 8M 25
Hayscastle. Pemb 4E 14
Hayscastle Cross. Pemb 4F 14
Hayshead. Ang 3K 67
Hay Street. Herts 1L 21
Hayton. Aber 5J 73
Hayton. Cumb
nr. Aspatria 7F 52
nr. Brampton 6K 53
Hayton. E Yor 3F 42
Hayton. Notts 1E 36
Hayton's Bent. Shrp 3D 26
Haytor Vale. Devn 8G 7
Haytown. Devn 4C 6
Haywards Heath. W Sus 3L 11
Haywood. S Lan 4H 59
Hazelbank. S Lan 5G 59
Hazelbury Bryan. Dors 5F 8
Hazeleigh. Essx 3E 22
Hazeley. Hants 8E 20
Hazel Grove. G Man 1H 35
Hazelhead. S Yor 7K 41
Hazelslade. Staf 8J 35
Hazel Street. Kent 2C 12
Hazelton Walls. Fife 5G 67
Hazelwood. Derbs 5M 35
Hazlemere. Buck 4F 20
Hazler. Shrp 2C 26
Hazlerigg. Tyne 4F 54
Hazles. Staf 5J 35
Hazleton. Glos 2J 19
Hazon. Nmbd 1E 54
Heacham. Norf 6C 38
Headbourne Worthy. Hants 2B 10
Headcorn. Kent 1E 12
Headingley. W Yor 4L 41
Headington. Oxon 3C 20
Headlam. Dur 4K 47
Headless Cross. Worc 5J 27
Headley. Hants
nr. Haslemere 2F 10
nr. Kingsclere 7C 20
Headley. Surr 8K 21
Headley Down. Hants 2F 10
Headley Heath. Worc 4J 27
Headley Park. Bris 7D 18
Head of Muir. Falk 1G 59
Headon. Notts 2E 36
Heads Nook. Cumb 6J 53
Heage. Derbs 4A 36
Healaugh. N Yor
nr. Grinton 6J 47
nr. York 3C 42
Heald Green. G Man 1G 35
Heale. Devn 1F 6
Healey. G Man 6G 41
Healey. Nmbd 6D 54
Healey. N Yor 7K 47
Healeyfield. Dur 7D 54
Healing. NE Lin 6K 43
Heamoor. Corn 5H 3
Heanish. Arg 3F 62
Heanor. Derbs 5B 36
Heanton Punchardon. Devn 2E 6
Heapham. Linc 1F 36
Heartsease. Powy 6L 25
Heasley Mill. Devn 2G 7
Heaste. High 4H 69
Heath. Derbs 3B 36
Heath, The. Norf
nr. Buxton 7J 39
nr. Fakenham 7F 38
nr. Hevingham 7H 39
Heath, The. Staf 6J 35
Heath, The. Suff 8H 31
Heath and Reach. C Beds 1G 21
Heath Common. W Sus 4J 11
Heathcote. Derbs 3K 35
Heath Cross. Devn 6G 7
Heathencote. Nptn 7E 28
Heath End. Hants 7C 20
Heath End. Leics 7A 36
Heath End. W Mid 1J 27
Heather. Leics 8A 36
Heatherfield. High 1F 68
Heatherton. Derb 6M 35
Heathfield. Cambs 7A 30
Heathfield. Cumb 7F 52
Heathfield. Devn 8H 7
Heathfield. E Sus 3B 12
Heathfield. Ren 3B 58
Heathfield. Som
nr. Lydeard St Lawrence 2L 7
nr. Norton Fitzwarren 3L 7
Heath Green. Worc 4J 27
Heathhall. Dum 4D 52
Heath Hayes. Staf 8J 35
Heath Hill. Shrp 8F 34
Heath House. Som 1C 8
Heathrow Airport. G Lon 6H 21
Heathstock. Devn 5M 7
Heathton. Shrp 2G 27
Heathtop. Derbs 6L 35
Heath Town. W Mid 2H 27
Heatley. Staf 7J 35
Heatley. Warr 1F 34
Heaton. Lanc 1C 40
Heaton. Staf 3H 35
Heaton. Tyne 5F 54
Heaton. W Yor 4K 41
Heaton Moor. G Man 8G 41
Heaton's Bridge. Lanc 6C 40
Heaverham. Kent 8B 22
Heavitree. Devn 6J 7
Hebburn. Tyne 5G 55
Hebden. N Yor 1J 41
Hebden Bridge. W Yor 5H 41
Hebden Green. Ches W 3E 34
Hebing End. Herts 1L 21
Hebron. Carm 4H 15
Hebron. Nmbd 3E 54
Heck. Dum 3E 52
Heckdyke. Notts 8E 42
Heckfield. Hants 7E 20
Heckfield Green. Suff 4H 31
Heckfordbridge. Essx 1F 22
Heckington. Linc 5J 37
Heckmondwike. W Yor 5L 41
Heddington. Wilts 7H 19
Heddle. Orkn 8C 88
Heddon. Devn 3F 6
Heddon-on-the-Wall. Nmbd 5E 54
Hedenham. Norf 2K 31
Hedge End. Hants 4B 10
Hedgerley. Buck 5G 21
Hedging. Som 3B 8
Hedley on the Hill. Nmbd 6D 54
Hednesford. Staf 8J 35
Hedon. E Yor 5J 43
Hegdon Hill. Here 6D 26
Heglibister. Shet 2D 90
Heighington. Darl 3L 47
Heighington. Linc 3H 37
Heightington. Worc 4F 26
Heights of Brae. High 7F 78
Heights of Fodderty. High 7F 78
Heights of Kinlochewe. High 7M 77
Heiton. Bord 6E 60
Hele. Devn
nr. Exeter 5J 7
nr. Holsworthy 6C 6
nr. Ilfracombe 1E 6
Hele. Torb 5M 5
Helen's Bay. Ards 4J 93
Helensburgh. Arg 1A 58
Helford. Corn 6L 3
Helhoughton. Norf 7E 38
Helions Bumpstead. Essx 7C 30
Helland. Corn 4C 4
Helland. Som 3B 8
Hellandbridge. Corn 4C 4
Hellesdon. Norf 8J 39
Hellesveor. Corn 4J 3
Hellidon. Nptn 6C 28
Hellifield. N Yor 2G 41
Hellingly. E Sus 4B 12
Hellington. Norf 1K 31
Hellister. Shet 3D 90
Helmdon. Nptn 7C 28
Helmingham. Suff 6H 31
Helmington Row. Dur 8E 54
Helmsdale. High 2L 79
Helmshore. Lanc 5F 40
Helmsley. N Yor 7D 48
Helperby. N Yor 1B 42
Helperthorpe. N Yor 8G 49
Helpringham. Linc 5J 37
Helpston. Pet 1J 29
Helsby. Ches W 2C 34
Helsey. Linc 2B 38
Helston. Corn 6K 3
Helstone. Corn 3C 4
Helton. Cumb 3D 46
Helwith. N Yor 5J 47
Helwith Bridge. N Yor 1G 41
Helygain. Flin 3M 33
Hem, The. Shrp 1F 26
Hemblington. Norf 8K 39
Hemel Hempstead. Herts 3H 21
Hemerdon. Devn 6H 5
Hemingbrough. N Yor 4D 42
Hemingby. Linc 2K 37
Hemingfield. S Yor 7A 42
Hemingford Abbots. Cambs 4K 29
Hemingford Grey. Cambs 4K 29
Hemingstone. Suff 6H 31
Hemington. Leics 7B 36
Hemington. Nptn 3H 29
Hemington. Som 8F 18
Hemley. Suff 7J 31
Hemlington. Midd 4B 48
Hempholme. E Yor 2H 43
Hempnall. Norf 2J 31
Hempnall Green. Norf 2J 31
Hempriggs. High 7E 86
Hemp's Green. Essx 1F 22
Hempstead. Essx 8C 30
Hempstead. Medw 7D 22
Hempstead. Norf
nr. Holt 6H 39
nr. Stalham 7L 39
Hempsted. Glos 2G 19
Hempton. Norf 7F 38
Hempton. Oxon 8B 28
Hemsby. Norf 8L 39
Hemswell. Linc 8G 43
Hemswell Cliff. Linc 1G 37
Hemsworth. Dors 5H 9
Hemsworth. W Yor 6B 42
Hemyock. Devn 4L 7
Henallt. Carm 4L 15
Henbury. Bris 6D 18
Henbury. Ches E 2G 35
Hendomen. Powy 3M 25
Hendon. G Lon 5K 21
Hendon. Tyne 6H 55
Hendra. Corn 6B 4
Hendre. B'end 6J 17
Hendreforgan. Rhon 6J 17
Hendy. Carm 4E 16
Heneglwys. IOA 3D 32
Henfeddau Fawr. Pemb 3J 15
Henfield. S Glo 6E 18
Henfield. W Sus 4K 11
Henford. Devn 6C 6
Hengoed. Cphy 5L 17
Hengoed. Shrp 6A 34
Hengrave. Suff 5E 30
Henham. Essx 1B 22
Heniarth. Powy 2L 25
Henlade. Som 3A 8
Henley. Dors 5E 8
Henley. Shrp
nr. Church Stretton 3C 26
nr. Ludlow 4D 26
Henley. Som 2C 8
Henley. Suff 6H 31
Henley. W Sus 3F 10
Henley Down. E Sus 4D 12
Henley-in-Arden. Warw 5K 27
Henley-on-Thames. Oxon 5E 20
Henley Street. Kent 7C 22
Henllan. Cdgn 2K 15
Henllan. Den 4K 33
Henllan. Mon 1A 18
Henllan Amgoed. Carm 5H 15
Henllys. Torf 4A 18
Henlow. C Beds 8J 29
Hennock. Devn 7H 7
Henny Street. Essx 8E 30
Henryd. Cnwy 3G 33
Henry's Moat. Pemb 4G 15
Hensall. N Yor 5C 42
Henshaw. Nmbd 5A 54
Hensingham. Cumb 3J 45
Henstead. Suff 3L 31
Hensting. Hants 3B 10
Henstridge. Som 4F 8
Henstridge Ash. Som 3F 8
Henstridge Bowden. Som 3E 8
Henstridge Marsh. Som 3F 8
Henton. Oxon 3E 20
Henton. Som 1C 8
Henwood. Corn 8B 6
Heogan. Shet 3E 90
Heolgerrig. Mer T 4K 17
Heol Senni. Powy 2J 17
Heol-y-Cyw. B'end 6J 17
Hepburn. Nmbd 7H 61
Hepple. Nmbd 1C 54
Hepscott. Nmbd 3F 54
Heptonstall. W Yor 5H 41
Hepworth. Suff 4F 30
Hepworth. W Yor 7K 41
Herbrandston. Pemb 6E 14
Hereford. Here 8D 26
Heribusta. High 6F 76
Heriot. Bord 4B 60
Hermiston. Edin 2K 59
Hermitage. Bord 2K 53
Hermitage. Dors 5E 8
Hermitage. W Ber 6C 20
Hermitage. W Sus 5E 10
Hermon. Carm
nr. Llandeilo 2F 16
nr. Newcastle Emlyn 3K 15
Hermon. IOA 4C 32
Hermon. Pemb 3J 15
Herne. Kent 7H 23
Herne Bay. Kent 7H 23
Herne Common. Kent 7H 23
Herne Pound. Kent 8C 22
Herner. Devn 3E 6
Hernhill. Kent 7G 23
Herodsfoot. Corn 5E 4
Heronden. Kent 8J 23
Herongate. Essx 4C 22
Heronsford. S Ayr 3G 51
Heronsgate. Herts 4H 21
Heron's Ghyll. E Sus 3A 12
Herra. Shet 4L 91
Herriard. Hants 1D 10
Herringfleet. Suff 2L 31
Herringswell. Suff 5D 30
Herrington. Tyne 6G 55
Hersden. Kent 7J 23
Hersham. Corn 5B 6
Hersham. Surr 7J 21
Herstmonceux. E Sus 4C 12
Herston. Dors 8J 9
Herston. Orkn 2F 86
Hertford. Herts 2L 21
Hertford Heath. Herts 2L 21
Hertingfordbury. Herts 2L 21
Hesketh. Lanc 5C 40
Hesketh Bank. Lanc 5C 40
Hesketh Lane. Lanc 3E 40
Hesket Newmarket. Cumb 8H 53
Heskin Green. Lanc 6D 40
Hesleden. Dur 8H 55
Hesleyside. Nmbd 3B 54
Heslington. York 2D 42
Hessay. York 2C 42
Hessenford. Corn 6F 4
Hessett. Suff 5F 30
Hessilhead. N Ayr 4B 58
Hessle. E Yor 5H 43
Hestaford. Shet 2C 90
Hest Bank. Lanc 1C 40
Hester's Way. Glos 1H 19
Hestinsetter. Shet 3C 90
Heston. G Lon 6J 21
Hestwall. Orkn 8B 88
Heswall. Mers 1A 34
Hethe. Oxon 1C 20
Hethelpit Cross. Glos 1F 18
Hethersett. Norf 1H 31
Hethersgill. Cumb 5J 53
Hetherside. Cumb 5J 53
Hethpool. Nmbd 7F 60
Hett. Dur 8F 54
Hetton. N Yor 2H 41
Hetton-le-Hole. Tyne 7G 55
Hetton Steads. Nmbd 6H 61
Heugh. Nmbd 4D 54
Heugh-head. Abers 4C 72
Heveningham. Suff 4K 31
Hever. Kent 1A 12
Heversham. Cumb 7C 46
Hevingham. Norf 7H 39
Hewas Water. Corn 7B 4
Hewelsfield. Glos 3D 18
Hewish. N Som 7C 18
Hewish. Som 5C 8
Hewood. Dors 5B 8
Heworth. York 2D 42
Hexham. Nmbd 5C 54
Hextable. Kent 6B 22
Hexton. Herts 8J 29
Hexworthy. Devn 8F 6
Heybridge. Essx
nr. Brentwood 4C 22
nr. Maldon 3E 22
Heybridge Basin. Essx 3E 22
Heybrook Bay. Devn 7G 5
Heydon. Cambs 7M 29
Heydon. Norf 7H 39
Heydour. Linc 6H 37
Heylipol. Arg 3E 62
Heyop. Powy 5M 25
Heysham. Lanc 1C 40
Heyshott. W Sus 4F 10
Heytesbury. Wilts 1H 9
Heythrop. Oxon 1A 20
Heywood. G Man 6G 41
Heywood. Wilts 8G 19
Hibaldstow. N Lin 7G 43
Hickleton. S Yor 7B 42
Hickling. Norf 7L 39
Hickling. Notts 7D 36
Hickling Green. Norf 7L 39
Hickling Heath. Norf 7L 39
Hickstead. W Sus 3K 11
Hidcote Bartrim. Glos 7K 27
Hidcote Boyce. Glos 7K 27
Higford. Shrp 1F 26
High Ackworth. W Yor 6B 42
Higham. Derbs 4A 36
Higham. Kent 6D 22
Higham. Lanc 4G 41
Higham. S Yor 7M 41
Higham. Suff
nr. Ipswich 8G 31
nr. Newmarket 5D 30
Higham Dykes. Nmbd 4E 54
Higham Ferrers. Nptn 5G 29
Higham Gobion. C Beds 8J 29
Higham on the Hill. Leics 2A 28
Highampton. Devn 5D 6
Higham Wood. Kent 1C 12
High Angerton. Nmbd 3D 54
High Auldgirth. Dum 3D 52
High Bankhill. Cumb 7K 53
High Banton. N Lan 1F 58
High Barnet. G Lon 4K 21
High Beech. Essx 4M 21
High Bentham. N Yor 1E 40
High Bickington. Devn 3F 6
High Biggins. Cumb 8D 46
High Birkwith. N Yor 8F 46
High Blantyre. S Lan 4E 58
High Bonnybridge. Falk 2G 59
High Borrans. Cumb 5C 46
High Bradfield. S Yor 8L 41
High Bray. Devn 2F 6
Highbridge. Cumb 7H 53
Highbridge. High 7C 70
Highbridge. Som 1B 8
Highbrook. W Sus 2L 11
High Brooms. Kent 1B 12
High Bullen. Devn 3E 6
Highburton. W Yor 6K 41
Highbury. Som 1E 8
High Buston. Nmbd 1F 54
High Callerton. Nmbd 4E 54
High Carlingill. Cumb 5E 46
High Catton. E Yor 2E 42
High Church. Nmbd 3E 54
Highclere. Hants 7B 20
Highcliffe. Dors 6L 9
High Cogges. Oxon 3A 20
High Common. Norf 1F 30
High Coniscliffe. Darl 4L 47
High Crosby. Cumb 6J 53
High Cross. Hants 3E 10
High Cross. Herts 2L 21
High Easter. Essx 2C 22
High Eggborough. N Yor 5C 42
High Ellington. N Yor 7K 47
Higher Alham. Som 1E 8
Higher Ansty. Dors 5F 8
Higher Ashton. Devn 7H 7
Higher Ballam. Lanc 4B 40
Higher Bartle. Lanc 4D 40
Higher Bockhampton. Dors 6F 8
Higher Bojewyan. Corn 5G 3
High Ercall. Telf 8D 34
Higher Cheriton. Devn 5L 7
Higher Clovelly. Devn 3C 6
Higher Compton. Plym 6G 5
Higher Dean. Devn 5K 5
Higher Dinting. Derbs 8J 41
Higher Dunstone. Devn 8G 7
Higher End. G Man 7D 40
Higherford. Lanc 3G 41
Higher Gabwell. Devn 5M 5
Higher Halstock Leigh. Dors 5D 8
Higher Heysham. Lanc 1C 40
Higher Hurdsfield. Ches E 2H 35
Higher Kingcombe. Dors 6D 8
Higher Kinnerton. Flin 3B 34
Higher Melcombe. Dors 5F 8
Higher Penwortham. Lanc 5D 40
Higher Porthpean. Corn 6C 4
Higher Poynton. Ches E 1H 35
Higher Shotton. Flin 3B 34
Higher Shurlach. Ches W 2E 34
Higher Slade. Devn 1E 6
Higher Tale. Devn 5K 7
Highertown. Corn 4M 3
Higher Town. IOS 1H 3
Higher Town. Som 1J 7
Higher Vexford. Som 2L 7
Higher Walton. Lanc 5D 40
Higher Walton. Warr 1D 34
Higher Whatcombe. Dors 5G 9
Higher Wheelton. Lanc 5E 40
Higher Whiteleigh. Corn 6B 6
Higher Whitley. Ches W 1E 34
Higher Wincham. Ches W 2E 34
Higher Wraxall. Dors 5D 8
Higher Wych. Ches W 5C 34
Higher Yalberton. Torb 6L 5
High Etherley. Dur 3K 47
High Ferry. Linc 5L 37
Highfield. E Yor 4E 42
Highfield. N Ayr 4B 58
Highfield. Tyne 6E 54
Highfields Caldecote.
Cambs 6L 29
High Gallowhill. E Dun 2E 58
High Garrett. Essx 1D 22
Highgate. G Lon 5K 21
Highgate. N Ayr 4B 58
Highgate. Powy 3L 25
High Grange. Dur 8E 54
High Green. Cumb 5C 46
High Green. Norf 1H 31
High Green. Shrp 3F 26
High Green. S Yor 8M 41
High Green. W Yor 6K 41
High Green. Worc 7G 27
Highgreen Manor. Nmbd 2B 54
High Halden. Kent 2E 12
High Halstow. Medw 6D 22
High Ham. Som 2C 8
High Harrington. Cumb 2K 45
High Haswell. Dur 7G 55
High Hatton. Shrp 7E 34
High Hawsker. N Yor 5G 49
High Hesket. Cumb 7J 53
High Hesleden. Dur 8H 55
High Hoyland. S Yor 6L 41
High Hunsley. E Yor 4G 43
High Hurstwood. E Sus 3A 12
High Hutton. N Yor 1E 42
High Ireby. Cumb 8G 53
High Keil. Arg 1B 50
High Kelling. Norf 6H 39
High Kilburn. N Yor 8C 48
High Knipe. Cumb 4D 46
High Lands. Dur 3K 47
Highlands, The. Shrp 3E 26
Highlane. Ches E 3G 35
Highlane. Derbs 1B 36
High Lane. G Man 1H 35
High Lane. Worc 5E 26
High Laver. Essx 3B 22
Highlaws. Cumb 7F 52
Highleadon. Glos 1F 18
High Legh. Ches E 1F 34
Highleigh. W Sus 6F 10
High Leven. Stoc T 4B 48
Highley. Shrp 3F 26
High Littleton. Bath 8E 18
High Longthwaite. Cumb 7G 53
High Lorton. Cumb 2L 45
High Marishes. N Yor 8F 48
High Marnham. Notts 2F 36
High Melton. S Yor 7C 42
High Mickley. Nmbd 5D 54
Highmoor. Cumb 7G 53
High Moor. Lanc 6D 40
Highmoor. Oxon 5E 20
Highmoor Cross. Oxon 5E 20
Highmoor Hill. Mon 5C 18
Highnam. Glos 2F 18
High Newport. Tyne 6G 55
High Newton. Cumb 7C 46
High Newton-by-the-Sea.
Nmbd 7K 61
High Nibthwaite. Cumb 7A 46
High Offley. Staf 7F 34
High Ongar. Essx 3B 22
High Onn. Staf 8G 35
High Orchard. Glos 2G 19
High Park. Mers 6B 40
High Roding. Essx 2C 22
High Row. Cumb 8H 53
High Salvington. W Sus 5J 11
High Scales. Cumb 7F 52
High Shaw. N Yor 6G 47
High Shincliffe. Dur 7F 54
High Side. Cumb 8G 53
High Spen. Tyne 5E 54
Highsted. Kent 7F 22
High Stoop. Dur 7E 54
High Street. Corn 6B 4
High Street. Suff
nr. Aldeburgh 6L 31
nr. Bungay 3K 31
nr. Yoxford 4L 31
Highstreet Green. Essx 8D 30
High Street Green. Suff 6G 31
Highstreet Green. Surr 2G 11
Hightae. Dum 4E 52
High Throston. Hart 8H 55
Hightown. Ches E 4G 35
Hightown. Mers 7A 40
High Town. Staf 8H 35
Hightown Green. Suff 6F 30
High Toynton. Linc 3K 37
High Trewhitt. Nmbd 1D 54
High Valleyfield. Fife 1J 59
Highway. Here 7C 26
Highweek. Devn 8H 7
High Westwood. Dur 6E 54
Highwood. Staf 6J 35
Highwood. Worc 5E 26
High Worsall. N Yor 5A 48
Highworth. Swin 4L 19
High Wray. Cumb 6B 46
High Wych. Herts 2A 22
High Wycombe. Buck 4F 20
Hilborough. Norf 1E 30
Hilcott. Wilts 8K 19
Hildenborough. Kent 1B 12
Hildersham. Cambs 7B 30
Hilderstone. Staf 6H 35
Hilderthorpe. E Yor 1J 43
Hilfield. Dors 5E 8
Hilgay. Norf 2C 30
Hill, The. Cumb 6L 45
Hill. S Glo 4E 18
Hill. Warw 5B 28
Hill. Worc 7H 27
Hillam. N Yor 5C 42
Hillbeck. Cumb 4F 46
Hillberry. IOM 7C 44
Hillborough. Kent 7J 23
Hillbourne. Pool 6J 9
Hillbrae. Abers
nr. Aberchirder 1F 72
nr. Inverurie 3G 73
nr. Methlick 2H 73
Hill Brow. Hants 3E 10
Hillbutts. Dors 5H 9
Hillclifflane. Derbs 5L 35
Hillcommon. Som 3L 7
Hill Deverill. Wilts 1G 9
Hilldyke. Linc 5L 37
Hill End. Dur 8D 54
Hill End. Fife 8D 66
Hillend. Fife 1K 59
Hillend. N Lan 3G 59
Hill End. N Yor 2J 41
Hillend. Shrp 2G 27
Hillend. Swan 7L 15
Hillersland. Glos 2D 18
Hillerton. Devn 6G 7
Hillesden. Buck 1D 20
Hillesley. Glos 5F 18
Hillfarrance. Som 3L 7
Hill Gate. Here 1C 18
Hill Green. Essx 8A 30
Hill Green. W Ber 6B 20
Hillhall. Lis 5H 93
Hillhead. Abers 2E 72
Hillhead. Devn 6M 5
Hill Head. Hants 5C 10
Hillhead. S Ayr 8C 58
Hillhead of Auchentumb.
Abers 8J 81
Hilliard's Cross. Staf 8K 35
Hilliclay. High 5C 86
Hillingdon. G Lon 5H 21
Hillington. Glas 3D 58
Hillington. Norf 7D 38
Hillmorton. Warw 4C 28
Hill of Beath. Fife 8E 66
Hill of Fearn. High 6J 79
Hill of Fiddes. Abers 3J 73
Hill of Keillor. Ang 3F 66
Hill of Overbrae. Abers 7H 81
Hill Ridware. Staf 8J 35
Hillsborough. Lis 6H 93
Hillsborough. S Yor 8M 41
Hillside. Abers 6J 73
Hillside. Ang 1L 67
Hillside. Devn 5K 5
Hillside. Mers 6B 40
Hillside. Orkn 7C 88
Hillside. Shet 1E 90
Hillside. Shrp 3E 26
Hill Side. W Yor 6K 41
Hillside. Worc 5F 26
Hillside of Prieston. Ang 4G 67
Hill Somersal. Derbs 6K 35
Hillstown. Derbs 3B 36
Hillstreet. Hants 4M 9
Hillswick. Shet 6G 91
Hill Top. Dur
nr. Barnard Castle 3H 47
nr. Durham 7F 54
nr. Stanley 6E 54

Hilltown—Key Green

Hilltown. *New M* 7H **93**
Hill View. *Dors* 6H **9**
Hillwell. *Shet* 6D **90**
Hill Wootton. *Warw* 5M **27**
Hillyland. *Per* 5D **66**
Hilmarton. *Wilts* 6J **19**
Hilperton. *Wilts* 8G **19**
Hilperton Marsh. *Wilts* 8G **19**
Hilsea. *Port* 5D **10**
Hilston. *E Yor* 4K **43**
Hiltingbury. *Hants* 3B **10**
Hilton. *Cambs* 5K **29**
Hilton. *Cumb* 3F **46**
Hilton. *Derbs* 6L **35**
Hilton. *Dors* 5F **8**
Hilton. *Dur* 3K **47**
Hilton. *High* 5H **79**
Hilton. *Shrp* 2F **26**
Hilton. *Staf* 1J **27**
Hilton. *Stoc T* 4B **48**
Hilton of Cadboll. *High* 6J **79**
Himbleton. *Worc* 6H **27**
Himley. *Staf* 2G **27**
Hincaster. *Cumb* 7D **46**
Hinchwick. *Glos* 1K **19**
Hinckley. *Leics* 2B **28**
Hinderclay. *Suff* 4G **31**
Hinderwell. *N Yor* 4E **48**
Hindford. *Shrp* 6B **34**
Hindhead. *Surr* 2F **10**
Hindley. *G Man* 7E **40**
Hindley. *Nmbd* 6D **54**
Hindley Green. *G Man* 7E **40**
Hindlip. *Worc* 6G **27**
Hindolveston. *Norf* 7G **39**
Hindon. *Wilts* 2H **9**
Hindringham. *Norf* 6F **38**
Hingham. *Norf* 1G **31**
Hinksford. *Staf* 3G **27**
Hinstock. *Shrp* 7E **34**
Hintlesham. *Suff* 7G **31**
Hinton. *Hants* 6L **9**
Hinton. *Here* 8B **26**
Hinton. *Nptn* 6C **28**
Hinton. *Shrp* 1C **26**
Hinton. *S Glo* 6F **18**
Hinton Ampner. *Hants* 3C **10**
Hinton Blewett. *Bath* 8D **18**
Hinton Charterhouse. *Bath* 8F **18**
Hinton-in-the-Hedges. *Nptn* 8C **28**
Hinton Martell. *Dors* 5J **9**
Hinton on the Green. *Worc* 7J **27**
Hinton Parva. *Swin* 5L **19**
Hinton St George. *Som* 4C **8**
Hinton St Mary. *Dors* 4F **8**
Hinton Waldrist. *Oxon* 4A **20**
Hints. *Shrp* 4E **26**
Hints. *Staf* 1K **27**
Hinwick. *Bed* 5G **29**
Hinxhill. *Kent* 1G **13**
Hinxton. *Cambs* 7A **30**
Hinxworth. *Herts* 7K **29**
Hipley. *Hants* 4D **10**
Hipperholme. *W Yor* 5K **41**
Hipsburn. *Nmbd* 8K **61**
Hipswell. *N Yor* 6K **47**
Hiraeth. *Carm* 4H **15**
Hirn. *Abers* 5G **73**
Hirnant. *Powy* 8K **33**
Hirst. *N Lan* 3G **59**
Hirst. *Nmbd* 3F **54**
Hirst Courtney. *N Yor* 5D **42**
Hirwaen. *Den* 4L **33**
Hirwaun. *Rhon* 4J **17**
Hiscott. *Devn* 3E **6**
Histon. *Cambs* 5M **29**
Hitcham. *Suff* 6F **30**
Hitchin. *Herts* 1J **21**
Hittisleigh. *Devn* 6G **7**
Hittisleigh Barton. *Devn* 6G **7**
Hive. *E Yor* 4F **42**
Hixon. *Staf* 7J **35**
Hoaden. *Kent* 8J **23**
Hoar Cross. *Staf* 7K **35**
Hoarwithy. *Here* 1D **18**
Hoath. *Kent* 7J **23**
Yr Hôb. *Flin* 4B **34**
Hobarris. *Shrp* 4B **26**
Hobbister. *Orkn* 1E **86**
Hobbles Green. *Suff* 6D **30**
Hobbs Cross. *Essx* 4A **22**
Hobkirk. *Bord* 8C **60**
Hobson. *Dur* 6E **54**
Hoby. *Leics* 8D **36**
Hockering. *Norf* 8G **39**
Hockering Heath. *Norf* 8G **39**
Hockerton. *Notts* 4E **36**
Hockley. *Essx* 4E **22**
Hockley. *Staf* 1L **27**
Hockley. *W Mid* 4L **27**
Hockley Heath. *W Mid* 4K **27**
Hockliffe. *C Beds* 1G **21**
Hockwold cum Wilton.
Norf 3D **30**
Hockworthy. *Devn* 4K **7**
Hoddesdon. *Herts* 3L **21**
Hoddlesden. *Bkbn* 5F **40**
Hoddomcross. *Dum* 4F **52**
Hodgeston. *Pemb* 7G **15**
Hodley. *Powy* 3L **25**
Hodnet. *Shrp* 7E **34**
Hodsoll Street. *Kent* 7C **22**
Hodson. *Swin* 5K **19**
Hodthorpe. *Derbs* 2C **36**
Hoe. *Norf* 8F **38**
Hoe, The. *Plym* 6G **5**
Hoe Gate. *Hants* 4D **10**
Hoff. *Cumb* 4E **46**
Hoffleet Stow. *Linc* 6K **37**
Hogaland. *Shet* 6H **91**
Hogben's Hill. *Kent* 8G **23**
Hoggard's Green. *Suff* 6E **30**
Hoggeston. *Buck* 1F **20**
Hoggrill's End. *Warw* 2L **27**
Hogha Gearraidh. *W Isl* 6J **75**
Hoghton. *Lanc* 5E **40**
Hoghton Bottoms. *Lanc* 5E **40**
Hognaston. *Derbs* 4L **35**
Hogsthorpe. *Linc* 2B **38**
Hogstock. *Dors* 5H **9**
Holbeach. *Linc* 7L **37**
Holbeach Bank. *Linc* 7L **37**
Holbeach Clough. *Linc* 7L **37**
Holbeach Drove. *Linc* 8L **37**
Holbeach Hurn. *Linc* 7L **37**
Holbeach St Johns. *Linc* 8L **37**
Holbeach St Marks. *Linc* 6L **37**
Holbeach St Matthew. *Linc* 6M **37**
Holbeck. *Notts* 2C **36**
Holbeck. *W Yor* 4L **41**
Holbeck Woodhouse. *Notts* 2C **36**
Holberrow Green. *Worc* 6J **27**
Holbeton. *Devn* 6J **5**
Holborn. *G Lon* 5L **21**
Holbrook. *Derbs* 5A **36**
Holbrook. *S Yor* 1B **36**
Holbrook. *Suff* 8H **31**
Holburn. *Nmbd* 6H **61**
Holbury. *Hants* 5B **10**
Holcombe. *Devn* 8J **7**
Holcombe. *G Man* 6F **40**
Holcombe. *Som* 1E **8**
Holcombe Brook. *G Man* 6F **40**
Holcombe Rogus. *Devn* 4K **7**
Holcot. *Nptn* 5E **28**
Holden. *Lanc* 3F **40**
Holdenby. *Nptn* 5D **28**
Holder's Green. *Essx* 1C **22**
Holdgate. *Shrp* 3D **26**
Holdingham. *Linc* 5H **37**
Holditch. *Dors* 5B **8**
Holemoor. *Devn* 5D **6**
Hole Street. *W Sus* 4J **11**
Holford. *Som* 1L **7**
Holker. *Cumb* 8B **46**
Holkham. *Norf* 5E **38**
Hollacombe. *Devn* 5C **6**
Holland. *Orkn*
on Papa Westray 4D **88**
on Stronsay 7F **88**
Holland Fen. *Linc* 5K **37**
Holland Lees. *Lanc* 7D **40**
Holland-on-Sea. *Essx* 2J **23**
Holland Park. *W Mid* 1J **27**
Hollandstoun. *Orkn* 4G **89**
Hollesley. *Suff* 7K **31**
Hollinfare. *Warr* 8E **40**
Hollingbourne. *Kent* 8E **22**
Hollingbury. *Brig* 5L **11**
Hollingdon. *Buck* 1F **20**
Hollingrove. *E Sus* 3C **12**
Hollington. *Derbs* 6L **35**
Hollington. *E Sus* 4D **12**
Hollington. *Staf* 6J **35**
Hollington Grove. *Derbs* 6L **35**
Hollingworth. *G Man* 8J **41**
Hollins. *Derbs* 2M **35**
Hollins. *G Man*
nr. Bury 7G **41**
nr. Middleton 7G **41**
Hollinsclough. *Staf* 3J **35**
Hollinswood. *Telf* 1F **26**
Hollinthorpe. *W Yor* 4A **42**
Hollinwood. *G Man* 7H **41**
Hollinwood. *Shrp* 6D **34**
Hollocombe. *Devn* 4F **6**
Holloway. *Derbs* 4M **35**
Hollowell. *Nptn* 4D **28**
Hollow Meadows. *S Yor* 1L **35**
Hollows. *Dum* 4H **53**
Hollybush. *Cphy* 4L **17**
Hollybush. *E Ayr* 8B **58**
Hollybush. *Worc* 8F **26**
Holly End. *Norf* 1A **30**
Holly Hill. *N Yor* 5K **47**
Hollyhurst. *Shrp* 5D **34**
Hollym. *E Yor* 5L **43**
Hollywood. *Worc* 4J **27**
Holmacott. *Devn* 3E **6**
Holmbridge. *W Yor* 7K **41**
Holmbury St Mary. *Surr* 1J **11**
Holmbush. *Corn* 6C **4**
Holmcroft. *Staf* 7H **35**
Holme. *Cambs* 3J **29**
Holme. *Cumb* 8D **46**
Holme. *N Lin* 7G **43**
Holme. *N Yor* 7A **48**
Holme. *Notts* 4F **36**
Holme. *W Yor* 7K **41**
Holmebridge. *Dors* 7G **9**
Holme Chapel. *Lanc* 5G **41**
Holme Hale. *Norf* 1E **30**
Holme Lacy. *Here* 8D **26**
Holme Marsh. *Here* 6B **26**
Holmend. *Dum* 1E **52**
Holme next the Sea. *Norf* 5D **38**
Holme-on-Spalding-Moor.
E Yor 4F **42**
Holme on the Wolds. *E Yor* 3G **43**
Holme Pierrepont. *Notts* 6D **36**
Holmer. *Here* 7D **26**
Holmer Green. *Buck* 4G **21**
Holmes. *Lanc* 6C **40**
Holme St Cuthbert. *Cumb* 7F **52**
Holmes Chapel. *Ches E* 3F **34**
Holmesfield. *Derbs* 2M **35**
Holmeswood. *Lanc* 6C **40**
Holmewood. *Derbs* 3B **36**
Holmfirth. *W Yor* 7K **41**
Holmhead. *E Ayr* 7D **58**
Holmisdale. *High* 1C **68**
Holm of Drumlanrig. *Dum* 2C **52**
Holmpton. *E Yor* 5L **43**
Holmrook. *Cumb* 5K **45**
Holmsgarth. *Shet* 3E **90**
Holmside. *Dur* 7F **54**
Holmwrangle. *Cumb* 7K **53**
Holne. *Devn* 5K **5**
Holsworthy. *Devn* 5C **6**
Holsworthy Beacon. *Devn* 5C **6**
Holt. *Dors* 5J **9**
Holt. *Norf* 6G **39**
Holt. *Wilts* 7G **19**
Holt. *Worc* 5G **27**
Holt. *Wrex* 4C **34**
Holtby. *York* 2D **42**
Holt End. *Hants* 2D **10**
Holt End. *Worc* 5J **27**
Holt Fleet. *Worc* 5G **27**
Holt Green. *Lanc* 7B **40**
Holt Heath. *Dors* 5J **9**
Holt Heath. *Worc* 5G **27**
Holton. *Oxon* 3C **20**
Holton. *Som* 3E **8**
Holton. *Suff* 4K **31**
Holton cum Beckering. *Linc* 1J **37**
Holton Heath. *Dors* 6H **9**
Holton le Clay. *Linc* 7K **43**
Holton le Moor. *Linc* 8H **43**
Holton St Mary. *Suff* 8G **31**
Holt Pound. *Hants* 1F **10**
Holtsmere End. *Herts* 2H **21**
Holtye. *E Sus* 2A **12**
Holwell. *Dors* 4F **8**
Holwell. *Herts* 8J **29**
Holwell. *Leics* 7E **36**
Holwell. *Oxon* 3L **19**
Holwell. *Som* 1F **8**
Holwick. *Dur* 3H **47**
Holworth. *Dors* 7F **8**
Holybourne. *Hants* 1E **10**
Holy City. *Devn* 5B **8**
Holy Cross. *Worc* 4H **27**
Holyfield. *Essx* 3L **21**
Holyhead. *IOA* 2B **32**
Holy Island. *Nmbd* 5J **61**
Holymoorside. *Derbs* 3M **35**
Holyport. *Wind* 6F **20**
Holystone. *Nmbd* 1C **54**
Holytown. *N Lan* 3F **58**
Holywell. *Cambs* 4L **29**
Holywell. *Corn* 3L **3**
Holywell. *Dors* 5D **8**
Holywell. *Flin* 3L **33**
Holywell. *Glos* 4F **18**
Holywell. *Nmbd* 4G **55**
Holywell. *Warw* 5K **27**
Holywell Green. *W Yor* 6J **41**
Holywell Lake. *Som* 3L **7**
Holywell Row. *Suff* 4D **30**
Holywood. *Ards* 5J **93**
Holywood. *Dum* 3D **52**
Homer. *Shrp* 1E **26**
Homer Green. *Mers* 7B **40**
Homersfield. *Suff* 3J **31**
Hom Green. *Here* 1D **18**
Homington. *Wilts* 3K **9**
Honeyborough. *Pemb* 6F **14**
Honeybourne. *Worc* 7K **27**
Honeychurch. *Devn* 5F **6**
Honeydon. *Bed* 6J **29**
Honey Hill. *Kent* 7H **23**
Honey Street. *Wilts* 7K **19**
Honey Tye. *Suff* 8F **30**
Honeywick. *C Beds* 1G **21**
Honiley. *Warw* 4L **27**
Honing. *Norf* 7K **39**
Honingham. *Norf* 8H **39**
Honington. *Linc* 5G **37**
Honington. *Suff* 4F **30**
Honington. *Warw* 7L **27**
Honiton. *Devn* 5L **7**
Honley. *W Yor* 6K **41**
Honnington. *Telf* 8F **34**
Hoo. *Suff* 6J **31**
Hoobrook. *Worc* 4G **27**
Hood Green. *S Yor* 7M **41**
Hooe. *E Sus* 5C **12**
Hooe. *Plym* 6H **5**
Hooe Common. *E Sus* 4C **12**
Hoo Green. *Ches E* 1F **34**
Hoohill. *Bkpl* 4B **40**
Hook. *Cambs* 2M **29**
Hook. *E Yor* 5E **42**
Hook. *G Lon* 7J **21**
Hook. *Hants*
nr. Basingstoke 8E **20**
nr. Fareham 5C **10**
Hook. *Pemb* 5F **14**
Hook. *Wilts* 5J **19**
Hook-a-Gate. *Shrp* 1C **26**
Hook Bank. *Worc* 7G **27**
Hooke. *Dors* 5D **8**
Hooker Gate. *Tyne* 6E **54**
Hookgate. *Staf* 6F **34**
Hook Green. *Kent*
nr. Lamberhurst 2C **12**
nr. Meopham 7C **22**
nr. Southfleet 6C **22**
Hook Norton. *Oxon* 8A **28**
Hook's Cross. *Herts* 1K **21**
Hook Street. *Glos* 4E **18**
Hookway. *Devn* 6H **7**
Hookwood. *Surr* 1K **11**
Hoole. *Ches W* 3C **34**
Hooley. *Surr* 8K **21**
Hooley Bridge. *G Man* 6G **41**
Hooley Brow. *G Man* 6G **41**
Hoo St Werburgh. *Medw* 6D **22**
Hooton. *Ches W* 2B **34**
Hooton Levitt. *S Yor* 8C **42**
Hooton Pagnell. *S Yor* 7B **42**
Hooton Roberts. *S Yor* 8B **42**
Hoove. *Shet* 3D **90**
Hope. *Derbs* 1K **35**
Hope. *Flin* 4B **34**
Hope. *High* 5G **85**
Hope. *Powy* 1A **26**
Hope. *Shrp* 1B **26**
Hope. *Staf* 4K **35**
Hope Bagot. *Shrp* 4D **26**
Hope Bowdler. *Shrp* 2C **26**
Hopedale. *Staf* 4K **35**
Hope Green. *Ches E* 1H **35**
Hopeman. *Mor* 7M **79**
Hope Mansell. *Here* 2E **18**
Hopesay. *Shrp* 3B **26**
Hope's Green. *Essx* 5D **22**
Hopetown. *W Yor* 5A **42**
Hope under Dinmore. *Here* 6D **26**
Hopley's Green. *Here* 6B **26**
Hopperton. *N Yor* 2B **42**
Hop Pole. *Linc* 8J **37**
Hopstone. *Shrp* 2F **26**
Hopton. *Derbs* 4L **35**
Hopton. *Powy* 3M **25**
Hopton. *Shrp*
nr. Oswestry 7B **34**
nr. Wem 7D **34**
Hopton. *Staf* 7H **35**
Hopton. *Suff* 4F **30**
Hopton Cangeford. *Shrp* 3D **26**
Hopton Castle. *Shrp* 4B **26**
Hoptonheath. *Shrp* 4B **26**
Hopton Heath. *Staf* 7H **35**
Hopton on Sea. *Norf* 1M **31**
Hopton Wafers. *Shrp* 4E **26**
Hopwas. *Staf* 1K **27**
Hopwood. *Worc* 4J **27**
Horam. *E Sus* 4B **12**
Horbling. *Linc* 6J **37**
Horbury. *W Yor* 6L **41**
Horcott. *Glos* 3K **19**
Horden. *Dur* 7H **55**
Horderley. *Shrp* 3C **26**
Hordle. *Hants* 6L **9**
Hordley. *Shrp* 6B **34**
Horeb. *Carm*
nr. Brechfa 4M **15**
nr. Llanelli 6L **15**
Horeb. *Cdgn* 2K **15**
Horfield. *Bris* 6D **18**
Horgabost. *W Isl* 4B **76**
Horham. *Suff* 4J **31**
Horkstow. *N Lin* 6G **43**
Horley. *Oxon* 7B **28**
Horley. *Surr* 1K **11**
Horn Ash. *Dors* 5B **8**
Hornblotton Green. *Som* 2D **8**
Hornby. *Lanc* 1D **40**
Hornby. *N Yor*
nr. Appleton Wiske 5A **48**
nr. Catterick Garrison 6L **47**
Horncastle. *Linc* 3K **37**
Hornchurch. *G Lon* 5B **22**
Horncliffe. *Nmbd* 5G **61**
Horndean. *Hants* 4E **10**
Horndean. *Bord* 5F **60**
Horndon. *Devn* 7E **6**
Horndon on the Hill. *Thur* 5C **22**
Horne. *Surr* 1L **11**
Horner. *Som* 1J **7**
Horning. *Norf* 8K **39**
Horninghold. *Leics* 2F **28**
Horninglow. *Staf* 7L **35**
Horningsea. *Cambs* 5A **30**
Horningsham. *Wilts* 1G **9**
Horningtoft. *Norf* 7F **38**
Hornsbury. *Som* 4B **8**
Hornsby. *Cumb* 6K **53**
Hornsbygate. *Cumb* 6K **53**
Horns Corner. *Kent* 3D **12**
Horns Cross. *Devn* 3C **6**
Hornsea. *E Yor* 3K **43**
Hornsea Burton. *E Yor* 3K **43**
Hornsey. *G Lon* 5L **21**
Hornton. *Oxon* 7A **28**
Horpit. *Swin* 5L **19**
Horrabridge. *Devn* 5H **5**
Horringer. *Suff* 5E **30**
Horringford. *IOW* 7C **10**
Horrocks Fold. *G Man* 6F **40**
Horrocksford. *Lanc* 3F **40**
Horsbrugh Ford. *Bord* 6L **59**
Horsebridge. *Devn* 8D **6**
Horsebridge. *Hants* 2M **9**
Horsebrook. *Staf* 8G **35**
Horsecastle. *N Som* 7C **18**
Horsehay. *Telf* 1E **26**
Horseheath. *Cambs* 7C **30**
Horsehouse. *N Yor* 7J **47**
Horsell. *Surr* 8G **21**
Horseman's Green. *Wrex* 5C **34**
Horsenden. *Buck* 3E **20**
Horseway. *Cambs* 3M **29**
Horsey. *Norf* 7L **39**
Horsey. *Som* 2B **8**
Horsford. *Norf* 8H **39**
Horsforth. *W Yor* 4L **41**
Horsham. *W Sus* 2J **11**
Horsham. *Worc* 6F **26**
Horsham St Faith. *Norf* 8J **39**
Horsington. *Linc* 3J **37**
Horsington. *Som* 3F **8**
Horsley. *Derbs* 5A **36**
Horsley. *Glos* 4G **19**
Horsley. *Nmbd*
nr. Prudhoe 5D **54**
nr. Rochester 2B **54**
Horsley Cross. *Essx* 1H **23**
Horsleycross Street. *Essx* 1H **23**
Horsleyhill. *Bord* 8C **60**
Horsleyhope. *Dur* 7D **54**
Horsley Woodhouse. *Derbs* 5A **36**
Horsmonden. *Kent* 1C **12**
Horspath. *Oxon* 3C **20**
Horstead. *Norf* 8J **39**
Horsted Keynes. *W Sus* 3L **11**
Horton. *Buck* 2G **21**
Horton. *Dors* 5J **9**
Horton. *Lanc* 2G **41**
Horton. *Nptn* 6F **28**
Horton. *Shrp* 6C **34**
Horton. *Som* 4B **8**
Horton. *S Glo* 5F **18**
Horton. *Staf* 4H **35**
Horton. *Swan* 8L **15**
Horton. *Wilts* 7J **19**
Horton. *Wind* 6H **21**
Horton Cross. *Som* 4B **8**
Horton-cum-Studley. *Oxon* 2C **20**
Horton Grange. *Nmbd* 4F **54**
Horton Green. *Ches W* 5C **34**
Horton Heath. *Hants* 4B **10**
Horton in Ribblesdale.
N Yor 8G **47**
Horton Kirby. *Kent* 7B **22**
Hortonwood. *Telf* 8E **34**
Horwich. *G Man* 6E **40**
Horwich End. *Derbs* 1J **35**
Horwood. *Devn* 3E **6**
Hoscar. *Lanc* 6C **40**
Hose. *Leics* 7E **36**
Hosh. *Per* 5B **66**
Hosta. *W Isl* 6J **75**
Hoswick. *Shet* 5E **90**
Hotham. *E Yor* 4F **42**
Hothfield. *Kent* 1F **12**
Hoton. *Leics* 7C **36**
Houbie. *Shet* 4L **91**
Hough. *Arg* 3E **62**
Hough. *Ches E*
nr. Crewe 4F **34**
nr. Wilmslow 2G **35**
Hougham. *Linc* 5F **36**
Hough Green. *Hal* 1C **34**
Hough-on-the-Hill. *Linc* 5G **37**
Houghton. *Cambs* 4K **29**
Houghton. *Cumb* 6J **53**
Houghton. *Hants* 2M **9**
Houghton. *Nmbd* 5E **54**
Houghton. *Pemb* 6F **14**
Houghton. *W Sus* 4H **11**
Houghton Bank. *Darl* 3L **47**
Houghton Conquest.
C Beds 7H **29**
Houghton Green. *E Sus* 3F **12**
Houghton-le-Side. *Darl* 3L **47**
Houghton-le-Spring. *Tyne* 6G **55**
Houghton on the Hill. *Leics* 1D **28**
Houghton Regis. *C Beds* 1H **21**
Houghton St Giles. *Norf* 6F **38**
Houlland. *Shet*
on Mainland 2D **90**
on Yell 6K **91**
Houlsyke. *N Yor* 5E **48**
Hound. *Hants* 5B **10**
Hound Green. *Hants* 8E **20**
Houndslow. *Bord* 5D **60**
Houndsmoor. *Som* 3L **7**
Houndwood. *Bord* 3F **60**
Hounsdown. *Hants* 4M **9**
Hounslow. *G Lon* 6J **21**
Housabister. *Shet* 2E **90**
Housay. *Shet* 6L **91**
Househill. *High* 8J **79**
Housetter. *Shet* 5H **91**
Houss. *Shet* 4D **90**
Houston. *Ren* 3C **58**
Housty. *High* 8C **86**
Houton. *Orkn* 1E **86**
Hove. *Brig* 5K **11**
Hoveringham. *Notts* 5D **36**
Hoveton. *Norf* 8K **39**
Hovingham. *N Yor* 8D **48**
How. *Cumb* 6K **53**
How Caple. *Here* 8E **26**
Howden. *E Yor* 5E **42**
Howden-le-Wear. *Dur* 8E **54**
Howe, The. *Cumb* 7C **46**
Howe. *High* 5E **86**
Howe, The. *IOM* 8A **44**
Howe. *Norf* 1J **31**
Howe. *N Yor* 7A **48**
Howe Green. *Essx* 3D **22**
Howegreen. *Essx* 3E **22**
Howe Green. *Warw* 3M **27**
Howell. *Linc* 5J **37**
How End. *C Beds* 7H **29**
Howe of Teuchar. *Abers* 1G **73**
Howes. *Dum* 5F **52**
Howe Street. *Essx*
nr. Chelmsford 2C **22**
nr. Finchingfield 8C **30**
Howey. *Powy* 7K **25**
Howgate. *Midl* 4L **59**
Howgill. *Lanc* 3G **41**
Howgill. *N Yor* 2J **41**
How Green. *Kent* 1A **12**
How Hill. *Norf* 8K **39**
Howick. *Nmbd* 8K **61**
Howle. *Telf* 7E **34**
Howle Hill. *Here* 1E **18**
Howleigh. *Som* 4M **7**
Howlett End. *Essx* 8B **30**
Howley. *Som* 5A **8**
Howley. *Warr* 1E **34**
Hownam. *Bord* 8E **60**
Howsham. *N Lin* 7H **43**
Howsham. *N Yor* 1E **42**
Howtel. *Nmbd* 6F **60**
Howt Green. *Kent* 7E **22**
Howton. *Here* 1C **18**
Howwood. *Ren* 3B **58**
Hoxne. *Suff* 4H **31**
Hoylake. *Mers* 2M **33**
Hoyland. *S Yor* 7A **42**
Hoylandswaine. *S Yor* 7L **41**
Hoyle. *W Sus* 4G **11**
Hubberholme. *N Yor* 8H **47**
Hubberston. *Pemb* 6E **14**
Hubbert's Bridge. *Linc* 5K **37**
Huby. *N Yor*
nr. Harrogate 3L **41**
nr. York 1C **42**
Hucclecote. *Glos* 2G **19**
Hucking. *Kent* 8E **22**
Hucknall. *Notts* 5C **36**
Huddersfield. *W Yor* 6K **41**
Huddington. *Worc* 6H **27**
Huddlesford. *Staf* 1K **27**
Hudswell. *N Yor* 5K **47**
Huggate. *E Yor* 2F **42**
Hugglescote. *Leics* 8B **36**
Hughenden Valley. *Buck* 4F **20**
Hughley. *Shrp* 2D **26**
Hughton. *High* 1E **70**
Hugh Town. *IOS* 1H **3**
Hugus. *Corn* 4L **3**
Huish. *Devn* 4E **6**
Huish. *Wilts* 7K **19**
Huish Champflower. *Som* 3K **7**
Huish Episcopi. *Som* 3C **8**
Huisinis. *W Isl* 2A **76**
Hulcote. *Nptn* 7E **28**
Hulcott. *Buck* 2F **20**
Hulham. *Devn* 7K **7**
Hull. *Hull* 5J **43**
Hulland. *Derbs* 5L **35**
Hulland Moss. *Derbs* 5L **35**
Hulland Ward. *Derbs* 5L **35**
Hullavington. *Wilts* 5G **19**
Hullbridge. *Essx* 4E **22**
Hulme. *G Man* 8G **41**
Hulme. *Staf* 5H **35**
Hulme End. *Staf* 4K **35**
Hulme Walfield. *Ches E* 3G **35**
Hulverstone. *IOW* 7A **10**
Hulver Street. *Suff* 3L **31**
Humber. *Devn* 8J **7**
Humber. *Here* 6D **26**
Humber Bridge. *N Lin* 5H **43**
Humberside Airport. *N Lin* 6H **43**
Humberston. *NE Lin* 7L **43**
Humberstone. *Leic* 1D **28**
Humbie. *E Lot* 3B **60**
Humbleton. *E Yor* 4K **43**
Humbleton. *Nmbd* 7G **61**
Humby. *Linc* 6H **37**
Hume. *Bord* 5E **60**
Humshaugh. *Nmbd* 4C **54**
Huna. *High* 4E **86**
Huncoat. *Lanc* 4F **40**
Huncote. *Leics* 2C **28**
Hundall. *Derbs* 2A **36**
Hunderthwaite. *Dur* 3H **47**
Hundleby. *Linc* 3L **37**
Hundle Houses. *Linc* 4K **37**
Hundleton. *Pemb* 6F **14**
Hundon. *Suff* 7D **30**
Hundred, The. *Here* 5D **26**
Hundred Acres. *Hants* 4C **10**
Hundred House. *Powy* 7L **25**
Hungarton. *Leics* 1D **28**
Hungerford. *Hants* 4K **9**
Hungerford. *Shrp* 3D **26**
Hungerford. *Som* 1K **7**
Hungerford. *W Ber* 7M **19**
Hungerford Newtown.
W Ber 6A **20**
Hunger Hill. *G Man* 7E **40**
Hungerton. *Linc* 6F **36**
Hungladder. *High* 6E **76**
Hungryhatton. *Shrp* 7E **34**
Hunmanby. *N Yor* 8H **49**
Hunmanby Sands. *N Yor* 8J **49**
Hunningham. *Warw* 5A **28**
Hunnington. *Worc* 3H **27**
Hunny Hill. *IOW* 7B **10**
Hunsdon. *Herts* 2M **21**
Hunsdonbury. *Herts* 2M **21**
Hunsingore. *N Yor* 2B **42**
Hunslet. *W Yor* 4M **41**
Hunslet Carr. *W Yor* 4M **41**
Hunsonby. *Cumb* 8K **53**
Hunspow. *High* 4D **86**
Hunstanton. *Norf* 5C **38**
Hunstanworth. *Dur* 7C **54**
Hunston. *Suff* 5F **30**
Hunston. *W Sus* 5F **10**
Hunstrete. *Bath* 7E **18**
Hunt End. *Worc* 5J **27**
Hunterfield. *Midl* 3M **59**
Hunters Forstal. *Kent* 7H **23**
Hunter's Quay. *Arg* 2L **57**
Huntham. *Som* 3B **8**
Hunthill Lodge. *Ang* 8D **72**
Huntingdon. *Cambs* 4K **29**
Huntingfield. *Suff* 4K **31**
Huntingford. *Wilts* 3G **9**
Huntington. *Ches W* 3C **34**
Huntington. *E Lot* 2B **60**
Huntington. *Here* 6A **26**
Huntington. *Staf* 8H **35**
Huntington. *Telf* 1E **26**
Huntington. *York* 2D **42**
Huntingtower. *Per* 5D **66**
Huntley. *Glos* 2F **18**
Huntley. *Staf* 5J **35**
Huntly. *Abers* 2E **72**
Huntlywood. *Bord* 5D **60**
Hunton. *Hants* 2B **10**
Hunton. *Kent* 1D **12**
Hunton. *N Yor* 6K **47**
Hunton Bridge. *Herts* 4H **21**
Hunt's Corner. *Norf* 3G **31**
Huntscott. *Som* 1J **7**
Hunt's Cross. *Mers* 1C **34**
Hunts Green. *Warw* 2K **27**
Huntsham. *Devn* 3K **7**
Huntshaw. *Devn* 3E **6**
Huntspill. *Som* 1B **8**
Huntstile. *Som* 2A **8**
Huntworth. *Som* 2B **8**
Hunwick. *Dur* 8E **54**
Hunworth. *Norf* 6G **39**
Hurcott. *Som*
nr. Ilminster 4B **8**
nr. Somerton 3D **8**
Hurdcott. *Wilts* 2K **9**
Hurdley. *Powy* 2A **26**
Hurdsfield. *Ches E* 2H **35**
Hurlet. *Glas* 3D **58**
Hurley. *Warw* 2L **27**
Hurley. *Wind* 5F **20**
Hurlford. *E Ayr* 6C **58**
Hurliness. *Orkn* 3D **86**
Hurlston Green. *Lanc* 6C **40**
Hurn. *Dors* 6K **9**
Hursey. *Dors* 5C **8**
Hursley. *Hants* 3B **10**
Hurst. *G Man* 7H **41**
Hurst. *N Yor* 5J **47**
Hurst. *Som* 4C **8**
Hurst. *Wok* 6E **20**
Hurstbourne Priors. *Hants* 1B **10**
Hurstbourne Tarrant. *Hants* 8A **20**
Hurst Green. *Ches E* 5D **34**
Hurst Green. *E Sus* 3D **12**
Hurst Green. *Essx* 2G **23**
Hurst Green. *Lanc* 4E **40**
Hurst Green. *Surr* 8L **21**
Hurstley. *Here* 7B **26**
Hurstpierpoint. *W Sus* 4K **11**
Hurstway Common. *Here* 7B **26**
Hurst Wickham. *W Sus* 4K **11**
Hurstwood. *Lanc* 4G **41**
Hurtmore. *Surr* 1G **11**
Hurworth-on-Tees. *Darl* 4M **47**
Hurworth Place. *Darl* 5L **47**
Hury. *Dur* 4H **47**
Husbands Bosworth. *Leics* 3D **28**
Husborne Crawley. *C Beds* 8G **29**
Husthwaite. *N Yor* 8C **48**
Hutcherleigh. *Devn* 6K **5**
Hut Green. *N Yor* 5C **42**
Huthwaite. *Notts* 4B **36**
Huttoft. *Linc* 2B **38**
Hutton. *Cumb* 3C **46**
Hutton. *E Yor* 2H **43**
Hutton. *Essx* 4C **22**
Hutton. *Lanc* 5C **40**
Hutton. *N Som* 8B **18**
Hutton. *Bord* 4G **61**
Hutton Bonville. *N Yor* 5M **47**
Hutton Buscel. *N Yor* 7G **49**
Hutton Conyers. *N Yor* 8M **47**
Hutton Cranswick. *E Yor* 2H **43**
Hutton End. *Cumb* 8J **53**
Hutton Gate. *Red C* 4C **48**
Hutton Henry. *Dur* 8H **55**
Hutton-le-Hole. *N Yor* 7E **48**
Hutton Magna. *Dur* 4K **47**
Hutton Mulgrave. *N Yor* 5F **48**
Hutton Roof. *Cumb*
nr. Kirkby Lonsdale 8D **46**
nr. Penrith 8H **53**
Hutton Rudby. *N Yor* 5B **48**
Huttons Ambo. *N Yor* 1E **42**
Hutton Sessay. *N Yor* 8B **48**
Hutton Village. *Red C* 4D **48**
Hutton Wandesley. *N Yor* 2C **42**
Huxham. *Devn* 6J **7**
Huxham Green. *Som* 2D **8**
Huxley. *Ches W* 3D **34**
Huxter. *Shet*
on Mainland 2B **90**
on Whalsay 1F **90**
Huyton. *Mers* 8C **40**
Hwlffordd. *Pemb* 5F **14**
Hycemoor. *Cumb* 6K **45**
Hyde. *Glos*
nr. Stroud 3G **19**
nr. Winchcombe 1J **19**
Hyde. *G Man* 8H **41**
Hyde Heath. *Buck* 3G **21**
Hyde Lea. *Staf* 8H **35**
Hyde Park. *S Yor* 7C **42**
Hydestile. *Surr* 1G **11**
Hyndford Bridge. *S Lan* 5H **59**
Hynish. *Arg* 4E **62**
Hyssington. *Powy* 2B **26**
Hythe. *Hants* 5B **10**
Hythe. *Kent* 2H **13**
Hythe End. *Wind* 6H **21**
Hythie. *Abers* 8K **81**
Hyton. *Cumb* 6K **45**

I

Ianstown. *Mor* 7D **80**
Iarsiadar. *W Isl* 8E **82**
Ibberton. *Dors* 5F **8**
Ible. *Derbs* 4L **35**
Ibrox. *Glas* 3D **58**
Ibsley. *Hants* 5K **9**
Ibstock. *Leics* 8B **36**
Ibstone. *Buck* 4E **20**
Ibthorpe. *Hants* 8A **20**
Iburndale. *N Yor* 5F **48**
Ibworth. *Hants* 8C **20**
Icelton. *N Som* 7B **18**
Ichrachan. *Arg* 4E **64**
Ickburgh. *Norf* 2E **30**
Ickenham. *G Lon* 5H **21**
Ickenthwaite. *Cumb* 7B **46**
Ickford. *Buck* 3D **20**
Ickham. *Kent* 8J **23**
Ickleford. *Herts* 8J **29**
Icklesham. *E Sus* 4E **12**
Ickleton. *Cambs* 7A **30**
Icklingham. *Suff* 4D **30**
Ickwell. *C Beds* 7J **29**
Icomb. *Glos* 1L **19**
Idbury. *Oxon* 2L **19**
Iddesleigh. *Devn* 5E **6**
Ide. *Devn* 6H **7**
Ideford. *Devn* 8H **7**
Ide Hill. *Kent* 8A **22**
Iden. *E Sus* 3F **12**
Iden Green. *Kent*
nr. Benenden 2E **12**
nr. Goudhurst 2D **12**
Idle. *W Yor* 4K **41**
Idless. *Corn* 4M **3**
Idlicote. *Warw* 7L **27**
Idmiston. *Wilts* 2K **9**
Idole. *Carm* 5L **15**
Idridgehay. *Derbs* 5L **35**
Idrigill. *High* 7E **76**
Idstone. *Oxon* 5L **19**
Iffley. *Oxon* 3C **20**
Ifield. *W Sus* 2K **11**
Ifieldwood. *W Sus* 2K **11**
Ifold. *W Sus* 2H **11**
Iford. *E Sus* 5M **11**
Ifton Heath. *Shrp* 6B **34**
Ightfield. *Shrp* 6D **34**
Ightham. *Kent* 8B **22**
Iken. *Suff* 6L **31**
Ilam. *Staf* 4K **35**
Ilchester. *Som* 3D **8**
Ilderton. *Nmbd* 7H **61**
Ilford. *G Lon* 5M **21**
Ilford. *Som* 4B **8**
Ilfracombe. *Devn* 1E **6**
Ilkeston. *Derbs* 5B **36**
Ilketshall St Andrew. *Suff* 3K **31**
Ilketshall St Lawrence. *Suff* 3K **31**
Ilketshall St Margaret. *Suff* 3K **31**
Ilkley. *W Yor* 3K **41**
Illand. *Corn* 8B **6**
Illey. *W Mid* 3H **27**
Illidge Green. *Ches E* 3F **34**
Illington. *Norf* 3F **30**
Illingworth. *W Yor* 5J **41**
Illogan. *Corn* 4K **3**
Illogan Highway. *Corn* 4K **3**
Illston on the Hill. *Leics* 2E **28**
Ilmer. *Buck* 3E **20**
Ilmington. *Warw* 7L **27**
Ilminster. *Som* 4B **8**
Ilsington. *Devn* 8G **7**
Ilsington. *Dors* 6F **8**
Ilston. *Swan* 5E **16**
Ilton. *N Yor* 8K **47**
Ilton. *Som* 4B **8**
Imachar. *N Ayr* 5H **57**
Imber. *Wilts* 1H **9**
Immingham. *NE Lin* 6J **43**
Immingham Dock. *NE Lin* 6K **43**
Impington. *Cambs* 5M **29**
Ince. *Ches W* 2C **34**
Ince Blundell. *Mers* 7B **40**
Ince-in-Makerfield. *G Man* 7D **40**
Inchbae Lodge. *High* 7E **78**
Inchbare. *Ang* 1K **67**
Inchberry. *Mor* 8C **80**
Inchbraoch. *Ang* 2L **67**
Inchbrook. *Glos* 3G **19**
Incheril. *High* 7M **77**
Inchinnan. *Ren* 3C **58**
Inchlaggan. *High* 5B **70**
Inchmichael. *Per* 5F **66**
Inchnadamph. *High* 1C **78**
Inchree. *High* 1E **64**
Inchture. *Per* 5F **66**
Inchyra. *Per* 5E **66**
Indian Queens. *Corn* 6B **4**
Ingatestone. *Essx* 4C **22**
Ingbirchworth. *S Yor* 7L **41**
Ingestre. *Staf* 7H **35**
Ingham. *Linc* 1G **37**
Ingham. *Norf* 7K **39**
Ingham. *Suff* 4E **30**
Ingham Corner. *Norf* 7K **39**
Ingleborough. *Norf* 8A **38**
Ingleby. *Derbs* 7M **35**
Ingleby Arncliffe. *N Yor* 5B **48**
Ingleby Barwick. *Stoc T* 4B **48**
Ingleby Greenhow. *N Yor* 5C **48**
Ingleigh Green. *Devn* 5F **6**
Inglemire. *Hull* 4H **43**
Inglesbatch. *Bath* 7F **18**
Ingleton. *Dur* 3K **47**
Ingleton. *N Yor* 8E **46**
Inglewhite. *Lanc* 3D **40**
Ingoe. *Nmbd* 4D **54**
Ingol. *Lanc* 4D **40**
Ingoldisthorpe. *Norf* 6C **38**
Ingoldmells. *Linc* 3B **38**
Ingoldsby. *Linc* 6H **37**
Ingon. *Warw* 6L **27**
Ingram. *Nmbd* 8H **61**
Ingrave. *Essx* 4C **22**
Ingrow. *W Yor* 4J **41**
Ings. *Cumb* 6C **46**
Ingst. *S Glo* 5D **18**
Ingthorpe. *Rut* 1G **29**
Ingworth. *Norf* 7H **39**
Inishrush. *M Ulst* 3F **93**
Inkberrow. *Worc* 6J **27**
Inkford. *Worc* 4J **27**
Inkpen. *W Ber* 7A **20**
Inkstack. *High* 4D **86**
Innellan. *Arg* 3L **57**
Inner Hope. *Devn* 8J **5**
Innerleith. *Fife* 6F **66**
Innerleithen. *Bord* 6M **59**
Innerleven. *Fife* 7G **67**
Innermessan. *Dum* 5F **50**
Innerwick. *E Lot* 2E **60**
Innerwick. *Per* 3K **65**
Innsworth. *Glos* 1G **19**
Insch. *Abers* 3F **72**
Insh. *High* 5J **71**
Inshegra. *High* 6E **84**
Inshore. *High* 4F **84**
Inskip. *Lanc* 4C **40**
Instow. *Devn* 2D **6**
Intwood. *Norf* 1H **31**
Inver. *Abers* 6B **72**
Inver. *High* 5J **79**
Inver. *Per* 3D **66**
Inverailort. *High* 7J **69**
Inveralligin. *High* 8K **77**
Inverallochy. *Abers* 7K **81**
Inveramsay. *Abers* 3G **73**
Inveran. *High* 4F **78**
Inveraray. *Arg* 7E **64**
Inverarish. *High* 2G **69**
Inverarity. *Ang* 3H **67**
Inverarnan. *Stir* 6H **65**
Inverarnie. *High* 2G **71**
Inverbeg. *Arg* 8H **65**
Inverbervie. *Abers* 8H **73**
Inverboyndie. *Abers* 7F **80**
Invercassley. *High* 3E **78**
Invercharnan. *High* 3F **64**
Inverchoran. *High* 8C **78**
Invercreran. *Arg* 3E **64**
Inverdruie. *High* 4K **71**
Inverebrie. *Abers* 2J **73**
Invereck. *Arg* 1L **57**
Inveresk. *E Lot* 2M **59**
Inveresragan. *Arg* 4D **64**
Inverey. *Abers* 7L **71**
Inverfarigaig. *High* 3F **70**
Invergarry. *High* 5D **70**
Invergeldie. *Per* 5M **65**
Invergordon. *High* 7H **79**
Invergowrie. *Per* 4G **67**
Inverguseran. *High* 5J **69**
Inverharroch. *Mor* 2C **72**
Inverie. *High* 5J **69**
Inverinan. *Arg* 6D **64**
Inverinate. *High* 3L **69**
Inverkeilor. *Ang* 3K **67**
Inverkeithing. *Fife* 1K **59**
Inverkeithny. *Abers* 1F **72**
Inverkip. *Inv* 2M **57**
Inverkirkaig. *High* 2A **78**
Inverlael. *High* 5B **78**
Inverliever Lodge. *Arg* 7C **64**
Inverliver. *Arg* 4E **64**
Inverlochlarig. *Stir* 6J **65**
Inverlochy. *High* 8B **70**
Inverlussa. *Arg* 1F **56**
Inver Mallie. *High* 7B **70**
Invermarkie. *Abers* 2D **72**
Invermoriston. *High* 4E **70**
Invernaver. *High* 5K **85**
Inverneil House. *Arg* 1H **57**
Inverness. *High* 1G **71**
Inverness Airport. *High* 8H **79**
Invernettie. *Abers* 1L **73**
Inverpolly Lodge. *High* 2A **78**
Inverquhomery. *Abers* 1K **73**
Inverroy. *High* 7C **70**
Inversanda. *High* 2D **64**
Invershiel. *High* 4L **69**
Invershin. *High* 4F **78**
Invershore. *High* 8D **86**
Inversnaid. *Stir* 7H **65**
Inverugie. *Abers* 1L **73**
Inveruglas. *Arg* 7H **65**
Inverurie. *Abers* 3G **73**
Invervar. *Per* 3L **65**
Inverythan. *Abers* 1G **73**
Inwardleigh. *Devn* 6E **6**
Inworth. *Essx* 2E **22**
Iochdar. *W Isl* 1D **74**
Iping. *W Sus* 3F **10**
Ipplepen. *Devn* 5L **5**
Ipsden. *Oxon* 5D **20**
Ipstones. *Staf* 5J **35**
Ipswich. *Suff* 7H **31**
Irby. *Mers* 1A **34**
Irby in the Marsh. *Linc* 3A **38**
Irby upon Humber. *NE Lin* 7J **43**
Irchester. *Nptn* 5G **29**
Ireby. *Cumb* 8G **53**
Ireby. *Lanc* 8E **46**
Ireland. *Shet* 5D **90**
Ireleth. *Cumb* 7M **45**
Ireshopeburn. *Dur* 8B **54**
Ireton Wood. *Derbs* 5L **35**
Irlam. *G Man* 8F **40**
Irnham. *Linc* 7H **37**
Iron Acton. *S Glo* 5E **18**
Iron Bridge. *Cambs* 2A **30**
Ironbridge. *Telf* 1E **26**
Iron Cross. *Warw* 6J **27**
Ironville. *Derbs* 4B **36**
Irstead. *Norf* 7K **39**
Irthington. *Cumb* 5J **53**
Irthlingborough. *Nptn* 4G **29**
Irton. *N Yor* 7H **49**
Irvine. *N Ayr* 6B **58**
Irvine Mains. *N Ayr* 6B **58**
Irvinestown. *Ferm* 6C **92**
Isabella Pit. *Nmbd* 3G **55**
Isauld. *High* 5A **86**
Isbister. *Orkn* 8C **88**
Isbister. *Shet*
on Mainland 4H **91**
on Whalsay 1F **90**
Isfield. *E Sus* 4A **12**
Isham. *Nptn* 4F **28**
Island Carr. *N Lin* 7G **43**
Islay Airport. *Arg* 4C **56**
Isle Abbotts. *Som* 3B **8**
Isle Brewers. *Som* 3B **8**
Isleham. *Cambs* 4C **30**
Isle of Man Airport. *IOM* 8B **44**
Isle of Thanet. *Kent* 7K **23**
Isle of Whithorn. *Dum* 8K **51**
Isle of Wight. *IOW* 7B **10**
Isleornsay. *High* 4J **69**
Islesburgh. *Shet* 1D **90**
Isles of Scilly (St Mary's) Airport.
IOS 1H **3**
Islesteps. *Dum* 4D **52**
Isleworth. *G Lon* 6J **21**
Isley Walton. *Leics* 7B **36**
Islibhig. *W Isl* 1A **76**
Islington. *G Lon* 5L **21**
Islington. *Telf* 7F **34**
Islip. *Nptn* 4G **29**
Islip. *Oxon* 2C **20**
Isombridge. *Telf* 8E **34**
Istead Rise. *Kent* 7C **22**
Itchen. *Sotn* 4B **10**
Itchen Abbas. *Hants* 2C **10**
Itchenor. *W Sus* 5E **10**
Itchen Stoke. *Hants* 2C **10**
Itchingfield. *W Sus* 3J **11**
Itchington. *S Glo* 5E **18**
Itlaw. *Abers* 8F **80**
Itteringham. *Norf* 6H **39**
Itteringham Common. *Norf* 7H **39**
Itton. *Devn* 6F **6**
Itton Common. *Mon* 4C **18**
Ivegill. *Cumb* 7J **53**
Ivelet. *N Yor* 6H **47**
Iverchaolain. *Arg* 2K **57**
Iver Heath. *Buck* 5H **21**
Iveston. *Dur* 6E **54**
Ivetsey Bank. *Staf* 8G **35**
Ivinghoe. *Buck* 2G **21**
Ivinghoe Aston. *Buck* 2G **21**
Ivington. *Here* 6C **26**
Ivington Green. *Here* 6C **26**
Ivybridge. *Devn* 6J **5**
Ivychurch. *Kent* 3G **13**
Ivy Hatch. *Kent* 8B **22**
Ivy Todd. *Norf* 1E **30**
Iwade. *Kent* 7F **22**
Iwerne Courtney. *Dors* 4G **9**
Iwerne Minster. *Dors* 4G **9**
Ixworth. *Suff* 4F **30**
Ixworth Thorpe. *Suff* 4F **30**

J

Jackfield. *Shrp* 1E **26**
Jack Hill. *N Yor* 2K **41**
Jacksdale. *Notts* 4B **36**
Jackton. *S Lan* 4D **58**
Jacobstow. *Corn* 6A **6**
Jacobstowe. *Devn* 5E **6**
Jacobs Well. *Surr* 8G **21**
Jameston. *Pemb* 7G **15**
Jamestown. *Dum* 2H **53**
Jamestown. *Fife* 1K **59**
Jamestown. *High* 8E **78**
Jamestown. *W Dun* 1B **58**
Janetstown. *High*
nr. Thurso 5B **86**
nr. Wick 6E **86**
Jarrow. *Tyne* 5G **55**
Jarvis Brook. *E Sus* 3B **12**
Jasper's Green. *Essx* 1D **22**
Jaywick. *Essx* 2H **23**
Jedburgh. *Bord* 7D **60**
Jeffreyston. *Pemb* 6G **15**
Jemimaville. *High* 7H **79**
Jenkins Park. *High* 5D **70**
Jersey Marine. *Neat* 5G **17**
Jesmond. *Tyne* 5F **54**
Jevington. *E Sus* 5B **12**
Jingle Street. *Mon* 2C **18**
Jockey End. *Herts* 2H **21**
Jodrell Bank. *Ches E* 2F **34**
Johnby. *Cumb* 8J **53**
John O'Gaunts. *W Yor* 5M **41**
John o' Groats. *High* 4E **86**
John's Cross. *E Sus* 3D **12**
Johnshaven. *Abers* 1L **67**
Johnson Street. *Norf* 8K **39**
Johnston. *Pemb* 5F **14**
Johnstone. *Ren* 3C **58**
Johnstonebridge. *Dum* 2E **52**
Johnstown. *Carm* 5L **15**
Johnstown. *Wrex* 5B **34**
Jonesborough. *New M* 7G **93**
Joppa. *Edin* 2M **59**
Joppa. *S Ayr* 8C **58**
Jordan Green. *Norf* 7G **39**
Jordans. *Buck* 4G **21**
Jordanston. *Pemb* 3F **14**
Jump. *S Yor* 7A **42**
Jumpers Common. *Dors* 6K **9**
Juniper. *Nmbd* 6C **54**
Juniper Green. *Edin* 3K **59**
Jurby East. *IOM* 5C **44**
Jurby West. *IOM* 5C **44**
Jury's Gap. *E Sus* 4F **12**

K

Kaber. *Cumb* 4F **46**
Kaimend. *S Lan* 5H **59**
Kaimes. *Edin* 3L **59**
Kaimrig End. *Bord* 5J **59**
Kames. *Arg* 2J **57**
Kames. *E Ayr* 7E **58**
Katesbridge. *Arm* 6H **93**
Kea. *Corn* 4M **3**
Keadby. *N Lin* 6F **42**
Keady. *Arm* 7F **93**
Keal Cotes. *Linc* 3L **37**
Kearsley. *G Man* 7F **40**
Kearsney. *Kent* 1J **13**
Kearstwick. *Cumb* 7E **46**
Kearton. *N Yor* 6H **47**
Kearvaig. *High* 4E **84**
Keasden. *N Yor* 1F **40**
Keason. *Corn* 5F **4**
Keckwick. *Hal* 1D **34**
Keddington. *Linc* 1L **37**
Keddington Corner. *Linc* 1L **37**
Kedington. *Suff* 7D **30**
Kedleston. *Derbs* 5M **35**
Kedlock Feus. *Fife* 6G **67**
Keekle. *Cumb* 3K **45**
Keelby. *Linc* 6J **43**
Keele. *Staf* 5G **35**
Keeley Green. *Bed* 7H **29**
Keeston. *Pemb* 5F **14**
Keevil. *Wilts* 8H **19**
Kegworth. *Leics* 7B **36**
Kehelland. *Corn* 4K **3**
Keig. *Abers* 4F **72**
Keighley. *W Yor* 3J **41**
Keilarsbrae. *Clac* 8B **66**
Keillmore. *Arg* 1F **56**
Keillor. *Per* 3F **66**
Keillour. *Per* 5C **66**
Keills. *Arg* 3D **56**
Keiloch. *Abers* 6A **72**
Keils. *Arg* 3E **56**
Keinton Mandeville. *Som* 2D **8**
Keir Mill. *Dum* 2C **52**
Keirsleywell Row. *Nmbd* 6A **54**
Keisby. *Linc* 7H **37**
Keisley. *Cumb* 3F **46**
Keiss. *High* 5E **86**
Keith. *Mor* 8D **80**
Keith Inch. *Abers* 1L **73**
Kelbrook. *Lanc* 3H **41**
Kelby. *Linc* 5H **37**
Keld. *Cumb* 4D **46**
Keld. *N Yor* 5G **47**
Keldholme. *N Yor* 7E **48**
Kelfield. *N Lin* 7F **42**
Kelfield. *N Yor* 4C **42**
Kelham. *Notts* 4E **36**
Kellacott. *Devn* 7D **6**
Kellan. *Arg* 3L **63**
Kellas. *Ang* 4H **67**
Kellas. *Mor* 8A **80**
Kellaton. *Devn* 8L **5**
Kelleth. *Cumb* 5E **46**
Kelling. *Norf* 5G **39**
Kellingley. *N Yor* 5C **42**
Kellington. *N Yor* 5C **42**
Kelloe. *Dur* 8G **55**
Kelloholm. *Dum* 8F **58**
Kells. *Cumb* 3J **45**
Kells. *ME Ant* 4G **93**
Kelly. *Devn* 7C **6**
Kelly Bray. *Corn* 8C **6**
Kelmarsh. *Nptn* 4E **28**
Kelmscott. *Oxon* 4L **19**
Kelsale. *Suff* 5K **31**
Kelsall. *Ches W* 3D **34**
Kelshall. *Herts* 8L **29**
Kelsick. *Cumb* 6F **52**
Kelso. *Bord* 6E **60**
Kelstedge. *Derbs* 3M **35**
Kelstern. *Linc* 8K **43**
Kelsterton. *Flin* 2A **34**
Kelston. *Bath* 7F **18**
Keltneyburn. *Per* 3A **66**
Kelton. *Dum* 4D **52**
Kelton Hill. *Dum* 6B **52**
Kelty. *Fife* 8E **66**
Kelvedon. *Essx* 2E **22**
Kelvedon Hatch. *Essx* 4B **22**
Kelvinside. *Glas* 3D **58**
Kelynack. *Corn* 5G **3**
Kemback. *Fife* 6H **67**
Kemberton. *Shrp* 1F **26**
Kemble. *Glos* 4H **19**
Kemerton. *Worc* 8H **27**
Kemeys Commander. *Mon* 3B **18**
Kemnay. *Abers* 4G **73**
Kempe's Corner. *Kent* 1G **13**
Kempley. *Glos* 1E **18**
Kempley Green. *Glos* 1E **18**
Kempsey. *Worc* 7G **27**
Kempsford. *Glos* 4K **19**
Kemps Green. *Warw* 4K **27**
Kempshott. *Hants* 1D **10**
Kempston. *Bed* 7H **29**
Kempston Hardwick. *Bed* 7H **29**
Kempton. *Shrp* 3B **26**
Kemp Town. *Brig* 5L **11**
Kemsing. *Kent* 8B **22**
Kemsley. *Kent* 7F **22**
Kenardington. *Kent* 2F **12**
Kenchester. *Here* 7C **26**
Kencot. *Oxon* 3L **19**
Kendal. *Cumb* 6D **46**
Kendleshire. *S Glo* 6E **18**
Kendray. *S Yor* 7A **42**
Kenfig. *B'end* 6H **17**
Kenfig Hill. *B'end* 6H **17**
Kengharair. *Arg* 3K **63**
Kenilworth. *Warw* 4L **27**
Kenknock. *Stir* 4J **65**
Kenley. *G Lon* 8L **21**
Kenley. *Shrp* 1D **26**
Kenmore. *High* 8J **77**
Kenmore. *Per* 3A **66**
Kenn. *Devn* 7J **7**
Kenn. *N Som* 7C **18**
Kennacraig. *Arg* 3H **57**
Kenneggy Downs. *Corn* 6J **3**
Kennerleigh. *Devn* 5H **7**
Kennet. *Clac* 8C **66**
Kennethmont. *Abers* 3E **72**
Kennett. *Cambs* 5D **30**
Kennford. *Devn* 7J **7**
Kenninghall. *Norf* 3G **31**
Kennington. *Kent* 1G **13**
Kennington. *Oxon* 3C **20**
Kennoway. *Fife* 7G **67**
Kennyhill. *Suff* 4C **30**
Kennythorpe. *N Yor* 1E **42**
Kenovay. *Arg* 3E **62**
Kensaleyre. *High* 8F **76**
Kensington. *G Lon* 6K **21**
Kenstone. *Shrp* 7D **34**
Kensworth. *C Beds* 2H **21**
Kensworth Common.
C Beds 2H **21**
Kentallen. *High* 2E **64**
Kentchurch. *Here* 1C **18**
Kentford. *Suff* 5D **30**
Kentisbeare. *Devn* 5K **7**
Kentisbury. *Devn* 1F **6**
Kentisbury Ford. *Devn* 1F **6**
Kentmere. *Cumb* 5C **46**
Kenton. *Devn* 7J **7**
Kenton. *G Lon* 5J **21**
Kenton. *Suff* 5H **31**
Kenton Bankfoot. *Tyne* 5F **54**
Kentra. *High* 1M **63**
Kentrigg. *Cumb* 6D **46**
Kents Bank. *Cumb* 8B **46**
Kent's Green. *Glos* 1F **18**
Kent's Oak. *Hants* 3M **9**
Kent Street. *E Sus* 4D **12**
Kent Street. *Kent* 8C **22**
Kent Street. *W Sus* 3K **11**
Kenwick. *Shrp* 6C **34**
Kenwyn. *Corn* 4M **3**
Kenyon. *Warr* 8E **40**
Keoldale. *High* 5F **84**
Keppoch. *High* 3L **69**
Kepwick. *N Yor* 6B **48**
Keresley. *W Mid* 3M **27**
Keresley Newland. *Warw* 3M **27**
Keristal. *IOM* 7C **44**
Kerne Bridge. *Here* 2D **18**
Kerridge. *Ches E* 2H **35**
Kerris. *Corn* 6H **3**
Kerrow. *High* 2D **70**
Kerry. *Powy* 4L **25**
Kerrycroy. *Arg* 3L **57**
Kerry's Gate. *Here* 8B **26**
Kersall. *Notts* 3E **36**
Kersbrook. *Devn* 7K **7**
Kerse. *Ren* 4B **58**
Kersey. *Suff* 7G **31**
Kershopefoot. *Cumb* 3J **53**
Kersoe. *Worc* 7H **27**
Kerswell. *Devn* 5K **7**
Kerswell Green. *Worc* 7G **27**
Kesgrave. *Suff* 7J **31**
Kesh. *Ferm* 5B **92**
Kessingland. *Suff* 3M **31**
Kessingland Beach. *Suff* 3M **31**
Kestle. *Corn* 7B **4**
Kestle Mill. *Corn* 6A **4**
Keston. *G Lon* 7M **21**
Keswick. *Cumb* 3A **46**
Keswick. *Norf*
nr. North Walsham 6K **39**
nr. Norwich 1J **31**
Ketsby. *Linc* 2L **37**
Kettering. *Nptn* 4F **28**
Ketteringham. *Norf* 1H **31**
Kettins. *Per* 4F **66**
Kettlebaston. *Suff* 6F **30**
Kettlebridge. *Fife* 7G **67**
Kettlebrook. *Staf* 1L **27**
Kettleburgh. *Suff* 5J **31**
Kettleholm. *Dum* 4F **52**
Kettleness. *N Yor* 4F **48**
Kettleshulme. *Ches E* 2H **35**
Kettlesing. *N Yor* 2L **41**
Kettlesing Bottom. *N Yor* 2L **41**
Kettlestone. *Norf* 6F **38**
Kettlethorpe. *Linc* 2F **36**
Kettletoft. *Orkn* 6F **88**
Kettlewell. *N Yor* 8H **47**
Ketton. *Rut* 1G **29**
Kew. *G Lon* 6J **21**
Kewaigue. *IOM* 7C **44**
Kewstoke. *N Som* 7B **18**
Kexbrough. *S Yor* 7L **41**
Kexby. *Linc* 1F **36**
Kexby. *York* 2E **42**
Keyford. *Som* 1F **8**
Key Green. *Ches E* 3G **35**
Key Green. *N Yor* 5F **48**

Keyham—Lifton

Keyham. *Leics* 1D 28
Keyhaven. *Hants* 6M 9
Keyhead. *Abers* 8K 81
Keyingham. *E Yor* 5K 43
Keymer. *W Sus* 4L 11
Keynsham. *Bath* 7E 18
Keysoe. *Bed* 5H 29
Keysoe Row. *Bed* 5H 29
Key's Toft. *Linc* 4A 38
Keyston. *Cambs* 4H 29
Key Street. *Kent* 7E 22
Keyworth. *Notts* 6D 36
Kibblesworth. *Tyne* 6F 54
Kibworth Beauchamp.
Leics 2D 28
Kibworth Harcourt. *Leics* 2D 28
Kidbrooke. *G Lon* 6M 21
Kidburngill. *Cumb* 2K 45
Kiddemore Green. *Staf* 1G 27
Kidderminster. *Worc* 4G 27
Kiddington. *Oxon* 1B 20
Kidd's Moor. *Norf* 1H 31
Kidlington. *Oxon* 2B 20
Kidmore End. *Oxon* 6D 20
Kidnal. *Ches W* 5C 34
Kidsgrove. *Staf* 4G 35
Kidstones. *N Yor* 7H 47
Kidwelly. *Carm* 6L 15
Kiel Crofts. *Arg* 4D 64
Kielder. *Nmbd* 2L 53
Kilbagie. *Fife* 8C 66
Kilbarchan. *Ren* 3C 58
Kilbeg. *High* 5H 69
Kilberry. *Arg* 3G 57
Kilbirnie. *N Ayr* 4B 58
Kilbride. *Arg* 5C 64
Kilbride. *High* 3G 69
Kilbucho Place. *Bord* 6J 59
Kilburn. *Derbs* 5A 36
Kilburn. *G Lon* 5K 21
Kilburn. *N Yor* 8C 48
Kilby. *Leics* 2D 28
Kilchattan. *Arg* 8J 63
Kilchattan Bay. *Arg* 4L 57
Kilchenzie. *Arg* 7F 56
Kilcheran. *Arg* 4C 64
Kilchiaran. *Arg* 3B 56
Kilchoan. *High*
nr. Inverie 6J 69
nr. Tobermory 1K 63
Kilchoman. *Arg* 3B 56
Kilchrenan. *Arg* 5E 64
Kilclief. *New M* 6J 93
Kilconquhar. *Fife* 7H 67
Kilcoo. *New M* 7H 93
Kilcot. *Glos* 1E 18
Kilcoy. *High* 8F 78
Kilcreggan. *Arg* 1M 57
Kildale. *N Yor* 5D 48
Kildary. *High* 6H 79
Kildermorie Lodge. *High* 6F 78
Kildonan. *Dum* 6F 50
Kildonan. *High*
nr. Helmsdale 1K 79
on Isle of Skye 8E 76
Kildonan. *N Ayr* 7K 57
Kildonnan. *High* 7F 68
Kildrummy. *Abers* 4D 72
Kildwick. *N Yor* 3J 41
Kilfillan. *Dum* 6H 51
Kilfinan. *Arg* 2J 57
Kilfinnan. *High* 6C 70
Kilgetty. *Pemb* 6H 15
Kilgour. *Fife* 7F 66
Kilgrammie. *S Ayr* 1H 51
Kilham. *E Yor* 1H 43
Kilham. *Nmbd* 6F 60
Kilkeel. *New M* 7H 93
Kilkenneth. *Arg* 3E 62
Kilkhampton. *Corn* 4B 6
Killadeas. *Ferm* 6C 92
Killamarsh. *Derbs* 1B 36
Killandrist. *Arg* 3C 64
Killay. *Swan* 5F 16
Killean. *Arg* 5F 56
Killearn. *Stir* 1D 58
Killeen. *M Ulst* 5F 93
Killellan. *Arg* 8F 56
Killen. *Derr* 4C 92
Killen. *High* 8G 79
Killerby. *Darl* 4K 47
Killeter. *Derr* 4C 92
Killichonan. *Per* 2K 65
Killiechronan. *Arg* 3L 63
Killiecrankie. *Per* 1C 66
Killilan. *High* 2L 69
Killimster. *High* 6E 86
Killin. *Stir* 4K 65
Killinchy. *Ards* 5J 93
Killinghall. *N Yor* 2L 41
Killington. *Cumb* 7E 46
Killingworth. *Tyne* 4F 54
Killin Lodge. *High* 5F 70
Killinochonoch. *Arg* 8C 64
Killochyett. *Bord* 5B 60
Killough. *New M* 7J 93
Killowen. *New M* 7G 93
Killundine. *High* 3L 63
Killylea. *Arm* 6E 92
Killyleagh. *New M* 6J 93
Killyrammer. *Caus* 2F 93
Kilmacolm. *Inv* 3B 58
Kilmahog. *Stir* 7L 65
Kilmahumaig. *Arg* 8B 64
Kilmalieu. *High* 2C 64
Kilmaluag. *High* 6F 76
Kilmany. *Fife* 5G 67
Kilmarie. *High* 4G 69
Kilmarnock. *E Ayr* 6C 58
Kilmaron. *Fife* 6G 67
Kilmartin. *Arg* 8C 64
Kilmaurs. *E Ayr* 5C 58
Kilmelford. *Arg* 6C 64
Kilmeny. *Arg* 3C 56
Kilmersdon. *Som* 8E 18
Kilmeston. *Hants* 3C 10
Kilmichael Glassary. *Arg* 8C 64
Kilmichael of Inverlussa.
Arg 1G 57
Kilmington. *Devn* 6A 8
Kilmington. *Wilts* 2F 8
Kilmoluaig. *Arg* 3E 62
Kilmorack. *High* 1E 70
Kilmore. *Arg* 5C 64
Kilmore. *Arm* 6F 93
Kilmore. *High* 5H 69
Kilmore. *New M* 6J 93
Kilmory. *Arg* 2G 57
Kilmory. *High*
nr. Kilchoan 8G 69
on Rùm 5E 68
Kilmory. *N Ayr* 7J 57
Kilmory Lodge. *Arg* 7B 64
Kilmote. *High* 2K 79
Kilmuir. *High*
nr. Dunvegan 1D 68
nr. Invergordon 6H 79
nr. Inverness 1G 71
nr. Uig 6E 76
Kilmun. *Arg* 1L 57
Kilnave. *Arg* 2B 56
Kilncadzow. *S Lan* 5G 59
Kilndown. *Kent* 2D 12
Kiln Green. *Here* 2E 18
Kiln Green. *Wok* 6F 20
Kilnhill. *Cumb* 8G 53
Kilnhurst. *S Yor* 8B 42
Kilninian. *Arg* 3J 63
Kilninver. *Arg* 5C 64
Kiln Pit Hill. *Nmbd* 6D 54
Kilnsea. *E Yor* 6M 43
Kilnsey. *N Yor* 1H 41
Kilnwick. *E Yor* 3G 43
Kiloran. *Arg* 8J 63
Kilpatrick. *N Ayr* 7J 57
Kilpeck. *Here* 8C 26
Kilpin. *E Yor* 5E 42
Kilpin Pike. *E Yor* 5E 42
Kilrea. *Caus* 3F 93
Kilrenny. *Fife* 7J 67
Kilsby. *Nptn* 4C 28
Kilspindie. *Per* 5F 66
Kilsyth. *N Lan* 2F 58
Kiltarlity. *High* 1F 70
Kilton. *Som* 1L 7
Kilton Thorpe. *Red C* 4D 48
Kilvaxter. *High* 7E 76
Kilve. *Som* 1L 7
Kilvington. *Notts* 5F 36
Kilwinning. *N Ayr* 5A 58
Kimberley. *Norf* 1G 31
Kimberley. *Notts* 5B 36
Kimblesworth. *Dur* 7F 54
Kimble Wick. *Buck* 3F 20
Kimbolton. *Cambs* 5H 29
Kimbolton. *Here* 5D 26
Kimcote. *Leics* 3C 28
Kimmeridge. *Dors* 8H 9
Kimmerston. *Nmbd* 6G 61
Kimpton. *Hants* 1L 9
Kimpton. *Herts* 2J 21
Kinallen. *Arm* 6H 93
Kinawley. *Ferm* 7C 92
Kinbeachie. *High* 7G 79
Kinbrace. *High* 8L 85
Kinbuck. *Stir* 7A 66
Kincaple. *Fife* 6H 67
Kincardine. *Fife* 1H 59
Kincardine. *High* 5G 79
Kincardine Bridge. *Falk* 1H 59
Kincardine O'Neil. *Abers* 6E 72
Kinchrackine. *Arg* 5F 64
Kincorth. *Aber* 5J 73
Kincraig. *High* 5J 71
Kincraigie. *Per* 3C 66
Kindallachan. *Per* 2C 66
Kineton. *Glos* 1J 19
Kineton. *Warw* 6M 27
Kinfauns. *Per* 5E 66
Kingairloch. *High* 2C 64
Kingarth. *Arg* 4K 57
Kingcoed. *Mon* 3C 18
King Edward. *Abers* 8G 81
Kingerby. *Linc* 8H 43
Kingham. *Oxon* 1L 19
Kingholm Quay. *Dum* 4D 52
Kinghorn. *Fife* 1L 59
Kingie. *High* 5B 70
Kinglassie. *Fife* 8F 66
Kingledores. *Bord* 7K 59
King o' Muirs. *Clac* 8B 66
Kingoodie. *Per* 5G 67
King's Acre. *Here* 7C 26
Kingsand. *Corn* 6G 5
Kingsash. *Buck* 3F 20
Kingsbarns. *Fife* 6J 67
Kingsbridge. *Devn* 7K 5
Kingsbridge. *Som* 2J 7
King's Bromley. *Staf* 8K 35
Kingsburgh. *High* 8E 76
Kingsbury. *G Lon* 5J 21
Kingsbury. *Warw* 2L 27
Kingsbury Episcopi. *Som* 3C 8
Kings Caple. *Here* 1D 18
Kingscavil. *W Lot* 2J 59
Kingsclere. *Hants* 8C 20
King's Cliffe. *Nptn* 2H 29
Kings Clipstone. *Notts* 3D 36
Kingscote. *Glos* 4G 19
Kingscott. *Devn* 4E 6
Kings Coughton. *Warw* 6J 27
Kingscross. *N Ayr* 7K 57
Kingsdon. *Som* 3D 8
Kingsdown. *Kent* 1K 13
Kingsdown. *Swin* 5K 19
Kingsdown. *Wilts* 7G 19
Kingseat. *Fife* 8E 66
Kingsey. *Buck* 3E 20
Kingsfold. *Lanc* 5D 40
Kingsfold. *W Sus* 2J 11
Kingsford. *E Ayr* 5C 58
Kingsford. *Worc* 3G 27
Kingsforth. *N Lin* 6H 43
Kingsgate. *Kent* 6K 23
King's Green. *Glos* 8F 26
Kingshall Street. *Suff* 5F 30
Kingsheanton. *Devn* 2E 6
King's Heath. *W Mid* 3J 27
Kings Hill. *Kent* 8C 22
Kingsholm. *Glos* 2G 19
Kingshouse. *High* 2G 65
Kingshouse. *Stir* 5K 65
Kingshurst. *W Mid* 3K 27
Kingskerswell. *Devn* 5L 5
Kingskettle. *Fife* 7G 67
Kingsland. *Here* 5C 26
Kingsland. *IOA* 2B 32
Kings Langley. *Herts* 3H 21
Kingsley. *Ches W* 2D 34
Kingsley. *Hants* 2E 10
Kingsley. *Staf* 5J 35
Kingsley Green. *W Sus* 2F 10
Kingsley Holt. *Staf* 5J 35
King's Lynn. *Norf* 7C 38
King's Meaburn. *Cumb* 3E 46
Kings Moss. *Mers* 7D 40
Kingsmuir. *Ang* 3H 67
Kingsmuir. *Fife* 7J 67
Kings Muir. *Bord* 6L 59
King's Newnham. *Warw* 4B 28
King's Newton. *Derbs* 7A 36
Kingsnorth. *Kent* 2G 13
Kingsnorth. *Medw* 6E 22
King's Norton. *Leics* 1D 28
Kings Norton. *W Mid* 4J 27
King's Nympton. *Devn* 4F 6
King's Pyon. *Here* 6C 26
Kings Ripton. *Cambs* 4K 29
King's Somborne. *Hants* 2A 10
King's Stag. *Dors* 4F 8
King's Stanley. *Glos* 3G 19
King's Sutton. *Nptn* 8B 28
Kingstanding. *W Mid* 2J 27
Kingsteignton. *Devn* 8H 7
Kingsteps. *High* 8K 79
King Sterndale. *Derbs* 2J 35
King's Thorn. *Here* 8D 26
Kingsthorpe. *Nptn* 5E 28
Kingston. *Cambs* 6L 29
Kingston. *Devn* 7J 5
Kingston. *Dors*
nr. Sturminster Newton 5F 8
nr. Swanage 8H 9
Kingston. *E Lot* 1C 60
Kingston. *Hants* 5K 9
Kingston. *IOW* 7B 10
Kingston. *Kent* 8H 23
Kingston. *Mor* 7C 80
Kingston. *W Sus* 5H 11
Kingston Bagpuize. *Oxon* 4B 20
Kingston Blount. *Oxon* 4E 20
Kingston by Sea. *W Sus* 5K 11
Kingston Deverill. *Wilts* 2G 9
Kingstone. *Here* 8C 26
Kingstone. *Som* 4B 8
Kingstone. *Staf* 7J 35
Kingston Lisle. *Oxon* 5M 19
Kingston Maurward. *Dors* 6F 8
Kingston near Lewes.
E Sus 5L 11
Kingston on Soar. *Notts* 7C 36
Kingston Russell. *Dors* 6D 8
Kingston St Mary. *Som* 3M 7
Kingston Seymour. *N Som* 7C 18
Kingston Stert. *Oxon* 3E 20
Kingston upon Hull. *Hull* 5J 43
Kingston upon Thames.
G Lon 7J 21
King's Walden. *Herts* 1J 21
Kingswear. *Devn* 6L 5
Kingswells. *Aber* 5H 73
Kingswinford. *W Mid* 3G 27
Kingswood. *Buck* 2D 20
Kingswood. *Glos* 4F 18
Kingswood. *Here* 6A 26
Kingswood. *Kent* 8E 22
Kingswood. *Per* 4D 66
Kingswood. *Powy* 2M 25
Kingswood. *Som* 2L 7
Kingswood. *S Glo* 6E 18
Kingswood. *Surr* 8K 21
Kingswood. *Warw* 4K 27
Kingswood Common. *Staf* 1G 27
Kings Worthy. *Hants* 2B 10
Kingthorpe. *Linc* 2J 37
Kington. *Here* 6A 26
Kington. *S Glo* 4E 18
Kington. *Worc* 6H 27
Kington Langley. *Wilts* 6H 19
Kington Magna. *Dors* 3F 8
Kington St Michael. *Wilts* 6H 19
Kingussie. *High* 5H 71
Kingweston. *Som* 2D 8
Kinharrachie. *Abers* 2J 73
Kinhrive. *High* 6G 79
Kinkell Bridge. *Per* 6C 66
Kinknockie. *Abers* 1K 73
Kinkry Hill. *Cumb* 4K 53
Kinlet. *Shrp* 3F 26
Kinloch. *High*
nr. Lochaline 2A 64
nr. Loch More 8F 84
on Rùm 6E 68
Kinloch. *Per* 3E 66
Kinlochard. *Stir* 7J 65
Kinlochbervie. *High* 6E 84
Kinlocheil. *High* 8L 69
Kinlochewe. *High* 7M 77
Kinloch Hourn. *High* 5L 69
Kinloch Laggan. *High* 7F 70
Kinlochleven. *High* 1F 64
Kinloch Lodge. *High* 6H 85
Kinlochmoidart. *High* 8J 69
Kinlochmore. *High* 1F 64
Kinloch Rannoch. *Per* 2L 65
Kinlochspelve. *Arg* 5A 64
Kinloid. *High* 7H 69
Kinloss. *Mor* 7L 79
Kinmel Bay. *Cnwy* 2J 33
Kinmuck. *Abers* 4H 73
Kinnadie. *Abers* 1J 73
Kinnaird. *Per* 5F 66
Kinneff. *Abers* 8H 73
Kinnelhead. *Dum* 1E 52
Kinnell. *Ang* 2K 67
Kinnerley. *Shrp* 7B 34
Kinnernie. *Abers* 5G 73
Kinnersley. *Here* 7B 26
Kinnersley. *Worc* 7G 27
Kinnerton. *Powy* 6M 25
Kinnerton. *Shrp* 2B 26
Kinnesswood. *Per* 7E 66
Kinninvie. *Dur* 3J 47
Kinnordy. *Ang* 2G 67
Kinoulton. *Notts* 6D 36
Kinross. *Per* 7E 66
Kinrossie. *Per* 4E 66
Kinsbourne Green. *Herts* 2J 21
Kinsey Heath. *Ches E* 5E 34
Kinsham. *Here* 5B 26
Kinsham. *Worc* 8H 27
Kinsley. *W Yor* 6B 42
Kinson. *Bour* 6J 9
Kintbury. *W Ber* 7A 20
Kintessack. *Mor* 7L 79
Kintillo. *Per* 6E 66
Kinton. *Here* 4C 26
Kinton. *Shrp* 8B 34
Kintore. *Abers* 4G 73
Kintour. *Arg* 4D 56
Kintra. *Arg* 5J 63
Kintraw. *Arg* 7C 64
Kinveachy. *High* 4K 71
Kinver. *Staf* 3G 27
Kinwarton. *Warw* 6K 27
Kiplingcotes. *E Yor* 3G 43
Kippax. *W Yor* 4B 42
Kippen. *Stir* 8L 65
Kippford. *Dum* 6C 52
Kipping's Cross. *Kent* 1C 12
Kirbister. *Orkn*
nr. Hobbister 1E 86
nr. Quholm 8B 88
Kirbuster. *Orkn* 7F 88
Kirby Bedon. *Norf* 1J 31
Kirby Bellars. *Leics* 8E 36
Kirby Cane. *Norf* 2K 31
Kirby Cross. *Essx* 1J 23
Kirby Fields. *Leics* 1C 28
Kirby Green. *Norf* 2K 31
Kirby Grindalythe. *N Yor* 1G 43
Kirby Hill. *N Yor*
nr. Richmond 5K 47
nr. Ripon 1A 42
Kirby Knowle. *N Yor* 7B 48
Kirby-le-Soken. *Essx* 1J 23
Kirby Misperton. *N Yor* 8E 48
Kirby Muxloe. *Leics* 1C 28
Kirby Sigston. *N Yor* 6B 48
Kirby Underdale. *E Yor* 2F 42
Kirby Wiske. *N Yor* 7A 48
Kircubbin. *Ards* 5K 93
Kirdford. *W Sus* 3H 11
Kirk. *High* 6D 86
Kirkabister. *Shet*
on Bressay 4E 90
on Mainland 2E 90
Kirkandrews. *Dum* 7M 51
Kirkandrews-on-Eden.
Cumb 6H 53
Kirkapol. *Arg* 3F 62
Kirkbampton. *Cumb* 6H 53
Kirkbean. *Dum* 6D 52
Kirk Bramwith. *S Yor* 6D 42
Kirkbride. *Cumb* 6G 53
Kirkbridge. *N Yor* 6L 47
Kirkbuddo. *Ang* 3J 67
Kirkburn. *E Yor* 2G 43
Kirkburton. *W Yor* 6K 41
Kirkby. *Linc* 8H 43
Kirkby. *Mers* 8C 40
Kirkby. *N Yor* 5C 48
Kirkby Fenside. *Linc* 3L 37
Kirkby Fleetham. *N Yor* 6L 47
Kirkby Green. *Linc* 4H 37
Kirkby-in-Ashfield. *Notts* 4C 36
Kirkby-in-Furness. *Cumb* 6M 45
Kirkby la Thorpe. *Linc* 5J 37
Kirkby Lonsdale. *Cumb* 8E 46
Kirkby Malham. *N Yor* 1G 41
Kirkby Mallory. *Leics* 1B 28
Kirkby Malzeard. *N Yor* 8L 47
Kirkby Mills. *N Yor* 7E 48
Kirkbymoorside. *N Yor* 7D 48
Kirkby on Bain. *Linc* 3K 37
Kirkby Overblow. *N Yor* 3M 41
Kirkby Stephen. *Cumb* 5F 46
Kirkby Thore. *Cumb* 3E 46
Kirkby Underwood. *Linc* 7H 37
Kirkby Wharfe. *N Yor* 3C 42
Kirkcaldy. *Fife* 8F 66
Kirkcambeck. *Cumb* 5K 53
Kirkcolm. *Dum* 5F 50
Kirkconnel. *Dum* 8F 58
Kirkconnell. *Dum* 5D 52
Kirkcowan. *Dum* 5J 51
Kirkcudbright. *Dum* 6A 52
Kirkdale. *Mers* 8B 40
Kirk Deighton. *N Yor* 2A 42
Kirk Ella. *E Yor* 5H 43
Kirkfieldbank. *S Lan* 5G 59
Kirkforthar Feus. *Fife* 7F 66
Kirkgunzeon. *Dum* 5C 52
Kirk Hallam. *Derbs* 5B 36
Kirkham. *Lanc* 4C 40
Kirkham. *N Yor* 1E 42
Kirkhamgate. *W Yor* 5L 41
Kirk Hammerton. *N Yor* 2B 42
Kirkharle. *Nmbd* 3D 54
Kirkheaton. *Nmbd* 4D 54
Kirkheaton. *W Yor* 6K 41
Kirkhill. *Ang* 1K 67
Kirkhill. *High* 1F 70
Kirkhope. *S Lan* 1D 52
Kirkhouse. *Bord* 6M 59
Kirkibost. *High* 4G 69
Kirkinch. *Ang* 3G 67
Kirkinner. *Dum* 6K 51
Kirkintilloch. *E Dun* 2E 58
Kirk Ireton. *Derbs* 4L 35
Kirkland. *Cumb*
nr. Cleator Moor 3K 45
nr. Penrith 8L 53
nr. Wigton 7G 53
Kirkland. *Dum*
nr. Kirkconnel 8F 58
nr. Moniaive 2C 52
Kirkland Guards. *Cumb* 7F 52
Kirk Langley. *Derbs* 6L 35
Kirklauchline. *Dum* 6F 50
Kirkleatham. *Red C* 3C 48
Kirklevington. *Stoc T* 5B 48
Kirkley. *Suff* 2M 31
Kirklington. *N Yor* 7M 47
Kirklington. *Notts* 4D 36
Kirklinton. *Cumb* 5J 53
Kirkliston. *Edin* 2K 59
Kirkmabreck. *Dum* 6K 51
Kirkmaiden. *Dum* 8G 51
Kirk Merrington. *Dur* 8F 54
Kirk Michael. *IOM* 5C 44
Kirkmichael. *Per* 1D 66
Kirkmichael. *S Ayr* 1J 51
Kirkmuirhill. *S Lan* 5F 58
Kirknewton. *Nmbd* 6G 61
Kirknewton. *W Lot* 3K 59
Kirkney. *Abers* 2E 72
Kirk of Shotts. *N Lan* 3G 59
Kirkoswald. *Cumb* 7K 53
Kirkoswald. *S Ayr* 1H 51
Kirkpatrick. *Dum* 2D 52
Kirkpatrick Durham. *Dum* 4B 52
Kirkpatrick-Fleming. *Dum* 4G 53
Kirk Sandall. *S Yor* 7D 42
Kirksanton. *Cumb* 6L 45
Kirk Smeaton. *N Yor* 6C 42
Kirkstall. *W Yor* 4L 41
Kirkstile. *Dum* 2H 53
Kirkstyle. *High* 4E 86
Kirkthorpe. *W Yor* 5A 42
Kirkton. *Abers*
nr. Alford 4F 72
nr. Insch 3F 72
nr. Turriff 1H 73
Kirkton. *Ang*
nr. Dundee 4H 67
nr. Forfar 3H 67
nr. Tarfside 7D 72
Kirkton. *Dum* 3D 52
Kirkton. *Fife* 5G 67
Kirkton. *High*
nr. Golspie 4H 79
nr. Kyle of Lochalsh 3K 69
nr. Lochcarron 1L 69
Kirkton. *Bord* 8C 60
Kirkton. *S Lan* 7H 59
Kirktonhill. *W Dun* 2B 58
Kirkton Manor. *Bord* 6L 59
Kirkton of Airlie. *Ang* 2G 67
Kirkton of Auchterhouse.
Ang 4G 67
Kirkton of Bourtie. *Abers* 3H 73
Kirkton of Collace. *Per* 4E 66
Kirkton of Craig. *Ang* 2L 67
Kirkton of Culsalmond.
Abers 2F 72
Kirkton of Durris. *Abers* 6G 73
Kirkton of Glenbuchat.
Abers 4C 72
Kirkton of Glenisla. *Ang* 1F 66
Kirkton of Kingoldrum. *Ang* 2G 67
Kirkton of Largo. *Fife* 7H 67
Kirkton of Lethendy. *Per* 3E 66
Kirkton of Logie Buchan.
Abers 3J 73
Kirkton of Maryculter. *Abers* 6H 73
Kirkton of Menmuir. *Ang* 1J 67
Kirkton of Monikie. *Ang* 4J 67
Kirkton of Oyne. *Abers* 3F 72
Kirkton of Rayne. *Abers* 2F 72
Kirkton of Skene. *Abers* 5H 73
Kirktown. *Abers*
nr. Fraserburgh 7J 81
nr. Peterhead 8K 81
Kirktown of Alvah. *Abers* 7F 80
Kirktown of Auchterless.
Abers 1G 73
Kirktown of Deskford. *Mor* 7E 80
Kirktown of Fetteresso.
Abers 7H 73
Kirktown of Mortlach. *Mor* 2C 72
Kirktown of Slains. *Abers* 3K 73
Kirkurd. *Bord* 5K 59
Kirkwall. *Orkn* 8D 88
Kirkwall Airport. *Orkn* 1F 86
Kirkwhelpington. *Nmbd* 3C 54
Kirk Yetholm. *Bord* 7F 60
Kirmington. *N Lin* 6J 43
Kirmond le Mire. *Linc* 8J 43
Kirn. *Arg* 2L 57
Kirriemuir. *Ang* 2G 67
Kirstead Green. *Norf* 2J 31
Kirtlebridge. *Dum* 4G 53
Kirtleton. *Dum* 4G 53
Kirtling. *Cambs* 6C 30
Kirtling Green. *Cambs* 6C 30
Kirtlington. *Oxon* 2C 20
Kirtomy. *High* 5K 85
Kirton. *Linc* 6L 37
Kirton. *Notts* 3D 36
Kirton. *Suff* 8J 31
Kirton End. *Linc* 5K 37
Kirton Holme. *Linc* 5K 37
Kirton in Lindsey. *N Lin* 8G 43
Kishorn. *High* 1K 69
Kislingbury. *Nptn* 6D 28
Kites Hardwick. *Warw* 5B 28
Kittisford. *Som* 3K 7
Kittle. *Swan* 6E 16
Kittybrewster. *Aber* 5J 73
Kitwood. *Hants* 2D 10
Kivernoll. *Here* 8C 26
Kiveton Park. *S Yor* 1B 36
Knaith. *Linc* 1F 36
Knaith Park. *Linc* 1F 36
Knaphill. *Surr* 8G 21
Knapp. *Hants* 3B 10
Knapp. *Per* 4F 66
Knapp. *Som* 3B 8
Knapperfield. *High* 6D 86
Knapton. *Norf* 6K 39
Knapton. *York* 2C 42
Knapton Green. *Here* 6C 26
Knapwell. *Cambs* 5L 29
Knaresborough. *N Yor* 2A 42
Knarsdale. *Nmbd* 6L 53
Knatts Valley. *Kent* 7B 22
Knaven. *Abers* 1H 73
Knayton. *N Yor* 7B 48
Knebworth. *Herts* 1K 21
Knedlington. *E Yor* 5E 42
Kneesall. *Notts* 3E 36
Kneesworth. *Cambs* 7L 29
Kneeton. *Notts* 5E 36
Knelston. *Swan* 8L 15
Knenhall. *Staf* 6H 35
Knightacott. *Devn* 2F 6
Knightcote. *Warw* 6B 28
Knightcott. *N Som* 8B 18
Knightley. *Staf* 7G 35
Knightley Dale. *Staf* 7G 35
Knightlow Hill. *Warw* 4B 28
Knighton. *Devn* 7H 5
Knighton. *Dors* 4E 8
Knighton. *Leic* 1C 28
Knighton. *Powy* 4A 26
Knighton. *Som* 1L 7
Knighton. *Staf*
nr. Eccleshall 7F 34
nr. Woore 5F 34
Knighton. *Wilts* 6L 19
Knighton. *Worc* 6J 27
Knighton Common. *Worc* 4E 26
Knight's End. *Cambs* 2M 29
Knightswood. *Glas* 3D 58
Knightwick. *Worc* 6F 26
Knill. *Here* 5A 26
Knipton. *Leics* 6F 36
Knitsley. *Dur* 7E 54
Kniveton. *Derbs* 4L 35
Knock. *Arg* 4L 63
Knock. *Cumb* 3E 46
Knock. *Mor* 8E 80
Knockally. *High* 1M 79
Knockan. *Arg* 5K 63
Knockan. *High* 2C 78
Knockandhu. *Mor* 3B 72
Knockando. *Mor* 1A 72
Knockarthur. *High* 3H 79
Knockbain. *High* 8G 79
Knockbreck. *High* 7D 76
Knockcloghrim. *M Ulst* 4F 93
Knockdee. *High* 5C 86
Knockdolian. *S Ayr* 3G 51
Knockdon. *S Ayr* 8B 58
Knockdown. *Glos* 5G 19
Knockenbaird. *Abers* 3F 72
Knockenkelly. *N Ayr* 7K 57
Knockentiber. *E Ayr* 6B 58
Knockfarrel. *High* 8F 78
Knockglass. *High* 5B 86
Knockholt. *Kent* 8A 22
Knockholt Pound. *Kent* 8A 22
Knockie Lodge. *High* 4E 70
Knockin. *Shrp* 7B 34
Knockinlaw. *E Ayr* 6C 58
Knockinnon. *High* 8C 86
Knocknacarry. *Caus* 2H 93
Knockrome. *Arg* 2E 56
Knocksharry. *IOM* 6B 44
Knockshinnoch. *E Ayr* 8C 58
Knockvennie. *Dum* 4B 52
Knockvologan. *Arg* 6J 63
Knodishall. *Suff* 5L 31
Knole. *Som* 3C 8
Knollbury. *Mon* 5C 18
Knolls Green. *Ches E* 2G 35
Knolton. *Wrex* 6B 34
Knook. *Wilts* 1H 9
Knossington. *Leics* 1F 28
Knott. *High* 8E 76
Knott End-on-Sea. *Lanc* 3B 40
Knotting. *Bed* 5H 29
Knotting Green. *Bed* 5H 29
Knottingley. *W Yor* 5B 42
Knotts. *Cumb* 3C 46
Knotty Ash. *Mers* 8C 40
Knotty Green. *Buck* 4G 21
Knowbury. *Shrp* 4D 26
Knowe. *Dum* 4J 51
Knowefield. *Cumb* 6J 53
Knowehead. *Dum* 2M 51
Knowes. *E Lot* 2D 60
Knowesgate. *Nmbd* 3C 54
Knoweside. *S Ayr* 8A 58
Knowes of Elrick. *Abers* 8F 80
Knowle. *Bris* 6E 18
Knowle. *Devn*
nr. Braunton 2D 6
nr. Budleigh Salterton 7K 7
nr. Crediton 5G 7
Knowle. *Shrp* 4D 26
Knowle. *W Mid* 4K 27
Knowle Green. *Lanc* 4E 40
Knowle St Giles. *Som* 4B 8
Knowlesands. *Shrp* 2F 26
Knowle Village. *Hants* 5C 10
Knowl Hill. *Wind* 6F 20
Knowlton. *Kent* 8J 23
Knowsley. *Mers* 8C 40
Knowstone. *Devn* 3H 7
Knucklas. *Powy* 4A 26
Knuston. *Nptn* 5G 29
Knutsford. *Ches E* 2F 34
Knypersley. *Staf* 4G 35
Krumlin. *W Yor* 6J 41
Kuggar. *Corn* 7L 3
Kyleakin. *High* 3J 69
Kyle of Lochalsh. *High* 3J 69
Kylerhea. *High* 3J 69
Kylesku. *High* 8E 84
Kyles Lodge. *W Isl* 5A 76
Kylesmorar. *High* 6K 69
Kylestrome. *High* 8E 84
Kymin. *Mon* 2D 18
Kynaston. *Here* 8E 26
Kynaston. *Shrp* 7B 34
Kynnersley. *Telf* 8E 34
Kyre Green. *Worc* 5E 26
Kyre Park. *Worc* 5E 26
Kyrewood. *Worc* 5E 26

L

Labost. *W Isl* 7F 82
Lacasaidh. *W Isl* 1E 76
Lacasdail. *W Isl* 8H 83
Laceby. *NE Lin* 7K 43
Lacey Green. *Buck* 3F 20
Lach Dennis. *Ches W* 2F 34
Lache. *Ches W* 3B 34
Lack. *Ferm* 5C 92
Lackagh. *Caus* 3E 92
Lackford. *Suff* 4D 30
Lacock. *Wilts* 7H 19
Ladbroke. *Warw* 6B 28
Laddingford. *Kent* 1C 12
Lade Bank. *Linc* 4L 37
Ladock. *Corn* 6A 4
Lady. *Orkn* 5F 88
Ladybank. *Fife* 6G 67
Ladycross. *Corn* 7C 6
Lady Green. *Mers* 7B 40
Lady Hall. *Cumb* 6L 45
Ladykirk. *Bord* 5F 60
Ladysford. *Abers* 7J 81
Ladywood. *W Mid* 3J 27
Ladywood. *Worc* 5G 27
Laga. *High* 1M 63
Lagavulin. *Arg* 5D 56
Lagg. *Arg* 2E 56
Lagg. *N Ayr* 7J 57
Laggan. *Arg* 4B 56
Laggan. *High*
nr. Fort Augustus 6C 70
nr. Newtonmore 6G 71
Laggan. *Mor* 2C 72
Lagganlia. *High* 5J 71
Lagganulva. *Arg* 3K 63
Laghey Corner. *M Ulst* 5F 93
Laglingarten. *Arg* 7F 64
Lagness. *W Sus* 5F 10
Laid. *High* 6G 85
Laide. *High* 4K 77
Laigh Fenwick. *E Ayr* 5C 58
Laindon. *Essx* 5C 22
Lairg. *High* 3F 78
Lairg Muir. *High* 3F 78
Laithes. *Cumb* 8J 53
Laithkirk. *Dur* 3H 47
Lake. *Devn* 2E 6
Lake. *IOW* 7C 10
Lake. *Wilts* 2K 9
Lakenham. *Norf* 1J 31
Lakenheath. *Suff* 3D 30
Lakesend. *Norf* 2B 30
Lakeside. *Cumb* 7B 46
Laleham. *Surr* 7H 21
Laleston. *B'end* 6H 17
Lamancha. *Bord* 4L 59
Lamarsh. *Essx* 8E 30
Lamas. *Norf* 7J 39
Lamb Corner. *Essx* 8G 31
Lambden. *Bord* 5E 60
Lamberhead Green. *G Man* 7D 40
Lamberhurst. *Kent* 2C 12
Lamberhurst Quarter. *Kent* 2C 12
Lamberton. *Bord* 4G 61
Lambeth. *G Lon* 6L 21
Lambfell Moar. *IOM* 6B 44
Lambhill. *Glas* 3D 58
Lambley. *Nmbd* 6L 53
Lambley. *Notts* 5D 36
Lambourn. *W Ber* 6M 19
Lambourne End. *Essx* 4A 22
Lambourn Woodlands.
W Ber 6M 19
Lambs Green. *Dors* 6H 9
Lambs Green. *W Sus* 2K 11
Lambston. *Pemb* 5F 14
Lamellion. *Corn* 5E 4
Lamerton. *Devn* 8D 6
Lamesley. *Tyne* 6F 54
Laminess. *Orkn* 6F 88
Lamington. *High* 6H 79
Lamington. *S Lan* 6H 59
Lamlash. *N Ayr* 6K 57
Lamonby. *Cumb* 8J 53
Lamorick. *Corn* 5C 4
Lamorna. *Corn* 6H 3
Lamorran. *Corn* 7A 4
Lampeter. *Cdgn* 8E 24
Lampeter Velfrey. *Pemb* 5H 15
Lamphey. *Pemb* 6G 15
Lamplugh. *Cumb* 2K 45
Lamport. *Nptn* 4E 28
Lamyatt. *Som* 2E 8
Lana. *Devn*
nr. Ashwater 6C 6
nr. Holsworthy 5C 6
Lanark. *S Lan* 5G 59
Lanarth. *Corn* 6L 3
Lancaster. *Lanc* 1C 40
Lanchester. *Dur* 7E 54
Lancing. *W Sus* 5J 11
Landbeach. *Cambs* 5A 30
Landcross. *Devn* 3D 6
Landerberry. *Abers* 5G 73
Landford. *Wilts* 4L 9
Land Gate. *G Man* 7D 40
Landhallow. *High* 8C 86
Landimore. *Swan* 7L 15
Landkey. *Devn* 2E 6
Landkey Newland. *Devn* 2E 6
Landore. *Swan* 5F 16
Landport. *Port* 5D 10
Landrake. *Corn* 5F 4
Landscove. *Devn* 5K 5
Land's End Airport. *Corn* 6G 3
Landshipping. *Pemb* 5G 15
Landulph. *Corn* 5G 5
Landywood. *Staf* 1H 27
Lane. *Corn* 2M 3
Laneast. *Corn* 7B 6
Lane Bottom. *Lanc* 4G 41
Lane End. *Buck* 4F 20
Lane End. *Hants* 3C 10
Lane End. *IOW* 7D 10
Lane End. *Wilts* 1G 9
Lane Ends. *Derbs* 6L 35
Lane Ends. *Dur* 8E 54
Lane Ends. *Lanc* 2F 40
Laneham. *Notts* 2F 36
Lane Head. *Dur*
nr. Hutton Magna 4K 47
nr. Woodland 3J 47
Lanehead. *Dur* 7B 54
Lane Head. *G Man* 8E 40
Lanehead. *Nmbd* 3A 54
Lane Head. *W Yor* 7K 41
Lane Heads. *Lanc* 4C 40
Lanercost. *Cumb* 5K 53
Laneshaw Bridge. *Lanc* 3H 41
Laney Green. *Staf* 1H 27
Langais. *W Isl* 7K 75
Langal. *High* 1B 64
Langar. *Notts* 6E 36
Langbank. *Ren* 2B 58
Langbar. *N Yor* 2J 41
Langburnshiels. *Bord* 1K 53
Langcliffe. *N Yor* 1G 41
Langdale End. *N Yor* 6G 49
Langdon. *Corn* 6B 6
Langdon Beck. *Dur* 8B 54
Langdon Cross. *Corn* 7C 6
Langdon Hills. *Essx* 5C 22
Langdown. *Hants* 5B 10
Langdyke. *Fife* 7G 67
Langenhoe. *Essx* 2G 23
Langford. *C Beds* 7J 29
Langford. *Devn* 5K 7
Langford. *Essx* 3E 22
Langford. *Notts* 4F 36
Langford. *Oxon* 3L 19
Langford. *Som* 3M 7
Langford Budville. *Som* 3L 7
Langham. *Dors* 3F 8
Langham. *Essx* 8G 31
Langham. *Norf* 5G 39
Langham. *Rut* 8F 36
Langham. *Suff* 5F 30
Langho. *Lanc* 4F 40
Langholm. *Dum* 3H 53
Langland. *Swan* 6F 16
Langleeford. *Nmbd* 7G 61
Langley. *Ches E* 2H 35
Langley. *Derbs* 5B 36
Langley. *Essx* 8M 29
Langley. *Glos* 1J 19
Langley. *Hants* 5B 10
Langley. *Herts* 1K 21
Langley. *Kent* 8E 22
Langley. *Nmbd* 5B 54
Langley. *Slo* 6H 21
Langley. *Som* 3K 7
Langley. *Warw* 5K 27
Langley. *W Sus* 3F 10
Langley Burrell. *Wilts* 6H 19
Langleybury. *Herts* 3H 21
Langley Common. *Derbs* 6L 35
Langley Green. *Derbs* 6L 35
Langley Green. *Norf* 1K 31
Langley Green. *Warw* 5K 27
Langley Green. *W Sus* 2K 11
Langley Heath. *Kent* 8E 22
Langley Marsh. *Som* 3K 7
Langley Moor. *Dur* 7F 54
Langley Park. *Dur* 7F 54
Langley Street. *Norf* 1K 31
Langney. *E Sus* 5C 12
Langold. *Notts* 1C 36
Langore. *Corn* 7B 6
Langport. *Som* 3C 8
Langrick. *Linc* 5K 37
Langridge. *Bath* 7F 18
Langridgeford. *Devn* 3E 6
Langrigg. *Cumb* 7F 52
Langrish. *Hants* 3E 10
Langsett. *S Yor* 7L 41
Langshaw. *Bord* 6C 60
Langstone. *Hants* 5E 10
Langthorne. *N Yor* 6L 47
Langthorpe. *N Yor* 1A 42
Langthwaite. *N Yor* 5J 47
Langtoft. *E Yor* 1H 43
Langtoft. *Linc* 8J 37
Langton. *Dur* 4K 47
Langton. *Linc*
nr. Horncastle 3K 37
nr. Spilsby 2L 37
Langton. *N Yor* 1E 42
Langton by Wragby. *Linc* 2J 37
Langton Green. *Kent* 2B 12
Langton Herring. *Dors* 7E 8
Langton Long Blandford.
Dors 5G 9
Langton Matravers. *Dors* 8H 9
Langtree. *Devn* 4D 6
Langwathby. *Cumb* 8K 53
Langwith. *Derbs* 2C 36
Langworth. *Linc* 2H 37
Lanivet. *Corn* 5C 4
Lanjeth. *Corn* 6B 4
Lank. *Corn* 4C 4
Lanlivery. *Corn* 6C 4
Lanner. *Corn* 5L 3
Lanreath. *Corn* 6D 4
Lansallos. *Corn* 6D 4
Lansdown. *Bath* 7F 18
Lansdown. *Glos* 1H 19
Lanteglos Highway. *Corn* 6D 4
Lanton. *Nmbd* 6G 61
Lanton. *Bord* 7D 60
Lapford. *Devn* 5G 7
Lapford Cross. *Devn* 5G 7
Laphroaig. *Arg* 5C 56
Lapley. *Staf* 8G 35
Lapworth. *Warw* 4K 27
Larachbeg. *High* 3A 64
Larbert. *Falk* 1G 59
Larden Green. *Ches E* 4D 34
Larel. *High* 6C 86
Largie. *Abers* 2F 72
Largiemore. *Arg* 1J 57
Largoward. *Fife* 7H 67
Largs. *N Ayr* 4M 57
Largue. *Abers* 1F 72
Largybeg. *N Ayr* 7K 57
Largymeanoch. *N Ayr* 7K 57
Largymore. *N Ayr* 7K 57
Larkfield. *Inv* 2M 57
Larkfield. *Kent* 8D 22
Larkhall. *Bath* 7F 18
Larkhall. *S Lan* 4F 58
Larkhill. *Wilts* 1K 9
Larling. *Norf* 3F 30
Larne. *ME Ant* 3J 93
Larport. *Here* 8D 26
Lartington. *Dur* 4J 47
Lary. *Abers* 5C 72
Lasham. *Hants* 1D 10
Lashenden. *Kent* 1E 12
Lasswade. *Midl* 3M 59
Lastingham. *N Yor* 6E 48
Latchford. *Herts* 1L 21
Latchford. *Oxon* 3D 20
Latchingdon. *Essx* 3E 22
Latchley. *Corn* 8D 6
Latchmere Green. *Hants* 8D 20
Lathbury. *Mil* 7F 28
Latheron. *High* 8C 86
Latheronwheel. *High* 8C 86
Lathom. *Lanc* 7C 40
Lathones. *Fife* 7H 67
Latimer. *Buck* 4H 21
Latteridge. *S Glo* 5E 18
Lattiford. *Som* 3E 8
Latton. *Wilts* 4J 19
Laudale House. *High* 2B 64
Lauder. *Bord* 5C 60
Laugharne. *Carm* 5K 15
Laughterton. *Linc* 2F 36
Laughton. *E Sus* 4B 12
Laughton. *Leics* 3D 28
Laughton. *Linc*
nr. Gainsborough 8F 42
nr. Grantham 6H 37
Laughton Common. *S Yor* 1C 36
Laughton en le Morthen.
S Yor 1C 36
Launcells. *Corn* 5B 6
Launceston. *Corn* 7C 6
Launcherley. *Som* 1D 8
Launton. *Oxon* 1D 20
Laurelvale. *Arm* 6G 93
Laurencekirk. *Abers* 8G 73
Laurieston. *Dum* 5A 52
Laurieston. *Falk* 2H 59
Lavendon. *Mil* 6G 29
Lavenham. *Suff* 7F 30
Laverhay. *Dum* 2F 52
Laversdale. *Cumb* 5J 53
Laverstock. *Wilts* 2K 9
Laverstoke. *Hants* 1B 10
Laverton. *Glos* 8J 27
Laverton. *N Yor* 8L 47
Laverton. *Som* 8F 18
Lavister. *Wrex* 4B 34
Law. *S Lan* 4G 59
Lawers. *Per* 4L 65
Lawford. *Essx* 8G 31
Lawhitton. *Corn* 7C 6
Lawkland. *N Yor* 1F 40
Lawley. *Telf* 1E 26
Lawnhead. *Staf* 7G 35
Lawrencetown. *Arm* 6G 93
Lawrenny. *Pemb* 6G 15
Lawshall. *Suff* 6E 30
Lawton. *Here* 6C 26
Laxey. *IOM* 6D 44
Laxfield. *Suff* 4J 31
Laxfirth. *Shet* 2E 90
Laxo. *Shet* 1E 90
Laxton. *E Yor* 5E 42
Laxton. *Nptn* 2G 29
Laxton. *Notts* 3E 36
Laycock. *W Yor* 3J 41
Layer Breton. *Essx* 2F 22
Layer-de-la-Haye. *Essx* 1F 22
Layer Marney. *Essx* 2F 22
Laymore. *Dors* 5B 8
Laysters Pole. *Here* 5D 26
Layter's Green. *Buck* 4G 21
Laytham. *E Yor* 4E 42
Lazenby. *Red C* 4C 48
Lazonby. *Cumb* 8K 53
Lea. *Derbs* 4M 35
Lea. *Here* 1E 18
Lea. *Linc* 1F 36
Lea. *Shrp*
nr. Bishop's Castle 3B 26
nr. Shrewsbury 1C 26
Lea. *Wilts* 5H 19
Leabrooks. *Derbs* 4B 36
Leac a Li. *W Isl* 4C 76
Leachd. *Arg* 8E 64
Leachkin. *High* 1G 71
Leachpool. *Pemb* 5F 14
Leadburn. *Midl* 4L 59
Leadenham. *Linc* 4G 37
Leaden Roding. *Essx* 2B 22
Leaderfoot. *Bord* 6C 60
Leadgate. *Cumb* 7M 53
Leadgate. *Dur* 6E 54
Leadgate. *Nmbd* 6E 54
Leadhills. *S Lan* 8G 59
Leadingcross Green. *Kent* 8E 22
Lea End. *Worc* 4J 27
Leafield. *Oxon* 2M 19
Leagrave. *Lutn* 1H 21
Lea Hall. *W Mid* 3K 27
Lea Heath. *Staf* 7J 35
Leake. *N Yor* 6B 48
Leake Common Side. *Linc* 4L 37
Leake Fold Hill. *Linc* 4M 37
Leake Hurn's End. *Linc* 5M 37
Lealholm. *N Yor* 5E 48
Lealt. *Arg* 8A 64
Lealt. *High* 7G 77
Leam. *Derbs* 2L 35
Lea Marston. *Warw* 2L 27
Leamington Hastings. *Warw* 5B 28
Leamington Spa, Royal.
Warw 5M 27
Leamonsley. *Staf* 1K 27
Leamside. *Dur* 7G 55
Leargybreck. *Arg* 2E 56
Lease Rigg. *N Yor* 5F 48
Leasgill. *Cumb* 7C 46
Leasingham. *Linc* 5H 37
Leasingthorne. *Dur* 8F 54
Leasowe. *Mers* 8A 40
Leatherhead. *Surr* 8J 21
Leathley. *N Yor* 3L 41
Leaths. *Dum* 5B 52
Leaton. *Shrp* 8C 34
Leaton. *Telf* 8E 34
Lea Town. *Lanc* 4C 40
Leaveland. *Kent* 8G 23
Leavenheath. *Suff* 8F 30
Leavening. *N Yor* 1E 42
Leaves Green. *G Lon* 7M 21
Lea Yeat. *Cumb* 7F 46
Leazes. *Dur* 6E 54
Lebberston. *N Yor* 7H 49
Lechlade on Thames. *Glos* 4L 19
Leck. *Lanc* 8E 46
Leckford. *Hants* 2A 10
Leckfurin. *High* 6K 85
Leckgruinart. *Arg* 3B 56
Leckhampstead. *Buck* 8E 28
Leckhampstead. *W Ber* 6B 20
Leckhampton. *Glos* 2H 19
Leckmelm. *High* 4B 78
Leckwith. *V Glam* 7L 17
Leconfield. *E Yor* 3H 43
Ledaig. *Arg* 4D 64
Ledburn. *Buck* 1G 21
Ledbury. *Here* 8F 26
Ledgemoor. *Here* 6C 26
Ledgowan. *High* 8B 78
Ledicot. *Here* 5C 26
Ledmore. *High* 2C 78
Lednabirichen. *High* 4H 79
Lednagullin. *High* 5L 85
Ledsham. *Ches W* 2B 34
Ledsham. *W Yor* 5B 42
Ledston. *W Yor* 5B 42
Ledstone. *Devn* 7K 5
Ledwell. *Oxon* 1B 20
Lee, The. *Buck* 3G 21
Lee. *Devn*
nr. Ilfracombe 1D 6
nr. South Molton 3H 7
Lee. *G Lon* 6L 21
Lee. *Hants* 4A 10
Lee. *Lanc* 2D 40
Lee. *Shrp* 6C 34
Leeans. *Shet* 3D 90
Leebotten. *Shet* 5E 90
Leebotwood. *Shrp* 2C 26
Lee Brockhurst. *Shrp* 7D 34
Leece. *Cumb* 8M 45
Leechpool. *Mon* 5D 18
Lee Clump. *Buck* 3G 21
Leeds. *Kent* 8E 22
Leeds. *W Yor* 4L 41
Leeds Bradford Airport.
W Yor 3L 41
Leedstown. *Corn* 5K 3
Leegomery. *Telf* 8E 34
Lee Head. *Derbs* 8J 41
Leek. *Staf* 4H 35
Leekbrook. *Staf* 4H 35
Leek Wootton. *Warw* 5L 27
Lee Mill. *Devn* 6H 5
Leeming. *N Yor* 7L 47
Leeming Bar. *N Yor* 6L 47
Lee Moor. *Devn* 5H 5
Lee Moor. *W Yor* 5M 41
Lee-on-the-Solent. *Hants* 5C 10
Lees. *Derbs* 6L 35
Lees. *G Man* 7H 41
Lees, The. *Kent* 8G 23
Lees. *W Yor* 4J 41
Leeswood. *Flin* 3A 34
Leetown. *Per* 5F 66
Leftwich. *Ches W* 2E 34
Legbourne. *Linc* 1L 37
Legburthwaite. *Cumb* 4B 46
Legerwood. *Bord* 5C 60
Legsby. *Linc* 1J 37
Leicester. *Leic* 1C 28
Leicester Forest East. *Leics* 1C 28
Leigh. *Dors* 5E 8
Leigh, The. *Glos* 1G 19
Leigh. *G Man* 7E 40
Leigh. *Kent* 1B 12
Leigh. *Shrp* 1B 26
Leigh. *Surr* 1K 11
Leigh. *Wilts* 4J 19
Leigh. *Worc* 6F 26
Leigham. *Plym* 6H 5
Leigh Beck. *Essx* 5E 22
Leigh Common. *Som* 3F 8
Leigh Delamere. *Wilts* 6G 19
Leigh Green. *Kent* 2F 12
Leighland Chapel. *Som* 2K 7
Leigh-on-Sea. *S'end* 5E 22
Leigh Park. *Hants* 5E 10
Leigh Sinton. *Worc* 6F 26
Leighterton. *Glos* 4G 19
Leighton. *N Yor* 8K 47
Leighton. *Powy* 2M 25
Leighton. *Shrp* 1E 26
Leighton. *Som* 1F 8
Leighton Bromswold.
Cambs 4J 29
Leighton Buzzard. *C Beds* 1G 21
Leigh-upon-Mendip. *Som* 1E 8
Leinthall Earls. *Here* 5C 26
Leinthall Starkes. *Here* 5C 26
Leintwardine. *Here* 4C 26
Leire. *Leics* 2C 28
Leirinmore. *High* 5G 85
Leishmore. *High* 1E 70
Leiston. *Suff* 5L 31
Leitfie. *Per* 3F 66
Leith. *Edin* 2L 59
Leitholm. *Bord* 5E 60
Leitrim. *New M* 7H 93
Lelant. *Corn* 5J 3
Lelant Downs. *Corn* 5J 3
Lelley. *E Yor* 4K 43
Lem Hill. *Shrp* 4F 26
Lemington. *Tyne* 5E 54
Lempitlaw. *Bord* 6E 60
Lemsford. *Herts* 2K 21
Lenacre. *Cumb* 7E 46
Lenchie. *Abers* 2E 72
Lenchwick. *Worc* 7J 27
Lendalfoot. *S Ayr* 3G 51
Lendrick. *Stir* 7K 65
Lenham. *Kent* 8E 22
Lenham Heath. *Kent* 1F 12
Lenimore. *N Ayr* 5H 57
Lennel. *Bord* 5F 60
Lennoxtown. *E Dun* 2E 58
Lenton. *Linc* 6H 37
Lentran. *High* 1F 70
Lenwade. *Norf* 8G 39
Lenzie. *E Dun* 2E 58
Leochel Cushnie. *Abers* 4E 72
Leogh. *Shet* 2M 89
Leominster. *Here* 6C 26
Leonard Stanley. *Glos* 3G 19
Lepe. *Hants* 6B 10
Lephenstrath. *Arg* 1B 50
Lephin. *High* 1C 68
Lephinchapel. *Arg* 8D 64
Lephinmore. *Arg* 8D 64
Leppington. *N Yor* 1E 42
Lepton. *W Yor* 6L 41
Lerryn. *Corn* 6D 4
Lerwick. *Shet* 3E 90
Lerwick (Tingwall) Airport.
Shet 3E 90
Lesbury. *Nmbd* 8K 61
Leslie. *Abers* 3E 72
Leslie. *Fife* 7F 66
Lesmahagow. *S Lan* 6G 59
Lesnewth. *Corn* 2D 4
Lessingham. *Norf* 7K 39
Lessonhall. *Cumb* 6G 53
Leswalt. *Dum* 5F 50
Letchmore Heath. *Herts* 4J 21
Letchworth Garden City.
Herts 8K 29
Letcombe Bassett. *Oxon* 5A 20
Letcombe Regis. *Oxon* 5A 20
Letham. *Ang* 3J 67
Letham. *Falk* 1G 59
Letham. *Fife* 6G 67
Lethanhill. *E Ayr* 8C 58
Lethenty. *Abers* 1H 73
Letheringham. *Suff* 6J 31
Letheringsett. *Norf* 6G 39
Lettaford. *Devn* 7G 7
Lettan. *Orkn* 5G 89
Letter. *Abers* 4G 73
Letterewe. *High* 6L 77
Letterfearn. *High* 3K 69
Lettermore. *Arg* 3K 63
Letters. *High* 5B 78
Lettershendoney. *Derr* 3D 92
Letterston. *Pemb* 4F 14
Letton. *Here*
nr. Kington 7B 26
nr. Leintwardine 4B 26
Letty Green. *Herts* 2K 21
Letwell. *S Yor* 1C 36
Leuchars. *Fife* 5H 67
Leumrabhagh. *W Isl* 2E 76
Leusdon. *Devn* 8G 7
Levaneap. *Shet* 1E 90
Levedale. *Staf* 8G 35
Leven. *E Yor* 3J 43
Leven. *Fife* 7G 67
Levencorroch. *N Ayr* 7K 57
Levenhall. *E Lot* 2A 60
Levens. *Cumb* 7C 46
Levens Green. *Herts* 1L 21
Levenshulme. *G Man* 8G 41
Levenwick. *Shet* 5E 90
Leverburgh. *W Isl* 5B 76
Leverington. *Cambs* 8M 37
Leverton. *Linc* 5L 37
Leverton. *W Ber* 6M 19
Leverton Lucasgate. *Linc* 5M 37
Leverton Outgate. *Linc* 5M 37
Levington. *Suff* 8J 31
Levisham. *N Yor* 6F 48
Levishie. *High* 4E 70
Lew. *Oxon* 3M 19
Lewaigue. *IOM* 5D 44
Lewannick. *Corn* 7B 6
Lewdown. *Devn* 7D 6
Lewes. *E Sus* 4M 11
Leweston. *Pemb* 4F 14
Lewisham. *G Lon* 6L 21
Lewiston. *High* 3F 70
Lewistown. *B'end* 6J 17
Lewknor. *Oxon* 4E 20
Leworthy. *Devn*
nr. Barnstaple 2F 6
nr. Holsworthy 5C 6
Lewson Street. *Kent* 7F 22
Lewthorn Cross. *Devn* 8G 7
Lewtrenchard. *Devn* 7D 6
Ley. *Corn* 5D 4
Leybourne. *Kent* 8C 22
Leyburn. *N Yor* 6K 47
Leycett. *Staf* 5F 34
Leyfields. *Staf* 1L 27
Ley Green. *Herts* 1J 21
Ley Hill. *Buck* 3G 21
Leyland. *Lanc* 5D 40
Leylodge. *Abers* 4G 73
Leymoor. *W Yor* 6K 41
Leys. *Per* 4F 66
Leysdown-on-Sea. *Kent* 6G 23
Leysmill. *Ang* 3K 67
Leyton. *G Lon* 5L 21
Leytonstone. *G Lon* 5M 21
Lezant. *Corn* 8C 6
Leziate. *Norf* 8C 38
Lhanbryde. *Mor* 7B 80
Lhen, The. *IOM* 4C 44
Liatrie. *High* 2C 70
Libanus. *Powy* 2J 17
Libberton. *S Lan* 5H 59
Libbery. *Worc* 6H 27
Liberton. *Edin* 3L 59
Liceasto. *W Isl* 4C 76
Lichfield. *Staf* 1K 27
Lickey. *Worc* 4H 27
Lickey End. *Worc* 4H 27
Lickfold. *W Sus* 3G 11
Liddaton. *Devn* 7D 6
Liddington. *Swin* 5L 19
Liddle. *Orkn* 3F 86
Lidgate. *Suff* 6D 30
Lidgett. *Notts* 3D 36
Lidham Hill. *E Sus* 4E 12
Lidlington. *C Beds* 8G 29
Lidsey. *W Sus* 5G 11
Lidstone. *Oxon* 1A 20
Lienassie. *High* 3L 69
Liff. *Ang* 4G 67
Lifford. *W Mid* 3J 27
Lifton. *Devn* 7C 6

Lower Weare—Moat

Lower Weare. *Som* 8C 18
Lower Welson. *Here* 6A 26
Lower Whatcombe. *Dors* 5G 9
Lower Whitley. *Ches W* 2E 34
Lower Wield. *Hants* 1D 10
Lower Withington. *Ches E* 3G 35
Lower Woodend. *Buck* 5F 20
Lower Woodford. *Wilts* 2K 9
Lower Wraxall. *Dors* 5D 8
Lower Wych. *Ches W* 5C 34
Lower Wyche. *Worc* 7F 26
Lowesby. *Leics* 1E 28
Lowestoft. *Suff* 2M 31
Loweswater. *Cumb* 2L 45
Low Etherley. *Dur* 3K 47
Lowfield Heath. *W Sus* 1K 11
Lowford. *Hants* 4B 10
Low Fulney. *Linc* 7K 37
Low Gate. *Nmbd* 5C 54
Lowgill. *Cumb* 6E 46
Lowgill. *Lanc* 1E 40
Low Grantley. *N Yor* 8L 47
Low Green. *N Yor* 2L 41
Low Habberley. *Worc* 4G 27
Low Ham. *Som* 3C 8
Low Hameringham. *Linc* 3L 37
Low Hawsker. *N Yor* 5G 49
Low Hesket. *Cumb* 7J 53
Low Hesleyhurst. *Nmbd* 2D 54
Lowick. *Cumb* 7A 46
Lowick. *Nptn* 3G 29
Lowick. *Nmbd* 6H 61
Lowick Bridge. *Cumb* 7A 46
Lowick Green. *Cumb* 7A 46
Low Knipe. *Cumb* 3D 46
Low Leighton. *Derbs* 1J 35
Low Lorton. *Cumb* 2L 45
Low Marishes. *N Yor* 8F 48
Low Marnham. *Notts* 3F 36
Low Mill. *N Yor* 6D 48
Low Moor. *Lanc* 3F 40
Low Moor. *W Yor* 5K 41
Low Moorsley. *Tyne* 7G 55
Low Newton-by-the-Sea.
Nmbd 7K 61
Lownie Moor. *Ang* 3H 67
Lowood. *Bord* 6C 60
Low Row. *Cumb*
nr. Brampton 5K 53
nr. Wigton 7F 52
Low Row. *N Yor* 6H 47
Lowsonford. *Warw* 5K 27
Low Street. *Norf* 1G 31
Lowther. *Cumb* 3D 46
Lowthorpe. *E Yor* 1H 43
Lowton. *Devn* 5F 6
Lowton. *G Man* 8E 40
Lowton. *Som* 4L 7
Lowton Common.
G Man 8E 40
Low Torry. *Fife* 1J 59
Low Toynton. *Linc* 2K 37
Low Valleyfield. *Fife* 1H 59
Low Westwood. *Dur* 6E 54
Low Whinnow. *Cumb* 6H 53
Low Wood. *Cumb* 7B 46
Low Worsall. *N Yor* 5A 48
Low Wray. *Cumb* 5B 46
Loxbeare. *Devn* 4J 7
Loxhill. *Surr* 2H 11
Loxhore. *Devn* 2F 6
Loxley. *S Yor* 1M 35
Loxley. *Warw* 6L 27
Loxley Green. *Staf* 6J 35
Loxton. *N Som* 8B 18
Loxwood. *W Sus* 2H 11
Lubcroy. *High* 3D 78
Lubenham. *Leics* 3E 28
Lubinvullin. *High* 5H 85
Luccombe. *Som* 1J 7
Luccombe Village. *IOW* 7C 10
Lucker. *Nmbd* 6J 61
Luckett. *Corn* 8C 6
Luckington. *Wilts* 5G 19
Lucklawhill. *Fife* 5H 67
Luckwell Bridge. *Som* 2J 7
Lucton. *Here* 5C 26
Ludag. *W Isl* 4D 74
Ludborough. *Linc* 8K 43
Ludchurch. *Pemb* 5H 15
Luddenden. *W Yor* 5J 41
Luddenden Foot. *W Yor* 5J 41
Luddenham. *Kent* 7F 22
Ludderburn. *Cumb* 6C 46
Luddesdown. *Kent* 7C 22
Luddington. *N Lin* 6F 42
Luddington. *Warw* 6K 27
Luddington in the Brook.
Nptn 3J 29
Ludford. *Linc* 1J 37
Ludford. *Shrp* 4D 26
Ludgershall. *Buck* 2D 20
Ludgershall. *Wilts* 8L 19
Ludgvan. *Corn* 5J 3
Ludham. *Norf* 8K 39
Ludlow. *Shrp* 4D 26
Ludstone. *Shrp* 2G 27
Ludwell. *Wilts* 3H 9
Ludworth. *Dur* 7G 55
Luffenhall. *Herts* 1K 21
Luffincott. *Devn* 6C 6
Lugar. *E Ayr* 7D 58
Luggate Burn. *E Lot* 2D 60
Lugg Green. *Here* 5C 26
Luggiebank. *N Lan* 2F 58
Lugton. *E Ayr* 4C 58
Lugwardine. *Here* 7D 26
Luib. *High* 3G 69
Luib. *Stir* 5J 65
Lulham. *Here* 7C 26
Lullington. *Derbs* 8L 35
Lullington. *E Sus* 5B 12
Lullington. *Som* 8F 18
Lulsgate Bottom. *N Som* 7D 18
Lulsley. *Worc* 6F 26
Lulworth Camp. *Dors* 7G 9
Lumb. *Lanc* 5G 41
Lumby. *N Yor* 4B 42
Lumphanan. *Abers* 5E 72
Lumphinnans. *Fife* 8E 66
Lumsdaine. *Bord* 3F 60
Lumsden. *Abers* 3D 72
Lunan. *Ang* 2K 67
Lunanhead. *Ang* 2H 67
Luncarty. *Per* 5D 66
Lund. *E Yor* 3G 43
Lund. *N Yor* 4D 42
Lundie. *Ang* 4F 66
Lundin Links. *Fife* 7H 67
Lundy Green. *Norf* 2J 31
Lunna. *Shet* 1E 90
Lunning. *Shet* 1F 90
Lunnon. *Swan* 8M 15
Lunsford. *Kent* 8C 22
Lunsford's Cross. *E Sus* 4D 12
Lunt. *Mers* 7B 40
Luppitt. *Devn* 5L 7
Lupridge. *Devn* 6K 5
Lupset. *W Yor* 6M 41
Lupton. *Cumb* 7D 46
Lurgan. *Arm* 6G 93
Lurganare. *New M* 7G 93
Lurgashall. *W Sus* 3G 11
Lurley. *Devn* 4J 7
Lusby. *Linc* 3L 37
Luscombe. *Devn* 6K 5
Luson. *Devn* 7J 5
Luss. *Arg* 8H 65
Lussagiven. *Arg* 1F 56
Lusta. *High* 8D 76
Lustleigh. *Devn* 7G 7
Luston. *Here* 5C 26
Luthermuir. *Abers* 1K 67
Luthrie. *Fife* 6G 67
Lutley. *Staf* 3G 27
Luton. *Devn*
nr. Honiton 5K 7
nr. Teignmouth 8J 7
Luton. *Lutn* 1H 21
Luton Airport. *Lutn* 1J 21
Lutterworth. *Leics* 3C 28
Lutton. *Devn*
nr. Ivybridge 6H 5
nr. South Brent 5J 5
Lutton. *Linc* 7M 37
Lutton. *Nptn* 3J 29
Lutton Gowts. *Linc* 7M 37
Lutworthy. *Devn* 4G 7
Luxborough. *Som* 2J 7
Luxley. *Glos* 1E 18
Luxulyan. *Corn* 6C 4
Lybster. *High* 8D 86
Lydbury North. *Shrp* 3B 26
Lydcott. *Devn* 2F 6
Lydd. *Kent* 3G 13
Lydd Airport. *Kent* 3G 13
Lydden. *Kent*
nr. Dover 1J 13
nr. Margate 7K 23
Lyddington. *Rut* 2F 28
Lydd-on-Sea. *Kent* 3G 13
Lydeard St Lawrence. *Som* 2L 7
Lyde Green. *Hants* 8E 20
Lydford. *Devn* 7E 6
Lydford Fair Place. *Som* 2D 8
Lydgate. *G Man* 7H 41
Lydgate. *W Yor* 5H 41
Lydham. *Shrp* 2B 26
Lydiard Millicent. *Wilts* 5J 19
Lydiate. *Mers* 7B 40
Lydiate Ash. *Worc* 4H 27
Lydlinch. *Dors* 4F 8
Lydmarsh. *Som* 5B 8
Lydney. *Glos* 3E 18
Lydstep. *Pemb* 7G 15
Lye, The. *Shrp* 2E 26
Lye. *W Mid* 3H 27
Lye Green. *Buck* 3G 21
Lye Green. *E Sus* 2B 12
Lye Head. *Worc* 4F 26
Lyford. *Oxon* 4A 20
Lyham. *Nmbd* 6H 61
Lylestone. *N Ayr* 5B 58
Lymbridge Green. *Kent* 1H 13
Lyme Regis. *Dors* 6B 8
Lyminge. *Kent* 1H 13
Lymington. *Hants* 6M 9
Lyminster. *W Sus* 5H 11
Lymm. *Warr* 1E 34
Lymore. *Hants* 6L 9
Lympne. *Kent* 2H 13
Lympsham. *Som* 8B 18
Lympstone. *Devn* 7J 7
Lynaberack Lodge. *High* 6H 71
Lynbridge. *Devn* 1G 7
Lynch. *Som* 1J 7
Lynchat. *High* 5H 71
Lynch Green. *Norf* 1H 31
Lyndhurst. *Hants* 5M 9
Lyndon. *Rut* 1G 29
Lyne. *Bord* 5L 59
Lyne. *Surr* 7H 21
Lyneal. *Shrp* 6C 34
Lyne Down. *Here* 8E 26
Lyneham. *Oxon* 1L 19
Lyneham. *Wilts* 6J 19
Lyneholmeford. *Cumb* 4K 53
Lynemouth. *Nmbd* 2F 54
Lyne of Gorthleck. *High* 3F 70
Lyne of Skene. *Abers* 4G 73
Lynesack. *Dur* 3J 47
Lyness. *Orkn* 2E 86
Lyng. *Norf* 8G 39
Lyngate. *Norf*
nr. North Walsham 6J 39
nr. Worstead 7K 39
Lynmouth. *Devn* 1G 7
Lynn. *Staf* 1J 27
Lynn. *Telf* 8F 34
Lynsted. *Kent* 7F 22
Lynstone. *Corn* 5B 6
Lynton. *Devn* 1G 7
Lynwilg. *High* 4J 71
Lyon's Gate. *Dors* 5E 8
Lyonshall. *Here* 6B 26
Lytchett Matravers. *Dors* 6H 9
Lytchett Minster. *Dors* 6H 9
Lyth. *High* 5D 86
Lytham. *Lanc* 5B 40
Lytham St Anne's. *Lanc* 5B 40
Lythe. *N Yor* 4F 48
Lythes. *Orkn* 3F 86
Lythmore. *High* 5B 86

M

Mabe Burnthouse. *Corn* 5L 3
Mabie. *Dum* 4D 52
Mablethorpe. *Linc* 1B 38
Macbiehill. *Bord* 4K 59
Macclesfield. *Ches E* 2H 35
Macclesfield Forest. *Ches E* 2H 35
Macduff. *Abers* 7G 81
Machan. *S Lan* 4F 58
Macharioch. *Arg* 1C 50
Machen. *Cphy* 6M 17
Machrie. *N Ayr* 6H 57
Machrihanish. *Arg* 7F 56
Machroes. *Gwyn* 8C 32
Machynlleth. *Powy* 2G 25
Mackerye End. *Herts* 2J 21
Mackworth. *Derb* 6M 35
Macmerry. *E Lot* 2B 60
Macosquin. *Caus* 2F 93
Madderty. *Per* 5C 66
Maddington. *Wilts* 1J 9
Maddiston. *Falk* 2H 59
Madehurst. *W Sus* 4G 11
Madeley. *Staf* 5F 34
Madeley. *Telf* 1E 26
Madeley Heath. *Staf* 5F 34
Madeley Heath. *Worc* 4H 27
Madford. *Devn* 4L 7
Madingley. *Cambs* 5L 29
Madley. *Here* 8C 26
Madresfield. *Worc* 7G 27
Madron. *Corn* 5H 3
Maenaddwyn. *IOA* 2D 32
Maenclochog. *Pemb* 4G 15
Maendy. *V Glam* 7K 17
Maenporth. *Corn* 6L 3
Maentwrog. *Gwyn* 6F 32
Maen-y-groes. *Cdgn* 1K 15
Maer. *Staf* 6F 34
Maerdy. *Carm* 2F 16
Maerdy. *Cnwy* 6K 33
Maerdy. *Rhon* 5J 17
Maesbrook. *Shrp* 7B 34
Maesbury. *Shrp* 7B 34
Maesbury Marsh. *Shrp* 7B 34
Maes-glas. *Flin* 3L 33
Maesgwyn-Isaf. *Powy* 1L 25
Maeshafn. *Den* 4M 33
Maes Llyn. *Cdgn* 2K 15
Maesmynis. *Powy* 8K 25
Maesteg. *B'end* 5H 17
Maestir. *Cdgn* 8E 24
Maesybont. *Carm* 3E 16
Maesycrugiau. *Carm* 2L 15
Maesycwmmer. *Cphy* 5L 17
Maesyrhandir. *Powy* 3K 25
Magdalen Laver. *Essx* 3B 22
Maggieknockater. *Mor* 1C 72
Maghaberry. *Lis* 5G 93
Magham Down. *E Sus* 4C 12
Maghera. *M Ulst* 3F 93
Maghera. *New M* 7H 93
Magherafelt. *M Ulst* 4F 93
Magheralin. *Arm* 6G 93
Magheramason. *Derr* 3C 92
Magheraveely. *Ferm* 7D 92
Maghery. *Arm* 5F 93
Maghull. *Mers* 7B 40
Magna Park. *Leics* 3C 28
Magor. *Mon* 5C 18
Magpie Green. *Suff* 4G 31
Maguiresbridge. *Ferm* 7C 92
Magwyr. *Mon* 5C 18
Maidenbower. *W Sus* 2K 11
Maiden Bradley. *Wilts* 2G 9
Maidencombe. *Torb* 5M 5
Maidenhayne. *Devn* 6A 8
Maidenhead. *Wind* 5F 20
Maiden Law. *Dur* 7E 54
Maiden Newton. *Dors* 6D 8
Maidens. *S Ayr* 1H 51
Maiden's Green. *Brac* 6F 20
Maidensgrove. *Oxon* 5E 20
Maidenwell. *Corn* 4D 4
Maidenwell. *Linc* 2L 37
Maiden Wells. *Pemb* 7F 14
Maidford. *Nptn* 6D 28
Maids Moreton. *Buck* 8E 28
Maidstone. *Kent* 8D 22
Maidwell. *Nptn* 4E 28
Mail. *Shet* 5E 90
Maindee. *Newp* 5B 18
Mainsforth. *Dur* 8G 55
Mains of Auchindachy. *Mor* 1D 72
Mains of Auchnagatt.
Abers 1J 73
Mains of Drum. *Abers* 6H 73
Mains of Edingight. *Mor* 8E 80
Mainsriddle. *Dum* 6D 52
Mainstone. *Shrp* 3A 26
Maisemore. *Glos* 1G 19
Major's Green. *Worc* 4K 27
Makeney. *Derbs* 5A 36
Makerstoun. *Bord* 6D 60
Malacleit. *W Isl* 6J 75
Malaig. *High* 6H 69
Malaig Bheag. *High* 6H 69
Malborough. *Devn* 8K 5
Malcoff. *Derbs* 1J 35
Malcolmburn. *Mor* 8C 80
Malden Rushett. *G Lon* 7J 21
Maldon. *Essx* 3E 22
Malham. *N Yor* 1H 41
Maligar. *High* 7F 76
Malinslee. *Telf* 1E 26
Mallaig. *High* 6H 69
Malleny Mills. *Edin* 3K 59
Mallows Green. *Essx* 1A 22
Malltraeth. *IOA* 4D 32
Mallusk. *Ant* 4H 93
Mallwyd. *Gwyn* 1H 25
Malmesbury. *Wilts* 5H 19
Malmsmead. *Devn* 1G 7
Malpas. *Ches W* 5C 34
Malpas. *Corn* 4M 3
Malpas. *Newp* 4B 18
Malswick. *Glos* 1F 18
Maltby. *S Yor* 8C 42
Maltby. *Stoc T* 4B 48
Maltby le Marsh. *Linc* 1A 38
Malt Lane. *Arg* 7E 64
Maltman's Hill. *Kent* 1F 12
Malton. *N Yor* 8E 48
Malvern Link. *Worc* 7F 26
Malvern Wells. *Worc* 7F 26
Mamble. *Worc* 4E 26
Mamhilad. *Mon* 3B 18
Manaccan. *Corn* 6L 3
Manafon. *Powy* 2L 25
Manais. *W Isl* 5C 76
Manaton. *Devn* 7G 7
Manby. *Linc* 1L 37
Mancetter. *Warw* 2M 27
Manchester. *G Man* 8G 41
Manchester Airport. *G Man* 1G 35
Mancot. *Flin* 3B 34
Manea. *Cambs* 3A 30
Maney. *W Mid* 2K 27
Manfield. *N Yor* 4L 47
Mangotsfield. *S Glo* 6E 18
Mangurstadh. *W Isl* 8D 82
Mankinholes. *W Yor* 5H 41
Manley. *Ches W* 2D 34
Manmoel. *Cphy* 4L 17
Mannal. *Arg* 3E 62
Mannerston. *Falk* 2J 59
Manningford Bohune.
Wilts 8K 19
Manningford Bruce. *Wilts* 8K 19
Manningham. *W Yor* 4K 41
Mannings Heath.
W Sus 3K 11
Mannington. *Dors* 5J 9
Manningtree. *Essx* 8H 31
Mannofield. *Aber* 5J 73
Manorbier. *Pemb* 7G 15
Manorbier Newton. *Pemb* 7G 15
Manordeilo. *Carm* 2F 16
Manorowen. *Pemb* 3F 14
Manor Park. *G Lon* 5M 21
Mansell Gamage. *Here* 7B 26
Mansell Lacy. *Here* 7C 26
Mansergh. *Cumb* 7E 46
Mansewood. *Glas* 3D 58
Mansfield. *E Ayr* 8E 58
Mansfield. *Notts* 3C 36
Mansfield Woodhouse.
Notts 3C 36
Mansriggs. *Cumb* 7A 46
Manston. *Dors* 4G 9
Manston. *Kent* 7K 23
Manston. *W Yor* 4A 42
Manswood. *Dors* 5H 9
Manthorpe. *Linc*
nr. Bourne 8H 37
nr. Grantham 6G 37
Manton. *N Lin* 7G 43
Manton. *Notts* 2C 36
Manton. *Rut* 1F 28
Manton. *Wilts* 7K 19
Manuden. *Essx* 1A 22
Maperton. *Som* 3E 8
Maplebeck. *Notts* 3E 36
Maple Cross. *Herts* 4H 21
Mapledurham. *Oxon* 6D 20
Mapledurwell. *Hants* 8D 20
Maplehurst. *W Sus* 3J 11
Maplescombe. *Kent* 7B 22
Mapleton. *Derbs* 5K 35
Mapperley. *Derbs* 5B 36
Mapperley. *Nott* 5C 36
Mapperley Park. *Nott* 5C 36
Mapperton. *Dors*
nr. Beaminster 6D 8
nr. Poole 6H 9
Mappleborough Green.
Warw 5J 27
Mappleton. *E Yor* 3K 43
Mapplewell. *S Yor* 7M 41
Mappowder. *Dors* 5F 8
Maraig. *W Isl* 3D 76
Marazion. *Corn* 5J 3
Marbhig. *W Isl* 2F 76
Marbury. *Ches E* 5D 34
March. *Cambs* 2M 29
Marcham. *Oxon* 4B 20
Marchamley. *Shrp* 7D 34
Marchington. *Staf* 6K 35
Marchington Woodlands.
Staf 7K 35
Marchwiel. *Wrex* 5B 34
Marchwood. *Hants* 4A 10
Marcross. *V Glam* 8J 17
Marden. *Here* 7D 26
Marden. *Kent* 1D 12
Marden. *Wilts* 8J 19
Marden Beech. *Kent* 1D 12
Marden Thorn. *Kent* 1D 12
Mardu. *Shrp* 3A 26
Mardy. *Mon* 2B 18
Marefield. *Leics* 1E 28
Mareham le Fen. *Linc* 3K 37
Mareham on the Hill. *Linc* 3K 37
Marehay. *Derbs* 5B 36
Marehill. *W Sus* 4H 11
Maresfield. *E Sus* 3A 12
Marfleet. *Hull* 5J 43
Marford. *Wrex* 4B 34
Margam. *Neat* 6G 17
Margaret Marsh. *Dors* 4G 9
Margaret Roding. *Essx* 2B 22
Margaretting. *Essx* 3C 22
Margaretting Tye. *Essx* 3C 22
Margate. *Kent* 6K 23
Margery. *Surr* 8K 21
Margnaheglish. *N Ayr* 6K 57
Marham. *Norf* 1D 30
Marhamchurch. *Corn* 5B 6
Marholm. *Pet* 1J 29
Marian Cwm. *Den* 3K 33
Mariandyrys. *IOA* 2F 32
Marian-glas. *IOA* 2E 32
Mariansleigh. *Devn* 3G 7
Marian-y-de. *Gwyn* 7C 32
Marian-y-mor. *Gwyn* 7C 32
Marine Town. *Kent* 6F 22
Marishader. *High* 7F 76
Marjoriebanks. *Dum* 3E 52
Mark. *Dum* 6G 51
Mark. *Som* 1B 8
Markbeech. *Kent* 1A 12
Markby. *Linc* 2A 38
Mark Causeway. *Som* 1B 8
Mark Cross. *E Sus* 2B 12
Markeaton. *Derb* 6M 35
Market Bosworth. *Leics* 1B 28
Market Deeping. *Linc* 8J 37
Market Drayton. *Shrp* 6E 34
Market End. *Warw* 3M 27
Market Harborough. *Leics* 3E 28
Markethill. *Arm* 7F 93
Markethill. *Per* 4F 66
Market Lavington. *Wilts* 8J 19
Market Overton. *Rut* 8F 36
Market Rasen. *Linc* 1J 37
Market Stainton. *Linc* 1K 37
Market Weighton. *E Yor* 3F 42
Market Weston. *Suff* 4F 30
Markfield. *Leics* 8B 36
Markham. *Cphy* 4L 17
Markinch. *Fife* 7F 66
Markington. *N Yor* 1L 41
Marksbury. *Bath* 7E 18
Mark's Corner. *IOW* 6B 10
Marks Tey. *Essx* 1F 22
Markwell. *Corn* 6F 4
Markyate. *Herts* 2H 21
Marlborough. *Wilts* 7K 19
Marlcliff. *Warw* 6J 27
Marldon. *Devn* 5L 5
Marle Green. *E Sus* 4B 12
Marlesford. *Suff* 6K 31
Marley Green. *Ches E* 5D 34
Marley Hill. *Tyne* 6F 54
Marlingford. *Norf* 1H 31
Mar Lodge. *Abers* 7L 71
Marloes. *Pemb* 6D 14
Marlow. *Buck* 5F 20
Marlow. *Here* 4B 26
Marlow Bottom. *Buck* 5F 20
Marlow Common. *Buck* 5F 20
Marlpit Hill. *Kent* 1M 11
Marlpits. *E Sus* 3M 11
Marlpool. *Derbs* 5B 36
Marnhull. *Dors* 4F 8
Marnoch. *Abers* 8E 80
Marnock. *N Lan* 3F 58
Marple. *G Man* 1H 35
Marr. *S Yor* 7C 42
Marrel. *High* 2L 79
Marrick. *N Yor* 6J 47
Marrister. *Shet* 1F 90
Marros. *Carm* 6J 15
Marsden. *Tyne* 5G 55
Marsden. *W Yor* 6J 41
Marsett. *N Yor* 7H 47
Marsh. *Buck* 3F 20
Marsh. *Devn* 4A 8
Marsh, The. *Powy* 2B 26
Marsh, The. *Shrp* 7E 34
Marshall Meadows. *Nmbd* 4G 61
Marshalsea. *Dors* 5B 8
Marshalswick. *Herts* 3J 21
Marsham. *Norf* 7H 39
Marshaw. *Lanc* 2D 40
Marsh Baldon. *Oxon* 4C 20
Marsh Benham. *W Ber* 7B 20
Marshborough. *Kent* 8K 23
Marshbrook. *Shrp* 3C 26
Marshchapel. *Linc* 8L 43
Marshfield. *Newp* 5A 18
Marshfield. *S Glo* 6F 18
Marshgate. *Corn* 6A 6
Marsh Gibbon. *Buck* 1D 20
Marsh Green. *Devn* 6K 7
Marsh Green. *Kent* 1M 11
Marsh Green. *Staf* 4G 35
Marsh Green. *Telf* 8E 34
Marsh Lane. *Derbs* 2B 36
Marshside. *Kent* 7J 23
Marshside. *Mers* 6B 40
Marsh Side. *Norf* 5D 38
Marsh Street. *Som* 1J 7
Marshwood. *Dors* 6B 8
Marske. *N Yor* 5K 47
Marske-by-the-Sea. *Red C* 3D 48
Marston. *Ches W* 2E 34
Marston. *Here* 6B 26
Marston. *Linc* 5F 36
Marston. *Oxon* 3C 20
Marston. *Staf*
nr. Stafford 7H 35
nr. Wheaton Aston 8G 35
Marston. *Warw* 2L 27
Marston. *Wilts* 8H 19
Marston Doles. *Warw* 6B 28
Marston Green. *W Mid* 3K 27
Marston Hill. *Glos* 4K 19
Marston Jabbett. *Warw* 3A 28
Marston Magna. *Som* 3D 8
Marston Meysey. *Wilts* 4K 19
Marston Montgomery.
Derbs 6K 35
Marston Moretaine. *C Beds* 7G 29
Marston on Dove. *Derbs* 7L 35
Marston St Lawrence.
Nptn 7C 28
Marston Stannett. *Here* 6D 26
Marston Trussell. *Nptn* 3D 28
Marstow. *Here* 2D 18
Marsworth. *Buck* 2G 21
Marten. *Wilts* 8L 19
Marthall. *Ches E* 2G 35
Martham. *Norf* 8L 39
Marthwaite. *Cumb* 6E 46
Martin. *Hants* 4J 9
Martin. *Kent* 1K 13
Martin. *Linc*
nr. Horncastle 3K 37
nr. Metheringham 4J 37
Martindale. *Cumb* 4C 46
Martin Dales. *Linc* 3J 37
Martin Drove End. *Hants* 3J 9
Martinhoe. *Devn* 1F 6
Martinhoe Cross. *Devn* 1F 6
Martin Hussingtree. *Worc* 5G 27
Martin Mill. *Kent* 1K 13
Martinscroft. *Warr* 1E 34
Martin's Moss. *Ches E* 3G 35
Martinstown. *Dors* 7E 8
Martinstown. *ME Ant* 3G 93
Martlesham. *Suff* 7J 31
Martlesham Heath. *Suff* 7J 31
Martletwy. *Pemb* 5G 15
Martley. *Worc* 5F 26
Martock. *Som* 4C 8
Marton. *Ches E* 3G 35
Marton. *Cumb* 7M 45
Marton. *E Yor*
nr. Bridlington 1K 43
nr. Hull 4J 43
Marton. *Linc* 1F 36
Marton. *Midd* 4C 48
Marton. *N Yor*
nr. Boroughbridge 1B 42
nr. Pickering 7E 48
Marton. *Shrp*
nr. Myddle 7C 34
nr. Worthen 1A 26
Marton. *Warw* 5B 28
Marton Abbey. *N Yor* 1C 42
Marton-le-Moor. *N Yor* 8A 48
Martyr's Green. *Surr* 8H 21
Martyr Worthy. *Hants* 2C 10
Marwick. *Orkn* 7B 88
Marwood. *Devn* 2E 6
Marybank. *High*
nr. Dingwall 8E 78
nr. Invergordon 6H 79
Maryburgh. *High* 8F 78
Maryfield. *Corn* 6G 5
Maryhill. *Glas* 3D 58
Marykirk. *Abers* 1K 67
Marylebone. *G Lon* 5K 21
Marylebone. *G Man* 7D 40
Marypark. *Mor* 2A 72
Maryport. *Cumb* 8E 52
Maryport. *Dum* 8G 51
Marystow. *Devn* 7D 6
Mary Tavy. *Devn* 8E 6
Maryton. *Ang*
nr. Kirriemuir 2G 67
nr. Montrose 2K 67
Marywell. *Abers* 6E 72
Marywell. *Ang* 3K 67
Masham. *N Yor* 7L 47
Mashbury. *Essx* 2C 22
Masongill. *N Yor* 8E 46
Masons Lodge. *Abers* 5H 73
Mastin Moor. *Derbs* 2B 36
Mastrick. *Aber* 5J 73
Matching. *Essx* 2B 22
Matching Green. *Essx* 2B 22
Matching Tye. *Essx* 2B 22
Matfen. *Nmbd* 4D 54
Matfield. *Kent* 1C 12
Mathern. *Mon* 4D 18
Mathon. *Here* 7F 26
Mathry. *Pemb* 3E 14
Matlaske. *Norf* 6H 39
Matlock. *Derbs* 4L 35
Matlock Bath. *Derbs* 4L 35
Matterdale End. *Cumb* 3B 46
Mattersey. *Notts* 1D 36
Mattersey Thorpe. *Notts* 1D 36
Mattingley. *Hants* 8E 20
Mattishall. *Norf* 8G 39
Mattishall Burgh. *Norf* 8G 39
Mauchline. *E Ayr* 7C 58
Maud. *Abers* 1J 73
Maudlin. *Corn* 5C 4
Maugersbury. *Glos* 1K 19
Maughold. *IOM* 5D 44
Maulden. *C Beds* 8H 29
Maulds Meaburn. *Cumb* 4E 46
Maunby. *N Yor* 7A 48
Maund Bryan. *Here* 6D 26
Mautby. *Norf* 8L 39
Mavesyn Ridware. *Staf* 8J 35
Mavis Enderby. *Linc* 3L 37
Mawbray. *Cumb* 7E 52
Mawdesley. *Lanc* 6C 40
Mawdlam. *B'end* 6H 17
Mawgan. *Corn* 6L 3
Mawgan Porth. *Corn* 2M 3
Maw Green. *Ches E* 4F 34
Mawla. *Corn* 4L 3
Mawnan. *Corn* 6L 3
Mawnan Smith. *Corn* 6L 3
Mawsley Village. *Nptn* 4E 28
Mawthorpe. *Linc* 2A 38
Maxey. *Pet* 1J 29
Maxstoke. *Warw* 3L 27
Maxted Street. *Kent* 1H 13
Maxton. *Kent* 1J 13
Maxton. *Bord* 6D 60
Maxwellheugh. *Bord* 6E 60
Maxwelltown. *Dum* 4D 52
Maxworthy. *Corn* 6B 6
Mayals. *Swan* 6F 16
Maybole. *S Ayr* 1J 51
Maybush. *Sotn* 4A 10
Maydown. *Derr* 3D 92
Mayes Green. *Surr* 2J 11
Mayfield. *E Sus* 3B 12
Mayfield. *Midl* 3A 60
Mayfield. *Per* 5D 66
Mayfield. *Staf* 5K 35
Mayford. *Surr* 8G 21
Mayhill. *Swan* 5F 16
Mayland. *Essx* 3F 22
Maylandsea. *Essx* 3F 22
Maynard's Green. *E Sus* 4B 12
Mayobridge. *New M* 7G 93
Maypole. *IOS* 1H 3
Maypole. *Kent* 7J 23
Maypole. *Mon* 2C 18
Maypole Green. *Norf* 2L 31
Maypole Green. *Suff* 6F 30
Maywick. *Shet* 5D 90
Mazetown. *Lis* 5H 93
Mead. *Devn* 4B 6
Meadgate. *Bath* 8E 18
Meadle. *Buck* 3F 20
Meadowbank. *Ches W* 3E 34
Meadowfield. *Dur* 8F 54
Meadow Green. *Here* 6F 26
Meadowmill. *E Lot* 2B 60
Meadows. *Nott* 6C 36
Meadowtown. *Shrp* 1B 26
Meadwell. *Devn* 7D 6
Meaford. *Staf* 6G 35
Mealabost. *W Isl*
nr. Borgh 6H 83
nr. Stornoway 8H 83
Mealasta. *W Isl* 1A 76
Meal Bank. *Cumb* 6D 46
Mealrigg. *Cumb* 7F 52
Mealsgate. *Cumb* 7G 53
Meanwood. *W Yor* 4L 41
Mearbeck. *N Yor* 1G 41
Meare. *Som* 1C 8
Meare Green. *Som*
nr. Curry Mallet 3A 8
nr. Stoke St Gregory 3B 8
Mears Ashby. *Nptn* 5F 28
Measham. *Leics* 8M 35
Meath Green. *Surr* 1K 11
Meathop. *Cumb* 7C 46
Meaux. *E Yor* 4H 43
Meavy. *Devn* 5H 5
Medbourne. *Leics* 2E 28
Medburn. *Nmbd* 4E 54
Meddon. *Devn* 4B 6
Meden Vale. *Notts* 3C 36
Medlam. *Linc* 4L 37
Medlicott. *Shrp* 2C 26
Medmenham. *Buck* 5F 20
Medomsley. *Dur* 6E 54
Medstead. *Hants* 2D 10
Medway Towns. *Medw* 7D 22
Meerbrook. *Staf* 3H 35
Meer End. *W Mid* 4L 27
Meers Bridge. *Linc* 1A 38
Meesden. *Herts* 8M 29
Meeson. *Telf* 7E 34
Meeth. *Devn* 5E 6
Meeting Green. *Suff* 6D 30
Meeting House Hill. *Norf* 7K 39
Meidrim. *Carm* 4J 15
Meifod. *Powy* 1L 25
Meigh. *New M* 7G 93
Meigle. *Per* 3F 66
Meikle Earnock. *S Lan* 4F 58
Meikle Kilchattan Butts.
Arg 4K 57
Meikleour. *Per* 4E 66
Meikle Tarty. *Abers* 3J 73
Meikle Wartle. *Abers* 2G 73
Meinciau. *Carm* 5L 15
Meir. *Stoke* 5H 35
Meir Heath. *Staf* 5H 35
Melbourn. *Cambs* 7L 29
Melbourne. *Derbs* 7A 36
Melbourne. *E Yor* 3E 42
Melbury Abbas. *Dors* 3G 9
Melbury Bubb. *Dors* 5D 8
Melbury Osmond. *Dors* 5D 8
Melbury Sampford. *Dors* 5D 8
Melby. *Shet* 2B 90
Melchbourne. *Bed* 5H 29
Melcombe Bingham. *Dors* 5F 8
Melcombe Regis. *Dors* 7E 8
Meldon. *Devn* 6E 6
Meldon. *Nmbd* 3E 54
Meldreth. *Cambs* 7L 29
Melfort. *Arg* 6C 64
Melgarve. *High* 6E 70
Meliden. *Den* 2K 33
Melinbyrhedyn. *Powy* 3H 25
Melincourt. *Neat* 4H 17
Melin-y-coed. *Cnwy* 4H 33
Melin-y-ddol. *Powy* 2K 25
Melin-y-wig. *Den* 6K 33
Melkington. *Nmbd* 5F 60
Melkinthorpe. *Cumb* 3D 46
Melkridge. *Nmbd* 5M 53
Melksham. *Wilts* 7H 19
Mellangaun. *High* 5K 77
Melldalloch. *Arg* 2J 57
Mellguards. *Cumb* 7J 53
Melling. *Lanc* 8D 46
Melling. *Mers* 7B 40
Melling Mount. *Mers* 7C 40
Mellis. *Suff* 4G 31
Mellon Charles. *High* 4K 77
Mellon Udrigle. *High* 4K 77
Mellor. *G Man* 1H 35
Mellor. *Lanc* 4E 40
Mellor Brook. *Lanc* 4E 40
Mells. *Som* 1F 8
Melmerby. *Cumb* 8L 53
Melmerby. *N Yor*
nr. Middleham 7J 47
nr. Ripon 8M 47
Melplash. *Dors* 6C 8
Melrose. *Bord* 6C 60
Melsetter. *Orkn* 3D 86
Melsonby. *N Yor* 5K 47
Meltham. *W Yor* 6K 41
Meltham Mills. *W Yor* 6K 41
Melton. *E Yor* 5G 43
Melton. *Suff* 6J 31
Meltonby. *E Yor* 2E 42
Melton Constable. *Norf* 6G 39
Melton Mowbray. *Leics* 8E 36
Melton Ross. *N Lin* 6H 43
Melvaig. *High* 5J 77
Melverley. *Shrp* 8B 34
Melverley Green. *Shrp* 8B 34
Melvich. *High* 5L 85
Membury. *Devn* 5A 8
Memsie. *Abers* 7J 81
Memus. *Ang* 2H 67
Menabilly. *Corn* 6C 4
Menai Bridge. *IOA* 3E 32
Mendham. *Suff* 3J 31
Mendlesham. *Suff* 5H 31
Mendlesham Green. *Suff* 5G 31
Menethorpe. *N Yor* 1E 42
Menheniot. *Corn* 5E 4
Menithwood. *Worc* 5F 26
Menna. *Corn* 6B 4
Mennock. *Dum* 1C 52
Menston. *W Yor* 3K 41
Menstrie. *Clac* 8B 66
Menthorpe. *N Yor* 4E 42
Mentmore. *Buck* 2G 21
Meole Brace. *Shrp* 8C 34
Meols. *Mers* 1M 33
Meon. *Hants* 5C 10
Meonstoke. *Hants* 3D 10
Meopham. *Kent* 7C 22
Meopham Green. *Kent* 7C 22
Meopham Station. *Kent* 7C 22
Mepal. *Cambs* 3M 29
Meppershall. *C Beds* 8J 29
Merbach. *Here* 7B 26
Mercaston. *Derbs* 5L 35
Merchiston. *Edin* 2L 59
Mere. *Ches E* 1F 34
Mere. *Wilts* 2G 9
Mere Brow. *Lanc* 6C 40
Mereclough. *Lanc* 4G 41
Mere Green. *W Mid* 2K 27
Mere Green. *Worc* 5H 27
Mere Heath. *Ches W* 2E 34
Mereside. *Bkpl* 4B 40
Meretown. *Staf* 7F 34
Mereworth. *Kent* 8C 22
Meriden. *W Mid* 3L 27
Merkadale. *High* 2E 68
Merkland. *S Ayr* 2H 51
Merkland Lodge. *High* 1D 78
Merley. *Pool* 6J 9
Merlin's Bridge. *Pemb* 5F 14
Merridge. *Som* 2M 7
Merrington. *Shrp* 7C 34
Merrion. *Pemb* 7F 14
Merriott. *Som* 4C 8
Merrivale. *Devn* 8E 6
Merrow. *Surr* 8H 21
Merrybent. *Darl* 4L 47
Merry Lees. *Leics* 1B 28
Merrymeet. *Corn* 5E 4
Mersham. *Kent* 2G 13
Merstham. *Surr* 8K 21
Merston. *W Sus* 5F 10
Merstone. *IOW* 7C 10
Merther. *Corn* 7A 4
Merthyr. *Carm* 4K 15
Merthyr Cynog. *Powy* 1J 17
Merthyr Dyfan. *V Glam* 7L 17
Merthyr Mawr. *B'end* 7H 17
Merthyr Tudful. *Mer T* 4K 17
Merthyr Tydfil. *Mer T* 4K 17
Merthyr Vale. *Mer T* 4K 17
Merton. *Devn* 4E 6
Merton. *G Lon* 7K 21
Merton. *Norf* 2F 30
Merton. *Oxon* 2C 20
Meshaw. *Devn* 4G 7
Messing. *Essx* 2E 22
Messingham. *N Lin* 7F 42
Metcombe. *Devn* 6K 7
Metfield. *Suff* 3J 31
Metherell. *Corn* 5G 5
Metheringham. *Linc* 3H 37
Methil. *Fife* 8G 67
Methilhill. *Fife* 8G 67
Methley. *W Yor* 5A 42
Methley Junction. *W Yor* 5A 42
Methlick. *Abers* 2H 73
Methven. *Per* 5D 66
Methwold. *Norf* 2D 30
Methwold Hythe. *Norf* 2D 30
Mettingham. *Suff* 3K 31
Metton. *Norf* 6H 39
Mevagissey. *Corn* 7C 4
Mexborough. *S Yor* 7B 42
Mey. *High* 4D 86
Meysey Hampton. *Glos* 4K 19
Miabhag. *W Isl* 4C 76
Miabhaig. *W Isl*
nr. Cliasmol 3B 76
nr. Timsgearraidh 8D 82
Mial. *High* 6J 77
Michaelchurch. *Here* 1D 18
Michaelchurch Escley. *Here* 8B 26
Michaelchurch-on-Arrow.
Powy 7M 25
Michaelston-le-Pit. *V Glam* 7L 17
Michaelston-y-Fedw. *Newp* 6M 17
Michaelstow. *Corn* 4C 4
Michelcombe. *Devn* 5J 5
Micheldever. *Hants* 2C 10
Micheldever Station. *Hants* 1C 10
Michelmersh. *Hants* 3M 9
Mickfield. *Suff* 5H 31
Micklebring. *S Yor* 8C 42
Mickleby. *N Yor* 4F 48
Micklefield. *W Yor* 4B 42
Micklefield Green. *Herts* 4H 21
Mickleham. *Surr* 8J 21
Mickleover. *Derb* 6M 35
Micklethwaite. *Cumb* 6G 53
Micklethwaite. *W Yor* 3K 41
Mickleton. *Dur* 3H 47
Mickleton. *Glos* 7K 27
Mickletown. *W Yor* 5A 42
Mickle Trafford. *Ches W* 3C 34
Mickley. *N Yor* 8L 47
Mickley Green. *Suff* 6E 30
Mickley Square. *Nmbd* 5D 54
Mid Ardlaw. *Abers* 7J 81
Midbea. *Orkn* 5D 88
Mid Beltie. *Abers* 5F 72
Mid Calder. *W Lot* 3J 59
Mid Clyth. *High* 8D 86
Middle Assendon. *Oxon* 5E 20
Middle Aston. *Oxon* 1B 20
Middle Barton. *Oxon* 1B 20
Middlebie. *Dum* 4G 53
Middle Chinnock. *Som* 4C 8
Middle Claydon. *Buck* 1E 20
Middlecliffe. *S Yor* 7B 42
Middlecott. *Devn* 7G 7
Middle Drums. *Ang* 2J 67
Middle Duntisbourne. *Glos* 3H 19
Middle Essie. *Abers* 8K 81
Middleforth Green. *Lanc* 5D 40
Middleham. *N Yor* 7K 47
Middle Handley. *Derbs* 2B 36
Middle Harling. *Norf* 3F 30
Middlehope. *Shrp* 3C 26
Middle Littleton. *Worc* 7J 27
Middle Maes-coed. *Here* 8B 26
Middlemarsh. *Dors* 5E 8
Middle Marwood. *Devn* 2E 6
Middle Mayfield. *Staf* 5K 35
Middlemoor. *Devn* 8D 6
Middlemuir. *Abers*
nr. New Deer 1H 73
nr. Strichen 8J 81
Middle Rainton. *Tyne* 7G 55
Middle Rasen. *Linc* 1H 37
Middles, The. *Dur* 6F 54
Middlesbrough. *Midd* 4B 48
Middlesceugh. *Cumb* 7H 53
Middleshaw. *Cumb* 7D 46
Middlesmoor. *N Yor* 8J 47
Middlestone. *Dur* 8F 54
Middlestone Moor. *Dur* 8F 54
Middle Stoughton. *Som* 1C 8
Middlestown. *W Yor* 6L 41
Middle Street. *Glos* 3F 18
Middle Taphouse. *Corn* 5D 4
Middleton. *Ang* 3J 67
Middleton. *Arg* 3E 62
Middleton. *Cumb* 7E 46
Middleton. *Derbs*
nr. Bakewell 3K 35
nr. Wirksworth 4L 35
Middleton. *Essx* 8E 30
Middleton. *G Man* 7G 41
Middleton. *Hants* 1B 10
Middleton. *Hart* 8J 55
Middleton. *Here* 5D 26
Middleton. *IOW* 7M 9
Middleton. *Lanc* 2C 40
Middleton. *Midl* 4A 60
Middleton. *Norf* 8C 38
Middleton. *Nptn* 3F 28
Middleton. *Nmbd*
nr. Belford 6J 61
nr. Morpeth 3D 54
Middleton. *N Yor*
nr. Ilkley 3K 41
nr. Pickering 7E 48
Middleton. *Per* 7E 66
Middleton. *Shrp*
nr. Ludlow 4D 26
nr. Oswestry 7B 34
Middleton. *Suff* 5L 31
Middleton. *Swan* 8L 15
Middleton. *Warw* 2K 27
Middleton. *W Yor* 5L 41
Middleton Cheney. *Nptn* 7C 28
Middleton Green. *Staf* 6H 35
Middleton-in-Teesdale.
Dur 3H 47
Middleton One Row. *Darl* 4A 48
Middleton-on-Leven. *N Yor* 5B 48
Middleton-on-Sea. *W Sus* 5G 11
Middleton on the Hill. *Here* 5D 26
Middleton-on-the-Wolds.
E Yor 3G 43
Middleton Priors. *Shrp* 2E 26
Middleton Quernhow.
N Yor 8M 47
Middleton St George. *Darl* 4M 47
Middleton Scriven. *Shrp* 3E 26
Middleton Stoney. *Oxon* 1C 20
Middleton Tyas. *N Yor* 5L 47
Middletown. *Arm* 7E 92
Middletown. *Cumb* 4J 45
Middle Town. *IOS* 1H 3
Middletown. *Powy* 8B 34
Middle Tysoe. *Warw* 7M 27
Middle Wallop. *Hants* 2L 9
Middlewich. *Ches E* 3F 34
Middle Winterslow. *Wilts* 2L 9
Middlewood. *Corn* 8B 6
Middlewood. *S Yor* 8M 41
Middle Woodford. *Wilts* 2K 9
Middlewood Green. *Suff* 5G 31
Middleyard. *Glos* 3G 19
Middlezoy. *Som* 2B 8
Middridge. *Dur* 3L 47
Midelney. *Som* 3C 8
Midfield. *High* 5H 85
Midford. *Bath* 7F 18
Mid Garrary. *Dum* 4L 51
Midge Hall. *Lanc* 5D 40
Midgeholme. *Cumb* 6L 53
Midgham. *W Ber* 7C 20
Midgley. *W Yor*
nr. Halifax 5J 41
nr. Horbury 6L 41
Mid Ho. *Shet* 4K 91
Midhopestones. *S Yor* 8L 41
Midhurst. *W Sus* 3F 10
Mid Kirkton. *N Ayr* 4L 57
Mid Lambrook. *Som* 4C 8
Midland. *Orkn* 1E 86
Mid Lavant. *W Sus* 5F 10
Midlem. *Bord* 7C 60
Midney. *Som* 3D 8
Midsomer Norton. *Bath* 8E 18
Midton. *Inv* 2M 57
Midtown. *High*
nr. Poolewe 5K 77
nr. Tongue 5H 85
Midville. *Linc* 4L 37
Mid Walls. *Shet* 3B 90
Mid Yell. *Shet* 4K 91
Migdale. *High* 4G 79
Migvie. *Abers* 5D 72
Milborne Port. *Som* 4E 8
Milborne St Andrew. *Dors* 6G 9
Milborne Wick. *Som* 3E 8
Milbourne. *Nmbd* 4E 54
Milbourne. *Wilts* 5H 19
Milburn. *Cumb* 3E 46
Milbury Heath. *S Glo* 4E 18
Milby. *N Yor* 1B 42
Milcombe. *Oxon* 8B 28
Milden. *Suff* 7F 30
Mildenhall. *Suff* 4D 30
Mildenhall. *Wilts* 7L 19
Milebrook. *Powy* 4B 26
Milebush. *Kent* 1D 12
Mile End. *Cambs* 3C 30
Mile End. *Essx* 1F 22
Mileham. *Norf* 8F 38
Mile Oak. *Brig* 5K 11
Miles Green. *Staf* 4G 35
Miles Hope. *Here* 5D 26
Milesmark. *Fife* 1J 59
Mile Town. *Kent* 6F 22
Milfield. *Nmbd* 6G 61
Milford. *Arm* 6F 93
Milford. *Derbs* 5A 36
Milford. *Devn* 3B 6
Milford. *Powy* 3K 25
Milford. *Staf* 7H 35
Milford. *Surr* 1G 11
Milford Haven. *Pemb* 6F 14
Milford on Sea. *Hants* 6L 9
Milkwall. *Glos* 3D 18
Milkwell. *Wilts* 3H 9
Milland. *W Sus* 3F 10
Millbank. *Ant* 4H 93
Millbank. *High* 5C 86
Mill Bank. *W Yor* 5J 41
Millbay. *ME Ant* 4J 93
Millbeck. *Cumb* 3A 46
Millbounds. *Orkn* 6E 88
Millbreck. *Abers* 1K 73
Millbridge. *Surr* 1F 10
Millbrook. *C Beds* 8H 29
Millbrook. *Corn* 6G 5
Millbrook. *G Man* 8H 41
Millbrook. *ME Ant* 3H 93
Millbrook. *Sotn* 4A 10
Mill Common. *Suff* 3L 31
Mill Corner. *E Sus* 3E 12
Milldale. *Staf* 4K 35
Millden Lodge. *Ang* 8E 72
Milldens. *Ang* 2J 67
Millearn. *Per* 6C 66
Mill End. *Buck* 5E 20
Mill End. *Cambs* 6C 30
Mill End. *Glos* 2K 19
Millend. *Glos* 4F 18
Mill End. *Herts* 8L 29
Millerhill. *Midl* 3M 59
Miller's Dale. *Derbs* 2K 35
Millers Green. *Derbs* 4L 35
Millerston. *Glas* 3E 58
Millfield. *Abers* 6D 72
Millfield. *Pet* 1J 29
Millgate. *Lanc* 6G 41
Mill Green. *Essx* 3C 22
Mill Green. *Norf* 3H 31
Mill Green. *Shrp* 7E 34
Mill Green. *Staf* 7J 35
Mill Green. *Suff* 7F 30
Millhalf. *Here* 7A 26
Millhall. *E Ren* 4D 58
Millhayes. *Devn*
nr. Honiton 5M 7
nr. Wellington 4L 7
Millhead. *Lanc* 8C 46
Millheugh. *S Lan* 4F 58
Mill Hill. *Bkbn* 5E 40
Mill Hill. *G Lon* 4K 21
Millholme. *Cumb* 6D 46
Millhouse. *Arg* 2J 57
Millhouse. *Cumb* 8H 53
Millhousebridge. *Dum* 3F 52
Millhouses. *S Yor* 1M 35
Millikenpark. *Ren* 3C 58
Millington. *E Yor* 2F 42
Millington Green. *Derbs* 5L 35
Millisle. *Ards* 5J 93
Mill Knowe. *Arg* 7G 57
Mill Lane. *Hants* 8E 20
Millmeece. *Staf* 6G 35
Mill of Craigievar. *Abers* 4E 72
Mill of Fintray. *Abers* 4H 73
Mill of Haldane. *W Dun* 1C 58
Millom. *Cumb* 6L 45
Millow. *C Beds* 7K 29
Millpool. *Corn* 4D 4
Millport. *N Ayr* 4L 57
Mill Side. *Cumb* 7C 46
Mill Street. *Norf*
nr. Lyng 8G 39
nr. Swanton Morley 8G 39
Millthorpe. *Derbs* 2M 35
Millthorpe. *Linc* 6J 37
Millthrop. *Cumb* 6E 46
Milltimber. *Aber* 5H 73
Milltown. *Abers*
nr. Corgarff 5B 72
nr. Lumsden 4D 72
Mill Town. *Ant* 4G 93
Milltown. *Ant* 4G 93
Milltown. *Arm*
nr. Banbridge 6G 93
nr. Coalisland 5F 93
nr. Richhill 6F 93
Milltown. *Corn* 6D 4
Milltown. *Derbs* 3A 36
Milltown. *Devn* 2E 6
Milltown. *Dum* 4H 53
Milltown of Aberdalgie. *Per* 5D 66
Milltown of Auchindoun.
Mor 1C 72
Milltown of Campfield.
Abers 5F 72
Milltown of Edinvillie. *Mor* 1B 72
Milltown of Rothiemay. *Mor* 1E 72
Milltown of Towie. *Abers* 4D 72
Milnacraig. *Ang* 2F 66
Milnathort. *Per* 7E 66
Milngavie. *E Dun* 2D 58
Milnholm. *Stir* 1F 58
Milnrow. *G Man* 6H 41
Milnthorpe. *Cumb* 7C 46
Milnthorpe. *W Yor* 6M 41
Milson. *Shrp* 4E 26
Milstead. *Kent* 8F 22
Milston. *Wilts* 1K 9
Milthorpe. *Nptn* 7C 28
Milton. *Ang* 3G 67
Milton. *Cambs* 5A 30
Milton. *Cumb*
nr. Brampton 5K 53
nr. Crooklands 7D 46
Milton. *Derbs* 7M 35
Milton. *Dum*
nr. Crocketford 4C 52
nr. Glenluce 6H 51
Milton. *Glas* 3D 58
Milton. *High*
nr. Achnasheen 8D 78
nr. Applecross 1J 69
nr. Drumnadrochit 2E 70
nr. Invergordon 6H 79
nr. Inverness 1F 70
nr. Wick 6E 86
Milton. *Mor*
nr. Cullen 7E 80
nr. Tomintoul 4A 72
Milton. *N Som* 7B 18
Milton. *Notts* 2E 36
Milton. *Oxon*
nr. Bloxham 8B 28
nr. Didcot 4B 20
Milton. *Pemb* 6G 15
Milton. *Port* 6D 10
Milton. *Som* 3C 8
Milton. *S Ayr* 7C 58
Milton. *Stir*
nr. Aberfoyle 7K 65
nr. Drymen 8J 65
Milton. *Stoke* 4H 35
Milton. *W Dun* 2C 58
Milton Abbas. *Dors* 5G 9
Milton Abbot. *Devn* 8D 6
Milton Auchlossan. *Abers* 5E 72
Milton Bridge. *Midl* 3L 59
Milton Bryan. *C Beds* 8G 29
Milton Clevedon. *Som* 2E 8
Milton Coldwells. *Abers* 2J 73
Milton Combe. *Devn* 5G 5
Milton Common. *Oxon* 3D 20
Milton Damerel. *Devn* 4C 6
Miltonduff. *Mor* 7A 80
Milton End. *Glos* 3K 19
Milton Ernest. *Bed* 6H 29
Milton Green. *Ches W* 4C 34
Milton Hill. *Devn* 8J 7
Milton Hill. *Oxon* 4B 20
Milton Keynes. *Mil* 8F 28
Milton Keynes Village. *Mil* 8F 28
Milton Lilbourne. *Wilts* 7K 19
Milton Malsor. *Nptn* 6E 28
Milton Morenish. *Per* 4L 65
Milton of Auchinhove.
Abers 5E 72
Milton of Balgonie. *Fife* 7G 67
Milton of Barras. *Abers* 8H 73
Milton of Campsie. *E Dun* 2E 58
Milton of Cultoquhey. *Per* 5B 66
Milton of Cushnie. *Abers* 4E 72
Milton of Finavon. *Ang* 2H 67
Milton of Gollanfield. *High* 8H 79
Milton of Lesmore. *Abers* 3D 72
Milton of Leys. *High* 1G 71
Milton of Tullich. *Abers* 6C 72
Milton on Stour. *Dors* 3F 8
Milton Regis. *Kent* 7E 22
Milton Street. *E Sus* 5B 12
Milton-under-Wychwood.
Oxon 2L 19
Milverton. *Som* 3L 7
Milverton. *Warw* 5M 27
Milwich. *Staf* 6H 35
Mimbridge. *Surr* 7G 21
Minard. *Arg* 8D 64
Minchington. *Dors* 4H 9
Minchinhampton. *Glos* 3G 19
Mindrum. *Nmbd* 6F 60
Minehead. *Som* 1J 7
Minera. *Wrex* 4A 34
Minerstown. *New M* 7J 93
Minety. *Wilts* 4J 19
Minffordd. *Gwyn* 7E 32
Mingarrypark. *High* 1A 64
Mingary. *High* 1L 63
Mingearraidh. *W Isl* 3D 74
Miningsby. *Linc* 3L 37
Minions. *Corn* 8B 6
Minishant. *S Ayr* 8B 58
Minllyn. *Gwyn* 1H 25
Minnigaff. *Dum* 5K 51
Minorca. *IOM* 6D 44
Minskip. *N Yor* 1A 42
Minstead. *Hants* 4L 9
Minsted. *W Sus* 3F 10
Minster. *Kent*
nr. Ramsgate 7K 23
Minster. *Kent*
nr. Sheerness 6F 22
Minsteracres. *Nmbd* 6D 54
Minsterley. *Shrp* 1B 26
Minster Lovell. *Oxon* 2M 19
Minsterworth. *Glos* 2F 18
Minterne Magna. *Dors* 5E 8
Minterne Parva. *Dors* 5E 8
Minting. *Linc* 2J 37
Mintlaw. *Abers* 1K 73
Minto. *Bord* 7C 60
Minton. *Shrp* 2C 26
Minwear. *Pemb* 5G 15
Minworth. *W Mid* 2K 27
Miodar. *Arg* 3F 62
Mirbister. *Orkn* 7C 88
Mirehouse. *Cumb* 3J 45
Mireland. *High* 5E 86
Mirfield. *W Yor* 6L 41
Miserden. *Glos* 3H 19
Miskin. *Rhon* 6K 17
Misson. *Notts* 8D 42
Misterton. *Leics* 3C 28
Misterton. *Notts* 8E 42
Misterton. *Som* 5C 8
Mistley. *Essx* 8H 31
Mistley Heath. *Essx* 8H 31
Mitcham. *G Lon* 7K 21
Mitcheldean. *Glos* 2E 18
Mitchell. *Corn* 6A 4
Mitchel Troy. *Mon* 2C 18
Mitcheltroy Common. *Mon* 3C 18
Mitford. *Nmbd* 3E 54
Mithian. *Corn* 3L 3
Mitton. *Staf* 8G 35
Mixbury. *Oxon* 8D 28
Mixenden. *W Yor* 5J 41
Mixon. *Staf* 4J 35
Moaness. *Orkn* 1D 86
Moarfield. *Shet* 3K 91
Moat. *Cumb* 4J 53

North End—Perlethorpe

North End. W Sus 5J 11
North End. Wilts 4J 19
North Erradale. High 5J 77
North Evington. Leic 1D 28
North Fambridge. Essx 4E 22
North Fearns. High 2G 69
North Featherstone. W Yor 5B 42
North Feorline. N Ayr 7J 57
North Ferriby. E Yor 5G 43
Northfield. Aber 5H 73
Northfield. E Yor 5H 43
Northfield. Som 2A 8
Northfield. W Mid 4J 27
Northfleet. Kent 6C 22
North Frodingham. E Yor 2J 43
Northgate. Linc 7J 37
North Gluss. Shet 6H 91
North Gorley. Hants 4K 9
North Green. Norf 3J 31
North Green. Suff
nr. Framlingham 5K 31
nr. Halesworth 4K 31
nr. Saxmundham 5K 31
North Greetwell. Linc 2H 37
North Grimston. N Yor 1F 42
North Halling. Medw 7D 22
North Hayling. Hants 5E 10
North Hazelrigg. Nmbd 6H 61
North Heasley. Devn 2G 7
North Heath. W Sus 3H 11
North Hill. Corn 8B 6
North Holmwood. Surr 1J 11
North Huish. Devn 6K 5
North Hykeham. Linc 3G 37
Northiam. E Sus 3E 12
Northill. C Beds 7J 29
Northington. Hants 2C 10
North Kelsey. Linc 7H 43
North Kelsey Moor. Linc 7H 43
North Kessock. High 1G 71
North Killingholme. N Lin 6J 43
North Kilvington. N Yor 7B 48
North Kilworth. Leics 3D 28
North Kyme. Linc 4J 37
North Lancing. W Sus 5J 11
Northlands. Linc 4L 37
Northleach. Glos 2K 19
North Lee. Buck 3F 20
North Lees. N Yor 8L 47
Northleigh. Devn
nr. Barnstaple 2F 6
nr. Honiton 6L 7
North Leigh. Kent 1H 13
North Leigh. Oxon 2A 20
North Leverton. Notts 1E 36
Northlew. Devn 6E 6
North Littleton. Worc 7J 27
North Lopham. Norf 3G 31
North Luffenham. Rut 1G 29
North Marden. W Sus 4F 10
North Marston. Buck 1E 20
North Middleton. Midl 4A 60
North Middleton. Nmbd 7H 61
North Molton. Devn 3G 7
North Moor. N Yor 7G 49
Northmoor. Oxon 3B 20
Northmoor Green. Som 2B 8
North Moreton. Oxon 5C 20
Northmuir. Ang 2G 67
North Mundham. W Sus 5F 10
North Murie. Per 5F 66
North Muskham. Notts 4E 36
North Ness. Orkn 2E 86
North Newbald. E Yor 4G 43
North Newington. Oxon 8B 28
North Newnton. Wilts 8K 19
North Newton. Som 2A 8
Northney. Hants 5E 10
North Nibley. Glos 4F 18
North Oakley. Hants 8C 20
North Ockendon. G Lon 5B 22
Northolt. G Lon 5J 21
Northop. Flin 4M 33
Northop Hall. Flin 3A 34
North Ormesby. Midd 4C 48
North Ormsby. Linc 8K 43
Northorpe. Linc
nr. Bourne 8H 37
nr. Donington 6K 37
nr. Gainsborough 8F 42
North Otterington. N Yor 7A 48
Northover. Som
nr. Glastonbury 2C 8
nr. Yeovil 3D 8
North Owersby. Linc 8H 43
Northowram. W Yor 5K 41
North Perrott. Som 5C 8
North Petherton. Som 2A 8
North Petherwin. Corn 7B 6
North Pickenham. Norf 1E 30
North Piddle. Worc 6H 27
North Poorton. Dors 6D 8
North Port. Arg 5E 64
Northport. Dors 7H 9
North Queensferry. Fife 1K 59
North Radworthy. Devn 2G 7
North Rauceby. Linc 5H 37
Northrepps. Norf 6J 39
North Rigton. N Yor 3L 41
North Rode. Ches E 3G 35
North Roe. Shet 5H 91
North Ronaldsay Airport. Orkn 4G 89
North Row. Cumb 8G 53
North Runcton. Norf 8C 38
North Sannox. N Ayr 5K 57
North Scale. Cumb 7L 45
North Scarle. Linc 3F 36
North Seaton. Nmbd 3F 54
North Seaton Colliery. Nmbd 3F 54
North Sheen. G Lon 6J 21
North Shian. Arg 3D 64
North Shields. Tyne 5G 55
North Shoebury. S'end 5F 22
North Shore. Bkpl 4B 40
North Side. Cumb 2K 45
North Skelton. Red C 4D 48
North Somercotes. Linc 8M 43
North Stainley. N Yor 8L 47
North Stainmore. Cumb 4G 47
North Stifford. Thur 5C 22
North Stoke. Bath 7F 18
North Stoke. Oxon 5D 20
North Stoke. W Sus 4H 11
Northstowe. Cambs 5M 29
North Street. Hants 2D 10
North Street. Kent 8G 23
North Street. Medw 6E 22
North Street. W Ber 6D 20
North Sunderland. Nmbd 6K 61
North Tamerton. Corn 6C 6
North Tawton. Devn 5F 7
North Thoresby. Linc 8K 43
North Tidworth. Wilts 1L 9
North Town. Devn 5E 6
Northtown. Orkn 2F 86
North Town. Shet 6D 90
North Tuddenham. Norf 8G 39
North Walbottle. Tyne 5E 54
Northwall. Orkn 5G 89
North Walney. Cumb 8K 45
North Walsham. Norf 6J 39
North Waltham. Hants 1C 10
North Warnborough. Hants 8E 20
North Water Bridge. Ang 1K 67
North Watten. High 6D 86
Northway. Glos 8H 27
Northway. Swan 6E 16
North Weald Bassett. Essx 3B 22
North Weston. N Som 6C 18
North Weston. Oxon 3D 20
North Wheatley. Notts 1E 36
North Whilborough. Devn 5L 5
Northwich. Ches W 2E 34
North Wick. Bath 7D 18
Northwick. Som 1B 8
Northwick. S Glo 5D 18
North Widcombe. Bath 8D 18
North Willingham. Linc 1J 37
North Wingfield. Derbs 3B 36
North Witham. Linc 7G 37
Northwold. Norf 2D 30
Northwood. Derbs 3L 35
Northwood. G Lon 4H 21
Northwood. IOW 6B 10
Northwood. Kent 7K 23
Northwood. Shrp 6C 34
Northwood. Stoke 5G 35
Northwood Green. Glos 2F 18
North Wootton. Dors 4E 8
North Wootton. Norf 7C 38
North Wootton. Som 1D 8
North Wraxall. Wilts 6G 19
North Wroughton. Swin 5K 19
North Yardhope. Nmbd 1C 54
Norton. Devn 6L 5
Norton. Glos 1G 19
Norton. Hal 1D 34
Norton. Herts 8K 29
Norton. IOW 7M 9
Norton. Mon 1C 18
Norton. Nptn 5D 28
Norton. Notts 2C 36
Norton. Powy 5B 26
Norton. Shrp
nr. Ludlow 3C 26
nr. Madeley 1F 26
nr. Shrewsbury 1D 26
Norton. S Yor
nr. Askern 6C 42
nr. Sheffield 1A 36
Norton. Stoc T 3B 48
Norton. Suff 5F 30
Norton. Swan 6F 16
Norton. W Sus
nr. Selsey 6F 10
nr. Westergate 5G 11
Norton. Wilts 5G 19
Norton. Worc
nr. Evesham 7J 27
nr. Worcester 6G 27
Norton Bavant. Wilts 1H 9
Norton Bridge. Staf 6G 35
Norton Canes. Staf 1J 27
Norton Canon. Here 7B 26
Norton Corner. Norf 7G 39
Norton Disney. Linc 4F 36
Norton East. Staf 1J 27
Norton Ferris. Wilts 2F 8
Norton Fitzwarren. Som 3M 7
Norton Green. IOW 7M 9
Norton Green. Stoke 4H 35
Norton Hawkfield. Bath 7D 18
Norton Heath. Essx 3B 22
Norton in Hales. Shrp 6F 34
Norton in the Moors. Stoke 4G 35
Norton-Juxta-Twycross. Leics 1M 27
Norton-le-Clay. N Yor 8B 48
Norton Lindsey. Warw 5L 27
Norton Little Green. Suff 5F 30
Norton Malreward. Bath 7E 18
Norton Mandeville. Essx 3B 22
Norton-on-Derwent. N Yor 8E 48
Norton St Philip. Som 8F 18
Norton Subcourse. Norf 2L 31
Norton sub Hamdon. Som 4C 8
Norton Woodseats. S Yor 1A 36
Norwell. Notts 3E 36
Norwell Woodhouse. Notts 3E 36
Norwich. Norf 1J 31
Norwich Airport. Norf 8J 39
Norwick. Shet 2L 91
Norwood. Derbs 1B 36
Norwood Green. W Yor 5K 41
Norwood Hill. Surr 1K 11
Norwood Park. Som 2D 8
Norwoodside. Cambs 2M 29
Noseley. Leics 2E 28
Noss. Shet 6D 90
Noss Mayo. Devn 7H 5
Nosterfield. N Yor 7L 47
Nostie. High 3K 69
Notgrove. Glos 1K 19
Nottage. B'end 7H 17
Nottingham. Nott 5C 36
Nottington. Dors 7E 8
Notton. Dors 6E 8
Notton. W Yor 6M 41
Notton. Wilts 7H 19
Nounsley. Essx 2D 22
Noutard's Green. Worc 5F 26
Nox. Shrp 8C 34
Noyadd Trefawr. Cdgn 2J 15
Nuffield. Oxon 5D 20
Nunburnholme. E Yor 3F 42
Nuncargate. Notts 4C 36
Nunclose. Cumb 7J 53
Nuneaton. Warw 2A 28
Nuneham Courtenay. Oxon 4C 20
Nun Monkton. N Yor 2C 42
Nunnerie. S Lan 8H 59
Nunney. Som 1F 8
Nunnington. N Yor 8D 48
Nunnykirk. Nmbd 2D 54
Nunsthorpe. NE Lin 7K 43
Nunthorpe. Midd 4C 48
Nunthorpe. York 2C 42
Nunton. Wilts 3K 9
Nunwick. Nmbd 4B 54
Nunwick. N Yor 8M 47
Nupend. Glos 3F 19
Nursling. Hants 4A 10
Nursted. Hants 3E 10
Nursteed. Wilts 7J 19
Nurston. V Glam 8K 17
Nutbourne. W Sus
nr. Chichester 5E 10
nr. Pulborough 4H 11
Nutfield. Surr 8L 21
Nuthall. Notts 5C 36
Nuthampstead. Herts 8M 29
Nuthurst. Warw 4K 27
Nuthurst. W Sus 3J 11
Nutley. E Sus 3M 11
Nuttall. G Man 6F 40
Nutwell. S Yor 7D 42
Nybster. High 5E 86
Nyetimber. W Sus 6F 10
Nyewood. W Sus 3F 10
Nymet Rowland. Devn 5G 7
Nymet Tracey. Devn 5G 7
Nympsfield. Glos 3G 19
Nynehead. Som 3L 7
Nyton. W Sus 5G 11

O

Oadby. Leics 1D 28
Oad Street. Kent 7E 22
Oakamoor. Staf 5J 35
Oakbank. Arg 4B 64
Oakbank. W Lot 3J 59
Oakdale. Cphy 5L 17
Oakdale. Pool 6J 9
Oake. Som 3L 7
Oaken. Staf 1G 27
Oakenclough. Lanc 3D 40
Oakengates. Telf 8E 34
Oakenholt. Flin 2A 34
Oakenshaw. Dur 8F 54
Oakenshaw. W Yor 5K 41
Oakerthorpe. Derbs 4A 36
Oakford. Cdgn 1L 15
Oakford. Devn 3J 7
Oakfordbridge. Devn 3J 7
Oakgrove. Ches E 3H 35
Oakham. Rut 1F 28
Oakhanger. Ches E 4F 34
Oakhanger. Hants 2E 10
Oakhill. Som 1E 8
Oakington. Cambs 5M 29
Oaklands. Powy 7K 25
Oakle Street. Glos 2F 18
Oakley. Bed 6H 29
Oakley. Buck 2D 20
Oakley. Fife 1J 59
Oakley. Hants 8C 20
Oakley. Suff 4H 31
Oakley Green. Wind 6G 21
Oakley Park. Powy 4J 25
Oakmere. Ches W 3D 34
Oakridge Lynch. Glos 3H 19
Oaks. Shrp 1C 26
Oaksey. Wilts 4H 19
Oaks Green. Derbs 6K 35
Oakshaw Ford. Cumb 4K 53
Oakshott. Hants 3E 10
Oakthorpe. Leics 8M 35
Oak Tree. Darl 4A 48
Oakwood. Derb 6A 36
Oakwood. W Yor 4M 41
Oakwoodhill. Surr 2J 11
Oakworth. W Yor 4J 41
Oape. High 3E 78
Oare. Kent 7G 23
Oare. Som 1H 7
Oare. W Ber 6C 20
Oare. Wilts 7K 19
Oareford. Som 1H 7
Oasby. Linc 6H 37
Oath. Som 3B 8
Oathlaw. Ang 2H 67
Oatlands. N Yor 2M 41
Oban. Arg 5C 64
Oban. W Isl 3C 76
Oborne. Dors 4E 8
Obsdale. High 7G 79
Obthorpe. Linc 8H 37
Occlestone Green. Ches W 3E 34
Occold. Suff 4H 31
Ochiltree. E Ayr 7D 58
Ochtermuthill. Per 6B 66
Ochtertyre. Per 5B 66
Ockbrook. Derbs 6B 36
Ockeridge. Worc 5F 26
Ockham. Surr 8H 21
Ockle. High 8G 69
Ockley. Surr 1J 11
Ocle Pychard. Here 7D 26
Octofad. Arg 4B 56
Octomore. Arg 4B 56
Octon. E Yor 1H 43
Odcombe. Som 4D 8
Odd Down. Bath 7F 18
Oddingley. Worc 6H 27
Oddington. Oxon 2C 20
Oddsta. Shet 4K 91
Odell. Bed 6G 29
Odie. Orkn 7F 88
Odiham. Hants 8E 20
Odsey. Cambs 8K 29
Odstock. Wilts 3K 9
Odstone. Leics 1A 28
Offchurch. Warw 5A 28
Offenham. Worc 7J 27
Offenham Cross. Worc 7J 27
Offerton. G Man 1H 35
Offerton. Tyne 6G 55
Offham. E Sus 4L 11
Offham. Kent 8C 22
Offham. W Sus 5H 11
Offleyhay. Staf 7G 35
Offley Hoo. Herts 1J 21
Offleymarsh. Staf 7F 34
Offord Cluny. Cambs 5K 29
Offord D'Arcy. Cambs 5K 29
Offton. Suff 7G 31
Offwell. Devn 6L 7
Ogbourne Maizey. Wilts 6K 19
Ogbourne St Andrew. Wilts 6K 19
Ogbourne St George. Wilts 6L 19
Ogden. G Man 6H 41
Ogle. Nmbd 4E 54
Ogmore. V Glam 7H 17
Ogmore-by-Sea. V Glam 7H 17
Ogmore Vale. B'end 5J 17
Okeford Fitzpaine. Dors 4G 9
Okehampton. Devn 6E 6
Okehampton Camp. Devn 6E 6
Okraquoy. Shet 4E 90
Okus. Swin 5K 19
Old. Nptn 4E 28
Old Aberdeen. Aber 5J 73
Old Alresford. Hants 2C 10
Oldany. High 8D 84
Old Arley. Warw 2L 27
Old Basford. Nott 5C 36
Old Basing. Hants 8D 20
Oldberrow. Warw 5K 27
Old Bewick. Nmbd 7H 61
Old Bexley. G Lon 6A 22
Old Blair. Per 1B 66
Old Bolingbroke. Linc 3L 37
Oldborough. Devn 5G 7
Old Brampton. Derbs 2M 35
Old Bridge of Tilt. Per 1B 66
Old Bridge of Urr. Dum 5B 52
Old Brumby. N Lin 7F 42
Old Buckenham. Norf 2G 31
Old Burghclere. Hants 8B 20
Oldbury. Shrp 2F 26
Oldbury. Warw 2M 27
Oldbury. W Mid 3H 27
Oldbury-on-Severn. S Glo 4E 18
Oldbury on the Hill. Glos 5G 19
Old Byland. N Yor 7C 48
Old Cassop. Dur 8G 55
Oldcastle. Mon 1B 18
Oldcastle Heath. Ches W 5C 34
Old Catton. Norf 8J 39
Old Clee. NE Lin 7K 43
Old Cleeve. Som 1K 7
Old Colwyn. Cnwy 3H 33
Oldcotes. Notts 1C 36
Old Coulsdon. G Lon 8L 21
Old Dailly. S Ayr 2H 51
Old Dalby. Leics 7D 36
Old Dam. Derbs 2K 35
Old Deer. Abers 1J 73
Old Dilton. Wilts 1G 9
Old Down. S Glo 5E 18
Oldeamere. Cambs 2L 29
Old Edlington. S Yor 8C 42
Old Eldon. Dur 3L 47
Old Ellerby. E Yor 4J 43
Old Fallings. W Mid 1H 27
Oldfallow. Staf 8H 35
Old Felixstowe. Suff 8K 31
Oldfield. Shrp 3E 26
Oldfield. Worc 5G 27
Old Fletton. Pet 2J 29
Oldford. Som 8F 18
Old Forge. Here 1D 18
Old Glossop. Derbs 8J 41
Old Goole. E Yor 5E 42
Old Gore. Here 1E 18
Old Graitney. Dum 5H 53
Old Grimsby. IOS 1G 3
Oldhall. High 6D 86
Old Hall Street. Norf 6K 39
Oldham. G Man 7H 41
Oldhamstocks. E Lot 2E 60
Old Heathfield. E Sus 3B 12
Old Hill. W Mid 3H 27
Old Hunstanton. Norf 5C 38
Oldhurst. Cambs 4K 29
Old Hutton. Cumb 7D 46
Old Kea. Corn 4M 3
Old Kilpatrick. W Dun 2C 58
Old Kinnernie. Abers 5G 73
Old Knebworth. Herts 1K 21
Oldland. S Glo 6E 18
Old Laxey. IOM 6D 44
Old Leake. Linc 4M 37
Old Lenton. Nott 6C 36
Old Llanberis. Gwyn 5F 32
Old Malton. N Yor 8E 48
Oldmeldrum. Abers 3H 73
Old Micklefield. W Yor 4B 42
Old Mill. Corn 8D 6
Oldmixon. N Som 8B 18
Old Monkland. N Lan 3F 58
Old Newton. Suff 5G 31
Old Park. Telf 1E 26
Old Pentland. Midl 3M 59
Old Philpstoun. W Lot 2J 59
Old Quarrington. Dur 8G 55
Old Radnor. Powy 6A 26
Old Rayne. Abers 3F 72
Oldridge. Devn 6H 7
Old Romney. Kent 3G 13
Old Scone. Per 5E 66
Oldshore Beg. High 6D 84
Oldshoremore. High 6E 84
Old Snydale. W Yor 5B 42
Old Sodbury. S Glo 5F 18
Old Somerby. Linc 6G 37
Old Spital. Dur 4H 47
Oldstead. N Yor 7C 48
Old Stratford. Nptn 7E 28
Old Swan. Mers 8B 40
Old Swarland. Nmbd 1E 54
Old Tebay. Cumb 5E 46
Old Town. Cumb 7J 53
Old Town. E Sus 6B 12
Oldtown. High 5F 79
Old Town. IOS 1H 3
Old Town. Nmbd 2B 54
Old Trafford. G Man 8G 41
Old Tupton. Derbs 3A 36
Oldwall. Cumb 5J 53
Oldwalls. Swan 7L 15
Old Warden. C Beds 7J 29
Oldways End. Som 3H 7
Old Westhall. Abers 3F 72
Old Weston. Cambs 4H 29
Oldwhat. Abers 8H 81
Old Windsor. Wind 6G 21
Old Wives Lees. Kent 8G 23
Old Woking. Surr 8H 21
Oldwood Common. Worc 5D 26
Old Woodstock. Oxon 2B 20
Olgrinmore. High 6B 86
Oliver's Battery. Hants 3B 10
Ollaberry. Shet 5H 91
Ollerton. Ches E 2F 34
Ollerton. Notts 3D 36
Ollerton. Shrp 7E 34
Olmarch. Cdgn 7F 24
Olmstead Green. Cambs 7C 30
Olney. Mil 6F 28
Olrig. High 5C 86
Olton. W Mid 3K 27
Olveston. S Glo 5E 18
Omagh. Ferm 5D 92
Ombersley. Worc 5G 27
Ompton. Notts 3D 36
Omunsgarth. Shet 3D 90
Onchan. IOM 7D 44
Onecote. Staf 4J 35
Onehouse. Suff 6G 31
Onen. Mon 2C 18
Ongar Hill. Norf 7B 38
Ongar Street. Here 5B 26
Onibury. Shrp 4C 26
Onich. High 1E 64
Onllwyn. Neat 3H 17
Onneley. Staf 5F 34
Onslow Green. Essx 2C 22
Onslow Village. Surr 1G 11
Onthank. E Ayr 6C 58
Openwoodgate. Derbs 5A 36
Opinan. High
nr. Gairloch 6J 77
nr. Laide 4K 77
Orasaigh. W Isl 2E 76
Orbost. High 1D 68
Orby. Linc 3A 38
Orchard Hill. Devn 3D 6
Orchard Portman. Som 3M 7
Orcheston. Wilts 1J 9
Orcop. Here 1C 18
Orcop Hill. Here 1C 18
Ord. High 4H 69
Ordale. Shet 3L 91
Ordhead. Abers 4F 72
Ordie. Abers 5D 72
Ordiquish. Mor 8C 80
Ordley. Nmbd 6C 54
Ordsall. Notts 2E 36
Ore. E Sus 4E 12
Oreton. Shrp 3E 26
Orford. Suff 7L 31
Orford. Warr 8E 40
Organford. Dors 6H 9
Orgil. Orkn 1D 86
Orgreave. Staf 8K 35
Oridge Street. Glos 1F 18
Orlestone. Kent 2F 12
Orleton. Here 5C 26
Orleton. Worc 5E 26
Orleton Common. Here 5C 26
Orlingbury. Nptn 4F 28
Ormacleit. W Isl 2D 74
Ormathwaite. Cumb 3A 46
Ormesby. Red C 4C 48
Ormesby St Margaret. Norf 8L 39
Ormesby St Michael. Norf 8L 39
Ormiscaig. High 4K 77
Ormiston. E Lot 3B 60
Ormsaigbeg. High 1K 63
Ormsaigmore. High 1K 63
Ormsary. Arg 2G 57
Ormsgill. Cumb 7L 45
Ormskirk. Lanc 7C 40
Orphir. Orkn 1E 86
Orpington. G Lon 7A 22
Orrell. G Man 7D 40
Orrell. Mers 8B 40
Orrisdale. IOM 5C 44
Orsett. Thur 5C 22
Orslow. Staf 8G 35
Orston. Notts 5E 36
Orthwaite. Cumb 8G 53
Orton. Cumb 5E 46
Orton. Mor 8C 80
Orton. Nptn 4F 28
Orton. Staf 2G 27
Orton Longueville. Pet 2J 29
Orton-on-the-Hill. Leics 1M 27
Orton Waterville. Pet 2J 29
Orton Wistow. Pet 2J 29
Orwell. Cambs 6L 29
Osbaldeston. Lanc 4E 40
Osbaldwick. York 2D 42
Osbaston. Leics 1B 28
Osbaston. Shrp 8B 34
Osbournby. Linc 6H 37
Osclay. High 8D 86
Oscroft. Ches W 3D 34
Ose. High 1E 68
Osgathorpe. Leics 8B 36
Osgodby. Linc 8H 43
Osgodby. N Yor
nr. Scarborough 7H 49
nr. Selby 4D 42
Oskaig. High 2G 69
Oskamull. Arg 4K 63
Osleston. Derbs 6L 35
Osmaston. Derb 6A 36
Osmaston. Derbs 5L 35
Osmington. Dors 7F 8
Osmington Mills. Dors 7F 8
Osmondthorpe. W Yor 4M 41
Osmondwall. Orkn 3E 86
Osmotherley. N Yor 6B 48
Osnaburgh. Fife 6H 67
Ospisdale. High 5H 79
Ospringe. Kent 7G 23
Ossett. W Yor 5L 41
Ossington. Notts 3E 36
Ostend. Essx 4F 22
Ostend. Norf 6K 39
Osterley. G Lon 6J 21
Oswaldkirk. N Yor 8D 48
Oswaldtwistle. Lanc 5F 40
Oswestry. Shrp 7A 34
Otby. Linc 8J 43
Otford. Kent 8B 22
Otham. Kent 8D 22
Otherton. Staf 8H 35
Othery. Som 2B 8
Otley. Suff 6J 31
Otley. W Yor 3L 41
Otterbourne. Hants 3B 10
Otterburn. Nmbd 2B 54
Otterburn. N Yor 2G 41
Otterburn Camp. Nmbd 2B 54
Otterburn Hall. Nmbd 2B 54
Otter Ferry. Arg 1J 57
Otterford. Som 4M 7
Otterham. Corn 6A 6
Otterhampton. Som 1M 7
Otterham Quay. Medw 7E 22
Ottershaw. Surr 7H 21
Otterspool. Mers 1B 34
Otterswick. Shet 5K 91
Otterton. Devn 7K 7
Otterwood. Hants 5B 10
Ottery St Mary. Devn 6K 7
Ottinge. Kent 1H 13
Ottringham. E Yor 5K 43
Oughterby. Cumb 6G 53
Oughtershaw. N Yor 7G 47
Oughterside. Cumb 7F 52
Oughtibridge. S Yor 8M 41
Oughtrington. Warr 1E 34
Oulston. N Yor 8C 48
Oulton. Cumb 6G 53
Oulton. Norf 7H 39
Oulton. Staf
nr. Gnosall Heath 7F 34
nr. Stone 6H 35
Oulton. Suff 2M 31
Oulton. W Yor 5A 42
Oulton Broad. Suff 2M 31
Oulton Street. Norf 7H 39
Oundle. Nptn 3H 29
Ousby. Cumb 8L 53
Ousdale. High 2L 79
Ousden. Suff 6D 30
Ousefleet. E Yor 5F 42
Ouston. Dur 6F 54
Ouston. Nmbd
nr. Bearsbridge 6A 54
nr. Stamfordham 4D 54
Outer Hope. Devn 7J 5
Outertown. Orkn 8B 88
Outgate. Cumb 6B 46
Outhgill. Cumb 5F 46
Outlands. Staf 6F 34
Outlane. W Yor 6J 41
Out Newton. E Yor 5L 43
Out Rawcliffe. Lanc 3C 40
Outwell. Norf 1B 30
Outwick. Hants 4K 9
Outwood. Surr 1L 11
Outwood. W Yor 5M 41
Outwood. Worc 4H 27
Outwoods. Leics 8B 36
Outwoods. Staf 8F 34
Ouzlewell Green. W Yor 5M 41
Ovenden. W Yor 5J 41
Over. Cambs 4L 29
Over. Ches W 3E 34
Over. Glos 2G 19
Over. S Glo 5D 18
Overbister. Orkn 5F 88
Over Burrows. Derbs 6L 35
Overbury. Worc 8H 27
Overcombe. Dors 7E 8
Over Compton. Dors 4D 8
Over End. Cambs 2H 29
Over Finlarg. Ang 3H 67
Overgreen. Derbs 2M 35
Over Green. Warw 2K 27
Over Haddon. Derbs 3L 35
Over Hulton. G Man 7E 40
Over Kellet. Lanc 8D 46
Over Kiddington. Oxon 1B 20
Overleigh. Som 2C 8
Overley. Staf 8K 35
Over Monnow. Mon 2D 18
Over Norton. Oxon 1M 19
Over Peover. Ches E 2F 34
Overpool. Ches W 2B 34
Overscaig. High 1E 78
Overseal. Derbs 8L 35
Over Silton. N Yor 6B 48
Oversland. Kent 8G 23
Overstone. Nptn 5F 28
Over Stowey. Som 2L 7
Overstrand. Norf 5J 39
Over Stratton. Som 4C 8
Over Street. Wilts 2J 9
Overthorpe. Nptn 7B 28
Overton. Aber 4H 73
Overton. Ches W 2D 34
Overton. Hants 1C 10
Overton. High 8D 86
Overton. Lanc 2C 40
Overton. N Yor 2C 42
Overton. Shrp
nr. Bridgnorth 3E 26
nr. Ludlow 4D 26
Overton. Swan 8L 15
Overton. W Yor 6L 41
Overton. Wrex 5B 34
Overtown. Lanc 8E 46
Overtown. N Lan 4G 59
Overtown. Swin 6K 19
Over Wallop. Hants 2L 9
Over Whitacre. Warw 2L 27
Over Worton. Oxon 1B 20
Oving. Buck 1E 20
Oving. W Sus 5G 11
Ovingdean. Brig 5L 11
Ovingham. Nmbd 5D 54
Ovington. Dur 4K 47
Ovington. Essx 7D 30
Ovington. Hants 2C 10
Ovington. Norf 1F 30
Ovington. Nmbd 5D 54
Owen's Bank. Staf 7L 35
Ower. Hants
nr. Holbury 5B 10
nr. Totton 4M 9
Owermoigne. Dors 7F 8
Owlbury. Shrp 2B 26
Owler Bar. Derbs 2L 35
Owlerton. S Yor 8M 41
Owlsmoor. Brac 7F 20
Owlswick. Buck 3E 20
Owmby. Linc 7H 43
Owmby-by-Spital. Linc 1H 37
Ownham. W Ber 6B 20
Owrytn. Wrex 5B 34
Owslebury. Hants 3C 10
Owston. Leics 1E 28
Owston. S Yor 6C 42
Owston Ferry. N Lin 7F 42
Owstwick. E Yor 4K 43
Owthorne. E Yor 5L 43
Owthorpe. Notts 6D 36
Owton Manor. Hart 3B 48
Oxborough. Norf 1D 30
Oxbridge. Dors 6C 8
Oxcombe. Linc 2L 37
Oxen End. Essx 1C 22
Oxenhall. Glos 1F 18
Oxenholme. Cumb 6D 46
Oxenhope. W Yor 4J 41
Oxen Park. Cumb 7B 46
Oxenpill. Som 1C 8
Oxenton. Glos 8H 27
Oxenwood. Wilts 8M 19
Oxford. Oxon 3C 20
Oxgangs. Edin 3L 59
Oxhey. Herts 4J 21
Oxhill. Warw 7M 27
Oxley. W Mid 1H 27
Oxley Green. Essx 2F 22
Oxley's Green. E Sus 3C 12
Oxlode. Cambs 3A 30
Oxnam. Bord 8E 60
Oxshott. Surr 7J 21
Oxspring. S Yor 7L 41
Oxted. Surr 8L 21
Oxton. Mers 1B 34
Oxton. N Yor 3C 42
Oxton. Notts 4D 36
Oxton. Bord 4B 60
Oxwich. Swan 8L 15
Oxwich Green. Swan 8L 15
Oxwick. Norf 7F 38
Oykel Bridge. High 3D 78
Oyne. Abers 3F 72
Oystermouth. Swan 6F 16
Ozleworth. Glos 4F 18

P

Pabail Iarach. W Isl 8J 83
Pabail Uarach. W Isl 8J 83
Pachesham Park. Surr 8J 21
Packers Hill. Dors 4F 8
Packington. Leics 8A 36
Packmoor. Stoke 4G 35
Packmores. Warw 5L 27
Packwood. W Mid 4K 27
Packwood Gullet. W Mid 4K 27
Padanaram. Ang 2H 67
Padbury. Buck 8E 28
Paddington. G Lon 5K 21
Paddington. Warr 1E 34
Paddlesworth. Kent 2H 13
Paddock. Kent 8F 22
Paddockhole. Dum 3G 53
Paddock Wood. Kent 1C 12
Paddolgreen. Shrp 6D 34
Padeswood. Flin 3A 34
Padiham. Lanc 4F 40
Padside. N Yor 2K 41
Padson. Devn 6E 6
Padstow. Corn 4B 4
Padworth. W Ber 7D 20
Page Bank. Dur 8F 54
Pagham. W Sus 6F 10
Paglesham Churchend. Essx 4F 22
Paglesham Eastend. Essx 4F 22
Paibeil. W Isl
on North Uist 7J 75
on Taransay 4B 76
Paiblesgearraidh. W Isl 7J 75
Paignton. Torb 5L 5
Pailton. Warw 3B 28
Paine's Corner. E Sus 3C 12
Painleyhill. Staf 6J 35
Painscastle. Powy 8L 25
Painshawfield. Nmbd 5D 54
Painsthorpe. E Yor 2F 42
Painswick. Glos 3G 19
Painter's Forstal. Kent 8F 22
Painthorpe. W Yor 6M 41
Pairc Shiaboist. W Isl 7F 82
Paisley. Ren 3C 58
Pakefield. Suff 2M 31
Pakenham. Suff 5F 30
Pale. Gwyn 7J 33
Palehouse Common. E Sus 4A 12
Palestine. Hants 1L 9
Paley Street. Wind 6F 20
Palgowan. Dum 3J 51
Palgrave. Suff 4H 31
Pallington. Dors 6F 8
Palmarsh. Kent 2H 13
Palmer Moor. Derbs 6K 35
Palmers Cross. W Mid 1G 27
Palmerstown. V Glam 8L 17
Palnackie. Dum 6C 52
Palnure. Dum 5K 51
Palterton. Derbs 3B 36
Pamber End. Hants 8D 20
Pamber Green. Hants 8D 20
Pamber Heath. Hants 7D 20
Pamington. Glos 8H 27
Pamphill. Dors 5H 9
Pampisford. Cambs 7A 30
Panborough. Som 1C 8
Panbride. Ang 4J 67
Pancrasweek. Devn 5B 6
Pandy. Gwyn
nr. Bala 7H 33
nr. Tywyn 2F 24
Pandy. Mon 1B 18
Pandy. Powy 2J 25
Pandy. Wrex 7L 33
Pandy Tudur. Cnwy 4H 33
Panfield. Essx 1D 22
Pangbourne. W Ber 6D 20
Pannal. N Yor 2M 41
Pannal Ash. N Yor 2L 41
Pannanich. Abers 6C 72
Pant. Shrp 7A 34
Pant. Wrex 5A 34
Pantasaph. Flin 3L 33
Pant Glas. Gwyn 6D 32
Pant-glas. Shrp 6A 34
Pantgwyn. Carm 2E 16
Pantgwyn. Cdgn 2J 15
Pant-lasau. Swan 4F 16
Panton. Linc 2J 37
Pant-pastynog. Den 4K 33
Pantperthog. Gwyn 2G 25
Pant-teg. Carm 4L 15
Pant-y-Caws. Carm 4H 15
Pant-y-dwr. Powy 5J 25
Pant-y-ffridd. Powy 2L 25
Pantyffynnon. Carm 3F 16
Pantygasseg. Torf 3A 18
Pant-y-llyn. Carm 3F 16
Pant-yr-awel. B'end 6J 17
Pant y Wacco. Flin 3L 33
Panxworth. Norf 8K 39
Papa Stour Airport. Shet 2B 90
Papa Westray Airport. Orkn 4D 88
Papcastle. Cumb 8F 52
Papigoe. High 6E 86
Papil. Shet 4D 90
Papple. E Lot 2C 60
Papplewick. Notts 4C 36
Papworth Everard. Cambs 5K 29
Papworth St Agnes. Cambs 5K 29
Par. Corn 6C 4
Paramour Street. Kent 7J 23
Parbold. Lanc 6C 40
Parbrook. Som 2D 8
Parbrook. W Sus 3H 11
Parc. Gwyn 7H 33
Parcllyn. Cdgn 1J 15
Parc-Seymour. Newp 4C 18
Pardown. Hants 1C 10
Pardshaw. Cumb 2K 45
Parham. Suff 5K 31
Park. Abers 6G 73
Park. Arg 3D 64
Park. Derr 3D 92
Park. Dum 2D 52
Park Bottom. Corn 4K 3
Parkburn. Abers 2G 73
Park Corner. E Sus 2B 12
Park Corner. Oxon 5D 20
Parkend. Glos 3E 18
Park End. Nmbd 4B 54
Parkeston. Essx 8J 31
Parkfield. Corn 5F 4
Parkgate. Ant 4H 93
Parkgate. Ches W 2A 34
Parkgate. Cumb 7G 53
Parkgate. Dum 3E 52
Park Gate. Hants 5C 10
Parkgate. Surr 1K 11
Park Gate. Worc 4H 27
Parkhall. W Dun 2C 58
Parkham. Devn 3C 6
Parkham Ash. Devn 3C 6
Parkhead. Cumb 7H 53
Parkhead. Glas 3E 58
Park Hill. Mers 7C 40
Parkhouse. Mon 3D 18
Parkhurst. IOW 6B 10
Park Lane. G Man 7F 40
Park Lane. Staf 1G 27
Parkmill. Swan 8M 15
Park Mill. W Yor 6L 41
Parkneuk. Abers 8G 73
Parkside. N Lan 4G 59
Parkstone. Pool 6J 9
Park Street. Herts 3J 21
Park Street. W Sus 2J 11
Park Town. Oxon 3C 20
Park Village. Nmbd 5L 53
Parkway. Here 8F 26
Parley Cross. Dors 6J 9
Parmoor. Buck 5E 20
Parr. Mers 8D 40
Parracombe. Devn 1F 6
Parrog. Pemb 3G 15
Parsonage Green. Essx 2D 22
Parsonby. Cumb 8F 52
Parson Cross. S Yor 8M 41
Parson Drove. Cambs 1L 29
Partick. Glas 3D 58
Partington. G Man 8F 40
Partney. Linc 3M 37
Parton. Cumb
nr. Whitehaven 2J 45
nr. Wigton 6G 53
Parton. Dum 4A 52
Partridge Green. W Sus 4J 11
Parwich. Derbs 4K 35
Passenham. Nptn 8E 28
Passfield. Hants 2F 10
Passingford Bridge. Essx 4B 22
Paston. Norf 6K 39
Pasturefields. Staf 7H 35
Patchacott. Devn 6D 6
Patcham. Brig 5L 11
Patchetts Green. Herts 4J 21
Patching. W Sus 5H 11
Patchole. Devn 1F 6
Patchway. S Glo 5E 18
Pateley Bridge. N Yor 1K 41
Pathe. Som 2B 8
Pathfinder Village. Devn 6H 7
Pathhead. Abers 1L 67
Pathhead. E Ayr 8E 58
Pathhead. Fife 8F 66
Pathhead. Midl 3A 60
Pathlow. Warw 6K 27
Path of Condie. Per 6D 66
Pathstruie. Per 6D 66
Patmore Heath. Herts 1M 21
Patna. E Ayr 8C 58
Patney. Wilts 8J 19
Patrick. IOM 6B 44
Patrick Brompton. N Yor 6L 47
Patrington. E Yor 5L 43
Patrington Haven. E Yor 5L 43
Patrixbourne. Kent 8H 23
Patterdale. Cumb 4B 46
Pattiesmuir. Fife 1J 59
Pattingham. Staf 2G 27
Pattishall. Nptn 6D 28
Pattiswick. Essx 1E 22
Patton Bridge. Cumb 6D 46
Paul. Corn 6H 3
Paulerspury. Nptn 7E 28
Paull. E Yor 5J 43
Paulton. Bath 8E 18
Pauperhaugh. Nmbd 2E 54
Pave Lane. Telf 8F 34
Pavenham. Bed 6G 29
Pawlett. Som 1A 8
Pawston. Nmbd 6F 60
Paxford. Glos 8K 27
Paxton. Bord 4G 61
Payhembury. Devn 5K 7
Paythorne. Lanc 2G 41
Payton. Som 3L 7
Peacehaven. E Sus 5M 11
Peak Dale. Derbs 2J 35
Peak Forest. Derbs 2K 35
Peak Hill. Linc 8K 37
Peakirk. Pet 1J 29
Pearsie. Ang 2G 67
Peasedown St John. Bath 8F 18
Peaseland Green. Norf 8G 39
Peasemore. W Ber 6B 20
Peasenhall. Suff 5K 31
Pease Pottage. W Sus 2K 11
Peaslake. Surr 1H 11
Peasley Cross. Mers 8D 40
Peasmarsh. E Sus 3E 12
Peasmarsh. Som 4B 8
Peasmarsh. Surr 1G 11
Peaston. E Lot 3B 60
Peastonbank. E Lot 3B 60
Peathill. Abers 7J 81
Peat Inn. Fife 7H 67
Peatling Magna. Leics 2C 28
Peatling Parva. Leics 3C 28
Peaton. Arg 1M 57
Peaton. Shrp 3D 26
Peats Corner. Suff 5H 31
Pebmarsh. Essx 8E 30
Pebworth. Worc 7K 27
Pecket Well. W Yor 5H 41
Peckforton. Ches E 4D 34
Peckham Bush. Kent 8C 22
Peckleton. Leics 1B 28
Pedair-ffordd. Powy 8L 33
Pedham. Norf 8K 39
Pedlinge. Kent 2H 13
Pedmore. W Mid 3H 27
Pedwell. Som 2C 8
Peebles. Bord 5L 59
Peel. IOM 6B 44
Peel. Bord 6B 60
Peel Common. Hants 5C 10
Peening Quarter. Kent 3E 12
Peggs Green. Leics 8B 36
Pegsdon. C Beds 8J 29
Pegswood. Nmbd 3F 54
Peinchorran. High 2G 69
Peinlich. High 8F 76
Pelaw. Tyne 5F 54
Pelcomb Bridge. Pemb 5F 14
Pelcomb Cross. Pemb 5F 14
Peldon. Essx 2F 22
Pelsall. W Mid 1J 27
Pelton. Dur 6F 54
Pelutho. Cumb 7F 52
Pelynt. Corn 6E 4
Pemberton. Carm 6M 15
Pembrey. Carm 6L 15
Pembridge. Here 6B 26
Pembroke. Pemb 6F 14
Pembroke Dock. Pemb 6F 14
Pembroke Ferry. Pemb 6F 14
Pembury. Kent 1C 12
Penallt. Mon 2D 18
Penally. Pemb 7H 15
Penalt. Here 1D 18
Penalum. Pemb 7H 15
Penare. Corn 7B 4
Penarth. V Glam 7L 17
Penbeagle. Corn 5J 3
Penberth. Corn 6H 3
Pen-bont Rhydybeddau. Cdgn 4F 24
Penbryn. Cdgn 1J 15
Pencader. Carm 3L 15
Pen-cae. Cdgn 1L 15
Pencaenewydd. Gwyn 6D 32
Pencaerau. Neat 5G 17
Pencaitland. E Lot 3B 60
Pencarnisiog. IOA 3C 32
Pencarreg. Carm 2M 15
Pencarrow. Corn 3D 4
Pencelli. Powy 2K 17
Pen-clawdd. Swan 7M 15
Pencoed. B'end 6J 17
Pencombe. Here 6D 26
Pencraig. Here 1D 18
Pencraig. Powy 8K 33
Pendeen. Corn 5G 3
Pendeford. W Mid 1G 27
Penderyn. Rhon 4J 17
Pendine. Carm 6J 15
Pendlebury. G Man 7F 40
Pendleton. G Man 8G 41
Pendleton. Lanc 4F 40
Pendock. Worc 8F 26
Pendoggett. Corn 4C 4
Pendomer. Som 4D 8
Pendoylan. V Glam 7K 17
Pendre. B'end 6J 17
Penegoes. Powy 2G 25
Penelewey. Corn 4M 3
Penffordd. Pemb 4G 15
Penffordd-Lâs. Powy 3H 25
Penfro. Pemb 6F 14
Pengam. Cphy 5L 17
Pengam. Card 7M 17
Penge. G Lon 7L 21
Pengelly. Corn 3C 4
Pengenffordd. Powy 1L 17
Pengersick. Corn 6J 3
Pengorffwysfa. IOA 1D 32
Pengover Green. Corn 5E 4
Pengwern. Den 3K 33
Penhale. Corn
nr. Mullion 7K 3
nr. St Austell 6B 4
Penhale Camp. Corn 3L 3
Penhallow. Corn 3L 3
Penhalvean. Corn 5L 3
Penhelig. Gwyn 3F 24
Penhill. Swin 5K 19
Penhow. Newp 4C 18
Penhurst. E Sus 4C 12
Peniarth. Gwyn 2F 24
Penicuik. Midl 3L 59
Peniel. Carm 4L 15
Penifiler. High 1F 68
Peninver. Arg 7G 57
Penisa'r Waun. Gwyn 4E 32
Penistone. S Yor 7L 41
Penketh. Warr 1D 34
Penkill. S Ayr 2H 51
Penkridge. Staf 8H 35
Penley. Wrex 6C 34
Penllech. Gwyn 7B 32
Penllergaer. Swan 5F 16
Pen-llyn. IOA 2C 32
Penmachno. Cnwy 5G 33
Penmaen. Swan 8M 15
Penmaenmawr. Cnwy 3G 33
Penmaenpool. Gwyn 1F 24
Penmaen Rhos. Cnwy 3H 33
Pen-marc. V Glam 8K 17
Penmark. V Glam 8K 17
Penmarth. Corn 5L 3
Penmon. IOA 2F 32
Penmorfa. Gwyn 6E 32
Penmynydd. IOA 3E 32
Penn. Buck 4G 21
Penn. Dors 6B 8
Penn. W Mid 2G 27
Pennal. Gwyn 2G 25
Pennan. Abers 7H 81
Pennant. Cdgn 6E 24
Pennant. Den 7K 33
Pennant. Gwyn 8J 33
Pennant. Powy 3H 25
Pennant Melangell. Powy 8K 33
Pennar. Pemb 6F 14
Pennard. Swan 6E 16
Pennerley. Shrp 2B 26
Pennington. Cumb 8A 46
Pennington. G Man 8E 40
Pennington. Hants 6M 9
Pennorth. Powy 2L 17
Penn Street. Buck 4G 21
Pennsylvania. Devn 6J 7
Pennsylvania. S Glo 6F 18
Penny Bridge. Cumb 7B 46
Pennycross. Plym 6G 5
Pennygate. Norf 7K 39
Pennyghael. Arg 5L 63
Penny Hill. Linc 7L 37
Pennylands. Lanc 7C 40
Pennymoor. Devn 4H 7
Pennyvenie. E Ayr 1K 51
Pennywell. Tyne 6G 55
Penparc. Cdgn 2J 15
Penparcau. Cdgn 4E 24
Pen-pedair-heol. Cphy 5L 17
Penperlleni. Mon 3B 18
Penpillick. Corn 6C 4
Penpol. Corn 5M 3
Penpoll. Corn 6D 4
Penponds. Corn 5K 3
Penpont. Corn 4C 4
Penpont. Dum 2C 52
Penpont. Powy 2J 17
Penprysg. B'end 6J 17
Penquit. Devn 6J 5
Penrherber. Carm 3J 15
Penrhiw. Pemb 2J 15
Penrhiwceiber. Rhon 5K 17
Pen-Rhiw-fawr. Neat 3G 17
Penrhiw-llan. Cdgn 2K 15
Penrhiw-pal. Cdgn 2K 15
Penrhos. Gwyn 7C 32
Penrhos. Here 6B 26
Penrhos. IOA 2B 32
Penrhos. Mon 2C 18
Penrhos. Powy 3H 17
Penrhos Garnedd. Gwyn 3E 32
Penrhyn. IOA 1C 32
Penrhyn Bay. Cnwy 2H 33
Penrhyn-coch. Cdgn 4F 24
Penrhyndeudraeth. Gwyn 7F 32
Penrhyn-side. Cnwy 2H 33
Penrice. Swan 8L 15
Penrith. Cumb 3D 46
Penrose. Corn 4A 4
Penruddock. Cumb 3C 46
Penryn. Corn 5L 3
Pen-sarn. Carm 5L 15
Pen-sarn. Gwyn 8E 32
Pensax. Worc 5F 26
Pensby. Mers 1A 34
Penselwood. Som 2F 8
Pensford. Bath 7E 18
Pensham. Worc 7H 27
Penshaw. Tyne 6G 55
Penshurst. Kent 1B 12
Pensilva. Corn 5E 4
Pensnett. W Mid 3H 27
Penston. E Lot 2B 60
Penstone. Devn 5G 7
Pentewan. Corn 7C 4
Pentir. Gwyn 4E 32
Pentire. Corn 2L 3
Pentlepoir. Pemb 6H 15
Pentlow. Essx 7E 30
Pentney. Norf 8D 38
Penton Mewsey. Hants 1M 9
Pentraeth. IOA 3E 32
Pentre. Powy
nr. Church Stoke 2A 26
nr. Kerry 4L 25
nr. Mochdre 4K 25
Pentre. Rhon 5J 17
Pentre. Shrp 8B 34
Pentre. Wrex
nr. Chirk 5A 34
nr. Llanarmon Dyffryn Ceiriog 7L 33
Pentrebach. Carm 1H 17
Pentre-bach. Cdgn 2M 15
Pentrebach. Mer T 4K 17
Pentre-bach. Powy 1J 17
Pentrebach. Swan 4F 16
Pentre Berw. IOA 3D 32
Pentre-bont. Cnwy 5G 33
Pentrecagal. Carm 2K 15
Pentre-celyn. Den 5L 33
Pentre-clawdd. Shrp 6A 34
Pentreclwydau. Neat 4H 17
Pentre-cwrt. Carm 3K 15
Pentre Dolau Honddu. Powy 8J 25
Pentre-dwr. Swan 5F 16
Pentrefelin. Carm 2E 16
Pentrefelin. Cdgn 8F 24
Pentrefelin. Cnwy 3H 33
Pentrefelin. Gwyn 7E 32
Pentrefoelas. Cnwy 5H 33
Pentre Galar. Pemb 3H 15
Pentregat. Cdgn 1K 15
Pentre Gwenlais. Carm 3F 16
Pentre Gwynfryn. Gwyn 8E 32
Pentre Halkyn. Flin 3M 33
Pentre Hodre. Shrp 4B 26
Pentre-Llanrhaeadr. Den 4K 33
Pentre Llifior. Powy 3L 25
Pentrellwyn. IOA 2E 32
Pentre-llwyn-llwyd. Powy 7J 25
Pentre-llyn-cymmer. Cnwy 5J 33
Pentre Meyrick. V Glam 7J 17
Pentre-piod. Gwyn 7H 33
Pentre-poeth. Newp 5A 18
Pentre'r beirdd. Powy 1L 25
Pentre'r-felin. Powy 1J 17
Pentre-tafarn-y-fedw. Cnwy 4H 33
Pentre-ty-gwyn. Carm 1H 17
Pentre-uchaf. Gwyn 7C 32
Pentrich. Derbs 4A 36
Pentridge. Dors 4J 9
Pen-twyn. Cphy 4M 17
Pentwyn. Cphy 4L 17
Pentwyn. Card 6M 17
Pentyrch. Card 6L 17
Pentywyn. Carm 6J 15
Penuwch. Cdgn 6E 24
Penwithick. Corn 6C 4
Penwyllt. Powy 3H 17
Pen-y-banc. Carm 2F 16
Penybanc. Carm 3F 16
Pen-y-bont. Carm 4K 15
Pen-y-bont. Powy 8M 33
Penybont. Powy 6L 25
Pen-y-Bont Ar Ogwr. B'end 6J 17
Penybontfawr. Powy 8K 33
Penybryn. Cphy 5L 17
Pen-y-bryn. Pemb 2H 15
Pen-y-bryn. Wrex 5A 34
Pen-y-cae. Powy 3H 17
Penycae. Wrex 5A 34
Pen-y-cae mawr. Mon 4C 18
Penycaerau. Gwyn 8A 32
Pen-y-cefn. Flin 3L 33
Pen-y-clawdd. Mon 3C 18
Pen-y-coedcae. Rhon 6K 17
Penycwm. Pemb 4E 14
Pen-y-Darren. Mer T 4K 17
Pen-y-fai. B'end 6H 17
Pen-y-ffordd. Flin 2L 33
Penyffordd. Flin 3B 34
Penyffridd. Gwyn 5E 32
Pen-y-garn. Cdgn 4F 24
Pen-y-garnedd. IOA 3E 32
Penygarnedd. Powy 8L 33
Pen-y-graig. Gwyn 7B 32
Penygraig. Rhon 5J 17
Penygraigwen. IOA 2D 32
Pen-y-groes. Carm 3E 16
Penygroes. Gwyn 5D 32
Penygroes. Pemb 3H 15
Pen-y-Mynydd. Carm 6L 15
Penymynydd. Flin 3B 34
Penyrheol. Cphy 6L 17
Pen-yr-heol. Mon 2C 18
Penyrheol. Swan 5E 16
Penysarn. IOA 1D 32
Pen-y-stryt. Den 5L 33
Penywaun. Rhon 4J 17
Penzance. Corn 5H 3
Peopleton. Worc 6H 27
Peover Heath. Ches E 2F 34
Peper Harow. Surr 1G 11
Peplow. Shrp 7E 34
Pepper Arden. N Yor 5L 47
Perceton. N Ayr 5B 58
Percyhorner. Abers 7J 81
Perham Down. Wilts 1L 9
Periton. Som 1J 7
Perkinsville. Dur 6F 54
Perlethorpe. Notts 2D 36

Perranarworthal—Ridsdale

Perranarworthal. Corn 5L 3
Perranporth. Corn 3L 3
Perranuthnoe. Corn 6J 3
Perranwell. Corn 5L 3
Perranzabuloe. Corn 3L 3
Perrott's Brook. Glos 3J 19
Perry. W Mid 2J 27
Perry Barr. W Mid 2J 27
Perry Crofts. Staf 1L 27
Perry Green. Essx 1E 22
Perry Green. Herts 2M 21
Perry Green. Wilts 5H 19
Perry Street. Kent 6C 22
Perry Street. Som 5B 8
Perrywood. Kent 8G 23
Pershall. Staf 7G 35
Pershore. Worc 7H 27
Pertenhall. Bed 5H 29
Perth. Per 5E 66
Perthy. Shrp 6B 34
Perton. Staf 2G 27
Pertwood. Wilts 2G 9
Peterborough. Pet 2J 29
Peterburn. High 5J 77
Peterchurch. Here 8B 26
Peterculter. Aber 5H 73
Peterhead. Abers 1L 73
Peterlee. Dur 7H 55
Petersfield. Hants 3E 10
Petersfinger. Wilts 3K 9
Peters Green. Herts 2J 21
Peters Marland. Devn 4D 6
Peterstone Wentlooge.
Newp 5A 18
Peterston-super-Ely. V Glam 7K 17
Peterstow. Here 1D 18
Peters Village. Kent 7D 22
Peter Tavy. Devn 8E 6
Petertown. Orkn 1E 86
Petham. Kent 8H 23
Petherwin Gate. Corn 7B 6
Petrockstowe. Devn 5E 6
Petsoe End. Mil 7F 28
Pett. E Sus 4E 12
Pettaugh. Suff 6H 31
Pett Bottom. Kent 8H 23
Petteridge. Kent 1C 12
Pettinain. S Lan 5H 59
Pettistree. Suff 6J 31
Petton. Devn 3K 7
Petton. Shrp 7C 34
Petts Wood. G Lon 7M 21
Pettycur. Fife 1L 59
Pettywell. Norf 7G 39
Petworth. W Sus 3G 11
Pevensey. E Sus 5C 12
Pevensey Bay. E Sus 5C 12
Pewsey. Wilts 7K 19
Pheasants Hill. Buck 5E 20
Philadelphia. Tyne 6G 55
Philham. Devn 3B 6
Philiphaugh. Bord 7B 60
Phillack. Corn 5J 3
Philleigh. Corn 8A 4
Philpstoun. W Lot 2J 59
Phocle Green. Here 1E 18
Phoenix Green. Hants 8E 20
Pibsbury. Som 3C 8
Pibwrlwyd. Carm 5L 15
Pica. Cumb 2K 45
Piccadilly. Warw 2L 27
Piccadilly Corner. Norf 3J 31
Piccotts End. Herts 3H 21
Pickering. N Yor 7E 48
Picket Piece. Hants 1A 10
Picket Post. Hants 5K 9
Pickford. W Mid 3L 27
Pickhill. N Yor 7M 47
Picklenash. Glos 1F 18
Picklescott. Shrp 2C 26
Pickletillem. Fife 5H 67
Pickmere. Ches E 2E 34
Pickstock. Telf 7F 34
Pickwell. Devn 1D 6
Pickwell. Leics 8E 36
Pickworth. Linc 6H 37
Pickworth. Rut 8G 37
Picton. Ches W 2C 34
Picton. Flin 2L 33
Picton. N Yor 5B 48
Pict's Hill. Som 3C 8
Piddinghoe. E Sus 5M 11
Piddington. Buck 4F 20
Piddington. Nptn 6F 28
Piddington. Oxon 2D 20
Piddlehinton. Dors 6F 8
Piddletrenthide. Dors 6F 8
Pidley. Cambs 4L 29
Pidney. Dors 5F 8
Pie Corner. Here 5E 26
Piercebridge. Darl 4L 47
Pierowall. Orkn 5D 88
Pigdon. Nmbd 3E 54
Pightley. Som 2M 7
Pikehall. Derbs 4K 35
Pikeshill. Hants 5L 9
Pilford. Dors 5J 9
Pilgrims Hatch. Essx 4B 22
Pilham. Linc 8F 42
Pill, The. Mon 5C 18
Pill. N Som 6D 18
Pillaton. Corn 5F 4
Pillaton. Staf 8H 35
Pillerton Hersey. Warw 7M 27
Pillerton Priors. Warw 7L 27
Pilleth. Powy 5A 26
Pilley. Hants 6M 9
Pilley. S Yor 7M 41
Pillgwenlly. Newp 5B 18
Pilling. Lanc 3C 40
Pilling Lane. Lanc 3B 40
Pillowell. Glos 3E 18
Pillwell. Dors 4F 8
Pilning. S Glo 5D 18
Pilsbury. Derbs 3K 35
Pilsdon. Dors 6C 8
Pilsgate. Pet 1H 29
Pilsley. Derbs
nr. Bakewell 2L 35
nr. Clay Cross 3B 36
Pilson Green. Norf 8K 39
Piltdown. E Sus 3M 11
Pilton. Edin 2L 59
Pilton. Nptn 3H 29
Pilton. Rut 1G 29
Pilton. Som 1D 8
Pilton Green. Swan 8L 15
Pimperne. Dors 5H 9
Pinchbeck. Linc 7K 37
Pinchbeck Bars. Linc 7J 37
Pinchbeck West. Linc 7K 37
Pinfold. Lanc 6B 40
Pinford End. Suff 6E 30
Pinged. Carm 6L 15
Pinhoe. Devn 6J 7
Pinkerton. E Lot 2E 60
Pinkneys Green. Wind 5F 20
Pinley. W Mid 4A 28
Pinley Green. Warw 5L 27
Pinmill. Suff 8J 31
Pinmore. S Ayr 2H 51
Pinner. G Lon 5J 21
Pins Green. Worc 7F 26
Pinsley Green. Ches E 5D 34
Pinvin. Worc 7H 27
Pinwherry. S Ayr 3G 51
Pinxton. Derbs 4B 36
Pipe and Lyde. Here 7D 26
Pipe Aston. Here 4C 26
Pipe Gate. Shrp 5F 34
Pipehill. Staf 1J 27
Piperhill. High 8J 79
Pipe Ridware. Staf 8J 35
Pipers Pool. Corn 7B 6
Pipewell. Nptn 3F 28
Pippacott. Devn 2E 6
Pipton. Powy 1L 17
Pirbright. Surr 8G 21
Pirnmill. N Ayr 5H 57
Pirton. Herts 8J 29
Pirton. Worc 7G 27
Pisgah. Stir 7A 66
Pishill. Oxon 5E 20
Pistyll. Gwyn 6C 32
Pitagowan. Per 1B 66
Pitcairn. Per 2B 66
Pitcairngreen. Per 5D 66
Pitcalnie. High 6J 79
Pitcaple. Abers 3G 73
Pitchcombe. Glos 3G 19
Pitchcott. Buck 1E 20
Pitchford. Shrp 1D 26
Pitch Green. Buck 3E 20
Pitch Place. Surr 8G 21
Pitcombe. Som 2E 8
Pitcox. E Lot 2D 60
Pitcur. Per 4F 66
Pitfichie. Abers 4F 72
Pitgrudy. High 4H 79
Pitkennedy. Ang 2J 67
Pitlessie. Fife 7G 67
Pitlochry. Per 2C 66
Pitmachie. Abers 3F 72
Pitmaduthy. High 6H 79
Pitmedden. Abers 3H 73
Pitminster. Som 4M 7
Pitnacree. Per 2C 66
Pitney. Som 3C 8
Pitroddie. Per 5F 66
Pitscottie. Fife 6H 67
Pitsea. Essx 5D 22
Pitsford. Nptn 5E 28
Pitsford Hill. Som 2L 7
Pitsmoor. S Yor 1A 36
Pitstone. Buck 2G 21
Pitt. Hants 3B 10
Pitt Court. Glos 4F 18
Pittentrail. High 3H 79
Pittenweem. Fife 7J 67
Pittington. Dur 7G 55
Pitton. Swan 8L 15
Pitton. Wilts 2L 9
Pittswood. Kent 1C 12
Pittulie. Abers 7J 81
Pittville. Glos 1H 19
Pitversie. Per 6E 66
Pityme. Corn 4B 4
Pity Me. Dur 7F 54
Pixey Green. Suff 4J 31
Pixley. Here 8E 26
Place Newton. N Yor 8F 48
Plaidy. Abers 8G 81
Plaidy. Corn 6E 4
Plain Dealings. Pemb 5G 15
Plains. N Lan 3F 58
Plainsfield. Som 2L 7
Plaish. Shrp 2D 26
Plaistow. Here 8E 26
Plaistow. W Sus 2H 11
Plaitford. Wilts 4L 9
Plastow Green. Hants 7C 20
Plas yn Cefn. Den 3K 33
Platt, The. E Sus 2B 12
Platt Bridge. G Man 7E 40
Platt Lane. Shrp 6D 34
Platts Common. S Yor 7A 42
Platt's Heath. Kent 8E 22
Plawsworth. Dur 7F 54
Plaxtol. Kent 8C 22
Playden. E Sus 3F 12
Playford. Suff 7J 31
Play Hatch. Oxon 6E 20
Playing Place. Corn 4M 3
Playley Green. Glos 8F 26
Plealey. Shrp 1C 26
Plean. Stir 1G 59
Pleasington. Bkbn 5E 40
Pleasley. Derbs 3C 36
Pledgdon Green. Essx 1B 22
Plenmeller. Nmbd 5M 53
Pleshey. Essx 2C 22
Plockton. High 2K 69
Plocrapol. W Isl 4C 76
Ploughfield. Here 7B 26
Plowden. Shrp 3B 26
Ploxgreen. Shrp 1B 26
Pluckley. Kent 1F 12
Plucks Gutter. Kent 7J 23
Plumbland. Cumb 8F 52
Plumbridge. Derr 4D 92
Plumgarths. Cumb 6C 46
Plumley. Ches E 2F 34
Plummers Plain. W Sus 3K 11
Plumpton. Cumb 8J 53
Plumpton. E Sus 4L 11
Plumpton. Nptn 7C 28
Plumpton Foot. Cumb 8J 53
Plumpton Green. E Sus 4L 11
Plumpton Head. Cumb 8K 53
Plumstead. G Lon 6M 21
Plumstead. Norf 6H 39
Plumtree. Notts 6D 36
Plumtree Park. Notts 6D 36
Plungar. Leics 6E 36
Plush. Dors 5F 8
Plushabridge. Corn 8C 6
Plwmp. Cdgn 1K 15
Plymouth. Plym 6G 5
Plympton. Plym 6H 5
Plymstock. Plym 6H 5
Plymtree. Devn 5K 7
Pockley. N Yor 7D 48
Pocklington. E Yor 3F 42
Pode Hole. Linc 7K 37
Podimore. Som 3D 8
Podington. Bed 5G 29
Podmore. Staf 6F 34
Poffley End. Oxon 2A 20
Point Clear. Essx 2G 23
Pointon. Linc 6J 37
Pokesdown. Bour 6K 9
Polbae. Dum 4H 51
Polbain. High 3M 77
Polbathic. Corn 6F 4
Polbeth. W Lot 3J 59
Polbrock. Corn 5C 4
Polchar. High 5J 71
Polebrook. Nptn 3H 29
Pole Elm. Worc 7G 27
Polegate. E Sus 5B 12
Pole Moor. W Yor 6J 41
Poles. High 4H 79
Polesworth. Warw 1L 27
Polglass. High 3M 77
Polgooth. Corn 6B 4
Poling. W Sus 5H 11
Poling Corner. W Sus 5H 11
Polio. High 6H 79
Polkerris. Corn 6C 4
Polla. High 6F 84
Pollard Street. Norf 6K 39
Pollicott. Buck 2E 20
Pollington. E Yor 6D 42
Polloch. High 1B 64
Pollok. Glas 3D 58
Pollokshaws. Glas 3D 58
Pollokshields. Glas 3D 58
Polmaily. High 2E 70
Polmassick. Corn 7B 4
Polmont. Falk 2H 59
Polnessan. E Ayr 8C 58
Polnish. High 7J 69
Polperro. Corn 6E 4
Polruan. Corn 6D 4
Polscoe. Corn 5D 4
Polsham. Som 1D 8
Polskeoch. Dum 1A 52
Polstead. Suff 8F 30
Polstead Heath. Suff 7F 30
Poltesco. Corn 7L 3
Poltimore. Devn 6J 7
Polton. Midl 3L 59
Polwarth. Bord 4E 60
Polyphant. Corn 7B 6
Polzeath. Corn 4B 4
Pomeroy. M Ulst 5E 92
Ponde. Powy 1L 17
Pondersbridge. Cambs 2K 29
Ponders End. G Lon 4L 21
Pond Street. Essx 8A 30
Pondtail. Hants 8F 20
Ponsanooth. Corn 5L 3
Ponsongath. Corn 7L 3
Ponsworthy. Devn 8G 7
Pontamman. Carm 3F 16
Pontantwn. Carm 5L 15
Pontardawe. Neat 4G 17
Pontarddulais. Swan 4E 16
Pontarfynach. Cdgn 5G 25
Pont-ar-gothi. Carm 4M 15
Pont ar Hydfer. Powy 2H 17
Pontarllechau. Carm 2G 17
Pontarsais. Carm 4L 15
Pontblyddyn. Flin 3A 34
Pontbren Llwyd. Rhon 4J 17
Pont-Cyfyng. Cnwy 5G 33
Pontdolgoch. Powy 3K 25
Pontefract. W Yor 5B 42
Ponteland. Nmbd 4E 54
Ponterwyd. Cdgn 4G 25
Pontesbury. Shrp 1C 26
Pontesford. Shrp 1C 26
Pontfadog. Wrex 7M 33
Pontfaen. Pemb 3G 15
Pont-faen. Powy 1J 17
Pont-Faen. Shrp 6A 34
Pontgarreg. Cdgn 1K 15
Pont-Henri. Carm 6L 15
Ponthir. Torf 4B 18
Ponthirwaun. Cdgn 2J 15
Pont-iets. Carm 6L 15
Pontllanfraith. Cphy 5L 17
Pontlliw. Swan 4F 16
Pont Llogel. Powy 1K 25
Pontllyfni. Gwyn 5D 32
Pontlottyn. Cphy 4L 17
Pontneddfechan. Powy 4J 17
Pont-newydd. Carm 6L 15
Pont-newydd. Flin 4L 33
Pontnewydd. Torf 4A 18
Ponton. Shet 2D 90
Pont Pen-y-benglog. Gwyn 4F 32
Pontrhydfendigaid. Cdgn 6G 25
Pont Rhyd-y-cyff. B'end 6H 17
Pontrhydyfen. Neat 5G 17
Pont-rhyd-y-groes. Cdgn 5G 25
Pontrhydyrun. Torf 4A 18
Pont-Rhythallt. Gwyn 4E 32
Pontrilas. Here 1B 18
Pontrilas Road. Here 1B 18
Pontrobert. Powy 1L 25
Pont-rug. Gwyn 4E 32
Ponts Green. E Sus 4C 12
Pontshill. Here 1E 18
Pont-Sian. Cdgn 2L 15
Pontsticill. Mer T 3K 17
Pont-Walby. Neat 4H 17
Pontwelly. Carm 3L 15
Pontwgan. Cnwy 3G 33
Pontyates. Carm 6L 15
Pontyberem. Carm 5M 15
Pontybodkin. Flin 4A 34
Pontyclun. Rhon 6K 17
Pontycymer. B'end 5J 17
Pontyglazier. Pemb 3H 15
Pontygwaith. Rhon 5K 17
Pont-y-pant. Cnwy 5G 33
Pontypool. Torf 4A 18
Pontypridd. Rhon 6K 17
Pontypwl. Torf 4A 18
Pontywaun. Cphy 5M 17
Pooksgreen. Hants 4A 10
Pool. Corn 4K 3
Pool. W Yor 3L 41
Poole. N Yor 5B 42
Poole. Pool 6J 9
Poole. Som 3L 7
Poole Keynes. Glos 4H 19
Poolend. Staf 4H 35
Poolewe. High 5K 77
Pooley Bridge. Cumb 3C 46
Poolfold. Staf 4G 35
Pool Head. Here 6D 26
Pool Hey. Lanc 6B 40
Poolhill. Glos 1F 18
Poolmill. Here 1D 18
Pool o' Muckhart. Clac 7D 66
Pool Quay. Powy 8A 34
Poolsbrook. Derbs 2B 36
Pool Street. Essx 8D 30
Pootings. Kent 1A 12
Pope Hill. Pemb 5F 14
Pope's Hill. Glos 2E 18
Popeswood. Brac 7F 20
Popham. Hants 1C 10
Poplar. G Lon 5L 21
Popley. Hants 8D 20
Porchfield. IOW 6B 10
Porin. High 8D 78
Poringland. Norf 1J 31
Porkellis. Corn 5K 3
Porlock. Som 1H 7
Porlock Weir. Som 1H 7
Portachoillan. Arg 4G 57
Port Adhair Bheinn na Faoghla.
W Isl 8J 75
Port Adhair Thirlodh. Arg 3F 62
Portadown. Arm 6G 93
Portaferry. Ards 6J 93
Port Ann. Arg 1J 57
Port Appin. Arg 3D 64
Port Asgaig. Arg 3D 56
Port Askaig. Arg 3D 56
Portavadie. Arg 3J 57
Portavogie. Ards 5K 93
Portballintrae. Caus 1F 93
Port Bannatyne. Arg 3K 57
Portbury. N Som 6D 18
Port Carlisle. Cumb 5G 53
Port Charlotte. Arg 4B 56
Portchester. Hants 5D 10
Port Clarence. Stoc T 3B 48
Port Driseach. Arg 2J 57
Port Dundas. Glas 3D 58
Port Ellen. Arg 5C 56
Port Elphinstone. Abers 3G 73
Portencalzie. Dum 4F 50
Portencross. N Ayr 5L 57
Port Erin. IOM 8A 44
Port Erroll. Abers 2K 73
Porter's Fen Corner. Norf 1B 30
Portesham. Dors 7E 8
Portessie. Mor 7D 80
Port e Vullen. IOM 5D 44
Port-Eynon. Swan 8L 15
Portfield. Som 3C 8
Portfield Gate. Pemb 5F 14
Portgate. Devn 7D 6
Port Gaverne. Corn 3C 4
Port Glasgow. Inv 2B 58
Portglenone. ME Ant 3F 93
Portgordon. Mor 7C 80
Portgower. High 2L 79
Porth. Corn 2M 3
Porth. Rhon 5K 17
Porthaethwy. IOA 3E 32
Porthallow. Corn
nr. Looe 6E 4
nr. St Keverne 6L 3
Porthcawl. B'end 7H 17
Porthceri. V Glam 8K 17
Porthcothan. Corn 4A 4
Porthcurno. Corn 6G 3
Port Henderson. High 6J 77
Porthgain. Pemb 3E 14
Porthgwarra. Corn 6G 3
Porthill. Shrp 8C 34
Porthkerry. V Glam 8K 17
Porthleven. Corn 6K 3
Porthllechog. IOA 1D 32
Porthmadog. Gwyn 7E 32
Porthmeor. Corn 5H 3
Porth Navas. Corn 6L 3
Portholland. Corn 7B 4
Porthoustock. Corn 6M 3
Porthtowan. Corn 4K 3
Porth Tywyn. Carm 6L 15
Porth-y-felin. IOA 2B 32
Porthyrhyd. Carm
nr. Carmarthen 5M 15
nr. Llandovery 1G 17
Porth-y-waen. Shrp 7A 34
Portincaple. Arg 8G 65
Portington. E Yor 4E 42
Portinnisherrich. Arg 6D 64
Portinscale. Cumb 3A 46
Port Isaac. Corn 3B 4
Portishead. N Som 6C 18
Portknockie. Mor 7D 80
Port Lamont. Arg 2K 57
Portlethen. Abers 6J 73
Portlethen Village. Abers 6J 73
Portling. Dum 6C 52
Port Lion. Pemb 6F 14
Portloe. Corn 8B 4
Port Logan. Dum 7F 50
Portmahomack. High 5K 79
Portmead. Swan 5F 16
Portmeirion. Gwyn 7E 32
Portmellon. Corn 7C 4
Port Mholair. W Isl 8J 83
Port Mor. High 8F 68
Portmore. Hants 6M 9
Port Mulgrave. N Yor 4E 48
Portnacroish. Arg 3D 64
Portnahaven. Arg 4A 56
Portnalong. High 2E 68
Portnaluchaig. High 7H 69
Portnancon. High 5G 85
Port Nan Giuran. W Isl 8J 83
Port nan Long. W Isl 6K 75
Port Nis. W Isl 5J 83
Portobello. Edin 2M 59
Portobello. W Yor 6M 41
Port of Menteith. Stir 7K 65
Porton. Wilts 2K 9
Portormin. High 8D 86
Portpatrick. Dum 6F 50
Port Quin. Corn 3B 4
Port Ramsay. Arg 3C 64
Portreath. Corn 4K 3
Portree. High 1F 68
Port Righ. High 1F 68
Portrush. Caus 2F 93
Portscatho. Corn 8A 4
Portsea. Port 5D 10
Port Seton. E Lot 2B 60
Portskerra. High 5L 85
Portskewett. Mon 5D 18
Portslade-by-Sea. Brig 5K 11
Portsmouth. Port 6D 10
Portsmouth. W Yor 5H 41
Port Soderick. IOM 7C 44
Port Solent. Port 5D 10
Portsonachan. Arg 5E 64
Portsoy. Abers 7E 80
Portstewart. Caus 2F 93
Port Sunlight. Mers 1B 34
Portswood. Sotn 4B 10
Port Talbot. Neat 6G 17
Porttannachy. Mor 7C 80
Port Tennant. Swan 5F 16
Portuairk. High 1K 63
Portway. Here 7C 26
Portway. Worc 4J 27
Port Wemyss. Arg 4A 56
Port William. Dum 7J 51
Portwrinkle. Corn 6F 4
Poslingford. Suff 7D 30
Postbridge. Devn 8F 6
Postcombe. Oxon 4E 20
Post Green. Dors 6H 9
Posting. Kent 1H 13
Postlip. Glos 1J 19
Post-Mawr. Cdgn 1L 15
Postwick. Norf 1J 31
Potarch. Abers 6F 72
Potsgrove. C Beds 1G 21
Potten End. Herts 3H 21
Potter Brompton. N Yor 8G 49
Pottergate Street. Norf 2H 31
Potterhanworth. Linc 3H 37
Potterhanworth Booths.
Linc 3H 37
Potter Heigham. Norf 8L 39
Potter Hill. Leics 7E 36
Potteries, The. Stoke 5G 35
Potterne. Wilts 8H 19
Potterne Wick. Wilts 8J 19
Potternewton. W Yor 4M 41
Potters Bar. Herts 3K 21
Potters Brook. Lanc 2C 40
Potter's Cross. Staf 3G 27
Potters Crouch. Herts 3J 21
Potter Somersal. Derbs 6K 35
Potterspury. Nptn 7E 28
Potter Street. Essx 3A 22
Potterton. Abers 4J 73
Potthorpe. Norf 7F 38
Pottle Street. Wilts 1G 9
Potto. N Yor 5B 48
Potton. C Beds 7K 29
Pott Row. Norf 7D 38
Pott Shrigley. Ches E 1H 35
Poughill. Corn 5B 6
Poughill. Devn 5H 7
Poulner. Hants 5K 9
Poulshot. Wilts 8H 19
Poulton. Glos 3K 19
Poulton-le-Fylde. Lanc 4B 40
Pound Bank. Worc 4F 26
Poundbury. Dors 6E 8
Poundfield. E Sus 2B 12
Poundgate. E Sus 3A 12
Pound Green. E Sus 3B 12
Pound Green. Suff 6D 30
Pound Hill. W Sus 2K 11
Poundland. S Ayr 3G 51
Poundon. Buck 1D 20
Poundsgate. Devn 8G 7
Poundstock. Corn 6B 6
Pound Street. Hants 7B 20
Pounsley. E Sus 3B 12
Powburn. Nmbd 8H 61
Powderham. Devn 7J 7
Powerstock. Dors 6D 8
Powfoot. Dum 5F 52
Powick. Worc 6G 27
Powmill. Per 8D 66
Poxwell. Dors 7F 8
Poyle. Slo 6H 21
Poynings. W Sus 4K 11
Poyntington. Dors 3E 8
Poynton. Ches E 1H 35
Poynton. Telf 8D 34
Poynton Green. Telf 8D 34
Poyntz Pass. Arm 7G 93
Poystreet Green. Suff 6F 30
Praa Sands. Corn 6J 3
Pratt's Bottom. G Lon 7A 22
Praze-an-Beeble. Corn 5K 3
Prees. Shrp 6D 34
Preesall. Lanc 3B 40
Preesall Park. Lanc 3B 40
Prees Green. Shrp 6D 34
Prees Higher Heath. Shrp 6D 34
Prendergast. Pemb 5F 14
Prendwick. Nmbd 8H 61
Pren-gwyn. Cdgn 2L 15
Prenteg. Gwyn 6E 32
Prenton. Mers 1B 34
Prescot. Mers 8C 40
Prescott. Devn 4K 7
Prescott. Shrp 7C 34
Preshute. Wilts 7K 19
Pressen. Nmbd 6F 60
Prestatyn. Den 2K 33
Prestbury. Ches E 2H 35
Prestbury. Glos 1H 19
Presteigne. Powy 5B 26
Presthope. Shrp 2D 26
Prestleigh. Som 1E 8
Preston. Brig 5L 11
Preston. Devn 8H 7
Preston. Dors 7F 8
Preston. E Lot
nr. East Linton 2C 60
nr. Prestonpans 2A 60
Preston. E Yor 4J 43
Preston. Glos 3J 19
Preston. Herts 1J 21
Preston. Kent
nr. Canterbury 7J 23
nr. Faversham 7G 23
Preston. Lanc 5D 40
Preston. Nmbd 7J 61
Preston. Rut 1F 28
Preston. Bord 4E 60
Preston. Shrp 8D 34
Preston. Suff 6F 30
Preston. Wilts
nr. Aldbourne 6L 19
nr. Lyneham 6J 19
Preston Bagot. Warw 5K 27
Preston Bissett. Buck 1D 20
Preston Bowyer. Som 3L 7
Preston Brockhurst.
Shrp 7D 34
Preston Brook. Hal 1D 34
Preston Candover. Hants 1D 10
Preston Capes. Nptn 6C 28
Preston Cross. Glos 8E 26
Preston Gubbals. Shrp 8C 34
Preston-le-Skerne. Dur 3M 47
Preston Marsh. Here 7D 26
Prestonmill. Dum 6D 52
Preston on Stour.
Warw 7L 27
Preston on the Hill. Hal 1D 34
Preston on Wye. Here 7B 26
Prestonpans. E Lot 2A 60
Preston Plucknett. Som 4D 8
Preston-under-Scar. N Yor 6J 47
Preston upon the Weald Moors.
Telf 8E 34
Preston Wynne. Here 7D 26
Prestwich. G Man 7G 41
Prestwick. Nmbd 4E 54
Prestwick. S Ayr 7B 58
Prestwold. Leics 7C 36
Prestwood. Buck 3F 20
Prestwood. Staf 5K 35
Price Town. B'end 5J 17
Prickwillow. Cambs 3B 30
Priddy. Som 8D 18
Priestcliffe. Derbs 2K 35
Priesthill. Glas 3D 58
Priest Hutton. Lanc 8D 46
Priestland. E Ayr 6D 58
Priest Weston. Shrp 2A 26
Priestwood. Brac 6F 20
Priestwood. Kent 7C 22
Primethorpe. Leics 2C 28
Primrose Green. Norf 8G 39
Primrose Hill. Glos 3E 18
Primrose Hill. Lanc 7B 40
Primrose Valley. N Yor 8J 49
Primsidemill. Bord 7F 60
Princes Gate. Pemb 5H 15
Princes Risborough.
Buck 3F 20
Princethorpe. Warw 4B 28
Princetown. Devn 8E 6
Prinsted. W Sus 5E 10
Prion. Den 4K 33
Prior Muir. Fife 6J 67
Prior's Frome. Here 8D 26
Priors Halton. Shrp 4C 26
Priors Hardwick.
Warw 6B 28
Priorslee. Telf 8F 34
Priors Marston. Warw 6B 28
Prior's Norton. Glos 1G 19
Priory, The. W Ber 7M 19
Priory Wood. Here 7A 26
Priston. Bath 7E 18
Pristow Green. Norf 3H 31
Prittlewell. S'end 5E 22
Privett. Hants 3D 10
Prixford. Devn 2E 6
Probus. Corn 7A 4
Prospect. Cumb 7F 52
Prospect Village. Staf 8J 35
Provanmill. Glas 3E 58
Prudhoe. Nmbd 5D 54
Publow. Bath 7E 18
Puckeridge. Herts 1L 21
Puckington. Som 4B 8
Pucklechurch. S Glo 6E 18
Puckrup. Glos 8G 27
Puddinglake. Ches W 3F 34
Puddington. Ches W 2B 34
Puddington. Devn 4H 7
Puddlebrook. Glos 2E 18
Puddledock. Norf 2G 31
Puddletown. Dors 6F 8
Pudleston. Here 6D 26
Pudsey. W Yor 4L 41
Pulborough. W Sus 4H 11
Puleston. Telf 7F 34
Pulford. Ches W 4B 34
Pulham. Dors 5F 8
Pulham Market. Norf 3H 31
Pulham St Mary. Norf 3J 31
Pulley. Shrp 1C 26
Pulloxhill. C Beds 8H 29
Pulpit Hill. Arg 5C 64
Pulverbatch. Shrp 1C 26
Pumpherston. W Lot 3J 59
Pumsaint. Carm 8F 24
Puncheston. Pemb 4G 15
Puncknowle. Dors 7D 8
Punnett's Town. E Sus 3C 12
Purbrook. Hants 5D 10
Purfleet. Thur 6B 22
Puriton. Som 1B 8
Purleigh. Essx 3E 22
Purley. G Lon 7L 21
Purley on Thames. W Ber 6D 20
Purlogue. Shrp 4A 26
Purl's Bridge. Cambs 3A 30
Purse Caundle. Dors 4E 8
Purslow. Shrp 3B 26
Purston Jaglin. W Yor 6B 42
Purtington. Som 5B 8
Purton. Glos
nr. Lydney 3E 18
nr. Sharpness 3E 18
Purton. Wilts 5J 19
Purton Stoke. Wilts 4J 19
Pury End. Nptn 7E 28
Pusey. Oxon 4A 20
Putley. Here 8E 26
Putney. G Lon 6K 21
Putsborough. Devn 1D 6
Puttenham. Herts 2F 20
Puttenham. Surr 1G 11
Puttock End. Essx 7E 30
Puttock's End. Essx 2B 22
Puxey. Dors 4F 8
Puxton. N Som 7C 18
Pwll. Carm 6L 15
Pwll. Powy 2L 25
Pwllcrochan. Pemb 6F 14
Pwll-glas. Den 5L 33
Pwllgloyw. Powy 1K 17
Pwllheli. Gwyn 7C 32
Pwllmeyric. Mon 4D 18
Pwlltrap. Carm 5J 15
Pwll-y-glaw. Neat 5G 17
Pyecombe. W Sus 4K 11
Pye Corner. Herts 2M 21
Pye Corner. Newp 5B 18
Pye Green. Staf 8H 35
Pyewipe. NE Lin 6K 43
Pyle. B'end 6H 17
Pyle. IOW 8B 10
Pyle Hill. Surr 8G 21
Pylle. Som 2E 8
Pymoor. Cambs 3A 30
Pymore. Dors 6C 8
Pyrford. Surr 8H 21
Pyrford Village. Surr 8H 21
Pyrton. Oxon 4D 20
Pytchley. Nptn 4F 28
Pyworthy. Devn 5C 6

Q

Quabbs. Shrp 4M 25
Quadring. Linc 6K 37
Quadring Eaudike. Linc 6K 37
Quainton. Buck 1E 20
Quaking Houses. Dur 6E 54
Quarley. Hants 1L 9
Quarndon. Derbs 5M 35
Quarrendon. Buck 2F 20
Quarrier's Village. Inv 3B 58
Quarrington. Linc 5H 37
Quarrington Hill. Dur 8G 55
Quarry, The. Glos 4F 18
Quarry Bank. W Mid 3H 27
Quarrywood. Mor 7A 80
Quartalehouse. Abers 1J 73
Quarter. N Ayr 3L 57
Quarter. S Lan 4F 58
Quatford. Shrp 2F 26
Quatt. Shrp 3F 26
Quebec. Dur 7E 54
Quedgeley. Glos 2G 19
Queen Adelaide. Cambs 3B 30
Queenborough. Kent 6F 22
Queen Camel. Som 3D 8
Queen Charlton. Bath 7E 18
Queen Dart. Devn 4H 7
Queenhill. Worc 8G 27
Queen Oak. Dors 2F 8
Queensbury. W Yor 4K 41
Queensferry Crossing. Edin 1K 59
Queensferry. Flin 3B 34
Queenstown. Bkpl 4B 40
Queen Street. Kent 1C 12
Queenzieburn. N Lan 2E 58
Quemerford. Wilts 7J 19
Quendale. Shet 6D 90
Quendon. Essx 8B 30
Queniborough. Leics 8D 36
Quenington. Glos 3K 19
Quernmore. Lanc 1D 40
Quethiock. Corn 5F 4
Quholm. Orkn 8B 88
Quick's Green. W Ber 6C 20
Quidenham. Norf 3G 31
Quidhampton. Hants 8C 20
Quidhampton. Wilts 2K 9
Quilquox. Abers 2J 73
Quina Brook. Shrp 6D 34
Quindry. Orkn 2F 86
Quine's Hill. IOM 7C 44
Quinton. Nptn 6E 28
Quinton. W Mid 3H 27
Quintrell Downs. Corn 2M 3
Quixhill. Staf 5K 35
Quoditch. Devn 6D 6
Quorn. Leics 8C 36
Quorndon. Leics 8C 36
Quothquan. S Lan 6H 59
Quoyloo. Orkn 7B 88
Quoyness. Orkn 1D 86
Quoys. Shet
on Mainland 1E 90
on Unst 2L 91

R

Rableyheath. Herts 2K 21
Raby. Cumb 6F 52
Raby. Mers 2B 34
Rachan Mill. Bord 6K 59
Rachub. Gwyn 4F 32
Rack End. Oxon 3B 20
Rackenford. Devn 4H 7
Rackham. W Sus 4H 11
Rackheath. Norf 8J 39
Racks. Dum 4E 52
Rackwick. Orkn
on Hoy 2D 86
on Westray 5D 88
Radbourne. Derbs 6L 35
Radcliffe. G Man 7F 40
Radcliffe. Nmbd 1F 54
Radcliffe on Trent. Notts 6D 36
Radclive. Buck 8D 28
Radernie. Fife 7H 67
Radfall. Kent 7H 23
Radford. Bath 8E 18
Radford. Nott 5C 36
Radford. Oxon 1B 20
Radford. W Mid 3M 27
Radford. Worc 6J 27
Radford Semele. Warw 5M 27
Radipole. Dors 7E 8
Radlett. Herts 4J 21
Radley. Oxon 4C 20
Radnage. Buck 4E 20
Radstock. Bath 8E 18
Radstone. Nptn 7C 28
Radway. Warw 7A 28
Radway Green. Ches E 4F 34
Radwell. Bed 6H 29
Radwell. Herts 8K 29
Radwinter. Essx 8C 30
Radyr. Card 6L 17
RAF Coltishall. Norf 7J 39
Rafford. Mor 8L 79
Raffrey. New M 6J 93
Ragdale. Leics 8D 36
Ragdon. Shrp 2C 26
Ragged Appleshaw. Hants 1M 9
Raggra. High 7E 86
Raglan. Mon 3C 18
Ragnall. Notts 2F 36
Raholp. New M 6J 93
Raigbeg. High 3J 71
Rainford. Mers 7C 40
Rainford Junction. Mers 7C 40
Rainham. G Lon 5B 22
Rainham. Medw 7E 22
Rainhill. Mers 8C 40
Rainow. Ches E 2H 35
Rainton. N Yor 8A 48
Rainworth. Notts 4C 36
Raisbeck. Cumb 5E 46
Raise. Cumb 7M 53
Rait. Per 5F 66
Raithby. Linc 1L 37
Raithby by Spilsby. Linc 3L 37
Raithwaite. N Yor 4F 48
Rake. W Sus 3F 10
Rake End. Staf 8J 35
Rakeway. Staf 5J 35
Rakewood. G Man 6H 41
Ralia. High 6H 71
Ram Alley. Wilts 7L 19
Ramasaig. High 1C 68
Rame. Corn
nr. Millbrook 7G 5
nr. Penryn 5L 3
Ram Lane. Kent 1F 12
Ramnageo. Shet 3L 91
Rampisham. Dors 5D 8
Rampside. Cumb 8M 45
Rampton. Cambs 5M 29
Rampton. Notts 2E 36
Ramsbottom. G Man 6F 40
Ramsburn. Mor 8E 80
Ramsbury. Wilts 6L 19
Ramscraigs. High 1M 79
Ramsdean. Hants 3E 10
Ramsdell. Hants 8C 20
Ramsden. Oxon 2A 20
Ramsden. Worc 7H 27
Ramsden Bellhouse. Essx 4D 22
Ramsden Heath. Essx 4D 22
Ramsey. Cambs 3K 29
Ramsey. Essx 8J 31
Ramsey. IOM 5D 44
Ramsey Forty Foot. Cambs 3L 29
Ramsey Heights. Cambs 3K 29
Ramsey Island. Essx 3F 22
Ramsey Mereside. Cambs 3K 29
Ramsey St Mary's. Cambs 3K 29
Ramsgate. Kent 7K 23
Ramsgill. N Yor 8K 47
Ramshaw. Dur 7C 54
Ramshorn. Staf 5J 35
Ramsley. Devn 6F 6
Ramsnest Common. Surr 2G 11
Ramstone. Abers 4F 72
Ranais. W Isl 1F 76
Ranby. Linc 2K 37
Ranby. Notts 1D 36
Rand. Linc 2J 37
Randalstown. Ant 4G 93
Randwick. Glos 3G 19
Ranfurly. Ren 3B 58
Rangag. High 7C 86
Rangemore. Staf 7K 35
Rangeworthy. S Glo 5E 18
Rankinston. E Ayr 8C 58
Rank's Green. Essx 2D 22
Ranmore Common. Surr 8J 21
Rannoch Station. Per 2J 65
Ranochan. High 7K 69
Ranskill. Notts 1D 36
Ranton. Staf 7G 35
Ranton Green. Staf 7G 35
Ranworth. Norf 8K 39
Raploch. Stir 8A 66
Rapness. Orkn 5E 88
Rapps. Som 4B 8
Rascal Moor. E Yor 4F 42
Rascarrel. Dum 7B 52
Rasharkin. Caus 3F 93
Rashfield. Arg 1L 57
Rashwood. Worc 5H 27
Raskelf. N Yor 8B 48
Rassau. Blae 3L 17
Rastrick. W Yor 5K 41
Ratagan. High 4L 69
Ratby. Leics 1C 28
Ratcliffe Culey. Leics 2M 27
Ratcliffe on Soar. Notts 7B 36
Ratcliffe on the Wreake.
Leics 8D 36
Rathen. Abers 7K 81
Rathfriland. Arm 7G 93
Rathillet. Fife 5G 67
Rathmell. N Yor 1G 41
Ratho. Edin 2K 59
Ratho Station. Edin 2K 59
Rathven. Mor 7D 80
Ratley. Hants 3M 9
Ratley. Warw 7A 28
Ratlinghope. Shrp 2C 26
Rattar. High 4D 86
Ratten Row. Cumb 7H 53
Ratten Row. Lanc 3C 40
Rattery. Devn 5K 5
Rattlesden. Suff 6F 30
Ratton Village. E Sus 5B 12
Rattray. Abers 8K 81
Rattray. Per 3E 66
Raughton. Cumb 7H 53
Raughton Head. Cumb 7H 53
Raunds. Nptn 4G 29
Ravenfield. S Yor 8B 42
Ravenfield Common. S Yor 8B 42
Ravenglass. Cumb 5K 45
Ravenhills Green. Worc 6F 26
Raveningham. Norf 2K 31
Ravenscar. N Yor 5G 49
Ravensdale. IOM 5C 44
Ravensden. Bed 6H 29
Ravenseat. N Yor 5G 47
Ravenshead. Notts 4C 36
Ravensmoor. Ches E 4E 34
Ravensthorpe. Nptn 4D 28
Ravensthorpe. W Yor 5L 41
Ravenstone. Leics 8B 36
Ravenstone. Mil 6F 28
Ravenstonedale. Cumb 5F 46
Ravenstown. Cumb 8B 46
Ravenstruther. S Lan 5H 59
Ravensworth. N Yor 5K 47
Ravernet. Lis 5H 93
Raw. N Yor 5G 49
Rawcliffe. E Yor 5D 42
Rawcliffe. York 2C 42
Rawcliffe Bridge. E Yor 5D 42
Rawdon. W Yor 4L 41
Rawgreen. Nmbd 6C 54
Rawmarsh. S Yor 8B 42
Rawnsley. Staf 8J 35
Rawreth. Essx 4D 22
Rawridge. Devn 5M 7
Rawson Green. Derbs 5A 36
Rawtenstall. Lanc 5G 41
Raydon. Suff 8G 31
Raylees. Nmbd 2C 54
Rayleigh. Essx 4E 22
Raymond's Hill. Devn 6B 8
Rayne. Essx 1D 22
Rayners Lane. G Lon 5J 21
Reach. Cambs 5B 30
Read. Lanc 4F 40
Reading. Read 6E 20
Reading Green. Suff 4H 31
Reading Street. Kent 2F 12
Readymoney. Corn 6D 4
Reagill. Cumb 4E 46
Rearquhar. High 4H 79
Rearsby. Leics 8D 36
Reasby. Linc 2H 37
Reaseheath. Ches E 4E 34
Reaster. High 5D 86
Reawick. Shet 3D 90
Reay. High 5A 86
Rechullin. High 8K 77
Reculver. Kent 7J 23
Redberth. Pemb 6G 15
Redbourn. Herts 2J 21
Redbourne. N Lin 7G 43
Redbrook. Glos 3D 18
Redbrook. Wrex 5D 34
Redburn. High 1K 71
Redburn. Nmbd 5A 54
Redcar. Red C 3D 48
Redcastle. High 1F 70
Redcliffe Bay. N Som 6C 18
Red Dial. Cumb 7G 53
Redding. Falk 2H 59
Reddingmuirhead. Falk 2H 59
Reddings, The. Glos 1H 19
Reddish. G Man 8G 41
Redditch. Worc 5J 27
Rede. Suff 6E 30
Redenhall. Norf 3J 31
Redesdale Camp. Nmbd 2B 54
Redesmouth. Nmbd 3B 54
Redford. Ang 3J 67
Redford. Dur 8D 54
Redford. W Sus 3F 10
Redfordgreen. Bord 8A 60
Redgate. Corn 5E 4
Redgrave. Suff 4G 31
Redhill. Abers 5G 73
Redhill. Herts 8K 29
Redhill. N Som 7D 18
Redhill. Shrp 8F 34
Redhill. Surr 8K 21
Red Hill. Warw 6K 27
Red Hill. W Yor 5B 42
Redhouses. Arg 3C 56
Redisham. Suff 3L 31
Redland. Bris 6D 18
Redland. Orkn 7C 88
Redlingfield. Suff 4H 31
Red Lodge. Suff 4C 30
Redlynch. Som 2F 8
Redlynch. Wilts 3L 9
Redmain. Cumb 8F 52
Redmarley. Worc 5F 26
Redmarley D'Abitot. Glos 8F 26
Redmarshall. Stoc T 3A 48
Redmile. Leics 6E 36
Redmire. N Yor 6J 47
Rednal. Shrp 7B 34
Redpath. Bord 6C 60
Redpoint. High 7J 77
Red Post. Corn 5B 6
Red Rock. G Man 7D 40
Red Roses. Carm 5J 15
Red Row. Nmbd 2F 54
Redruth. Corn 4L 3
Red Street. Staf 4G 35
Redvales. G Man 7G 41
Red Wharf Bay. IOA 2E 32
Redwick. Newp 5C 18
Redwick. S Glo 5D 18
Redworth. Darl 3L 47
Reed. Herts 8L 29
Reed End. Herts 8L 29
Reedham. Linc 4K 37
Reedham. Norf 1L 31
Reedness. E Yor 5F 42
Reeds Beck. Linc 3K 37
Reemshill. Abers 1G 73
Reepham. Linc 2H 37
Reepham. Norf 7G 39
Reeth. N Yor 6J 47
Regaby. IOM 5D 44
Regil. N Som 7D 18
Regoul. High 8J 79
Reiff. High 2L 77
Reigate. Surr 8K 21
Reighton. N Yor 8J 49
Reilth. Shrp 3A 26
Reinigeadal. W Isl 3D 76
Reisque. Abers 4H 73
Reiss. High 6E 86
Rejerrah. Corn 3L 3
Releath. Corn 5K 3
Relubbus. Corn 5J 3
Relugas. Mor 1K 71
Remenham. Wok 5E 20
Remenham Hill. Wok 5E 20
Rempstone. Notts 7C 36
Rendcomb. Glos 3J 19
Rendham. Suff 5K 31
Rendlesham. Suff 6K 31
Renfrew. Ren 3D 58
Renhold. Bed 6H 29
Renishaw. Derbs 2B 36
Rennington. Nmbd 8K 61
Renton. W Dun 2B 58
Renwick. Cumb 7K 53
Repps. Norf 8L 39
Repton. Derbs 7M 35
Rescassa. Corn 7B 4
Rescobie. Ang 2J 67
Rescorla. Corn
nr. Penwithick 6C 4
nr. Sticker 7B 4
Resipole. High 1B 64
Resolfen. Neat 4H 17
Resolis. High 7G 79
Resolven. Neat 4H 17
Rest and be thankful. Arg 7G 65
Reston. Bord 3F 60
Restrop. Wilts 5J 19
Retford. Notts 1E 36
Retire. Corn 5C 4
Rettendon. Essx 4D 22
Revesby. Linc 3K 37
Rew. Devn 8K 5
Rewe. Devn 6J 7
Rew Street. IOW 6B 10
Rexon. Devn 7D 6
Reybridge. Wilts 7H 19
Reydon. Suff 4M 31
Reymerston. Norf 1G 31
Reynalton. Pemb 6G 15
Reynoldston. Swan 8L 15
Rezare. Corn 8C 6
Rhadyr. Mon 3B 18
Rhaeadr Gwy. Powy 6J 25
Rhandirmwyn. Carm 8G 25
Rhayader. Powy 6J 25
Rheindown. High 1F 70
Rhemore. High 2L 63
Rhenetra. High 8F 76
Rhewl. Den
nr. Llangollen 6L 33
nr. Ruthin 4L 33
Rhewl. Shrp 6B 34
Rhewl-Mostyn. Flin 2L 33
Rhian. High 2F 78
Rhian Breck. High 3F 78
Rhicarn. High 1A 78
Rhiconich. High 6E 84
Rhicullen. High 6G 79
Rhidorroch. High 4B 78
Rhifail. High 7K 85
Rhigos. Rhon 4J 17
Rhilochan. High 3H 79
Rhiroy. High 5B 78
Rhitongue. High 6J 85
Rhiw. Gwyn 8B 32
Rhiwabon. Wrex 5B 34
Rhiwbina. Card 6L 17
Rhiwbryfdir. Gwyn 6F 32
Rhiwderin. Newp 5A 18
Rhiwlas. Gwyn
nr. Bala 7J 33
nr. Bangor 4E 32
Rhiwlas. Powy 7L 33
Rhodes. G Man 7G 41
Rhodesia. Notts 1C 36
Rhodes Minnis. Kent 1H 13
Rhodiad-y-Brenin. Pemb 4D 14
Rhondda. Rhon 5J 17
Rhonehouse. Dum 6B 52
Rhoose. V Glam 8K 17
Rhos. Carm 3K 15
Rhos. Neat 4G 17
Rhos, The. Pemb 5G 15
Rhosaman. Carm 3G 17
Rhoscefnhir. IOA 3E 32
Rhoscolyn. IOA 3B 32
Rhos Common. Powy 8A 34
Rhoscrowther. Pemb 6F 14
Rhos-ddu. Gwyn 7B 32
Rhosdylluan. Gwyn 8H 33
Rhosesmor. Flin 4M 33
Rhos-fawr. Gwyn 7C 32
Rhosgadfan. Gwyn 5E 32
Rhosgoch. IOA 2D 32
Rhosgoch. Powy 8L 25
Rhos Haminiog. Cdgn 6E 24
Rhos-hill. Pemb 2H 15
Rhoshirwaun. Gwyn 8A 32
Rhoslan. Gwyn 6D 32
Rhoslefain. Gwyn 2E 24
Rhosllanerchrugog. Wrex 5A 34
Rhôs Lligwy. IOA 2D 32
Rhosmaen. Carm 2F 16
Rhosmeirch. IOA 3D 32
Rhosneigr. IOA 3C 32
Rhôs-on-Sea. Cnwy 2H 33
Rhossili. Swan 8L 15
Rhosson. Pemb 4D 14
Rhostrenwfa. IOA 3D 32
Rhostryfan. Gwyn 5D 32
Rhostyllen. Wrex 5B 34
Rhoswiel. Shrp 6A 34
Rhosybol. IOA 2D 32
Rhos-y-brithdir. Powy 8L 33
Rhos-y-garth. Cdgn 5F 24
Rhos-y-gwaliau. Gwyn 7J 33
Rhos-y-llan. Gwyn 7B 32
Rhos-y-meirch. Powy 5A 26
Rhu. Arg 1A 58
Rhuallt. Den 3K 33
Rhubha Stoer. High 8C 84
Rhubodach. Arg 2K 57
Rhuddall Heath. Ches W 3D 34
Rhuddlan. Cdgn 2L 15
Rhuddlan. Den 3K 33
Rhue. High 4A 78
Rhulen. Powy 8L 25
Rhunahaorine. Arg 5G 57
Rhuthun. Den 5L 33
Rhuvoult. High 6E 84
Y Rhws. V Glam 8K 17
Rhyd. Gwyn 6F 32
Rhydaman. Carm 3F 16
Rhydargaeau. Carm 4L 15
Rhydcymerau. Carm 1E 16
Rhydd. Worc 7G 27
Rhyd-Ddu. Gwyn 5E 32
Rhydding. Neat 5G 17
Rhydfudr. Cdgn 6E 24
Rhydlanfair. Cnwy 5H 33
Rhydlewis. Cdgn 2K 15
Rhydlios. Gwyn 7A 32
Rhydlydan. Cnwy 5H 33
Rhyd-meirionydd. Cdgn 4F 24
Rhydowen. Cdgn 2L 15
Rhyd-Rosser. Cdgn 6E 24
Rhydspence. Here 8M 25
Rhydtalog. Flin 5M 33
Rhyd-uchaf. Gwyn 7J 33
Rhydwyn. IOA 2C 32
Rhyd-y-clafdy. Gwyn 7C 32
Rhydycroesau. Powy 7M 33
Rhydyfelin. Cdgn 5E 24
Rhydyfelin. Rhon 6K 17
Rhyd-y-foel. Cnwy 3J 33
Rhyd-y-fro. Neat 4G 17
Rhydymain. Gwyn 8H 33
Rhyd-y-meudwy. Den 5L 33
Rhydymwyn. Flin 4M 33
Rhyd-yr-onen. Gwyn 2F 24
Rhyd-y-sarn. Gwyn 6F 32
Rhyl. Den 2K 33
Rhymney. Cphy 4L 17
Rhymni. Cphy 4L 17
Rhynd. Per 5E 66
Rhynie. Abers 3D 72
Ribbesford. Worc 4F 26
Ribbleton. Lanc 4D 40
Ribby. Lanc 4C 40
Ribchester. Lanc 4E 40
Riber. Derbs 4M 35
Ribigill. High 6H 85
Riby. Linc 7J 43
Riccall. N Yor 4D 42
Riccarton. E Ayr 6C 58
Richards Castle. Here 5C 26
Richborough Port. Kent 7K 23
Richhill. Arm 6F 93
Richings Park. Buck 6H 21
Richmond. G Lon 6J 21
Richmond. N Yor 5K 47
Rickarton. Abers 7H 73
Rickerby. Cumb 6J 53
Rickerscote. Staf 7H 35
Rickford. N Som 8C 18
Rickham. Devn 8K 5
Rickinghall. Suff 4G 31
Rickleton. Tyne 6F 54
Rickling. Essx 8A 30
Rickling Green. Essx 1B 22
Rickmansworth. Herts 4H 21
Riddings. Derbs 4B 36
Riddlecombe. Devn 4F 6
Riddlesden. W Yor 3J 41
Ridge. Dors 7H 9
Ridge. Herts 3K 21
Ridge. Wilts 2H 9
Ridgebourne. Powy 6K 25
Ridge Lane. Warw 2L 27
Ridgeway. Derbs
nr. Alfreton 4A 36
nr. Sheffield 1B 36
Ridgeway. Staf 4G 35
Ridgeway Cross. Here 7F 26
Ridgeway Moor. Derbs 1B 36
Ridgewell. Essx 7D 30
Ridgewood. E Sus 3A 12
Ridgmont. C Beds 8G 29
Ridgwardine. Shrp 6E 34
Riding Mill. Nmbd 5D 54
Ridley. Kent 7C 22
Ridley. Nmbd 5A 54
Ridlington. Norf 6K 39
Ridlington. Rut 1F 28
Ridsdale. Nmbd 3C 54

Shawwood—Stickford

Shawwood. E Ayr 7D 58
Shearington. Dum 5E 52
Shearsby. Leics 2D 28
Shearston. Som 2A 8
Shebbear. Devn 5D 6
Shebdon. Staf 7F 34
Shebster. High 5B 86
Sheddocksley. Aber 5H 73
Shedfield. Hants 4C 10
Shedog. N Ayr 6J 57
Sheen. Staf 3K 35
Sheepbridge. Derbs 2A 36
Sheep Hill. Dur 6E 54
Sheepscar. W Yor 4M 41
Sheepscombe. Glos 2G 19
Sheepstor. Devn 5H 5
Sheepwash. Devn 5D 6
Sheepwash. Nmbd 3F 54
Sheepway. N Som 6C 18
Sheepy Magna. Leics 1M 27
Sheepy Parva. Leics 1M 27
Sheering. Essx 2B 22
Sheerness. Kent 6F 22
Sheerwater. Surr 7H 21
Sheet. Hants 3E 10
Sheffield. S Yor 1A 36
Sheffield Bottom. W Ber 7D 20
Sheffield Green. E Sus 3M 11
Shefford. C Beds 8J 29
Shefford Woodlands.
W Ber 6A 20
Sheigra. High 5D 84
Sheinton. Shrp 1E 26
Shelderton. Shrp 4C 26
Sheldon. Derbs 3K 35
Sheldon. Devn 5L 7
Sheldon. W Mid 3K 27
Sheldwich. Kent 8G 23
Sheldwich Lees. Kent 8G 23
Shelf. W Yor 5K 41
Shelfanger. Norf 3H 31
Shelfield. Warw 5K 27
Shelfield. W Mid 1J 27
Shelford. Notts 5D 36
Shelford. Warw 3B 28
Shell. Worc 6H 27
Shelley. Suff 8G 31
Shelley. W Yor 6L 41
Shell Green. Hal 1D 34
Shellingford. Oxon 4M 19
Shellow Bowells. Essx 3C 22
Shelsley Beauchamp. Worc 5F 26
Shelsley Walsh. Worc 5F 26
Shelthorpe. Leics 8C 36
Shelton. Bed 5H 29
Shelton. Norf 2J 31
Shelton. Notts 5E 36
Shelton. Shrp 8C 34
Shelton Green. Norf 2J 31
Shelton Lock. Derb 6A 36
Shelve. Shrp 2B 26
Shelwick. Here 7D 26
Shelwick Green. Here 7D 26
Shenfield. Essx 4C 22
Shenington. Oxon 7A 28
Shenley. Herts 3J 21
Shenley Brook End. Mil 8F 28
Shenleybury. Herts 3J 21
Shenley Church End. Mil 8F 28
Shenmore. Here 8B 26
Shennanton. Dum 5J 51
Shenstone. Staf 1K 27
Shenstone. Worc 4G 27
Shenstone Woodend. Staf 1K 27
Shenton. Leics 1A 28
Shenval. Mor 3B 72
Shepeau Stow. Linc 8L 37
Shephall. Herts 1K 21
Shepherd's Bush. G Lon 5K 21
Shepherd's Gate. Norf 8B 38
Shepherd's Green. Oxon 5E 20
Shepherd's Port. Norf 6C 38
Shepherdswell. Kent 1J 13
Shepley. W Yor 7K 41
Sheppardstown. High 7C 86
Shepperdine. S Glo 4E 18
Shepperton. Surr 7H 21
Shepreth. Cambs 7L 29
Shepshed. Leics 8B 36
Shepton Beauchamp. Som 4C 8
Shepton Mallet. Som 1E 8
Shepton Montague. Som 2E 8
Shepway. Kent 8D 22
Sheraton. Dur 8H 55
Sherborne. Dors 4E 8
Sherborne. Glos 2K 19
Sherborne. Som 8D 18
Sherborne Causeway. Dors 3G 9
Sherborne St John. Hants 8D 20
Sherbourne. Warw 5L 27
Sherburn. Dur 7G 55
Sherburn. N Yor 8G 49
Sherburn Hill. Dur 7G 55
Sherburn in Elmet. N Yor 4B 42
Shere. Surr 1H 11
Shereford. Norf 7E 38
Sherfield English. Hants 3L 9
Sherfield on Loddon. Hants 8D 20
Sherford. Devn 7K 5
Sherford. Dors 6H 9
Sheriffhales. Shrp 8F 34
Sheriff Hutton. N Yor 1D 42
Sheriffston. Mor 7B 80
Sheringham. Norf 5H 39
Sherington. Mil 7F 28
Shermanbury. W Sus 4K 11
Shernal Green. Worc 5H 27
Shernborne. Norf 6D 38
Sherrington. Wilts 2H 9
Sherston. Wilts 5G 19
Sherwood. Nott 5C 36
Sherwood Green. Devn 3E 6
Shettleston. Glas 3E 58
Shevington. G Man 7D 40
Shevington Moor. G Man 6D 40
Shevington Vale. G Man 7D 40
Sheviock. Corn 6F 4
Shide. IOW 7B 10
Shiel Bridge. High 4L 69
Shieldaig. High
nr. Charlestown 6K 77
nr. Torridon 8K 77
Shieldhill. Dum 3E 52
Shieldhill. Falk 2G 59
Shieldhill. S Lan 5J 59
Shieldmuir. N Lan 4F 58
Shielfoot. High 8H 69
Shielhill. Abers 8K 81
Shielhill. Ang 2H 67
Shifnal. Shrp 1F 26
Shilbottle. Nmbd 1E 54
Shilbottle Grange. Nmbd 1F 54
Shildon. Dur 3L 47
Shillford. E Ren 4C 58
Shillingford. Devn 3J 7
Shillingford. Oxon 4C 20
Shillingford St George. Devn 7J 7
Shillingstone. Dors 4G 9
Shillington. C Beds 8J 29
Shillmoor. Nmbd 1B 54
Shilton. Oxon 3L 19
Shilton. Warw 3B 28
Shilvinghampton. Dors 7E 8
Shilvington. Nmbd 3E 54
Shimpling. Norf 3H 31
Shimpling. Suff 6E 30
Shimpling Street. Suff 6E 30
Shincliffe. Dur 7F 54
Shiney Row. Tyne 6G 55
Shinfield. Wok 7E 20
Shingay. Cambs 7L 29
Shingham. Norf 1D 30
Shingle Street. Suff 7K 31
Shinner's Bridge. Devn 5K 5
Shinness. High 2F 78
Shipbourne. Kent 8B 22
Shipdham. Norf 1F 30
Shipham. Som 8C 18
Shiphay. Torb 5L 5
Shiplake. Oxon 6E 20
Shipley. Derbs 5B 36
Shipley. Nmbd 8J 61
Shipley. Shrp 2G 27
Shipley. W Sus 3J 11
Shipley. W Yor 4K 41
Shipley Bridge. Surr 1L 11
Shipmeadow. Suff 3K 31
Shippon. Oxon 4B 20
Shipston-on-Stour. Warw 7L 27
Shipton. Buck 1E 20
Shipton. Glos 2J 19
Shipton. N Yor 2C 42
Shipton. Shrp 2D 26
Shipton Bellinger. Hants 1L 9
Shipton Gorge. Dors 6C 8
Shipton Green. W Sus 6F 10
Shipton Moyne. Glos 5G 19
Shipton-on-Cherwell. Oxon 2B 20
Shiptonthorpe. E Yor 3F 42
Shipton-under-Wychwood.
Oxon 2L 19
Shirburn. Oxon 4D 20
Shirdley Hill. Lanc 6B 40
Shire. Cumb 8L 53
Shirebrook. Derbs 3C 36
Shiregreen. S Yor 8A 42
Shirehampton. Bris 6D 18
Shiremoor. Tyne 4G 55
Shirenewton. Mon 4C 18
Shireoaks. Notts 1C 36
Shires Mill. Fife 1J 59
Shirkoak. Kent 2F 12
Shirland. Derbs 4A 36
Shirley. Derbs 5L 35
Shirley. Sotn 4A 10
Shirley. W Mid 4K 27
Shirleywich. Staf 7H 35
Shirl Heath. Here 6C 26
Shirrell Heath. Hants 4C 10
Shirwell. Devn 2E 6
Shiskine. N Ayr 7J 57
Shobdon. Here 5B 26
Shobnall. Staf 7L 35
Shobrooke. Devn 5H 7
Shoby. Leics 7D 36
Shocklach. Ches W 5C 34
Shoeburyness. S'end 5F 22
Sholden. Kent 8K 23
Sholing. Sotn 4B 10
Sholver. G Man 7H 41
Shoot Hill. Shrp 8C 34
Shop. Corn
nr. Bude 4B 6
nr. Padstow 4A 4
Shop. Devn 4C 6
Shopford. Cumb 4K 53
Shoreditch. G Lon 5L 21
Shoreditch. Som 3M 7
Shoregill. Cumb 5F 46
Shoreham. Kent 7B 22
Shoreham-by-Sea. W Sus 5K 11
Shoresdean. Nmbd 5G 61
Shoreswood. Nmbd 5G 61
Shorncote. Glos 4J 19
Shorne. Kent 6C 22
Shorne Ridgeway. Kent 6C 22
Shortacombe. Devn 7E 6
Shortbridge. E Sus 3A 12
Shortgate. E Sus 4A 12
Short Green. Norf 3G 31
Shorthampton. Oxon 1M 19
Short Heath. Derbs 8M 35
Short Heath. W Mid
nr. Erdington 2J 27
nr. Wednesfield 1H 27
Shortlanesend. Corn 4M 3
Shorton. Torb 5L 5
Shortstown. Bed 7H 29
Shortwood. S Glo 6E 18
Shorwell. IOW 7B 10
Shoscombe. Bath 8F 18
Shotesham. Norf 2J 31
Shotgate. Essx 4D 22
Shotley. Suff 8J 31
Shotley Bridge. Dur 6D 54
Shotleyfield. Nmbd 6D 54
Shotley Gate. Suff 8J 31
Shottenden. Kent 8G 23
Shottermill. Surr 2F 10
Shottery. Warw 6K 27
Shotteswell. Warw 7B 28
Shottisham. Suff 7K 31
Shottle. Derbs 5M 35
Shotton. Dur
nr. Peterlee 8H 55
nr. Sedgefield 3A 48
Shotton. Flin 3B 34
Shotton. Nmbd
nr. Morpeth 4F 54
nr. Town Yetholm 6F 60
Shotton Colliery. Dur 7G 55
Shotts. N Lan 3G 59
Shotwick. Ches W 2B 34
Shouldham. Norf 1C 30
Shouldham Thorpe. Norf 1C 30
Shoulton. Worc 6G 27
Shrawardine. Shrp 8C 34
Shrawley. Worc 5G 27
Shreding Green. Buck 5H 21
Shrewley. Warw 5L 27
Shrewsbury. Shrp 8C 34
Shrewton. Wilts 1J 9
Shrigley. New M 6J 93
Shripney. W Sus 5G 11
Shrivenham. Oxon 5L 19
Shropham. Norf 2F 30
Shroton. Dors 4G 9
Shrub End. Essx 1F 22
Shucknall. Here 7D 26
Shudy Camps. Cambs 7C 30
Shulishadermor. High 1F 68
Shulista. High 6F 76
Shurdington. Glos 2H 19
Shurlock Row. Wind 6F 20
Shurrery. High 6B 86
Shurton. Som 1M 7
Shustoke. Warw 2L 27
Shute. Devn
nr. Axminster 6A 8
nr. Crediton 5H 7
Shutford. Oxon 7A 28
Shut Heath. Staf 7G 35
Shuthonger. Glos 8G 27
Shutlanehead. Staf 5G 35
Shutlanger. Nptn 7E 28
Shutt Green. Staf 1G 27
Shuttington. Warw 1L 27
Shuttlewood. Derbs 2B 36
Shuttleworth. G Man 6G 41
Siabost. W Isl 7F 82
Siabost bho Dheas. W Isl 7F 82
Siabost bho Thuath. W Isl 7F 82
Siadar. W Isl 6G 83
Siadar Uarach. W Isl 6G 83
Sibbaldbie. Dum 3F 52
Sibbertoft. Nptn 3D 28
Sibdon Carwood. Shrp 3C 26
Sibertswold. Kent 1J 13
Sibford Ferris. Oxon 8A 28
Sibford Gower. Oxon 8A 28
Sible Hedingham. Essx 8D 30
Sibsey. Linc 4L 37
Sibsey Fen Side. Linc 4L 37
Sibson. Cambs 2H 29
Sibson. Leics 1A 28
Sibster. High 6E 86
Sibthorpe. Notts 5E 36
Sibton. Suff 5K 31
Sicklesmere. Suff 5E 30
Sicklinghall. N Yor 3A 42
Sid. Devn 7L 7
Sidbury. Devn 6L 7
Sidbury. Shrp 3E 26
Sidcot. N Som 8C 18
Sidcup. G Lon 6A 22
Siddick. Cumb 8E 52
Siddington. Ches E 2G 35
Siddington. Glos 4J 19
Side of the Moor. G Man 6F 40
Sidestrand. Norf 6J 39
Sidford. Devn 6L 7
Sidlesham. W Sus 6F 10
Sidley. E Sus 5D 12
Sidlow. Surr 1K 11
Sidmouth. Devn 7L 7
Sigford. Devn 8G 7
Sigglesthorne. E Yor 3J 43
Sighthill. Edin 2K 59
Sigingstone. V Glam 7J 17
Signet. Oxon 2L 19
Silchester. Hants 7D 20
Sildinis. W Isl 2D 76
Sileby. Leics 8D 36
Silecroft. Cumb 6L 45
Silfield. Norf 2H 31
Silian. Cdgn 7E 24
Silkstone. S Yor 7L 41
Silkstone Common. S Yor 7L 41
Silksworth. Tyne 6G 55
Silk Willoughby. Linc 5H 37
Silloth. Cumb 6F 52
Sills. Nmbd 1B 54
Sillyearn. Mor 8E 80
Silpho. N Yor 6G 49
Silsden. W Yor 3J 41
Silsoe. C Beds 8H 29
Silverbank. Abers 6G 73
Silverbridge. New M 7F 93
Silverburn. Midl 3L 59
Silverdale. Lanc 8C 46
Silverdale. Staf 5G 35
Silverdale Green. Lanc 8C 46
Silver End. Essx 2E 22
Silver End. W Mid 3H 27
Silvergate. Norf 7H 39
Silver Green. Norf 2J 31
Silverhillocks. Abers 7G 81
Silverley's Green. Suff 4J 31
Silverstone. Nptn 7D 28
Silverton. Devn 5J 7
Silverton. W Dun 2C 58
Silvington. Shrp 4E 26
Simm's Cross. Hal 1D 34
Simm's Lane End. Mers 7D 40
Simonburn. Nmbd 4B 54
Simonsbath. Som 2G 7
Simonstone. Lanc 4F 40
Simprim. Bord 5F 60
Simpson. Pemb 5E 14
Simpson Cross. Pemb 5E 14
Sinclairston. E Ayr 8C 58
Sinclairtown. Fife 8F 66
Sinderby. N Yor 7M 47
Sinderhope. Nmbd 6B 54
Sindlesham. Wok 7E 20
Sinfin. Derb 6M 35
Singleborough. Buck 8E 28
Singleton. Kent 1F 12
Singleton. Lanc 4B 40
Singleton. W Sus 4F 10
Singlewell. Kent 6C 22
Sinkhurst Green. Kent 1E 12
Sinnahard. Abers 4D 72
Sinnington. N Yor 7E 48
Sinton Green. Worc 5G 27
Sion Mills. Derr 4C 92
Sipson. G Lon 6H 21
Sirhowy. Blae 3L 17
Sisland. Norf 2K 31
Sissinghurst. Kent 2D 12
Siston. S Glo 6E 18
Sithney. Corn 6K 3
Sittingbourne. Kent 7F 22
Six Ashes. Staf 3F 26
Six Bells. Blae 4M 17
Six Hills. Leics 7D 36
Sixhills. Linc 1J 37
Six Mile Bottom. Cambs 6B 30
Sixmilecross. Ferm 5D 92
Sixpenny Handley. Dors 4H 9
Sizewell. Suff 5L 31
Skail. High 7K 85
Skaill. Orkn 8B 88
Skaills. Orkn 1G 87
Skares. E Ayr 8D 58
Skateraw. E Lot 2E 60
Skaw. Shet 1F 90
Skeabost. High 1F 68
Skeabrae. Orkn 7B 88
Skeeby. N Yor 5K 47
Skeffington. Leics 1E 28
Skeffling. E Yor 6L 43
Skegby. Notts
nr. Mansfield 3B 36
nr. Tuxford 2E 36
Skegness. Linc 3B 38
Skelberry. Shet
nr. Boddam 6D 90
nr. Housetter 5H 91
Skelbo. High 4H 79
Skelbo Street. High 4H 79
Skelbrooke. S Yor 6C 42
Skeldyke. Linc 6L 37
Skelfhill. Bord 1J 53
Skellingthorpe. Linc 2G 37
Skellister. Shet 2E 90
Skellorn Green. Ches E 1H 35
Skellow. S Yor 6C 42
Skelmanthorpe. W Yor 6L 41
Skelmersdale. Lanc 7C 40
Skelmorlie. N Ayr 3L 57
Skelpick. High 6K 85
Skelton. Cumb 8J 53
Skelton. E Yor 5E 42
Skelton. N Yor
nr. Richmond 5J 47
nr. Ripon 1A 42
Skelton. Red C 4D 48
Skelton. York 2C 42
Skelton Green. Red C 4D 48
Skelwick. Orkn 5D 88
Skelwith Bridge. Cumb 5B 46
Skendleby. Linc 3M 37
Skendleby Psalter. Linc 2M 37
Skenfrith. Mon 1C 18
Skerne. E Yor 2H 43
Skeroblingarry. Arg 7G 57
Skerray. High 5J 85
Skerricha. High 6E 84
Skerries Airport. Shet 6L 91
Skerton. Lanc 1C 40
Sketchley. Leics 2B 28
Sketty. Swan 5F 16
Skewen. Neat 5G 17
Skewsby. N Yor 8D 48
Skeyton. Norf 7J 39
Skeyton Corner. Norf 7J 39
Skiall. High 5B 86
Skidbrooke. Linc 8M 43
Skidbrooke North End.
Linc 8M 43
Skidby. E Yor 4H 43
Skilgate. Som 3J 7
Skillington. Linc 7F 36
Skinburness. Cumb 6F 52
Skinflats. Falk 1H 59
Skinidin. High 1D 68
Skinnet. High 5H 85
Skinningrove. Red C 4E 48
Skipness. Arg 4H 57
Skippool. Lanc 3B 40
Skiprigg. Cumb 7H 53
Skipsea. E Yor 2J 43
Skipsea Brough. E Yor 2J 43
Skipton. N Yor 2H 41
Skipton-on-Swale. N Yor 8A 48
Skipwith. N Yor 4D 42
Skirbeck. Linc 5L 37
Skirbeck Quarter. Linc 5L 37
Skirlaugh. E Yor 4J 43
Skirling. Bord 6J 59
Skirmett. Buck 4E 20
Skirpenbeck. E Yor 2E 42
Skirwith. Cumb 8L 53
Skirwith. N Yor 8F 46
Skirza. High 5E 86
Skitby. Cumb 5J 53
Skitham. Lanc 3C 40
Skittle Green. Buck 3E 20
Skroo. Shet 2M 89
Skulamus. High 3H 69
Skullomie. High 5J 85
Skyborry Green. Shrp 4A 26
Skye Green. Essx 1E 22
Skye of Curr. High 3K 71
Slack, The. Dur 3K 47
Slack. W Yor 5H 41
Slackhall. Derbs 1J 35
Slack Head. Cumb 8C 46
Slackhead. Mor 7D 80
Slackholme End. Linc 2B 38
Slacks of Cairnbanno.
Abers 1H 73
Slad. Glos 3G 19
Slade. Swan 8L 15
Slade, The. W Ber 7C 20
Slade End. Oxon 4C 20
Slade Field. Cambs 3L 29
Slade Green. G Lon 6B 22
Slade Heath. Staf 1H 27
Slade Hooton. S Yor 1C 36
Sladesbridge. Corn 4C 4
Slaggyford. Nmbd 6L 53
Slaidburn. Lanc 2F 40
Slaid Hill. W Yor 3M 41
Slaithwaite. W Yor 6J 41
Slaley. Derbs 4L 35
Slaley. Nmbd 6C 54
Slamannan. Falk 2G 59
Slapton. Buck 1G 21
Slapton. Devn 7L 5
Slapton. Nptn 7D 28
Slattocks. G Man 7G 41
Slaugham. W Sus 3K 11
Slaughterbridge. Corn 3D 4
Slaughterford. Wilts 6G 19
Slawston. Leics 2E 28
Sleaford. Hants 2F 10
Sleaford. Linc 5H 37
Sleagill. Cumb 4D 46
Sleap. Shrp 7C 34
Sledmere. E Yor 1G 43
Sleightholme. Dur 4H 47
Sleights. N Yor 5F 48
Slepe. Dors 6H 9
Slickly. High 5D 86
Sliddery. N Ayr 7J 57
Sligachan. High 3F 68
Slimbridge. Glos 3F 18
Slindon. Staf 6G 35
Slindon. W Sus 5G 11
Slinfold. W Sus 2J 11
Slingsby. N Yor 8D 48
Slip End. C Beds 2H 21
Slipton. Nptn 4G 29
Slitting Mill. Staf 8J 35
Slochd. High 3J 71
Slockavullin. Arg 8C 64
Sloley. Norf 7J 39
Sloncombe. Devn 7G 7
Sloothby. Linc 2A 38
Slough. Slo 6G 21
Slough Green. Som 3A 8
Slough Green. W Sus 3K 11
Sluggan. High 3J 71
Slyne. Lanc 1C 40
Smailholm. Bord 6D 60
Smallbridge. G Man 6H 41
Smallbrook. Devn 6H 7
Smallburgh. Norf 7K 39
Smallburn. E Ayr 7E 58
Smalldale. Derbs 2J 35
Small Dole. W Sus 4K 11
Smalley. Derbs 5B 36
Smallfield. Surr 1L 11
Small Heath. W Mid 3J 27
Smallholm. Dum 4F 52
Small Hythe. Kent 2E 12
Smallrice. Staf 6H 35
Smallridge. Devn 5B 8
Smallwood Hey. Lanc 3B 40
Smallworth. Norf 3G 31
Smannell. Hants 1A 10
Smardale. Cumb 5F 46
Smarden. Kent 1E 12
Smarden Bell. Kent 1E 12
Smart's Hill. Kent 1B 12
Smeatharpe. Devn 4M 7
Smeeth. Kent 2G 13
Smeeth, The. Norf 8B 38
Smeeton Westerby. Leics 2D 28
Smeircleit. W Isl 4D 74
Smerral. High 8C 86
Smestow. Staf 2G 27
Smethwick. W Mid 3J 27
Smirisary. High 8H 69
Smisby. Derbs 8M 35
Smitham Hill. Bath 8D 18
Smith End Green. Worc 6F 26
Smithfield. Cumb 5J 53
Smith Green. Lanc 2C 40
Smithies, The. Shrp 2E 26
Smithincott. Devn 4K 7
Smith's Green. Essx 1B 22
Smithstown. High 6J 77
Smithton. High 1H 71
Smithwood Green. Suff 6F 30
Smithy Bridge. G Man 6H 41
Smithy Green. Ches E 2F 34
Smithy Lane Ends. Lanc 6C 40
Smockington. Leics 3B 28
Smoogro. Orkn 1E 86
Smythe's Green. Essx 2F 22
Snaigow House. Per 3D 66
Snailbeach. Shrp 1B 26
Snailwell. Cambs 5C 30
Snainton. N Yor 7G 49
Snaith. E Yor 5D 42
Snape. N Yor 7L 47
Snape. Suff 6K 31
Snape Green. Lanc 6B 40
Snapper. Devn 2E 6
Snarestone. Leics 1M 27
Snarford. Linc 1H 37
Snargate. Kent 3F 12
Snave. Kent 3G 13
Sneachill. Worc 6H 27
Snead. Powy 2B 26
Snead Common. Worc 5F 26
Sneaton. N Yor 5F 48
Sneatonthorpe. N Yor 5G 49
Snelland. Linc 1H 37
Snelston. Derbs 5K 35
Snetterton. Norf 2F 30
Snettisham. Norf 6C 38
Snibston. Leics 8B 36
Sniseabhal. W Isl 2D 74
Snitter. Nmbd 1D 54
Snitterby. Linc 8G 43
Snitterfield. Warw 6L 27
Snitton. Shrp 4D 26
Snodhill. Here 7B 26
Snodland. Kent 7D 22
Snods Edge. Nmbd 6D 54
Snowshill. Glos 8J 27
Snow Street. Norf 3G 31
Snydale. W Yor 5B 42
Soake. Hants 4D 10
Soar. Carm 2F 16
Soar. Gwyn 7F 32
Soar. IOA 3C 32
Soar. Powy 1J 17
Soberton. Hants 4D 10
Soberton Heath. Hants 4D 10
Sockbridge. Cumb 3D 46
Sockburn. Darl 5M 47
Sodom. Den 3K 33
Sodom. Shet 1F 90
Soham. Cambs 4B 30
Soham Cotes. Cambs 4B 30
Solas. W Isl 6K 75
Soldon Cross. Devn 4C 6
Soldridge. Hants 2D 10
Solent Breezes. Hants 5C 10
Sole Street. Kent
nr. Meopham 7C 22
nr. Waltham 1G 13
Solihull. W Mid 3K 27
Sollers Dilwyn. Here 6C 26
Sollers Hope. Here 8E 26
Sollom. Lanc 6C 40
Solva. Pemb 4D 14
Somerby. Leics 8E 36
Somerby. Linc 7H 43
Somercotes. Derbs 4B 36
Somerford. Dors 6K 9
Somerford. Staf 1G 27
Somerford Keynes. Glos 4J 19
Somerley. W Sus 6F 10
Somerleyton. Suff 2L 31
Somersal Herbert. Derbs 6K 35
Somersby. Linc 2L 37
Somersham. Cambs 4L 29
Somersham. Suff 7G 31
Somerton. Oxon 1B 20
Somerton. Som 3C 8
Somerton. Suff 6E 30
Sompting. W Sus 5J 11
Sonning. Wok 6E 20
Sonning Common. Oxon 5E 20
Sonning Eye. Oxon 6E 20
Sookholme. Notts 3C 36
Sopley. Hants 6K 9
Sopworth. Wilts 5G 19
Sorbie. Dum 7K 51
Sordale. High 5C 86
Sorisdale. Arg 1H 63
Sorn. E Ayr 7D 58
Sornhill. E Ayr 6D 58
Sortat. High 5D 86
Sotby. Linc 2K 37
Sots Hole. Linc 3J 37
Sotterley. Suff 3L 31
Soudley. Shrp
nr. Church Stretton 2C 26
nr. Market Drayton 7F 34
Soughton. Flin 4M 33
Soulbury. Buck 1F 20
Soulby. Cumb
nr. Appleby 4F 46
nr. Penrith 3C 46
Souldern. Oxon 8C 28
Souldrop. Bed 5G 29
Sound. Ches E 5E 34
Sound. Shet
nr. Lerwick 3E 90
nr. Tresta 2D 90
Soundwell. S Glo 6E 18
Sourhope. Bord 7F 60
Sourin. Orkn 6D 88
Sour Nook. Cumb 7H 53
Sourton. Devn 6E 6
Soutergate. Cumb 6M 45
South Acre. Norf 8E 38
Southall. G Lon 6J 21
South Allington. Devn 8K 5
South Alloa. Falk 8B 66
Southam. Glos 1H 19
Southam. Warw 5B 28
South Ambersham. W Sus 3G 11
Southampton. Sotn 4B 10
Southampton Airport.
Hants 4B 10
Southannan. N Ayr 4M 57
South Anston. S Yor 1C 36
South Ascot. Wind 7G 21
South Baddesley. Hants 6A 10
South Balfern. Dum 6K 51
South Ballachulish. High 2E 64
South Bank. Red C 3C 48
South Barrow. Som 3E 8
South Benfleet. Essx 5D 22
South Bents. Tyne 5H 55
South Bersted. W Sus 5G 11
Southborough. Kent 1B 12
Southbourne. Bour 6K 9
Southbourne. W Sus 5E 10
South Bowood. Dors 6C 8
South Brent. Devn 6J 5
South Brewham. Som 2F 8
South Broomage. Falk 1G 59
South Broomhill. Nmbd 2F 54
Southburgh. Norf 1F 30
South Burlingham. Norf 1K 31
Southburn. E Yor 2G 43
South Cadbury. Som 3E 8
South Carlton. Linc 2G 37
South Cave. E Yor 4G 43
South Cerney. Glos 4J 19
South Chailey. E Sus 4L 11
South Chard. Som 5B 8
South Charlton. Nmbd 7J 61
South Cheriton. Som 3E 8
South Church. Dur 3L 47
Southchurch. S'end 5F 22
South Cleatlam. Dur 4K 47
South Cliffe. E Yor 4F 42
South Clifton. Notts 2F 36
South Clunes. High 1F 70
South Cockerington. Linc 1L 37
South Common. Devn 5B 8
South Cornelly. B'end 6H 17
Southcott. Devn
nr. Great Torrington 4D 6
nr. Okehampton 6E 6
Southcott. Wilts 8K 19
Southcourt. Buck 2F 20
South Cove. Suff 3L 31
South Creagan. Arg 3D 64
South Creake. Norf 6E 38
South Crosland. W Yor 6K 41
South Croxton. Leics 8D 36
South Dalton. E Yor 3G 43
South Darenth. Kent 7B 22
Southdean. Bord 1L 53
Southdown. Bath 7F 18
South Duffield. N Yor 4D 42
Southease. E Sus 5M 11
South Elkington. Linc 1K 37
South Elmsall. W Yor 6B 42
Southend. Arg 1B 50
South End. Cumb 8M 45
Southend. Glos 4F 18
South End. N Lin 5J 43
Southend. W Ber 6C 20
Southend Airport. Essx 5E 22
Southend-on-Sea. S'end 5E 22
Southerfield. Cumb 7F 52
Southerhouse. Shet 4D 90
Southerly. Devn 7E 6
Southernden. Kent 1E 12
Southerndown. V Glam 7H 17
Southerness. Dum 6D 52
South Erradale. High 6J 77
Southerton. Devn 6K 7
Southery. Norf 2C 30
Southey Green. Essx 8D 30
South Fambridge. Essx 4E 22
South Fawley. W Ber 5A 20
South Feorline. N Ayr 7J 57
South Ferriby. N Lin 5G 43
South Field. E Yor 5H 43
Southfleet. Kent 6C 22
South Garvan. High 8L 69
Southgate. Cdgn 4E 24
Southgate. G Lon 4L 21
Southgate. Norf
nr. Aylsham 7H 39
nr. Fakenham 6E 38
Southgate. Swan 6E 16
South Gluss. Shet 6H 91
South Godstone. Surr 1L 11
South Gorley. Hants 4K 9
South Green. Essx
nr. Billericay 4C 22
nr. Colchester 2G 23
South Green. Kent 7E 22
South Hanningfield. Essx 4D 22
South Harting. W Sus 4E 10
South Hayling. Hants 6E 10
South Hazelrigg. Nmbd 6H 61
South Heath. Buck 3G 21
South Heath. Essx 2H 23
South Heighton. E Sus 5M 11
South Hetton. Dur 7G 55
South Hiendley. W Yor 6A 42
South Hill. Corn 8C 6
South Hill. Som 3C 8
South Hinksey. Oxon 3C 20
South Hole. Devn 3B 6
South Holme. N Yor 8E 48
South Holmwood. Surr 1J 11
South Hornchurch. G Lon 5B 22
South Huish. Devn 7J 5
South Hykeham. Linc 3G 37
South Hylton. Tyne 6G 55
Southill. C Beds 7J 29
Southington. Hants 1C 10
South Kelsey. Linc 8H 43
South Kessock. High 1G 71
South Killingholme. N Lin 6J 43
South Kilvington. N Yor 7B 48
South Kilworth. Leics 3D 28
South Kirkby. W Yor 6B 42
South Kirkton. Abers 5G 73
South Knighton. Devn 8H 7
South Kyme. Linc 5J 37
South Lancing. W Sus 5J 11
South Ledaig. Arg 4D 64
Southleigh. Devn 6M 7
South Leigh. Oxon 3A 20
South Leverton. Notts 1E 36
South Littleton. Worc 7J 27
South Lopham. Norf 3G 31
South Luffenham. Rut 1G 29
South Malling. E Sus 4M 11
South Marston. Swin 5K 19
South Middleton. Nmbd 7G 61
South Milford. N Yor 4B 42
South Milton. Devn 7K 5
South Mimms. Herts 3K 21
Southminster. Essx 4F 22
South Molton. Devn 3G 7
South Moor. Dur 6E 54
Southmoor. Oxon 4A 20
South Moreton. Oxon 5C 20
South Mundham. W Sus 5F 10
South Muskham. Notts 4E 36
South Newbald. E Yor 4G 43
South Newington. Oxon 8B 28
South Newsham. Nmbd 4G 55
South Newton. N Ayr 4J 57
South Newton. Wilts 2J 9
South Normanton. Derbs 4B 36
South Norwood. G Lon 7L 21
South Nutfield. Surr 1L 11
South Ockendon. Thur 5B 22
Southoe. Cambs 5J 29
Southolt. Suff 5H 31
South Ormsby. Linc 2L 37
Southorpe. Pet 1H 29
South Otterington. N Yor 7A 48
South Owersby. Linc 8H 43
Southowram. W Yor 5K 41
South Oxhey. Herts 4J 21
South Perrott. Dors 5C 8
South Petherton. Som 4C 8
South Petherwin. Corn 7C 6
South Pickenham. Norf 1E 30
South Pool. Devn 7K 5
South Poorton. Dors 6D 8
South Port. Arg 5E 64
Southport. Mers 6B 40
Southpunds. Shet 6E 90
South Queensferry. Edin 2K 59
South Radworthy. Devn 2G 7
South Rauceby. Linc 5H 37
South Raynham. Norf 7E 38
Southrepps. Norf 6J 39
South Reston. Linc 1M 37
Southrey. Linc 3J 37
Southrop. Glos 3K 19
Southrope. Hants 1D 10
South Runcton. Norf 1C 30
South Scarle. Notts 3F 36
Southsea. Port 6D 10
South Shields. Tyne 5G 55
South Shore. Bkpl 4B 40
Southside. Orkn 7E 88
South Somercotes. Linc 8M 43
South Stainley. N Yor 1M 41
South Stainmore. Cumb 4G 47
South Stifford. Thur 6B 22
South Stoke. Bath 7F 18
South Stoke. Oxon 5C 20
South Stoke. W Sus 5H 11
South Street. E Sus 4L 11
South Street. Kent
nr. Faversham 8G 23
nr. Whitstable 7H 23
South Tawton. Devn 6F 6
South Thoresby. Linc 2M 37
South Tidworth. Wilts 1L 9
South Town. Devn 7J 7
South Town. Hants 2D 10
Southtown. Norf 1M 31
Southtown. Orkn 2F 86
South View. Shet 3D 90
Southwaite. Cumb 7J 53
South Walsham. Norf 8K 39
South Warnborough. Hants 1E 10
Southwater. W Sus 3J 11
Southwater Street. W Sus 3J 11
Southway. Som 1D 8
South Weald. Essx 4B 22
South Weirs. Hants 5L 9
Southwell. Dors 8E 8
Southwell. Notts 4E 36
South Weston. Oxon 4E 20
South Wheatley. Corn 6B 6
South Wheatley. Notts 1E 36
Southwick. Hants 5D 10
Southwick. Nptn 2H 29
Southwick. Tyne 6G 55
Southwick. W Sus 5K 11
Southwick. Wilts 8G 19
South Widcombe. Bath 8D 18
South Wigston. Leics 2C 28
South Willingham. Linc 1J 37
South Wingfield. Derbs 4A 36
South Witham. Linc 8G 37
Southwold. Suff 4M 31
South Wonston. Hants 2B 10
Southwood. Norf 1K 31
Southwood. Som 2D 8
South Woodham Ferrers.
Essx 4E 22
South Wootton. Norf 7C 38
South Wraxall. Wilts 7G 19
South Zeal. Devn 6F 6
Soval Lodge. W Isl 1E 76
Sowerby. N Yor 7B 48
Sowerby. W Yor 5J 41
Sowerby Bridge. W Yor 5J 41
Sowerby Row. Cumb 7H 53
Sower Carr. Lanc 3B 40
Sowley Green. Suff 6D 30
Sowood. W Yor 6J 41
Sowton. Devn 6J 7
Soyal. High 4F 78
Soyland Town. W Yor 5J 41
Spa, The. New M 6H 93
Spacey Houses. N Yor 2M 41
Spa Common. Norf 6J 39
Spalding. Linc 7K 37
Spaldington. E Yor 4E 42
Spaldwick. Cambs 4J 29
Spalford. Notts 3F 36
Spamount. Derr 4C 92
Spanby. Linc 6H 37
Sparham. Norf 8G 39
Sparhamhill. Norf 8G 39
Spark Bridge. Cumb 7B 46
Sparket. Cumb 3C 46
Sparkford. Som 3E 8
Sparkwell. Devn 6H 5
Sparrow Green. Norf 8F 38
Sparrowpit. Derbs 1J 35
Sparrow's Green. E Sus 2C 12
Sparsholt. Hants 2B 10
Sparsholt. Oxon 5M 19
Spartylea. Nmbd 7B 54
Spath. Staf 6J 35
Spaunton. N Yor 7E 48
Spaxton. Som 2M 7
Spean Bridge. High 7C 70
Spear Hill. W Sus 4J 11
Speen. Buck 4F 20
Speen. W Ber 7B 20
Speeton. N Yor 8J 49
Speke. Mers 1C 34
Speldhurst. Kent 1B 12
Spellbrook. Herts 2A 22
Spelsbury. Oxon 1A 20
Spencers Wood. Wok 7E 20
Spennithorne. N Yor 7K 47
Spennymoor. Dur 8F 54
Spernall. Warw 5J 27
Sperrin. Derr 4E 92
Spetchley. Worc 6G 27
Spetisbury. Dors 5H 9
Spexhall. Suff 3K 31
Speybank. High 5J 71
Spey Bay. Mor 7C 80
Speybridge. High 3L 71
Speyview. Mor 1B 72
Spilsby. Linc 3M 37
Spindlestone. Nmbd 6J 61
Spinkhill. Derbs 2B 36
Spinney Hills. Leic 1D 28
Spinningdale. High 5G 79
Spital. Mers 1B 34
Spitalhill. Derbs 5K 35
Spital in the Street. Linc 8G 43
Spithurst. E Sus 4M 11
Spittal. Dum 6J 51
Spittal. E Lot 2B 60
Spittal. High 6C 86
Spittal. Nmbd 4H 61
Spittal. Pemb 4F 14
Spittalfield. Per 3E 66
Spittal of Glenmuick.
Abers 7C 72
Spittal of Glenshee. Per 8M 71
Spittal-on-Rule. Bord 7C 60
Spixworth. Norf 8J 39
Splatt. Corn 7B 6
Spofforth. N Yor 2A 42
Spondon. Derb 6B 36
Spon End. W Mid 4M 27
Spooner Row. Norf 2G 31
Sporle. Norf 8E 38
Spott. E Lot 2D 60
Spratton. Nptn 4E 28
Spreakley. Surr 1F 10
Spreyton. Devn 6G 7
Spridlington. Linc 1H 37
Springburn. Glas 3E 58
Springfield. Dum 5H 53
Springfield. Ferm 6B 92
Springfield. Fife 6G 67
Springfield. High 7G 79
Springfield. W Mid 3J 27
Springhill. Staf 1H 27
Spring Hill. W Mid 2G 27
Springholm. Dum 5C 52
Springside. N Ayr 6B 58
Springthorpe. Linc 1F 36
Spring Vale. IOW 6D 10
Spring Valley. IOM 7C 44
Springwell. Tyne 6F 54
Sproatley. E Yor 4J 43
Sproston Green. Ches W 3F 34
Sprotbrough. S Yor 7C 42
Sproughton. Suff 7H 31
Sprouston. Bord 6E 60
Sprowston. Norf 8J 39
Sproxton. Leics 7F 36
Sproxton. N Yor 7D 48
Sprunston. Cumb 7J 53
Spurstow. Ches E 4D 34
Squires Gate. Bkpl 4B 40
Sraid Ruadh. Arg 3E 62
Srannda. W Isl 5B 76
Sron an t-Sithein. High 1C 64
Sronphadruig Lodge. Per 8H 71
Sruth Mor. W Isl 7L 75
Stableford. Shrp 2F 26
Stackhouse. N Yor 1G 41
Stackpole. Pemb 7F 14
Stackpole Elidor. Pemb 7F 14
Stacksford. Norf 2G 31
Stacksteads. Lanc 5G 41
Staddiscombe. Plym 6H 5
Staddlethorpe. E Yor 5F 42
Staddon. Devn 5C 6
Stadhampton. Oxon 4D 20
Stadhlaigearraidh. W Isl 2D 74
Stafainn. High 7F 76
Staffield. Cumb 7K 53
Staffin. High 7F 76
Stafford. Staf 7H 35
Stafford Park. Telf 1F 26
Stagden Cross. Essx 2C 22
Stagsden. Bed 7G 29
Stag's Head. Devn 3F 6
Stainburn. Cumb 2K 45
Stainburn. N Yor 3L 41
Stainby. Linc 7G 37
Staincliffe. W Yor 5L 41
Staincross. S Yor 6M 41
Staindrop. Dur 3K 47
Staines-upon-Thames.
Surr 6H 21
Stainfield. Linc
nr. Bourne 7H 37
nr. Lincoln 2J 37
Stainforth. N Yor 1G 41
Stainforth. S Yor 6D 42
Staining. Lanc 4B 40
Stainland. W Yor 6J 41
Stainsacre. N Yor 5G 49
Stainton. Cumb
nr. Carlisle 6H 53
nr. Kendal 7D 46
nr. Penrith 3C 46
Stainton. Dur 4J 47
Stainton. Midd 4B 48
Stainton. N Yor 6K 47
Stainton. S Yor 8C 42
Stainton by Langworth.
Linc 2H 37
Staintondale. N Yor 6G 49
Stainton le Vale. Linc 8J 43
Stainton with Adgarley.
Cumb 8A 46
Stair. Cumb 2M 45
Stair. E Ayr 7C 58
Stairhaven. Dum 6H 51
Staithes. N Yor 4E 48
Stakeford. Nmbd 3F 54
Stake Pool. Lanc 3C 40
Stakes. Hants 5D 10
Stalbridge. Dors 4F 8
Stalbridge Weston. Dors 4F 8
Stalham. Norf 7K 39
Stalham Green. Norf 7K 39
Stalisfield Green. Kent 8F 22
Stallen. Dors 4E 8
Stallingborough. NE Lin 6K 43
Stalling Busk. N Yor 7H 47
Stallington. Staf 6H 35
Stalmine. Lanc 3B 40
Stalybridge. G Man 8H 41
Stambourne. Essx 8D 30
Stamford. Linc 1H 29
Stamford. Nmbd 8K 61
Stamford Bridge. Ches W 3C 34
Stamford Bridge. E Yor 2E 42
Stamfordham. Nmbd 4D 54
Stamperland. E Ren 4D 58
Stanah. Lanc 3B 40
Stanborough. Herts 2K 21
Stanbridge. C Beds 1G 21
Stanbridge. Dors 5J 9
Stanbury. W Yor 4J 41
Stand. N Lan 3F 58
Standburn. Falk 2H 59
Standeford. Staf 1H 27
Standen. Kent 1E 12
Standen Street. Kent 2E 12
Standerwick. Som 8G 19
Standford. Hants 2F 10
Standford Bridge. Telf 7F 34
Standingstone. Cumb 7G 53
Standish. Glos 3G 19
Standish. G Man 6D 40
Standish Lower Ground.
G Man 7D 40
Standlake. Oxon 3A 20
Standon. Hants 3B 10
Standon. Herts 1L 21
Standon. Staf 6G 35
Standon Green End. Herts 2L 21
Stane. N Lan 4G 59
Stanecastle. N Ayr 6B 58
Stanfield. Norf 7F 38
Stanfield. Suff 6D 30
Stanford. C Beds 7J 29
Stanford. Kent 2H 13
Stanford Bishop. Here 6E 26
Stanford Bridge. Worc 5F 26
Stanford Dingley. W Ber 6C 20
Stanford in the Vale. Oxon 4M 19
Stanford-le-Hope. Thur 5C 22
Stanford on Avon. Nptn 4C 28
Stanford on Soar. Notts 7C 36
Stanford on Teme. Worc 5F 26
Stanford Rivers. Essx 3B 22
Stanfree. Derbs 2B 36
Stanghow. Red C 4D 48
Stanground. Pet 2K 29
Stanhoe. Norf 6E 38
Stanhope. Dur 8C 54
Stanhope. Bord 7K 59
Stanion. Nptn 3G 29
Stanley. Derbs 5B 36
Stanley. Dur 6E 54
Stanley. Per 4E 66
Stanley. Shrp 3F 26
Stanley. Staf 4H 35
Stanley. W Yor 5M 41
Stanley Common. Derbs 5B 36
Stanley Crook. Dur 8E 54
Stanley Hill. Here 7E 26
Stanlow. Ches W 2C 34
Stanmer. Brig 5L 11
Stanmore. G Lon 4J 21
Stanmore. Hants 3B 10
Stanmore. W Ber 6B 20
Stannersburn. Nmbd 3M 53
Stanningfield. Suff 6E 30
Stannington. Nmbd 4F 54
Stannington. S Yor 1M 35
Stansbatch. Here 5B 26
Stanshope. Staf 4K 35
Stanstead. Suff 7E 30
Stanstead Abbotts. Herts 2L 21
Stansted. Kent 7C 22
Stansted Airport. Essx 1B 22
Stansted Mountfitchet.
Essx 1B 22
Stanthorne. Ches W 3E 34
Stanton. Derbs 8L 35
Stanton. Glos 8J 27
Stanton. Nmbd 2E 54
Stanton. Staf 5K 35
Stanton. Suff 4F 30
Stanton by Bridge. Derbs 7A 36
Stanton-by-Dale. Derbs 6B 36
Stanton Chare. Suff 4F 30
Stanton Drew. Bath 7D 18
Stanton Fitzwarren. Swin 4K 19
Stanton Harcourt. Oxon 3B 20
Stanton Hill. Notts 3B 36
Stanton in Peak. Derbs 3L 35
Stanton Lacy. Shrp 4C 26
Stanton Long. Shrp 2D 26
Stanton-on-the-Wolds.
Notts 6D 36
Stanton Prior. Bath 7E 18
Stanton St Bernard. Wilts 7J 19
Stanton St John. Oxon 3C 20
Stanton St Quintin. Wilts 6H 19
Stanton Street. Suff 5F 30
Stanton under Bardon.
Leics 8B 36
Stanton upon Hine Heath.
Shrp 7D 34
Stanton Wick. Bath 7E 18
Stanwardine in the Fields.
Shrp 7C 34
Stanwardine in the Wood.
Shrp 7C 34
Stanway. Essx 1F 22
Stanway. Glos 8J 27
Stanwell. Surr 6H 21
Stanwell Green. Suff 4H 31
Stanwell Moor. Surr 6H 21
Stanwick. Nptn 4G 29
Stanydale. Shet 2C 90
Staoinebrig. W Isl 2D 74
Stape. N Yor 6E 48
Stapehill. Dors 5J 9
Stapeley. Ches E 5E 34
Stapenhill. Staf 7L 35
Staple. Kent 8J 23
Staple Cross. Devn 3K 7
Staplecross. E Sus 3D 12
Staplefield. W Sus 3K 11
Staple Fitzpaine. Som 4A 8
Stapleford. Cambs 6A 30
Stapleford. Herts 2L 21
Stapleford. Leics 8F 36
Stapleford. Linc 4F 36
Stapleford. Notts 6B 36
Stapleford. Wilts 2J 9
Stapleford Abbotts. Essx 4B 22
Stapleford Tawney. Essx 4B 22
Staplegrove. Som 3M 7
Staplehay. Som 3M 7
Staple Hill. S Glo 6E 18
Staplehurst. Kent 1D 12
Staplers. IOW 7C 10
Stapleton. Bris 6E 18
Stapleton. Cumb 4K 53
Stapleton. Here 5B 26
Stapleton. Leics 2B 28
Stapleton. N Yor 4L 47
Stapleton. Shrp 1C 26
Stapleton. Som 3C 8
Stapley. Som 4L 7
Staploe. Bed 5J 29
Staplow. Here 7E 26
Star. Fife 7G 67
Star. Pemb 3J 15
Starbeck. N Yor 2M 41
Starbotton. N Yor 8H 47
Starcross. Devn 7J 7
Stareton. Warw 4M 27
Starkholmes. Derbs 4M 35
Starling. G Man 6F 40
Starling's Green. Essx 8A 30
Starston. Norf 3J 31
Start. Devn 7L 5
Startforth. Dur 4J 47
Start Hill. Essx 1B 22
Startley. Wilts 5H 19
Stathe. Som 3B 8
Stathern. Leics 6E 36
Station Town. Dur 8H 55
Staughton Green. Cambs 5J 29
Staughton Highway. Cambs 5J 29
Staunton. Glos
nr. Cheltenham 1F 18
nr. Monmouth 2D 18
Staunton in the Vale. Notts 5F 36
Staunton on Arrow. Here 5B 26
Staunton on Wye. Here 7B 26
Staveley. Cumb 6C 46
Staveley. Derbs 2B 36
Staveley. N Yor 1A 42
Staveley-in-Cartmel. Cumb 7B 46
Staverton. Devn 5K 5
Staverton. Glos 1G 19
Staverton. Nptn 5C 28
Staverton. Wilts 7G 19
Stawell. Som 2B 8
Stawley. Som 3K 7
Staxigoe. High 6E 86
Staxton. N Yor 8H 49
Staylittle. Powy 3H 25
Staynall. Lanc 3B 40
Staythorpe. Notts 4E 36
Stean. N Yor 8J 47
Stearsby. N Yor 8D 48
Steart. Som 1A 8
Stebbing. Essx 1C 22
Stebbing Green. Essx 1C 22
Stedham. W Sus 3F 10
Steel. Nmbd 6C 54
Steel Cross. E Sus 2B 12
Steelend. Fife 8D 66
Steele Road. Bord 2K 53
Steel Heath. Shrp 6D 34
Steen's Bridge. Here 6D 26
Steep. Hants 3E 10
Steep Lane. W Yor 5J 41
Steeple. Dors 7H 9
Steeple. Essx 3F 22
Steeple Ashton. Wilts 8H 19
Steeple Aston. Oxon 1B 20
Steeple Barton. Oxon 1B 20
Steeple Bumpstead. Essx 7C 30
Steeple Claydon. Buck 1D 20
Steeple Gidding. Cambs 3J 29
Steeple Langford. Wilts 2J 9
Steeple Morden. Cambs 7K 29
Steeton. W Yor 3J 41
Stein. High 8D 76
Steinmanhill. Abers 1G 73
Stelling Minnis. Kent 1H 13
Stembridge. Som 3C 8
Stemster. High
nr. Halkirk 5C 86
nr. Westfield 5B 86
Stenalees. Corn 6C 4
Stenhill. Devn 4K 7
Stenhouse. Edin 2L 59
Stenhousemuir. Falk 1G 59
Stenigot. Linc 1K 37
Stenscholl. High 7F 76
Stenso. Orkn 7C 88
Stenson. Derbs 7M 35
Stenson Fields. Derbs 6M 35
Stenton. E Lot 2D 60
Stenwith. Linc 6F 36
Steòrnabhagh. W Isl 8H 83
Stepaside. Pemb 6H 15
Stepford. Dum 3C 52
Stepney. G Lon 5L 21
Steppingley. C Beds 8H 29
Stepps. N Lan 3E 58
Sterndale Moor. Derbs 3K 35
Sternfield. Suff 5K 31
Stert. Wilts 8J 19
Stetchworth. Cambs 6C 30
Stevenage. Herts 1K 21
Stevenston. N Ayr 5A 58
Stevenstone. Devn 4E 6
Steventon. Hants 1C 10
Steventon. Oxon 4B 20
Steventon End. Essx 7B 30
Stevington. Bed 6G 29
Stewartby. Bed 7H 29
Stewarton. Arg 8F 56
Stewarton. E Ayr 5C 58
Stewartstown. M Ulst 5F 93
Stewkley. Buck 1F 20
Stewkley Dean. Buck 1F 20
Stewley. Som 4B 8
Stewton. Linc 1L 37
Steyning. W Sus 4J 11
Steynton. Pemb 6F 14
Stibb. Corn 4B 6
Stibbard. Norf 7F 38
Stibb Cross. Devn 4D 6
Stibb Green. Wilts 7L 19
Stibbington. Cambs 2H 29
Stichill. Bord 6E 60
Sticker. Corn 6B 4
Stickford. Linc 3L 37

Willesden. G Lon 5K 21
Willesley. Wilts 5G 19
Willett. Som 2L 7
Willey. Shrp 2E 26
Willey. Warw 3B 28
Willey Green. Surr 8G 21
Williamscot. Oxon 7B 28
Williamsetter. Shet 5D 90
Willian. Herts 8K 29
Willingale. Essx 3B 22
Willingdon. E Sus 5B 12
Willingham. Cambs 4M 29
Willingham by Stow. Linc 1F 36
Willingham Green. Cambs 6C 30
Willington. Bed 7J 29
Willington. Derbs 7L 35
Willington. Dur 8E 54
Willington. Tyne 5G 55
Willington. Warw 8L 27
Willington Corner. Ches W 3D 34
Willisham Tye. Suff 6G 31
Willitoft. E Yor 4E 42
Williton. Som 1K 7
Willoughbridge. Staf 5F 34
Willoughby. Linc 2A 38
Willoughby. Warw 5C 28
Willoughby-on-the-Wolds. Notts 7D 36
Willoughby Waterleys. Leics 2C 28
Willoughton. Linc 8G 43
Willow Green. Worc 6F 26
Willows Green. Essx 2D 22
Willsbridge. S Glo 6E 18
Willslock. Staf 6J 35
Wilmcote. Warw 6K 27
Wilmington. Bath 7E 18
Wilmington. Devn 6M 7
Wilmington. E Sus 5B 12
Wilmington. Kent 6B 22
Wilmslow. Ches E 1G 35
Wilnecote. Staf 1L 27
Wilney Green. Norf 3G 31
Wilpshire. Lanc 4E 40
Wilsden. W Yor 4J 41
Wilsford. Linc 5H 37
Wilsford. Wilts
nr. Amesbury 2K 9
nr. Devizes 8J 19
Wilsill. N Yor 1K 41
Wilsley Green. Kent 2D 12
Wilson. Here 1D 18
Wilson. Leics 7B 36
Wilsontown. S Lan 4H 59
Wilstead. Bed 7H 29
Wilsthorpe. E Yor 1J 43
Wilsthorpe. Linc 8H 37
Wilstone. Herts 2G 21
Wilton. Cumb 3K 45
Wilton. N Yor 7F 48
Wilton. Red C 4C 48
Wilton. Bord 8C 60
Wilton. Wilts
nr. Marlborough 7L 19
nr. Salisbury 2J 9
Wimbish. Essx 8B 30
Wimbish Green. Essx 8C 30
Wimblebury. Staf 8J 35
Wimbledon. G Lon 6K 21
Wimblington. Cambs 2M 29
Wimboldsley. Ches W 3E 34
Wimborne Minster. Dors 5J 9
Wimborne St Giles. Dors 4J 9
Wimbotsham. Norf 1C 30
Wimpole. Cambs 7L 29
Wimpstone. Warw 7L 27
Wincanton. Som 3F 8
Winceby. Linc 3L 37
Wincham. Ches W 2E 34
Winchburgh. W Lot 2J 59
Winchcombe. Glos 1J 19
Winchelsea. E Sus 4F 12
Winchelsea Beach. E Sus 4F 12
Winchester. Hants 3B 10
Winchet Hill. Kent 1D 12
Winchfield. Hants 8E 20
Winchmore Hill. Buck 4G 21
Winchmore Hill. G Lon 4L 21
Wincle. Ches E 3H 35
Windermere. Cumb 6C 46
Winderton. Warw 7M 27
Windhill. High 1F 70
Windle Hill. Ches W 2B 34
Windlesham. Surr 7G 21
Windley. Derbs 5M 35
Windmill. Derbs 2K 35
Windmill Hill. E Sus 4C 12
Windmill Hill. Som 4B 8
Windrush. Glos 2K 19
Windsor. Wind 6G 21
Windsor Green. Suff 6E 30
Windyedge. Abers 6H 73
Windygates. Fife 7G 67
Windyharbour. Ches E 2G 35
Windyknowe. W Lot 3H 59
Wineham. W Sus 3K 11
Winestead. E Yor 5L 43
Winfarthing. Norf 3H 31
Winford. IOW 7C 10
Winford. N Som 7D 18
Winforton. Here 7A 26
Winfrith Newburgh. Dors 7G 9
Wing. Buck 1F 20
Wing. Rut 1F 28
Wingate. Dur 8H 55
Wingates. G Man 7E 40
Wingates. Nmbd 2E 54
Wingerworth. Derbs 3A 36
Wingfield. C Beds 1H 21
Wingfield. Suff 4J 31
Wingfield. Wilts 8G 19
Wingfield Park. Derbs 4A 36
Wingham. Kent 8J 23
Wingmore. Kent 1H 13
Wingrave. Buck 2F 20
Winkburn. Notts 4E 36
Winkfield. Brac 6G 21
Winkfield Row. Brac 6F 20
Winkhill. Staf 4J 35
Winklebury. Hants 8D 20
Winkleigh. Devn 5F 6
Winksley. N Yor 8L 47
Winkton. Dors 6K 9
Winlaton. Tyne 5E 54
Winlaton Mill. Tyne 5E 54
Winless. High 6E 86
Winmarleigh. Lanc 3C 40
Winnal Common. Here 8C 26
Winnard's Perch. Corn 5B 4
Winnersh. Wok 6E 20
Winnington. Ches W 2E 34
Winnington. Staf 6F 34
Winnothdale. Staf 5J 35
Winscales. Cumb 2K 45
Winscombe. N Som 8C 18
Winsford. Ches W 3E 34
Winsford. Som 2J 7
Winsham. Devn 2D 6
Winsham. Som 5B 8
Winshill. Staf 7L 35
Winsh-wen. Swan 5F 16
Winskill. Cumb 8K 53
Winslade. Hants 1D 10
Winsley. Wilts 7G 19
Winslow. Buck 1E 20
Winson. Glos 3J 19
Winson Green. W Mid 3J 27
Winsor. Hants 4M 9
Winster. Cumb 6C 46
Winster. Derbs 3L 35
Winston. Dur 4K 47
Winston. Suff 5H 31
Winstone. Glos 3H 19
Winswell. Devn 4D 6
Winterborne Clenston. Dors 5G 9
Winterborne Herringston. Dors 7E 8
Winterborne Houghton. Dors 5G 9
Winterborne Kingston. Dors 6G 9
Winterborne Monkton. Dors 7E 8
Winterborne St Martin. Dors 7E 8
Winterborne Stickland. Dors 5G 9
Winterborne Whitechurch. Dors 5G 9
Winterborne Zelston. Dors 6G 9
Winterbourne. S Glo 5E 18
Winterbourne. W Ber 6B 20
Winterbourne Abbas. Dors 6E 8
Winterbourne Bassett. Wilts 6K 19
Winterbourne Dauntsey. Wilts 2K 9
Winterbourne Earls. Wilts 2K 9
Winterbourne Gunner. Wilts 2K 9
Winterbourne Monkton. Wilts 6K 19
Winterbourne Steepleton. Dors 7E 8
Winterbourne Stoke. Wilts 1J 9
Winterbrook. Oxon 5D 20
Winterburn. N Yor 2H 41
Winter Gardens. Essx 5D 22
Winterhay Green. Som 4B 8
Winteringham. N Lin 5G 43
Winterley. Ches E 4F 34
Wintersett. W Yor 6A 42
Winterton. N Lin 6G 43
Winterton-on-Sea. Norf 8L 39
Winthorpe. Linc 3B 38
Winthorpe. Notts 4F 36
Winton. Bour 6J 9
Winton. Cumb 4F 46
Winton. E Sus 5B 12
Wintringham. N Yor 8F 48
Winwick. Cambs 3J 29
Winwick. Nptn 4D 28
Winwick. Warr 8E 40
Wirksworth. Derbs 4L 35
Wirswall. Ches E 5D 34
Wisbech. Cambs 8A 38
Wisbech St Mary. Cambs 1M 29
Wisborough Green. W Sus 3H 11
Wiseton. Notts 1E 36
Wishaw. N Lan 4F 58
Wishaw. Warw 2K 27
Wisley. Surr 8H 21
Wispington. Linc 2K 37
Wissenden. Kent 1F 12
Wissett. Suff 4K 31
Wistanstow. Shrp 3C 26
Wistanswick. Shrp 7E 34
Wistaston. Ches E 4E 34
Wiston. Pemb 5G 15
Wiston. S Lan 6H 59
Wiston. W Sus 4J 11
Wistow. Cambs 3K 29
Wistow. N Yor 4C 42
Wiswell. Lanc 4F 40
Witcham. Cambs 3A 30
Witchampton. Dors 5H 9
Witchford. Cambs 4B 30
Witham. Essx 2E 22
Witham Friary. Som 1F 8
Witham on the Hill. Linc 8H 37
Witham St Hughs. Linc 3F 36
Withcall. Linc 1K 37
Witherenden Hill. E Sus 3C 12
Withergate. Norf 7J 39
Witheridge. Devn 4H 7
Witheridge Hill. Oxon 5D 20
Witherley. Leics 2M 27
Withermarsh Green. Suff 8G 31
Withern. Linc 1M 37
Withernsea. E Yor 5L 43
Withernwick. E Yor 3J 43
Withersdale Street. Suff 3J 31
Withersfield. Suff 7C 30
Witherslack. Cumb 7C 46
Withiel. Corn 5B 4
Withiel Florey. Som 2J 7
Withington. Glos 2J 19
Withington. G Man 8G 41
Withington. Here 7D 26
Withington. Shrp 8D 34
Withington. Staf 6J 35
Withington Green. Ches E 2G 35
Withington Marsh. Here 7D 26
Withleigh. Devn 4J 7
Withnell. Lanc 5E 40
Withnell Fold. Lanc 5E 40
Withybrook. Warw 3B 28
Withycombe. Som 1K 7
Withycombe Raleigh. Devn 7K 7
Withyham. E Sus 2A 12
Withypool. Som 2H 7
Witley. Surr 1G 11
Witnesham. Suff 6H 31
Witney. Oxon 2A 20
Wittering. Pet 1H 29
Wittersham. Kent 3E 12
Witton. Norf 1K 31
Witton. Worc 5G 27
Witton Bridge. Norf 6K 39
Witton Gilbert. Dur 7F 54
Witton-le-Wear. Dur 8E 54
Witton Park. Dur 8E 54
Wiveliscombe. Som 3K 7
Wivelrod. Hants 2D 10
Wivelsfield. E Sus 3L 11
Wivelsfield Green. E Sus 4L 11
Wivenhoe. Essx 1G 23
Wiveton. Norf 5G 39
Wix. Essx 1H 23
Wixford. Warw 6J 27
Wixhill. Shrp 7D 34
Wixoe. Suff 7D 30
Woburn. C Beds 8G 29
Woburn Sands. Mil 8G 29
Woking. Surr 8H 21
Wokingham. Wok 7F 20
Wolborough. Devn 8H 7
Woldingham. Surr 8L 21
Wold Newton. E Yor 8H 49
Wold Newton. NE Lin 8K 43
Wolferlow. Here 5E 26
Wolferton. Norf 7C 38
Wolfhill. Per 4E 66
Wolf's Castle. Pemb 4F 14
Wolfsdale. Pemb 4F 14
Wolgarston. Staf 8H 35
Wollaston. Nptn 5G 29
Wollaston. Shrp 8B 34
Wollaston. W Mid 3G 27
Wollaton. Nott 5C 36
Wollerton. Shrp 6E 34
Wollescote. W Mid 3H 27
Wolseley Bridge. Staf 7J 35
Wolsingham. Dur 8D 54
Wolstanton. Staf 5G 35
Wolston. Warw 4B 28
Wolsty. Cumb 6F 52
Wolterton. Norf 6H 39
Wolvercote. Oxon 3B 20
Wolverhampton. W Mid 2H 27
Wolverley. Shrp 6C 34
Wolverley. Worc 4G 27
Wolverton. Hants 8C 20
Wolverton. Mil 7F 28
Wolverton. Warw 5L 27
Wolverton. Wilts 2F 8
Wolverton Common. Hants 8C 20
Wolvesnewton. Mon 4C 18
Wolvey. Warw 3B 28
Wolvey Heath. Warw 3B 28
Wolviston. Stoc T 3B 48
Womaston. Powy 5A 26
Wombleton. N Yor 7D 48
Wombourne. Staf 2G 27
Wombwell. S Yor 7A 42
Womenswold. Kent 8J 23
Womersley. N Yor 6C 42
Wonersh. Surr 1H 11
Wonson. Devn 7F 6
Wonston. Dors 5F 8
Wonston. Hants 2B 10
Wooburn. Buck 5G 21
Wooburn Green. Buck 5G 21
Wood. Pemb 4E 14
Woodacott. Devn 5C 6
Woodale. N Yor 8J 47
Woodall. S Yor 1B 36
Woodbank. Ches W 2B 34
Woodbastwick. Norf 8K 39
Woodbeck. Notts 2E 36
Woodborough. Notts 5D 36
Woodborough. Wilts 8K 19
Woodbridge. Devn 6L 7
Woodbridge. Dors 4F 8
Woodbridge. Suff 7J 31
Wood Burcote. Nptn 7D 28
Woodbury. Devn 7K 7
Woodbury Salterton. Devn 7K 7
Woodchester. Glos 3G 19
Woodchurch. Kent 2F 12
Woodchurch. Mers 1A 34
Woodcock Heath. Staf 7J 35
Woodcombe. Som 1J 7
Woodcote. Oxon 5D 20
Woodcote Green. Worc 4H 27
Woodcott. Hants 8B 20
Woodcroft. Glos 4D 18
Woodcutts. Dors 4H 9
Wood Dalling. Norf 7G 39
Woodditton. Cambs 6C 30
Woodeaton. Oxon 2C 20
Wood Eaton. Staf 8G 35
Wood End. Bed 5H 29
Woodend. Cumb 5L 45
Wood End. Herts 1L 21
Woodend. Nptn 7D 28
Woodend. Staf 7K 35
Wood End. Warw
nr. Bedworth 3L 27
nr. Dordon 2L 27
nr. Tanworth-in-Arden 4K 27
Woodend. W Sus 5F 10
Wood Enderby. Linc 3K 37
Woodend Green. Essx 1B 22
Woodfalls. Wilts 3K 9
Woodfield. Oxon 1C 20
Woodfields. Lanc 4E 40
Woodford. Corn 4B 6
Woodford. Devn 6K 5
Woodford. Glos 4E 18
Woodford. G Lon 4L 21
Woodford. G Man 1G 35
Woodford. Nptn 4G 29
Woodford. Plym 6H 5
Woodford Green. G Lon 4M 21
Woodford Halse. Nptn 6C 28
Woodgate. Norf 8G 39
Woodgate. W Mid 3H 27
Woodgate. W Sus 5G 11
Woodgate. Worc 5H 27
Wood Green. G Lon 4K 21
Woodgreen. Hants 4K 9
Woodgreen. Oxon 2A 20
Woodhall. Inv 2B 58
Woodhall. Linc 3K 37
Woodhall. N Yor 6H 47
Woodhall Spa. Linc 3J 37
Woodham. Surr 7H 21
Woodham Ferrers. Essx 4D 22
Woodham Mortimer. Essx 3E 22
Woodham Walter. Essx 3E 22
Woodhaven. Fife 5H 67
Wood Hayes. W Mid 1H 27
Woodhead. Abers
nr. Fraserburgh 7J 81
nr. Fyvie 2G 73
Woodhill. N Som 6C 18
Woodhill. Shrp 3F 26
Woodhill. Som 3B 8
Woodhorn. Nmbd 3F 54
Woodhouse. Leics 8C 36
Woodhouse. S Yor 1B 36
Woodhouse. W Yor
nr. Leeds 4L 41
nr. Normanton 5A 42
Woodhouse Eaves. Leics 8C 36
Woodhouses. Ches W 2D 34
Woodhouses. G Man
nr. Failsworth 7H 41
nr. Sale 8F 40
Woodhouses. Staf 8K 35
Woodhuish. Devn 6M 5
Woodhurst. Cambs 4L 29
Woodingdean. Brig 5L 11
Woodland. Devn 5K 5
Woodland. Dur 3J 47
Woodland Head. Devn 6G 7
Woodlands. Abers 6G 73
Woodlands. Dors 5J 9
Woodlands. Hants 4M 9
Woodlands. Kent 7B 22
Woodlands. N Yor 2M 41
Woodlands. S Yor 7C 42
Woodlands Park. Wind 6F 20
Woodlands St Mary. W Ber 6M 19
Woodlane. Shrp 7E 34
Woodlane. Staf 7K 35
Woodleigh. Devn 7K 5
Woodlesford. W Yor 5A 42
Woodley. G Man 8H 41
Woodley. Wok 6E 20
Woodmancote. Glos
nr. Cheltenham 1H 19
nr. Cirencester 3J 19
Woodmancote. W Sus
nr. Chichester 5E 10
nr. Henfield 4K 11
Woodmancote. Worc 7H 27
Woodmancott. Hants 1C 10
Woodmansey. E Yor 4H 43
Woodmansgreen. W Sus 3F 10
Woodmansterne. Surr 8K 21
Woodmanton. Devn 7K 7
Woodmill. Staf 7K 35
Woodminton. Wilts 3J 9
Woodnesborough. Kent 8K 23
Woodnewton. Nptn 2H 29
Woodnook. Linc 6G 37
Wood Norton. Norf 7G 39
Woodplumpton. Lanc 4D 40
Woodrising. Norf 1F 30
Woodrow. Cumb 7G 53
Woodrow. Dors
nr. Fifehead Neville 4F 8
nr. Hazelbury Bryan 5F 8
Wood Row. W Yor 5A 42
Woods Eaves. Here 7A 26
Woodseaves. Shrp 6E 34
Woodseaves. Staf 7G 35
Woodsend. Wilts 6L 19
Woodsetts. S Yor 1C 36
Woodsford. Dors 6F 8
Wood's Green. E Sus 2C 12
Woodshaw. Wilts 5J 19
Woodside. Aber 5J 73
Woodside. Brac 6G 21
Woodside. Derbs 5A 36
Woodside. Dum 4E 52
Woodside. Dur 3K 47
Woodside. Fife 7H 67
Woodside. Herts 3K 21
Woodside. Per 4F 66
Wood Stanway. Glos 8J 27
Woodstock. Oxon 2B 20
Woodstock Slop. Pemb 4G 15
Woodston. Pet 2J 29
Wood Street. Norf 7K 39
Wood Street Village. Surr 8G 21
Woodthorpe. Derbs 2B 36
Woodthorpe. Leics 8C 36
Woodthorpe. Linc 1M 37
Woodthorpe. Notts 5C 36
Woodthorpe. York 3C 42
Woodton. Norf 2J 31
Woodtown. Devn
nr. Bideford 3D 6
nr. Littleham 3D 6
Woodvale. Mers 6B 40
Woodville. Derbs 8M 35
Woodwalton. Cambs 3K 29
Woodwick. Orkn 7C 88
Woodyates. Dors 4J 9
Woody Bay. Devn 1F 6
Woofferton. Shrp 5D 26
Wookey. Som 1D 8
Wookey Hole. Som 1D 8
Wool. Dors 7G 9
Woolacombe. Devn 1D 6
Woolage Green. Kent 1J 13
Woolage Village. Kent 8J 23
Woolavington. Som 1B 8
Woolbeding. W Sus 3F 10
Woolcotts. Som 2J 7
Wooldale. W Yor 7K 41
Wooler. Nmbd 7G 61
Woolfardisworthy. Devn
nr. Bideford 3C 6
nr. Crediton 5H 7
Woolfords. S Lan 4J 59
Woolgarston. Dors 7H 9
Woolhampton. W Ber 7C 20
Woolhope. Here 8E 26
Woolland. Dors 5F 8
Woolley. Bath 7F 18
Woolley. Cambs 4J 29
Woolley. Corn 4B 6
Woolley. Derbs 3A 36
Woolley. W Yor 6M 41
Woolley Green. Wilts 7G 19
Woolmere Green. Worc 5H 27
Woolmer Green. Herts 2K 21
Woolminstone. Som 5C 8
Woolpit. Suff 5F 30
Woolridge. Glos 1G 19
Woolscott. Warw 5B 28
Woolsery. Devn 3C 6
Woolsington. Tyne 5E 54
Woolstaston. Shrp 2C 26
Woolsthorpe By Belvoir. Linc 6F 36
Woolsthorpe-by-Colsterworth. Linc 7G 37
Woolston. Devn 7K 5
Woolston. Shrp
nr. Church Stretton 3C 26
nr. Oswestry 7B 34
Woolston. Som 3E 8
Woolston. Sotn 4B 10
Woolston. Warr 1E 34
Woolstone. Glos 8H 27
Woolstone. Oxon 5L 19
Woolston Green. Devn 5K 5
Woolton. Mers 1C 34
Woolton Hill. Hants 7B 20
Woolverstone. Suff 8H 31
Woolverton. Som 8F 18
Woolwell. Devn 5H 5
Woolwich. G Lon 6M 21
Woonton. Here
nr. Kington 6B 26
nr. Leominster 5D 26
Wooperton. Nmbd 7H 61
Woore. Shrp 5F 34
Wooth. Dors 6C 8
Wooton. Shrp 3F 26
Wootton. Bed 7H 29
Wootton. Hants 6L 9
Wootton. IOW 6C 10
Wootton. Kent 1J 13
Wootton. Nptn 6E 28
Wootton. N Lin 6H 43
Wootton. Oxon
nr. Abingdon 3B 20
nr. Woodstock 2B 20
Wootton. Shrp
nr. Ludlow 4C 26
nr. Oswestry 7B 34
Wootton. Staf
nr. Eccleshall 7G 35
nr. Ellastone 5K 35
Wootton Bassett, Royal. Wilts 5J 19
Wootton Bridge. IOW 6C 10
Wootton Common. IOW 6C 10
Wootton Courtenay. Som 1J 7
Wootton Fitzpaine. Dors 6B 8
Wootton Rivers. Wilts 7K 19
Wootton St Lawrence. Hants 8C 20
Wootton Wawen. Warw 5K 27
Worcester. Worc 6G 27
Worcester Park. G Lon 7K 21
Wordsley. W Mid 3G 27
Worfield. Shrp 2F 26
Work. Orkn 8D 88
Workhouse Green. Suff 8F 30
Workington. Cumb 2J 45
Worksop. Notts 2C 36
Worlaby. N Lin 6H 43
World's End. W Ber 6B 20
Worlds End. Hants 4D 10
Worldsend. Shrp 2C 26
Worlds End. W Mid 3K 27
World's End. W Sus 4L 11
Worle. N Som 7B 18
Worleston. Ches E 4E 34
Worlingham. Suff 3L 31
Worlington. Suff 4C 30
Worlingworth. Suff 5J 31
Wormbridge. Here 8C 26
Wormegay. Norf 8C 38
Wormelow Tump. Here 8C 26
Wormhill. Derbs 2K 35
Wormingford. Essx 8F 30
Worminghall. Buck 3D 20
Wormington. Glos 8J 27
Worminster. Som 1D 8
Wormit. Fife 5G 67
Wormleighton. Warw 6B 28
Wormley. Herts 3L 21
Wormley. Surr 2G 11
Wormshill. Kent 8E 22
Wormsley. Here 7C 26
Worplesdon. Surr 8G 21
Worrall. S Yor 8M 41
Worsbrough. S Yor 7A 42
Worsley. G Man 7F 40
Worstead. Norf 7K 39
Worsthorne. Lanc 4G 41
Worston. Lanc 3F 40
Worth. Kent 8K 23
Worth. W Sus 2K 11
Wortham. Suff 4G 31
Worthen. Shrp 1B 26
Worthenbury. Wrex 5C 34
Worthing. Norf 8F 38
Worthing. W Sus 5J 11
Worthington. Leics 7B 36
Worth Matravers. Dors 8H 9
Worting. Hants 8D 20
Wortley. Glos 4F 18
Wortley. S Yor 8M 41
Wortley. W Yor 4L 41
Worton. N Yor 7H 47
Worton. Wilts 8H 19
Wortwell. Norf 3J 31
Wotherton. Shrp 1A 26
Wothorpe. Pet 1H 29
Wotter. Devn 5H 5
Wotton. Glos 2G 19
Wotton. Surr 1J 11
Wotton-under-Edge. Glos 4F 18
Wotton Underwood. Buck 2D 20
Wouldham. Kent 7D 22
Wrabness. Essx 8H 31
Wrafton. Devn 2D 6
Wragby. Linc 2J 37
Wragby. W Yor 6B 42
Wramplingham. Norf 1H 31
Wrangbrook. W Yor 6B 42
Wrangle. Linc 4M 37
Wrangle Lowgate. Linc 4M 37
Wrangway. Som 4L 7
Wrantage. Som 3B 8
Wrawby. N Lin 7H 43
Wraxall. N Som 6C 18
Wraxall. Som 2E 8
Wray. Lanc 1C 40
Wraysbury. Wind 6H 21
Wrayton. Lanc 8E 46
Wrea Green. Lanc 4B 40
Wreay. Cumb
nr. Carlisle 7J 53
nr. Penrith 3C 46
Wrecclesham. Surr 1F 10
Wrecsam. Wrex 4B 34
Wrekenton. Tyne 6F 54
Wrelton. N Yor 7E 48
Wrenbury. Ches E 5D 34
Wreningham. Norf 2H 31
Wrentham. Suff 3L 31
Wrenthorpe. W Yor 5M 41
Wrentnall. Shrp 1C 26
Wressle. E Yor 4E 42
Wressle. N Lin 7G 43
Wrestlingworth. C Beds 7K 29
Wretton. Norf 2C 30
Wrexham. Wrex 4B 34
Wreyland. Devn 7G 7
Wrickton. Shrp 3E 26
Wrightington Bar. Lanc 6D 40
Wright's Green. Essx 2B 22
Wrinehill. Staf 5F 34
Wrington. N Som 7C 18
Writtle. Essx 3C 22
Wrockwardine. Telf 8E 34
Wroot. N Lin 7E 42
Wrotham. Kent 8C 22
Wrotham Heath. Kent 8C 22
Wroughton. Swin 5K 19
Wroxall. IOW 7C 10
Wroxall. Warw 4L 27
Wroxeter. Shrp 1D 26
Wroxham. Norf 8K 39
Wroxton. Oxon 7B 28
Wyaston. Derbs 5K 35
Wyatt's Green. Essx 4B 22
Wybers Wood. NE Lin 7K 43
Wyberton. Linc 5L 37
Wyboston. Bed 6J 29
Wybunbury. Ches E 5E 34
Wychbold. Worc 5H 27
Wych Cross. E Sus 2M 11
Wychnor. Staf 8K 35
Wychnor Bridges. Staf 8K 35
Wyck. Hants 2E 10
Wyck Hill. Glos 1K 19
Wyck Rissington. Glos 1K 19
Wycliffe. Dur 4K 47
Wycombe Marsh. Buck 4F 20
Yr Wyddgrug. Flin 4M 33
Wyddial. Herts 8L 29
Wye. Kent 1G 13
Wyesham. Mon 2D 18
Wyfold. Oxon 5D 20
Wyfordby. Leics 8E 36
Wyke. Devn 6H 7
Wyke. Dors 3F 8
Wyke. Shrp 1E 26
Wyke. Surr 8G 21
Wyke. W Yor 5K 41
Wyke Champflower. Som 2E 8
Wykeham. Linc 7K 37
Wykeham. N Yor
nr. Malton 8F 48
nr. Scarborough 7G 49
Wyken. Shrp 2F 26
Wyken. W Mid 3A 28
Wyke Regis. Dors 8E 8
Wykey. Shrp 7B 34
Wykin. Leics 2B 28
Wylam. Nmbd 5E 54
Wylde Green. W Mid 2K 27
Wylye. Wilts 2J 9
Wymering. Port 5D 10
Wymeswold. Leics 7D 36
Wymington. Bed 5G 29
Wymondham. Leics 8F 36
Wymondham. Norf 1H 31
Wyndham. B'end 5J 17
Wynford Eagle. Dors 6D 8
Wyng. Orkn 2E 86
Wynyard Village. Stoc T 3B 48
Wyre Piddle. Worc 7H 27
Wysall. Notts 7D 36
Wyson. Here 5D 26
Wythall. Worc 4J 27
Wytham. Oxon 3B 20
Wythenshawe. G Man 1G 35
Wythop Mill. Cumb 2L 45
Wyton. Cambs 4K 29
Wyton. E Yor 4J 43
Wyverstone. Suff 5G 31
Wyverstone Street. Suff 5G 31
Wyville. Linc 7F 36
Wyvis Lodge. High 6E 78

Y

Yaddlethorpe. N Lin 7F 42
Yafford. IOW 7B 10
Yafforth. N Yor 6M 47
Yalding. Kent 8C 22
Yanley. N Som 7D 18
Yanwath. Cumb 3D 46
Yanworth. Glos 2J 19
Yapham. E Yor 2E 42
Yapton. W Sus 5G 11
Yarburgh. Linc 8L 43
Yarcombe. Devn 5M 7
Yarde. Som 2K 7
Yardley. W Mid 3K 27
Yardley Gobion. Nptn 7E 28
Yardley Hastings. Nptn 6F 28
Yardley Wood. W Mid 3K 27
Yardro. Powy 7M 25
Yarhampton. Worc 5F 26
Yarkhill. Here 7E 26
Yarlet. Staf 7H 35
Yarley. Som 1D 8
Yarlington. Som 3E 8
Yarm. Stoc T 4B 48
Yarmouth. IOW 7A 10
Yarnbrook. Wilts 8G 19
Yarnfield. Staf 6G 35
Yarnscombe. Devn 3E 6
Yarnton. Oxon 2B 20
Yarpole. Here 5C 26
Yarrow. Nmbd 3M 53
Yarrow. Bord 7A 60
Yarrow. Som 1B 8
Yarrow Feus. Bord 7M 59
Yarrow Ford. Bord 6B 60
Yarsop. Here 7C 26
Yarwell. Nptn 2H 29
Yate. S Glo 5F 18
Yateley. Hants 7F 20
Yatesbury. Wilts 6J 19
Yattendon. W Ber 6C 20
Yatton. Here
nr. Leominster 5C 26
nr. Ross-on-Wye 8E 26
Yatton. N Som 7C 18
Yatton Keynell. Wilts 6G 19
Yaverland. IOW 7D 10
Yawl. Devn 6B 8
Yaxham. Norf 8G 39
Yaxley. Cambs 2J 29
Yaxley. Suff 4H 31
Yazor. Here 7C 26
Yeading. G Lon 5J 21
Yeadon. W Yor 3L 41
Yealand Conyers. Lanc 8D 46
Yealand Redmayne. Lanc 8D 46
Yealand Storrs. Lanc 8C 46
Yealmpton. Devn 6H 5
Yearby. Red C 3D 48
Yearngill. Cumb 7F 52
Yearsett. Here 6F 26
Yearsley. N Yor 8C 48
Yeaton. Shrp 8C 34
Yeaveley. Derbs 5K 35
Yeavering. Nmbd 6G 61
Yedingham. N Yor 8F 48
Yeldersley Hollies. Derbs 5L 35
Yelford. Oxon 3A 20
Yelland. Devn 2D 6
Yelling. Cambs 5K 29
Yelsted. Kent 7E 22
Yelvertoft. Nptn 4C 28
Yelverton. Devn 5H 5
Yelverton. Norf 1J 31
Yenston. Som 3F 8
Yeoford. Devn 6G 7
Yeolmbridge. Corn 7C 6
Yeo Mill. Devn 3H 7
Yeovil. Som 4D 8
Yeovil Marsh. Som 4D 8
Yeovilton. Som 3D 8
Yerbeston. Pemb 6G 15
Yesnaby. Orkn 8B 88
Yetlington. Nmbd 1D 54
Yetminster. Dors 4D 8
Yett. N Lan 4F 58
Yett. S Ayr 7C 58
Yettington. Devn 7K 7
Yetts o' Muckhart. Clac 7D 66
Yielden. Bed 5H 29
Yieldshields. S Lan 4G 59
Yiewsley. G Lon 5H 21
Ynysboeth. Rhon 5K 17
Ynysddu. Cphy 5L 17
Ynysforgan. Swan 5F 16
Ynyshir. Rhon 5K 17
Ynyslas. Cdgn 3F 24
Ynysmaerdy. Rhon 6K 17
Ynysmeudwy. Neat 4G 17
Ynystawe. Swan 4F 16
Ynyswen. Powy 3H 17
Ynys-wen. Rhon 5J 17
Ynys y Barri. V Glam 8L 17
Ynysybwl. Rhon 5K 17
Ynysymaerdy. Neat 5G 17
Yockenthwaite. N Yor 8H 47
Yockleton. Shrp 8C 34
Yokefleet. E Yor 5F 42
Yoker. Glas 3D 58
Yonder Bognie. Abers 1E 72
Yonderton. Abers 2J 73
York. York 2D 42
Yorkletts. Kent 7G 23
Yorkley. Glos 3E 18
Yorton. Shrp 7D 34
Yorton Heath. Shrp 7D 34
Youlgreave. Derbs 3L 35
Youlthorpe. E Yor 2E 42
Youlton. N Yor 1B 42
Young's End. Essx 2D 22
Young Wood. Linc 2J 37
Yoxall. Staf 8K 35
Yoxford. Suff 5K 31
Ysbyty Cynfyn. Cdgn 5G 25
Ysbyty Ifan. Cnwy 6H 33
Ysbyty Ystwyth. Cdgn 5G 25
Ysceifiog. Flin 3L 33
Yspitty. Carm 5E 16
Ystalyfera. Neat 4G 17
Ystrad. Rhon 5J 17
Ystrad Aeron. Cdgn 1M 15
Ystradfellte. Powy 3J 17
Ystradffin. Carm 8G 25
Ystradgynlais. Powy 3G 17
Ystradmeurig. Cdgn 6G 25
Ystrad Mynach. Cphy 5L 17
Ystradowen. Carm 3G 17
Ystradowen. V Glam 7K 17
Ystumtuen. Cdgn 5G 25
Ythanbank. Abers 2J 73
Ythanwells. Abers 2F 72

Z

Zeal Monachorum. Devn 5G 7
Zeals. Wilts 2F 8
Zelah. Corn 3M 3
Zennor. Corn 5H 3
Zouch. Notts 7C 36

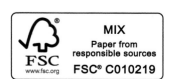